THE PAPERS OF

WOODROW WILSON

VOLUME 42
APRIL 7–JUNE 23, 1917

SPONSORED BY THE WOODROW WILSON
FOUNDATION
AND PRINCETON UNIVERSITY

THE PAPERS OF

WOODROW WILSON

ARTHUR S. LINK, *EDITOR*

DAVID W. HIRST, *SENIOR ASSOCIATE EDITOR*

JOHN E. LITTLE, *ASSOCIATE EDITOR*

FREDRICK AANDAHL, *ASSOCIATE EDITOR*

MANFRED F. BOEMEKE, *ASSISTANT EDITOR*

PHYLLIS MARCHAND AND MARGARET D. LINK,
EDITORIAL ASSISTANTS

Volume 42
April 7–June 23, 1917

PRINCETON UNIVERSITY PRESS
PRINCETON, NEW JERSEY
1983

Note to scholars: Princeton University Press sub-
scribes to the Resolution on Permissions of the Association of American University Presses, defining what
we regard as "fair use" of copyrighted works. This
Resolution, intended to encourage scholarly use of
university press publications and to avoid unnecessary
applications for permission, is obtainable from the Press
or from the A.A.U.P. central office. Note, however, that
the scholarly apparatus, transcripts of shorthand, and
the texts of Wilson documents as they appear in this
volume are copyrighted, and the usual rules about the
use of copyrighted materials apply.

Publication of this book has been aided by a grant
from the National Historical Publications and Records
Commission.

Printed in the United States of America
by Princeton University Press
Princeton, New Jersey

INTRODUCTION

As this volume begins, the United States has just entered the World War, and Wilson and his administration face the awesome task of mobilizing the American economy, people, and an army and navy in order, first, to stem the tide of war weariness in France and Russia, and, second, eventually to defeat Imperial Germany. To make matters worse, the German submarine campaign during these months succeeds even beyond the earlier predictions of the German Admiralty and threatens to bring Great Britain to her knees.

The documents in this volume vividly illustrate the Wilson administration's early plans for nationwide mobilization and actions to set it into motion. More important, they reveal clearly that Wilson is the commander in chief, as much in military affairs as in domestic mobilization. By the time that this volume ends, he has pushed through a reluctant Congress a Selective Service Act to raise a large National Army. Wilson has also stood off Theodore Roosevelt's demand that he be permitted to organize an army corps of his own. Admiral Sims and American destroyers are on their way to Queenstown to participate in the war against the submarine. General Pershing has arrived in France with the first contingent of his American Expeditionary Force on June 13, 1917. Congress has approved a huge bond issue, part of which rescues the Allies from bankruptcy, and a large emergency shipbuilding program is mired in controversy between its two chief directors. Wilson establishes a Committee on Public Information to rally public opinion behind the war; becomes entangled with newspaper publishers, editors, and reporters over the issue of censorship; and, just as this volume ends, finally wins passage, after much controversy (but without effective sanctions over the press) of the Espionage Act to control domestic subversion. June 23, 1917, finds Wilson still struggling with Congress for passage of legislation to control the prices and distribution of coal and food. Moreover, as the documents in this volume reveal, Wilson does all that he can during the early months of American belligerency to encourage the nascent Russian democracy but is still suspicious of Allied war aims. Formidable tasks lie ahead, and one of them is effective coordination of the American and Allied military efforts and agreement on common war objectives.

THE WARTIME VOLUMES

We continue to adhere to the principles of selection which we set forth and explained in the special introduction, "Editing the

Presidential Volumes," to Volume 27. However, the volume of materials which fall within our definition of a "Wilson paper" increases almost exponentially once the United States enters the World War, and this fact means that volumes from this one forward will of course cover a shorter time span than the preceding ones have done. To put the matter another way, we have not become more selective for the wartime volumes. We will continue to print all documents which relate significantly to Wilson's personal life, his general political leadership at home, his direction of American economic and military mobilization, and his conduct of wartime diplomacy.

A special word about the latter may be helpful here. Once the United States entered the war, Wilson increasingly bypassed the Department of State and conducted diplomacy directly through the agencies, mainly, of the British and French ambassadors and special agents, most particularly Sir William Wiseman (1885-1962), whose role has been portrayed in W. B. Fowler, *British-American Relations, 1917-1918: The Role of Sir William Wiseman* (Princeton University Press, 1969). We have of course combed the archives of the British Foreign Office and the private papers of British leaders of this period (just as we have searched the archives of numerous other governments and their principals). But we, and all historians of this period, owe a debt to Sir William Wiseman which cannot be adequately described. Officials in the Foreign Office destroyed large numbers of sensitive dispatches and documents very soon after they were written. Wiseman, in contrast, kept copies of everything of a diplomatic nature which passed through his office (and most important dispatches between the British embassy in Washington and the Foreign Office did). He also kept copies of all of his own important correspondence with the Foreign Office and British officials. Wiseman lived in New York from 1916 until his death. He remained a close friend of Colonel House and gave his papers for the wartime period to Yale University to be alongside those of his friend. Historians in general and students of Woodrow Wilson would be bereft of thousands of vital documents without what we think was Wiseman's farsighted action.

"VERBATIM ET LITERATIM"

In earlier volumes of this series, we have said something like the following: "All documents are reproduced *verbatim et literatim*, with typographical and spelling errors corrected in square brackets only when necessary for clarity and ease of reading." The following essay explains our textual methods and review procedures.

We have never printed and do not intend to print critical, or corrected, versions of documents. We print them exactly as they are, with a few exceptions which we always note. We never use *sic*, except to denote the repetition of words in a document; in fact, we think that a succession of *sics* defaces a page.

We usually repair words in square brackets when letters are missing. As we have said, we also repair words in square brackets for clarity and ease of reading. Our general rule is to do this when we, ourselves, cannot read the word without stopping to determine its meaning. Jumbled words and names misspelled beyond recognition of course have to be repaired. We correct the misspelling of a name in the footnote which identifies the person.

However, when an old man writes to Wilson saying that he is glad to hear that Wilson is "comming" to Newark, or a semiliterate farmer from Texas writes phonetically to complain of the low price of cotton, we see no reason to correct spellings in square brackets when the words are perfectly understandable. We do not correct Wilson's misspellings unless they are unreadable, except to supply in square brackets letters missing in words. For example, for some reason he insisted upon spelling "belligerent" as "belligerant." Nothing would be gained by correcting "belligerant" in square brackets.

We think that it is very important for several reasons to follow the rule of *verbatim et literatim*. Most important, a document has its own integrity and power, particularly when it is not written in a perfect literary form. There is something very moving in seeing a Texas dirt farmer struggling to express his feelings in words, or a semiliterate former slave doing the same thing. Second, in Wilson's case it is crucially important to reproduce his errors in letters which he typed himself, since he usually typed badly when he was in an agitated state. Third, since style is the essence of the person, we would never correct grammar or make tenses consistent, as one correspondent has urged us to do. Fourth, we think that it is obligatory to print typed documents *verbatim et literatim*. For example, we think that it is very important that we print exact transcripts of Charles L. Swem's copies of Wilson's letters. Swem made many mistakes (we correct them in footnotes from a reading of his shorthand books), and Wilson let them pass. We thus have to assume that Wilson did not read his letters before signing them, and this, we think, is a significant fact. Finally, printing typed letters and documents *verbatim et literatim* tells us a great deal about the educational level of the stenographic profession in the United States during Wilson's time.

We think that our series would be worthless if we produced unreliable texts, and we go to some effort to make certain that the texts are authentic.

Our typists are highly skilled and proofread their transcripts carefully as soon as they have typed them. The Editor sight proofreads documents once he has assembled a volume and is setting its annotation. The Editors who write the notes read through the documents several times and are careful to check any anomalies. Then, once the manuscript volume has been completed and all notes checked, the Editor and Senior Associate Editor orally proofread the documents against the copy. They read every comma, dash, and character. They note every absence of punctuation. They study every nearly illegible word in written documents.

Once this process of "establishing the text" is completed, the manuscript volume goes to our editor at Princeton University Press, who checks the volume carefully and sends it to the printing plant. The volume is set by linotype by a typographer who has been working on the Wilson volumes for years. The galley proofs go to the proofroom, where they are read orally against copy. And we must say that the proofreaders at the Press are extraordinarily skilled. Some years ago, before we found a way to ease their burden, they used to query every misspelled word, absence of punctuation, or other such anomalies. Now we write "O.K." above such words or spaces on the copy.

We read the galley proofs three times. Our copyeditor gives them a sight reading against the manuscript copy to look for remaining typographical errors and to make sure that no line has been dropped. The Editor and Senior Associate Editor sight read them against documents and copy. We then get the page proofs, which have been corrected at the Press. We check all the changes three times. In addition, we get *revised* pages and check them twice.

This is not the end. Our indexer of course reads the pages word by word. Before we return the pages to the Press, she comes in with a list of queries, all of which are answered by reference to the documents.

Our rule in the Wilson Papers is that our tolerance of error is zero. No system and no person can be perfect. We are sure that there are errors in our volumes. However, we believe that we have done everything humanly possible to avoid error; the chance is remote that what looks at first glance like a typographical error is indeed an error.

Professors John Milton Cooper, Jr., William H. Harbaugh, and Richard W. Leopold read the manuscript of this volume carefully and critically; their contributions were, as always, invaluable. Our editor at Princeton University Press, Judith May, continues to be helpful in countless ways. We thank them sincerely.

THE EDITORS

Princeton, New Jersey
September 14, 1982

CONTENTS

Collateral Materials

ILLUSTRATIONS

From the collections of Princeton University Library.

Following page 294

ABBREVIATIONS

ALI	autograph letter initialed
ALS	autograph letter signed
CC	carbon copy
CCL	carbon copy of letter
CLS	Charles Lee Swem
CLSsh	Charles Lee Swem shorthand
CLST	Charles Lee Swem typed
EBW	Edith Bolling Wilson
EMH	Edward Mandell House
FR	*Papers Relating to the Foreign Relations of the United States*
FR-WWS 1917	Papers Relating to the Foreign Relations of the United States, 1917, Supplement, The World War
Hw, hw	handwriting, handwritten
JD	Josephus Daniels
JPT	Joseph Patrick Tumulty
JRT	Jack Romagna typed
MS	manuscript
MSS	manuscripts
NDB	Newton Diehl Baker
RG	record group
RL	Robert Lansing
T	typed
TC	typed copy
TCL	typed copy of letter
TCLS	typed copy of letter signed
TI	typed initialed
TL	typed letter
TLI	typed letter initialed
TLS	typed letter signed
TS	typed signed
TWG	Thomas Watt Gregory
WGM	William Gibbs McAdoo
WHP	Walter Hines Page
WJB	William Jennings Bryan
WW	Woodrow Wilson
WWhw	Woodrow Wilson handwriting, handwritten
WWsh	Woodrow Wilson shorthand
WWT	Woodrow Wilson typed
WWTL	Woodrow Wilson typed letter
WWTLI	Woodrow Wilson typed letter initialed
WWTLS	Woodrow Wilson typed letter signed
WWTS	Woodrow Wilson typed signed

ABBREVIATIONS FOR COLLECTIONS
AND REPOSITORIES

Following the National Union Catalog
of the Library of Congress

A-Ar	Alabama Department of Archives and History
AFL-CIO-Ar	American Federation of Labor-Congress of Industrial Organizations Archives
CDR	Commerce Department Records
CGSR	Coast and Geodetic Survey Records
CtY	Yale University
DLC	Library of Congress
DNA	National Archives
FFM-Ar	French Foreign Ministry Archives
FMD-Ar	French Ministry of Defense Archives
FO	British Foreign Office
HPL	Hoover Presidential Library
IEN	Northwestern University
JDR	Justice Department Records
MeB	Bowdoin College
MH	Harvard University
MH-Ar	Harvard University Archives
Nc-Ar	North Carolina State Department of Archives and History
NIC	Cornell University
NjP	Princeton University
NN	New York Public Library
NNZI	Zionist Archives and Library of Palestine Foundation Fund
OHi	Ohio State Historical Society
OkU	University of Oklahoma
PHC	Haverford College
PRO	Public Record Office
RSB Coll., DLC	Ray Stannard Baker Collection of Wilsoniana, Library of Congress
SDR	State Department Records
WC, NjP	Woodrow Wilson Collection, Princeton University
WP, DLC	Woodrow Wilson Papers, Library of Congress
WU	University of Wisconsin

SYMBOLS

[May 1, 1917]	publication date of a published writing; also date of document when date is not part of text
[*April 16, 1917*]	composition date when publication date differs
[[June 3, 1917]]	delivery date of speech if publication date differs
* * * * * * *	text deleted by author of document

THE PAPERS OF
WOODROW WILSON
VOLUME 42
APRIL 7–JUNE 23, 1917

A Memorandum

7 Apr. '17

PROGRAMME.

Measures for war:

The Additional Forces Bill,

The additional navy Bill,

And all legislation needed to put the country in a thorough state of defense and preparation for action.

Bills for the safeguarding of the nation:

These include the bills recentcy [recently] submitted to the Judiciary Committee by the Department of Justice.

Some further suggestions, affecting, for example, various restrictions on trading with the enemy, will presently be forthcoming from the Council for National Defense.

Webb Bill.

Amendments to Shipping Bill.

Amendments to Federal Reserve Act.

Strike legislation, particularly control of the Railroads for military purposes and the increase of the Interstate Commerce Commission.

WWT MS (WP, DLC).

To John Avery McIlhenny

My dear Mr. Chairman: [The White House] 7 April, 1917

I trust that the Commission will not think that my choice casts any reflection upon their judgments if I prefer to sign the second alternative form of the enclosed order rather than the first.[1] I think that the more inclusive measure is probably in the circumstances the best.

Cordially and sincerely yours,   [Woodrow Wilson]

CCL (WP, DLC).

[1] See J. A. McIlhenny *et al.* to WW, April 5, 1917 (first letter of that date), Vol. 41.

To Charles William Eliot

My dear Doctor Eliot: The White House 7 April, 1917
    Thank you for your letter of April third.[1]
    I feel, as I said in the statement given to the Press yesterday, that it is not wise or opportune now to choose a permanent system for the country in the matter of our military defense, because we must not delay our immediate preparation for the purpose of making plans which cannot be wisely made until we know what the future policy of the world is going to be, but I agree with you that when the time of the choice comes there is a vast deal to learn from the experience of Switzerland and I am sure I among others will be glad to learn it.
        Cordially and sincerely yours,   Woodrow Wilson

TLS (C. W. Eliot Papers, MH-Ar).
    [1] C. W. Eliot to WW, April 3, 1917, Vol. 41.

To William Jennings Bryan

                    The White House 1917 Apr 7
    Thank you very warmly for your telegram[1] I am sure that the whole country will believe that you are ready to serve in any way that may set its interests forward   Woodrow Wilson.

T telegram (W. J. Bryan Papers, DLC).
    [1] WJB to WW, April 6, 1917, Vol. 41.

To Walter Lippmann

My dear Mr. Lippmann: The White House 7 April, 1917
    Thank you warmly for your generous letter of April third.[1]
    The interesting and important suggestion it embodies about registering all men of military age will necessarily, I take it, be part of the plan, or, rather, necessarily accompany the plan in practice which has been proposed by the General Staff of the Army to the Congress for the raising of the additional forces that will be needed. It is certainly a very wise and necessary thing to do.
        Cordially and faithfully yours,   Woodrow Wilson

TLS (W. Lippmann Papers, CtY).
    [1] W. Lippmann to WW, April 3, 1917, Vol. 41.

To John Sharp Williams

My dear Senator: The White House 7 April, 1917

Allow me to acknowledge with sincere appreciation your two letters of April third and fourth.[1] I hope that when you have occasion to write again to Mr. Scales you will tell him how genuinely I appreciate his personal attitude and the resolutions passed by the Confederate Veterans of the City of Memphis.[2] Such things are very delightful to receive.

You speak, I feel, more generously of my recent address to the Congress than it at all deserves. If it deserves any of the praise you give it, it is because it was really and truly spoken from the heart and with a simplicity of conviction which must have robbed it of all false elements of expression.

Colonel Montgomery's letter pleased me very much, and your reply to it was of course admirable.[3] I hope that you will give him, when you have the opportunity, my personal thanks and regards.

     Cordially and sincerely yours,   Woodrow Wilson

TLS (J. S. Williams Papers, DLC).
  [1] J. S. Williams to WW, April 3 and 4, 1917, both TLS (WP, DLC).
  [2] Both the letter from Dabney M. Scales to Williams and the resolutions enclosed were returned to Williams.
  [3] J. S. Williams to W. A. Montgomery, April 3, 1917, CCL (WP, DLC). The letter from Montgomery to Williams was returned to Williams.

To Francis Bowes Sayre

My dear Frank: The White House 7 April, 1917

Bless your heart for your letter of April fifth![1] Of course, I knew how you would feel and how ready you would stand to do anything that you could do in this time of the country's need for every man who can think straight and act effectively. I do not now see just what advice to give you, but you may be sure that I will keep your offer in my mind as I do in my heart.

I long very constantly to see dear Jessie and you and the baby. I am sure you do not need to be told how constantly I am thinking of you and how warmly I love you all.

In necessary haste, with deep love for all,

     Affectionately yours,   Woodrow Wilson

TLS (received from Francis B. Sayre).
  [1] F. B. Sayre to WW, April 5, 1917, Vol. 41.

To Melancthon Williams Jacobus

My dear Friend: [The White House] 7 April, 1917

Your letter of April fifth[1] sounds a very deep and a very true note about the present interests and problems of the world. You are undoubtedly right in thinking that at bottom there lies the spiritual problem which is the spring of life. You letter has moved me very deeply and I thank you for it with all my heart.

Cordially and faithfully yours,   Woodrow Wilson

TLS (Letterpress Books, WP, DLC).
 [1] M. W. Jacobus to WW, April 5, 1917, Vol. 41.

To Elihu Root

My dear Mr. Root: [The White House] 7 April, 1917

May I not thank you for your very gracious and generous letter of April third?[1] It has given me real gratification.

I am glad that you see what seemed to me to be the implication of my action but what most of the newspapers have missed, that instead of abrogating the Monroe Doctrine the position I have taken plants it more securely than ever upon the very principles upon which the whole world is invited to act.

Sincerely yours,   Woodrow Wilson

TLS (Letterpress Books, WP, DLC).
 [1] It is missing in both WP, DLC, and the E. Root Papers, DLC.

To John Pierpont Morgan, Jr.

My dear Mr. Morgan: [The White House] 7 April, 1917

Your letter of April fourth[1] is certainly a most generous one and I want to express my warm appreciation of the spirit of service in which it is written. I am sure I can count upon you and your associates in this emergency.

Cordially and sincerely yours,   Woodrow Wilson

TLS (Letterpress Books, WP, DLC).
 [1] It is missing in WP, DLC; however, it is printed in the extract from the Brahany Diary printed at April 5, 1917, Vol. 41.

From Joseph Patrick Tumulty, with Enclosure

[The White House, April 7, 1917]

The Secretary begs to lay the attached correspondence before the President, and to ask his opinion as to the reply to be made.

The Secretary does not think it advisable for the President to express any opinion on the matter contained in Mr. Kahn's letter.

TL (WP, DLC).

ENCLOSURE

From Otto Hermann Kahn[1]

Dear Mr. President,   New York, April 6, 1917

Amidst the vast responsibilities and cares resting upon you, may I be permitted to intrude for a very few minutes with a matter of small moment in itself, but which your well known interest in affairs of art and culture emboldens me to bring to your attention and which, moreover, in its wider aspect and effect, may deserve to be considered as of some weightier significance.

The Board of Directors of the Metropolitan Opera Co., of which I am Chairman, is confronted with the question whether Opera in German sung by German artists shall continue to be given at the Metropolitan Opera House during the war.

The views and preferences of the patrons of the House appear to be divided on this subject. Some feel strongly that, until Germany shall have purged itself from the acts, and banished the spirit, which have made it an outlaw amongst nations, it would be an affront to the feelings and the patriotism of Americans to expect them to listen, not so much to German music, as to artists whose brothers are engaged in warfare against the United States, a warfare, moreover, characterized by inhuman and illegitimate methods.

Others take the view that, however deep and justified our resentment and however intolerable Germany's course of action, the flag of art should still be considered neutral and the passions of war and the strident voices of conflict should remain hushed in the house of art, belonging as it does to all mankind. Moreover, they point to the fact that in your magnificent and inspiring utterance of April 2nd, you particularly emphasize that our quarrel is with the Imperial German Government and not with the German people, and that your "own thought has not been driven from its habitual and normal course by the unhappy events of the last two months," and that you "do not believe that the thought of the nation has been altered or clouded by them."

It would seem likely that the action of the Metropolitan Opera Company in the premises will, to a considerable extent, be followed by other organizations throughout the country in respect of their attitude towards German art and artists.

It is for this reason, and because of the actual and spiritual significance of our conclusion and because of the interpretation which will be given to it here and perhaps even amongst the German people, that I venture to hope that you may see fit to let us have the privilege of a word of guidance on your part.

Should it be your pleasure to indicate to us your views, you would perhaps grant us permission to publish what you may say, because a word of light and leading from you on the subject of the attitude which America should maintain during the war towards this and kindred questions would be of far-reaching importance and would, I am sure, be eagerly and gratefully welcomed by many thousands who, whilst fully realizing that the supreme task before the nation is, under your leadership, to bring the war to a successful ending, yet believe that it is peculiarly the function of America, even in times of war, and perhaps *especially* in times of war, to hold up side by side with the beacon of liberty, the torch of the things of art and of the spirit.

It is needless to add, on the other hand, that if it should be more agreeable to you that such expressions as you may favor us with be not published, they will be treated by us in the strictest confidence.

I have the honor to remain, dear Mr. President, with the expression of my highest respect and regard,

Most sincerely yours,   Otto H. Kahn

TLS (WP, DLC).
¹ German-born partner in the banking firm of Kuhn, Loeb & Co. of New York; for many years chairman of the board and the principal stockholder of the Metropolitan Opera Co.

To Joseph Patrick Tumulty

Dear Tumulty: The White House [c. April 7, 1917].

I think you are right. It would not be wise to express an opinion in regard to this matter, and yet personally I should hate to see them stop German opera. I wish you would thank Mr. Kahn for his letter and for the considerate spirit in which it is written, and tell him that I take advantage of his generosity to say that I think it would not be wise for me to express a judgment in the matter. I have no doubt that I can trust to the good sense and moderation of the directors of the Metropolitan Opera Company not to take any extreme or unnecessary action.[1]

The President.

TL (WP, DLC).

[1] J. P. Tumulty to O. H. Kahn, April 9, 1917, TLS (O. H. Kahn Papers, NjP), paraphrased the latter part of Wilson's letter. The board of directors of the Metropolitan Opera Co. voted in November not to present any performances in the German language "during the present season." *New York Times*, Nov. 3, 1917.

From Robert Lansing

My dear Mr. President: Washington April 7, 1917.

Referring to the disposition to be made of the German refugee ships in American ports, about which we conversed yesterday, I wish to set forth my further views on the subject. They have the character of enemy private property within the jurisdiction of a belligerent. It might be argued that inasmuch as they are subsidized by the German Government and are more or less under its control, they partake of the nature of enemy public property, which is confiscable by the belligerent in whose possession it is found; but I think this would be regarded as a strained interpretation of their character, and I would, therefore, rather regard them as privately owned enemy property. As to the disposition of enemy private property thus situated, there are two views among authorities. According to the one view, there is an obligation that they should be exempt from confiscation except in the exigency of military necessity, public safety, or reprisal. This is the European Continental view. According to the Anglo-American view, the sovereign possesses the right to require confiscation if this should be found necessary, but leans toward a general policy of exemption. The difference in effect between these two views is not very great. In practice, however, nations as a rule seem to recognize the exemption of private property as a policy which ought to be followed save in exceptional cases.

In view of the foregoing, it has, I believe, become the modern custom to requisition enemy private property when necessary upon the payment of compensation. This is the rule agreed to by the nations at The Hague in Convention Six, 1907, relating to the status of enemy merchant ships at the outbreak of hostilities. The United States, however, did not sign this Convention on the ground, among others, that it did not give complete freedom for vessels of the enemy in port at the outbreak of hostilities to depart. As these vessels are generally so disabled as to be unable to depart, and as they would be immediately seized on the ocean by Allied cruisers if they did depart, it seems this policy of the United States need not interfere with any policy of requisition which may be adopted.

It may be argued that the Treaties of 1828, 1799, and 1785 would be violated by requisitioning the German refugee vessels. The only stipulation of these treaties bearing on this point is Article 23 of the Treaty of 1799 providing that in case of war "The merchants of either country then residing in the other shall be allowed to remain nine months to collect their debts and settle their affairs, and may depart freely, carrying off all their effects without molestation or hindrance." As most of the German vessels are owned by non-resident German corporations, with only operating agents here, only two or three vessels lying in our insular ports being possibly owned by Germans residing there, it would seem that this stipulation of the treaty would, as a practical matter, have little application to vessels in United States ports. I have not exact data, however, as to the resident ownership of these vessels.

As to the authority of the President to requisition the German ships without an act of Congress, I have considerable doubt, except possibly in the event that they are to be used directly in warlike operations, in which case the President might be regarded as exercising his powers as commander-in-chief. I have not had opportunity to examine this point thoroughly.

I think that, outside of the purely legal questions involved, there is strong moral right on our side in taking possession of these German vessels and using them in our merchant marine. The German submarine warfare has very materially decreased the shipping of the world and has caused very serious embarrassment to this country in the matter of transportation. I do not feel that we are bound to let these ships lie idle in our ports while the tonnage of the world is being from day to day reduced by the German Government. If you hold the same view as to the matter, I have no doubt that the legal difficulties can all be removed and the vessels can be repaired and sent forth with cargoes.   Faithfully yours,   Robert Lansing.

TLS (SDR, RG 59, 862.85/61A, DNA).

From George Jan Sosnowski[1]

Dear Mr. President: New York, 7 April, 1917.

"Not the entry of America, but the degeneration of Russia, is the decisive element in the war."

Such is the opinion of the German Government at this time, and, knowing it, we must exert our best energy to frustrate the plans of Germany in this direction. We must expect that the German Imperial Government will not spare their best talent in men and money in dealing the newly established Russian democracy a crushing blow. We have already a sign of this activity, when we note that Count von Bernstorff, Germany's best and crookedest diplomat and plotter, has been assigned as Ambassador to Sweden.

A new German consulate has been established at Haparanda, a small town on the frontier of Finland and Sweden, although there is no trade between Russia and Germany at this time.

Obviously, all these preparations are being made to institute a propaganda of intrigue, unrest and discontent in the interior and elsewhere in Russia where they may be able to develop it and provoke a separate peace.

The German General Staff will shift practically all of their activity to the Eastern front, and a big drive may reasonably be expected there into Russia, and I am quite certain that it will meet with considerable success, the Germans being today at the height of their military power; and to achieve this object, the German Government will do its utmost.

With a reverse of the Russian army, would come von Bernstorff's opportunity to launch a peace proposition. In the meantime, he will have ample time to promote and develop his intrigues inside of Russia, hoping to dishearten the people and force them to demand a cessation of hostilities.

The danger is obviously great, but, being aware of it, we might in a way partly contravene it. I say partly, because it will be a physical impossibility to avert military reverses.

The way, in my estimation, to meet this condition, is to uphold the Russian morale and let them know that we are coming to their aid and will help them in their necessity.

What Russia mostly needs is war material, but her communications with the outside world are very bad. The submarine menace is as great in the White Sea as in the danger zone.

The Trans-Siberian Railway is a single track affair and very badly managed. What should be done, is to lend Russia some able American traffic managers. If the largest railroads in Great

Britain were improved under American management, it is obvious that the Trans-Siberian Railway would be similarly bene-fitted, and it is difficult to measure the enormous help this would be to Russia; I do not think I exaggerate when I say fifty per cent. benefit or increased efficiency. American railroad interests should, through the good offices of the Administration, get in touch with the Russian Government and get contracts to double track the Trans-Siberian Railway at such points as would best insure better traffic, and eliminate the inadequacy of a single track railway.

After improving their transportation in this way, we can speed war material and troops to Russia. The presence of American troops on Russian soil is of the utmost importance, not for fight-ing the Germans on the front, *but to support the Government of the new Republic and help preserve its existence.* This is a most vital question, and I beg of you, Mr. President, to give to this suggestion *your most careful consideration.*

The presence of American troops will work wonders in the minds and on the morale of the Russian people. It will inspire their confidence in the ultimate victory of the Allies, and give them a feeling of safety. It will further upset any effect of Ger-man propaganda established to poison the mind of the Russian people with the slogan "that the Allies will fight Germany to the last drop of Russian blood!" And above all, it will give to the Russian National Government a strong hand in all their actions, —to say nothing of paving the way for American capital and trade possibilities.

The offer of the Polish Falconers of 100,000 men for service in this war is also available for this service and affords the very best material for an expeditionary force to Russia, especially on account of the similarity of languages.

In a previous communication dated March 1st,[2] I offered to you my services for the organization of a corps to be known as the "Kosciuszko Corps" of 40,000 of the Poles who have pledged themselves to the United States Army. Some General of the United States Army should be placed at the head of this Corps after its organization. If it would be your pleasure to commis-sion me under him, I would gratefully accept.

I am, Your Excellency,

Most respectfully,   G. J. Sosnowski.

TLS (WP, DLC).

[1] A spokesman for the National Defense Committee (K.O.N.) of Poland, a socialist and left-wing organization headed by Jósef Klemens Pilsudski. Sosnow-ski had recently arrived in the United States as a member of a Russian pur-

chasing team. See Piotr S. Wandycz, *The United States and Poland* (Cambridge, Mass., 1980), pp. 114-15.
² The Editors have been unable to find this letter.

From the Diary of Thomas W. Brahany

Saturday, April 7, 1917

Fewer telegrams, but many letters. It is impossible for our stenographic and clerical force to send individual replies to all letters. The President has several forms for replies for those who send congratulations, those who tender service, those who offer factories, etc. These forms have been engraved on cards; and by means of these engraved cards, which are quite attractive, we are able to keep well abreast our correspondence. The President and Dr. Grayson went to the vaudeville show at Keiths Theatre tonight. The President and Mrs. Wilson played golf this morning.

T MS (F. D. Roosevelt Papers, NHpR).

Two Letters to Robert Lansing

My dear Mr. Secretary,　　　　The White House. 8 April, 1917.

I must say that this matter gives me grave concern. Undoubtedly we need the ships, and some of them could be got in shape for use, no doubt, within a month or two, when, perhaps, they would be even more needed than they are now; and yet I *despise* the spirit of seizure.

Inasmuch as, so far as I know, they are not, at any rate immediately, needed for military purposes, I take it from your memorandum that the only course open to us is requisition for other transportation uses or seizure by way of reprisal. I suppose either of these courses would require authorization by the Congress (may I not have your advice on that point?)

I believe that seizure (*ship for ship, for the American ships sunk*) by way of reprisal would, in the extraordinary circumstances of this submarine warfare, be morally justifiable. This would be confiscation and would hardly fall under my general war powers.

I shall await your further advice on the points of law, domestic as well as international, with the greatest interest.

Faithfully Yours,　W.W.

WWTLI (SDR, RG 59, 862.85/61½, DNA).

My dear Mr. Secretary,   The White House. 8 April, 1917.

Your letter[1] convinces me that I had become confused, by the different despatches and their apparently different meanings, as to the character of the commissions contemplated, and that you are right in the conclusion to which you have come.

I would be obliged if you would intimate to each of the governments in very cordial terms that we would welcome these visits, endeavouring, at the same time, to have it arranged so that the social activities that must necessarily attend our reception of the French visitors may not interfere with the serious business we must transact with the Englishmen.

So far as the English mission is concerned, it seems to me that the sooner it comes the better: our *plans* cannot wait. There is no choice, apparently, but to let each group come when it will: we shall have to do the rest on this side the water.

I hope that you will let Sharp tell the Foreign Office in Paris at once of the English visit and Page the Foreign Office in London of the French. It may be that they can arrange the sequence for themselves.   Faithfully Yours,   W.W.

WWTLI (SDR, RG 59, 763.72/3670½, DNA).
  [1] RL to WW, April 6, 1917, Vol. 41.

From Robert Lansing, with Enclosure

PERSONAL AND CONFIDENTIAL:

My dear Mr. President: Washington April 8, 1917.

I enclose for your consideration the report of a conversation which Mr. Polk had Saturday with the Brazilian Ambassador[1] in regard to the Pan-American Treaty.

I assume from what Mr. Polk told me of his interview that Müller[2] desired speedy action, that is, a negotiation of the treaty prior to Brazil's entering the war. It is just possible that the Brazilian Government would like to use the treaty as another excuse for declaring war against Germany, a course of action which it seems certain will be pursued, though I do not think so.

I am not prepared yet to give you my opinion as to the wisdom of signing such a treaty at the present time. It might in certain circumstances (for example, Argentina's friendliness for Germany) cause much embar[r]assment. It might of course draw some of the smaller American Republics into the war, but I am not at all sure that would be a benefit as we might have to aid them.

It requires, I think very careful consideration before we decide.

Faithfully yours,   Robert Lansing

TLS (R. Lansing Papers, DLC).
¹ That is, Domicio da Gama.
² That is, Lauro Severiano Müller, Brazilian Minister of Foreign Affairs.

E N C L O S U R E

Frank Lyon Polk to Robert Lansing

My dear Mr. Secretary: [Washington] April 7, 1917.

In response to the request of the Brazilian Ambassador, I called at his house this morning. He read to me a despatch which he had just received from his Government, to the effect that the President¹ and Mr. Lauro Muller had come to the conclusion that the time had come for the United States and Brazil to sign the Pan American treaty with such countries as were ready to sign and that other countries might follow. The suggestion made by Mr. Lauro Muller is that after the enumeration of the countries that do sign should be inserted "and the other American nations that successively subscribe this Treaty."

Mr. Lauro Muller said that sentiment in Brazil was now ripe for putting through the treaty, that his Government had sounded out Chile and the Argentine. The Minister from Chile² reported that public sentiment in Chile was not quite ready for action, but it might sign later. There has been no reply from Argentina. The Ambassador also told me that he thought his country would probably declare war on Germany.

In view of the very friendly attitude of Brazil and some other Latin American countries, it might be just as well to line up our friends at this time, and probably several of the governments not so friendly would sign rather than be left out.

The Ambassador said he would send an aide memoir on the subject, but he seemed to want some word from us that the suggestion would meet with a favorable reception.

Frank L Polk

TLS (R. Lansing Papers, DLC).
¹ Wenceslao Braz Pereira Gomes, President of Brazil.
² Santiago Aldunate.

Two Letters from Robert Lansing

MOST CONFIDENTIAL:

My dear Mr. President: Washington April 8, 1917.

There is one matter of very great importance which it seems to me ought to be decided at once, and that is the coordination of the secret service work of this Government, of which the secret service office of the Department of State has been for eight or nine months the "Clearing house" or at least the depository of information gathered from various sources.

There are two general divisions of the work, the foreign and the domestic. The foreign division naturally is under this Department, the information coming from special agents employed by the Department in this country and abroad, from our diplomatic and consular officers, from the Bureau of Naval Intelligence and from friendly foreign governments. The domestic division obtains its information chiefly from the Secret Service of the Treasury, from the special agents of the Department of Justice and of the Post Office Department, and from the detective forces of several of our cities. Of course the domestic division obtains much information which is most useful to the foreign division, and vice versa.

Manifestly it is important that in some way these two general divisions and the various groups of secret agents should work in complete harmony otherwise there will be duplication of work and frequent "crossing of wires." This will be even more evident if the plans of increasing the channels of info[r]mation, which I have in mind, are carried out.

It seemed advisable to me to have these various activities under the general control of one efficient man, and with that idea in view I spoke to Secretary McAdoo on the subject. He advocated strongly the appointment of Chief Flynn of the Secret Service. I did not have time to go into the matter with him, but I felt at once that this selection would be most embar[r]assing for two principal reasons; first, Chief Flynn cannot possess the requisite knowledge of foreign affairs to direct work in that field; and, second, there is unfortunately extreme jealousy between the secret agents of Justice and those of the Treasury. They both seem willing to report to the State Department but not to each other. There is another reason which seems to me sufficient in itself to preclude Flynn's selection and that it would make the Treasury the head office of this work, which ought to be under the Department of State.

On the other hand, Bielaski,[1] head of special agents of Justice would not do at all because he would lack the knowledge of international affairs and would be entirely unacceptable to Flynn and his men.

I am not courting additional responsibilities but I do feel that the central office of secret information of all sorts should be in the State Department because this is a time when the safety of the state is threatened from without, and because the head of the service must confer constantly with the Embassies of the Allied powers and with the missions of certain Latin-American countries, and because it is only by a thoroughly experienced and trustworthy man who is expert in international matters and to whom the Department archives are open, that the information gathered can be properly valued. I believe that on the nucleus already formed in this Department a very efficient organization can be built up.

The chief difficulty lies in harmonizing the domestic work. I do not think that it can be done if either the chief of the Treasury [or] of the Department of Justice is given control. It will result in friction and jealousy. My suggestion is to select a man entirely outside the service and let all of the present secret service branches act under him through their respective chiefs. Moreover, he should be selected and employed by neither the Department of Justice nor the Treasury, for otherwise the same feeling of envy will exist.

You will understand of course that I am in no way criticizing the ability of the chiefs of the two secret service offices, both of whom are men of experience, efficiency, and energy, possessing rare talents. That is not my purpose. I am only seeking a way to get the best results and to bring into accord under one head the entire work of collecting information and making investigations.

This is the problem to be solved and it ought to be solved at once. I would not trouble you with it except for the fact that I fear the Departments interested cannot be brought into agreement otherwise.

My letter is of course for your eyes alone but I will be glad to discuss the subject with others if you think that is the advisable way.   Faithfully yours,   Robert Lansing.

TLS (WP, DLC).
[1] That is, Alexander Bruce Bielaski.

My dear Mr. President: Washington April 8, 1917.

In accordance with the letter which I received from you this morning I have sent the enclosed telegrams to London and Paris,[1] and also a letter to the French Ambassador, a copy of which is enclosed.[2] Faithfully yours, Robert Lansing.

TLS (WP, DLC).

[1] RL to WHP, April 8, 1917, and RL to W. G. Sharp, April 8, 1917, CC telegrams (WP, DLC). Lansing advised the Ambassadors that the proposed British and French missions to visit the United States would be "most welcome" and instructed each to inform the government to which he was accredited of the mission to be sent by the other in order that they might coordinate their respective visits.

[2] RL to J. J. Jusserand, April 8, 1917, TCL (WP, DLC). This letter conveyed the same message as the telegrams cited above, but in a warmer and more personal tone.

From Edward Mandell House

Dear Governor: New York. April 8, 1917.

Wiseman who has just returned from Washington tells me in confidence that he saw a cable from Balfour saying that the British Cabinet unanimously agreed that it would be wise for him to come to America immediately. The cable also said that he, Balfour, had received an intimation that you approved his coming. Just where he got this word, Wiseman did not know.

Wiseman also said that he read a cable in which they wanted to know whether or not it would be a good time to begin a vigorous propoganda here. At Spring-Rice's suggestion, Wiseman answered this last cable himself and told them it would be a mistake to do anything of the kind.

In discussing the situation with him we agreed that if Balfour was discouraged about coming it would have a bad effect, not only with the Government, but throughout the Empire generally. We thought it would have been better if the suggestion had not come so soon, but having come, it would be well to cordially acquiesce.

We thought it inadvisable to have a visit at this time from any prominent British or French military or naval men. Those that come should do so quietly and be of minor reputation so that their coming would not be heralded. Balfour's visit, we thought, could be interpreted as having to do with trade, blockade and other matters connected with the Foreign Office.

I am afraid it will give offense unless I am able to answer Balfour's cable by tomorrow or next day.

I am glad to tell you that the general impression as to what is being done in both the Army and Navy is one of satisfaction.

Affectionately yours,   E. M. House

TLS (WP, DLC).

From Charles William Eliot

Dear Mr. President: Cambridge, Mass., 8 April 1917.

Now that you have brought the people up to entrance into the war on firm moral grounds, and pledged the country to an effective membership in a durable league to enforce peace, the next immediate problem is the creation of a permanent military and naval force which rests on a solid moral basis, and is easily expansible or reducible.

Voluntary enlistment is urged on individuals in peace times on all sorts of delusive grounds; in war times it soon fails to yield the number of recruits required. The draft by lot or selection leaves the unwilling recruit under the impression that he has been lamentably unlucky—not that he is fulfilling a universal obligation. It is inequitable and in practice immoral.

You have doubtless assented to the General Staff's Bill under the impression that a million men can be got under arms more quickly by that legislation than by any other. Yesterday Mr. Daniel Willard should have received a letter from me in which I tried to demonstrate that legislation copied from the Swiss would produce a large army of trained men sooner than any other method. The Swiss system has also the inestimable advantage of providing every soldier with the only motives that can justify him in committing the ferocious acts which the German methods of carrying on war compel him to perform. Those motives are love of home and country and obedience to his country's equitable law on universal military service.

The Swiss law will provide quickly an American army of any required size with the least possible interference with the national industries, with positive benefit to the schools of the country, and on frugal terms, since the pay of officers and men is nominal only. In these days, it is immoral to hire any man to do such work as soldiers must do.

The army created under the Swiss legislation can be suddenly reduced at will; and every soldier will return to civil life with joy and with no tendency to militarism; but also while in active service every man will have had a substantial moral motive for doing the horrible things he has had to do.

I cannot but hope that for the sake of the whole people, and in the cause of liberty now and in the future, you will soon lead Congress to the legislation which has proved effective in the Swiss Republic to prevent invasion and to increase the vigor and productiveness of the people. I fully realize that you have been surrounded by official military and naval advisers who think the Swiss system inadequate, and that it has been almost inevitable that you should yield at first to their professional views. They naturally desire and advocate a professional standing army. During the discussions in Congress may you not have opportunity to state the moral and educational value of the Swiss system, and its complete fulfillment of all legitimate American purposes or objects now and for the next ten years? I am, with the highest regard, Sincerely yours Charles W. Eliot

TLS (WP, DLC).

From Brand Whitlock

Beaurivage Ouchy, April 8, 1917.

I have just read your noble message with the emotion, the pride and the solemn joy it must inspire in every lover of democracy. Stop. It takes its place at once among the classic charters of human liberty . Brand Whitlock.

T telegram (WP, DLC).

To Edward Mandell House

Dear House, The White House. 9 April, 1917.

I fear from your letter of yesterday, just received, that a letter of mine to you must have miscarried. In it I said that of course we must say to Balfour's Private Secretary that he and his associates would be welcome. We have conveyed that intimation already to Page, in reply to a cable of his to the same effect.

There is a French commission (apparently only of compliment), headed by Viviani,[1] Joffre[2] et al., who are also coming!

In haste, Affectionately, W.W

WWTLI (E. M. House Papers, CtY).
    [1] René Viviani; veteran Socialist politician; Premier, 1914-1915; at this time Minister of Justice and Keeper of the Seals.
    [2] Marshal Joseph-Jacques Césaire Joffre, former commander in chief of the French armies on the western front.

To Carter Glass

My dear Glass: [The White House] 9 April, 1917

I beg that you will not think of enlisting in the Army.[1] You are one of the men I shall most depend upon to keep the counsels of the country steady and the Congress efficient in the performance of its fundamental and all-important duties. Surely, you are just as much serving the colors there as you could be in the ranks of the Army. We are mobilizing the nation as well as creating an Army, and that means that we must keep every instrumentality in it at its highest pitch of efficiency and guided by thoughtful intelligence. In my own view, it is clearly your duty to stay where you are.[2]

In haste, with warm regard and admiration,

Faithfully yours,   Woodrow Wilson

TLS (Letterpress Books, WP, DLC).
[1] See C. Glass to WW, April 6, 1917, Vol. 41.
[2] Wilson wrote similar letters to all congressmen and senators who said that they intended or desired to enlist in the armed services. E.g., WW to J. T. Heflin, April 9, 1917; to Pat Harrison, April 9, 1917; to J. M. Evans, April 9, 1917; to Clement Brumbaugh, April 9, 1917; to M. M. Neely, April 9, 1917; to D. V. Stephens, April 9, 1917; to J. N. Garner, April 9, 1917; to H. T. Rainey, April 10, 1917; and to Dudley Doolittle, April 10, 1917, all TLS (Letterpress Books, WP, DLC).

To Macmillan and Company

My dear Sirs: [The White House] 9 April, 1917

I certainly owe you an apology for not having replied sooner to your request conveyed on behalf of Sir T.[1] Tagore that he have my permission to dedicate his book to me, the book of which you were kind enough to send me the proofs.

Will you not express to Sir R. Tagore my warm appreciation of the motives which prompted him to make this request and my regret that it seems unwise for me to comply with it, not because of any lack of sympathy on my part for the principles which he so eloquently supports in his book, but because just now I have to take all sorts of international considerations into my thought and must err if I err at all on the side of tact and prudence?

Very sincerely yours,   Woodrow Wilson

TLS (Letterpress Books, WP, DLC).
[1] Wilson dictated "R."

To Agnes Thomas Olney

[The White House] 9 April, 1917

I am sure that I am expressing the opinion of the whole country when I express to you my heartfelt grief at the death of your distinguished husband.[1] I had relied upon him for counsel and the whole nation honored his wisdom and patriotism in affairs. A great citizen has passed away.   Woodrow Wilson

T telegram (Letterpress Books, WP, DLC).
[1] Richard Olney had died on April 8.

From Edward Mandell House, with Enclosure

Dear Governor: New York. April 9, 1917.

Upon receipt of your letter this morning I got the cable off to Balfour.

The enclosed copy of cable is one received by the Evening Mail. This man Odell[1] is close to the Germans and it seems significant that he should send such a message. Would you advise my getting Rumely[2] to ask for something more specific?
                    Affectionately yours,   E. M. House

TLS (WP, DLC).
[1] George Talbot Odell, Berlin correspondent of the New York *Evening Mail.*
[2] Edward Aloysius Rumely, publisher of the New York *Evening Mail.*

E N C L O S U R E

Copenhagen, April 7, 1917.

Odell says it is important to see Colonel House. His presence at the Hague is desirable.   Egan.

T telegram (WP, DLC).

From Albert Sidney Burleson

My dear Mr. President: Washington April 9, 1917.

Referring to your note[1] returning my letter addressed to Senator Culberson and the other matter accompanying it which I submitted to you, allow me to say that the changes which you suggest and the proposed amendment to the Espionage Bill are entirely satisfactory to me. I feel sure that this amendment in the form which meets your approval will accomplish the purposes in view.

I am,   Faithfully yours,   A. S. Burleson

TLS (WP, DLC).

¹ Wilson's "note" is missing in both WP, DLC, and in the Burleson Papers, DLC. No evidence in congressional documents or the newspapers sheds any light on Wilson's suggested changes and proposed amendment. The exchange between Daniels and Wilson of April 11-12 would seem to indicate that Wilson's proposed amendment did not relate to censorship.

From the Diary of Josephus Daniels

1917 Monday 9 April

5 p.m. Saw the President—decided to approve the site of armor plate factory recommended by the Board—Charleston, W Va.

Named the 5 battle-cruisers after famous ships of early era.

Talked about censorship. He will appoint George Creel as head.

Talked about Com. of Munitions—would Baruch do? Yes, I said. He is somewhat vain. President: Did you ever see a Jew who was not? Told story about North Carolina—how he would bury Benedict Arnold

Bound diary (J. Daniels Papers, DLC).

From the Diary of Thomas W. Brahany

Monday, April 9, 1917

A quiet day at the office. Plenty of correspondence, but few callers. The President talked with Representative Dent,¹ chairman of the committee on military affairs. The Austrian Charge d'Affaires, Baron Zwiedinek, called at the State Department this morning and asked for passports for himself and the Embassy Staff. J. M. Nye,² one of our Secret Service men, called to see Baron Zwiedinck this afternoon and told him he was instructed by the State Department to make all necessary arrangements to insure the safe departure of the Austrian Embassy Staff. The Baron thanked him and said he would let him know if any special protection was desired. At present there seemed to be no need of the precaution for safety suggested by Nye. "They all seem to be very sad that they have to leave this country," Nye told me. There seems to be no bitter feeling in this country toward Austria. When the German Ambassador left Washington, Nye had a big force of special agents for protection purposes. Among the cablegrams received today was the following from Paris: "I respectfully salute the champion of the liberty of humanity and the world. Marquis de Lafayette." This is a free translation of the cablegram.³

1 Stanley Hubert Dent, Jr., Democrat of Alabama.
2 Joseph M. Nye.
3 Marquis de Lafayette to WW, April 8, 1917, T translation of telegram (SDR, RG 59, 763.72/3757½, DNA). This State Department translation reads as follows: "I respectfully salute the chamipon [champion] of individual and world wide liberty." Wilson replied as follows: "Your message is doubly gratifying coming from one of the illustrious race revered and honored by all liberty-loving Americans." WW to the Marquis de Lafayette, April 12, 1917, T telegram (SDR, RG 59, 763.72/3757½, DNA).

To Edward Mandell House

The White House April 10 1917

Yours of yesterday received I would certainly ask for something more specific   Woodrow Wilson

T telegram (E. M. House Papers, CtY).

To Robert Lansing

My dear Mr. Secretary,   The White House. 10 April, 1917.

The recent debates on the war resolution in Congress lead to [*sic*] me to suggest that you send the following confidential message to Ambassador Page in London:

Take an early opportunity in conversation with the Prime Minister to convey to him in the most confidential manner the information that the only circumstance which seems now to stand in the way of an absolutely cordial cooperation with Great Britain by practically all Americans who are not influenced by ties of blood directly associating them with Germany is the failure so far to find a satisfactory method of self-government for Ireland. This appeared very strikingly in the recent debates in Congress upon the war resolution and appeared in the speeches of opponents of that resolution who were not themselves Irishmen or representatives of constituencies in which Irish voters were influential, notably several members from the South. If the people of the United States could feel that there was an early prospect of the establishment for Ireland of substantial self-government a very great element of satisfaction and enthusiasm would be added to the cooperation now about to be organized between this country and Great Britain. Convey this information unofficially of course but as having no little significance. Successful action now would absolutely divorce our citizens of Irish birth and sympathy from the German sympathizers here with whom many of them have been inclined to make common cause.[1]

Page now knows the Prime Minister well enough to know how to say these things to him frankly, and if a way could be found now to grant Ireland what she has so often been promised, it would be felt that the real programme of government by the consent of the governed had been adopted everywhere in the anti-Prussian world.   Faithfully Yours,   W.W.

WWTLI (SDR, RG 59, 841D.oo/103½, DNA).
 ¹ This was sent as RL to WHP, April 11, 1917, T telegram (SDR, RG 59, 841D.oo/105a, DNA).

From William Gibbs McAdoo, with Enclosure

Dear Mr. President: Washington April 10, 1917.

The Ways and Means Committee of the House will meet this afternoon to consider the bond bill. Mr. Kitchin has returned and I think it very important that you should write him a letter this morning, urging the importance of the prompt passage of this measure. I enclose copy of a brief statement I gave out to the press last night, which may be of service to you in this connection. I hope you will communicate with Mr. Kitchin immediately.   Cordially yours,   W G McAdoo

TLS (WP, DLC).

E N C L O S U R E

Secretary McAdoo said: Washington, D. C., April 9, 1917.

The Administration will ask Congress for authority to issue $5,000,000,000 of Government bonds to meet the situation created by the war with Germany. The proposed bonds will be exempt from taxation and bear interest probably at three and one-half (3½) per centum per annum. Two billion dollars of these bonds will be required to finance, in part, the expenditures involved in the proper organization and operation of the army and navy and the conduct of the war generally. Of course, a large amount of additional revenue will have to be raised by taxation, but this part of the problem is under consideration by the Ways and Means Committee of the House of Representatives. It will naturally take a reasonable time to discuss and agree upon the new items for taxation, which should not and, I am confident, will not become the subject of partisan treatment.

Three billion dollars of the proposed issue of bonds should be used to supply credit to the Governments making common cause with us against Germany to enable them to secure essential supplies in the United States and carry on the war with increased effect. The most serviceable thing we can do immediately for the common cause is to furnish credit to these foreign Governments who, in conjunction with us, are fighting Germany. This financial aid ought to be extended at the earliest possible moment. It will be trebly valuable and effective if extended now.

The purpose is to purchase the obligations of the foreign Governments to which credit is given—such obligations to bear the same rate of interest and, in other essentials, to contain the same terms and conditions as the bonds of the United States.

The bonds of the United States will be offered as a great popular loan and the widest opportunity will be given to the public to subscribe, and, by subscribing, to perform one of the most patriotic services that can be rendered to the country at this time.

In view of the fact that the laws of the United States forbid the payment of commissions on sales of Government bonds, it is extremely gratifying to have received so many offers from bankers and others throughout the country, of the free use of their services and facilities in making the proposed bond issue a success. It is the purpose of the Department to make use of these offers and to seek the assistance of the Federal Reserve Banks, the National banks, the State banks and trust companies, the savings banks, insurance companies, private bankers and investment bankers throughout the country in the public offering that will be made of the Government's bonds. Every governmental agency, such as the Internal Revenue offices and post-offices, will be asked to assist in this patriotic work.

When the Congress shall have granted the necessary authority to make public offer of the bonds, I shall take the benefit of the counsel of the most experienced bankers and investors in the country as to the best means of making the offering a pronounced success.

The wealth of the United States is so great, the investment resources of the country are so large, the strength of our banking situation is so phenomenal, and the patriotism of our people is so aroused, that I am confident that when the Government offers its bonds for public subscription, the amount will be overwhelmingly subscribed.

So many offers have been received from bankers, organizations and individuals tendering their services and facilities to the Government free of expense in placing the bonds at the disposal of the public, that it has been absolutely impossible for me to make personal acknowledgment and express my deep appreciation and gratification at this genuine manifestation of patriotic interest in the efforts to finance the war. So I am asking the newspapers of the country to indulge me to the extent of advising the senders of the many telegrams and letters which have poured into the Department of the Government's appreciation of the loyal impulse and splendid spirit which inspired them.

Mimeographed MS (WP, DLC).

Two Letters to Claude Kitchin

My dear Mr. Kitchin: [The White House] 10 April, 1917

I cannot send you the accompanying official letter without writing you a line of deep and sincere sympathy upon the death of your brother.[1] The news was very tardy in reaching me that you had suffered this bereavement, and I want you to know how sincerely my sympathy goes out to you in this trial.

Cordially and sincerely yours,   [Woodrow Wilson]

[1] Samuel Boaz Kitchin, farmer and proprietor of a lumber company in Scotland Neck, N. C., who had died on April 6, 1917.

My dear Mr. Kitchin: [The White House] 10 April, 1917

I have been in constant consultation with the Secretary of the Treasury with regard to the suggestions he has made to the Committee of Ways and Means about the financial legislation necessary for the conduct of the war and concerning the methods of raising the necessary funds, and write you this line to say that those suggestions have my entire approval.

May I express the hope that the Committee may accept these suggestions in substance as embodying the best thought of the administration, and that it may be able to present this legislation at an early date to the Congress?

Cordially and respectfully yours,   [Woodrow Wilson]

CCL (WP, DLC).

From Josephus Daniels

Dear Mr. President: Washington. Apr. 10. 1917.

I am enclosing you two statements, prepared in the division of Operations bearing upon the interned ships and refugee ships, suggesting a policy and method of carrying it into execution, for your consideration.[1] I thought you would wish this before the meeting of the cabinet.

Sincerely yours,   Josephus Daniels

ALS (WP, DLC).
   [1] Two T MS dated April 8, 1917 (WP, DLC). The first provided a carefully argued rationale for its conclusions: (1) that German naval vessels now in American ports should be made prizes of war and their officers and crews interned as prisoners of war; (2) that German merchant vessels in American ports should be seized and used in the American war effort; and (3) that their private owners should have their property rights protected by appropriate legislation. The second statement argued that the German merchant vessels, when seized, should be repaired, armed, and manned by the United States Navy as naval auxiliary vessels so that they might better be able to carry out their mission to get supplies across the ocean in the face of enemy attack.

From Robert Lansing

My dear Mr. President: Washington April 10, 1917.

In your note of April 8th you asked me whether the requisition of German ships for transportation uses or the seizure of such ships by way of reprisal requires authorization by Congress. In reply, I should say that both requisition and reprisal, in the circumstances, require action by Congress.

Reprisal is a well-established method in international practice by which one nation obtains redress for injuries inflicted by another nation when other means of satisfaction have failed. A reprisal in the nature of seizure of property may amount to, and in this case I assume that it is desired that it should amount to, confiscation of the property in question. The confiscation of enemy private property within the jurisdiction of the United States at or after the outbreak of war has been in several cases held by the Supreme Court of the United States to be contrary to "the modern usage of nations which has become law." As this usage of nations has thus been declared to be the law in the United States, it is necessary to have Congress authorize the confiscation. That such confiscatory acts by Congress are necessary is shown by the history of the United States in the War of Independence and the Civil War, when special acts of confiscation were passed—the Acts of August 6, 1861, July 17, 1862, the Joint Resolution of same date, and the Act of March 3, 1863. Moreover, the Constitution delegates to the Congress the power to make rules concerning "captures on land and water," and power to grant letters of marque and reprisal. It was the opinion of Jefferson, Clay, and Gallatin that an act of Congress was necessary to vest in the President authority for making reprisals.

As to requisitions of private property, I find no case in which, as commander-in-chief, the President has requisitioned property of the enemy within United States territory. Many cases of requisitions of goods for the use of American forces have occurred, of course, but these have been within territory occupied by the army in the Mexican and Civil Wars. The right of requisition under military occupation is, I take it, different from the right of requisition of goods in the United States for commercial purposes in time of war. In the Mexican and Civil Wars, goods were requisitioned without an Act of Congress by order of the President as commander-in-chief, but receipts for the goods taken or money payments were generally made, though the right was asserted that requisition might be made without compensation. The Supreme Court of the United States has held in cases coming before it that compensation must be made for taking private property by the armed forces during military occupation. There appear to be on the books no statutes giving the President direct authority to requisition enemy property, and I am of the opinion that such authority by Congress in the circumstances is necessary.

I have turned over to the War Trade Committee[1] the task of drafting an appropriate act to cover the seizure of German and Austrian ships, by way of reprisal, ship for ship for the American ships sunk, and for purposes of requisitioning the remaining ships.　　　　Faithfully yours,　Robert Lansing.

TLS (WP, DLC).
[1] An advisory group composed of representatives of the State, Justice, and Commerce departments.

From Edward Mandell House

Dear Governor:　　　　　　　　New York. April 10, 1917.

Your telegram has just come. It seems risky asking the Mail to get further information through the open cable; therefore, I am asking the State Department to have Egan find if there is anything in it.

Egan seems indiscreet in sending such cables in the open to, what is considered, a German paper.

I am glad you saw Roosevelt.[1] I hope you will send for Lodge also. It looks as if you would have to depend largely upon republican support to carry through your war measures. Did you see the admirable speech that Root made last night at the Republican Club?[2]

The English and French are very worried over the Russian situation and with cause. Some distinguished Frenchmen[3] asked me today to suggest to you the sending of an American commission to Russia at once. They think it important that Russia be told authoritatively that if they are to have the good will and financial support of this country, they must compose their internal differences and not make a separate peace at this time. These men thought that a prominent Jew, a business man, a labor leader and an educator should compose the commission.

If you think well of this, how would Oscar Straus, Willard Straight, Gompers and Benj. Ide Wheeler do? It seems to me to be good policy at this time to give republicans a voice in these ways since they are not represented in the government.

Affectionately yours,   E. M. House

P.S. I saw Whitehouse again today. He is wondering whether you will see him for a minute. His idea is that if he goes back to England without at least having seen you, it will make a bad impression and lessen his influence. He does not leave until Tuesday of next week.

TLS (WP, DLC).
[1] Theodore Roosevelt called upon Wilson at the White House at noon on April 10. The extract from the diary of Thomas W. Brahany, printed as the next document, well conveys both the tone of the meeting and the topics discussed. Other accounts of the meeting, which conflict somewhat in detail but really add little to Brahany's discussion, include those in the *New York Times*, April 11, 1917; John J. Leary , Jr., *Talks with T.R.* (Boston and New York, 1920), pp. 95-98; and Joseph P. Tumulty, *Woodrow Wilson as I Know Him* (Garden City, N. Y., 1921), pp. 285-86.
The only other account of the meeting which, if accurate, adds significant details is T. Roosevelt to John Callan O'Laughlin, April 13, 1917, printed in Elting E. Morison *et al.*, eds., *The Letters of Theodore Roosevelt* (8 vols., Cambridge, Mass., 1951-54), VIII, 1173-74. In this letter, Roosevelt described the meeting as follows: "I put before the President my proposals and the reasons therefor, substantially as I have put them in public. He evidently felt pleased that I was going to support his bill [for a selective-service draft] and·to ask for action supplementary to it, and not contradictory to it. He suddenly entered into a defense of his past conduct, saying that he had for a long time felt what he now said in his speech to Congress, but that the American people were not awake to the need, and that he had to bide his time; and he added that many people had misunderstood him (hastily interpolating, with obvious insincerity, that he did not mean me). I answered in substance, and almost in words, as follows: 'Mr. President, what I have said and thought, and what others have said and thought, is all dust in a windy street, if now we can make your message good. Of course, it amounts to nothing, if we cannot make it good. But, if we can translate it into fact, then it will rank as a great state paper, with the great state papers of Washington and Lincoln. Now, all that I ask is that I be allowed to do all that in me is to help make good this speech of yours—to help get the nation to act, so as to justify and live up to the speech, and the declaration of war that followed.' I added that I felt that the situation was as if Jefferson, after the *Leopard* attacked *Chesapeake*, had gone to war with Great Britain, in which case it would have been Light-Horse Harry Lee's duty instantly to support to the best of his power and ability such action; and that I wished to act toward him as in such case I would have felt it the duty of Light-Horse Harry Lee to act toward Jefferson."

2 Elihu Root had spoken to a large meeting at the Republican Club of New York on April 9. He declared that it was the duty of all Republicans to stand squarely behind the President in the present war, no matter what mistakes might be made or how much the party in power was criticized. He said that a coalition cabinet was not necessary but did urge vigorous prosecution of the war and the sending of an American army, "great if possible and small if it must be," to Europe as a tangible sign of American support of the Allies. Extensive extracts from Root's speech are printed in the *New York Times*, April 10, 1917.

3 Stéphane Joseph Vincent Lauzanne and Marcel Knecht. Lauzanne, former editor in chief of the Paris *Matin*, had served in the French army, 1914-1915, and had come to the United States in October 1916 to head an information office sponsored by the French government. Knecht, an Alsatian, was his assistant.

From the Diary of Thomas W. Brahany

Tuesday, April 10, 1917

The President and Mrs. Wilson played golf this morning. At noon the President received Col. Theodore Roosevelt. As far as I know they had never met before.[1] Col. Roosevelt wishes to raise a division for service in France and his White House call was made to lay his plans before the President. The President and the former President met in the Green Room, Col. Roosevelt being presented to the President by I. H. Hoover, Chief Usher. The President doesn't like Theodore Roosevelt and he was not one bit effusive in his greeting. This did not disconcert the Colonel who in his usual vigorous manner proceeded to outline his plans; but first he commended in the warmest terms the President's message to Congress and gave his entire approval to the administration's program for the raising of an army by selective conscription. The interview lasted twenty-five minutes and before it closed the President had thawed out and was laughing and "talking back." They had a real good visit. On taking leave of the President, the Colonel said he wished to go to the Executive Office to see Tumulty with a view to having him arrange a meeting with Mr. Underwood and several other members of the Council of National Defense. "No," said the President, "You make yourself comfortable here and I'll have Tumulty come over from the office." Tumulty went over at once. All the White House men who served under Theodore Roosevelt have the greatest admiration for him. Forster worships him. He was a hard taskmaster—long hours and driving work—but he was so appreciative of good work and so explosively generous and personal in his compliments that his force from messengers to secretaries enjoyed their long hours and hard work. Today he spoke of the fine service Hoover had given him and his family, and he took occasion to say this where it would do Hoover good, viz, in the presence of the President. When he was leaving he saw Wilson Jackson, a little colored fellow who for many years has been a White House messenger. "Hello Jack," said the Colonel shaking Jackson's hand and patting him on the back. We relaxed the rule today against newspapermen and motion picture men gathering in front of the North entrance. The Colonel was filmed and interviewed to his heart's content.

Cabinet meeting this afternoon. All members present.

1 Brahany was mistaken. Wilson and Roosevelt had met on at least five previous occasions. They met in Baltimore on March 4, 1896, when both men spoke at a rally on behalf of municipal reform. See the newspaper report printed at that date in Vol. 9. They met again when Roosevelt lectured in Princeton on January 21, 1897. See the extract from Wilson's diary printed at that date in Vol. 10. Wilson was Roosevelt's guest at Oyster Bay on July 26-27, 1901. See WW to T. Roosevelt, July 28, 1901, Vol. 12. On the fourth occasion, Roosevelt was Wilson's luncheon guest on the occasion of the Army-Navy football game played in Princeton on December 2, 1905. See the news report printed at Dec. 4, 1905, Vol. 16. Finally, Wilson entertained Roosevelt informally at the White House during the afternoon of May 26, 1914. See Head Usher's Diary, T MS (WP, DLC), entry for May 26, 1914.

To George Washington Goethals

My dear General Goethals: The White House 11 April, 1917

Acting under the provisions of Section[s] 5 and 7 of the Shipping Act, I have given my approval to the plan of the United States Shipping Board for the construction of a large emergency wooden fleet to assist in the carriage of supplies and munitions to the Allies and for other services during the war. When this undertaking was conceived, the Board entertained the hope that they might have the use of your directing genius in the marshaling of the resources of the country for the rapid construction of the tonnage required; indeed it was in part upon that hope that they formed the plan. I am informed that they have spoken to you of the plan and that it has received your enthusiastic endorsement and that you indicated to members of the Board that you would be willing to accept in directing the enterprise in cooperation with them. I am writing these lines to express my own personal hope that you will do so. I would be very much obliged if you would kindly get into communication with the Board at your earliest convenience about this, for I think it is one of the most pressing pieces of business connected with the successful prosecution of the war.

I personally would like to see the weight of your connection with this enterprise added to the answer which we will thus be giving to the challenge of the submarine.

Cordially and sincerely yours,   Woodrow Wilson

TLS (G. W. Goethals Papers, DLC).

From Newton Diehl Baker

(CONFIDENTIAL)

Dear Mr. President: Washington. April 11, 1917

I hand you a memorandum made by the War College for your information.[1] Unless you direct otherwise, I shall not take the matter up with the Secretary of State, but will await directions from you in the matter. I have had the feeling that the initial relations of cooperation ought to be worked out through diplomatic channels rather than through military channels and that only after the broad basis of our cooperation is established would it be wise to allow military commissions to consider the subject.

Respectfully yours,   Newton D. Baker

TLS (N. D. Baker Papers, DLC).

[1] Brig. Gen. Joseph E. Kuhn to Maj. Gen. Hugh L. Scott, "Military missions of liaison with belligerent countries," April 10, 1917, TS MS (N. D. Baker Papers, DLC). Kuhn reported that the British government was prepared to send a military mission to the United States and that the American military mission in France had requested additional personnel. Kuhn recommended that these matters be referred to Baker and proposed that Baker ask Lansing to have the American ambassadors in London and Paris ascertain whether the governments there were willing to exchange military missions with the United States.

Three Letters to Newton Diehl Baker

My dear Mr. Secretary,   The White House. 11 April, 1917.

I am glad that you think it wise to go slowly in this matter. We are in danger of creating too much machinery.

If the officers already on the other side are to constitute a chief part of the personnel of such commissions (and they, by the way, are out of touch with conditions on this side the water), why are they not the proper and suitable instruments through which to obtain advice as to what means of communication and information would be most desirable and most immediately practicable between our military authorities and those with whom we are to cooperate. It seems to me much more practical to use the few officers we have in getting troops ready here and creating the materials for cooperation than to send them parlening [parleying] to England anf [and] France. I would like to have a personal talk with you about this.

Faithfully Yours,   W.W.

WWTLI (N. D. Baker Papers, DLC).

My dear Mr. Secretary: The White House 11 April, 1917

Enclosed is the draft of the Executive order which was laid before me at the last Cabinet meeting by the Secretary of State.[1] In looking it over this query occurs to me: Would not the creation of such a committee be apt to cross wires with the present activities of the Advisory Board of the Council of National Safety? I would be very much obliged to you for your reply to that question, and also for your opinion as to the general advisability of creating this extra piece of machinery.

This is the matter that we discussed during the Cabinet meeting yesterday.

Cordially and faithfully yours,   Woodrow Wilson

[1] It is printed as an Enclosure with NDB to WW, April 12, 1917.

My dear Mr. Secretary: The White House 11 April, 1917

The enclosed is indeed impressive and delightful.[1] I thank you for having given me the encouragement of reading it.

Cordially and faithfully yours,   Woodrow Wilson

TLS (N. D. Baker Papers, DLC).
[1] A. J. Hieber to NDB, April 7, 1917, T telegram (N. D. Baker Papers, DLC). On behalf of the German Club of Cleveland, Ohio, Hieber took note of Wilson's statement that the war was against German militarism, not against the German people, and he pledged to the President and Congress the club's loyal support and cooperation.

To William Charles Adamson

My dear Judge: [The White House] 11 April, 1917

It seems to me that this bill as here drawn[1] is entirely in line with our conversation of the other day, and I thank you for it sincerely.

Cordially and faithfully yours,   [Woodrow Wilson]

CCL (WP, DLC).
[1] Confidential committee print, Committee on Interstate and Foreign Commerce, House of Representatives, 65th Cong., 1st sess. The bill, introduced by Adamson on April 13, 1917, as H.R. 2901, enlarged the Interstate Commerce Commission from seven to eleven members, amended some of the I.C.C.'s procedures, and provided penalties for obstructing the mails and interstate or foreign commerce in wartime. The bill also authorized the President to employ the armed forces of the United States to prevent such obstruction and, in various emergencies, to take possession of and operate telephone and telegraph facilities and railroad lines and to draft their officers and employees into the service of the United States.

To Washington Gladden

[The White House]

My dear Doctor Gladden: 11 April, 1917

I am assuming that you will still be in California when this letter has crossed the continent.

I want to tell you how deep my gratification was at receiving your generous letter.[1] It helps me mightily to know that you think of me in the midst of my struggles to do the right thing, and your approval is very dear to me.

Cordially and sincerely yours,   Woodrow Wilson

TLS (Letterpress Books, WP, DLC).
[1] It is missing in both WP, DLC, and the Gladden Papers, OHi.

To Harry Augustus Garfield

My dear Garfield: The White House 11 April, 1917

If I did not heed the advice of your letter of March twenty-eighth,[1] you may be sure it was only because I could not. I hope with all my heart that my address to the Congress has convinced you that I had good reasons and that the course I pursued was not pursued either in haste or in vexation. I should not like to feel that I was going against the judgment of a man whose judgment I so highly and sincerely value.

In haste, with the warmest regard,

Faithfully yours,   Woodrow Wilson

TLS (H. A. Garfield Papers, DLC).
[1] H. A. Garfield to WW, March 28, 1917, Vol. 41.

To Charles William Eliot

My dear Doctor Eliot: The White House 11 April, 1917

I appreciate the force of your argument for the Swiss system and you may be sure that nothing that you have written me has been overlooked. I have simply been obliged to devote so much of my time to public business that it has seemed almost impossible to answer the letters that I receive as well as read them.

If you were here, I think I could make you realize very vividly the elements I am dealing with and the impossibility which exists at present of bringing the Congress to the adoption of any sort of permanent system. When the time does come, if I am here to share in the solution of the question, you may be sure that the weighty arguments you have submitted to me will have my most serious consideration.

In haste, with great regret that I cannot return worthier replies to your letters.

Cordially and sincerely yours,   Woodrow Wilson

TLS (C. W. Eliot Papers, MH-Ar).

To Harry Fielding Reid

My dear Reid: [The White House] 11 April, 1917

Thank you warmly for your letter of April tenth.[1] It renders me not a little uneasy to learn that you are going to venture upon the seas at this time. I wish I knew of some way of adding to your security.

It is generous of you to ask whether there is anything I can suggest that you could do. I am sorry to say that my mind is barren upon that matter at present, but I shall trust to your own knowledge of affairs and of the opportunity to find out the things that will be of greatest service. I am heartily glad that you should be actively associated with the National Research Council.

Please give my warm regards to Mrs. Reid.

It is very lonely sometimes when I must go for so long without seeing my friends, but my absorption just now is so great that fortunately I do not have time to think of my bereavement.

With the best wishes,

Cordially and sincerely yours,   Woodrow Wilson

TLS (Letterpress Books, WP, DLC).
[1] It is missing.

From Robert Lansing, with Enclosure

My dear Mr. President: Washington April 11, 1917.

I call your attention to the enclosed despatch just received from Ambassador Francis. It causes me serious concern. I wish we could do something to prevent the socialistic element in Russia from carrying out any plan which would destroy the efficiency of the Allied Powers.

My suggestion would be that a Commission, say of three men be sent at once to Russia, if agreeable to that Government, and that one of the Commissioners be Samuel Gompers who would have a very decided influence with the labor element in Russia and prevent in a large measure, I believe, the tendency of the socialists toward a separate peace with Germany.

From despatches we have received, as you know, the German socialists are seeking to meet the Russian socialists, undoubtedly for the purpose of influencing them to support a separate peace between Germany and Russia.

Faithfully yours,   Robert Lansing

TLS (SDR, RG 59, 763.72/3771, DNA).

ENCLOSURE

Petrograd, April 10, 1917.

1169. Naval attache cables his Department 13010 (*): I hear authoritatively that naval conditions precarious, military not wholly satisfactory. Social circles urging peace and fears are entertained by some that army will be influenced thereby. Desirable that everything possible be promptly done to strengthen situation.   Francis.

* April 10, 1 p.m.

T telegram (SDR, RG 59, 763.72/3771, DNA).

From Robert Lansing, with Enclosure

My dear Mr. President: Washington April 11, 1917.

I call your attention to the disquieting telegram of the 10th from Mr. Fletcher. If there is an attempt to prevent the shipment of oil from Tampico I see no way but to occupy the territory with troops or else to allow the British naval forces to do so, even though it would be a technical violation of the Monroe Doctrine.

Might I suggest that a definite policy be determined upon at once in the event of Mexico's imposing an embargo so that tentative plans could be made to prevent a serious disaster? I think that both Secretary Baker and Secretary Daniels should be consulted. I have already shown Fletcher's telegram to Baker.

Faithfully yours,   Robert Lansing.

TLS (SDR, RG 59, 600.129/7, DNA).

ENCLOSURE

Mexico, April 10, 1917.

74. It is rumored that the Mexican Government is contemplating prohibiting exportations of articles of first necessity includ-

ing petroleum and there are leading editorials in the PUEBLO, the Government organ, and the EXCELSIOR today which seem to indicate that a move of this sort is under consideration. Some fear that the Mexican Government may put into effect the idea suggested by Carranza in his peace note of February eleventh forbidding exports to belligerents.   Fletcher.

T telegram (SDR, RG 59, 600.129/7, DNA).

To Robert Lansing

My dear Mr. Secretary,   The White House. 11 April, 1917.

Unfortunately, the Mexican government has, no doubt, a legal right to prohibit exports; and I feel quite clear that we could not make such action on its part a justification for invasion and (virtual) war.

On the other hand, the property in the oil fields at Tampico is largely, I understand, the property of British subjects. I have also understood that the military commander there[1] (whose connection with either Carranza or Villa is shawody [shadowy] and hard to trace) is probably subsidized by the British owners. We have more than once allowed European governments to oblige Latin American governments to meet their financial obligations by a show of force, without deeming their action a violation of the Monroe Doctrine, because it involved no attempt at political control. The violation of British rights at Tampico might, on the same principle, without any disrespect to us, be prevented by a show of naval force on the part of the British government. In this instance, in view of the circumstances of the war, such action on their part would seem to be justified by necessity if not by the consideration that such a policy as they would be seeking to prevent on the part of the Mexican authorities, not being justified by the economic necessities of Mexico, would seem to be directed against Great Britain in hostile spirit.

I hope that you will communicate the circumstances to the British government, through the most direct channel available, and intimate to them that we would feel justified in leaving them free to take the necessary steps to safeguard their indispensable sources of oil supply against inimical action by the Mexicans.[2]

Faithfully Yours,   W.W.

WWTLI (SDR, RG 59, 600.129/12½, DNA).
  [1] That is, Manuel Peláez.
  [2] It was reported from Washington on April 12 that the Mexican government would place no embargo on the exportation of oil by the British from the Tampico oil district. The report added that the State Department had received definite

assurance that there would be no interference with the oil industry, and that the Royal Navy would continue to receive its oil supplies from Mexico. Alberto J. Pani, Minister of Commerce and Industry, gave official notification to this effect on April 13. *New York Times*, April 13 and 14, 1917.

From Josephus Daniels, with Enclosure

Dear Mr. President: Washington. April 11, 1917.

I am enclosing herewith two drafts of a censorship bill, the main provisions of which were drawn up at the Army War College.[1] I think the one you decide upon should be introduced early.

After our conversation about appointing George Creel as Chief of Publicity, with an army and military assistant, I wrote him and he will be over to-day. His ideas are summed up in the enclosed memorandum. Inasmuch as the work to be done will accelerate enlistment I hope you will feel that the appointment should be made to-day.   Sincerely,   Josephus Daniels

I will thank you to return enclosures unless you wish to keep them.   JD

ALS (J. Daniel Papers, DLC).
    [1] T MSS, n.d. (J. Daniels Papers, DLC). Both drafts authorized the President, in time of war, to issue a proclamation prohibiting publication of information about the armed forces and defense measures, except when duly authorized, and to issue implementing regulations. Both drafts also provided penalties for unauthorized publication and empowered the President to revoke the proclamation when it was no longer needed. One of the drafts also specified that nothing in the proposed act should limit "discussion, comment or criticism of the acts or policies of the government or its representatives," so long as this discussion did not convey information prohibited in the act.

E N C L O S U R E

A Memorandum by George Creel

Department of Publicity.

1. Censorship is a word to be avoided. It is offensive to Americans, and likewise misleading. While there is much that is properly secret, the total is small compared to the vast amount of information that it is right and necessary for the people to have. The *suppressive* features of the work must be so overlaid by the publicity policy that they will go unregarded and unresented. Administration activities must be dramatized and staged, and every energy exerted to arouse ardor and enthusiasm. Recruiting can be stimulated and public confidence gained; extortion can be exposed and praise given to the patriotism that abates

its profits; and in the rush of generous feeling much that is evil and nagging will disappear.

2. The Department must have a single civilian head. A military management suggests the censorship we are trying to avoid. Also, since the work is to cover every governmental department, no single department should have control of it.

3. Navy, Army and State should each assign a representative to the Department of Publicity. With the civilian head, they would constitute the board of censors.

4. A small, carefully picked force of newspaper men must be gathered together. Not only will they prepare for publication the matter presented by Army, Navy and State, but it will also be a daily task to visit Agriculture, Labor, Commerce, Interior, Treasury and Justice to "*get the news*," to develop "stories," and to aid the Department in an expert way to put the best foot forward.

5. The civilian head should form the famous writers of the country into a committee. I have fifty promises already. Each man will be asked to consider some phase of governmental activity, the signed articles to be placed in certain magazines, or else syndicated for free publication.

6. Only a Washington office is necessary. I would insist upon small salaries. Not only do we want to get the idea of patriotic service, but small pay would discourage the "political" hack.

7. Branch offices are not needed. There must be no attempt to pass upon everything that is written for papers and periodicals. The law and its penalties are plain. Matter that the authors consider within the meaning of the law will be sent in to the Publicity Department for approval. Either that, or they must be prepared to take the chance of punishment. Through Washington contact with the press associations, news agencies and bureaus, cables, wireless, etc., the great news channels are guarded.

8. Either through letters, or, better still, by personal explanation to groups and associations, the general policy of the Publicity Department can be made clear. I am convinced that the policy outlined, when made clear, will elicit a tremendous response, and that space devoted now to "knocking" will be given over to "boosting."

9. If, by reason of partisanship or prejudice, vicious attacks continue, they may be handled easily without exercise of despotic power. Such articles will be ordered sent in to the Department of Publicity in advance of publication, and all assertions and attacks will be checked up. If criticism is honest, delay will be requested pending efforts at rectification. If dishonest, the error

will be pointed out. In this manner, I feel that we can end the whole ugly business of lying, malicious nagging.

10. The whole spirit of the Bureau of Publicity must be one of absolute co-operation. It must go upon the assumption that the press is eager and willing to do the handsome thing, and its attitude must be one of frankness, friendship and entire openness.

T MS (J. Daniels Papers, DLC).

From Stephen Samuel Wise

My dear Mr. President: New York City, April 11, 1917.

I am moved by your message of April 2nd to the Congress and the American people to point out what of course you clearly understand—how regrettable it is that there should be any element of discord among the American people, which makes impossible a unanimous support of our Government in its decision on behalf of the American people to co-operate with the Allied Peoples. I have in mind the altogether explicable attitude of those elements of the American population, which cannot reconcile the British championship of democracy the world over with the facts that obtain touching the denial of self-government to the Irish people. I venture to ask the question whether this were not an opportune time to appeal in such a way as may commend itself to you to the British Government to do that which the best thought of the Britain [British] has long been prepared to do,—namely, to accord home rule to the Irish people. Such an act at this time on the part of Great Britain would not merely answer the question touching Britain's right to stand out as the champion of smaller and oppressed nationalities, would not only end disaffection among the Irish people as well as compose the unrest which obtains among the Irish elements of the American people, but would, like the self-liberation of Russia, justify anew the position taken by you on behalf of our country, that we are battling for the freedom and democracy of the peoples of earth.

Have we not by our entry into the war, not for profit and not for conquest, but in order to serve and to liberate, have we not earned the right to speak in the terms of understanding and comradeship to the heads of the British Government? Has not the recent action of the Cuban Government shown forth how true it is that "nobleness enkindleth nobleness,"[1] and that an act of justice on the part of the British Government at this time, though unhappily belated, would give a new meaning and a new dignity to the warfare of the Allied Peoples, including our own, for the liberation of those peoples whose freedom is yet to be achieved.

Is it not true that the leadership of the British Government is such as to offer every reason for confidence that it will be prepared to solve this problem in the spirit of statesmanship and magnanimity, knowing that no sacrifice is too great to be made upon the altar of national unity and to the end of regaining the complete loyalty of a great and long-wronged people?

All men know how deeply you are concerned with the hope of freedom for the lesser peoples, how real is your passion for freedom for all nations. You have led the way with such high wisdom that you have earned, as no man of our day and generation, the right to set forth, in the terms of friendship to an allied nation, the wisdom and rightfulness of an act which would do more than aught else to unite the peoples of Great Britain and all the groupings of the American people in an irresistible struggle for the precious things of democracy and self-determination.

I belong to a people, who, for centuries, have known the meaning and burden of this struggle. Every liberty-loving and liberty-seeking people has a peculiar place in the sympathy of my own people, which hail with unique joy your message to the Congress of the United States, destined to become a Magna Charta for all the peoples and races of earth.

Faithfully yours,   Stephen S. Wise

TLS (WP, DLC).

1 Wise referred to Cuba's declaration of war against Germany on April 7.

Edward William Pou to Joseph Patrick Tumulty

Dear Mr. Tumulty: Washington April 11, 1917.

For the last two days I have made a sort of canvass of the members of the House with respect to the proposed Conscription Act.

The sentiment is overwhelmingly in favor of giving the boys a chance to volunteer first.

If an attempt is made to put through a bill providing for Conscription without affording opportunity to volunteer such attempt would, in my judgment, provoke a bitter fight on the floor with the result in doubt.

The influence of the President is so powerful and the confidence of his supporters so absolute he can get almost any thing he asks, but I should hate to see issue raised upon the proposition of immediate Conscription.

I have discussed the matter with members of the Committee on Rules. I think a majority is opposed. I have felt so deeply concerned that I venture to volunteer this letter for whatever it may be worth from one who has consistantly supported the President.

Sincerely your friend,   Edward W. Pou.

TCL (WP, DLC).

To Josephus Daniels

My dear Mr. Secretary,   The White House. 12 April, 1917.

I prefer the No. 1 of these bills, but think that section 3 of No. 2[1] should be inserted between sections two and three of No. 1.

Do I understand that I now have the authority to designate Creel? If so, I shall be glad to do so. I like his memorandum very much.

Would it not be well for him to associate with him in counsel as much as possible such men as Frederick Palmer, who have been abroad and seen the machine work on the other side of the water?   Faithfully Yours,   W.W.

WWTLI (J. Daniels Papers, DLC).
[1] Section 3 of the second draft, which provided that nothing in the proposed act should limit discussion or criticism of governmental acts or policies so long as this did not disclose information prohibited in the act.

Three Letters to Robert Lansing

My dear Mr. Secretary,   The White House. 12 April, 1917.

The suggestion of a commission to Russia has come to me from a number of querters [quarters] and I am inclined to think that it would be a good plan to send one, and send it practically at once.

The important, perhaps the all-important thing is the personnel. Men of large view, tested discretion, and a sympathetic appreciation of just what it is they have been sent over for are the sort we need; and it is necessary, besides, that they should *look* the part?

House has suggested a prominent Jew (Oscar Strauss), a business man (Willard Straight), a labor leader (Samuel Gompers), and an educator (Benjamin Ide Wheeler). What do you think, and whom would you suggest? Wheeler has always seemed to me a bit too ladylike. Crane has already gone to Russia and ought to be over there by this time, if his ship has escaped the submarines. Professor Harper of Chicago is widely known and trusted in Russia.

We must find the right men, and they must not all be Democrats,—need not any of them be Democrats,—but should be all genuinely enthusiastic for the success of the Russian revolution.

Faithfully Yours,   W.W.

WWTLI (SDR, RG 59, 763.72/3800½, DNA).

My dear Mr. Secretary,   The White House. 12 April, 1917.

I am inclined to think that it would be well to go forward with the Pan-American treaty at this time, as Brazil suggests.[1] It might turn out to be the psychological moment, and the treaty might serve in part to show the European peoples a way to secure peace when this war is over.

I say this tentatively, awaiting an expression of your own view. It would, I dare say, be wise, in case we should decide to go ahead, to consult with leading members of the Committee on Foreign Relations of both parties.

Faithfully Yours,   W.W.

WWTLI (R. Lansing Papers, DLC).
  [1] See RL to WW, April 8, 1917 (first letter of that date).

My dear Mr. Secretary,   The White House. 12 April, 1917.

I want you to read the enclosed most interesting letter.[1] After you have read it will you not be kind enough to hand it to the Secretary of War, for the suggestion about the Polish Falconers?

Faithfully Yours,   W.W.

WWTLI (N. D. Baker Papers, DLC).
  [1] G. J. Sosnowski to WW, April 7, 1917.

To Stephen Samuel Wise

Personal.

My dear Rabbi Wise: [The White House] 12 April, 1917

You may be sure that, though I have only time for a line in reply to it, I deeply appreciated your letter of April eleventh and that I share the thought that you express in it. It may be that I can find some diplomatic and suggestive way of putting the idea into the minds of those across the water.

I was sincerely sorry not to be able to see you when you were here. These are days when I do not and cannot choose my engagements.

Cordially and sincerely yours,   [Woodrow Wilson]

CCL (WP, DLC).

To Edward Mandell House

The White House. April 12, 1917.

Shall be very glad to see Whitehouse at two Saturday. Brazil is pressing for an immediate signing of our Pan American treaty by us and as many of the Latin American States as will be willing to come in at this time. What do you think?

Woodrow Wilson.

T decode of T telegram (E. M. House Papers, CtY).

From Robert Lansing

My dear Mr. President: Washington April 12, 1917.

I have your note of today in relation to the suggested Russian Commission and have been thinking over the personnel of such Commission. I think we may agree that Samuel Gompers is as available a man as we could get. In regard to Oscar Straus I should doubt very much the advisability of sending another Jew and I believe there is a measure of danger in overplaying the Jew element. I do not think Willard Straight is the man at all for the place and I doubt very much from my acquaintance with Dr. Wheeler whether he would be suitable.

I should think we ought to have, in addition to a labor leader, such a man as Doctor John R. Mott; a businessman like Cyrus McCormick or Howard Elliott;[1] a financier like Bertrand;[2] and a lawyer of prominence.

In regard to Professor Harper of Chicago, I have heard from several different sources that he is not as popular as I had supposed in Russia. I am therefore afraid to advise his selection. Of course I assume Mr. Crane would be joined to any Commission that might be sent.

As soon as you determine upon the make-up of the commission I will take it up with the individuals if you so desire, or, possibly, it would be more effective if you communicated directly with them.[3]   Faithfully yours,   Robert Lansing.

TLS (WP, DLC).
[1] President of the New Haven Railroad.

From Robert Lansing, with Enclosure

My dear Mr. President: [Washington] April 12, 1917.

Although you have received a copy of this message I desire to call your attention particularly to it and to receive from you directions as to what reply we should make.

I believe that it would be for our interest to have Guatemala in the war, and very possibly Honduras, as it would offer a constant check upon Mexico in case its Government should adopt any measures in the interest of Germany.

Faithfully yours,   Robert Lansing

CCL (SDR, RG 59, 763.72/3773, DNA).

ENCLOSURE

Guatemala, April 10, 1917.

The Minister for Foreign Affairs[1] under instructions of the President[2] and Government of Guatemala has brought to me a secret memorandum, the first part of which states that the Government of Guatemala is resolved to cooperate with the United States in the present emergency, and to that end a decree has been published declaring Guatemala to be in a state of siege, effecting in this way the ingress and egress of all strangers. The Minister for Foreign Affairs informs me that the President requests me to telegraph the following words in strict confidence: "The Government of Guatemala is ready to sever its diplomatic relations with the Imperial German Government, and to do everything which may be considered necessary for the triumph of the American arms. In all those measures or resolutions which the American Government may deem conducive to the success of the above purpose it will be aided by the Government of Guatemala with the greatest promptitude, energy and efficiency.

The Government of the United States can readily understand that the Government of Guatemala in taking this attitude not only brings upon itself the hatred and ill will of the German element residing in this republic, an element which with hostile purposes is working in Mexico and in the neighboring Central American countries, but exposes itself to the attacks of the Governments of the above mentioned countries which have been waiting for a long time for a favorable opportunity to disturb the present conditions, and thus accomplish its loss of prestige and ruin.

Therefore the Government of Guatemala in order to safeguard the sacred interests entrusted to it, and to be able to take upon itself before the nation and before history the great responsibilities which the present situation entails, proposes to the American Government the entering into a pact of alliance which could be offensive and defensive or only defensive, and which taking into consideration present circumstances could be concerted by a simple exchange of binding notes by diplomatic representatives duly authorized for that purpose."

There is no doubt that President Cabrera is very anxious to take sides openly with the United States and there is every reason to believe that he is in danger of being attacked whenever he takes the step unless his Government and every one here are mistaken.   Leavell.

T telegram (SDR, RG 59, 763.72/3773, DNA).
1 Luis Toledo Herrarte.
2 Manuel Estrada Cabrera.

From Newton Diehl Baker, with Enclosure

My dear Mr. President: Washington. April 12, 1917.

I return herewith the draft of the Executive Order inclosed with your note of yesterday.

The proposed committee would deal with exports from the points of view of:

1. Preventing the goods from reaching the enemy;

2. Economic considerations;

3. The relative needs of the domestic market and of the entente allies.

These subjects are necessarily considered by the Council of National Defense and subordinate bodies have already been created and are actively at work collecting economic information, surveying the available supplies of raw material, devising modes of limiting improvident uses of raw material, arranging for efficient distribution of raw material, quantity production of useful articles, and price regulation. These committees undertake to establish priorities of importance as between the needs of the entente allies, the several branches of the government service, and the domestic demand. The committee of which

Mr. Hoover is to be chairman will have the whole food problem for consideration from all of these points of view. The Munitions Board, which is in effect a committee of supply and purchase, is dealing with the metal situation, both domestic and foreign, and I am quite sure that the creation of a new committee of the kind suggested would overlap in its activities with work now actively in hand in various departments of the Council of National Defense.

It occurs to me to suggest as a possible solution of this difficulty, one or the other of the following courses:

Either by legislation to include the whole Cabinet in the Council of National Defense, which at present contains but six Members of the Cabinet, leaving out the Secretaries of State and the Treasury, the Postmaster General and the Attorney General. This course, I think, would make the Council more cumbersome merely from being larger, but it would bring the whole thing under the presidency of the Secretary of State, and assure the consideration of the international aspects of all questions presented; or

A second possible plan would be to have you instruct us as a Council of National Defense informally to include the Secretary of State as our counsellor and guide in the consideration of any matters having an international relation. We could then instruct the Director to include formal notice and invitation to the Secretary of State whenever any such matter was to be brought up, and we could, of course, accommodate ourselves in the matter of time and place of meeting to the convenience of the Secretary of State.

I think, too, that the question here presented would not be solved by the appointment of this particular committee. A specific situation, perhaps, could be so met, but it would recur constantly in another form. Some other question would be presented involving inter-departmental relations, and either including more departments in its scope than are represented in the Council of National Defense or including a less number than those so represented, and again the problem would arise as to whether you should create by Executive Order another inter-departmental board to deal with it. There would, therefore, be the precedent for the constant multiplication of formally created inter-departmental boards of a continuing character. Up to the present time the policy has been to create such boards only for the consideration and determination of a specific fact, like the board on the location of the nitrate plant, and I have assumed that as to all other inter-departmental questions it was your desire that the departments affected should informally consult one another, reach a conclusion, and draft their conclusion into a law or report for your final determination. This plan, as I have understood it, seems to me most elastic and flexible, allowing the composition of the informal conference to be changed with the scope of the question presented.

Respectfully yours,   Newton D. Baker

TLS (WP, DLC).

ENCLOSURE

EXECUTIVE ORDER

It is hereby ordered that the Departments of State, Treasury, War, Justice, Navy, and Commerce shall each appoint an officer as a representative on an inter-departmental committee to be designated as the WAR TRADE COMMITTEE to confer upon and make recommendations regarding matters of interest to two or more Departments relating to trade during the war in which the United States is engaged. This Committee may call in from time to time other officials or members of their own or other departments of the Government for purposes of consultation and assistance.

The recommendations of this Committee will be presented to the appropriate cabinet officer or officers for their consideration and if they deem it necessary for presentation to the President.

The White House, April 10, 1917.

T MS (WP, DLC).

From John Milton Waldron[1]

My dear Mr. President: Washington, D. C. April 12, 1917.

While the members of my Race (the Colored people) everywhere in this Country are loyal citizens, not many of them are enthusiastic in their support of yourself and the party in charge of the Government. There are many reasons for this coldness on the part of the Colored citizens towards the National Democratic Administration, which will readily occur to any intelligent American Statesman, who will give the matter even a little serious thought.

The Colored people make up one tenth of the entire population of America and in the perilous times now facing our Nation it would appear that everything possible should be done to have this large class of loyal American citizens become hearty, earnest and intelligent supporters of the President and the Party charged with the duty of carrying on the War that Germany and her Allies have forced upon Our Country.

In my humble judgment the time has come when the President of our great Republic should assure the Colored American Citizens that he and his Administration desire their hearty, united and enthusiastic support in carrying on the War which is upon us, and that no discrimination or injustice will be practiced by the Government or the Administration upon Colored American citizens because of their race, color, politics, previous condition of servitude or because of the locality in which the majority of them now reside.

The above expressed opinion is not only mine but it is the opinion of most—if not all—of the intelligent, loyal and thoughtful leaders of the Race everywhere in this Country. While this opinion is generally held by my people, it is seldom, if ever, expressed in the newspapers or in public gatherings as the Colored American citizen does not wish to give comfort and encouragement to the enemies of his Country.

A few words of reassurance from you, Mr. President, to my people at this time would be of untold value to Our threatened and war[r]ing nation and would set at rest the fears of ten millions of loyal American Citizens and turn them into enthusiastic and earnest supporters of the President and his Administration.

If you desire, Sir, an occasion and an opportunity to make a public address—long or short—to the Colored American Citizens of the Country, both the occasion and the opportunity are placed at your disposal in the Patriotic Meeting to be held at Shiloh Baptist Church ("Strangers' Home") L St. bet. 16th & 17th Sts., N.W. at 8 P.M. Sunday, April 22nd A.D. 1917. At this meeting the Shiloh Church and her Pastor will publicly pledge themselves to loyally and heartily support the President and his Administration and the Nation in the prosecution of the present War to a successful issue, and will urge the members of the Race everywhere in America to take the same stand. Your presence at this meeting and a word from you would make this meeting a thousand times more effective and would set at rest the fears and doubts of my people.

I await your pleasure, Mr. President, in this matter, and I

stand ready to serve you and our Country in any and every way I may be needed, and I beg to remain,

Yours in the King's business,   J. Milton Waldron

TLS (WP, DLC).
[1] Pastor of Shiloh Baptist Church in Washington.

Robert Lansing to William Elliott Gonzales

Washington, April 12, 1917.

Your April 7, 10 pm[1] has been considered by the President who is sending direct the following message to the President of Cuba quote I am greatly impressed by the unanimity with which the Cuban people through their constituted Congress have unhesitatingly cast in their lot with the nations of the world who are championing the rights and liberties, not alone of neutrals, but of all mankind. We rejoice [that] Cuba, having gained the prize of self-government through sacrifice and blood, is in a position to appraise, as all regenerated peoples do, the worth of that prize, and stands ready to aid in confirming its existence for the welfare of mankind. Woodrow Wilson End quote.   Lansing.

T telegram (SDR, RG 59, 763.72/3723, DNA).
[1] W. E. Gonzales to RL, April 7, 1917, T telegram (SDR, RG 59, 763.72/3723, DNA). Both houses of the Cuban Congress had just voted unanimously to authorize the President to declare war against Germany, and he had done so.

Robert Lansing to William Jennings Price[1]

Washington, April 12, 1917.

Inform Government of Panama that action of President[2] in issuing proclamation of cooperation with the United States against any hostile acts in Panama affecting this Government is viewed with great satisfaction. You may say further that the President has expressed his personal gratification at this spontaneous action on the part of Panama in allying itself with the Government of the United States in the protection of independence and justice for the Americas and accepts this action as an additional token of the steadfast friendship already existing between our two republics.   Lansing

T telegram (SDR, RG 59, 763.72/3729, DNA).
[1] United States Minister to Panama.
[2] Dr. Ramón M. Valdés.

From the Diary of Josephus Daniels

April Thursday 12 1917

Council of National Defense. Shall we take ships off coastwise trade to send them on trips to carry cargoes to Europe? Aeroplane 2 yr program

I had tentatively agreed to send colliers to carry rails to France where they are greatly needed. The President thinks better that we send to Chile for nitrates so that farmers may have fertilizer. Shall we send destroyers to England & France.

Baker & I sent letter to W.W. as to Committee of Publicity,[1] & suggested appointment of George Creel. He approved his appointment but waits for the method & the pay.

[1] RL *et al.* to WW, April 13, 1917.

To Edward William Pou

My dear Mr. Pou: The White House 13 April, 1917

Your letter of the eleventh[1] gratifies me as one of the best evidences you could have given for your real friendship and helpfulness.

I feel that the adoption of the principle of universal liability to service embodied in the proposed army bill is quite vital to the success of this grim undertaking we are now addressing ourselves to, and I hope sincerely that a more thorough discussion of the many aspects of the matter will show the necessity of this legislation.

I think perhaps it is forgotten that the recruiting of the regular army and the National Guard involves the calling for nearly 500,000 volunteers and upon a more liberal margin as to age than the proposed draft.

I wish I could find some proper means of conveying to the members of Congress the profound feeling I have that it is only by the adoption of such measures as those proposed that we can make the conclusive impression of strength and determination that is so necessary to the immediate moral effect of what we are doing. The more business-like determination we use now the less likelihood there is that our men will have to be sacrificed in any great numbers.

Cordially and sincerely yours,   Woodrow Wilson

TLS (E. W. Pou Papers, Nc-Ar).
[1] E. W. Pou to JPT, April 11, 1917.

To Robert Lansing, with Enclosures

My dear Mr. Secretary,   The White House. 13 April, 1917.

I have taken this matter up with the Secretary of the Treasury and, in case China enters the war, there will be no trouble about making a loan to her. The only difficulties will arise in keeping Japan at arm's length.   Faithfully Yours,   W.W.

WWTLI (SDR, RG 59, 893.51/3008, DNA).

E N C L O S U R E   I

From Robert Lansing

My dear Mr. President: Washington April 12, 1917.

I enclose a memorandum from Mr. Williams of the Far Eastern Division in regard to a loan to China in case China should enter the war. From the point of view of our relations in the far East it would seem to me very desirable to make this loan if possible, and it would cure a great deal of the uncertainty which now exists in regard to loans to China. Believing that it would put our relations upon a very substantial basis if we could aid the Chinese Republic in this emergency—for that Government is in serious financial straits—I am of the opinion that China's entrance into the war would be beneficial rather than detrimental and we would then be in the position of treating her upon the same basis as we will treat other belligerent nations who are at war with Germany.   Faithfully yours,   Robert Lansing.

TLS (SDR, RG 59, 893.51/3008, DNA).

E N C L O S U R E   I I

FOR THE SECRETARY.   April 12, 1917.

Mr. Reinsch, in his telegram of February 6, eleven p.m., reported the Chinese Minister of Finance[1] as saying that the sentiment in favor of joining the United States was gaining strength but that an obstacle was the fear concerning the Chinese arsenals. Mr. Reinsch asked authority to assure the Chinese Government that ten million dollars would be loaned from American sources to improve the arsenals.

At that time the Department was not in a position to give such assurance, but now in case Congress should decide to loan the

Allies three billion dollars it would seem easy to find the sum of ten millions or more if necessary to assist China.

Mr. Abbott of the Continental and Commercial Trust and Savings Bank has gone to China to negotiate a loan of twenty-five millions, but he said before leaving that they could float no loan in the United States for China if Japan opposed it. He is in favor of giving Japan participation if China will consent.

His negotiations, however, will require much time and Chinese consent to Japanese participation may be difficult to obtain. In case the United States makes the loan or gives China credit to the amount named there would be no need of delay and Japan would be unable by a publicity campaign in the United States to hinder it.

It would seem to be necessary to have the loan expended under the direction of the United States Government.

Should complications with Japan arise arrangement could be made to internationalize control of the arsenals and military resources of China by having representatives of all the entente powers cooperate with us.

One of the conditions made by China when first approached by Mr. Reinsch was that we guarantee her against Japanese control of her arsenals and army. This is the delicate feature of the proposed programme.   E.T.W.

TI MS (SDR, RG 59, 893.51/3008, DNA).
[1] Ch'en Chin-t'ao.

To Robert Lansing

My dear Mr. Secretary,   The White House. 13 April, 1917.

I think that we should meet Guatemala half-way in this matter. I am ready to enter into the understanding she suggests.

And the more I think the matter over the more I am convinced that this is a good time to go forward with our Pan-American treaty with such countries as are able to come in. There would be a rather substantial advantage in having Brazil come in first, for the German influence has been supposed to be stronger there, and the German plans for immigration and control more definite, than anywhere else in Latin America.

I would be very much obliged to you if you would take both these matters up with the purpose of putting them through as promptly as possible. The initial impressions being made now seem to me more influential than any can be that will come later.   Faithfully Yours,   W.W.

WWTLI (SDR, RG 59, 763.72/3801½, DNA).

From Robert Lansing and Others

Dear Mr. President: Washington April 13, 1917.

Even though the co-operation of the press has been generous and patriotic, there is a steadily developing need for some authoritative agency to assure the publication of all the vital facts of national defense. Premature or ill-advised announcements of policies, plans and specific activities, whether innocent or otherwise, would constitute a source of danger.

While there is much that is properly secret in connection with the departments of the Government, the total is small compared to the vast amount of information that it is right and proper for the people to have.

America's great present needs are confidence, enthusiasm and service, and these needs will not be met completely unless every citizen is given the feeling of partnership that comes with full, frank statements concerning the conduct of the public business.

It is our opinion that the two functions—censorship and publicity—can be joined in honesty and with profit, and we recommend the creation of a Committee on Public Information. The Chairman should be a civilian, preferably some writer of proved courage, ability and vision, able to gain the understanding co-operation of the press and at the same time rally the authors of the country to a work of service. Other members should be the Secretary of State, the Secretary of War, and the Secretary of the Navy, or an officer or officers detailed to the work by them.

We believe you have the undoubted authority to create this Committee on Public Information without waiting for further legislation, and because of the importance of the task, and its pressing necessity, we trust that you will see fit to do so.

The Committee, upon appointment, can proceed to the framing of regulations and the creation of machinery that will safeguard all information of value to an enemy, and at the same time open every department of government to the inspection of the people as far as possible. Such regulations and such machinery will, of course, be submitted for your approval before becoming effective.   Respectfully,   Robert Lansing.
                                       Newton D. Baker
                                       Josephus Daniels[1]

TLS (WP, DLC).
  [1] For the background of the creation of the C.P.I. and of Creel's appointment, see Stephen Vaughn, *Holding Fast the Inner Lines: Democracy, Nationalism, and the Committee on Public Information* (Chapel Hill, N. C., 1980), pp. 3-22.

From Newton Diehl Baker, with Enclosure

Dear Mr. President:　　　　　　　Washington. April 13, 1917

Just for your files and information, I inclose a copy of a letter written to Mr. Roosevelt in the form in which it was sent. I discovered the War College recommendation quoted in the letter and thought it better to use that than to ask the General Staff to pass upon a question involving the personnel of the selection of a general officer, which is a function not ordinarily committed to them, and consulting upon it in this instance might create an embarrassing precedent in the future.

Respectfully yours,　Newton D. Baker

TLS (WP, DLC).

ENCLOSURE

Newton Diehl Baker to Theodore Roosevelt

My dear Mr. Roosevelt:　　　　　[Washington] April 13, 1917

I have thought earnestly about the subject of our conversation the night before last, and have reached some conclusions which I think, in frankness, I ought to indicate to you.

The War College Division of the General Staff has repeatedly reaffirmed a recommendation to me in the following language:

"The War College Division earnestly recommends that no American troops be employed in active service in any European theater until after an adequate period of training, and that during this period all available trained officers and men in the Regular Army or National Guard be employed in training the new levees called into service. It should, therefore, be our policy at first to devote all our energies to raising troops in sufficient numbers to exert a substantial influence in a later stage of the war. Partially trained troops will be entirely unfit for such duty, and even if our regular forces and National Guard could be spared from training duty, their number is too small to exert any influence."

This policy I have a number of times approved. It is, of course, a purely military policy, and does not undertake to estimate what, if any, sentimental value would attach to a representation of the United States in France by a former President of the United States, but there are doubtless other ways in which that value could be contributed apart from a military expedition.

Cooperation between the United States and the Entente Allies has not yet been so far planned as that any decision has been reached upon the subject of sending an expeditionary force; but should any such force be sent, I should feel obliged to urge that it be placed under the command of the ablest and most experienced professional military man in our country, and that it be officered by and composed of men selected because of their previous military training and, as far as possible, actual military experience. My judgment reaches this conclusion for the reason that any such expedition will be made up of young Americans who will be sent to expose their lives in the bloodiest war yet fought in the world, and under conditions of warfare involving applications of science to the art, of such a character that the very highest degree of skill and training and the largest experience are needed for their guidance and protection. I could not reconcile my mind to a recommendation which deprived our soldiers of the most experienced leadership available, in deference to any mere sentimental consideration, nor could I consent to any expedition being sent until its members have been seasoned by most thorough training for the hardships which they would have to endure. I believe, too, that should any expeditionary force be sent by the United States, it should appear from every aspect of it that military considerations alone had determined its composition, and I think this appearance would be given rather by the selection of the officers from the men of the Army who have devoted their lives exclusively to the study and pursuit of military matters and have made a professional study of the recent changes in the art of war. I should, therefore, be obliged to withhold my approval from an expedition of the sort you propose.

I say these things, my dear Mr. Roosevelt, as the result of very earnest reflection and because I think you will value a frank expression of my best judgment rather than an apparent acquiescence in a plan which I do not approve, drawn from my failure to comment.

With assurances of appreciation of your patriotic intentions, I beg leave, with great respect, to remain,

Sincerely yours,   Newton D. Baker

TCL (WP, DLC).

From Newton Diehl Baker

Dear Mr. President: Washington. April 13, 1917
I think you will be interested in the following facts:
In the Civil War the persons who volunteered in the armies of the United States of 21 years of age and under numbered 2,159,798. Among these there were twenty-five of 10 years of age and under. Those of eighteen years and under were 1,151,-438.
The total of those of 22 years and over was 618,511, and of these only 46,626 were more than 25 years of age.
This, of course, was the largest test the volunteer system has ever had in the United States, and the results seem to me to point to the fact that military material must be drawn from the young men of the country, and that probably those who believe that a denial of the volunteer spirit to men over 25 years will be serious, are misled in their judgment as to the number of such men in the country desiring to volunteer.
                    Respectfully yours,   Newton D. Baker

TLS (WP, DLC).

From Edward Mandell House

Dear Governor: New York. April 13, 1917.
It occurred to me today that McAdoo would be a good man to head the Russian Commission. Not wishing to bother you I made the suggestion to Lansing. I hope you think well of it.
I also hope you will put on a leading Jew that is pro-Ally in sentiment—a man like Morganthau or Straus.
I shall try to get the Jews tomorrow to organize their people towards influencing the Russian Jews in the direction desired. I am told that many of the German Jews are urging the Russian Jews to make a separate peace.
                    Affectionately yours,   E. M. House

TLS (WP, DLC).

From the Diary of Josephus Daniels

                                1917 Friday 13 April
Cabinet—Lane had letter from Ala. quoting statute that any person who furnished intoxicants to an Indian was guilty of a crime, & that Mrs Wilson was an Indian[1] & the President violated the law when he served wine at White House dinner.

Pres. agreed that I at once order work on German war ships. They are damaged and cannot easily be put in commission. The officers evidently intended to make it impossible to use them.

Knight[2] telegraphed from China he would intern ships. We ordered him (Lansing & I) not to intern without specific orders. We have prevented revolution in China & protected people, & hope still to do so. Japs may demand to go in if we stay. Delicate question

President appointed George Creel as Chief of Information & Lansing, Baker & I to control. Creel went to L to sign letter whereupon L wanted it written on State Dept. paper & he sign *first*. Precedence!

1 Mrs. Wilson was a descendant of Pocahontas and John Rolfe.
2 Admiral Austin Melvin Knight, U.S.N., commander in chief of the Asiatic Fleet. Following the outbreak of the war in 1914, American gunboats had taken over the patrol duties to protect foreign lives and property on the Yangtze River and other Chinese waters formerly undertaken by vessels of Great Britain and other belligerent nations. When the United States entered the conflict, the Chinese government, fearful of Japanese intrusion into these areas, insisted upon at least nominal internment of all American naval ships remaining in Chinese waters. Their crews would be allowed to remain on board, but their breech blocks had to be deposited with the nearest American consulate. As the above text suggests, Admiral Knight had reluctantly agreed to this action but was overruled by Lansing and Daniels. However, in early May, the two secretaries reversed themselves and permitted the limited internment to take place. This policy remained in effect only until China declared war on Germany on August 14, 1917, whereupon the American gunboats returned to active duty. See William Reynolds Braisted, *The United States Navy in the Pacific, 1900-1922* (Austin, Tex., 1971), pp. 313-15.

A Press Release

[April 14, 1917]

I hereby create a Committee on Public Information to be composed of the Secretary of State, the Secretary of War, the Secretary of the Navy, and a civilian who shall be charged with the executive direction of the Committee.

As Civilian Chairman of this Committee, I appoint Mr. George Creel.

The Secretary of State, the Secretary of War, and the Secretary of the Navy are authorized each to detail an officer or officers to the work of the Committee.

T MS (WP, DLC).

From Newton Diehl Baker

Dear Mr. President: Washington. April 14, 1917

The Secretary of State has just handed me the letter from General Sosnowski, which I herewith return. I am much impressed with what the General says, and feel that if there is to be any sentimental effort anywhere in Europe, it ought to be made in Russia rather than in France. I think there would be great value in an American military expedition passing through Russia on railroad trains decorated with the American flag, and spreading the news from Vladivostok to the front that the Americans were there and were cooperating with the Russians. This sort of news would, in a country like Russia, spread from person to person, even though the newspaper publicity which we should rely upon in this country were unavailable.

I think it would be possible, with General Sosnowski's assistance, to organize, with fair rapidity, a considerable body of Polish Falcons for such an expedition, and it would seem to me that an American General at their head would be highly desirable. I find myself wondering, however, what the effect of an expedition so composed would be upon our own people. Might it not be said among our foreign-born people that we were planning to send them to do the fighting, while the native Americans stayed at home, and might not such an expedition in Russia be less obviously an American expedition to the Russian people, who would soon discover that we were, after all, sending only Poles? It would be necessary, of course, to organize the force so as to exclude German and Austrian Poles, and the force, when organized, would be obliged to fight against Austrians as well as Germans, since they are indiscriminately mixed on the Austrian front, but if it is your judgment that such an expedition is sufficiently safe from misunderstanding and sufficiently valuable to be sent, if possible, I will be glad to have General Sosnowski get into immediate touch with the General Staff and make an accurate determination as to the possibility of such a movement.   Respectfully yours,   Newton D. Baker

TLS (WP, DLC).

From Jeremiah Whipple Jenks[1]

New York City
My dear Mr. President: April fourteenth 1917

Since my return from the Far East last Fall I have been in almost constant touch with the best foreign observers as well as with the Chinese in Peking. Late conditions there touch most closely the interests of the United States and to my mind should determine in certain particulars its policy.

China, in severing diplomatic relations with Germany, announced deliberately that she was following the lead of the United States. Everyone familiar with the situation in China knows that that country is eager to follow the United States and not to be driven into action by the European powers who have already possessed themselves of Chinese territory, and especially by the power that has apparently been using the exigencies of the war to strengthen her grip on China.

According to all the late newspaper reports, as well as from personal letters, I learn that tremendous pressure is being brought to bear upon the Chinese government to join the Entente on terms to be arranged between China and Japan. My advices show that the Prime Minister[2] acting with Liang Chi-chao[3] or under his influence, has sent telegrams to Japan consulting her as to the Chinese action in the German crisis. The President[4] says that the Cabinet crisis of a few weeks ago came from the desire of the Prime Minister to state definitely to Japan through the Cabinet that China would sever relations with Germany and in proper time join the Entente on terms to be arranged between China and Japan. Practically all the Americans and English, apparently, in Peking feel that this clearly means that China is to be placed definitely under the leadership of Japan and that the final upshot of the matter would be that China must concede practically all of the demands in Group V of the Japanese demands of two years ago which she was finally able, under helping pressure of the United States and of the world's public opinion, to resist at that time. There can be no doubt that the majority of the thinking Chinese including the ablest and clearest headed thinkers in the Cabinet, will prefer to go into the war under the leadership of the United States.

My latest advices indicate that both the Germans and the Japanese are spending a great deal of money in Peking attempting to influence high military officials and the members of the Parliament. The result has been, according to the latest mails, that substantially three hundred members of Parliament are in favor of China following America, some two hundred would vote for China to join the Allies, while the remaining—some three hundred perhaps—are still open to conviction, either by honest argument, in doubtless many cases, or by receiving special advantages of some sort.

So far as I can gather from all sources the situation has not at this time of writing changed materially for the last three weeks, although at almost any moment we may expect to learn of some decision. In the interests of democratic government the world over, in the interests of China, in the interests of the United States both during the war and after the war, and if we take a far look ahead, in the interests, also, of all of the rest of the world, ought not the United States to encourage in China a sentiment favorable to action with the United States?

Apparently the United States government will have three billions of dollars to loan to the Allies on favorable terms. Ought not China to have at least a modicum of a few millions out of these billions? One per cent of this huge sum would put China into position to straighten out her own internal affairs reasonably well. Five per cent would enable China to prove a very important factor in actually fighting in the war if transportation for men and troops can be furnished, and if those for whom China would be fighting could furnish arms and munitions; still further also, if in counsel with us the Allies wished her to furnish either laborers in large numbers for the European countries or fighting men, China could now put into the field a half a million men well trained, in probably half the time that the United States could do so. She has about that many men under arms, many of them trained reasonably well under European instructors.

If the war lasts and the Allies try to make use of China, it will be American money that will outfit China. Would it not be wiser for this American money to be furnished, not indirectly through others, but directly by our government?

The government, through you, has already stated that the United States in this war wishes no indemnity, is seeking no advantage. The history of our relations with China proves beyond all cavil that the United States, by dealing with China direct, will seek no advantage. Is this not now a unique opportunity, and is it not also an act of loyalty to the European Allies to see to it that money furnished by the United States to be used in the war shall be so used that it will not give any other nation (of course, I mean Japan in his case), an opportunity of seizing an undue advantage at the expense of not only ourselves but of the European Allies?

During my stay of several months in Peking, I was profoundly impressed with the most remarkable progress made by China during the dozen years that had intervened since my earlier visit. The progress in Peking equalled the marvellous progress seen in Manila. I do not believe that Japan in the best years of her wonderful progress ever surpassed, if she even equalled, the progress made by China during the last dozen years. I could give you numerous specific illustrations of not only material progress but of even more remarkable progress in the training of citizens, in the training of officials, in the methods of governmental administration, in the progress toward honest and upright government, in the methods of judicial process and in almost innumerable other ways. China is just on the verge of becoming really independent. There can be no doubt that her ablest and best trained citizens desire a real democracy. It will take some time to get it, but they are on the right road.

When they heard that the American International Corporation was likely to try to share with the Japanese its concession to improve the Grand Canal, the Chinese felt that such an act would be a treacherous betrayal of confidence of the Chinese government. The concession was to Americans alone and would never have been made to Japanese and Americans together.[5] We cannot afford, if we care for the future interests of China or of ours in China, not to recognize clearly the Chinese feelings. China does not need today the tutelage of Japan or of any other foreign nation. So far as she needs guides let her seek her own guides. She is competent to do so.

If America will seize the present opportunity and without any hostile action of any nature or without attempting to seek any advantage will simply take the ground that she will stand by China directly with financial support, to my mind she can render the greatest service to the cause of democracy the world over and to the progress of the highest civilization, mental and moral. With the preparations that the United States is now making she has nothing to fear.

I spoke this week to Secretary Daniels about a possible opportunity of asking a favor of China in connection with the transfer of ships if some could be bought from the South American powers. I have official evidence that China would welcome an opportunity to render a service to the United States of any nature that was possible. If we should be in a position to ask a favor of China, it would be helpful as a means of approach to present our effort to be of substantial assistance to her.

I am very well aware of the strenuous efforts being made by the Japanese to prevent our taking any independent action, but as long as we are ourselves conscious that we are seeking no undue advantage, it seems to me clear that we ought to seize this opportunity to render this great service not only to China but to the world. I say nothing about the future advantage to ourselves

—that would be great—but to my mind the chief argument should be the higher one of promoting the cause of democracy and civilization.

Having lately come from China and being in constant touch with both the officials there and with private persons, native and foreign, I feel confident that I am representing clearly the feelings of the Chinese. I shall be very glad to take the matter up in person with you if you so desire.

Very respectfully and sincerely yours,

Jeremiah W. Jenks

TLS (SDR, RG 59, 763.72/3891, DNA).
¹ At this time, director of the Division of Public Affairs of the School of Commerce of New York University; an adviser to the Chinese Ministry of Finance.
² That is, Tuan Ch'i-jui.
³ Liang Ch'i-ch'ao, journalist, educator, and intellectual leader of republican China; he served briefly in several ministries.
⁴ That is, Li Yüan-Hung.
⁵ The American International Corp., an overseas investment firm headed by Frank A. Vanderlip and Willard D. Straight, had, on April 19, 1916, reached an agreement with the Chinese government under which the company would float a large loan for the purpose of dredging and improving the South Grand Canal located in Shantung and Kiangsu provinces. Following much further negotiation to modify the terms of the agreement, the A.I.C., without consulting the Chinese at all, signed an agreement on March 8, 1917, with the Industrial Bank of Japan which provided for a joint loan of $6,000,000 for the canal project, $3,500,000 to be floated in New York, the rest in Tokyo. The agreement also called for joint management and operation of the project. As Jenks suggests, the Chinese were very disturbed by this turn of events but had little choice but to accede to the new arrangement in November 1917. As it turned out, the project never materialized. See Noel H. Pugach, *Paul S. Reinsch: Open Door Diplomat in Action* (Millwood, N. Y., 1979), pp. 177, 205-12 *passim*.

From the Diary of Thomas W. Brahany

Saturday, April 14, 1917

Mr. Whitehouse, M.P., saw the President today. I think this appointment was made either at the instance of or through Col. House. Col. House writes the President three or four times a week. All his letters are marked "Confidential" and go to the President unopened. Under a recent order all letters to the President from the State, War or Navy Departments go to the President unopened.

The President went to the Belasco Theatre tonight. He was not feeling well this morning.

A Memorandum by John Howard Whitehouse

14th April 1917.

I reached Washington at 7.30 this morning and breakfasted with Walter Lippman[n] at the Cosmos Club. Later in the morning he told me that all the newspaper men in Washington were aware of my appointment with the President.

I went to the White House at a few minutes before two o'clock. The President entered the room into which I was shown at 2 o'clock precisely. He received me with very great kindness and began by saying that he wished first of all to thank me for the very great help I had been to him. I had placed him under a very great obligation both for the advice and the constructive suggestions I had made to him. He emphasized this so much that I felt greatly emba[r]rassed and told him that I much appreciated his words and could only count it a great privilege to have had the opportunity of being the slightest use to him.

He then plunged into a discussion of many matters connected with the war. He began by saying that there was one important subject which had been greatly occupying his thoughts lately but which of course "we" cannot speak of outside. That was a question of signing the Allies agreement not to make a separate peace. He said that after considering the matter most carefully he felt that he must remain outside that agreement. He said that the position of America would be one of much more general helpfulness and influence if he remained, in this sense, detached from the Allies, but he asked my views. I replied that I had heard what he said with great relief. I felt that by signing the agreement he would lose the special position of power which he now held not only with regard to the ending of the war but the world settlement upon a permanent peace basis. Moreover if he signed the agreement he would be giving his approval both to the statement of the Allies' terms and to the policy of the Paris Economic Pact. Some of the interpretations put upon the statement of the Allies terms would make them inconsistent with his own declared policy.

The President expressed his agreement and added that he understood that the statement of the Allies terms were understood in Austria to mean that their country was to be forcibly dismembered and blocks of their population handed over to other countries. Public opinion in Austria had hardened in consequence. Such dismemberment was not what he stood for. He had distinguished most carefully between rulers and their peoples. It was the peoples who should decide the form of government they would have. Forcibly to transfer people from one ruler to another, without their assent, was not a policy with which he had sympathy.

Reverting to the question of the compact with the Allies he said that the latter must have sufficient faith in him to believe that he would not desert them. He would not assent to a peace inimical to them.

The President then introduced a number of subjects with the object apparently of hearing my views and he again referred to the information I had already given him. I reminded him that in anything I had said in the past I had tried to express certain phases of English feeling without exaggeration, and without regard to my personal views.

He mentioned present feeling in England. I said I thought two main channels of thought were either forming or soon would do so. The more moderate school would now feel that in coming to a negotiated settlement, whenever that was possible, their fear for the future would be removed since America would be at the back of the settlement, a permanent guarantee for future peace. The argument used in the past was that a negotiated peace was impossible because there was no guarantee of future peace. The fact that America would be a party to the settlement gave that guarantee.

There was however a great danger in the present position. The extreme militarist party would be inclined to say that they had now almost inexhaustible stores of men and munitions to draw upon in America and that they could therefore carry on indefinitely until they could dictate on the field of battle the terms of a conqueror. If this spirit spread it would be a great disaster. The President agreed.

The President touched upon the terms of settlement. He said that having just entered the war he was not prepared at this moment to make any public suggestions to the allies. It would lay him open to the charge of desiring to dominate policy before the country had bourne any of the burdens of war. But the problems of the settlement were urgent.

I replied that I thought it fair to assert that the statesmen in England, and I presumed the same was true of other countries in the war, had no time to think. The President replied that he thought that was true at least so far as thinking in advance was concerned. The daily needs of the situation must absorb their energy.

I said it was therefore to him that we had to look for constructive suggestion. He said that this was one of the questions which he had decided to discuss with Mr Balfour. He thought that whilst for the time being he must not say anything more on these lines in public, he felt that much could be done in a private or semi-official way in educating public opinion on the problems of the settlement, and preparing them for its terms. He thought that much could be done both in America and in England on these lines.

He next discussed the question of Russia. He said the position of Russia was very uncertain. It was too early yet to know what was going to happen there. It might be that in setting up their new form of Government and working out domestic reforms they would find the war an intolerable evil and would desire to get to an end of it on any reasonable terms. It would be a serious blow to the Allies if that took place. He was being asked to advance loans to Russia and he was making a stipulation that the money lent should be spent upon the war. He was not prepared to finance Russia at this point in order that she might get out of the war.

I asked him whether he had the means of knowing what the present feeling was in Russia amongst the people generally. He said that he intended to send an agent to find out. He had been considering the right man to send. He had thought of Senator Knox. The matter was rather complicated however because he had been told that anyone sent to Russia must be of commanding physical appearance. The Senator would not answer this description and he feared he had not yet found the man.

I suggested to the President that the movement in favour of public diplomacy as against secret diplomacy would gain great strength in the future. He said he was sure that it would do so and assented to the view that people who were called upon to offer their lives should at least be parties to the policies which led to their sacrifice. He said he had sometimes wondered whether he would be reduced to sending messages to the peoples in Austria and Hungary by means of aeroplanes. He had had one experience before of a message arriving from the sky. At his old college it was made a rule that a knowledge of the shorter catechism was necessary for graduation. It was further provided that every student must buy a copy from the college at a charge of 50 cents. There was a big supply at the college and the help of some of the students was requisitioned shortly before Commencement to move the stock to another room. They appropriated a number of these copies and at the ceremony they sent them fluttering down on to the heads of the congregation through the ventilating holes in the ceiling. The venerable and very orthodox

Head[1] who was presiding thought that these fluttering papers were copies of a scurrilous attack upon the Professors which had been secretly circulated, and cried out from the chair, "Do not touch the foul thing."

The President touched upon war passions and panics. He said that the newspaper press in America was less responsible than the press of England. They were always inventing stories of himself which had no basis of fact, and were wholly unreliable. They (the papers) were also very ignorant. A few nights ago he had gone to bed very tired and was awakened in the night because the editor of one of the daily papers insisted that he had a secret of the utmost importance which he could impart only to the President. He went to the telephone and was told by this editor that there was a fleet of sub-marines which had set up a complete blockade of New York, Boston, and another port. He asked the editor whether he believed the tale himself and was told he did. The President then told him that he hoped he would not print such nonsense in his paper.

He had been urged to give his authority for the preparation of a list of aliens in America. The preparation of such a list would simply mean that the public would be invited to look upon these people with suspicion as possible traitors. They were for the most part perfectly loyal and good and inoffensive citizens. He had refused to allow any such course to be adopted. Unfortunately he could not control the State legislatures in this matter and some of them were adopting this very foolish policy.

The internment of the aliens in England was a double loss to the country. It withdrew these people from economic use and gave the country the expense of feeding them. I said that this was yielding to popular passion. The President replied that no Government got rid of mob passion by yielding to it—only by resisting it.

He went on to say that a curious problem had arisen in connection with the break with Austria—a break which had been forced upon Austria by Germany. The Austrians in America were probably the most numerous of all the nationalities in the country and there were one million Austrians who made regular remittances to relatives in Austria. These remittances amounted to 25 million dollars annually. These must now cease and it would be very interesting to see what influence this had in Austria.

He had been very much touched by the position of many Poles in America who had come to his government praying to be allowed to send money to friends and relatives in Poland, but they

[1] One of the early presidents, before the incumbency of James McCosh.

had no means whatever as a government for transmitting this money, and the problem of sending help to these people appeared insoluble.

He mentioned as an instance of the spread of war panic an incident which had occurred at the White House that morning when one of the servants had told Mrs Wilson that there was a German in the cellar. There was, but he was an old and very faithful servant.

He touched upon the approaching visit of Mr Balfour and of his character. He was much interested in the description I gave him of the way in which he was regarded in England. He said he was greatly looking forward to making his acquaintance. He had been greatly surprised to find that the mission which was being sent from France was a mission of compliment only. He did not think this was a time for the exchange of compliments and it appeared to him very inappropriate to send Joffre on a sort of triumphal tour through America to be feted and acclaimed.

With the President's permission I put before him fully the present position of the conscientious objectors in England, particularly those who remained in prison because they would not undertake civil work under direction. He expressed his sympathy, and shewed also surprise at the procedure adopted. I said that the example of America would have a great influence in England on the settlement of this question. He agreed, and gave me every encouragement as to the way in which the question would be treated in America.

At the end of our conference the President again repeated the expressions of his indebtedness. He wrote an inscription in his book on the Presidency of the United States[2] and gave it to me, and said many kind things.

From J. H. Whitehouse, "The House Report, 14 November 1916 to 14 April 1917," T MS in the Papers of J. Howard Whitehouse, Bembridge School, Isle of Wight.

[2] That is, *The President of the United States* (New York, 1916). This was a reprint of Chapter III of *Constitutional Government in the United States*, printed in Vol. 18 of this series.

Jean Jules Jusserand to the Foreign Ministry

Washington, reçu le 14 avril 1917

No. 433 Suite du no. précédent.

Je suis revenu, auprès du Président Wilson que j'ai vu tout à l'heure, sur cette question et sur celle de la guerre aux sous-marins, les deux n'en faisant qu'une puisqu'il s'agit d'annuler leur effort, d'une part en détruisant ces engins, et d'autre part en remplaçant les navires qu'ils coulent.

Le Président a fait à mon plaidoyer le meilleur accueil; il m'a dit qu'il était tout à fait d'accord que c'était la guerre d'aide la plus urgente et la plus utile que les Etats-Unis pouvaient nous prêter.

Je lui ai exposé mes motifs pour (souhaiter) que les navires en construction soient placés sous notre pavillon, question qu'il étudiera (mais il n'a pas fait de promesse formelle).

Il m'a assuré que ses instructions à tous les services compétents étaient de nous assister le mieux et le plus promptement possible et qu'il les renouvellerait.

J'ai parlé des navires saisis: pour les allemands, on (les) répare; pour les autrichiens dont plusieurs n'ont pas été endommagés, comme il n'y a pas état de guerre, on va procéder par voie d'achat de ces navires par une compagnie américaine qui les fera ensuite naviguer au profit des alliés. J'ai insisté pour que nous ne soyons pas oubliés, ce dont il m'a été assuré qu'il n'y avait nulle chance.   Jusserand.

T telegram (Guerre 1914-1918, États-Unis, Vol. 506, p. 229, FFM-Ar).

T R A N S L A T I O N

Washington, received April 14, 1917

No. 433 Continuation of preceding No.

I brought up again with President Wilson, whom I have just seen, the same question and also the question of submarine warfare, the two really being one, since it is a question of counteracting the submarines' activity, on the one hand by destroying these devices, and, on the other, by replacing the ships that they sink.

The President warmly welcomed my appeal; he told me that he agreed entirely that a war of logistical aid was the most urgent and most useful thing that the United States could give us.

I explained to him my grounds for hoping that the ships under construction would be placed under our flag, a question that he will study (but he made no formal promise).

He assured me that his instructions to all the services involved were to assist us in the best and promptest way possible, and he will renew these instructions.

I spoke of the seized ships: the German ships will be repaired; as for the Austrian ships, several of which are undamaged because they are not in a state of war, these will be bought by an

American company that will sail them right away for the benefit of the Allies. I urged that we not be forgotten, and he assured me that there was no chance of that.   Jusserand.

From the Diary of Thomas W. Brahany

Sunday, April 15, 1917

Today we gave to the press for publication tomorrow morning an appeal by the President to "My Fellow Countrymen." The President's appeal, which is in his best style, was written Friday and yesterday, and sent to the Public Printer last night. The President calls on all citizens to do his or her utmost to serve the country with strenuous industry and economy, in factory, field, mine and forest; on land and sea, and in commerce, and especially to promote and produce the largest supply of non-perishable food-stuffs possible for the ensuing year.

We gave to the press yesterday for publication this morning, the President's Executive Order of Friday designating the Secretaries of State, War and Navy, and George Creel, a well known magazine writer to serve as a board of news censorship. The letter of Secretaries Lansing, Baker and Daniels recommending this was given to the press also. This letter was drafted by Creel after consultation with the President. When he took it to Lansing for approval following its approval by Baker and Daniels, with whom he had talked fully, Creel was very cooly received. Lansing insisted that the letter be written on a State Department letterhead, and that his signature appear above the signatures of Baker and Daniels. Creel didn't want Lansing on the Board. It was the President's suggestion that Lansing's name be added. Creel was disgusted with what he termed Lansing's "petty sensitiveness." Baker and Daniels laughed heartily, Creel said, when he told them they would have to sign a second letter because Lansing wanted his name to appear first.

An Appeal to the American People

The White House, April 15, 1917

My Fellow-Countrymen: The entrance of our own beloved country into the grim and terrible war for democracy and human rights which has shaken the world creates so many problems of national life and action which call for immediate consideration and settlement that I hope you will permit me to address to you a few words of earnest counsel and appeal with regard to them.

We are rapidly putting our navy upon an effective war footing and are about to create and equip a great army, but these are the simplest parts of the great task to which we have addressed ourselves. There is not a single selfish element, so far as I can see, in the cause we are fighting for. We are fighting for what we believe and wish to be the rights of mankind and for the future peace and security of the world. To do this great thing worthily and successfully we must devote ourselves to the service without regard to profit or material advantage and with an energy and intelligence that will rise to the level of the enterprise itself. We must realize to the full how great the task is and how many things, how many kinds and elements of capacity and service and self-sacrifice it involves.

These, then, are the things we must do, and do well, besides fighting—the things without which mere fighting would be fruitless:

We must supply abundant food for ourselves and for our armies and our seamen, not only, but also for a large part of the nations with whom we have now made common cause, in whose support and by whose sides we shall be fighting.

We must supply ships by the hundreds out of our shipyards to carry to the other side of the sea, submarines or no submarines, what will every day be needed there, and abundant materials out of our fields and our mines and our factories with which not only to clothe and equip our own forces on land and sea, but also to clothe and support our people, for whom the gallant fellows under arms can no longer work; to help clothe and equip the armies with which we are cooperating in Europe, and to keep the looms and manufactories there in raw material; coal to keep the fires going in ships at sea and in the furnaces of hundreds of factories across the sea; steel out of which to make arms and ammunition both here and there; rails for wornout railways back of the fighting fronts; locomotives and rolling stock to take the place of those every day going to pieces; mules, horses, cattle for labor and for military service; everything with which the people of England and France and Italy and Russia have usually supplied themselves, but cannot now afford the men, the materials, or the machinery to make.

It is evident to every thinking man that our industries, on the farms, in the shipyards, in the mines, in the factories, must be made more prolific and more efficient than ever, and that they must be more economically managed and better adapted to the particular requirements of our task than they have been; and what I want to say is that the men and the women who devote their thought and their energy to these things will be serving the country and conducting the fight for peace and freedom just as truly and just as effectively as the men on the battlefield or in the trenches. The industrial forces of the country, men and women alike, will be a great national, a great international service army—a notable and honored host engaged in the service of the nation and the world, the efficient friends and saviors of free men everywhere. Thousands, nay, hundreds of thousands, of men otherwise liable to military service will of right and of necessity be excused from that service and assigned to the fundamental, sustaining work of the fields and factories and mines, and they will be as much part of the great patriotic forces of the nation as the men under fire.

I take the liberty, therefore, of addressing this word to the farmers of the country and to all who work on the farms: The supreme need of our own nation and of the nations with which we are cooperating is an abundance of supplies, and especially of foodstuffs. The importance of an adequate food supply, especially for the present year, is superlative. Without abundant food, alike for the armies and the peoples now at war, the whole great enterprise upon which we have embarked will break down and fail. The world's food reserves are low. Not only during the present emergency, but for some time after peace shall have come, both our own people and a large proportion of the people of Europe must rely upon the harvests in America.

Upon the farmers of this country, therefore, in large measure rests the fate of the war and the fate of the nations. May the nation not count upon them to omit no step that will increase the production of their land or that will bring about the most effectual cooperation in the sale and distribution of their products? The time is short. It is of the most imperative importance that everything possible be done, and done immediately, to make sure of large harvests. I call upon young men and old alike and upon the ablebodied boys of the land to accept and act upon this duty— to turn in hosts to the farms and make certain that no pains and no labor is lacking in this great matter.

I particularly appeal to the farmers of the South to plant abundant foodstuffs, as well as cotton. They can show their patriotism in no better or more convincing way than by resisting the great temptation of the present price of cotton and helping, helping upon a great scale, to feed the nation and the peoples everywhere who are fighting for their liberties and for our own.

The variety of their crops will be the visible measure of their comprehension of their national duty.

The Government of the United States and the governments of the several states stand ready to cooperate. They will do everything possible to assist farmers in securing an adequate supply of seed, an adequate force of laborers when they are most needed, at harvest time, and the means of expediting shipments of fertilizers and farm machinery, as well as of the crops themselves when harvested. The course of trade shall be as unhampered as it is possible to make it, and there shall be no unwarranted manipulation of the nation's food supply by those who handle it on its way to the consumer. This is our opportunity to demonstrate the efficiency of a great democracy, and we shall not fall short of it!

This, let me say to the middlemen of every sort, whether they are handling our foodstuffs or our raw materials of manufacture or the products of our mills and factories: The eyes of the country will be especially upon you. This is your opportunity for signal service, efficient and disinterested. The country expects you, as it expects all others, to forego unusual profits, to organize and expedite shipments of supplies of every kind, but especially of food, with an eye to the service you are rendering and in the spirit of those who enlist in the ranks, for their people, not for themselves. I shall confidently expect you to deserve and win the confidence of people of every sort and station.

To the men who run the railways of the country, whether they be managers or operative employees, let me say that the railways are the arteries of the nation's life and that upon them rests the immense responsibility of seeing to it that those arteries suffer no obstruction of any kind, no inefficiency or slackened power. To the merchant let me suggest the motto, "Small profits and quick services," and to the shipbuilder the thought that the life of the war depends upon him. The food and the war supplies must be carried across the seas, no matter how many ships are sent to the bottom. The places of those that go down must be supplied, and supplied at once. To the miner let me say that he stands where the farmer does: the work of the world waits on him. If he slackens or fails, armies and statesmen are helpless. He also is enlisted in the great Service Army. The manufacturer does not need to be told, I hope, that the nation looks to him to speed and perfect every process; and I want only to remind his employees that their service is absolutely indispensable and is counted on by every man who loves the country and its liberties.

Let me suggest, also, that every one who creates or cultivates a garden helps, and helps greatly, to solve the problem of the feeding of the nations; and that every housewife who practices strict economy puts herself in the ranks of those who serve the nation. This is the time for America to correct her unpardonable fault of wastefulness and extravagance. Let every man and every woman assume the duty of careful, provident use and expenditure as a public duty, as a dictate of patriotism which no one can now expect ever to be excused or forgiven for ignoring.

In the hope that this statement of the needs of the nation and of the world in this hour of supreme crisis may stimulate those to whom it comes and remind all who need reminder of the solemn duties of a time such as the world has never seen before, I beg that all editors and publishers everywhere will give as prominent publication and as wide circulation as possible to this appeal. I venture to suggest, also, to all advertising agencies that they would perhaps render a very substantial and timely service to the country if they would give it widespread repetition. And I hope that clergymen will not think the theme of it an unworthy or inappropriate subject of comment and homily from their pulpits.

The supreme test of the nation has come. We must all speak, act, and serve together!   Woodrow Wilson.[1]

Printed in the *New York Times*, April 16, 1917.
[1] There is a WWsh draft and a WWT draft of this statement in WP, DLC.

To Newton Diehl Baker, with Enclosure

My dear Mr. Secretary: The White House 16 April, 1917

The enclosed letter from Doctor Eliot raises a very important point.

I have been very uneasy at the thought that at the close of the war, according to the terms of the bill now proposed in the Congress, we would be practically left without military forces altogether, even without an organized National Guard. I had not realize[d] until lately that this was the effect of the bill.

I would be obliged to you for your advice as to the best way of preventing this, for surely it ought to be prevented.

In haste

Cordially and faithfully yours,   Woodrow Wilson

TLS (N. D. Baker Papers, DLC).

ENCLOSURE

From Charles William Eliot

Dear Mr. President: Cambridge, Mass., 14 April 1917.

I am sending you as a night letter the following telegram:

Yours of 11th received. General Staff Bill and Chamberlain Bill unfit for adoption. Can general consent be procured for Swiss system as compromise? Unless some form of universal service be adopted, membership of United States in alliance to enforce peace and effect armaments reduction will be unworthy of country. That alliance not necessarily permanent; but for ten years at least. Swiss system important aid to education and human conservation.

The situation in Congress is obviously very difficult; and public opinion about universal military training and service is just chaotic. The serious aspect of this condition of things is this,—unless some just and acceptable system of universal military training can be adopted promptly and put into effect, you will be left helpless when the time comes to make the United States an effective member of the alliance to enforce peace, and bring about the reduction of armaments. That is the most beneficent of the policies to which you have led the country. If the military forces which we are compelled to use temporarily—the Regular Army, the National Guard, and a force raised by lot conscription—be the only ones now organized, the country will have no considerable armed force at the end of the War, since present enlistments are for the War. All the other allies will have large armies on foot; we shall have nothing to speak of.

The Swiss method is the only one now in existence of demonstrated efficiency, and yet just and tolerable in a democracy. It is more than tolerable because it works a great improvement in the vigor and health of the population. We very much need in this country precisely the physical training which the Swiss legislation provides, and the practice it gives in cooperative discipline and team-play.

I would not add to your burdens by writing thus if I did not believe that the immediate adoption of some system of universal service is essential to the carrying out of some of the most beneficent of your policies.

I marvel that you are able to answer letters at all. The reply you have just sent me is more than adequate.

I am, with high regard,

Sincerely yours   Charles W. Eliot

TLS (WP, DLC).

To Margaret Woodrow Wilson

[The White House] 16 April, 1917

All of us join in sending you birthday greetings and more love than the wires can carry. May you have not only many happy returns but may each year bring greater and greater happiness. We will celebrate when you get back.[1]   Woodrow Wilson.

T telegram (Letterpress Books, WP, DLC).
[1] She was on a concert tour of the Middle West and South on behalf of the American Red Cross.

From the Diary of Thomas W. Brahany

Monday, April 16, 1917

Secretary Daniels advised the President this morning that William J. Bryan was in the city and wished to see the President. The President said he would see the former Secretary of State at 10 o'clock. Mr. Bryan was with the President nearly half an hour. On leaving he told the newspapermen that his call was to offer his services "either as a private in the ranks or as a soldier in the commissary." He was behind the government in anything it might determine to do, he said. He refused to discuss with the newspapermen, conscription or any other of the bills now before the Congress.

Half a dozen members of the Senate and House had conferences with the President this afternoon.

A Proclamation[1]

[*April 16, 1917*]

Whereas, All persons in the United States, citizens as well as aliens, should be informed of the penalties which they will incur for any failure to bear true allegiance to the United States;

Now, therefore, I, Woodrow Wilson, President of the United States, hereby issue this proclamation to call especial attention to the following provisions of the Constitution and the laws of the United States:

Section 3 of Article III of the Constitution provides, in part:

Treason against the United States shall consist only in levying war against them, or in adhering to their enemies, giving them aid and comfort.

The Criminal Code of the United States provides:

Section 1—Whoever, owing allegiance to the United States, levies war against them or adheres to their enemies, giving them aid and comfort within the United States or elsewhere, is guilty of treason.

Sec. 2—Whoever is convicted of treason shall suffer death; or, at the discretion of the court, shall be imprisoned not less than five years and fined not less than $10,000, to be levied on and collected out of any or all of his property, real and personal, of which he was the owner at the time of committing such treason, any sale or conveyance to the contrary notwithstanding; and every person so convicted of treason shall, however, be incapable of holding any office under the United States.

Sec. 3—Whoever, owing allegiance to the United States and having knowledge of the commission of any treason against them, conceals and does not, as soon as may be, disclose and make known the same to the President or to some Judge or Justice of a particular State, is guilty of misprision of treason and shall be imprisoned not more than seven years and fined not more than $1,000.

Sec. 6—If two or more persons in any State or territory or in any place subject to the jurisdiction of the United States, conspire to overthrow, put down, or to destroy by force the Government of the United States, or to levy war against them, or to oppose by force the authority thereof, or by force to prevent, hinder, or delay the execution of any law of the United States, or by force to seize, take, or possess any property of the United States, contrary to the authority thereof, they shall each be fined not more than $5,000 or imprisoned not more than six years, or both.

The courts of the United States have stated the following acts to be treasonable:

The use or attempted use of any force or violence against the Government of the United States, or its military or naval forces.

The acquisition, use, or disposal of any property with knowledge that it is to be, or with intent that it shall be, of assistance to the enemy in their hostilities against the United States.

The performance of any act or the publication of statements or information which will give or supply in any way aid and comfort to the enemies of the United States.

The direction, aiding, counseling, or contenancing of any of the foregoing acts.

Such acts are held to be treasonable, whether committed within the United States or elsewhere; whether committed by a citizen of the United States or by an alien domiciled, or residing, in the United States, inasmuch as resident aliens, as well as citizens, owe allegiance to the United States and its laws.

Any such citizen or alien who has knowledge of the commission of such acts and conceals and does not make known the facts to the officials named in Section 3 of the Penal Code is guilty of misprision of treason.

And I hereby proclaim and warn all citizens of the United States and all aliens, owing allegiance to the Government of the United States, to abstain from committing any and all acts which would constitute a violation of any of the laws herein set forth; and I further proclaim and warn all persons who may commit such acts that they will be vigorously prosecuted therefor.

In witness whereof I have hereunto set my hand and caused the seal of the United States to be affixed.

Done at the City of Washington, this sixteenth day of April, in the year of our Lord one thousand nine hundred and seventeen, and of the independence of the United States of America the one hundred and forty-first.   WOODROW WILSON,

By the President:
ROBERT LANSING, Secretary of State.

Printed in the *New York Times*, April 17, 1917.
[1] The following document was drafted in the Department of Justice and approved by the Attorney General, the Solicitor General, and the Secretary of State. Lansing sent it to Wilson in RL to WW, April 16, 1917, TLS (WP, DLC).

A News Report

[*April 17, 1917*]

PRESIDENT RECEIVES MEXICAN AMBASSADOR

Washington, April 17.—Ignacio Bonillas, the newly accredited Ambassador of Mexico to the United States, was formally presented to President Wilson at the White House at 2 o'clock this afternoon by Secretary Lansing. The Mexican envoy, in an address to the President, said:

"The First Chief of the Constitutionalist Army, in charge of the executive power of the nation, duly elected President, has instructed me to convey to your Excellency his sincerest desire for your personal happiness and for the prosperity of the people of the United States. I entreat your Excellency, in behalf of the Mexican people, and in my own name, to accept the same cordial salutation."

The President's reply to the remarks of Señor Bonillas was in part:

"The close neighborhood of the United States and Mexico makes it most desirable that there should be between the two countries relations of friendly trust and confidence. It has been my endeavor in these years of unrest and strife in Mexico to impress upon the Mexican people that the United States has none but the best interests of Mexico at heart, and has no wish more selfish than to see its people placed in the enjoyment of the blessings of peace, happiness, and prosperity by the establishment of a constitutional and stable government capable, among other things, of affording due protection to American citizens and property and of meeting all other international requirements.

"I take note of your statement that constitutional order will be re-established in Mexico on May 1. I shall welcome the day that brings me convincing evidence that a constitutional government has been established in Mexico both willing and able to afford to American citizens and their property the same measure of protection and to apply to them the same impartial administration of justice that is afforded and is applied to nationals or the citizens or subjects of other foreign countries. The United States asks no more, and can, of course, accept no less."[1]

Printed in the *New York Times*, April 18, 1917.

[1] The foregoing was undoubtedly based upon a press release prepared by the State Department, and the reply attributed to Wilson was of the kind which the department usually prepared for Wilson's use on such ceremonial occasions. Bonillas, in his report on this affair, said only that Wilson sent his cordial regards to the First Chief and his best wishes for the peace and prosperity of the Mexican people. I. Bonillas to the Foreign Ministry, No. 1106, TLS (L-e 1351, pp. 73-76, Mexican Ministry of Foreign Affairs-Ar).

From Edward Mandell House

[New York, April 17, 1917]

I would advise signing with Brazil. The immediate effect will be good, and it all should lead eventually to a United America

Whitehouse is delighted at appointment.

EBWhw decode (WP, DLC).

From William Gibbs McAdoo

PERSONAL

Dear Mr. President: Washington April 17, 1917.

Referring to the proposed Russian Commission, I feel certain that Mr. Root is the right man to head this Commission, and that his appointment would be highly regarded by the entire country. I am assuming, of course, that he is in full sympathy with our plans and that this would be verified before the matter is broached to him.

Messrs. Charles R. Crane, Cyrus McCormick and S. R. Bertron would make excellent members.

Mr. Eugene Meyer, Jr.,[1] of New York City is a prominent Hebrew of strong pro-Ally sympathies and of French descent. He speaks French fluently and is a business man and banker of unusual ability, and Mr. Justice Brandeis thinks he would prove one of the most useful men you could send to Russia. Mr. Brandeis says that Mr. Meyer has great influence with the Russian Jews outside of the socialist element. Mr. Meyer is a Republican.

For a railroad man I think A. H. Smith,[2] President of the New York Central Railroad is one of the best men you could choose. I have known Smith for fifteen years. He has risen from track hand to the presidency of this great system, is a man of great energy and capacity and knows the operating side of railroad problems from the ground up. His prestige as the head of one of the greatest railroad systems in America would be very helpful in the work he would be expected to do in Russia. I do not know whether he could be secured or not. If you could get him I am sure that you could depend upon his loyalty and full co-operation. Smith is also a Republican. If you should select these men the Commission would be composed equally of Republicans and Democrats.

I think you might well consider making the Commission larger by adding to it representatives of the Army and Navy. The larger number is to my mind more to be desired than the smaller. Of course, a representative socialist in full sympathy with our programme, if he could be found, would be highly desirable.

Affectionately yours, W G McAdoo

TLS (WP, DLC).
[1] Head of the stockbrokerage firm of Eugene Meyer, Jr. & Co.
[2] Alfred Holland Smith.

From Robert Lansing

My dear Mr. President: Washington April 17, 1917

Ambassador da Gama has been absent from the city and also ill so that I have not taken up with him the Pan American Treaty. This enforced delay has given me time to think the matter over carefully, and there are some difficulties which seem involved if a general invitation is issued to all the countries to the south of us.

For example, it might be that a signatory to the Treaty would become an ally of Germany against her European enemies (I am thinking particularly of Mexico where the oil wells at Tampico may cause trouble). In that event would we be bound under the Treaty to maintain the guarantee of territorial integrity with force of arms? Or it might be that a signatory might permit its territory to become the base of German military or naval operations (as might be the case of Ecuador in regard to the Galapagos Islands, or of Colombia in regard to her coasts). Could we observe the territorial integrity of the nation permitting this? Or could we do so if a Latin American country permitted its territory to become a refuge for Germans where they could conspire and carry on their propaganda in this country and other countries?

Possibly this difficulty could be cured by limiting at present the signatories to such governments as declare war against Germany, sever relations with that Government, or declare a benevolent neutrality with the assurance that they will only enter the war on our side or as our ally.

Furthermore under the guarantee of territorial integrity and political independence would the other signatories be bound to declare war against Germany? If it could be so interpreted, what I have said above has no weight. But could it be, unless our territory or waters were actually invaded by the Germans?

These are the questions which have been running through my mind and I would like your opinion upon them.

Faithfully yours,   Robert Lansing

TLS (SDR, RG 59, 710.11/319B, DNA).

From Walter Hines Page

London, England, April 17, 1917.

CONFIDENTIAL.

6018. For the President.

The King summoned me to Windsor Castle to spend last night and gave me a private audience of more than an hour and talked with me again at some length after dinner. He is most appreciative of our help which he very frankly confessed is much needed. He hoped the naval, military, and technical men of both countries will so fully and frankly confer as to prevent our repeating British mistakes. The most serious submarine situation, the dire need of ships and the fear lest Russia make a separate peace were his chief topics. He expressed high appreciation of Admiral Sims' visit[1] and spoke of Mr. Balfour's mission for which I thanked him. He remarked "I do not know how Balfour can now be spared but nothing else is so important as giving your Government all the information we have." He feels content with the present military situation in France but he is much concerned, as everybody here is who knows the facts, about the submarine warfare. He spoke with the greatest appreciation of your last speech to Congress and of your leadership. He added "People are talking much about absolute monarchs; there is no monarch, thank God, in Europe who has the power of the President." His conversation throughout was full of appreciation.   Page.

T telegram (WP, DLC).
 1 Rear Admiral William Sowden Sims, President of the Naval War College, had arrived in England on April 9 on a secret mission for the United States Navy. The exact nature of his oral instructions from Secretary Daniels and others remains unclear even today, but he, himself, later recalled that he was instructed to confer with the Allied admiralties on how "America could best cooperate with the Allies in the event of war." Sims immediately began to confer with high British political and naval officials and was to play a key role in bringing about the reluctant British decision to adopt the convoy system of defense against German submarines. On April 28, Sims was ordered to assume command of six American destroyers just sent to operate from British bases; on May 26, he was promoted to vice admiral; and, on June 9, he was appointed Commander, United States Naval Forces Operating in European Waters, the position which he held throughout the remainder of the war. See Elting E. Morison, *Admiral Sims and the Modern American Navy* (Boston, 1942), pp. 337-66 *passim*.

From Henry Lewis Stimson

Dear Mr. President: [New York] April 17, 1917.

After a trip involving testing public sentiment in the States of Michigan, Illinois, Iowa, Minnesota, Nebraska, Kansas, Missouri and Indiana, I have no doubt whatever of the hearty and overwhelming support of your policy by the people of those sections, including the very people who are represented by some of the Congressmen who are now opposing your army policy.[1]

We spoke in all to somewhat over 50,000 people, our meetings comprising both luncheon meetings with representative men of the various States, such as Chambers of Commerce, and mass meetings open to the public at large. While mainly urban, the audiences comprised all classes and, at such places as Des Moines and Topeka, there was a large rural element present.

In each meeting we aimed to make the following points:

First: That the real issue of the war was between Prussian autocracy and democracy which you so admirably epitomized in your address to the Congress when you stated: "The World must be made a safe place for democracy."

Second: The duty of sympathy towards all Americans of German birth who are proving their loyalty under difficult circumstances and that this Nation's quarrel was not with the German people but with its government.

Third: The serious nature of the war and the necessity of meeting it in a spirit of utmost earnestness; the necessity for close cooperation with the Allies and the danger and absurdity of an independent war by America.

Fourth: The necessity not only of financial and maritime support but of raising a powerful army and of sending a force abroad both as a moral and probably, eventually, as a much needed physicial [physical] support.

Fifth: That universal training and liability to service was the only way by which such a force could be raised and that such training was not a mere military cost like the other proposed expenditures of the war, but was in the nature of an investment, good in time of peace as well as war and bringing in returns in national democracy, character and health as well as safety.

The attitude of our audiences was such as to leave no doubt upon each of these points. In nearly all of the meetings resolutions covering them were passed by unanimous or nearly unanimous votes. Enthusiasm for France was marked everywhere. The very general support received by the proposition to send men abroad was the surprise of the trip to me. At Des Moines, Iowa, where we had anticipated a hostile meeting, a great audience of 8,000 people, completely filling the auditorium on a stormy night, fairly shouted their approval of that sentiment and similar approval was manifested at all the other meetings. The West is not only perfectly loyal, but desires that this nation shall perform creditably its part in the great task. There is an inclination in some parts of the West to think the war will be an easy one and not to appreciate the vulnerability of this country. This is the only danger and it can be met by a campaign of education. For this reason I was rather sorry to find that evidently under governmental instruction, the newspapers were not reporting the news of various treasonable attacks upon our lines of transportation and upon our western food supply. Reports of such attacks were brought privately to us but nothing appeared in the newspapers. The West is very sensitive as to such matters and news that their grain elevators and railroad bridges were in danger would do much towards making them alive to the serious character of the war. I think your proclamation published this morning will be of material benefit in this direction.

As soon as opposition in Congress definitely developed to your proposal that the necessary armies should be chosen upon the principle of universal liability to service, we made this issue prominent in each meeting and insisted upon resolutions being presented which brought it specifically before such meetings. The result was uniform and striking. Resolutions supporting you and specifically condemning the volunteer system were passed in Topeka, Kansas City, St. Louis and Indiana and in each case were practically unanimous. In Topeka, we were told beforehand by the leaders of the meeting that they thought it would be impossible to pass such resolutions in view of the opposition of Governor Capper and Congressman Anthony[2] but that the meeting would be glad to hear from us on the subject. After the discussion the resolutions were adopted without a dissenting vote and, by direction of the meeting itself, were sent to Mr. Anthony and his colleagues in Congress as well as to yourself.

The result of the trip left no doubt in my mind of the readiness of the people in that section of the country to support your proposals. In one respect they are more keenly against the volunteer system than even here in the East. They themselves pointed out to us that the application of the volunteer system would play havoc with their food supplies and transportation by calling out men who are already employed in places of vital usefulness and by leaving the management of national activities to chance instead of intelligent government control. I feel very clear that the Congressmen who are opposing you on this matter do not represent their constituents and that it only needs that the issue be clearly presented to carry conviction.

The proposition to try a general call for volunteers with a view to falling back on conscription, after it has failed, involved not only all the evils of the first system but several others peculiar to such a compromise. It invites failure with the consequent encouragement to our enemies. I was told in Indianapolis that Mr. Anthony's plans were being supported there by men who were known to be pro-German in their sympathies, with the evident purpose of trying to show that your war policy was unpopular with the Country. In the second place, such a compromise instantly creates an issue between two sets of patriotic people in the country. It puts the men who believe in universal service in the dilemma where they must either abandon their convictions or appear to be unpatriotic towards recruiting. Many people on our trip spoke to me of this dilemma.

I believe that there is a real opportunity for volunteers in this war but that it should be confined strictly and narrowly within such limits. It should be confined solely to men who from age or other reason would be exempt from liability and should be offered merely as a means of permitting such men to waive their exemption and to go. In the case of men within the prescribed age, the method of universal and common liability should be rigidly applied from the very beginning.

I trust you will pardon this long letter and permit me to say again, as I did in my telegram to you,[3] that I believe that in your message to the Congress, you expressed the true desire of the American conscience and that in acting along the lines of that message, you will be heartily supported by the Nation. Certainly I shall do my best at all times to support you.

Yours very sincerely,   [Henry L. Stimson]

CCL (H. L. Stimson Papers, CtY).

[1] Stimson, together with Frederic René Coudert, lawyer of New York, and Frederic Collin Walcott, banker and manufacturer of New York and Norfolk, Connecticut, had made a speaking tour of the states mentioned above in March and April under the auspices of the National Security League. See Elting E. Morison, *Turmoil and Tradition: A Study of the Life and Times of Henry L. Stimson* (Boston, 1960), pp. 228-29.

[2] Arthur Capper, Governor of Kansas, and Daniel Read Anthony, Jr., congressman from Kansas, both Republicans.

[3] It is missing in both WP, DLC, and in the H. L. Stimson Papers, CtY.

From James Sprunt, with Enclosures

Dear Mr. President: [Wilmington, N. C.] April 17th 1917.

My brother-in-law, Mr. B. F. Hall,[1] and I, and the other members of the Session of the First Presbyterian Church, have thought that you would like to read some of the beautiful things which were said of you during the Centennial Celebration of your beloved father's church here, and I now enclose them, with the endorsement of our whole congregation, which crowded our church building, and rose as one man upon the mention of your name, in sympathetic response to these expressions, which found an echo in every heart.

Believe me to be, dear Mr. President, always,

Yours faithfully,   James Sprunt

TLS (WP, DLC).

[1] Benjamin Franklin · Hall, wholesale grocer and commission merchant of Wilmington.

E N C L O S U R E   I

Extracts from sermon preached by Rev. Peyton H. Hoge, D.D.[1] in the First Presbyterian Church, Wilmington N. C., April 1st, 1917.

"But there is one of whom I must speak, of whom in this solemn hour of our country's history it is a duty to speak. We had hoped that he would be here. As we think of the last great anniversary of this church, we miss the commanding presence, the benignant countenance, the mellow voice, and the tender, loving words of the father who was with us then. But we hoped that instead of the father would be the son, whom God has made a Prince in all the earth. We expected that in speaking of his father, he would pay a tribute to the christian ministry and to the christian home that would become a classic in our literature, and the influence of which would go forth through all the land. But if we are to be disappointed in that, it is only because God has greater work for him to do. This week he speaks, not to us alone, but to the nation and to the world. His words will be momentous. They will decide the course of history, and the future of the world. And we, who know him, know that he will speak in righteousness and the fear of God. None of us perhaps can fully appreciate how cold and solitary has been the lofty path he has marked out for himself. But amid all the storms of passion, amid all the sneers and criticisms of lesser minds who could not rise to his heights, or see with his vision, he has kept true to his course, never swept from his feet, never hurried to unripe decisions, calm, patient, confident, the captain of his soul, reverencing his conscience as his king, and wearing the white flower of a blameless life in that fierce light which beats upon a throne. It is something to know that in this wild crisis of the world's history, the head of one great nation has sought to rule and lead according to the principles of Jesus Christ. And it will be to the perpetual honor of this church that in this high endeavor he was guided by the teachings received from this pulpit, and in the home of a pastor of this church. 'Instead of the fathers shall be the children whom thou mayest make princes in all the earth.' "

1 Peyton Harrison Hoge, Dr. Wilson's successor at the First Church, 1885-1899; at this time pastor of the Pewee Valley, Ky., Presbyterian Church.

E N C L O S U R E   I I

Extracts from an address delivered April 4th 1917 by Rev. W. W. Moore, D.D.,[1] President Union Theological Seminary, Richmond Va., at the Centennial celebration of the First Presbyterian Church, Wilmington N. C.

"I share the universal regret that the most eminent of all the useful men whom this church has given to the world has been prevented, by the grave conditions which confront the country, from being present on this occasion, and paying in person his tribute of gratitude and affection to the venerable mother, who to day celebrates the one hundreth anniversary of her birth. His duty, as the head of the nation, requires him to be at his post in Washington, but we know that his heart turns lovingly to the home of his boyhood to day. The first time I ever met Mr. Wilson, which happened to be in Scotland, he showed by his very first remark how he felt towards Wilmington. Many of you remember that as a boy he was known in the community as Tommy Wilson. Well, in 1896 Dr. Alexander Sprunt and I were travelling together in Europe. We were in the regalia room of the castle at Edinburgh, where the various crowns of the Kings of Scotland are shown to the visitors.[2] They are mounted on velvet cushions and surrounded by a circular glass case. There was a crowd in the room, and as they walked round this case with eyes on these ancient crowns, a gentleman jostled Dr. Sprunt, and looked up to beg his pardon. This caused them to look each other in the face, and the stranger stepping forward said, 'Is not this Mr. Sprunt of Wilmington?', to which Mr. Sprunt answered, 'Yes, sir.' 'Well, Mr. Sprunt,' said he, 'I am Tommy Wilson.' Do you catch the significance of that manner of introduction? Here was a man of international renown, an author, whose books were read on both sides of the sea, but when he met an old friend from Wilmington, those things were nothing to him. He immediately put their relations back on the boyhood basis. I have always remembered that incident with pleasure. It revealed to me for the first time that simplicity and genuineness of character, and warmth of heart with which the whole world has since become acquainted. Since that time he has been elevated to the highest position on earth, but there too he continues to be the same quiet, unassuming gentleman, and to his old friends in Wilmington he is still in his own mind Tommy Wilson.

Another incident illustrating the same qualities is related by Prof. Stockton Axson, Mr. Wilson's brother-in-law. He says that when Mr. Wilson was Professor in Wesleyan University at Middletown, Conn., Mrs. Wilson's uncle, the late Rev. Thos. A. Hoyt, formerly of Nashville, and then of Philadelphia, paid them a visit. The morning after his arrival, when Mr. Axson and Mr. Wilson were sitting alone, the latter broke into a soft chuckle. 'What are you laughing at?' asked Mr. Axson, and the future President replied 'To think how I blacked Uncle Tom's boots this morning. Passing his bed room door, I saw that he had put his boots outside, naturally assuming that all self-respecting people keep a man. I knew Bridget would not black them, and Annie couldn't, so there was nothing to do but tackle the job myself.' 'So,' says the narrator, 'there is a presidential picture to go along with Lincoln splitting rails, Garfield on the canal boat, and Grant driving a dray—Wilson blacking Uncle Tom's boots.'

When Mr. Wilson was Governor of New Jersey, he made an address on the importance of Bible study, in which he said that nearly all his life he had been engaged in educational work, and that he had always had the same conception of it, namely, that education was a fundamental part of progress, that you can't make progress unless you tie one generation in with another. Any disconnection between one generation and another will be a break, and may be a fatal break in the continuity of progress. You can't make progress in disconnected groups. There is a sense in which education may be said to be the memory of the race—recollecting its experiences, building upon the things that it has done. Well, that is what you are doing, my friends, in this celebration. You are connecting up this century with the last. You are tying this generation in with those that have gone before.

When your committee of arrangements invited me to take some part in these exercises, I accepted the invitation with alacrity and pleasure, partly because when Dr. Jos. R. Wilson gave up his charge here, the congregation had done me the honor to call me to the pastorate as his successor,[3] and as a consequence, I have ever since felt a peculiar interest in this church; partly because for more than thirty years, I have had many dear friends here, whose fellowship has been one of the green oases of life; and partly because I recognize the significance to this city of a hundred years of service by such a congregation as this, and was glad to take a part in the exercises by which you proposed to celebrate the centennial anniversary of the beginning of its organized work.["]

T MSS (WP, DLC).
  [1] Walter William Moore.
  [2] Wilson was in Holyrood Palace on June 13, 1896.
  [3] He did not accept the call and remained at Union Theological Seminary.

Herbert David Croly to Edward Mandell House

My dear Colonel House: New York City April 17, 1917

Some days ago we received a cablegram from Mr. Norman Angell in which he expressed a very lively desire to come to this country and help us over here in explaining to American public opinion some of the ideas which underly the League of Nations, and the President's general scheme of international policy. You may remember that when Mr. Angell was last here he spent practically all of his time in delivering lectures in different parts of the country in favor of these general ideas, and contributed enormously not merely to their understanding by the large number of audiences whom he addressed, but also in making those audiences feel that their country had a direct responsibility in going into the war in order to make those ideas prevail. It would, consequently, I think, be of great assistance to the general propaganda for the kind of war for which the American people are fighting at the present time in case Mr. Angell could return and help to disseminate those ideas. I am not quite sure what the obstacles are to his returning, but he seems from his cablegram to have some difficulty about obtaining the necessary passports from his own government. I am wondering whether you would think it worth while to suggest to the people in authority in Washington that Mr. Angell's presence in this country at the present time might be of great service in the explanation to the American people of the policy which underlies its participation in the war. I do not know of any man in either country who would be more useful to us in that way than Mr. Angell would be.   Sincerely yours,   Herbert Croly

Can anything be done about this?   E.M.H.

TLS (E. M. House Papers, CtY).

From the Diary of Josephus Daniels

1917 Tuesday 17 April

10 a.m. meeting with Lansing and Baker and Creel & Polk in L's office to talk about censorship. "We know nothing about it" said L & P "Let us ask England to send an experienced man. Page says they are willing to do so." All mail to South America should be censored, said L. "The Germans have subsidized S. American papers. We should do the same." Idea of L & P was for following E's plan to create a great censorship, touching all countries to the South of us and Europe—to cost millions of dollars. Not so B & I, & later we talked to the President who said he wished nobody brought over from E.—& did not wish c'sorship to be big. . . .

W.W. How the English mind works. In Oxford wished to buy single ticket to hear one lecture & not whole course. Could not let him have one. He walked in with speaker & sat on stage. . . .

Lord Balfour coming. "I believe in a personal God to which I can pray & who answers prayer"

A practical statesman with touch of mysticism

Pres said: "Let Destroyers go to other side

From the Diary of Thomas W. Brahany

Tuesday, April 17, 1917

Cabinet meeting at 2:30 today. This afternoon, late, the President saw Representative Dent, Chairman of the Committee on Military Affairs, regarding the Army bill. Later he had a talk with Representatives Mann and Lenroot, the Republican leaders.

From Newton Diehl Baker

My dear Mr. President: Washington. April 18, 1917.

I return Dr. Eliot's letter. I yesterday arranged with the House Committee on Military Affairs to have him appear before them on either the 19th or 20th, when I understand he is to be in Washington for that purpose. He will doubtless present the arguments in favor of the Swiss system as he has given very earnest and effective thought to it.

In the matter of the suggestion of your note that the proposed Bill will practically leave the Country without any military forces at the end of the war, I beg leave to say that of course I have been aware of this difficulty for some time. For that reason, the pending legislation does not disband all these forces at the end of the war but at the end of the *emergency*. Its purpose being to allow the President to disband the forces gradually, even though peace be declared, saving at all times in the service of the Government an adequate force for any holdover duty there may be. In the meantime it leaves for subsequent legislation the whole question of our future military organization and that I think is essential in the present situation if we want to avoid the heated feelings which the controversy over universal compulsory training and service engenders. I have told the Committees of the Congress very frankly what the effect of this Bill would be and have explained to them that I thought there would be little difficulty in recruiting a national army out of the veterans of these trained forces, either by enlistment or by such partial discharge as might be determined to be wise later on.

I think it would be well to have in mind a policy which we could ask Congress to adopt looking to a permanent peace-time military establishment; but I think it would be unwise to open that subject up until after these temporary forces have been authorized and a little better atmosphere has been created for the consideration of the problem.

Respectfully yours,   Newton D. Baker

TLS (WP, DLC).

From Robert Lansing

My dear Mr. President: Washington April 18, 1917.

It is with increasing anxiety that I have seen the trend of recent reports from Mexico. It appears to me that the military party in the Mexican Government is controlling its policies and that that party is intensely pro-German or at least anti-American. Whatever may be Carranza's personal views I do not think that he will be strong enough to resist the pressure of the element hostile to us, and that we ought to expect and be prepared for eventualities.

The danger spots of course are Tampico and the border, and possibly the Tehuantapec railway which I believe is English owned and operated. The trouble will very likely arise over Mexico's alleged effort to enforce neutrality by denying Mexican ports to American naval vessels and those of Great Britain and France. This will be a very plausible ground for demanding that any naval vessels at Tampico be withdrawn. Technically they will have right on their side, but from a practical point of view we cannot respect Mexican neutrality so far as Tampico is concerned. Our refusal to withdraw our protection from the oil wells, which I assume will be your view, may result in an open declaration of war or in an ultimatum which will result in war.

There is no doubt that the Mexican sympathizers with Germany have obtained very distorted views of the progress of events. We know the Germans are furnishing false information to the Mexicans as to the successes and intentions of their government. The people through this propaganda are becoming daily more insolent and hostile to Americans. The Government is moving troops to the north near the border. These seem to me significant of what we may anticipate at no distant day.

In this connection we know that from points in Mexico wireless messages are being sent undoubtedly to ships, possibly to Germany. We are allowing telegrams in code to go to Mexico and in all probability they contain shipping information and other news of value to Germany in her submarine campaign. Doubtless other information of value is going forward by the same channel. I think that we should act promptly to prevent this. We need to stop all code messages and to scrutinize carefully all plain messages which on their face are harmless. Unless we do this, it seems to me great damage may be done.

While I am dealing particularly with the Mexican situation, the matter of censorship of telegrams to other Latin American countries is equally important.

Faithfully yours,   Robert Lansing.

TLS (SDR, RG 59, 711.12/43A, DNA).

From Walter Hines Page

London, April 18, 1917

6030, April 18, Confidential for the President.
Your 4670, April 11, 2 p.m.[1]
I took up this subject in a confidential conversation with the Prime Minister at my house last night. He instantly understood and showed that he already knew the facts that I presented and was glad that the President had instructed me to bring the subject up. He had had the American situation in mind during the whole discussion of home rule and he was doing his best. Then he asked me to request the President to give his views to Mr. Balfour as soon as possible after his arrival. Our country has no better English friend than Mr. Balfour and he belongs to the party that before the war opposed home rule. The enlistment of his influence would be a great help and the Prime Minister feels sure of a good result of a frank explanation to him by the President.

I am [have] on my own account, without mentioning the President's instructions, expressed my private opinion to the same effect to other influential members of the Government.

Page.

T telegram (SDR, RG 59, 841D.00/106, DNA).
1 See WW to RL, April 10, 1917.

From the Diary of Thomas W. Brahany

Wednesday, April 18, 1917

The big fight is on for the so-called selective conscription bill. The President is strong for [it] and every effort the administration can make will be exerted to put it through. Representative

Dent (Democratic) Chairman of the Committee on Military Affairs is against the bill, which has the approval of the General Staff, and will have the support of a majority of his committee. Representative Kahn (Republican) will lead the fight for the bill. Speaker Champ Clark is against the bill.

Three Letters to Robert Lansing

My dear Mr. Secretary,   The White House. 19 April, 1917.

The answers to the important questions you here raise are reasonably clear to me. (By the way, I do not find among my papers here the Brazilian proposals you spoke of the other day).

If any one of the signatories to our proposed Pan-American treaty should become an ally of Germany against her European enemies, we would undoubtedly be bound to protect her against any loss of territory or any curtailment of her political independence that any of the Entente group might attempt; but we would be obliged to do that in any case, under the Monroe Doctrine.

Should any one of the signatories permit its territory to be used as a base of military or naval operations against us, it would manifestly be acting in contravention of the patent meaning of the pact and we would be free to act as if there were no pact.

As for "influences" and propaganda, we could not prevent them, any more than Great Britain has been able to prevent them in the United States, where they were very formidable, though they of course did not have the countenance of the Government.

I do not see that the other signatories would in the present circumstances be obligated to declare war on Germany. They would be obligated to come to our assistance with arms only when our political independence or territorial integrity were evidently and immediately threatened.

These questions do not seem to me to constitute difficulties of practical importance. If we can meet Brazil's wishes sufficiently to get her adherence to the pact, I shall feel warranted in pressing on. It seems to me that this is the very time when such a league would make the deepest impression and have the greatest moral effect on both sides of the water.

Faithfully Yours,   W.W.

WWTLI (SDR, RG 59, 710.11/319⅙, DNA).

My dear Mr. Secretary,　　The White House [April 19, 1917].

I have been thinking a great deal about the personnel of the Russian Commission. I hope that in your conference with him to-day you will find Mr. Root a real friend of the revolution. If you do, the Commission that has framed itself in my mind would be as follows:

Elihu Root, New York,
John R. Mott, New York,
Charles R. Crane,
Cyrus H. McCormick, Chicago,
Eugene Meyer, jr., New York,
S. R. Bertron, New York,
John F. Stevens, New York,[1]

and a representative of Labour whom I would suggest that we choose in this way: seek the advice of Mr. Gompers as to whom we could send whom the Socialists over there would not regard as an active opponent of Socialism. Gompers himself and the leaders immediately associated with him are known to be pronounced opponents of Socialism and would hardly be influential in the present ruling circles of labour at Petrograd. And yet we shall have to be careful, if we are to send a real representative of American Labour, not to send a Socialist.

　　　　　　Faithfully Yours,　W.W.

If you see no objection to this list, from an international or from a Russian point of view, I will be glad to write to these gentlemen and ask them to serve.　　　　　W.W.

WWTLI (SDR, RG 59, 763.72/4031½, DNA).
　[1] John Frank Stevens, civil engineer who specialized in railroad building; also chief engineer of the Panama Canal project, 1905-1907; at this time a private consultant in New York.

My dear Mr. Secretary,　　The White House. 19 April, 1917.

I do not know what to make out of the despatches from Mexico. It is by no means clear (matching the information of the War Department from General Pershing with the information of the State Department) which is the Anti-American party, Carranza's or that which is forming under the leadership of disaffected military men. We shall have to await developments before we come to a conclusion about that.

Carranza will, no doubt, in any case, be stiff and technical in insisting upon his authority to enforce neutrality, and will in all likelihood, as you anticipate, demand the removal of any armed ships we may have within Mexican territorial waters.

All of our larger ships lie, of necessity, beyond the three mile limit.

The United States cannot afford to be too "practical." She is the leading champion of the right of self-government and of political independence everywhere. Only the most extraordinary circumstances of arbitrary injustice on the part of the Mexican government would make me feel that we had the right to take control at Tampico or at the Tehuantapec R.R.

As I suggested, in a previous letter on this subject, there is reason to believe that the government at Mexico City is not in real control of the Tampico district itself and that English influences are. The same may be true at Tehuantapec.

I would be very much obliged if you would confer very fully with the British Ambassador about this whole situation. There is absolutely no breach of the Monroe doctrine in allowing the British to exercise an influence there which anti-American sentiment in Mexico for the time prevents our exercising. After you have ascertained the British plans and intentions thereabout we should have a conference (you and I) about what we may and can do,—I mean can consistintly with our principles and with our predominant influence just now in Latin America.

Faithfully Yours,   W.W.

WWTLI (SDR, RG 59, 711.12/43½, DNA).

From Guy Tresillian Helvering[1]

My dear Mr. President,   Washington, D. C. April 19, 1917.

The next few weeks—possibly days—will decide as to the policy which the country will adopt in securing the necessary forces which will be needed to protect the interests of the country.

Of course I am aware that you favor what is familiarly termed a "selective draft," but that term is not generally understood by the people and I feel that if you would but express your views, as clearly as you have on many other occasions, so that all may understand, much of the doubt would disappear and we would be able to get together for the common good much more readily.

I trust that you will realize that in writing you I am doing so in no captious spirit. We are all aiming for a common goal and I believe with the same earnestness of purpose, but we cannot overlook the fact that a great many of our people have a decided objection to anything which could be construed as "conscription" or "draft" and I am certain that a statement from you to the country would quickly clear away much of the misunderstanding which is now in existence.

Sincerely yours,   Guy T Helvering

TLS (WP, DLC).
  1 Democratic congressman from Kansas.

To Guy Tresillian Helvering

My dear Mr. Helvering: [The White House] 19 April, 1917

I welcome the inquiry of your letter of April nineteenth because I have realized the truth of what you say from my own observation, namely, that what is meant to be understood by the selective draft is not generally understood throughout the country.

The process of the draft is, I think, very clearly set forth in the bill drafted by the War Department and which I so earnestly hope the Congress will adopt, but it is worth while to state the idea which underlies the bill a little more fully.

I took occasion the other day in an address to the people of the country to point out the many forms of patriotic service that were open to them and to emphasize the fact that the military part of the service was by no means the only part, and perhaps, all things considered, not the most vital part. Our object is a mobilization of all the productive and active forces of the nation and their development to the highest point of cooperation and efficiency, and the idea of the selective draft is that those should be chosen for service in the Army who can be most readily spared from the prosecution of the other activities which the country must engage in and to which it must devote a great deal of its best energy and capacity.

The volunteer system does not do this. When men choose themselves, they sometimes choose without due regard to their other responsibilities. Men may come from the farms or from the mines or from the factories or centers of business who ought not to come but ought to stand back of the armies in the field and see that they get everything that they need and that people of the country are sustained in the meantime.

The principle of the selective draft, in short, has at its heart this idea, that there is a universal obligation to serve and that a public authority should choose those upon whom the obligation of military service shall rest, and also in a sense choose those who shall do the rest of the nation's work. The bill if adopted will do more, I believe, than any other single instrumentality to create the impression of universal service in the Army and out of it, and if properly administered will be a great source of stimulation.

Those who feel that we are turning away altogether from the voluntary principle seem to forget that some 600,000 men will be needed to fill the ranks of the Regular Army and the National Guard and that a very great field of individual enthusiasm lies there wide open.

Cordially and sincerely yours,   Woodrow Wilson

TLS (Letterpress Books, WP, DLC).

To John Humphrey Small

My dear Mr. Small: [The White House] 19 April, 1917

I have your letter of April seventeenth and have read it with not a little sympathy.[1] I am sure that whatever we do with regard to the refugee German ships, and under whatever form of law we do it, we should be careful that the real owners suffer no injuries. I have been in consultation with the Attorney General as to the form and have not received his final advice.

In haste

Cordially and sincerely yours,   Woodrow Wilson

TLS (Letterpress Books, WP, DLC).
  [1] J. H. Small to WW, April 17, 1917, TLS (WP, DLC).

To John Milton Waldron

My dear Mr. Waldron: [The White House] 19 April 1917.

Thank you sincerely for writing me. Your letter was the first notice I had that many of the members of the colored race were not enthusiastic in their support of the Government in this crisis. I am sure their conduct throughout this great emergency will show that there is little if any basis for a statement of this sweeping character.

I am sorry that because of the present situation which hourly demands my attention, it will not be possible for me to attend the meeting to which you have kindly invited me.

Sincerely yours,   Woodrow Wilson

TLS (Letterpress Books, WP, DLC).

To James Sprunt

My dear Mr. Sprunt: [The White House] 19 April, 1917

It was certainly a very gracious act of thoughtful friendship on your part to send me the remarks about myself made at the centennial celebration of the church. I have read them with the deepest appreciation and send you my most grateful thanks.

Cordially and sincerely yours,   Woodrow Wilson

TLS (Letterpress Books, WP, DLC).

From Robert Lansing, with Enclosures

My dear Mr. President: Washington April 19, 1917.

I enclose to you the proposal of the Brazilian Government as to a protocol or declaration complementary to the Pan American Treaty of guarantee to which I referred in a letter to you of two or three days ago. I also enclose a proposal of the Brazilian Ambassador as a substitute for the preamble of the Treaty. He made this proposal personally stating specifically that it was not made under instructions from his Government. He also desired to have it considered confidential.

I do not see how we could possibly accept the proposal of the Brazilian Government or the change suggested by the Ambassador. I think it would be better to proceed on our former lines and stick very closely to the original articles submitted. In order to refresh your memory I submit the four Articles which were proposed. I am a little doubtful as to whether we should press Article III at all or whether we should submit it to the Brazilian Government again. I am afraid that in certain circumstances it might be found very embar[r]assing. Please advise me as to your judgment in regard this Article.

Faithfully yours,   Robert Lansing.

TLS (R. Lansing Papers, DLC).

E N C L O S U R E   I

PROPOSAL OF BRAZILIAN GOVERNMENT.

["]Whereas, upon the respect shown by every American Nation for the rights of the others greatly depends the continuation of political harmony and solidarity in this Continent, the High Contracting Parties agree to declare: *First*, that they adopt as a fundamental rule of conduct in international relations the principle of non-intervention in the political affairs of the others; *Second*, that the guarantees that are the subject of the first article of the Treaty shall be rendered only after the High Contracting Party directly interested shall have requested their fulfillment by the others through the regular diplomatic channels; *Third*, that on recognizing foreign governments, the American Nations continue to be guided by the principle that *de facto* governments are regularly recognizable; *Fourth*, that the present Declaration shall be submitted to the other American Governments to be constitutionally ratified as a part of the Treaty."

SUGGESTION BY THE BRAZILIAN AMBASSADOR.

The Republics of America, considering (having in view) the identity of their political institutions and their common interest in maintaining harmony and amity between themselves, have deemed wise to celebrate a convention with the purpose of pledging mutual aid in the preservation of a continental system assuring them liberty, independence and autonomy in government and to this end agreed and signed, through their respective representatives, the following articles:

E N C L O S U R E I I

ARTICLE I.

That the High Contracting Parties to this solemn covenant and agreement hereby join one another in a common and mutual guarantee of territorial integrity and of political independence under republican forms of government.

ARTICLE II.

To give definitive application to the guarantee set forth in Article I the High Contracting Parties severally covenant to endeavor forthwith to reach a settlement of all disputes as to boundaries or territory now pending between them by amicable agreement or by means of international arbitration.

ARTICLE III.

That the High Contracting Parties further agree, First, that all questions, of whatever character, arising between any two or more of them which cannot be settled by the ordinary means of diplomatic correspondence shall, before any declaration of war or beginning of hostilities, be first submitted to a permanent international commission for investigation, one year being allowed for such investigation; and, Second, that if the dispute is not settled by investigation, to submit the same to arbitration, provided the question in dispute does not affect the honour, independence, or vital interests of the nations concerned or the interests of third parties.

ARTICLE IV.

To the end that domestic tranquility may prevail within their territories the High Contracting Parties further severally covenant and agree that they will not permit the departure from their respective jurisdictions of any military or naval expedition hostile to the established government of any of the High Contracting Parties, and that they will prevent the exportation from their respective jurisdictions of arms, ammunition or other munitions of war destined to or for the use of any person or persons notified to be in insurrection or revolt against the established government of any of the High Contracting Parties.

CC MSS (R. Lansing Papers, DLC).

From Robert Lansing, with Enclosure

My dear Mr. President: Washington April 19, 1917.

We ought to issue a list of contraband. We are receiving inquiries in regard to the matter and are unable to answer.

The Allied Governments have issued lists detailing numerous articles, the lists being very long, increasingly long because of the constant additions made from time to time.

After consideration of the subject it seemed to me that a general rather than a detailed list of contraband could be issued which would not require frequent change and consequent confusion.

If this method meets with your approval I would suggest the issuance of a contraband list like the one enclosed. It covers I believe all the articles included in the lists issued by the Allies, and at the same time it will not require constant amendments as their lists have.   Faithfully yours,   Robert Lansing

TLS (SDR, RG 59, 763.72112/3527A, DNA).

E N C L O S U R E

CONTRABAND OF WAR.

(1) All kinds of arms, guns, ammunition, explosives, and machines for their manufacture; component parts thereof; materials or ingredients used in their manufacture; articles necessary or convenient for their use.

(2) All contrivances for or means of transportation on land, in the water or air, and machines used in their manufacture; component parts thereof; materials or ingredients used in their manufacture; articles or animals necessary or convenient for their use.

(3) All kinds of food and clothing destined to come into possession or control of the enemy government or its officers or agents; articles and materials for the manufacture thereof.

(4) Tools, implements, instruments, equipment, maps, correspondence, papers and other articles, machines, or documents necessary or convenient for carrying on hostile operations.

(5) Coin, bullion, currency, evidences of debt; metals, materials, dies, plates, machinery or other articles necessary or convenient for their manufacture.

T MS (SDR, RG 59, 763.72112/3527A, DNA).

From George Washington Goethals

Dear Mr. President: New York April 19, 1917.

I have the honor to acknowledge the receipt of your letter of the 11th instant, requesting me to take charge of the construction of the large emergency wooden fleet to assist in the carriage of supplies and munitions to the Allies and for other services during the war, and in compliance with your wishes I proceeded to Washington on receipt of your letter for a conference with the United States Shipping Board.

I appreciate the evidence of confidence reposed in me by my selection for this duty, realizing the magnitude of the task and its difficulties.

A company for the handling of the project has been incorporated, and I am proceeding with the plans and necessary organization. From the consideration I have already given to the subject, I question whether the rosy views entertained by the Shipping Board as to the rapidity with which wooden ships in large numbers may be constructed can be realized. As I infer that perhaps the possibilities have been represented to you more hopefully than the situation apparently justifies, I feel that I ought to acquaint you with my view, at the same time pledging every effort of which I am capable to the fulfillment of the duty and the accomplishment of the best and quickest results.

Again assuring you of my appreciation of the honor conferred by this important duty and the very complimentary manner in which you have called upon me to be of assistance, I remain, Yours sincerely, Geo. W. Goethals

TLS (WP, DLC).

From Charles Pope Caldwell[1]

Washington, D. C.
My dear President Wilson: April 19th, 1917.

It has been my desire to and I have at all times since becoming a member of the Congress to support your administration in every particular, and I am anxious to do so in reference to the Army Bill.

The Amendment to sub-division three, section 1, of the bill handed to the Committee by the War Department, to my mind, does this and nothing more, namely: It gives you authority to accept for service men who volunteer pending the time that the draft provision can be put into effect, and who after selection, the same as by draft, you would like to have serve in the National Army. There is no obligation imposed on you to accept them, nor is there any hinderance to nor delay of the draft plan.

I am heartily in favor of using the draft at the earliest possible moment, but it seems to be [me] that the authority given by the amendment might well be used so you can accept those companies and individuals who want to serve their country, who have had military experience, and who can be spared from the industrial persuits.

I realize that they could enlist in the National Guard and Regular Army at present, but owing to the prejudice that has risen in the minds of a considerable number, I am sure that many will refuse to go into those two organizations.

I have sought an interview with you to get your opinion on this point, and to ask you this question.

First, Do you object to having this authority?

If you could accept this provision, I have no doubt but that the bill would be carried unanimously.

I am writing this letter in the greatest friendship, and if you answer the question in the affirmative, I will probably vote against the provision.[2]

Sincerely yours,   Chas Pope Caldwell.

TLS (WP, DLC).
    [1] Democratic congressman from New York, member of the Committee on Military Affairs.
    [2] Caldwell had voted with the majority of the House Committee on Military Affairs on April 18 to report out an amended bill which included the amendment which he discussed in the above letter. *New York Times*, April 19, 1917.

From William Royal Wilder

My dear Wilson: New York April 19, 1917.

My Polish friend, Sosnowski, has a very just and proper appreciation of you and your ideals at this crisis. It is worth your while to read the enclosure[1] if you can possibly spare the time. His former communications I called to the attention of Mr. Tumulty, and suggested that they be sent to the State Department. Mr. Lansing has met Mr. Sosnowski, and I understand lunched with him lately at the Metropolitan Club. He is a man of considerable influence among the Poles and assures me that within six months there could be raised an efficient force of 100,-000 Poles for service in Russia. His real anxiety, however, is in regard to the coming conference. His faith in you and your ideals is unbounded, and he fervently hopes, as do we all, that you will be able to keep as you now hold, the "whip-hand" on the situation. As I look at it, it boils down to this:

If the English statesmen adopt your views as expressed in your message and welcome the idea of a Republic in Russia, the war should be over in sixty days. There must be no dissension among the Allies, and they must follow your lead despite the fact that the English may regard you as too idealistic. For that matter, many of our own people and your best friends think so,— but you are absolutely right. Wars will never cease if we are to be regulated by the *lex talionis*. There must be 'peace on earth for *peaceful* men.' Part at least of the punishment of Prussia can safely be deferred to the Day of Judgment. If Britain thoroughly understands what the Russians want and will subscribe to your views, and you insist upon it, the inevitable revolution in Germany will come right speedily. You must not lose the control and America needs no 'honest broker' in directing and concluding the pending negotiations.

I sincerely wish I could be of some real assistance to you, but I know what you are after and devoutly hope that you will not be swerved from your purpose.

Faithfully yours,   Wm. R. Wilder

TLS (WP, DLC).
¹ G. J. Sosnowski to WW, April 18, 1917, TLS (WP, DLC). This is a long and somewhat florid letter which appealed to Wilson to broaden his moral leadership of the world and, especially, to reconstitute Poland as it existed before the first partition. Sosnowski also included maps of Poland through the third partition and other documents.

Two Letters to Robert Lansing

My dear Mr. Secretary,   The White House. 20 April, 1917.

I see no particular objection to the first and third of the Brazilian suggestions. The second would, of course, be a virtual repudiation of the Monroe Doctrine and could not be accepted by us. The fourth I do not fully understand.

Mr. de Gama's preamble I see no particular point to.

I am clear that we should urge upon Brazil and the other states now in a friendly attitude of cooperation with us the adoption of the articles as drafted, and I would certainly press Article III. along with the rest unless or until it should prove a definite obstacle. In view of the fact that more than twenty of the other nations of the world have entered into such an agreement with us (a fact which should be very persuasive in argument) I should be surprised if that Article proved the stumbling block.

It seems to me that we are clearly in a more favourable position than before in dealing with this matter with Brazil and with many of the other Latin American states. Brazil evidently desires very much to effect a definite rapprochement with us and her example would, in the present circumstances, be a very persuasive fact throughout Latin America. If Morgan¹ is in earnest, it ought to be possible to push the matter through before things grow cold. He ought by this time to know how to deal with the Government there.

I hope that you will organize our diplomatic forces all along the lines to bring this great thing about.

Faithfully Yours,   W.W.

WWTLI (R. Lansing Papers, DLC).
¹ That is, Edwin Vernon Morgan, Ambassador of the United States to Brazil.

My dear Mr. Secretary,   The White House. 20 April, 1917.

I agree with you that this form is the best in which to announce our list of contraband and that we should make an immediate announcement; but I am not clear as to the meaning of all of the enclosed statement.

No. 1 is clear. Under No. 2, is it your idea that all vehicles, of whatever kind, should be considered contraband *no matter whither bound?* Under 3 I assume that the words "destined to come into the possession or control of the enemy government or its officers or agents" is meant to apply to "articles and materials for the manufacture thereof" as well as to "all kinds of food and clothing," but the language does not make that clear. No. 4 is clear. Under 5 I assume that it is meant only to include materials and metals useful in the manufacture of coin, currency, etc., but the section might be read to inclued [include] all metals of all kinds and uses. Of course these points can all be made clear. They do not go to the merits.

Faithfully Yours,   W.W.

WWTLI (SDR, RG 59, 763.72112/3527½, DNA).

From Joseph Patrick Tumulty, with Enclosure

Dear Governor: The White House April 20, 1917.

I hope you will read the letter enclosed from Mr. Brisbane.[1] There has been a good deal of criticism with reference to this legislation[2] and an attempt is now being made by Senator Borah and others (see excerpt from Borah's speech enclosed)[3] to give the country the impression that the real purpose of this legislation is to afford us a shield against criticism of all kinds. Of course this is not the fact, nor is it the purpose of this legislation; but the idea has been industriously circulated and is now being used throughout the country, (see the clippings enclosed).

I think you might use the reply to Mr. Brisbane's letter as a means of putting this idea to sleep forever. You might say to Mr. Brisbane that it is hardly necessary for you to say that you will not request or permit any part of this law to be applied to you or in any way to be used as a bar against just criticism of every kind. "I can imagine no greater disservice than to establish any system of censorship that would deny to the people of a free republic like our own their right to criticise their public officials. I would regret to lose the benefits of just criticism that would flow to me while exercising the functions of the high office to which I have been elected. In these times I can be sure only of the motives which actuate me. I shall try to purge them of selfishness of every kind." The quoted sentences are merely by way of suggestion as to your reply to Mr. Brisbane.

Sincerely yours,   J P Tumulty

TLS (WP, DLC).

[1] Arthur Brisbane, editor of William Randolph Hearst's *New York Evening Journal.*

[2] He referred to a section of the so-called "espionage" bill which, as amended by the Senate Committee on the Judiciary, read as follows:

"Whoever, in time of war, in violation of regulations to be prescribed by the President, which he is hereby authorized to make and promulgate, shall collect, record, publish, or communicate, or attempt to elicit any information with respect to the movement, numbers, description, condition, or disposition of any of the armed forces, ships, aircraft, or war materials of the United States, or with respect to the plans, or conduct, or supposed plans or conduct of any naval or military operations, or with respect to any works or measures undertaken for or connected with, or intended for the fortification or defense of any place, or any other information relating to the public defense calculated to be, or which might be, useful to the enemy, shall be punished by a fine of not more than $10,000 or by imprisonment for not more than 10 years, or by both such fine and imprisonment: *Provided*, That nothing in this section shall be construed to limit or restrict, nor shall any regulation herein provided for limit or restrict, any discussion, comment, or criticism of the acts or policies of the Government or its representatives, or the publication of the same: *Provided*, That no discussion, comment, or criticism shall convey information prohibited under the provisions of this section." *Cong. Record*, 65th Cong., 1st sess., p. 782.

As the enclosed letter from Brisbane suggests, it was widely argued that this paragraph permitted the President to silence all criticism of the administration in time of war, and that, although the first proviso (added by the Judiciary Committee) seemed to safeguard the right of criticism, the second (also added by the committee) appeared to nullify the first. As it happened, after three days of heated debate, the Senate, on April 20, abandoned all efforts to find a compromise and later took up the Espionage bill adopted by the House of Representatives on May 4.

[3] This and the other enclosures mentioned below are missing.

E N C L O S U R E

From Arthur Brisbane

My dear Mr. President: Washington. April 20th, 1917.

I write concerning the proposition to nullify, by war legislation, the Constitutional Amendment guaranteeing freedom of the press.

Freedom of the press does not, of course, mean freedom for editors, but freedom for READERS, freedom for the public to know what is happening, what public servants are doing, what editors and others think on public questions.

Yesterday Senators Borah, Johnson[1] and others, discussing the proposed nullification of the Constitutional Amendment, quoted some of your most distinguished predecessors, including Abraham Lincoln. He was quoted to the effect that "The administrators and administration had better suffer some of the evils and some of the sorrows which accompany such work than that the people should lose control of or forfeit the great benefit flowing from the absolute freedom of the press."

If you had been present at that debate, you would surely have had something important to say. For newspaper men know, as the energetic David Lawrence puts it, that you WANT criticism, and wish to know what even your most unjust critics are thinking, as the pilot is anxious to know about rocks below the water.

Some statesmen appear eager that the nation should embark on the present serious enterprise with comment and criticism muzzled in advance.

Well informed newspaper workers are firm in their belief that desire to nullify the Constitutional Amendment does not at all reflect your state of mind. The newspaper men of the country and the public generally would be glad to hear from you on the subject before the interesting debate goes any farther.

Yours very sincerely,   Arthur Brisbane

TLS (WP, DLC).
¹ Hiram Warren Johnson of California.

To Joseph Patrick Tumulty

Dear Tumulty: [The White House, c. April 20, 1917]

I like your suggestion here and would be grateful if you would formulate a letter for me.   The President.

TL (WP, DLC).

From Robert Lansing, with Enclosure

PERSONAL AND SECRET:

My dear Mr. President: Washington April 20, 1917.

I enclose a copy of a very confidential telegram from Mr. Hoover which I think should receive your immediate attention. In view of what Mr. Hoover says I have had all copies of the despatch destroyed except the original and would suggest that it would be well to destroy this one.

Faithfully yours,   Robert Lansing.

TLS (MH).

E N C L O S U R E

London, April 19, 1917.

6035. Confidential, to be kept secret.

At Hoover's request I send the following important facts:

"Careful investigation present food situation Allied countries shows position is most critical, especially regarding breadstuffs. Stocks Italy, France and England do not average more than eight weeks of which at least four weeks are required for circulation, leaving only one month's real reserve, so that until next March harvest minimum three months' supply must be provided from overseas. The total minimum three months' requirement of breadstuffs, cereal imports for all Allies about eighty million bushels of wheat and thirty million bushels of corn. Approximately ten million bushels of wheat and corn can probably be drawn from India and Argentina, leaving one hundred million bushels required from United States and Canada. This does not include fodder. Disregarding shipping question, these are very close to minimums on which it can be hoped to maintain public tranquility. In view of this I strongly advise that all shipping should be devoted to this end regardless of other uses and all export of cereals to neutrals from the United States sent forth at once. There is a large stock of wheat in Australia which cannot be moved owing to the shortage of shipping not permitting the long haul and as neutrals are giving very little shipping to Allies they should be required to go to Australia for their supplies which they can probably arrange with the British Government and who will thus be enabled to press neutrals to cease food imports into Germany. It should further be remembered that bidding of neutrals in American markets in competition with each other and the Allies forces up prices not only to our own people but to the other Allies.

"Under no circumstances must these facts be made public. Herbert Hoover."   Page.

T telegram (MH).

From Robert Lansing, with Enclosure

My dear Mr. President: [Washington] April 20, 1917.

In connection with the enclosed dispatch from Mr. Page at Rome, which relates to the Russian situation, I have been wondering whether it might not be well for you to send to Prince Lvoff[1] a message which would in reality be an address to the

Russian people, expressing the confidence of the American people in the success of the democratic government which they have established and of our very sincere desire to aid them in their struggle against Germany.[2]

I believe at the present time this would be a most helpful document to be published throughout Russia because of the very high regard in which the United States is held by the liberal element in Russia. Of course if it is to be done at all it should be done at once as I believe the situation is serious and the present Government needs support.

Faithfully yours,   Robert Lansing

CCL (SDR, RG 59, 763.72/3965, DNA).
   [1] Prince Georgii Evgen'evich L'vov, at this time Minister-President of the provisional government.
   [2] Wilson's message to the provisional government is printed at May 22, 1917.

E N C L O S U R E

Rome, April 20, 1917.

926. Prime Minister and Minister for Foreign Affairs[1] left Rome unexpectedly night before last, incognito. Just learned they have gone France, believed for conference touching Russia, where situation considered extremely grave and for greater Italian interests in Eastern Mediterranean.

Nelson Page.

T telegram (SDR, RG 59, 763.72/3965, DNA).
   [1] That is, Paolo Boselli and Baron Sidney Sonnino.

From Edward Mandell House

Dear Governor: New York. April 20, 1917.

A Norwegian architect[1] of some distinction living here and who for the past six months has been with the Belgian Relief Commission in France and Belgium, gave me a message to you from the King of Norway[2] whom he claims to know well.

The King bade him say to you that Norway was entirely in sympathy with the Allies and that the reason she had not come in was because England did not think it wise. He said you could count upon the sympathy and cooperation of Norway in every way possible even to the extent of her entering the war if it were thought advisable. He thoroughly detests the Germans and their methods.[3]

If you could hear the stories these Americans bring back from the occupied portions of France and Belgium you would feel that any sacrifice that America might make was well worth while in order to crush German militarism. The concensus of opinion is that it is not the common soldier but the officer over him that directs the brutality. The German common people seem sick at heart and would be glad to rid themselves of the pest.

I wrote you sometime ago about the Russian Commission. I know more about that situation now than then and I think it it [*sic*] would be well to be careful in the selection of its perso[n]nel. Gompers, I am told, is persona non grata with the labor people.

The best informed Russian that I know, Prof. Simkovitch of Columbia,[4] tells me that he does not so much fear a separate peace as an insistence that peace be made before the German autocracy is finished. The Russians are eager to be rid of the war in order that they may devote themselves to their new internal problems.   Affectionately yours,   E. M. House

TLS (WP, DLC).

[1] Unidentified. House does not mention him in his diary, and the Historian of the Norwegian Royal Ministry of Foreign Affairs, Erik-Wilhelm Norman, has been unable to find anything about the alleged architect.

[2] Haakon VII.

[3] Mr. Norman writes: "After having examined in vain all the relevant source material available at this Ministry I turned for help to Mr. Tim Greve, who quite recently published an extensive and well documented biography of the late King Haakon VII. Mr. Greve said most emphatically that in his research on King Haakon he had never come across information that even remotely could lend verisimilitude to the allegations contained in the letter from Colonel House. While it is true that as a private person the King harbored strong pro-Allies sentiments, he was as a monarch the very model of constitutional correctitude. So, Mr. Greve found it highly improbable that the King would ever dream of delivering to the President of the United States through private channels a message the contents of which ran counter to the policy of neutrality adopted by his Government. I can only add that I share Mr. Greve's feelings in this respect." E.-W. Norman to F. Aandahl, March 23, 1981, TLS (WC, NjP).

[4] Vladimir Grigorievitch Simkhovitch, Professor of Economic History at Columbia University.

From Joseph Patrick Tumulty, with Enclosure

Dear Governor: The White House April 20, 1917.

I just had a little talk with Sydney Brooks who says he has been in correspondence with Lloyd George and Lord Northcliffe with reference to the Home Rule question. He says that just a little push by you in your private talk with Balfour would put over Home Rule. He says if you could bring home to Balfour the amount of American public sentiment which favors it and that how a denial of it is working to the disadvantage of England in this country, it would make a great impression. He says after the war there will of course be great and generous cooperation between England and this country; but that there will never be genuine cooperation between the people of America and the people of England until the Irish question is settled.

I am sending you herewith a letter from Mr. Brooks which he penned today.   Sincerely yours,   Tumulty

TLS (J. P. Tumulty Papers, DLC).

E N C L O S U R E

From Sydney Brooks

Dear Mr. President,   The White House Friday [April 20, 1917]

After several months in America I am now returning to England—& returning, I need not say, in a very happy mood & with the consciousness that the relations between our two countries are at length set fair. There is nothing nearer to my heart than improving them & I believe I see how they could be improved & particularly how the last great obstacle to their betterment—I mean of course, Ireland—could be lessened, if not removed.

I should very greatly value an opportunity of setting before you some views I have formed on this matter, if an opportunity could be found before the arrival of the British Commission.

I leave Washington on Sunday & sail for England on the following Saturday but not, I trust, without being able to pay to you my respects & say my adieux in person.

Believe me, dear Mr. President,
                    Yours very sincerely   Sydney Brooks

ALS (J. P. Tumulty Papers, DLC).

From Sir Cecil Arthur Spring Rice

Dear Mr President   Washington. 20 Ap 1917

These are the words read today at St Paul's Cathedral (Isaiah LXI)

"The spirit of the Lord God is upon me: because the Lord hath anointed me to preach good tidings unto the meek: he hath sent me to bind up the broken hearted: to proclaim liberty to the captives: to proclaim the acceptable year of the Lord, and the day of vengeance of our God: to comfort all that mourn * * * *

And they shall build old wastes: they shall raise up the former desolations and they shall repair the waste cities* * * *

For I the Lord love judgement, I hate robbery: and I will direct their work in truth and I will make an everlasting covenant with them. And their seed shall be known among the Gentiles and their offspring among the people: all that see them shall acknowledge them that they are the seed which the Lord hath blessed* * * *

For as the earth bringeth forth her bud, and as the garden causeth the things that are sown in it to spring forth: so the Lord God will cause righteousness and praise to spring forth before all the nations."

Yours respectfully   Cecil Spring Rice.

ALS (WP, DLC).

From Thomas Watt Gregory

Dear Mr. President: Washington, D. C. April 20, 1917.

In accordance with our understanding I herewith send you three copies of the joint resolution authorizing you to take over the German merchant vessels.[1] I suggest that you send one copy of the resolution to Chairman Culberson of the Senate Judiciary Committee, and one copy to Chairman Webb of the same Committee of the House. This will leave one for your private files.

I assume you will drop a personal line to each of these gentlemen urging the passage of the resolution.

Faithfully yours,   T. W. Gregory

TLS (WP, DLC).
[1] T MS (WP, DLC). The draft resolution authorized the President to "take over to the United States the possession and title" of any vessel within the jurisdiction of the United States which belonged to any subject or citizen of any nation with which the United States was at war and to make use of it, through the United States Shipping Board or any other agency of the government, in any way that he saw fit.

A Memorial to the President

Sir,   Boston, Mass. April 20, 1917.

When this European war began the world involuntarily speculated whether the Irish would be loyal and the Russian Jews, because of the denial of home rule by England, and of civil and political rights by Russia. As the United States of America enters this awful war the world speculates whether

Americans of color will be loyal because of the denial of rights to a majority of them.

Since Colored Americans in the past have offered their lives in every way for the country, if Germany is seeking to induce them to revolt, it but proves how notorious is their proscription. If this nation, knowing the active loyalty of the Americans in the past, believes this alleged plotting could succeed, it shows that the government and people believe that Colored Americans are most unjustly treated.

The Boston Branch of the National Equal Rights League, meeting when the country is at war, realizing its responsibility as a branch of the only nation-wide organization formed by and of and led by Colored citizens to oppose race and color discrimination, declares false all charges of disloyalty.

Colored Americans would be less than human if they did not feel bitterly every bar from employment, from public accommodation because of our race and color. Deep is the resentment against enforced segregation by city, state, or the federal government whether in the civil or military service. But we have no thought of taking up arms against this country. Ours it has been to save the government from rebellion. This work of our fathers we shall not destroy. There is not gold enough in all the treasuries of the nation[s] of the earth to corrupt us, for it is not a question of money, but of equality of rights.

Let neither white nor Colored Americans seek to deny the truths of human nature. Soldiers of democracies fight better than soldiers of autocracies. The same men fight better if in time of peace they can sell their labor in the open market than if denied work because of race; fight better if public accommodation in peace depends on conduct and the price, than if it is denied for color; fight more eagerly if in peace encouraged by possession of a free man's ballot, than if repressed by its denial; fight with more heart if in peace they have court protection than if their very race means possible murder by the mob.

To the national government which calls us all to war, to our fellow Americans of every race variety we would appeal in the name of fairplay, of justice and humanity. We are all citizens of a common country.

There is need no longer of subjection of Americans to the race prejudices of fellow Americans. In the presence of a common danger and a common obligation, with a war devasting Europe caused by racial clanishness and racial hatred, under Almighty God, let the United States of America and the people thereof give up race proscription and persecution at home. Let the door of the workshop, the school, the college, the civil service, the army, the navy, the military school, the naval school, now and henceforth open alike to every citizen of the Republic without regard to race and without distinction of color. Let the right to travel, to vote, to have court protection be free, without barrier or denial.

Give, Mr. President and all our Governors, the same encouragement for volunteering or enlisting to white, to brown, to yellow, to black, Americans all, by vouchsafing the same free chance to enlist, to rise by merit, and on return home, the same right to civil service, and to civil rights without bar or segregation.

With our great Republic entering a world war for humanity, remove the need for the Colored mother and father to suffer under the feeling that their son will return to find the color line drawn at factory, eating place, playhouse, and ballot-box; make it not necessary for the Colored soldier in the trenches to suffer with the thought that as he bares his breast to the bullet his sister is segregated in the government service at Washington and his mother in danger of the lynching mob.

Recognizing the world honored ethics of national defense, as England promised home-rule to the Irish and Russia abolition of restriction and the ghetto to her Jews, the United States of America is now called upon to grant the abolition of federal segregation and of disfranchisement to her Colored citizens.

As this nation goes forth to fight the "natural foe of liberty," let Americans highly resolve that all shall have liberty within her borders. As she fights for democracy as against autocracy let there be a democracy at home 100%, not 90% strong. As our President declares we "fight for the right of those who submit to authority to have a voice in their own government," let us all resolve that when the war is over such shall be the privilege of 100% of our people, not 90%.

Now is the time for all in authority to declare for the abolition of all racial discriminations and proscriptions and for all to join in our unhyphenated Americanism for victory under the favor of the God of all mankind.

Emery T. Morris 30 Parker St. Cambridge Mass.
William D. Brigham, 41 Wheatland Ave. Dorchester, Mass.
Allen W. Whatley 40 Warwick St Boston Mass.
William Monroe Trotter, 34 Cornhill, Boston, Mass.
Matthew A Neil Shaw DD MD. 16 Allston Hghts Boston Mass
Theodore Drury 20 Kendall St Boston Mass.
Mrs. Cravath Simpson, 21 Tappan St. Everett

R. McCants Andrews, 69 Dana St., Cambridge, Mass.
Mr. Wesley J. Furlong, Melrose, Mass.
Mrs Mary E. Gibson 49 Hammond St Roxbury Mass
Mrs Mary C. Hall 96 Kendall St Boston Mass
Mrs J. G Street 75 Camden St Roxbury District Boston Mass
Mrs. L. C. Parrish 95 Camden St. Boston Mass.
(Rev) Montrose W. Thornton Boston Mass., 102 Camden St.
Rev. Johnson W. Hill #313 Columbus Ave., Boston Mass.
Curtis J. Wright Atty. #39 Court St., Boston, Mass.
Mrs. Emeline Sport.

TS MS (WP, DLC).

To Henry Prather Fletcher

Washington, April 21, 1917.

The President desires that you take an early opportunity to discuss the present situation very frankly with General Carranza. You may say that this Government[,] relying [on] his declaration of Mexico's neutrality in the war between the United States and Germany confidently expects his Government to prevent Mexican territory from becoming a base of hostile acts toward the United States. General Carranza is, of course, aware that numbers of German subjects have passed and are passing from the United States to Mexico. Their known activities in the latter country cause this Government to be apprehensive of complications which the President is anxious to avoid. Appreciating the frank avowal of neutrality by General Carranza it seems needless to express the hope that he will take prompt and effective steps to prevent illegal acts of German subjects in Mexico which may interrupt or injure the trade of countries friendly with Mexico, jeopardize the lives and property of their citizens or in any way compromise the neutrality of Mexico.   Lansing

T telegram (SDR, RG 59, 862.20212/270a, DNA).

To Charles Allen Culberson

My dear Senator: [The White House] 21 April, 1917

I am taking the liberty of sending you enclosed a suggestion for a Joint Resolution which I think of capital importance and of immediate necessity. I hope that you will think it of as much consequence as I do, and I sincerely hope that its early passage will be possible. Just now our relation to the German ships which are in our custody is a very anomalous one and I think the public opinion of the country would justify the action I am suggesting.

I hope that in sending you suggestions of this sort in this way I am acting in the way that is agreeable to you. I, of course, hold myself ready to have a personal conference upon any matter of this sort at any time and hope that you will indicate your wishes to me if a personal conference should seem to you necessary and desirable.

Cordially and sincerely yours   [Woodrow Wilson][1]

CCL (WP, DLC).
[1] WW to E. Y. Webb, April 21, 1917, CCL (WP, DLC), is the same letter, *mutatis mutandis.*

From Robert Lansing, with Enclosure

My dear Mr. President: Washington April 21, 1917.

Owing to the mass of business which is accumulating and for the transaction of which it is necessary to confer with representatives of other departments, it has been deemed advisable to appoint an inter-departmental committee. So far, the only departments which have members on this committee are State, Justice, and Commerce, and it is impossible to get the other departments to take the initiative in appointing men to represent them on this committee. It has been thought advisable by the Attorney-General, the Secretary of Commerce, and myself, to bring about the completion of this committee by an executive order, a draft of which I enclose. There are many matters, such as censorship of mails, restrictions on entrance of aliens, regulations to govern exports under the bill pending in Congress, regulations to govern censorship of land and cable wires, etc., which, for their prompt disposition, require consultation with members of the departments concerned, not possible without a standing committee of subordinate officers authorized to present the views of their departments.

If you approve of the enclosed draft executive order, I would suggest that it be issued at the earliest possible moment, in order that the amount of pressing business which is increasing may be disposed of.

Faithfully yours,   Robert Lansing.

TLS (WP, DLC).

ENCLOSURE

EXECUTIVE ORDER

It is hereby ordered that the Departments of State, Treasury, War, Justice, Navy, and Commerce shall each appoint an officer as a representative on an inter-departmental committee to be designated as the *War Trade Committee* to confer upon and make recommendations regarding matters of interest to two or more departments relating to trade during the war in which the United States is engaged. This Committee may call in from time to time other officials or members of their own or other departments of the Government for purposes of consultation and assistance.

The recommendations of this Committee will be presented to the appropriate cabinet officer or officers for their consideration and if they deem it necessary for presentation to the President. The White House, April 21, 1917.

T MS (WP, DLC).

From Lillian D. Wald, with Enclosure

Dear President Wilson: New York City. April 21st, 1917.

Mrs. Willard Straight's[1] name would have appeared among the signatures attached to the enclosed copy of the letter sent to you a few days ago, had we been able to reach you before forwarding the communication to you.

Mrs. Straight was one of the first people we thought of who would sign this appeal for a re-statement of our democratic principles. I should be glad if you would, as a matter of record, attach her name to the letter sent to you.

Mrs. Willard Straight will perhaps add a note to this letter.
          Very sincerely yours,   Lillian D. Wald.

TLS (WP, DLC).
[1] Dorothy Payne Whitney Straight.

ENCLOSURE

From Lillian D. Wald and Others[1]

Dear Mr. President: Washington, D. C., April 16, 1917.

We are deeply concerned lest America, having declared a state of war, should sacrifice certain safeguards fundamental to the life of her democracy.

Several bills are now before Congress, or may come before it, seeking to punish those who designedly use military information for the benefit of foreign governments.

With this purpose we, of course, are entirely sympathetic but the administration of such laws, purposely made comprehensive, so as to include a wide range of possible offenders, may easily lend itself to the suppression of free speech, free assemblage, popular discussion and criticism.

We believe that you would deem it essential, perhaps more at this time than at any other, that the truth should not be withheld or concealed from the American people whose interests after all are the most vital consideration.

Even by this time, we have seen evidence of the breaking down of immemorial rights and privileges. Halls have been refused for public discussion; meetings have been broken up; speakers have been arrested and censorship exercised, not to prevent the transmission of information to enemy countries, but to prevent the free discussion by American citizens of our own problems and policies. As we go on, the inevitable psychology of war will manifest itself with increasing danger, not only to individuals but to our cherished institutions. It is possible that the moral damage to our democracy in this war may become more serious than the physical or national losses incurred.

What we ask of you, Mr. President, whose utterances at this time must command the earnest attention of the country, is to make an impressive statement that will reach, not only the officials of the federal government scattered throughout the union, but the officials of the several states and of the cities, towns and villages of the country, reminding them of the peculiar obligation devolving upon all Americans in this war to uphold in every way our constitutional rights and liberties. This will give assurance that in attempting to administer war-time laws, the spirit of democracy will not be broken. Such a statement sent throughout the country would reinforce your declaration that this is a war for democracy and liberty. It is only because this matter seems of paramount public importance that we venture to bring it to you at this time for your attention.

Very sincerely yours,

TCL (WP, DLC).

¹ This is the only copy of this letter in WP, DLC. A note on the first page reads "Letter sent by a group of people." The signers included, among others, Herbert Croly, Matthew Hale, Ben B. Lindsey, Charles C. Burlingham, Charles J. Rhoads, Lillian D. Wald, Jane Addams, Amos R. E. Pinchot, Owen R. Lovejoy, Paul U. Kellogg, and Elizabeth Gardiner (Mrs. Glendower) Evans. This letter and Wilson's reply were published in early May. See the *New York Times*, May 6, 1917.

From Edward Mandell House

Dear Governor: New York. April 22, 1917.

At the suggestion of Sir William Wiseman who, I believe, spoke also for Sir Cecil, I met Balfour as he passed through this morning and had an interesting talk with him.

Wiseman was afraid that he might get a wrong viewpoint because of his association with certain people he knows over here whom he was likely to meet before he saw you. I am glad I did so for some unlucky person thought to have General Wood meet the party yesterday.

I told Balfour that unless you advised to the contrary, I thought it would be well to minimize the importance of his visit here to the extent of a denial that it was for the purpose of forming some sort of agreement with the Allies. I find there is a feeling that this country is about to commit itself to a secret alliance with them.

Such men as Lippman[n] and Croly have been to see me, and I could not convince them that the object of the visit of the British and French was not for this purpose.

I hope you will agree with me that the best policy now is to avoid a discussion of peace settlements. Balfour concurs in this. If the Allies begin to discuss terms among themselves, they will soon hate one another worse than they do Germany, and a situation will arise similar to that in the Balkan States after the Turkish War. It seems to me that the only thing to be considered at present is how to beat Germany in the quickest way.

I told Balfour I hoped England would consider that a peace which was best for all the nations of the world would be the one best for England. He accepted this with enthusiasm.

If you have a tacit understanding with him not to discuss peace terms with the other allies, later, this country and England, will be able to dictate broad and generous terms—terms that will mean permanent peace.

Balfour was kind enough to remember all the things I had told him about you, and which he knows now are true. I know you will like him and I envy you the pleasure you will have in exchanging views with him.

Affectionately yours,   E. M. House

TLS (WP, DLC).

From the Diary of Thomas W. Brahany

Sunday, April 22, 1917

Washington cheered, clapped, honked, tooted and in other noisy ways showed its approval this afternoon when Arthur James Balfour and his colleagues of the British Mission reached Washington. They arrived by special train at the Union Station at 3 o'clock where they were met by the Secretary of State and other high officials of the government. A great crowd cheered them at the station and their journey, under cavalry escort, from the station to the Franklin McVeagh Home in 16th Street, was through streets lined with admiring thousands who greeted them warmly. British and French flags are flying over many homes and on thousands of automobiles.

From Josephus Daniels, with Enclosure

Dear Mr. President: Washington. Apr. 23. 1917.

Enclosed is a telegram from Admiral Sims. As you will recall, after the visit of Admiral Browning and Admiral Grasset[1] last week, it was decided to send five destroyers at once across the ocean to the place the two governments deemed most necessary. They have not reported, but the destroyers are ready and we expect their answer to-day. I sent a cable to Admiral Sims and upon his answer to-day ordered the six destroyers to the point [to] be designated by him.   Sincerely,   Josephus Daniels

ALS (WP, DLC).
[1] Vice Admiral Sir Montague Edward Browning, commander in chief of the North American and West Indies Station of the Royal Navy; Rear Admiral R. A. Grasset, commander of the French fleet in the Caribbean.

E N C L O S U R E

London April 21, 1917.

PERSONAL. 6056. Following is of extreme urgency and vitally confidential.

Admiral Sims says Quote: Situation here is critically serious and daily growing worse. During last twenty-four hours thirteen ships forty-four thousand tons lost not counting four mine sweepers mostly southwest of Ireland. April first to eighteenth inclusive four hundred and eight thousand tons sunk. Of utmost urgency that we give maximum assistance immediately. Every other consideration should be subordinated. I urge the immediate sailing of all available destroyers followed at earliest moment by reenforcement of destroyers and all light draft craft available. Fuel is available on this side. Vitally important that this information be treated with utmost secrecy and urgency. End quote   Page.

T telegram (WP, DLC).

From Frederic René Coudert

[New York]
April Twenty-Third
Dear Mr. President: Nineteen-Seventeen.

Mr. Henry L. Stimson has been good enough to send me copy of the letter of April 17th, which he has sent to you in regard to our trip through the Middle West. Let me send this line in confirmation and reiteration of all that he there says. It was a source of very real gratification to Mr. Stimson, Mr. Walcott and myself to find how strong and earnest the people were in their desire to support the policy of the Administration as so admirably outlined in your historic message. We can assure you from personal experience that the great mass of opinion favors the plan therein proposed and the policy of your Administration in recommending military service based upon the obligation of all citizens to serve the nation. The justice and democratic nature of this programme is beginning to be thoroughly understood in the States of Michigan, Illinois, Iowa, Minnesota, Nebraska, Kansas, Missouri and Indiana.

I feel confident that whatever the occasional utterances of a few Congressmen the mass of the people of these States will earnestly, sincerely and persistently support you in obtaining the desired legislation. May I also add that public opinion in these sections seem[s] fully to grasp the vital significance underlying the great conflict and is no longer deflected or confused by controversial matter; as their questionings and discussions indicated, they are now beginning to realize, owing largely to your message, that the conflict is not over questions of law, but over the much more vital question of the existence of law rather than force, as the governing factor in future world politics.

Believe me, my dear Mr. President, with expressions of very sincere regard,   Faithfully yours,   Frederic R. Coudert

TLS (WP, DLC).

From the Diary of Thomas W. Brahany

Monday, April 23, 1917

Mr. Balfour was received by the President this morning. He was accompanied by the Secretary of State. All of the available military and naval aides of the White House were on duty. The meeting took place in the Blue Room. Mr. Balfour and Secretary Lansing talked with the President more than a half hour. Tonight the President will entertain at dinner in compliment to Mr. Balfour's party.

The members of the French Mission will reach Hampton Roads on a French cruiser tomorrow where they will board the Mayflower, the President's yacht. They will reach Washington Wednesday morning. Breckinridge Long, Third Assistant Secretary of State, who is to meet the party at Hampton Roads, is "up in the air" today. He planned on furnishing the best of food and drink as part of the entertainment on the Mayflower when he was reminded of the order of the Secretary of the Navy against taking intoxicating liquor aboard Navy vessels. He appealed to Secretary Daniels who said he would not modify the order. Accordingly the distinguished French visitors will have no wine for dinner tomorrow night. It will be a novel experience for them, I dare say.

To Joseph Patrick Tumulty, with Enclosure

Dear Tumulty: [The White House, c. April 24, 1917]

The real answer to this letter I think it would perhaps be better for you to write than me. It is that I believe that such action as they suggest would do the cause more harm than good. As a one-time member of the Jersey Legislature, I think you can yourself imagine how you would feel about a letter from the President of the United States urging action by the State Legislature in the way of domestic policy of this sort. I am sure you will know how to intimate this difficulty to these ladies.

The President.

TL (WP, DLC).

E N C L O S U R E

April 24th [1917].

The Secretary promised a committee from The Just Government League of Maryland to call these resolutions to the attention of the President.[1]

T MS (WP, DLC).
[1] Two resolutions adopted by the annual convention of the Just Government League of Maryland, April 23, 1917, T MSS (WP, DLC). The first requested Wilson to send a message to the Governor and General Assembly of Maryland urging the immediate introduction and passage of a bill granting the suffrage to the women of the state in presidential, congressional, and municipal elections. The second asked Wilson, as the leader of the Democratic party, to "interpret" the suffrage plank of the platform of 1916 for the "enlightenment" of the Governor, Assembly, and people of Maryland.

From Stephen Samuel Wise

My dear Mr. President: New York April 24, 1917

I know you will understand and pardon me if I say to you with perfect frankness that I trust there is no ground for the rumor in the press that you are thinking of naming Mr. Elihu Root as the chief of our special Embassy to Russia. It is beyond dispute that Mr. Root is a man of trained mind and of distinguished accomplishments as a lawyer. At the same time, whatever be Mr. Root's repute as a lawyer, he stands out before the American people as the most eminent and powerful representative of those theories of government and political life to which you as the leader of the American democracy are opposed. It would seem to me that much of the great service which you have rendered the Russian people by your heartening reference in the Message of April 2nd would be lost if Mr. Root should be singled out as the chief representative of the American government and American opinion in the matter of co-operating with the Russian people as one of our Allies in the battle for the security of democratic peoples. Mr. Root has sometimes given of his pre-eminent gifts to the service of the country, but his talents have always been at the command of those reactionary influences in our political and industrial life to free the American people from which you have been twice elected President of the United States.

Mr. Root might, I dare say, be trusted to carry out your injunctions if you should commission him to be your representative. But I venture to ask,—why should a man be singled out for this great opportunity of service to a fellow-democracy in the making who is not of your mind, who is not a sharer of your own spirit touching the fundamental issues of democracy?

I must say to you in utmost frankness that I do not believe you have seriously considered naming Mr. Root for that post. Believing as I do that you were not only the first to greet the liberated Russian people but that the great weight of your influence has since the beginning of the war been exerted in behalf of a new regime to the end that Russia might be fitted to march side by side with her democratic Allies, it seems to me that it would be altogether unfitting to send to Russia a man who may find his voice now in greeting to the Russian people after their freedom has been achieved but who in his personality and practice throughout a lifetime has, above all, represented those very influences and powers from which the Russian people have at last liberated themselves.

Surely there must be men, not a few, who could be named as your representatives in connection with the Embassy to Russia, men who would speak out of the heart of the American people, men who by reason of innate convictions, not improvised views, would be fitted to voice your own will to further the hopes of democracy throughout the world.

I am, my dear Mr. President,

Very Faithfully yours,   Stephen S. Wise

TLS (WP, DLC).

From the Diary of Thomas W. Brahany

Tuesday, April 24, 1917

The dinner at the White House last night was strictly formal. Tumulty didn't like it because there was no music. I asked him this morning "How about it?" He replied, "Stupid; no music, no speeches and not enough soup." The guests included all the members of the British Mission except eight or ten of the less important officials, the members of the Cabinet, the Advisory Council of National Defense, ranking Army and Navy Officers, a few of the Assistant Secretaries of Departments, the Chairman of the Shipping Board, the Comptroller of the Currency and a few others. Mrs. Wilson and Miss Bones were the only women at the dinner. Mr. Balfour sat at Mrs. Wilson's right. Spring Rice, the British Ambassador, sat at the President's right. No members of Congress were invited.

The newspapermen had a talk today with Lieut. General Bridges[1] of the British Mission. He made a distinct hit. "Every inch a soldier," "I'd feel confidence with such a man as my superior," "He's a pippin," "A modest and capable man." These were some of the comments of the enthusiastic newspapermen when they returned from their talk with General Bridges.

Tonight I shall attend the reception which Secretary Lansing is giving in honor of Mr. Balfour in the Pan American Building. It is for men only—all members of Congress have been invited. The hour of the reception is 10 o'clock. The invitation reads, "To meet the Right Honorable Arthur James Balfour, M.P.Q.M. His Britan[n]ic Majesty's Principal Secretary of State for Foreign Affairs."

The President this morning signed the seven billion dollar bond bill. Secretary McAdoo asked for and received the pen used by the President in approving this bill.

Attended the reception last night at the Pan American Union Building. The line consisted of Secretary Lansing, Mr. Balfour and the British Ambassador. Mr. Balfour is very gracious and looked the part of the high class statesman that he is. He was warm in his greeting to everybody. The President arrived about 10:30 and his entrance was a signal for loud applause. In a few minutes the President was the centre of attraction. Dozens of Senators and Representatives greeted him, many of them informing him of their purpose to vote for the conscription bill. Former Senator Root had a minute or two with the President— their first meeting in a long time. The President was very cordial. I understand the President wishes Root to go to Russia as a member of a special American Commission and I think Root advised the President last night of his willingness to go. Next to the President the ablest statesman in this country, in my opinion, is Elihu Root. If he goes to Russia I hope he, and not Charles R. Crane, will be Chairman of the American Commission. The President did not stay at the reception more than fifteen or twenty minutes. Nearly all members of the Diplomatic Corps were at the reception. I had an interesting talk with Mr. Koo,[2] the Chinese Minister. My friend Sam Blythe has been writing some powerful pieces on political affairs in China for the Saturday Evening Post. I asked Mr. Koo if he had read Blythe's articles, and with true oriental diplomacy and a sly smile he replied: "Yes, he is a very witty writer." Miss Rankin,[3] member of Congress from Montana, was the only woman at the reception.

[1] Maj. Gen. George Tom Molesworth Bridges, commander of the 19th division of the British army.

[2] Ku Wei-chün, usually known in western countries as Vi Kyuin Wellington Koo.

[3] Jeannette Rankin.

From the Diary of William Phillips

Tuesday, April 24th.

A frightful day of details. The French party will arrive in Washington at noon to-morrow and all arrangements have been made for their reception, following the precedent of the Balfour party.

I saw the President in his library to-day regarding the dinner which he will give for the French on Thursday. Referring to the dinner at the White House last night for Balfour and his party, the President said he tried hard to talk to everybody—and he certainly did—but that everybody he spoke to got so frightened that he himself became very nervous.

The British Commission met in conference most of the morning to arrange their own program. I am glad that they are not prepared for action, for we are certainly not.

Balfour called this afternoon on Mrs. Wilson and Mrs. Lansing.

The dinner last night at the White House for Balfour was about sixty people, and members of the British Embassy and junior members of the Commission were invited in afterwards. The President forgot to give a toast to the King, which was a bad error. The seating of the table was atrocious—never saw anything so bad in my life, not one person at the table in his proper place.

Denman of the Shipping Board called and said his information showed that the sinking by submarines was increasing and that the German million-tons-a-month mark is rapidly being reached.

T MS (W. Phillips Papers, MH).

Jean Jules Jusserand to the Foreign Ministry

Washington, sans date reçu le 24 Avril 1917

CONFIDENTIEL

No. 497 M. Balfour a déjeuné dans l'intimité à l'Ambassade après avoir fait visite au Président.

Il s'est montré très satisfait de l'accueil reçu et des dispositions dans lesquelles il a trouvé M. Wilson. Il le croit (et je pense de même) décidé à continuer la guerre jusqu'à ce que l'Allemagne soit réellement vaincue.

Le Ministre anglais n'estime pas que des arrangements écrits soient utiles ou souhaitables. Bon vouloir réciproque, la communauté d'intérêts et d'intentions suffiront et vaudront mieux qu'un traité. On pratiquera ce qu'on appelle ici un "gentleman's agreement."

Un des points les plus difficiles à régler dans son opinion et sur lequel des divergences de vues sont le plus à craindre est le sort de l'Autriche.

J'ai fait connaître déjà à V. Exc. comment le Président Wilson incline à l'envisager. M. Balfour m'a paru ne pas s'écarter sensiblement de cette manière de voir selon laquelle il pourrait y avoir, à tout prendre plus d'avantage à laisser subsister une Autriche affaiblie par la quasi-indépendance de plusieurs de ses provinces que de risquer un démembrement à la suite duquel les partis allemands complètement manarchiques [monarchiques] subiraient l'attraction de l'Empire voisin et finiraient par s'agglomérer à lui. Le noyau germanique serait grand et sa puissance serait d'autant plus redoutable qu'on ne peut prévoir encore quel genre de contrepoids pourrait représenter la Russie.

Il va sans dire que ce sont là des vues exposées dans l'intimité sans caractère officiel ni définitives mais il me parait utile de les rapporter à titre confidentiel.   Jusserand

T telegram (Guerre 1914-1918, États-Unis, Vol. 506, p. 281, FFM-Ar).

T R A N S L A T I O N

Washington, no date
received April 24, 1917

CONFIDENTIAL

No. 497 Mr. Balfour had lunch privately at the embassy after visiting the President.

He showed himself well satisfied with the reception he had received and with Mr. Wilson's intentions. He believes (and I agree with him) that he has made up his mind to carry on the war until Germany is really beaten.

The English Minister does not believe that written arrangements would be useful or desirable. Reciprocal good will and a community of interests and intentions will suffice and be worth more than a treaty. They will effect what is called here a "gentleman's agreement."

One of the most difficult points to settle, in his view, and one on which there is most to fear from differences of opinion, is the fate of Austria.

I have already informed Your Excellency how President Wilson is inclined to view this question. Mr. Balfour does not seem to me to diverge very much from this way of looking at it—

that, on the whole, it is better to let survive an Austria that is enfeebled by the quasi-independence of several of its provinces than to risk a dismemberment with the result that the thoroughly monarchical German parties would be subject to the attraction of the neighboring empire and end up by joining it. The Germanic nucleus would be great, and its power even more redoubtable, since we still cannot foresee what sort of counterweight Russia could offer.

It goes without saying that these views, expressed privately, have no official character and are not definitive, but it appears useful for me to report them on a confidential basis.

Jusserand

To Arthur Brisbane[1]

My dear Mr. Brisbane: [The White House] 25 April, 1917.

I sincerely appreciate the frankness of your interesting letter of April twentieth with reference to the so-called Espionage Bill now awaiting action of the Congress.

I approve of this legislation but I need not assure you and those interested in it that, whatever action the Congress may decide upon, so far as I am personally concerned, I shall not expect or permit any part of this law to apply to me or any of my official acts, or in any way to be used as a shield against criticism.

I can imagine no greater disservice to the country than to establish a system of censorship that would deny to the people of a free republic like our own their indisputable right to criticize their own public officials. While exercising the great powers of the office I hold, I would regret in a crisis like the one through which we are now passing to lose the benefit of patriotic and intelligent criticism.

In these trying times one can feel certain only of his motives, which he must strive to purge of selfishness of every kind, and await with patience for the judgment of a calmer day to vindicate the wisdom of the course he has tried conscientiously to follow.

Thank you for having written me.

Cordially and sincerely yours,   Woodrow Wilson

TLS (Letterpress Books, WP, DLC).

[1] The following letter was based upon a draft by Tumulty, a Hw and T copy of which are in WP, DLC.

To George Sibley Johns

My dear Johns: [The White House] 25 April, 1917
Thank you for your letter of April seventeenth.[1] It certainly
warmed my heart, my dear fellow. The approval of old friends
is mighty dear to me just now.
From present indications, I think we will win with the fight in
the House, and there is no doubt we shall win it in the Senate for
the selective draft. Your suggestion about a Congressional commission to go abroad and study the matter is a very interesting
one and in ordinary circumstances I should not hesitate to suggest it to the leaders in Congress, but in the actual circumstances
it is so imperative that we should get to work at once to raise and
drill an army that I am afraid there isn't time for it. We must
do the most practicable thing and do it quickly.
In haste, with warmest regards and appreciation,
                    Faithfully yours,   Woodrow Wilson

TLS (Letterpress Books, WP, DLC).
  [1] It is missing.

From Robert Lansing, with Enclosures

My dear Mr. President: Washington April 25, 1917.
On May 1st General Carranza will be inaugurated as President of Mexico. The question arises whether Fletcher's presence
at the ceremony will be a recognition of the *de jure* character
of the Government and an acceptance of the Constitution.
I am enclosing a memorandum on the subject which recites
in a general way the salient features of the situation.
It would seem as if it were advisable as a matter of policy that
Fletcher should attend the inaugural ceremonies for we ought to
do everything possible to avoid any action which can be seized
upon as a pretext by the Mexicans for complaint.
If Carranza adopts the method referred to in the enclosed
telegram from Fletcher a reply can be drafted making the
proper reservations as to American vested rights affected by the
new Constitution. I enclose a form of reservation which might
be employed.
As to whether Fletcher's presence would be a formal recognition of the *de jure* character of the Government, I think that the
words "*de facto*" may be employed before and after the inauguration in such a way as to indicate that we consider the character
of the Government has not changed by the ceremony of inaugura-

tion but only the title of the head of the Government who will be "the *de facto* President" instead of "The Chief of the Constitutionalist Army."

Of course the advantage to be gained in preserving the *de facto* status is that the obligation to obey any mandate relating to neutrality issued by such a Government is far less than if it is *de jure*. Against an obligation of that sort we should endeavor to guard ourselves as far as possible. Furthermore it would be consistent with the reservation of rights improperly impaired by the new Constitution.

As the time is very short will you please give me your views on this important matter as soon as possible so that I may telegraph instructions to Fletcher?

Faithfully yours,   Robert Lansing.

TLS (WP, DLC).

E N C L O S U R E   I[1]

Confiscation of foreign owned properties in Mexico is the undoubted purpose of the new constitution which is designed to accomplish that purpose by the expropriation of property by executive act and by the retroactive application of its provisions, and by discrimination against foreign interests. Confiscation was the purpose also of many of the decrees of the provisional government, some of which are ratified and adopted by the new constitution. If, therefore, the Government of the United States determines to recognize Carranza as the *de jure* president of Mexico after his inauguration on May 1st, under the new constitution it is essential, if the rights of American owners of property in Mexico are to be preserved and protected that a statement should be incorporated in the letter of recognition to the following effect.

Apr. 25, 1917. Extract from letter of April 13, 1917 from Chandler P. Anderson to Hon. Frank L. Polk in which is pointed out some of the reasons in addition to the above for withholding *de jure* recognition.

CC MS (SDR, RG 59, 812.01/A, DNA).
  [1] The following memorandum and "FORM OF RESERVATION," which follow, had actually been drafted by Chandler P. Anderson. His initialed draft, a T and Hw MS, bears the same file number as the other Enclosures.

E N C L O S U R E   I I

FORM OF RESERVATION.

Recognition is extended to General Carranza as the *de facto* President of Mexico on the understanding and with the reservation that he is recognized without prejudice to the position heretofore taken by the Government of the United States in regard to the decrees of the provisional government and the provisions of the new constitution, if interpreted and applied so as to impair vested rights of foreign owners of properties in Mexico, as to which the Government of the United States reserves full liberty of action, because, as already stated by the Government of the United States, (see instructions to Ambassador Fletcher of January 22, 1917) it cannot acquiesce in the confiscation of or discrimination against the rights and interests of American citizens acquired either under the constitution of 1857 and the laws emanating therefrom or otherwise.

T MS (WP, DLC).

E N C L O S U R E   I I I

Mexico City. April 23, 1917.

122. My telegram number 76 was sent because my presence might constitute recognition de facto Government but in view of the fact that I am informed Carranza expects to announce his election and inauguration in formal letter to the heads of nations the question of recognition will be decided when the President receives this letter and I believe in view of the incidents reported in my telegram 100 my absence might be misunderstood and otherwise generally have a bad effect.   Fletcher.

T telegram (WP, DLC).

From the Diary of Thomas W. Brahany

[Wednesday, April 25, 1917]

We are all delighted at the way the people of Washington turned out to greet the French Mission today. The greeting was more spontaneous and warmer than that given the British Commission on Sunday. There can be no doubt of the deep affection of the people of this country for the French. Minister Viviani was in the first motor with Secretary Lansing, and he was warmly greeted by the cheering crowd which lined the streets from the Navy Yard to Henry White's home on Meridian Hill. The hero of the day was Marshal Joffre who was in the second motor with General Scott, Chief of Staff, U.S.A. Everybody wanted to see the man who planned the battle of the Marne and probably never before has Washington given such a tribute to a foreign visitor as that represented in today's greeting. Forster and I see too many big men to get excited, but we left the office early today and stood at the East entrance of the White House grounds until the French party motored by. And we were thrilled and caught the spirit of the admiring crowd.

Tomorrow at 11 o'clock the President is to receive the French Mission, and tomorrow night he will be host at a dinner in honor of the distinguished guests. We are receiving many letters and telegrams asking good offices to have the British and French Missions visit various cities.

Today Mr. Balfour met the newspapermen. Like General Bridges he made a hit—a decided hit.

The President is now a great National Hero—I think he has greater strength in the country than ever before.

To William Denman

My dear Mr. Denman: [The White House] 26 April, 1917

Since we are all working together for a common end, may I not urge that as fast as the German ships can be put in repair, crews be obtained for them and the necessary equipment, and they be put at once into operation in the trans-Atlantic transportation? I have no doubt at all that Congress will give me the necessary authority in this matter and that they will understand and approve my acting in the meantime if their action should be in any way delayed.

May I not suggest also that, besides sending the COLUMBIA to Honolulu to bring back the German ships lying there, the Shipping Board if practicable send six sea-going tugs also to Honolulu to assist so that we may at the very earliest possible date get the ships there also into operation?

It seems to me highly important, also, that the exact condition of the German ships lying in the harbors of the Philippines should be ascertained as soon as possible and whether it would be practicable to bring them to the United States in the tow of tugs. It has occurred to me that it might perhaps be feasible to bring them home with a certain amount of freight aboard and so contribute to defray the expenses of the operation.

I think it advisable that the Board should apply as promptly as possible and with as exact specifications as possible to the Navy Department with a view to securing the proper and necessary armaments for the ships that are to take part in the trans-Atlantic traffic.

If you will be kind enough to communicate with the Secretary of the Treasury as the work of repair on the vessels is completed, he will issue the necessary orders for their delivery into the hands of the representatives of the Board.

Cordially and sincerely yours,   Woodrow Wilson

TLS (Letterpress Books, WP, DLC).

To William Royal Wilder

My dear Wilder: [The White House] 26 April, 1917

Will you not thank Mr. Sosnowski for his letter which you sent to me enclosed in yours of April nineteenth? I have had my attention called to a number of Mr. Sosnowski's opinions and suggestions and want him to know how very welcome they are.

Cordially and sincerely yours,   Woodrow Wilson

TLS (Letterpress Books, WP, DLC).

To Thomas Watt Gregory

[The White House]
My dear Mr. Attorney General: 26 April, 1917

I know that you will not mind my sending to you the enclosed letter.[1] I am sure Mr. Redfield makes the suggestion in the best spirit, but I am equally sure that there has been no failure on the part of your department to press this suit.

Cordially and faithfully yours,   Woodrow Wilson

TLS (Letterpress Books, WP, DLC).
    [1] It is missing; however, it was W. C. Redfield to WW, April 23, 1917. Redfield urged the expedition of the government's antitrust suit against the United States Steel Corp. T memorandum (WP, DLC), attached to WW to T. W. Gregory, April 26, 1917, CCL (WP, DLC).

To Samuel Gompers

My dear Mr. Gompers: The White House 26 April, 1917

I thank you sincerely for calling my attention to the article in the New Republic, and I am handing it on where I hope many of its suggestions may bear fruit.

In haste

Cordially and sincerely yours,   Woodrow Wilson

TLS (S. Gompers Corr., AFL-CIO-Ar).

To Newton Diehl Baker, with Enclosures

My dear Mr. Secretary: The White House 26 April, 1917

The article from the New Republic which Mr. Gompers encloses in the letter which I am sending you has some very interesting material in it and I thought you might wish to have it considered by the proper committee of the Council for National Defense.

Always   Faithfully yours,   Woodrow Wilson

TLS (N. D. Baker Papers, DLC).

E N C L O S U R E   I

From Samuel Gompers

Sir: Washington, D. C., April 20, 1917.

Apprehension that in the great rush of work and the duties devolving upon you at the present time the article published in the April 14 issue of The New Republic entitled "A Program for Labor" may not have reached your attention, I am sending you the enclosed copy in the earnest hope that you will find a few minutes to read it. The importance of the article is such that I have had a copy made for your convenience.

Respectfully yours,   Saml. Gompers.

TLS (N. D. Baker Papers, DLC).

E N C L O S U R E   I I

A PROGRAM FOR LABOR

Mr. Gompers has repeatedly assured the country of the loyalty of labor. Last Monday, he recommended that the Council of National Defense should "issue a statement to employers and employees in our industrial plants and transportation systems advising that neither employers nor employees shall endeavor to take advantage of the country's necessities to change existing standards." With singular unanimity, the press has magnified this recommendation into a guaranty against strikes and all forms of industrial unrest.

But patriotic manifestos, unsupported by definite administrative plans, offer no such guaranty. Existing standards are changed day by day through the rising cost of food. Workers cannot do efficient work on a diet of loyalty. The government has entered into contracts with certain manufacturers to deliver munitions at a fixed price. These prices are based upon existing rates of wages. The contracts, which are for a definite period, apparently make no provision for an adjustment of prices to increased cost of production. Already the Department of Agriculture forecasts a serious shortage in the wheat crop. If the cost of food rises sharply, the workers in these plants may be forced to demand an increase in wages. Ought not the Council of National Defense to provide against such contingencies? Would not the government be wise to include in these contracts a provision for the establishment of joint conciliation committees upon whose recommendation the terms of the contracts might be made flexibly adjustable to changing market conditions? It was almost a year after the outbreak of war that England created her Munitions Tribunals to deal with just such problems. In their absence, strikes were frequent notwithstanding the patriotism of labor. Ought we not to profit by England's experience?

Unless Mr. Gompers and the Council of National Defense offer specific guidance, the local and state authorities and the official representatives of organized labor are likely to repeat other well intentioned blunders that hampered England during the first eighteen months of the war. On March 28, the New York State Federation of Labor, speaking "for the men and women, aye, and the children of labor * * * who will cheerfully make not only this but other sacrifices on our country's altar" gave advance approval to the suspension of "those statutes that safeguard our industrial population." A few days later, a bill appeared in the state assembly designed to sweep away all restrictions, not only upon the employment of men, but also upon the hours and night work of women and children. This is sheer bathos of misguided sentiment. The experience of England proves that men who work overtime and especially those who sacrifice their one day of rest in seven suffer a steady loss of productive capacity. The records of the English factory inspectors show that for the coldly practical purpose of sustained output, night work for women and children is bad policy. One manager reported that fatigue prevented many of the women from making the effort to go from their work to the mess-room. In another factory, also visited at night, several women spent the meal hour lying beside their piles of heaped-up work, while others were later found asleep beside their machines. "Taking the country as a whole," says the English Health of Munition Workers' Committee, "we are bound to record our impression that the munition workers in general have been allowed to reach a state of reduced efficiency and lowered health which might have been avoided" by reasonable precautions.

We shall blunder seriously if we proceed on the assumption that our factory laws were designed to hamper employers in the efficient conduct of their business. They are founded not on sentiment but on science and economic intelligence. Health and efficiency alike depend upon their enforcement. For this reason, it would be practical folly to entrust their suspension to well meaning amateurs. No modifications, even for short periods, should be permitted except upon the advice and under the control of physiological experts. The industrial army needs its trained medical corps quite as much as the regiments at the front.

As precautionary measures against labor unrest and deterioration, we venture the following suggestions:

1. Conciliation or adjustment committees should be established in all government plants and in all private plants under contract with the government. Upon these committees, employers and employees should have equal representation. It would be their duty to deal with disputes at the original point of friction. In case of their inability to bring about a satisfactory adjustment, appeal should be taken to a Conciliation Board expressly provided by the Council of National Defense.

The urgent need for some such machinery is shown by the history of a strike reported last week from Memphis, Tennessee. The Continental Piston Ring Company manufactures piston rings for aeroplanes used at the government aviation school. The federal court granted an injunction restraining the leaders in charge of the strike from interfering with the operation of the plant. "Federal agents," says the news item, "have started an investigation and arrests may follow if it can be shown that the strike was called with a view to embarrassing the company in filling war orders." Nothing is said about wages, hours or other conditions of employment. No reference is made to any possible valid grievance of the workers. Are detectives and injunctions the best means of developing the loyalty of labor? At this time of national tension would not a system of cooperative adjustment and conciliation be a better risk?

2. A Health Conservation Board, corresponding to the General Munitions Board announced last Tuesday by the Council of National Defense, is imperatively needed to supervise health conditions in government plants and to cooperate with similar state boards in the regulation of private plants under contract with the government. Dr. Frederick Martin of the Council of National Defense[1] is thoroughly qualified to head such an organization. No labor laws should be suspended or modified except after investigation and approval by this body of experts. Indeed, it would be to the best interest of the nation if the government could be persuaded to make minimum standards of hours, wages and shop conditions integral parts of all munition contracts. In wartime the workers will be willing to forego comforts and to work nearer the margin of physical exhaustion than in times of peace, but the country cannot afford the extravagance of paying for work done during incapacity from fatigue or the further extravagance of urging armies of workmen toward relative incapacity by neglect of proved physiological law.

No doubt the Council of National Defense has some such program under consideration. Judging from the experience of England, the effect of measures such as we have suggested would be a great increase in the volume and continuity of output. They would provide a substantial safeguard against industrial unrest.

NEW REPUBLIC, April 14, 1917.

T MS (N. D. Baker Papers, DLC).
[1] Actually, Dr. Franklin Henry Martin.

From Edith Houghton Hooker[1]

My dear Mr. Wilson: Baltimore April 26. 17

We appreciate very deeply your good wishes for the Maryland Suffrage Bill transmitted to us by Mr. Tumulty. We are convinced, however, that it would greatly strengthen our cause in the state if you would, as you did in the case of the Tennessee Legislature,[2] state your opinion of the significance of the suffrage plank in the Democratic Platform.

I had yesterday an interview with Governor Harrington,[3] and he said to me that he did not think the delegates who were elected prior to the adoption of the present National Democratic Platform would feel in any wise bound by this platform. This point of view seems so directly opposed to your splendid statement that I am writing you again to urge you to communicate directly with Governor Harrington and our General Assembly and express your interpretation of the Democratic suffrage plank.

You will remember that your telegram to W. R. Crabtree, President of the Tennessee Senate read as follows: "May I not express my earnest hope that the Senate of Tennessee will reconsider the vote by which it rejected the legislation extending the suffrage to women? Our Party is so distinctly pledged to its passage that it seems to me the moral obligation is complete."

There is a strong sentiment for the suffrage bill among the delegates, and there is no doubt at all but that it will pass with great ease if Governor Harrington, who, you will remember, is a Democratic Governor, would cease blocking its progress.

The delegation of Maryland suffragists that waited upon you on Tuesday, April 24th, was most disappointed at not being permitted an audience with you, but was highly appreciative of Mr. Tumulty's friendliness and charming courtesy.

Thanking you in advance for your cooperation, believe me,

Faithfully yours,   Edith Houghton Hooker

TLS (WP, DLC).
¹ President of the Just Government League of Maryland.
² WW to W. R. Crabtree, Feb. 28, 1917, Vol. 41.
³ Emerson Columbus Harrington.

From Andrew Dickson White

My dear Mr. President: Ithaca, N. Y. April 26, 1917.

I cannot resist the impulse to present a suggestion which may be of use in the present crisis.

As to conscription, the main outcry against it will arise, it seems to me, when the fathers and mothers of our young men, especially those from the universities, colleges, shops and stores, realize that their sons are to be carried off across the ocean and put into the trenches to fight the hardened, well-trained and brutal soldiery of Germany, Hungary, Croatia, and the like.

Why not, under a "selective conscription" take for this foreign service volunteers such as Roosevelt, Funston, Fitzhugh Lee, and their like could raise by tens and perhaps hundreds of thousands, men such as were the riflemen, sharpshooters and ranchmen with whom Andrew Jackson won the battle of New Orleans? And why not in that case train younger men thoroughly and even severely as a Reserve for defence of our country at home, at first at least? At a later period probably very many of these more youthful men of the Reserve would become ambitious to enter the volunteer foreign service.

It seems to me that with some understanding of this sort conscription would be comparatively easy and would not awaken the desperate and perhaps bloody opposition which it is likely to meet unless the "selective feature" is carefully used in some such manner as that above suggested. I remain, Mr. President,

Most respectfully and sincerely yours,

Andrew D. White

TLS (WP, DLC).

Sir Cecil Arthur Spring Rice to David Lloyd George

Washington April 26th, 1917.

No. 1119. Confidential. Following from Mr. Arthur Balfour for Prime Minister:

On Monday April 23rd, I went, by appointment, to see Secretary of State and after some conversation we proceeded together to visit President.

No questions of detail were discussed at either interview; they were indeed rather sedulously avoided both by President and Secretary of State.

This is not surprising since it is quite clear that not very much has been attempted and nothing completed in the way of reforming and expanding organization required to deal with the problems of a great war. Government are indeed fully acquainted with character of these problems and are determined to cope with them in large and useful spirit but mechanism for effectually carrying out this policy is still in large measure lacking.

Most important pronouncement made by President was a two-sided declaration that he did not think it would be expedient to bind himself by any Treaty obligations such as those into which other allies had already entered with each other but that nevertheless having joined us in conflict he meant to throw himself wholeheartedly into it and to see it through to a finish.

He evidently had 2 reasons for adopting line of policy indicated in first of these two statements. He thinks Treaties with European powers, merely because they are treaties, will be unpopular in the country.

I did not gather he shared this prejudice himself but he had to count it as political factor which could not be wisely neglected. He had, however, another reason which from our point of view is of (? utmost) importance. He is of course aware of general tenour of mutual engagements by which European Allies have bound themselves and he contemplates possibility that a time might come when though all essential objects of war had been attained one or other of allies relying on strict letter of treaties would show themselves uncompromising and unpractical over some questions of detail.

He evidently thought in that event United States being themselves unfettered might exercise powerful and valuable influence.

Were I in his place I should have decided as he has done.

He has very clearly grasped fact that Germany inspired by militarism is real enemy, an enemy which he will spare no effort to defeat but both he and Mr. Lansing evidently entertained strong hopes that it may be possible to detach Austria from her domineering partner.

Mr. Lansing confided to me that he was still in communication with Count Tarnowski, Austrian Ambassador elect. He is still in the country and I gather that in conversations with him Mr. Lansing takes the line that United States have no real quarrel with Austria whom they know is far too chivalrous to adopt in practice submarine methods of warfare, in which they have nominally to acquiesce, by their German Ally.

I told Mr. Lansing and President that we had had indications of Austria's anxiety for a separate peace, though practical difficulty she evidently felt in separating herself from Germany was for the present apparently overwhelming.

On the subject of Russia, President like the rest of us is anxious. It is no doubt true as Mr. House told me in so many words that but for Russian Revolution and famous German telegram to Mexico President would have found it very difficult to take decisive step but he is perfectly aware that Russian Revolution with all its possibilities for good is full of dangers for Allied Cause and he is resolved to exercise his whole influence to prevent her under influence of extreme party from making a separate peace. He proposes to send a mission to give advice and to promise assistance.

General Tanners' [The general tenor of the][1] conversation was friendly in the extreme and left upon me not the slightest misgiving as to (? enormous) energy with which administration proposes to carry on war or confidence which we may feel in their promises of co-operation.

T telegram (FO 371/3119, No. 86512, PRO).
[1] Correction from C. A. Spring Rice to D. Lloyd George, April 26, 1917, T telegram (FO 115/2202, pp. 3-7, PRO).

From the Diary of Colonel House

Washington, D. C. April 26, 1917.

Frank Lane was my first and longest caller. We went over the work of the Council for National Defence. He thought it an admirable body but it was not doing effective work because the President would give them no authority. He said, in the early days of his administration of the Interior Department, he took several matters to the President which delayed him in their execution so long that he determined to act upon his own judgment and take the consequence.

He asked if the President relied upon my advice as much as ever, and whether I saw him as frequently as in former days. I gently evaded this, and left him under the impression that, perhaps, I was not consulted more than the Cabinet. I was glad to see that he was pleased with himself and the work of the Council. I shall make inquiries from others on the inside to see how well they agree with his view.

I had lunch with the President and we talked for an hour or more afterward. He said his first conference with Balfour, at which Lansing was present, was not satisfactory for the reason, as he expressed it, "Lansing has a wooden mind and continually blocked what I was trying to convey. I would like to have a conversation with Balfour, you being present. How would it do to invite him to a family dinner and then go into a conference afterward. Do you think this could be done without hurting the sensibilities of anyone?"

My reply was that it could easily be done and it was therefore arranged. He wrote a note to Balfour and asked me to hand it to Drummond with whom he knew I had a four o'clock engagement. In this letter he said substantially this:

My dear Mr. Balfour:

I would like you to dine with me informally next Monday evening at eight o'clock. I have asked House to spend the weekend with me so the three of us may discuss matters together.

Sincerely yours,

The President then told me the substance of his first interview with Balfour and the ground covered. I argued against discussing peace terms with the Allies, just as I did in my first conversation with Mr. Balfour, and in my letter to the President.[1] The President thought it would be a pity to have Balfour go home without a discussion of the subject. My thought was that there was no harm in discussing it between themselves if it was distinctly understood and could be said, that there was no official discussion of the subject, and if neither Government would discuss peace terms with any of the other Allies. It was agreed that this should be done.

In my conference with Sir Eric Drummond, it was thought advisable for me to see Mr. Balfour again before he saw the President, so I might know how to guide the conversation and make it effective and harmonious. Drummond discussed with me quite frankly the situation which faces them as to Spring-Rice. They see he is nervously unfit for his duties. Drummond thought they would take him back to England for a rest. I expressed the hope that it would be merely for a rest, and that they would not replace him by another man who would disturb existing conditions. The fact that Spring-Rice has not been fit has forced us to work with his subordinates, and this arrangement is now quite satisfactory, and we do not wish it interrupted. He promised nothing would be done to upset the method now in force.

We talked of the unsatisfactory condition of the submarine warfare. I thought that whatever they were doing they should try something else, for they could not do worse than at present. It interested me to have him explain the "funnel idea" which I gave Gaunt some two months ago and which he has evidently passed on and which they are planning to adopt.

We worked out an arrangement by which we were to keep in close communication through Wiseman.

T MS (E. M. House Papers, CtY).

1 The meeting which took place on April 22. As House himself said in his diary entry of that date, the letter that he wrote to Wilson on the same day told "much of the conversation though not all." House advised Balfour to be "entirely frank" in his statement to Wilson of the "difficulties" of the Allies: "I suggested that he might exaggerate rather than minimize them which would cause the President to feel that it was necessary for this country to go in up to the hilt rather than in a desultory way." Balfour asked House's opinion about attempting to negotiate separate peace with Austria, Turkey, and Bulgaria. House replied that he "thought well" of Austria and Bulgaria but believed "that we should put Turkey into the scrapheap along with German militarism." Balfour agreed. The two men also discussed the problem of British diplomatic representation in Washington. In response to Balfour's question as to whether Spring Rice "got on well" with Wilson, House replied that the British Ambassador "never saw the President." However, House urged that Spring Rice not be recalled "for the reason that his subordinates like Wiseman, Gaunt and Sir Richard Crawford were working in such close harmony with us that it would be a pity to disturb existing relations by putting in a new man no matter how efficient he might be." House Diary, April 22, 1917.

To Cyrus Hall McCormick, Jr.

My dear Cyrus: The White House 27 April, 1917

You may have seen in the papers that we are thinking of sending a commission to Russia. I am very anxious that the commission should be really representative of what we are and of what we are thinking and I am writing to ask if it will not be possible for you to be a member of the commission. I hope most sincerely that it will be, for I believe that your cooperation will be of the highest value.

The plan would be for the commission to start as soon as its members could get ready for the journey and to take a government vessel at San Francisco and proceed directly to Vladivostok.

This route has been adopted not merely because it is the safer route, but also because it is thought that the impression made in Russia would be all the deeper if the commission crossed Siberia where the most dramatic effects of the recent revolution have been witnessed.

The object of the commission is, primarily, to show our interest and sympathy at this critical juncture in Russian affairs and, secondly, to associate ourselves in counsel and in all friendly services with the present Government of Russia. It is the opinion of those best acquainted with Russia that the time is most opportune for a visit of this sort from commissioners of the United States and that the effect of it will be in every way helpful and stimulating.

Cordially and sincerely yours,   Woodrow Wilson[1]

TLS (WP, DLC).
[1] Wilson wrote the same letter, *mutatis mutandis*, on April 27 to Eugene Meyer, Jr., and Samuel R. Bertron.

To Charles Pope Caldwell

My dear Mr. Caldwell: [The White House] 27 April, 1917

I beg that you will pardon my not having replied sooner to your letter of April nineteenth. The coming of the two foreign delegations has crowded my days beyond measure and I have found it impossible to keep up with my correspondence.

It is now, I am sorry to say, too late to reply to the questions put to me in your letter,[1] but I hope that you will understand why it does not seem possible to me to accept any compromise in the matter of the pending army bill.

I think, in the first place, that you are under a wrong impression as to the time it will take to get the draft process into action. In the second place, I am heartily opposed to having two classes of men in the service and seeming to create some moral difference between them.

In haste, with sincere regard,

Very truly yours,   Woodrow Wilson

TLS (Letterpress Books, WP, DLC).

[1] The House was to vote on the following day on a motion by Julius Kahn, the floor manager of the bill, to strike out the amendment which authorized the recruitment of volunteers, and the administration was standing firm in support of Kahn. The vote on Kahn's motion on April 28 was 313 for to 109 against. *New York Times*, April 28 and 29, 1917; *Cong. Record*, 65 Cong., 1st sess., p. 1555.

To George Washington Goethals

My dear General Goethals: The White House 27 April, 1917

Thank you for your letter of April nineteenth. Its frankness I greatly appreciate.

I am heartily glad you have undertaken the superintendence of the very important work which the Shipping Board is attempting and I have every confidence that the utmost will be made out of it under your superintendence that can be made in the circumstances. I had the pleasure of learning something more of your views the other day through our common friend, Colonel House.

Cordially and sincerely yours,   Woodrow Wilson

TLS (G. W. Goethals Papers, DLC).

To James Cardinal Gibbons

My dear Cardinal Gibbons: The White House 27 April, 1917

The demands upon my time incident to the arrival and entertainment of the foreign commissions now in Washington have delayed my replying to your gracious letter of April nineteenth.[1] I am sure you will understand, and I beg that you will pardon the delay.

The very remarkable resolutions unanimously adopted by the Archbishops of the United States at their annual meeting in the Catholic University on April eighteenth last, a copy of which you were kind enough to send me,[2] warms my heart and makes me very proud indeed that men of such large influence should act in so large a sense of patriotism and so admirable a spirit of devotion to our common country.

Cordially and sincerely yours,   Woodrow Wilson

TLS (Baltimore Cathedral-Ar).

[1] It is missing.

[2] The text of the letter signed by Cardinal Gibbons and the other archbishops present at the meeting is printed in the *New York Times*, April 20, 1917.

From Paul Oscar Husting

My dear Mr. President: Washington, D. C. Apr. 27, 1917.

On Apr. 12th last, I had the honor of discussing with you the question of the advisability of raising troops by conscription or volunteering and I then made the suggestion that it be done by combining both. At that time, I did not know, nor was it generally known, that the drafting machinery could not be perfected before three months after the passage of the Bill. It is plain from the statements of Senator Chamberlain and others that no soldiers can be brought to the colors by conscription until or about August 1st. This means that we shall lose the months of May, June and July, when time seems to me to be of the very essence.

Since seeing you, I have talked with men who have been and now are your warm supporters and all of whom off-hand were quite enthusiastically in favor of conscription because they believed that the volunteer system meant delay and that conscription meant immediate results. Upon being informed, however, that the draft machinery could not be perfected and that men could not be brought to the colors until on or about August 1st, these men, almost without exception, at once agreed with me that it not only would be wise but essential that pending the perfection of the draft machinery, we secure all the men possible by voluntary enrollment. They agreed with me most emphatically that the thing of first importance was to get men. I, therefore, beg to state that, in my judgment, if the people of the United States who favor conscription were informed that conscription meant three months' delay, or for that matter meant even one month's delay, they would favor the voluntary enrollment pending the time that the draft machinery can be put in practical operation.

So strongly have I become convinced that the insistence on a draft at the expense of valuable and precious time would be a mistake that I have sought to enlist the interest and co-operation of Senators who, like myself, have been friends and supporters of the Administration thru thick and thin and who have nothing but the welfare of the country and of the Administration at heart, and who feel that the defeat of the Government in its war policy would be not only unfortunate but perhaps disastrous. We find ourselves in this awkward and unfortunate dilemma, viz: We must either sustain the Government by voting for a Bill which we think is unwise and may work out disastrously or we must (may) defeat the Government which also may mean disaster by voting for a Bill that accords with our own convictions. I realize that to defeat the Government in this crisis would weaken it in the eyes of the world and particularly in the eyes of our enemies and we thereby would in a way aid and comfort our enemy. I have felt and often reiterated that the want of solidarity of the country—the failure of the people to back up our Government in its negotiations had much to do finally in bringing us into war with Germany. And, therefore, now that we are at war with Germany, I feel it would be most unfortunate for this Congress to defeat the Government. I will go further and say that I think it would be most unfortunate if there should be any substantial opposition to the Government or any substantial vote against the Army Bill now pending before both Houses.

That there is a very strong and substantial sentiment in Congress and amongst the people in favor of volunteering is quite manifest and this sentiment is not confined to those who from motives not friendly but hostile to the Government have obstructed, hindered and delayed this Government in all of its controversies with Germany. On the contrary, this sentiment is deep in the hearts of many of the members of Congress and of the people who have strongly supported the Government in all its controversies with Germany. The reason for this is not far to seek. The American volunteer has fought to a successful issue every war in which this country has been engaged and the Volunteer Army is an institution of 134 years of standing. While it is true that the universal service idea has taken root and is spreading rapidly, yet public opinion has not had the opportunity or the time to crystallize into anything like a unanimous sentiment in favor of it. Moreover, the universal service system has never been put into effect or has even been tried. If we had adopted the universal service system—say four or five years ago—and we thereby had put thru a course of training several million men of proper age whose names, addresses and qualifications were known and these men had been properly catalogued and classified, we would now have the foundation for an intelligent selective conscription such as is now contemplated. But the fact is that we have had no universal service and the question that is now confronting us has nothing to do with universal military service. It is proposed to tear up by the roots an old and tried, and at least with us, successful system of volunteering for an untried draft system which will like a drag-net take in by lot or chance young men, many of whom may physically be fit for military duty but who may temper[a]mentally or constitutionally be of no fighting value and, vica versa, leave out men who not only are temper[a]mentally and constitutionally fit for military duty but who are anxious and desirous of fighting for their country.

I am not unaware and unconscious of the arguments used that patriotic young men would enlist and less patriotic men would shirk under the volunteer system. But even so, my idea is that we want an Army that can fight and want it as soon as we can get it; that we want to start out with a nucleus of an Army that is made up of fighting men and who can be depended upon, and that when such an Army is obtained to begin with, it can then be safely recruited with men of the conscriptive type.

I repeat that there is a substantial sentiment in and out of Congress in favor of volunteering and that there are some very good and substantial reasons for it. People are seldom prepared to abandon, at a moment's notice, without opportunity for due and careful consideration, a system which they have been taught to believe and do believe to be the best in the world. They particularly hesitate to do so in a great crisis like this. I submit, therefore, that this sentiment is something that should and must be reckoned with because in order to have any system work out it must, of course, have the great mass of the people back of it.

Another thing to be considered in this connection is that this country has been seriously divided on the question of war itself. While there never was any doubt in my mind that the people of the country in the end would support our Government in whatever course it thought necessary to take, even to the extent of war, yet it must be remembered that many people are supporting the Government not because they like war but only because they have faith in their President, their Government and are patriotic citizens.

We must also remember that there are organized forces abroad and in our land that at heart are dissatisfied with the Government and anxious to stir up dissatisfaction, dissension and trouble. The Socialists in Convention assembled have passed a resolution counseling forcible opposition to the draft.[1] The dis-

[1] At a so-called "emergency convention" in St. Louis, April 7-14, 1917, delegates of the Socialist party adopted what later became known as the "St. Louis Proclamation." This document was a stinging denunciation of the war and of American participation in it. Among the actions which it recommended to Socialists were public demonstrations against the war; opposition to conscription, the sale of war bonds, and taxes upon the necessities of life; propaganda against military training; and resistance to all measures which curtailed civil liberties. The proclamation was soon ratified by a mail referendum of all party members in good standing. This manifesto caused the defection from the party of many moderate Socialists such as Charles Edward Russell, William English Walling, John Spargo, Allan Benson, Upton Sinclair, and Gustavus Myers. See David A. Shannon, *The Socialist Party of America: A History* (New York, 1955), pp. 93-100, and James Weinstein, *The Decline of Socialism in America, 1912-1925* (New York and London, 1967), pp. 125-29.

loyal pro-German elements, while quiet, are nevertheless secretly and busily intriguing and working against the Government. Some of the extreme pacifists are not in harmony with the Government's war measures. All these have been quick to see that the detested draft will be unpopular in the extreme in many states and, therefore, have aligned themselves against conscription. I fear that we are placing into their hands the most effective weapon that we can give them to promote their nefarious and treasonable purposes; in other words, I think this Conscription Bill is "water on their wheel."

Now, may I take the liberty to suggest a proposition which I believe would unite all of the friends of the Administration and disarm the opposition and at the same time accomplish better and quicker results than the Bill now before the Senate?

I enclose herewith a letter written by me to Senator Hollis on Apr. 24th, which sets out my proposition and my reasons for suggesting it as well as my reasons for writing it to him.[2] May I ask you to be good enough to read the letter and consider the arguments which I have attempted to make therein?

If the Administration could see its way clear to suggest, that is to say, initiate a proposition like this as a compromise, it would, in my opinion, involve no surrender whatever of a single idea embraced in the Senate Bill and at the same time would give the opponents of the Bill everything that they can reasonably ask for. I say this would involve no surrender whatever if the proposition came from the White House and if accepted by both Houses (as I am quite positive it almost unanimously would be), the world would understand that Congress and the people are unitedly back of the Government's program. Not only that, but it would give the most convincing assurance to Germany that we had laid the foundation for an Army that would grow to any proportions that the exigencies might require. It would allay all ill feeling and dissatisfaction in the nation and would disarm our enemies at home. If we secured by selective voluntary enrollment all the soldiers required by the call, we could furnish no more convincing proof that the people were solidly back of the Government. If we did not secure the entire number on the first call within the time limited, all arguments in favor of another volunteer call would fall to the ground and the draft would justify itself. Every member of Congress and all the people know that

[2] P. O. Husting to H. F. Hollis, April 24, 1917, TCLS (WP, DLC). Husting proposed that the President be authorized to call immediately for 1,000,000 volunteers. This would give the volunteer system a good trial; if it failed and more men were needed, then Congress could fall back upon selective service.

we must get the men by the draft if sufficient numbers do not volunteer and in the event that the initial call for volunteers should bring to the colors an insufficient number of men, there could be no argument left why another call for volunteers should be issued because everybody would understand then that all additional soldiers would have to be gotten under the draft. Consequently, in that event the initial call for voluntary enrollment and enlistment would constitute the bridge upon which we could pass from the old system to the new without first burning the bridge before we got across. Those favoring the volunteer system would not only be satisfied to have had their judgment and sentiments respected but, convinced that volunteering will not produce the necessary soldiers, they would be quick to join with the others in making the draft successful. And in addition to this, an Army of at least several hundreds of thousands of soldiers would actually be in esse—a force sufficient to discourage any draft riot and enough to "pacify" any and every potential trouble maker.

Now, Mr. President, I want to say in conclusion that while I feel that the passage of the Bill now before the Senate would be a grave mistake, yet, at the same time, I feel that the defeat of the Government might even involve this country in still graver consequences because of the moral effect it might have in Europe and also among our own people. I have directed myself, therefore, to you in the belief that whatever is proposed at this stage should emanate from the Government so that whatever is done would be done in full accord with the Government's wishes and would and could in no wise be construed as a defeat of the Government's purposes.

With assurances of my highest respect and esteem, I remain,
Sincerely yours,   Paul O Husting

TLS (WP, DLC).

From Albert Shaw

Dear Mr. President: New York April 27, 1917

In these busy times that keep your mind fully taxed with great affairs, I have not written you or made any venture at communication. But I must now tell you in a word that I have read your message of April 2, not once only but a number of times at intervals between readings. I am not much given to enthusiasm over messages and state papers, but I approve of this paper of yours in a very high degree. I read it as a necessary sequel to the peace address of January 22. I look upon your present policies as intended to offer to the German people precisely as fair and honorable a place in the world as you assign to the French or Italian or Russian people.

I was extremely reluctant to have the United States enter the war, and I was greatly out of sympathy with certain New York interests, in the press and in business, that were clamoring for war on grounds that did not seem to me to be constructive. I had differed with State Department policies quite strongly at times, because I was perhaps too insistently of opinion that we ought to take practical steps to enforce neutral maritime rights upon all belligerents.

All those things, however, lie in the past. The force of events has justified your course, as you have now helped the Allies and the neutrals to see a constructive outcome to what otherwise might have been a merely destructive war. I have tried in the editorial pages of the Review for May to express my approval of this entrance on our part into an immediate league for the establishment in the world of peace on enduring principles.[1]

Working out the vast and complicated details which follow our momentous decision will be a taxing and trying business for you at times. I am confident that you will have the main end in view; and have the most ardent hope that your leadership in the league of democracies for justice and harmony in the world may have two great effects: (1) to shorten the war, and (2) to reconstruct affairs on sound and progressive lines.

There may be nothing at all that I personally can do, because I am not exactly military timber. But if there should be anything of any sort, you will know that I am wholly at your service.

With great regard,   Faithfully yours,   Albert Shaw

TLS (WP, DLC).
[1] "America Now in 'League to Enforce Peace,' " *American Review of Reviews*, LV (May, 1917), 451.

Helen Woodrow Bones to Jessie Woodrow Wilson Sayre

Dearest Jessie,   The White House April 27, 1917

Do you mean to say you have never received my letter about your father's scornful remarks concerning your Committee of Safety—or whatever it is called—in Williamstown? I wrote to you as soon as I had a chance to talk to him about it and I *know* I sent the letter because I was in doubt as to whether to send it to you at Williamstown or in care of Mrs. Tedcastle at Hyde Park.

It was just about the time you were to go to her for the Easter holiday visit.

I am so sorry, dear, that you have been worrying—for evidently your father feels it was worse than foolish of the Committee to scare you about the children. Bless their hearts! Why should any one wish them harm! They are too far away from their grandfather to be in danger.

When I hear the whispered tales about spies that one hears at every luncheon here I feel that people are losing their minds. Goodness knows I am not brave, but I have to laugh at the hysterical state of mind Washington people are in. And I suppose you hear the same sort of talk.

I am just starting out to a luncheon this minute but I *must* stop for just a word of reassurance to you. I hate to think of your worrying, sweetness, and I hope you will stop when you know your father says *not to!*

I'll write you to-morrow. Meanwhile love, love, love from us all, especially   Your devoted Helen

ALS (received from Eleanor Axson Sayre).

To Stephen Samuel Wise

Personal.

My dear Rabbi Wise: [The White House] 28 April, 1917

Before your letter about Mr. Root came, I had already asked him to serve as the head of the commission we are about to send to Russia. Before doing so I convinced myself that he was genuinely and heartily in sympathy with the revolution in Russia, and his experience is such, his tact so great, and his appreciation of the object of the commission so clear that I cannot but feel that he will prove to have been an admirable choice.

I, of course, appreciate the considerations which you urge and indeed had them in mind before making the choice, but I believe, all things weighed together, my choice has been the wise one. It distresses me that your judgment should be different.

    Cordially and sincerely yours,   [Woodrow Wilson]

CCL (WP, DLC).

To Lillian D. Wald

My dear Miss Wald: The White House 28 April, 1917

The letter signed by yourself and others under date of April sixteenth has, of course, chimed in with my own feelings and sentiments. I do not know what steps it will be practicable to take in the immediate future to safeguard the things which I agree with you in thinking ought in any circumstances to be safeguarded, but you may be sure I will have the matter in mind and will act, I hope, at the right time in the spirit of your suggestion.

Cordially and sincerely yours,   Woodrow Wilson[1]

TLS (L. Wald Papers, NN).
[1] Miss Wald wrote to Tumulty on May 1, 1917 (TLS, WP, DLC) to ask if this exchange might be published. Wilson approved, and the correspondence was published, e.g., in the *New York Times*, May 6, 1917.

To Albert Shaw

My dear Shaw: The White House 28 April, 1917

Thank you warmly indeed for your letter of April twenty-seventh. I have always valued your judgment and such a letter does me a lot of good, particularly since I know you do not form such judgments as you have expressed in it without deliberation.

The task before us is a long one and a grim one, but I am sure we shall all stand together now with a similar purpose and in a like spirit.

I wish I had time for a real letter, but you will know the things which this letter is meant to express but which I have not time to put into it.

Cordially and sincerely yours,   Woodrow Wilson

TLS (A. Shaw Coll., NjP).

To Joseph Patrick Tumulty

The White House [c. April 28, 1917].

I do not see my way clear to pay this bill[1] under any existing appropriation, but it certainly is not fair that Mr. Lane should pay it as the services which he rendered were rendered at my request. I shall be very glad to pay it myself, and instruct that nothing should be said to Mr. Lane or conveyed to him in any way.

I suggest that Mr. Webster[2] send a memorandum to this effect to Miss Bones, saying that I request that she draw up a check payable to him (Mr. Webster) and that he then draw his own check to Mr. Lane and send it with a statement that he does so under my instructions.[3]   The President.

TL (WP, DLC).
   [1] A bill for $72.90, Franklin K. Lane's expenses for the trip which he and William B. Wilson took to New York, March 16-19, 1917, to assist in the settlement of the threatened railroad strike.
   [2] Nelson P. Webster, disbursing clerk at the White House.
   [3] Wilson also personally paid William B. Wilson's expenses of $43.45 in June.

From Meyer London[1]

Dear President Wilson: Washington, D. C. April 28, 1917.

If it can possibly be done I would earnestly ask you to revoke the appointment of Mr. Root as Chairman of the American Commission which is to visit Russia. He is the last person in the world to command the confidence of that awakened country. The type of the lawyer for whom the Russian people have respect is not represented by Root. The Russian bar represents not only the intellect but the conscience of the Russian people. Mr. Root may have a very practical mind, but new Russia has her own standards of the practical. Unless a man's life is associated with some noble ideal, he is not looked upon as a practical man.

The revolution could not have been accomplished without the Socialists, nor can the change be a lasting one without their cooperation. They will look upon the sending of Root as a calamity.

I know the Russian language and Russian literature. I have closely followed revolutionary events and in a modest way I have for years helped along Russia's struggle for liberty.

Assuring you of my very best wishes, and with a deep sympathy for our chief executive whom history has placed at the head of this republic when the world is being remade, I am,
                    Very sincerely yours,   Meyer London

TLS (WP, DLC).
   [1] Socialist congressman from New York.

Robert Lansing to Henry Prather Fletcher

                    Washington, April 28, 1917.

Your 76 April 10, 7 p.m. You may attend the festivities in connection with the inauguration of President-elect Carranza.

In felicitating General Carranza, you will be careful to say or do nothing that would indicate a recognition of his government as de jure in character.

Strictly confidential. For your guidance: everything should be done to hold the confidence and friendship of Carranza at this time. Although it may be impossible to accept those provisions of the new constitution which are in contravention of the international obligations of Mexico, it is desired for reasons of high policy not to force an issue on these questions. They will be met when they arise.

The Department relies upon your every effort to prevent matters of vital military importance coming to a head, in particular as regards the withdrawal of United States ships of war now in Mexican waters. Lansing

T telegram (SDR, RG 59, 123 F 63/151, DNA).

From the Diary of Colonel House

April 28, 1917.

My most important conference today was with Mr. Balfour. I made no secret of it and went directly to Breckenridge Long's house, which he is occupying. No one else was present and we talked for an hour and a half without interruption. And this reminds me that Sir Eric asked yesterday whether it would be convenient for Balfour to continue to be a guest of the Government rather than go to the British Embassy as planned. I told him it would be. I later spoke to the officials in the State Department and told them of Balfour's request and my reply.

I asked Drummond, and Balfour as well, to open their minds to me as freely as to one another so that things might go without friction. They promised to do so and this is an evidence of it.

Balfour wished to know where we should begin our discussion, whether we should first take up peace terms to be imposed in the event of a decisive defeat of Germany, or whether to take it up on a basis of a stalemate or partial defeat. I thought we had better discuss the first proposition.

He had a large map of Europe and of Asia Minor and we began this most important and interesting discussion, the understanding being that he and I would go through with it first, letting me convey our conclusions to the President before the three of us had our conference on Monday.

We took for granted that Alsace and Lorraine would go to France, and that France, Belgium, and Serbia would be restored.

We first discussed Poland and outlined what its boundaries should be. Of course, the stumbling block was the outlet to the sea. There can be no other excepting Danzig, and to take Danzig would be to go through East Prussia. This, I thought, would be a mistake because it would leave an Alsace and Lorraine to rankle and fester for future trouble. Balfour thought it might be made a free port, and in that way satisfy Poland. At the moment, I do not look upon this with favor, particularly since the Germans and Poles would be antagonistic and ready upon the slightest provocation, to find grievances against one another. We came to no conclusion upon this point because none could be arrived at. However, I warmly advocated a restored and rejuvenated Poland—a Poland big enough and potential enough to serve as a buffer state between Germany and Russia.

Serbia came next, and it was agreed that Austria must return Bosnia and Herzegovinia, but that Serbia, on her part, should give to Bulgaria that part of Macedonia which the first Balkan agreement gave her, and which was lost by her greediness in trying to grab additional territory which was not rightfully hers. Balfour thought Serbia would object to this, but that she must be forced to do so in the solution of a peaceful settlement.

Roumania, we thought, should have a small part of Russia which her people inhabited and also a part of Hungary for the same reason.

We thought Austria should be composed of three states, such as Bohemia, Hungary and Austria proper.

We came to no conclusion as to Trieste. I did not consider it best or desirable to shut Austria from the Adriatic. Balfour argued that Italy claims she should have protection for her east coast by having Dalmatia. She has no seaport from Venice to Brindisi, and she claims she must have the coast opposite in order to protect herself. Balfour referred to Italy as being greedy.

This led me to ask what treaties were out between the Allies as to the division of spoils after the war. He said they had treaties with one another, and that when Italy came in they made one with her in which they had promised pretty much what she demanded.

Balfour spoke with regret at the spectacle of great nations sitting down and dividing the spoils of war or, as he termed it, "dividing up the bearskin before the bear was killed." I asked him if he did not think it proper for the Allies to give copies of these treaties to the President for his confidential information. He thought such a request entirely reasonable and said he would have copies made for that purpose. He was not certain they had brought them over, but if not, he would send for them.

I asked if he did not consider it wise for us to keep clear of any promises so that at the peace conference we could exert an influence against greed and an improper distribution of territory. I said to him, what I once said to Grey, that if we are to justify our being in the war, we should free ourselves entirely from petty, selfish thoughts and look at the thing broadly and from a world viewpoint. Balfour agreed to this with enthusiasm. He was good enough to say: "I like to confer with you; I like your mind. It is so clear and direct." He spoke with much feeling, which surprised me, for he is not given to emotion.

Constantinople was our next point. We agreed that it should be internationalized. Crossing the Bosphorus we came to Anatolia. It is here that the secret treaties between the Allies come in most prominently. They have agreed to give Russia a sphere of influence in Armenia and the northern part. The British take in Mesopotamia which is contiguous to Egypt. France and Italy each have their spheres embracing the balance of Anatolia up to the Straits.

It is all bad and I told Balfour so. They are making it a breeding place for future war. I asked what the spheres of influence included. Balfour was hazy concerning this; whether it meant permanent occupation, or whether it meant that each nation had the exclusive right to develop the resources within their own sphere, he was not altogether clear.

We did not touch upon the German colonies, neither did we touch upon Japan, China, or the Eastern question generally.

We went back to Poland. His objection to a Polish state, cutting off Russia from Germany, was whether it would not hurt France more than Germany for the reason it would prevent Russia from coming to France's aid in the event of an attack by Germany. I thought we had to take into consideration the Russia of fifty years from now rather than the Russia of today. While we might hope it would continue democratic and cease to be aggressive, yet if the contrary happened, Russia would be the menace to Europe and not Germany. I asked him not to look upon Germany as a permanent enemy. If we did this, it would confuse our reasoning, and mistakes would likely be made. Balfour, however, was more impressed with the German menace than he was by the possible danger from Russia.

I stated with emphasis that I believed a right solution could only come by the British and American Governments taking a stand together for the right. In this I thought we might be joined by Russia under the new control.

As I left the house a number of photographers tried to photograph me. The secret service men prevented them from doing so unless I gave my consent which I did not do. I walked back to

Wallace's where I was to have lunch with Secretary Baker. The photographers had driven down the street and were awaiting me when I arrived. A few feet in front of me were some six or eight negro laborers striking off for lunch. I walked into the midst of them. They began to give way but I begged them not to do so and to allow me to walk with them. The newspaper photographers grinned and said "All right Colonel, if you do not want us to take you we wont do it."

There was no one present at lunch except Mr. Taft, Baker, Wallace and myself. The conversation at the table was general and Baker and I excused ourselves afterward and went into private conference. I wished to go through army matters with him, and to exchange views with him. I told him of the many criticisms I had heard of his department, particularly what General Wood had said. He met most of the criticism satisfactorily. I like Baker so much that I hope he may succeed in carrying through his difficult undertaking. While he is not the man for the place, it is evident that the President will keep him, and, if retained, I want him to excel.

Woolley, Gregory, McAdoo and many others took up the afternoon. I dined alone with the President and Mrs. Wilson. After dinner we went to the theater and then to bed without having any serious discussion.

I moved over to the White House today.

From Francis Bowes Sayre, with Enclosure

Dearest Father,   Williamstown, Massachusetts April 29, 1917.

My brother, Nevin, has asked me to forward the enclosed letter to you. Although I generally refuse all requests to forward letters to you personally, I hope you will forgive me for breaking my rule in this case.

Jessie and the children are splendidly well. We think so constantly of you; sometimes it seems hard to think that we can do nothing to lighten the wearying load which you have to bear. But all the country now is beginning to understand as never before your ideal of America; and the time is coming when those ideals will be made into realities.

We have taken a cottage for the summer at Siasconset on Nantucket Island. I hope to take Jessie and the babies down there early in June, and leave them there in case I am called to do Army Y.M.C.A. work for the summer, or in the event that you write that I can be of service to you personally or in the State Department.

    With hearts full of love from the four of us,

                         Ever affectionately your son,   Frank

TLS (WP, DLC).

E N C L O S U R E

From John Nevin Sayre

                                        Suffern, New York
My dear Mr. President: April 27, 1917.

    I wrote you on April 23rd with regard to the bill now being debated in Congress for a selective draft, but as I am not sure that this letter has reached you,[1] I am taking the liberty of writing again and asking my brother to forward this second letter. In case you should have already received my first letter, I hope you will pardon the seeming importunity of this second appeal.

    I have been informed by a friend in Washington that the proposed Selective Draft Legislation provides exemption from military service for members of religious organizations which have definitely expressed principles opposed to war, but that no provision for a similar exemption is made in the case of individual conscientious objectors. To put the matter concretely, Quakers might be excused from going to the front, but individual Jews, socialists, or Episcopalians like myself, who have equally strong objections to military service, might be drafted into it.

    Now if such be the case, I beg you to consider whether the exemption clause should not be extended to individuals rather than organizations? It seems to me that freedom of conscience can be safeguarded only in this way, for conscience is always an individual and personal thing, and in the Protestant view at least, the creed or principles of a religious organization cannot be substituted for it. I myself believe that all war goes against the direct teachings of Jesus, and therefore I could not conscientiously engage in it. But my Church takes no such positive stand. If, therefore, the Selective Draft Bill in its present form should be passed, it might force me and others in a similar position to a choice between obedience to conscience or our country's laws. I am sure you will realize how deplorable this would be and how fundamentally un-American.

    It may be said that such individual exemption as I speak of

would provide a loophole through which slackers and cowards would seek to evade military service. It is true that in some instances men might thus perjure themselves, but I submit that such persons, even if compelled to go to the front, would be of small use there. They would be cowards at heart, and possibly a demoralizing force to those around them. If we must have a selective draft, would it not be far better to let some of these slackers escape rather than force the consciences of many good, true men?

I am enclosing a statement of the Fellowship of Reconciliation,[2] explaining the position of its members with regard to war. Some of these are Christians of such recognized standing as Dr. John R. Mott. It would be very tragic for the country to conscript their consciences.

Trusting that you will give this matter your earnest consideration, I am,

Respectfully and sincerely yours,   John Nevin Sayre

TLS (WP, DLC).
  [1] It is missing.
  [2] *The Fellowship of Reconciliation*, printed pamphlet (WP, DLC).

From the Diary of Colonel House

April 29, 1917.

I devoted my morning to going through mail and telegrams which have poured in upon me and which I have not even had the time to open.

At one o'clock, Frank Polk, Miss Bones, Miss Brennan[1] and I drove to the Navy Yard to board the Mayflower which Secretary Daniels had commissioned to take the French and British Commissions to Mount Vernon. In addition to the personel[!] of the Missions the members of the Cabinet were present. I was busy from the time I boarded ship until I returned with discussions with different people. The most interesting person aboard was Marechal Joffre. I decided not to ask him any questions but, on the contrary, I told him something of political conditions as I had found them in Germany preceding the war and since.

He seemed interested, especially in my description of the intrigues of von Falkenhayn and von Tirpitz, and the manner in which von Hindenburg had superseded them. When I stated that Ludendorff was the master mind behind Hindenburg, he wanted to know if it was not a fact that Hindenburg was the ruthless executor. That is, Ludendorff's plans would perhaps be

futile from the Prussian viewpoint, if Hindenburg was not there
to brutally execute them.

Lansing, Spring-Rice, Jusserand and I had an interesting conversation. Lansing told me of Japan's desire to purchase the
Philippines.[2] We discussed this at some length. My view was
that it might be done, provided safe-guards be thrown around
the Islands for their protection and for their political independence. Lansing concurred in this view and we wondered what view
the President would take of it. I thought of Philip Dru and the
solution I made there of this question.[3]

The British Ambassador spoke of me in the most affectionate
terms, and insisted that our coming into the war and the good
relations existing between our countries was largely due to me.
He looked ill and I was touched by his pathetic look and condition.

The French Ambassador was equally complimentary. He lifted
his hat and said: "you have prophesied correctly concerning recent events. I wrote my government about you and told them
that, while you had prophesied accurately, it must be remembered that you had the making of events in your hands."

I concluded not to leave the boat at Mount Vernon, thinking I
would have a rest of an hour or so while the ceremonies took
place. After everyone had left the ship, I leaned over the rail to
see the last boat cast away. Baruch, who was about to board it
caught sight of me and asked if I were not coming. When I replied
in the negative, he scrambled back and remained with me the
entire time. I was so fretted that it occurred to me that it would
be a good opportunity to ask him to let Seitz,[4] of the New York
World, have $8500.00 for his Portland Argus, the unpaid part of
$15,000.00 which Crane has been carrying for a year or more
and now wishes to have paid. So the visit with me cost Baruch
$8500.00 which, I must say, he seemed entirely willing to pay.

The President, Mrs. Wilson, Miss Bones and I had dinner
alone. After dinner we went to the upstairs sitting room and
talked upon general subjects for awhile. The President read several chapters from Oliver's "Ordeal by Battle."[5] He was interested
in what I had to tell him of Oliver, and we discussed the different
points Oliver made in the chapters read, agreeing to some and
disagreeing as to others.

The President declared his intention of writing some things
which were on his mind after he retired from office. I su[r]prised
him by advising against his writing at all. Mrs. Wilson said,
"You astonish me. Why, that is was [what] he does best." The
President spoke up, saying: "You do not understand, House is

afraid to have me write." This accusation I had to acknowledge was true. I thought he would go out of office with such a tremendous reputation that it would be a pity to endanger it by writing or doing anything that might make people think less of him. The President agreed in general to this, and said he had no notion of writing about his administration, but expressed a desire to write one book which he has had long in mind and which he thought might have an influence for good.

He said, "I write with difficulty and it takes everything out of me." This estimate of himself in that field of his endeavors would surprise the general public since he is considered such a fluent writer. I asked how long it took him to write his April second Address to Congress. He said ten hours. I offered the opinion that his January 22nd speech to the Senate was a much abler document because it had more original thought. His April 2nd speech pleased, I thought, because it reflected the public mind, both here and in the Allied countries. He concurred entirely in this conclusion.

We talked of the proposed book and its contents. I thought if he would bring out clearly the necessity for a more responsive form of government, and the necessity for having Cabinet members sit in the House of Representatives, it would be worth while. We agreed that if the Cabinet officers sat in the House, the outcome would be that the President would have to take his material for the Cabinet from Congress. This, in the end, would give the Cabinet more power, and would have the further effect of bringing into Congress the best talent in the country. It would eventuate into something like the British system.

I arranged with the President to see Cleveland Dodge and Harry Davison, of Morgan & Co. on Wednesday. Dodge wants Davison to be the executive head of the Red Cross during the war, believing it will mean a difference between a five million proposition and a fifty million. I also asked the President for authority to send a despatch to Sir Horace Plunkett thanking him for the good work he has been doing on both sides of the Atlantic. The President said he would sanction anything I cared to say.

1 That is, Edith Benham.

2 House was probably fantasizing at this point.

3 [Edward Mandell House], *Philip Dru: Administrator; A Story of Tomorrow, 1920-1935* (New York, 1912), pp. 162-63, 275-76. Administrator Dru established cordial relations with Japan by "announcing the intention of the United States to give the Philippines their independence under the protection of Japan, reserving for America and the rest of the world the freest of trade relations with the Islands." *Ibid.*, p. 276.

4 Don Carlos Seitz.

5 Frederick Scott Oliver, *Ordeal by Battle* (London, 1915). There is a copy of this book in the Wilson Library, DLC.

Four Letters from Robert Lansing

My dear Mr. President: Washington April 30, 1917.

As the existence of a state of war makes it essential for the public safety that no communication of a character which would aid the enemy or its allies should be permitted I wish to lay before you the great necessity of preparing some plan for the censorship of postal correspondence. I understand that at the present time there is no bar to sending by mail from the United States communications, plain or in cipher, from Germans or German agents here, to Germans in Mexico or other neutral countries for their information and transmission by various means to Germany and her allies. The dangers to the country inherent in this form of communication are obvious—the present channel is open to the transmittal of military information, trans-ferrence of money and credit, and manipulation of intrigues, etc. I enclose a copy of a memorandum of the British Embassy dated April 12th pointing out the transferrence of German securities to the nominal value of $1,250,000, by a letter of Kuhn-Loeb and Company.[1]

In these circumstances I have to suggest that a plan of censor-ship of postal correspondence should be formulated at the earliest moment—in the first instance by the Post Office Department which is familiar with our postal laws and regulations, and later in cooperation with the State Department and possibly the Department of Justice.

On April 20th I laid the urgency of this matter before the Postmaster General but as I have not as yet received any indica-tion as to the attitude of his Department in the matter and as I regard the matter as of the utmost importance I take the liberty of calling it to your particular attention.

Faithfully yours,   Robert Lansing

[1] British Embassy, memorandum, April 12, 1917, T MS (WP, DLC).

My dear Mr. President: Washington April 30, 1917.

I think that we should anticipate two moves on the part of Germany and be prepared to deal with them promptly and deci-sively.

From our various sources of information, which are of course more or less uncertain, it appears that Germany may in the near future directly or indirectly through Austria outline terms of peace, which the German Government practically declined to do. I do not believe that the terms will be such that they can be considered nor do I think that they will be *bona fide*. They will be made to influence public opinion in this country and Russia.

The other move on the part of the German Government will be to indicate the success of democracy in Germany either by concessions by the Government or by an apparent revolution carefully staged. This step will also be taken to influence public opinion here and in Russia. It will of course be artificial and manufactured for the occasion. I am convinced that the sentiment for democracy in Germany is entirely under the control of the Government, which will take every means to give it the appearance of genuine[ne]ss and the movement an appearance of irresistable popular pressure.

I am writing of these possible, and I believe probable, steps by Germany because it seems to be advisable to consider in advance the policy to be adopted in meeting them. Would it be well to let the impression get abroad through the press that Germany may possibly make such moves, but that the American people ought not to be deceived as to their purpose, which is of course to cause reaction against a vigorous war policy and arouse false hopes of an early peace?

Faithfully yours,   Robert Lansing.

My dear Mr. President: Washington April 30, 1917.

I had a brief conversation this noon with Stanley Washburn,[1] whom I think you know as a man very closely in touch with Russian affairs.

He told me that he thought it would be a great mistake to send any Jew at all on the Commission to Russia, that, while the new Government were endeavoring to impress the idea of liberalism in the treatment of the Jews, there was never a more intense bitterness and hostility to the race than at present, and that this feeling was especially [strong?] among the soldiers at the front, the workmen and the peasantry. It was Washburn's idea that a Jew on the Commission would cast popular suspicion on the purpose of the Commission and very materially impair its usefulness.

I believe that Mr. Washburn's knowledge and his judgment as an observer entitle his opinion to careful consideration. He is a man of real discernment and not at all prejudiced or superficial in drawing conclusions.

In this connection I would call your attention to the latter part of the enclosed telegram from Ambassador Francis which you have doubtless seen.[2] It bears out Mr. Washburn's statement as to facts.

If it seems best not to send a Jew and if Mr. Myer has been asked to serve, the situation ought to be explained to him at once with a request that he withdraw.

Faithfully yours,   Robert Lansing.

TLS (WP, DLC).
[1] Foreign and war correspondent, whose experience in Russia went back to the Russo-Japanese War. He had most recently spent some twenty-six months covering the Russian front as a correspondent for the London *Times*.
[2] D. R. Francis to RL, April 28, 1917, T telegram (WP, DLC). Francis discussed a proposed Russian mission to the United States and press reports in Moscow speculating on the personnel of the United States mission to Russia. He also noted "nervousness among people generally, many of the wealthier classes leaving Petrograd." "I do not anticipate excesses," he concluded, "but they are rumored and if should come very likely be directed against Jews first."

My dear Mr. President: Washington April 30, 1917.

I enclose for your consideration a telegram which I think should be sent to Mr. Francis.[1] I learned from the Russian Chargé that his Government had cabled him as to this matter, and that the belief that joint conferences were being held here without Russia being a party was causing suspicion and a measure of offense. This unfortunate and ill-founded attitude had been first aroused by the recent conference between the premiers of Great Britain, France and Italy, to which Russia was not invited.

It is my opinion that no time is to be lost in removing the false impression which has been created. I have already told the French Ambassador and Mr. Balfour of this situation and they will act at once.   Faithfully yours,   Robert Lansing.

TLS (SDR, RG 59, 763.72/4377A, DNA).
[1] The Enclosure printed with WW to RL, May 1, 1917.

From William Bauchop Wilson

My dear Mr. President: Washington April 30, 1917.

Referring to the selection of a representative of labor on the Russian Commission, I take the liberty of suggesting the name of James Duncan,[1] of Quincy, Massachusetts. After discussing the matter with Mr. Gompers and others, I am of the opinion that, all things considered, Mr. Duncan is the best selection that could be made. For your convenience I am sending herewith a brief sketch of him taken from "Who's Who."

If you finally come to the conclusion that it is advisable to send an American Socialist in the group of Commissioners, may I suggest the name of William English Walling, of Greenwich, Connecticut. I know of no Socialist in this country who has been more in touch with the Socialistic group of Russia or understands them better than Mr. Walling, and the fact that he suffered indignities at the hands of the old secret police system of Russia, which is well known to Russian Socialists,[2] would make him a much more influential man than one who had not had that experience. I am also sending for your convenience a brief sketch of him taken from "Who's Who."[3]

                              Faithfully yours,   W B Wilson

TLS (SDR, RG 59, 763.72/4386½, DNA).
    [1] President of the Granite Cutter's International Association and first vice-president of the American Federation of Labor.
    [2] Walling spent many months from 1905 to 1907 in Russia, where he studied the revolutionary movements of that period. Near the end of his stay there, he and his wife were arrested and detained for approximately twenty-four hours by the Russian police, allegedly because of their contacts with revolutionaries. See William English Walling, *Russia's Message: The True World Import of the Revolution* (New York, 1908), p. x.
    [3] The two biographies from *Who's Who in America* not printed.

From Newton Diehl Baker

Dear Mr. President: Washington. April 30, 1917.

    You will be interested to know, although the incident is a minor one, that the big engine at the Springfield Arsenal broke down a week ago and required two days for repairs—one of them being Sunday, when the Arsenal is otherwise at rest. Inquiry developed the fact that emery had been put into the bearings of the big engine. This is the first instance of destruction in any of our Government arsenals which is obviously malicious.

                              Respectfully yours,   Newton D. Baker

TLS (WP, DLC).

From Cyrus Hall McCormick, Jr., with Enclosure

My dear Woodrow: [Chicago] April 30. 1917

    Your letter of the 27th was received this morning. I appreciate fully the compliment you pay me in feeling that I can be of service on this Commission to Russia.

    After consulting with my Wife[1] I telegraphed you that I am at your service in any way in which I can be useful to the Government. I now confirm the message and will be ready to go whenever you may desire.

Will you be good enuf to let Mr. Tumulty advise me whether you wish me to see anyone to receive information or instructions before going and also when it is expected the Commission should be ready to start.

Faithfully and sincerely yours   Cyrus H. McCormick

By a strange misadventure I find today among some of my papers a letter I wrote you on the 22nd which was not posted offering my services in any way they might be desired. I did not suppose the answer would come as swiftly and as forcibly as this request has come. Such a call cannot be declined if one has the health and the strength for the service.   C. H. McC.

ALS (WP, DLC).
[1] Harriet Bradley Hammond McCormick.

E N C L O S U R E

From Cyrus Hall McCormick, Jr.

My dear Woodrow: [Chicago] April 22. 1917.

Even at this late date I hope a word of personal sympathy and support may not be amiss.

Your eloquent appeal to the Congress giving the reasons why we must declare this country in a state of war with Germany will constitute one of the soul-stirring events in our history. The people of the Nation are with you and will support you in the great constructive work which lies before you.

I want you to know the loyal admiration I have for the stand you have taken for universal military training and service which is the only logical and fair method of raising the Army.

I am ready with all the force of personal effort, and the influence and usefulness of the Harvester Company, to contribute, in every way I can, to our military, industrial and agricultural preparedness. And I am proud to find that my son Cyrus[1] has worked out a plan for mobilizing the business brains of the Country in co[n]venient groups and centers, so that when the Government or the Council of Defense desire quick coöperation or information along any line the machinery for attending to it will be ready. He explained something of this to Secretary Lane a few days ago, and offered himself for any service for which he might be wanted.

I mention these things to assure you that you may count upon us to do our full share in support of the principles you have so forcibly laid down.

Do not take the trouble to reply to this letter. In these days your strength must be conserved for the largest things.

I am,   Faithfully yours,   Cyrus H. McCormick

I congratulate you on sending Charles Crane to Russia. He will be of great help to our Country's interests there.

ALS (WP, DLC).
[1] He signed himself Cyrus McCormick, Jr.

From the Diary of Josephus Daniels

April Monday 30 1917

12.40: Went to see President. Talked about sending our ships to England & France & decided to send 36 & try to secure other small craft. Must act now. He did not like Com. named by L & W[1]—all of them had fought shipping bill. Lunched with the President and Mrs. Wilson & he had good stories. Discussed "Damn." He told of a Judge, a Federalist, the Democrats wished to impeach—Chase I think. It was charged he used profanity on the bench—said damn. His lawyer argued that Damn was not profane—just emphatic. Acquitted. Pres. said he saw Jefferson Davis being taken to prison. Waffler—don't stop to print em. Dr. McCosh showed Garrett[2] plans of a new building. Got $10000 & it was reported & asked him while a guest in his house. Mrs. McC resented it & said "My husband merely showed him the plans, & added: 'I have all the money needed, except $10,000. What do you say?' "—Say Mr. Yankee!

[1] That is, the committee on transportation and communication headed by Daniel Willard, one of the committees of the Advisory Commission of the Council of National Defense, formed in February at the instigation of Franklin K. Lane. In his diary entry of April 25, Daniels indicated that this committee was in conflict with the Shipping Board. See also Robert D. Cuff, *The War Industries Board: Business-Government Relations During World War I* (Baltimore, 1973), p. 46.
[2] That is, Thomas Harrison Garrett, Princeton 1868.

From the Diary of Colonel House

April 30, 1917.

This has been a day filled with important work. I will not mention State Department officials, Cabinet members, etc. etc. but will go directly to the conversations I have had with the French and British Missions and with the President and Mr. Balfour.

I lunched at the French Embassy. The other guests besides

the Ambassador and Madame Jusserand were, Marechal Joffre, Viviani, Admiral Chochresprat,[1] Henry White, Myron T. Herrick, Marquis de Chambrun,[2] Frank Polk and myself. Before lunch there was a very pretty ceremony. The household servants and some neighborhood children brought flowers to Joffre and presented him with a small souvenir. He thanked them in a few sentences. There was no conversation of importance either at the table or afterward. My next engagement was with Sir Eric Drummond which we filled by a drive in a White House motor. Since our last talk he had thought of Viscount Grey of Falloden as a special envoy to the United States to remain indefinitely. This I considered an admirable suggestion. He wondered whether Grey would accept. I was sure he would. It would mean that they would have a member of the British Government here with whom I, at least, and I believed the President as well, would talk to as frankly as to a member of our own Government, so much confidence did we have in Grey.

I again expressed the hope that they would not recall Spring-Rice or humiliate him in any way. The occasion should be made one of compliment to him rather than otherwise, and he should be brought home, given a peerage, and have all the badges pinned upon him as having completed a great work for his government. Drummond assured me this would be done.

We arranged to keep in constant communication through Wiseman, and I urged him to let me know of any difficulties which might arise, or of any annoyances however petty which might come up and would not be known unless he dealt frankly with me.

My next engagement was with Emile Hovelaque.[3] This also was filled by a drive with him through Rock Creek Park. He desired to tell of the differences between Joffre and Viviani. Viviani, he said, has no sympathy with military men or their methods, and he and Joffre are continually quarrelling over the most trivial matters. The fault he laid to Viviani. Joffre's nerves are as steady as a rock, while Viviani is as jumpy as Spring-Rice. Viviani, being a socialist, never wished France to prepare for war and he is impatient of the entire propaganda. Then, too, he is jealous of the marked difference between the receptions given

[1] Vice Admiral Paul Louis Albert Chocheprat, the senior officer of the French navy.

[2] Charles Louis Antoine Pierre Gilbert Pineton, Marquis de Chambrun, a descendant of Lafayette, who represented the French parliament in the mission to the United States.

[3] Émile Lucien Hovelaque, Inspector General of Public Instruction, who served the French mission as translator.

Joffre and himself. Hovelaque told of how serious conditions were in France and how necessary it was to send our troops at once. It is very evident to me now that if the United States had not entered the war when we did, Germany would have had more than an even chance of success. The Allies seem to be pretty much at the end of their tether, and it is to be hoped Germany is in an even more depleted condition.

Although I had seen Joffre at lunch, he sent me an earnest request for another interview. It was unfortunate that a half hour was all I could give him as the request came so late that my remaining time was completely filled.

I went to Henry White's residence, where the French Mission is quartered, and was shown into the Marechal's bedroom where we had our conference. Joffre began by saying that he was anxious to explain the condition of France and how necessary it was for American soldiers to be sent over at once. He thought he could put them in condition to go to the front within five weeks after they arrived, provided they knew the rudiments of military tactics. He merely wanted them to be disciplined and to know the manual of arms.

We passed the usual compliments, both as to our countries and personally, he not falling behind me in expressions of admiration. To me Joffre looks more of the German than the French type. He must have been quite blonde when young. His hair is now so streaked with grey that it is difficult to know its original color. His eyes are peculiar and, to me, the most striking feature he has. He seems to have a well ordered mind, and appears to be the type of General well suited to the French in the time of stress which they were under when he was in general command. I constantly compared him, in my own mind, to General Grant. I told him this, and he seemed not displeased at the comparison.

I had to leave before we had finished since I had an engagement with McAdoo, and it was after six o'clock and the President had asked him to request Balfour to move up the White House dinner engagement from eight o'clock to seven in order to give us more time.

I have asked the President to see Joffre and Viviani separately in order to allay whatever feeling they might have because he had invited Balfour for tonight. My reason for this was that the importance of the Balfour conference should be minimized, not only with the public, but with Lansing so he might feel it was merely a social courtesy.

Besides the President, Mr. Balfour and myself there was no one present at dinner excepting Mrs. Wilson and Miss Bones. The President did most of the talking. I could see that he was nervous although I doubt whether it was apparent to Balfour. The conversation was along general lines, mostly educational, historical and architectural. The President told several stories of Lincoln, and Balfour listened with interest. He said Lincoln was not ready for the Presidency when it came to him; that up to that time he was not sufficiently educated and had not had adequate public experience. He spoke of the difficulty Lincoln had in acquiring an education and of his manner of obtaining it. They both thought it little less than marvellous, with his antecedents and limited opportunities, that he should develop a distinct literary flavor. Without saying so, I disagreed with them, for such things are given one at birth and not acquired except in a mediocre way.

In talking of education, the President expressed himself as not being in agreement with the general modern trend against the Classics. He thought the world had gained as much by the untruths of history as by the truth. He did not believe the human mind should be held down to facts and material matters. He considered that the trouble with Germany today. German thought expressed itself in terms of machinery and gasses. The reading of the romance languages and of the higher flights of fancy in literature led one into spiritual realms which, to say the least, was as advantageous to the world as its material progress. Balfour said he had never heard this view expressed but agreed with it, whether from politeness or not I do not know.

We took our coffee in the oval sitting room and when it was finished we went to the President's study and began a conference, the importance of which cannot be over-estimated. The President continued to do most of the talking. It was evident to me that he was keyed up for this conference as he had been resting most of the afternoon, not taking his usual exercise. To my mind, he was not at his best because of an apparent eagerness to excel. I had talked of Balfour so often to him and had given such a high estimate of his quality of mind, that he wished to make a good impression. As a matter of fact, he more than held his own, and presented a remarkable process of reasoning throughout the interview. But it seemed to me that I had seen him appear better, though I may have been over critical because I was anxious that he should appear as I had represented him to Balfour.

The ground we covered was exactly the same as Balfour and I had covered in our conference Saturday.[4] I did but little talking, but tried to steer the conversation so as to embrace what Balfour had said to me and what the President and I had agreed upon in former conferences.

When we touched upon the internationalization of Constantinople I suggested that it might lead to trouble. Neither Balfour nor the President caught the point and seemed to think I objected to that future for Constantinople. It was with some difficulty that I made them understand that I thoroughly agreed with the general idea, but desired to point out that it would inevitably lead to an attempt to internationalize the Straits between Sweden and Norway, and Continental Europe, and the Suez and Panama Canals. They caught the point but did not agree with me that the two questions had much in common. I find that statesmen are apt to look upon the interests of their own countries from one viewpoint, and the interests of other countries from quite another. They cannot see clearly the relationship of two similar problems when one touches their own interests and the other the interests of someone else.

The conclusions arrived at were exactly the conclusions which Balfour and I had reached in Saturday's conference, so it is unnecessary to re-state them. The discussion ran from shortly before eight o'clock until nearly half past ten when the President was due at a reception given by the Secretary of State to the members of Congress to meet the British and French Missions.

I asked Balfour again about the Allies' treaties with each other and the desirability of his giving copies to the President. He again agreed to do so.

In all the conferences I have had with the French and British I feel that they do not altogether trust one another. Joffre indicated it in our conference this afternoon, and when I told him I had met the King of the Belgians he remarked that the King had requested that the French rather than the British troops should be in touch with the Belgian troops.

The French have used bad judgment in sending envoys here who cannot speak English, for it makes it impossible for us to have as complete an understanding with them as with the English. One hesitates to entirely trust an interpreter. I can see more and more clearly the danger of friction between the Allies. Distrust lies close beneath the surface, and a little difference between them would bring it from under cover. I feel

[4] That is, April 28.

that this danger is not being well guarded. The Japanese, Russians and Italians are being left out of English, French and American calculations. As far as one can see, they do not appear at any of the functions in Washington except the larger ones, and there is a lack of Russian, Japanese and Italian flags which might easily hurt sensibilities. The British and ourselves are not unlike the Germans in that our manner indicates that other nations do not much matter.

When the conference broke up I walked down stairs with Mr. Balfour and asked if he felt that his mind and that of the President had touched at all points. He was quite enthusiastic and said he had never had a more interesting interview. He spoke of the President as having a wonderful combination of human philosophy and political sagacity.

The President and Mr. Balfour went to the reception together and I went to my room to prepare for taking the train. Before I left the President had returned and we had a few minutes further conversation. He was delighted at Balfour's comments, and seemed happy over the result of the evening's work.

From a Narrative by An Unknown Person

[April 30, 1917]

30 *Avril*—Le Président Wilson avait dit à M. Viviani l'autre jour: "J'espère que nous parlerons [d']affaires." (*I hope that we shall talk business*) Cette conversation capitale a eu lieu aujourdhui. Accompagné de M. Jusserand[,] le Chef de la Mission Française s'est rendu à la Maison Blanche où il a longuement parlé de la situation internationale[.] Il a envisagé la manière dont les États-Unis pouraient abréger le conflit en jetant dans la balance le poids de leurs ressources et la puissance de leurs hommes. Sur l'envoi de troupes américaines en France M. Viviani a exprimé l'avis que ce serait là une acte d'une haute portée morale et qu'au point de vue pratique le Maréchal Joffre considérait le projet comme rapidement réalisable.

Le Président Wilson, qui se propose de demander directment au Maréchal des explications detaillées a ce sujet, s'est declaré prêt à prendre les décisions les plus utiles à la cause des Alliés. Le ton de ses paroles quand il s'agissait de la France était particulièrement "affectueux." Cet adjectif n'est pas exageré. Le Président Wilson sous une apparence un peu froide cache une âme sensible qu'il met au service d'une logique politique dont on a pu mesurer la vigueur par le Message qui suivit la déclaration de guerre. Il a été sincèrement ému par la noblesse de notre pays au cours de ses épreuves et il n'a jamais caché son admiration pour les vertus françaises[.] Mais il a su, sous un masque d' impassibilité, attendre l'heure politique où il pouvait s'engager à fond et nous apporter un concours vraiment efficace. Cette entrevue de M. Wilson et de M. Viviani où ont été definés les buts de guerre et où la coopération franco-américaine a été precisé marquera une date dans l'histoire.

Et quel contraste entre les deux hommes d'état qui se sont ainsi face à face! Le Président Wilson d'un type très anglo saxon, maigre[,] la figure longue et osseuse[,] l'oeil calme et perçant derrière son lorgnon, mesuré dans ses gestes[,] précis comme un juriste dans ses paroles[,] ne laissant passer en son verbe la flamme intérieure qui l'anime qu'en de rares occasions. M. Viviani au contraire petri de généreux latinité est l'homme des frourailles lyriques, des formules spontanées, des élans oratoires qui parent magnifiquement une pensée realiste. Le geste chez lui appuie la mot. L'attitude complète la pensée. C'est merveille de le voir exposer ses idées et imposer aux autres la propre émotion.

Là, dans le cadre intime du Cabinet presidentiel[,] il ne s'agissait pas de plaider une cause. Elle était entendue d'avance. Il s'agissait d'organiser la victoire d'un idéal commun. On peut être certain qu'avec leurs qualités si differentes et au demeurant unis par les sympathies nationales qui renforcaient leur sympathie personnelle—les deux interlocuteurs ont fait de bonne besogne.

Au Ministère de la Guerre le travail continue. Une fois de plus le Maréchal Joffre se rencontre avec le Secrétaire d'Etat M. Baker et avec le Chef d'Etat Major. "L'atmosphère de la guerre a vraiment pénétré dans nos bureaux depuis que vous êtes là,["] me confie un officier. ["]La présence du Maréchal stimule toutes les énergies et nous invite à l'action. Il fallait cette visite pour nous sortir de notre passivité et nous donner le véritable élan."

A la fin de ces journées bien remplies, les receptions reprennent. M. Lansing offre un dîner en l'honneur des deux Missions française et britannique. Plus tard dans la soirée la Mission Viviani se transporte dans les salons du Palais Pan-Américain. C'est un "great event" pour Washington. Le Garde des Sceaux et le Maréchal Joffre soient pendant deux heures défiler d'innombrables amis qui leur présentent les compliments les plus flatteuses. Ils serrent des milliers de mains.

Et le lendemain les reporters qui aiment les exercices de

statistique calculent le nombre des "Shake-hand" distribués par M. Viviani et le Maréchal Joffre ainsi que la force musculaire dépensée de la sorte * * * Et cela fait un joli total!

Hw MS (État-Major de l'Armée de Terre, 14 N 25, FMD-Ar).

T R A N S L A T I O N

April 30. President Wilson had told Mr. Viviani the other day: "I hope that we shall talk business." This important conversation took place today. Accompanied by Mr. Jusserand, the Chief of the French Mission went to the White House where he spoke at length about the international situation. He envisaged the way in which the United States could shorten the conflict by throwing into the balance the weight of its resources and the strength of its men. As for sending American troops to France, Mr. Viviani expressed the view that this would be an act of high moral significance, and, from the practical point of view, Marshal Joffre considered the project as capable of being realized very quickly.

President Wilson, who intends to ask the Marshal directly for a detailed explication of the subject, said that he was ready to make whatever decisions were most useful for the cause of the Allies. The tone of his words when he spoke of France were particularly "affectionate." This adjective is not exaggerated. Under a somewhat cold exterior, President Wilson conceals a sensitive soul that he puts at the service of a political logic whose strength can be measured in his message which accompanied the declaration of war. Our country's noble bearing throughout its trials have sincerely moved him, and he has never concealed his admiration for the French virtues. But he has known, under a mask of impassivity, how to wait for the politic time really to commit himself and bring us truly effective help. This interview of Mr. Wilson and Mr. Viviani, which defined war aims and clarified Franco-American cooperation, will rank as a date in history.

And what a contrast between the two statesmen thus face to face! President Wilson is of a very Anglo-Saxon type—lean, with a long and bony face, eyes calm and piercing behind his pinc-nez, measured in his gestures, precise as a lawyer in his words, only rarely allowing the inner flame that animates him to appear in his language. Mr. Viviani, on the contrary, overflowing with generous latinity, is a man of lyrical flights, spontaneous formulations, and oratorical outbursts that reveal magnificently a realistic intellect. His gesture reinforces his word. His attitude completes his thought. It is marvelous to watch him set forth his ideas and impose on others the proper emotion.

There, in the intimate confines of the presidential office, there was no need to plead a cause. That had been agreed beforehand. It was a matter of organizing the victory of a common ideal. One can be sure that, having such different qualities and yet being united by national sympathies that reenforce their personal sympathy, the two speakers have done a great job.

At the War Department, the work continues. Marshal Joffre meets once more with Secretary Baker and with the Chief of Staff. "The atmosphere of war has truly penetrated into our office since you have been here," one officer confided to me. "The Marshal's presence stimulates all energies and calls us to action. It took this visit to pull us out of our passivity and give us real élan."

At the end of these very full days, the receptions resume. Mr. Lansing gave a dinner in honor of the French and British missions. Later in the evening, the Viviani mission went to the reception hall of the Pan American Building. It was a "great event" for Washington. For two hours, the Keeper of the Seals and Marshal Joffre received innumerable friends who gave them the most flattering compliments. They shook thousands of hands.

The next day, reporters who enjoy statistical exercises, calculated that the number of handshakes given by Mr. Viviani and Marshal Joffre amounted to muscular force on the order of * * * * And that was a jolly total!

To Robert Lansing, with Enclosure

Dear Mr. Secretary, [The White House, May 1, 1917]
I hope this admirable despatch will be sent at once.
W.W.

WWhwLI (SDR, RG 59, 763.72/4377A, DNA).

E N C L O S U R E E[1]

Amembassy Petrograd. Washington, April 30, 1917.
From various sources there have come to the Department certain reports as to the views held by the Russian Government and people concerning the British and French commissions now

in this country. These reports have been confirmed by a conversation which I had on Saturday, April twenty-eighth, with Mr. Onou,[2] the Russian Chargé.

It appears that the Russian Government has the impression that the British and French representatives came to this country, presumably at the invitation or suggestion of this Government, to hold a joint conference as to the conduct of the war and as to the objects to be attained. It is natural that having this impression the Russian Government should feel that it had been ignored in not being invited to participate in so important a conference which would deal with subjects of vital interest to Russia.

The impression is, however, founded entirely upon error. Independently and *each acting* without the knowledge of the other the British and French Governments asked this Government if it would be acceptable to it if they sent missions to this country to express to the President and the American people their gratification at the entry of the United States into the war and to give to our authorities information which would prevent them from making the mistakes which were made by the Allied Governments at the beginning of the conflict. To these inquiries this Government *of course* answered in the affirmative. It then advised each Government of the intention of the other, which I am informed was the first intimation of the fact ⟨which⟩ either had received.

The two missions came to this capital independently and all intercourse between this Government and the two groups of Commissioners has been several and never joint. There is no purpose to consider matters jointly.

It is understood that the Italian Government contemplates sending a commission of a similar nature, which will also be treated independently. If the Russian Government had intimated a desire to send a commission to this country it would have been welcomed in the same cordial spirit as have those which have arrived.

I would further point out that we are sending to Russia and to no other country at the present time a commission of prominent men because of the intense sympathy of the American Government and people for the great nation which has become a democracy. The commission will be headed by Honorable Elihu Root, a most distinguished statesman, who is devoted to the cause of political liberty and to the sovereign rights of the people. It is the primary purpose of this commission to convey to the Russian Government the friendship and good will of this nation and to express the confident hope that the Russian people, having developed a political system founded on the principle of democracy, will join with the free people of America in resisting with firmness and fortitude the ambitious designs of the German Government which by force, intrigue and deception they are striving to attain. The commission will further be charged with the duty of finding the most efficient means of cooperating with the Russian Government in the prosecution of the war with the united purpose of accomplishing the overthrow of military autocracy, which menaces human liberty and all democratic institutions.

You may, as soon as opportunity offers, state the foregoing to the Minister of Foreign Affairs and assure him that I have learned of the erroneous impression held by the Russian Government with deep concern, and am most desirous that it should be removed not only because of the ancient friendship of our two countries but because of the frankness and confidence with which one democracy can always communicate with another.

Lansing[3]

T telegram (SDR, RG 59, 763.72/4377A, DNA).
[1] Words in italics in the following document added by Wilson; words in angle brackets deleted by him.
[2] Constantin Onou, Chargé d'Affaires of the Russian embassy in Washington.
[3] This telegram was sent as RL to D. R. Francis, May 1, 1917, T telegram (SDR, RG 59, 763.72/4377A, DNA); it is printed in FR-WWS 1917, 2, I, 50-51.

To Cyrus Hall McCormick, Jr.

My dear Cyrus: The White House 1 May, 1917

Your reply to my request about Russia is thoroughly characteristic of you and I thank you with all my heart.

We are getting one of the government vessels ready and it will be a week or so before she can be ready and available in San Francisco, but I will keep you apprised and can only ask, in the meantime, that you will make such preparations as are possible for an early departure.

This is just a hasty line but it is full of deep and sincere appreciation.

Always   Faithfully yours,   Woodrow Wilson

TLS (WP, DLC).

To Meyer London

My dear Mr. London: [The White House] 1 May, 1917

I am sorry to say that my attention was called to your letter of April twenty-eighth after all the arrangements for the Commission to Russia had been made and those who are to compose it invited. I am sorry that I did not have a chance to see you before the object of the interview was rendered futile.

Cordially and sincerely yours, Woodrow Wilson

TLS (Letterpress Books, WP, DLC).

To John Nevin Sayre

My dear Nevin: [The White House] 1 May, 1917

Frank has sent me your letter of April twenty-seventh. Before it came the draft bill had passed both houses except for a little carpentering necessary to finish its details, which will be done in conference between the two houses, but I can assure you that the point you raise as to individual conscientious scruple has by no means been overlooked. I know it has been called to the attention of the two houses more than once and it has seemed impossible to make the exceptions apply to individuals because it would open the door to so much that was unconscientious on the part of persons who wished to escape service. I think you can see how that would be. At any rate, the committee felt the difficulty unsuperable[1] and thought the arrangement they did make the best feasible.[2]

Cordially and faithfully yours, Woodrow Wilson

TLS (Letterpress Books, WP, DLC).
[1] Wilson dictated "insuperable."
[2] As Wilson suggests in the above letter, the selective draft bill as finally adopted provided only for the exemption of persons who belonged to a "well-organized religious sect or organization at present organized and existing and whose existing creed or principles forbid its members to participate in war in any form." Persons so exempted might be obliged to serve in any capacity that the President should declare to be noncombatant. 40 *Statutes at Large* 78.

From Newton Diehl Baker

My dear Mr. President: Washington. May 1, 1917.

I am exceedingly anxious to have the registration and selection by draft under the military bill conducted under such circumstances as to create a strong patriotic feeling and relieve as far as possible the prejudice which remains to some extent in the popular mind against the draft by reason of Civil War memories. With this end in view, I am using a vast number of agencies throughout the country to make the day of registration a festival and patriotic occasion. Several Governors and some Mayors of cities are entering already heartily into this plan, and the Chamber of Commerce of the United States is taking it up through their affiliated bodies with the cities throughout the country.

As a part of this program, I am anxious to have you issue a proclamation when you sign the bill, and I submit herewith a draft for your revision. This proclamation ought not now to be executed, nor, indeed, should the bill be signed, when passed by the two houses, until certain preliminary arrangements necessary to start the registration machinery simultaneously throughout the country have been perfected. The only purpose of submitting the draft proclamation at the present moment is that it may, by lying on your table, find a moment of convenient leisure for your consideration.

Respectfully yours,   Newton D. Baker

TLS (N. D. Baker Papers, DLC).

A Draft of a Proclamation[1]

[c. May 1, 1917]

WHEREAS, Congress on the ——— day of ———— has enacted the following law.

Now, therefore, I, Woodrow Wilson, President of the United States, do call upon the Governor of each of the several States and territories, the Board of Commissioners of the District of Columbia and ⟨the⟩ *all* officers and agents of the several States *and* territories, ⟨and⟩ *of* the District of Columbia, and of the counties and municipalities therein to perform certain duties in the execution of the foregoing law, which duties ⟨shall⟩ *will* be communicated to them directly in regulations of even date herewith.

And I do further proclaim and give notice to all persons subject to registration in accordance with the above law that the time and place of such registration shall be between 7 A.M. and 9 P.M. on the ——— day of ———— 1917 at the customary voting place in the voting precinct wherein they have their permanent homes.

And I do charge those who, through sickness, shall be unable to present themselves for registration *upon the day named* and those who expect *then* to be absent from the counties in which they have their permanent homes that they apply to the County Clerk of the county in which they may be on the Sixth day after the date ⟨hereof⟩ *of this proclamation* for instructions as to how they may be registered on the date prescribed herein. In case such persons ⟨who⟩ *as*, through sickness or absence, may be unable to present themselves for registration as in the law provided shall be sojourning in cities of over thirty thousand population, they shall apply to the City Clerk of the city wherein they may be sojourning rather than to the Clerk of the county.

The power against which we are arrayed has sought to impose its will upon the world by force. To this end it has increased armament until it has changed the face of war. In the sense in which we have been wont to think of armies there are no armies in this struggle. There are ⟨only whole⟩ *entire* nations armed. Thus, the men beneath the battle flags are no ⟨less⟩ *more* a part of the army that is France than the men who remain to till the soil and man the factories. It must be so with us. It is ⟨, then,⟩ not an army that we must shape and train for war; it is a nation. To this end our people must draw close in one compact front against a common foe. But this cannot be if each man pursues a private purpose. All must pursue one purpose. The nation needs all men; but *it* needs each man, not in the field that will most pleasure him, but in the endeavor that will best serve the common good. Thus, though a sharpshooter pleases to operate a trip-hammer for the forging of great guns, and an expert machinist desires to march with the flag, the nation is being served only when the sharpshooter marches and the machinist remains at his levers. ⟨In brief,⟩ *T*he whole nation must be a team in which each man shall play the part for which he is best fitted. To this end, Congress has provided that ⟨this⟩ *the* nation *shall* be organized for war by selection and that each man *shall* be classified ⟨in that⟩ *for service in the* place ⟨where⟩ *to which* it shall best serve the general good to call him.

The significance of this ⟨could⟩ *can* not be overstated. It is a new thing in our history and a landmark in our progress. It is a *new* manner of accepting ⟨thoughtful and devoted self-giving⟩ *and vitalizing our duty to give ourselves with thoughtful devotion* to the common purpose of us all. It is in no sense *a* conscription of the unwilling; it is ⟨a⟩ , *rather*, selection from a nation which has volunteered in mass. It is no ⟨less than⟩ *more* a choosing of those who shall march with the colors than it is a selection of those who shall serve an equally necessary and devoted purpose in the industries *that lie* behind the battle line.

The day here named is the time upon which all shall present themselves for assignment to their tasks. ⟨In this sense it is⟩ *It is for that reason* destined to be remembered as one of the most conspicuous moments in our history. It is nothing less than the day upon which the manhood of ⟨this⟩ *the* country shall step forward in one solid rank in defense of the ideals to which this nation is consecrated. It is important to those ideals no less than to the pride of this generation in *manifesting* its devotion to them, that there be no gaps in ⟨this⟩ *the* ranks.

It is essential ⟨, then,⟩ that the day be approached in thoughtful apprehension of its significance and that we accord to it the honour and the meaning that it deserves. Our industrial need prescribes that it be not made a technical holiday, but the stern sacrifice that is before us urges that it be carried in all our hearts as a great day of patriotic devotion and obligation when the duty shall lie upon every man, whether he is himself to be registered or not, to see to it that the name of every male person of the designated ages is written on these lists of honor.[2]

T MS (WP, DLC).
[1] This proclamation was prepared by Baker. In the draft printed below, Wilson's deletions are printed in angle brackets, his additions in italics.
[2] This proclamation was issued in this revised form on May 18, 1917.

From Edward William Bok

                                        Merion Station, Pennsylvania
My dear Mr. President: May 1, 1917

I am going to publish this in my next number.[1] It is not likely that you will see it. But it seems to me you should: it strikes me as being well done. And where any doubt still exists in the mind of any woman as to the wisdom of your action, I think it will remove it.

With highest personal regard
                        Very sincerely yours   Edward Bok

ALS (WP, DLC).
[1] Christopher Morley, "The Man," *Ladies' Home Journal*, XXXIV (June 1917), 14. This was a fictionalized and rather melodramatic account of Wilson's alleged thoughts and emotions as he wrote his war message to Congress.

Jean Jules Jusserand to the Foreign Ministry

                                    Washington—reçu le 1 mai 1917
No. 531 Le Mtre de la Justice à Président du Conseil:[1]
J'ai été reçu ce matin avec notre ambassadeur pendant plus

d'une heure par le président. Je lui ai dit que l'Amérique était entrée dans la guerre pour l'abréger et qu'il fallait pour cela la mener fortement et prendre les mesures immédiates. J'ai ajouté que sans retarder les autres mesures la principale était celle qui avait pour conséquence d'abolir ou d'atténuer la guerre sous-marine en appliquant à la destruction des sous-marins les procédés trouvés et en construisant un nombre important de navires pour compenser ou égaler les pertes subies. Le Président a déclaré que son avis (était) (aussi) de mener la guerre avec force et que tout étant conditionné pour la faculté de transporter il fallait que les alliés indiquassent un ordre d'urgence dans leurs besoins; que l'Amérique était disposée à les satisfaire avec empressement; qu'il croyait savoir que les céréales devraient passer avant tout. J'ai répondu qu'il avait raison, mais qu'il était difficile de préciser d'une manière permanente la même urgence pour chaque besoin, que le blé, le maïs, les rails nous étaient indispensables; que je l'acceptais d'autant plus que les transports de troupe[s] étant impossibles pour les quelques jours qui allaient suivre, l'envoi des céréales était indispensable. Mais j'ai insisté sur l'envoi de troupes tant au point de vue moral que matériel pour frapper l'Allemagne et réconforter les alliés. Il m'a dit qu'il y était résolu; qu'une division était assez entraînée pour partir; qu'il n' (indiquait) pas la date pour ne pas créer de déceptions se réservant de la faire connaître quand le Congrès aurait voté toutes les mesures nécessaires. (à suivre)

No. 532 Suite du No. précédent:

Je lui ai demandé d'envoyer ensuite d'autres formations échelonnées. Il a répondu que c'était son désir et qu'il le ferait sans attendre l'organisation de l'énorme armée dont la levée a été votée. J'ai insisté, pour l'essence en lui donnant les chiffres de notre consommation militaire et en précisant les restrictions dont nous frappions l'élément civil.

Je suis entré dans les détails de (notre) crise de charbon. Je lui ai demandé, en outre, de l'envoi de charbon de terre, l'envoi de 10.000 (mineurs) pour intensifier notre production. Je ne crois pas pouvoir les promettre parceque le syndicat des mineurs est très peu accessible. Il faut ajouter qu'une grande proportion des mineurs sont hongrois. Je me suis tu sur les détails du concours pour les navires de guerre parce que la queston est en partie dégagée par l'Amiral Chocheprat.

Mais le président, au cours de la conversation, a indiqué qu'il avait l'intention de faire entrer en ligne les cuirassés américains et qu'il n'en ferait pas construire de nouveaux pour reporter toute la production sur les patrouilleurs. De même, je me suis tu sur la question financière que j'examinerai ce soir avec le Ministre des finances.

L'impression que je retire est plus que satisfaisante. La cordialité du ton et la fermeté de l'accent ne peuvent pas se redire; en me donnant congé le président m'a dit être à ma disposition. Je reviendrai lui dire adieu avant de quitter l'Amérique. Signé: Viviani.   Jusserand.

T telegrams (Guerre 1914-1918, États-Unis, Vol. 511, pp. 82-83, FFM-Ar).
   [1] Alexandre Félix Joseph Ribot, Premier and Minister of Foreign Affairs. He had succeeded Briand on March 20, 1917.

T R A N S L A T I O N

Washington—received May 1, 1917

531. The Minister of Justice to the President of the Council:

With our Ambassador I was received for over an hour this morning by the President. I said to him that America had entered the war to shorten it and, in order to do this, one needed to wage it strongly and take immediate steps. I added that, without delaying other measures, the main thing must be whatever would defeat or weaken the submarine war by applying newly discovered methods to the destruction of submarines and by building a large number of ships to compensate for or equal those lost. The President said that he, too, wanted to wage the war forcefully and, since everything depended on the ability to transport, the Allies must indicate the order of urgency of their needs; that America was prepared to satisfy these willingly; that he was reasonably sure that grains must come first. I replied that he was correct, but that it was difficult to define in any permanent way the same urgency for each need; that, for us, wheat, corn, and rails were indispensable; that I agreed even more that, because the transportation of troops was impossible in the near future, it was indispensable to send grains. But I insisted on the sending of troops, for moral reasons as much as for material ones—to strike Germany and cheer the Allies. He told me that he was resolved to do this; that one division was well on the way toward departure; that he would not give the date in order not to create false hopes and would undertake to make this known when Congress had voted all the necessary measures. (More to follow.)

532. Continuation of preceding number.

I asked him to send other formations afterward at intervals. He replied that this was his desire and that he would do it without waiting for the enormous army just voted for to be organized.

I emphasized that this was the essence of the matter by giving him the figures on our casualties and by describing the limitations that our losses have imposed upon our civilian population.

I gave details of our coal crisis. I asked him, moreover, to send, along with coal, 10,000 miners to intensify our production. I do not think this can be promised because the miners' union is not very receptive to the idea. One must add that a large proportion of the miners are Hungarian. I shall not comment on the details of cooperation regarding naval vessels because this question has in part been handled separately by Admiral Chocheprat.

But the President, in the course of the conversation, indicated that he intended to commit the American capital ships to active service and that he would do nothing to build new ones in order to transfer all production to patrol vessels. Also, I shall not comment on financial matters, which I am to discuss this evening with the Secretary of the Treasury.

The impression I have formed is more than satisfactory. The cordial tone and the resolute accent cannot be conveyed; as I left him, the President said he was at my disposal. I shall return to take leave of him before departing from America. Signed Viviani.   Jusserand.

Remarks at the White House[1]

2 May, 1917.

Mr. Secretary and gentlemen: It goes without saying that I am very glad to see you, and very glad to see you on such an errand. I have no homily to deliver to you, because I know you are as intensely interested as I am in drawing all of our efforts and energies together in a common action. My function has not of recent days been to give advice, but to get things coordinated so that there will not be any, or at any rate too much, lost motion, and in order that things should not be done twice by different bodies or done in conflict.

It is for that reason that I particularly welcome a conference such as this you are holding today and tomorrow—the conference which will acquaint you with exactly the task as it is conceived here in Washington and with the ways in which cooperation can be best organized. For, after all, the task is comparatively simple. The means of accomplishing the task are very complicated, because we must draw many pieces of machinery together, and we must see that they act, not only to a common object, but at the same time and in a common spirit. My function, therefore, today is the very pleasant function of saying how much obliged to you I am for having come here and associated yourself with us in the great task of making good what the nation has promised to do—go to the defense and vindication of the rights of people everywhere to live as they have a right to live under the very principles of our nation.

It is a thing one does not dare to talk about because a certain passion comes into one's thought and one's feeling as one thinks of the nature of the task—the ideal nature of it—of the opportunity that America has now to show to all the world what it means to have been a democracy for one hundred and forty-five years and to mean every bit of the creed which we have so long professed. And in this thing it ought to be easy to act and delightful to cooperate.

I thank you very much indeed for your courtesy in coming here.

T MS (WP, DLC).
[1] Wilson was speaking, at 2 P.M., to Newton D. Baker and a group of governors and representatives of state councils of national defense.

A Conversation with Josef-Jacques-Césaire Joffre

[*May 2, 1917*]

Marshal Joffre, accompanied by Colonel Cosby[1] (who had been assigned to serve as his interpreter) arrived at the White House at two minutes before 4 o'clock. The meeting was to take place at 4 o'clock. The Marshal was conducted into the Green Room, where President Wilson met him at exactly 4 o'clock. After exchanging salutations, they were seated and the conversation began.

The President expressed pleasure at having the opportunity to speak privately with the Marshal, who thanked him cordially for his friendly reception. The President asked the Marshal to tell him quite frankly how, in his view, the American army should be used in the conduct of the war.

Marshal Joffre: Germany is still strong, but its power is steadily diminishing. To maintain its troop strength, it is forced to call up all kinds of men, of whom many are not physically fit for service. It has deployed the class of 1918, which provides

[1] Lt. Col. Spencer Cosby, Corps of Engineers, U.S.A., had been in charge of public buildings and grounds in Washington from 1909 to 1913 and military attaché at the United States Embassy in Paris from 1913 to 1917. The English text of Cosby's memorandum of this conversation is missing. The text printed here was retranslated by the Editors.

about 400,000 recruits, which has reinforced its troops appreciably.

The President: Is France in the same situation as Germany with regard to effectives and manpower resources?

Marshal Joffre: No, our class of 1918 has just been called to the colors and will not go into the line for at least three or four months. It will provide about 170,000 men for the French army. So far, the German class of 1918 is probably not fully committed. We do know that a goodly number of the recruits of this class are already engaged at the front.

For the United States, the first and most important of things is to send to France a unit, for example, a division. When the American flag flies beside the French flag and the English flag, the moral effect will be considerable.

The President: How long will it take to prepare a division such as you envisage?

Marshal Joffre: This division could leave the United States almost immediately and complete its training in France within the space of a month. After this period of intense training, it could gradually take its place in one of the sectors of the front. We know that that is possible. It is the method that we have followed with success, when we employed the Russian troops that were landed in France.

The President: If I understand you correctly, it would require less time to prepare troops for trench warfare than to prepare them for a war of movement?

Marshal Joffre: Precisely; this is above all true for the officers.

The President: I don't quite see—

Marshal Joffre: The time needed to train the enlisted men for the two kinds of war is about the same. As for officers serving with troops, it takes them about three months of training in order to become *au courant* with the methods required in trench warfare. It takes longer, however, for staff officers.

The President: Thus, the Marshal means that our first division must be composed of regular soldiers who would have no need of basic military training?

Marshal Joffre: Just so. The essential thing will be to complete their training by instructing them in the specialties that modern war demands and that we can teach them right behind our front. By specialties, I mean the use of equipment and arms such as hand grenades, V.-B. rifle grenades, thanks to which the barrages are effective at the front at distances varying from 50 to 100 meters, or, again, machine guns. This means showing the American soldiers the tactical use of these weapons as they are being used right now by the French army.

The President: The Marshal's idea, I presume, is that we should prepare ourselves to provide certain auxiliary services in France, for example, ambulances. The grave question is the one of transportation. Given the great number of ships which have been destroyed, we have only a reduced number of vessels at our disposal. The transport of troops must be so regulated as not to interfere with the transport of food, munitions, and other supplies. How does the Marshal see this problem?

The Marshal: The transport of men or matériel could be worked out simultaneously. The transport of two or three regiments requires, in reality, only two or three ships (that depends on their capacity) and, in sum, that would involve only a very few other transports.

The President: Can't we send troops and supplies on the same ship?

The Marshal: Yes, that can be arranged. My proposal to send only one division at first, with other divisions progressively joining them in France later, as your units become ready, is designed to serve this very purpose, that is, to hamper your transport of all sorts of things to us as little as possible.

The President: Does the Marshal think that the American troops should debark at first in England or go directly to a port on France's south Atlantic coast?

Marshal Joffre: Debarking in England would require a double transport of troops. Debarking directly in France would avoid that. The ports of Dunkerque, Calais, and Boulogne have been made available to the English and are already badly jammed.

The President: I understand perfectly. But if I raise this question, it is because I thought that the methods of debarkation would perhaps be better developed in England than in France.

Marshal Joffre: I can make a study of the two systems of debarkation and compare the results obtained. If we debark American troops in England, then they must be taken by rail to another port, taken in ships across the Channel, and then landed at a French port, where, in any case, it will be necessary to provide quarters to receive them. If, on the contrary, we send the American units directly to France, to a port where necessary arrangements have already been made, it will only be a matter of transporting them by train to their training camp. The English ports are extremely congested. The railways of northern France are no less so, and we also would have to abandon all commercial traffic to take care of military needs, which would hinder us greatly.

The President: Has the Marshal chosen a French port?

Marshal Joffre: La Rochelle and its inner harbors. We have studied the possibility of using the port of La Pallice. In this connection, I wish to call your attention to the extreme importance of sending the general who will command the American troops and the staff ahead of the troops themselves.

The President: Then, would it not be opportune to debark all of them at the same time?

Marshal Joffre: No. The general must see that quarters for his men are ready at the port of debarkation and that all unloading facilities are ready. He must reconnoiter the site chosen for the training camp. He must study the sector that he will later occupy. He must see to it that, when the troops arrive, they will find everything ready to receive them. I call your attention to the choice of the general, particularly from the point of view of character and capabilities. It is extremely important that he be designated after the closest scrutiny.

The President: So he must be a perfectly trained soldier?

Marshal Joffre: Assuredly, yes.

The President: I ask that because the question of sending volunteers has come up. Since the general will have only a rather limited command at first, shouldn't he be a man chosen according to his aptitude for training troops rather than according to his aptitude for conceiving strategic plans and preparing vast enterprises of war?

Marshal Joffre: You are right. Later, after the first division has been reinforced by a second, a third division, and so on, and when a group of five divisions will have been formed, the American general will exercise an important command. The services of supply will also require strong leadership, and this will call for a very well trained general in order to carry out his functions.

The President: At this moment we would have five or six generals who have been tried under fire, and it will be possible to designate the aptest of these to command all the American forces.

Marshal Joffre: Just so. And not only will things work out in this manner, but also one must envisage the case in which, perhaps of twenty generals, ten will not be able to exercise their commands satisfactorily and will need to be recalled. Promotions must be by selection and not by seniority, so that colonels and even majors—if they distinguish themselves by their valor—could receive higher commands.

The President: I agree with you completely. However, our law sets requirements of seniority, up to the grade of colonel. Above that grade, it is a matter of choice.

Marshal Joffre: Our law likewise imposes limits on choices. I have arranged to broaden these and have established promotions to temporary rank, which give a grade for the duration of the war. In this fashion, many colonels command divisions. General Micheler,[2] who commands a group of three armies, was a brigadier general a few months ago.

The President: I think that we can also solve the difficulty by similar means. Moreover, Congress will probably find it necessary to modify the existing laws.

Marshal Joffre: After the war, our parliament, for its part, no doubt will have to vote laws that will confirm in their grades the officers with temporary appointments. As this is for the good of the country, that will be done.

As for the constitution of the division you intend to send to France, I must point out to you that we have adopted the type of division of three regiments (instead of the previous four). The American division, as now constituted, is too large, if one considers present methods of combat. The effectives of a division must be arranged in such a way that the infantry are effectively protected by the division's own artillery. Otherwise, experience has shown us, the losses of infantrymen are too heavy.

The President: I fear that, in the case of the present war, our army does not have enough artillery.

Marshal Joffre: France can provide all you need for the first division, from trench cannon from 58 to 75 [meters], all the way to the heavy artillery which you lack. We are also in a position to give you grenades, machine guns, and the special weapons which you don't have.

The composition of an American company, which includes only 150 men, is too small. A company now must encompass enough specialists trained to operate the equipment I mentioned and be able to fight in small units.

The President: I fear that our law limits the number of effectives in a company. It can be modified, however. Do you think our first American division should be constituted according to the American model, or according to the French model?

Marshal Joffre: In my view, this first division could have

---

2 Joseph Alfred Micheler.

the strength of an American division, with extra men to bring each company up to 250 men.

The President: Have you explained this to the Secretary of War?

Marshal Joffre: The day after I arrived, I had an interview with the Secretary of War and General Scott. The following day, I went with my staff officers to the War College, where I set forth my ideas as fully as possible. Since then, a great number of conferences have taken place between the officers of the American army and my officers. I hope that their collaboration will soon produce the best results.

The President: I hope you were pleased with your meetings. Did the Secretary of War get a good understanding of your ideas?

Marshal Joffre: I expressed myself carefully when I was with him. The Secretary's face lit up, and he said: "I understand." I also gave the officers of the War College six complete sets of all secret instructions which have been given to the various branches of the French army. I also gave them by hand a document showing my plan of cooperation and another document in which I give some indications concerning the possible organization of an American division.

The President: I have seen one of these documents, the one which presents your plan for cooperation. I read it last night.

Marshal Joffre: I am going to leave three officers in Washington during my tour across your country, so that they can work in concert with the American officers. I plan to spend a day in Washington on my return, and I hope that we can then reach a definitive agreement for the cooperation of the American army.

The President: I hope that can be done. I thank you very sincerely for the occasion which has been afforded me to talk with you. We hope to give you all possible support as soon as possible. I wish you good luck, and a happy return to France.

Marshal Joffre left the White House at 5:05.

T translation (WC, NjP) of Jean Fabry, *Joffre et son destin* (Paris, 1931), pp. 253-60.

Two Letters from Newton Diehl Baker

My dear Mr. President: Washington. May 2, 1917.

I have just had a long conference with General Bridges. We discussed the following subjects with the following results:

1. The United States is to extend medical aid to the British forces on the French front by the dispatch of hospital units, doctors and nurses, from time to time, with the understanding that these units are to be subject to collection as a part of our own military forces as they may be needed when our military expeditions arrive on the French front. A similar arrangement dealing with ambulance service as distinguished from hospital service has been undertaken with the French.

2. I am considering with the British Mission the question of sending a number of air-squadrons to England, there to be equipped with war-planes and given the finishing touches of air drill for war service and to be used in connection with the British air-squadrons as soon as properly schooled; with a like reservation of the right on our part to withdraw them for our own military expedition when needed. The question of doing this has not yet been determined but it is recommended by General Squier[1] and I think ought to be done, if it can be, speedily.

3. General Bridges took up with me the question of an expeditionary force, urging that it would be better for such a force from the United States to cooperate with the English because of similarity of language. But I told him frankly that there were many considerations to be weighed in this matter and that the likelihood was that our first expeditionary forces would cooperate more directly with the French. He seemed entirely satisfied and apparently had been directed not to stress this point. My reasons in the matter are as follows: (a) I think popular sentiment in our own country would approve cooperation with the French first rather than with the English; (b) our naval cooperation is necessarily with the English; our aircraft cooperation preferably with the English; our medical and hospital cooperation about equally with each and it would seem more equal to have our direct military cooperation first with the French.

4. The question of aid from America in the operation of English and French railroads in France was taken up. Both the English and French Commissions are urging their need of trained railroad men—not so much engineers as constructors and expert repair-mechanics. I asked General Bridges whether cooperation from us with the French in that regard would not be equally helpful to both British and French. He said it would—that the British were already obliged to aid the French in maintaining their railroad operation and that any aid we could give the French there would both help and relieve the British. This proposition involves the assembling in this country of regiments

of special troops which are already authorized by law and could be quickly assembled. Mr. Willard says the railroads could supply the men without interfering with their own efficiency. In all, perhaps, as many as 10,000 men would be needed. General Black,[2] under whom this work would be organized, thinks it an entire feasible form of cooperation, and both the French and British Commissions urge it as of very great value to them. I have withheld any expression of opinion on the matter, subject to your direction. If you care to have me go into further detail about it, I will be glad, of course, to come to you at any time. These troops if assembled and sent would be American troops under the American flag; paid by us as troops and subsisted by the French and English respectively at our charge.

5. General Bridges took up with me the question of their being allowed to recruit for British service in this country—first, as to British-born subjects resident here and, second, as to citizens of the United States. I told him that we could in no event allow the opening of recruiting offices here for the recruitment of American citizens as that would take from us the whole power of exempting persons indispensable to the industry of the country, upon which the success of all parties interested depended; that if Congress passes the bill now pending, there would be no objection from the War Department as a military matter to the voluntary recruitment of British subjects in the United States. The number would not in any event be large and, as it would be voluntary, it would hardly seem to be objectionable. He then asked me whether we would object to their putting their conscription act into effect in this country through the medium of our courts solely upon British subjects resident here. Their conscription act applies only to persons born in the United Kingdom and not to persons born in Ireland. I told him that that question was one of international policy and one of political policy in our Government and not a military question, and that I could not give any answer beyond saying that further legislation from Congress would be needed before any such enforced application of the obligation of British-born subjects resident here could be effected.

Out of the foregoing, the only question arising for immediate consideration by you is the advisability of cooperation in the railroad maintenance and operation and upon that I should like to have your direction.

Respectfully yours,   Newton D. Baker

[1] Brig. Gen. George Owen Squier, chief signal officer, U.S.A.
[2] Brig. Gen. William Murray Black, chief of engineers, U.S.A.

My dear Mr. President: Washington. May 2, 1917

In my talk with General Bridges this afternoon, I asked him to express quite frankly his view as to the effect in England, France and Germany of our sending an expeditionary force, and particularly with reference to the composition of the force. He told me that he thought the presence of even a brigade would be enormously stimulating; that it made very little difference whether they went first to England and then to France, or directly to France; that in both England and France there were many people who professed to expect America to make war at long range, and that there would be an instant and very great value from the fact of arrival of American troops. He went further and said that the English, French and German armies had all settled down to the conviction that this is too serious a kind of warfare for untrained men or amateurs of any sort, and that he had taken the liberty of telegraphing to the Chief of the British Staff and protesting against any favor being shown from them toward the organization of any form of volunteer group from America for such an expedition. He thought the Germans would ridicule a hastily-organized expedition of non-professionals and that both the British and French would be depressed by such an expedition as an evidence of our failing to appreciate the seriousness of the situation; but that if such an expedition were made up of regulars and led by one of our professional soldiers, it would command instant respect in spite of being small.

I know that you have entertained these views, and I have felt them very strongly. This frank statement from General Bridges is an interesting confirmation of our instinctive judgment on the subject.   Respectfully yours,   Newton D. Baker

TLS (WP, DLC).

From Edward Mandell House

Dear Governor: New York. May 2, 1917.

The suggestion of Root for the Russian Commission has raised something of a storm of criticism among the ultra liberals throughout the country. When they hear of McCormick and Eugene Meyer, it may become worse. It will be felt that the commission is to be sent to Russia for the commercial benefit of American [America] and not to steady the republic there.

I find it is generally known that you have Meyer in mind, and the protest against him is stronger than that against Root. They say he is reactionary and a stock broker of doubtful reputation whose only qualification is the friendship Brandeis has for him.

I doubt whether the commission with the perso[n]nel thought of could be made acceptable to Russia as now constituted, but it might be done by adding such men as Max Eastman or George Lunn.[1]

I do not think I have ever had a pleasanter time in Washington than upon my last visit, and I thank Mrs. Wilson and you very, very much.   Affectionately yours,   E. M. House

TLS (WP, DLC).
[1] George Richard Lunn, former Presbyterian minister; Socialist mayor of Schenectady, 1912-1913; elected mayor again as a Socialist, 1915. He was expelled from the Socialist party in March 1916 in a dispute over patronage but completed his term as mayor, 1916-1917. He was elected to Congress as a Democrat in November 1916 and served until 1919.

To Robert Lansing, with Enclosure

My dear Mr. Secretary,   The White House. 3 May, 1917.

After receiving your letter herein with regard to censoring the mails I not only had a conversation with the Postmaster General but also asked him to state to me in writing what he then said to me. The enclosed letter from him to me is the result.

I have given the matter a great feal [deal] of thought and have discussed it with a number of persons who are familiar with the circumstances of our communications by post with the countries to the south of us, and I fully agree with the conclusions of the Postmaster General. At any rate for the present. Circumstances which we do not know may come to light and existing circumstances may change.

Faithfully Yours,   W.W.

WWTLI (WP, DLC).

E N C L O S U R E

From Albert Sidney Burleson

My dear Mr. President: [Washington] May 3, 1917.

I am returning herewith the letter addressed to you under date of the 30th ultimo by the Secretary of State in regard to the censorship of the mails. I do not regard such censorship in this country as necessary for the reasons stated below:

On the 7th of April, 1917, the despatch from the United States of mail for Germany, Austria, Hungary, Luxembourg, Bulgaria and Turkey was suspended; such suspension applying to mail originating in the United States and also to that originating in other countries and forwarded via the United States.

All mail, whether originating in the United States or elsewhere, despatched from the United States to Europe and Africa and that which is despatched to Asia via the Atlantic route, is despatched via ports of the Entente Allies and is subject to the rigid and skilled censorship exercised by the censorship agencies organized and perfected by the Governments of those countries since the commencement of the war. Mail for Asia that is despatched via the Pacific route is despatched via Japan or Hongkong and consequently is subject to the censorship maintained either by Japan or the British Colony of Hongkong.

Censorship by the United States of mail for or from the destinations above mentioned would be duplicating work which is being performed by those who by reason of long and practical experience are experts in the business.

The only mail from the United States not subject to the censorship of the Entente Allies is that for Mexico and neutral countries and colonies in the West Indies, Central and South America. Any mail which might be despatched from the West Indies, Central or South America direct to Europe, Africa and Asia would be subject to censorship by the Entente Allies except possibly some mail which might be despatched direct to Spain and mail could not be despatched from Spain to the Central Powers or to any other country without passing through territory or waters controlled by the Entente Allies.

From the foregoing, it will be seen that censorship of the mails in the United States would be a duplication of work that is being better performed by our allies and would therefore be unnecessary and futile.   Faithfully yours,   A. S. Burleson

TLS (WP, DLC).

To Robert Lansing, with Enclosures

My dear Mr. Secretary: The White House 3 May, 1917

Secretary Wilson has been kind enough to send me the enclosed. I am sure you will read it with interest. It seems to me to show that Mr. Walling is the man we want.

Cordially and faithfully yours,   Woodrow Wilson

TLS (SDR, RG 59, 763.72/4390½, DNA).

ENCLOSURE   I

From William Bauchop Wilson

My Dear Mr. President: Washington May 3, 1917.

Anent the appointment of a Socialist on the Russian Commission, I am inclosing herewith a very interesting personal letter from Mr. William English Walling, which, I think, is important in determining the selection of a Socialist on the Commission. It should be said that the letter has no connection with my suggestion of his name for appointment on the Commission, as he had no knowledge of my having presented his name for consideration.   Faithfully yours,   W B Wilson

TLS (SDR, RG 59, 763.72/4390½, DNA).

ENCLOSURE   II

William English Walling to William Bauchop Wilson

PERSONAL

Dear Mr. Wilson: Greenwich Connecticut May 2, 1917.

I sent you yesterday an important clipping marked "Personal" without an accompanying letter, protesting against the possible appointment of Hillquit[1] as a member of the international commission to Russia, and urging that a member of the American Federation of Labor be sent to represent the American working class. I also pointed out the extreme danger of the effort to win the Russian working people for a purely German peace under the very plausible but deceptive slogan of "no annexation, no indemnities." This has been the program of pro-Kaiser Socialists from the very first day of the war—I refer, of course, to the Scheidemann group.[2] Unfortunately it is also the program of the German Socialist Minority (Kautsky, Bernstein, Ledebour, et al.).[3] Of course, this group is far more influential among the Socialists of the world outside of Germany. Undoubtedly its opposition to the German government at home is far more radical and sincere, but it does not differ in any important respect whatever from the Majority on international questions. A third faction, the very small Liebknecht-Rosa Luxembourg group,[4] is to be put in a somewhat different class, although we have no way of knowing whether its position is satisfactory to the non-German democracies of the world.

I write now to point out that none of the official leaders of the Majority now in control of the American Party can be trusted. On the contrary, all of them are in bitter opposition to the American government and American people, and all are for immediate peace absolutely regardless of the question as to whether it would be favorable to German militarism or not. While Meyer London, for example, is somewhat less rabid than Hillquit and Berger,[5] he has been notoriously pro-German throughout the war. Just one illustration—he advocated a plebiscite on Alsace Lorraine, but this on the assumption, as publicly confessed by Hillquit, that Alsace and Lorraine, if considered as one unit, have been so packed with Germans in recent years that there would be a German majority. All the other foreign leaders here are of the same pro-German point of view.

The case is scarcely bettered with the relatively small ultra-pacifist, American-born group, composed of such men as Debs and Benson. These have been won over absolutely by the German Minority to the program of immediate peace (which means a peace at any price), and to the peace policy of "no annexation, no indemnities," which gains importance from the fact that it is adopted, unanimously I believe, by the Russian Councils of Workmen and Soldier Deputies. It was adopted doubtless with the understanding that it meant exactly what it said. Kerenski, it is true, has given it an interpretation as meaning no *punitive* indemnities and no *forcible* annexation, a principle which would probably be accepted by all the world's leading democracies. But such an interpretation is obviously strained. Both the German and the Russian Socialists mean that not only Germany, but also Austria, Bulgaria and Turkey are to keep absolutely every one of the conquests they had made previously to the present war—leaving the French, Polish, Ruthenian, Rumanian, Italian, Armenian and Syrian populations, now under the Central Empires, in the same position as before.

Pardon this rather long letter, for its object is entirely practical and can be put in a single sentence. The official Socialist Majority should not be represented in the delegation to Russia; the American Federation of Labor alone should represent our working people.

Very sincerely yours,   Wm. English Walling

P.S. I have a letter from A. M. Simons[6] today stating that he will shortly leave the Party. Gaylord[7] it seems takes the same position, as does also John Spargo, one of the five members of the National Executive Committee. You are already aware that J. G. Phelps Stokes,[8] Charles Edward Russell, Upton Sinclair,

W. J. Ghent,[9] and many others of the best known American Socialists without foreign connections are in complete and absolute opposition to the Party and that all will leave it in case the treasonable resolutions of the recent St. Louis Convention are passed by referendum.

Allen Benson, A. M. Simons, Winfield Gaylord and Job Harriman have all openly expressed the view that the St. Louis resolutions are nothing more nor less than treason under the statutes of the United States. To send a supporter of these resolutions to Russia would obviously be insane.

J. G. Phelps Stokes has just written a careful letter to Polk of the State Department, giving at length the most urgent reasons why Hillquit and Berger should not even be permitted to sail for the so-called "international" Socialist conference at Stockholm now being engineered by Berlin.[10]

TLS (SDR, RG 59, 763.72/4390½, DNA).

[1] W. E. Walling, "The Pro-Hyphen German Socialist," New York *Globe,* May 1, 1917. Morris Hillquit, New York lawyer, trade-union organizer, and Socialist party leader; he was a principal drafter of the "St. Louis Proclamation," about which see P. O. Husting to WW, April 27, 1917, n. 1.

[2] That is, the Majority Socialists in the Reichstag, led by Friedrich Ebert and Philipp Scheidemann.

[3] The Independent Socialists, led by Karl Kautsky, Eduard Bernstein, and Georg Ledebour, who had just split off from the Majority.

[4] At this time, a small left-wing faction within the Independent Socialists, who centered around Karl Liebknecht and Rosa Luxemburg. Later the nucleus of the Spartacus League and the German Communist party.

[5] Victor Luitpold Berger, journalist of Milwaukee, a founder of the American Socialist party, served from 1911 to 1913 as the first Socialist congressman.

[6] Algie Martin Simons.

[7] Winfield Romeo Gaylord.

[8] James Graham Phelps Stokes.

[9] William James Ghent. All persons mentioned in this paragraph were prominent Socialist intellectuals and writers.

[10] In April 1917, Danish and Dutch Socialist leaders had taken the initiative in calling an international conference of representatives of socialist and labor parties of all countries to express their collective desire for peace and to formulate peace terms. The date of the beginning of the proposed conference, originally set for May 15, was repeatedly postponed into the summer and autumn of 1917, as the enthusiasm of the various socialist and labor parties and their respective national governments waxed and waned for a variety of reasons. As it turned out, the conference never took place, largely because of the refusal of the governments of the United States, Great Britain, France, and Italy to issue passports to the proposed delegates from their respective countries. While the Majority and Minority Socialists of Germany had agreed to participate, they did not in any way initiate or "engineer" the conference. See Merle Fainsod, *International Socialism and the World War* (Cambridge, Mass., 1935), pp. 124-46.

To Andrew Dickson White

My dear Mr. White: The White House 3 May, 1917

Thank you for your letter of April twenty-sixth.

I dare not accept the suggestion which it conveys. I have been authorized and directed by the Congress of the United States to use the whole force and manhood of the United States in this grim and terrible war. I could not venture in the circumstances to act upon any advice but that of the professional soldiers who have either witnessed or taken part in the struggle. It is their unanimous advice that any other course than that which we are pursuing in our preparations for securing an Army would be a fatal mistake, a mistake registered in dead men, in unnecessary and cruel loss of life. My recent conversations with the military men accompanying the two commissions from France and England have confirmed me in this conviction, and I must act upon it.   Sincerely yours,   Woodrow Wilson

TLS (A. D. White Papers, NIC).

To Paul Oscar Husting

My dear Senator: [The White House] 3 May, 1917

I feel very derelict in not having replied sooner to your interesting and important letter of April twenty-seventh, but I am sure you will understand and forgive when I say that I was so rushed from one thing to another that it was only when the debate on the Army bill was nearing its conclusion I was able to turn to your letter and give it the attention which it deserved. If I had known its subject matter, I would, of course, have sacrificed something else and read it sooner.

I am sure, my dear Senator, that the initial supposition upon which what you urge is based is a mistaken one. I think that later consideration of the matter and a fuller plan with regard to the methods to be adopted have convinced the War Department that it will not take anything like so long as they had at first supposed to effect the enrollment and the draft. As a matter of fact, it can probably be effected quite as fast as camps and materials can be supplied.

It is important to remember that in addition to the force of 500,000 men which we have principally been discussing, it will be necessary to raise a force of over 600,000 men to bring the Regular Army and the National Guard up to the authorized war strength. These men must be taken care of as well as the

500,000 and I dare say (though in this matter I have not yet conferred with the Secretary of War) that it may not be possible prudently to call the additional 500,000 men into camp for training at once.

My own feeling and position has been simply this: We are undertaking the grimmest business of war that the world has ever known, the Congress has authorized me to put the whole force and power of the United States into this war, and I would not dare in the circumstances to turn away from the unanimous advice of our own trained soldiers and of the soldiers who have been through the extraordinary experiences of the last three years in France and England. Their advice is unanimously in favor of the plan proposed to the Congress by the War Department and I feel that I have no choice in the matter but to follow experts in a war of experts.

I share the sentiments expressed in your letter and the predilections, but stern experience is an inexorable tutor.

With much regard and appreciation,

Cordially and sincerely yours,   Woodrow Wilson

TLS (Letterpress Books, WP, DLC).

Three Letters to Newton Diehl Baker

My dear Mr. Secretary,   The White House. 3 May, 1917.

I fully approve of this. Only one question: Does the army bill now about to pass authorize and provide for this use of the election machinery of the States and authorize [us] to thus to call [*sic*] on the state officials, or is all of this just a friendly summons to cooperate?

I return the draft of a proclamation, and thank you for having prepared it. I have made a few unimportant changes in the phrasing of it.   Faithfully Yours,   Woodrow Wilson

My dear Mr. Secretary,   The White House. 3 May, 1917.

I have your letter of yesterday in which you give me, enumerated, the topics of your discussion with General Bridges of the various matters proposed for immediate action.

As you say, we have already agreed with regard to all but one of them, namely, the advisability of active and immediate cooperation in the maintenance and operation of the railways of France which are being used for the support of the armies

at the front. I approve of the plan proposed for such cooperation and hope that one of the first things done will be to carry
it out.   Faithfully Yours,   Woodrow Wilson

My dear Mr. Secretary,   The White House. 3 May, 1917.

I have your letter of yesterday in which you give me the views
expressed by General Bridges when you invited him "to express
quite frankly his view as to the effect in England, France, and
Germany of our sending an expeditionary force" to the western
front. I had a similar conversation with General Joffre. I entirely
agree with the conclusions arrived at, and I allowed General
Joffre to take it for granted that such a force would be sent just
as soon as we could send it.
                 Faithfully Yours,   Woodrow Wilson

WWTLS (N. D. Baker Papers, DLC).

To George Holden Tinkham[1]

My dear Mr. Tinkham: [The White House] May 3, 1917.

I have received and shall carefully note the memorial signed
by Mr. Emery T. Morris and others, which you brought to my
office today.[2]

May I not thank you for your courtesy in the matter?
        Cordially and sincerely yours,   Woodrow Wilson

TLS (Letterpress Books, WP, DLC).
[1] Republican congressman from Massachusetts.
[2] E. T. Morris et al. to WW, April 20, 1917.

To Edward William Bok

My dear Mr. Bok: The White House 3 May, 1917

It was very kind of you to send me the advanced sheets of Mr.
Christopher Morley's sketch, "The Man." All the physical part of,
—I mean his really very beautiful descriptions of where I was
and how I acted and how I looked,—is fiction. I wish that I did
act with such dramatic propriety, but it is all very finely conceived and I have no objection to being so represented.

Seriously speaking, I feel myself very much Mr. Morley's
debtor for his very sympathetic and illuminating treatment of
the matter.
        Cordially and sincerely yours,   Woodrow Wilson

TLS (E. W. Bok Papers, PHC).

To Cyrus Hall McCormick, Jr.

My dear Cyrus: The White House 3 May, 1917

I wrote you a short letter the other day but want to add a line now because of the delightful letter you were kind enough to write me on April twenty-second. It was certainly very generous of you and I want you to know how it has warmed my heart.

In haste

Cordially and faithfully yours,   Woodrow Wilson

TLS (WP, DLC).

To John Dalziel Sprunt[1]

My dear Friend: [The White House] 3 May, 1917

It was a source of very great gratification to me to receive your letter.[2] Tragical as the story is which it conveys, there is a touch of steadfastness and heroism about the whole thing which touches me very deeply. It shows in you in these latter days of supreme trial the same quality that I used to perceive in you when I was a youngster and shared my dear father's admiration for all the sterling traits which we perceived in you. My thoughts often go back to the days in Wilmington and no figure of those days is more distinct than your own.

We have ourselves now gone into this grim and terrible war and there will be many a home no doubt in this country to which the same sort of story will come that has pulled at my heart-strings as I have read your letter. God grant that the common experience may breed steadfast, common purposes!

My heart goes out to you.

Cordially and sincerely yours,   Woodrow Wilson

TLS (Letterpress Books, WP, DLC).
[1] Younger brother of Wilson's old friend, James Sprunt of Wilmington, N. C. John D. Sprunt had gone to England many years before to represent the family's firm of Alexander Sprunt & Son. He married an English woman and remained in England permanently.
[2] J. D. Sprunt to WW, April 5, 1917, ALS (WP, DLC). Sprunt expressed his gratification that Wilson had made the decision for war and described in detail the circumstances of the deaths of two of his sons in combat while serving with the British army.

Two Letters from Robert Lansing

My dear Mr. President: Washington May 3, 1917.

I have examined William English Walling's book written in May, 1915, and entitled "The Socialists and the War"[1] and find

it a compilation of the views of other socialists of various countries. There is no editorial comment by Walling so I got from the
book no idea of his attitude.

He quotes quite extensively from other American socialists
and also summarizes their views. Of these I find that the ideas of
Charles Edward Russell are more in accord with what I conceive to be the best suited to influence Russian socialists. Walling
says of Russell:

> "He does not want peace until Germany is sufficiently beaten
> to ensure respect for treaties and the rights of small nations
> in the future or until her aggressive military party and
> absolute form of government have received a blow that will
> bring about their overthrow."

The quotations which he gives bear out this statement, Russell saying there is no way "but to fight through to the end."

Russell, as you probably know, is 56 years old, a journalist and
author, who in 1910 and again in 1912 was the Socialist candidate for Governor of New York.

I am sorry not to be able to tell you more of Walling but his
book helped me not at all.

Faithfully yours,   Robert Lansing.

1 William English Walling, *The Socialists and the War: A Documentary
Statement of the Position of the Socialists of All Countries* (New York, 1915).

My dear Mr. President: Washington May 3, 1917.

I saw Justice Brandeis yesterday morning about Eugene Meyer
and explained to him the situation. Meyer arrived in Washington
this morning and came to the Department with Brandeis who
had gone over the matter with him. He was very pleasant about
it and at once declared his willingness to withdraw his acceptance.

It will be easy to explain to those whom he has told that he
was going on the Commission, but the fact that we do not send
a Jew will have to be explained in some way because of its effect
in this country. It is a delicate question and needs very careful
handling.   Faithfully yours,   Robert Lansing.

TLS (WP, DLC).

From John Franklin Fort

My Dear Mr. President: Washington May 3, 1917.

When I wrote you some days ago and told you that the bituminous coal inquiry, to which you called the attention of this Commission,[1] had been referred to me for investigation, I promised to advise you of anything that seemed to me might be of interest to you. I beg to call your attention, as briefly as I can, to a few matters that I really think you should know.

It is not necessary to state to you how important the fuel problem is to all interests,—transportation, manufacturing, domestic, etc. I have had six full days hearings of the coal operators in Pennsylvania and in the South and West; and of the largest consumers, such as railroads, public utilities, manufacturers, etc. Six days may [not?] seem long, but every hour from 10 to 5:30 each day has been profitably used in conference with these people,—representing the very largest business interests of the country.

In the anthracite coal problem we yesterday finished a two days hearing before the whole Commission. As I see it, the whole question as to coal,—both bituminous and anthracite,—resolves itself into the solving of three propositions,—

(1) Its production
(2) Its transportation
(3) Its distribution.

Production, of course, is almost solely a labor problem. The labor problem is vital. The large wages being paid in other industries,—such as munitions and the like, is undoubtedly drawing laborers from the mines. Mine labor in many sections, especially in the anthracite regions of Pennsylvania, if lost is almost impossible to be replaced. To be an anthracite miner, a man must have learned the business by not less than two years experience, and have a certificate showing such service before, under the State law, I think, he can work at this work in the mine. The mine operators say that if these men enlist and they cannot replace them,—that is very serious. They are anxious that these men shall be made to feel, by some statement from the Government, that their patriotic duty is to stay at the mine; that they can better serve their country in this way than by enlisting; in fact, the mine operators hope there [their] men will not be permitted to enlist, and that those who may already have done so shall be released and sent back to the mine, with the assurance that they will serve their country best by going back. This question, it seems to me, is one for your careful thought.

What is said here applies equally to the laborers who operate the railway engines and car service *in the mine*. They must also be skilled to hold their job. The labor problem in West Virginia, Virginia, Alabama, Tennessee and Kentucky is also dangerous, because so many colored miners in some of these States have already gone North. That movement, however, has probably stopped. If labor conditions can be held as they are as much coal as was mined in 1916 can be mined in 1917, and by the proof, probably 20% more, because the wage increase, the operators think, will spur the miners to greater efficiency and output. All the additional labor they can get will also increase it. The operators hope for a considerable increase. The bituminous coal mined last year was 509,000,000 tons, an increase of 66,000,000 tons over 1915.

(2) The Transportation.

This is largely a railroad problem for the Interstate Commerce Commission. The facts disclosed show that not exceeding 75% of the allotment of cars to each mine has been given the operators during 1916, except in the case of two railroads, yet all promise more in 1917.

However, this touches what is, perhaps the gravest question— the matter of holding coal in cars by speculators. Thousands of cars are held out of use; coal shortage artificially created and huge demurrage charges piled upon indefensible speculative prices. The whole bill to be paid by the public. These speculators perform no useful function. Their activities are the outstanding abuse in the situation.

Water transportation is greatly reduced owing to the fact that every coal carrying barge, boat or ship that has heretofore beenin [been] in coastwise service has gone into other lines, because of the larger profits; with the result that water freight rates from say, New York to Boston, have risen from 60 cents to $3.75 and $4.00 per ton, and hence water freight is as high, if not higher, than rail transportation. But the freight rate is not so troublesome as the reduction of the transportation capacity. New England is in a serious situation as a result. Bituminous coal for factory use is now, in the Eastern States, $7.25 per ton (including freight) against $3.25 to $4.00 last year. The consumers there are willing to pay this if they can only be assured of getting it at that price as needed. The failure to transport coal by rail is defended because of the vast amount of other freight the roads were compelled to carry and which they have considered had a preferential right over coal. Coal is among the slowest moved freight. It has been left for days at terminals, sidings and in congested districts.

How to relieve this situation is for the Interstate Commerce Commission to suggest; but if I may be pardoned, I would say that if coal could be classed as continuous freight, which is not preferential, but only such freight as should be kept moving reasonably expeditiously, that would give great relief. I am convinced after hearing the views of the operators, carriers and consumers, that if this had been the classification of coal freight by the railways in 1916, that thousands of cars held under embargo or that other freight might pass them, in 1916 would have been moved on and the shortage of coal at the place of consumption, would have been much less and the scare as to coal for 1917 would have been largely removed. There is much more that can be said under this head, but I do not want to make this letter too long.

(3) Distribution.

On this subject much that was said on transportation also applies because, if the coal cannot reach the retailer, it cannot be delivered to the customer. But one unquestioned cause, in my view, for the present high price, is the speculating jobber who in many cases, as one retailer expressed it, is "A mere 'scalper,' as useless as a deck hand on a submarine." The scalper often has his office in his hat. The honest jobber has his place because his capital aids the retailer who is not of sufficient financial credit to buy direct from the operator at the mines. If the jobber takes his recognized commission of 10 cents a ton, only, he is not injurious to the trade. But if he speculates and holds cars of coal on the tracks or coal in storage for a rise in price, he is a dangerous factor in the increase of the price of coal to the consumer. Another element in the cost of distribution is the increase in the cost of harbor freight transportation from terminals to local dealers which has gone up from 20 to 60 cents per ton at New York. The remedy is not easy to suggest. The new increase in the wage scale, (which is just,) and which went into effect May first, will increase the cost of production of anthracite coal at the mine. The operators will announce this increase, no doubt, in the next five days. This, however, will not affect bituminous. The freight increase just allowed by the Interstate Commerce Commission (rightly no doubt) may also increase the cost to the consumer. But the scare heads in newspapers is doing the greatest damage. It seems to be scaring the people into accepting the prices now, and likely hereafter to be charged by those who use these statements to get all they can. The fact is that there is no justification for the present panic conditions. The bituminous operators say they have an abundant supply of coal (if they can get it in to market), that all demands can be met at a fair price if two conditions are remedied;—(1) sufficient transportation facilities, which can be reasonably assured if speculators are forbidden to use cars as warehouses, and (2) that the public be patient and await until their needs actually exist and not "bull" the market by trying to buy all the coal they can far in advance of their needs.

Enough will be mined each month this year to meet all the actual needs of trade as they arise.

It is my hope that a preliminary report can be gotten into Congress, by the Commission, next week. There is much to be said on the various phases of this subject, but it is not right to burden you with it. I apologize for sending you this long statement, but I thought that it might be helpful to you personally in thinking over the matter.

It is a new field for me, and I am only on the edges of this important question, but such as I have, I give to you for your wiser and more suggestive judgment. In the report of the Commission next week, I hope we shall have some carefully drafted suggestions for a legislative or other remedy. With these I do not feel at liberty to bother you now.

With great respect,
                    Very sincerely yours,   John Franklin Fort

P.S. Since writing the above, at a conference with a few leading operators this morning, a new circular for anthracite will [be] got out and will not show an increase of more than 30 cents per ton in view of the increased wage schedule of May 1st. We propose to issue a notice at once to the public and I feel very sure that we can keep any increase in the price of anthracite coal beyond the present, which I think is very much of a gain over what it looked like when we began.   F.

TLS (WP, DLC).
¹ That is, the Federal Trade Commission.

From Elizabeth Merrill Bass[1]

Dear Mr. President: Washington, D. C. [May 3, 1917]

As you know, women like Jane Addams, Lillian Wald, Florence Kell[e]y and Mrs. Glendower Evans, have been much disturbed over conscription etc. I have been holding conferences with them, and in New York Saturday, they agreed to waive the whole matter and follow you wherever you had to lead them. *But*, they asked me to see you in person and get a re-assurance from you on one or two of the to them most vital questions of social legislation—danger of the breaking down of the standards of labor, enforcement of Child Labor Law, preserving the social structure during war.

I realize what it means to ask a five minute interview with you now, but I want to keep these women. May I have it?

Respectfully   Elizabeth Bass

ALS (WP, DLC).
[1] Elizabeth Merrill (Mrs. George) Bass, "chairman" of the Women's Bureau of the Democratic National Committee.

From Robert Seymour Bridges, with Enclosure

Dear Mr President   Oxford England May 3rd 1917

I am exercising my privilege as Poet Laureate, to send you a copy of the sonnet that I have just contributed to The Times newspaper.

I wish that the expression were worthier, but you will kindly make allowance for a poet in his 73rd year, and I hope that the sentiments will have your full approval.

It is a pleasure to me to think that my nephew General Bridges, who is now on the Mission to America, may be at this time having the honour of a personal interview with you.

I am with great respect

yours truly   Robert Bridges (F.R.C.P.)[1]

ALS (WP, DLC).
[1] Fellow of the Royal College of Physicians.

E N C L O S U R E

To the United States of America
May 1. 1917.

Brothers in blood! They who this wrong began
To wreck our commonwealth, will rue the day
When first they challenged freemen to the fray
And with the Briton dared the American.
   Now are we pledged to win the Rights of Man;
Labour and Justice now shall have their way,
And in a League of Peace—God grant we may—

Transform the earth, not patch up the old plan.
　Sure is our hope since he who led your nation
Spake for mankind, & ye arose in awe
Of that high call to work the world's salvation;
　Clearing your minds of all estranging blindness
In the vision of Beauty and the Spirit; Law,
Freedom and Honour and sweet Lovingkindness.

　　　　　　　　　　　　　　　　　　　　RB

Hw MS (WP, DLC).

Jean Jules Jusserand to the Foreign Ministry

　　　　　　　　　　　Washington, reçu le 3 Mai 1917
　No. 551 Le Ministre de la Justice à Président du Conseil.
　Après le déjeuner[1] où j'étais seul lé Président m'a parlé de
l'après-guerre. Il m'a demandé si les Français ne resteraient pas
dans un état de haine incoërcible contre l'Allemagne. Je lui ai
répondu que la victoire et la restitution de nos provinces et les
indemnités payées réconforteraient et exalteraient l'âme natio-
nale, mais que les atrocités et les dévastations étrangères à la
guerre laisseraient un souvenir prolongé et passioné. Il m'a dit
que personne plus que lui n'avait été remué par ces atrocités,
mais qu'il fallait envisager une paix durable et m'a expliqué sa
formule "la paix sans victoire." Il voulait dire une paix basée sur
une victoire qui ne serait pas l'anéantissement d'une nation, car,
alors, la revanche est toujours certaine et la paix jamais sûre
[sûr].
　Je lui ai répondu que nous étions d'accord mais que tant que le
militarisme prussien existerait, il n'y aurait pas de paix durable.
C'est son avis et voici en propres termes, ses paroles: "Deux cas
sont possibles: ou le militarisme prussien sera abattu et la nation allemande démocratisée. Alors elle doit faire partie de la
société des nations. Ou nous ne pourrons pas l'écraser, alors, rien
n'est possible et il faudra mettre l'Allemagne au ban des nations."
Signé: René Viviani.　　　　　　　　　　　　　　Jusserand

T telegram (Guerre 1914-1918, États-Unis, Vol. 511, p. 94, FFM-Ar).
　[1] The luncheon took place on May 2, with Mrs. Wilson, Miss Benham, and
Hovelaque also present. The ladies withdrew after the luncheon, but Hovelaque
remained as interpreter. Hovelaque's description of Wilson on this occasion follows (our translation):
　"Nothing could be more simple or more cordial than this intimate encounter
in which the President revealed something of himself. During a rather long
conversation after dinner on April 29, I had already scrutinized with curiosity
this long, straight, bony, and clean-shaven face, which lit up at times with a quick
ironic smile. Even from afar, strength manifests itself in the stern bone of this
obstinate brow, in this heavy prominent jaw, these tight lips, the salient of a

dominating nose. But the extraordinary vitality of his blue gray eyes, hidden by pince-nez, reveal themselves only close-up. In this gray face of the jurist and of the professor, with thin hair, thin ears, a face that in portraits seems somewhat dour and uncommunicative, his unexpected fervor is disconcerting. This sudden intensity of life is astonishing in this impassive mask, and, moreover, the sparkling eyes, which one might think were devoted to study, have, I would say, youthfulness and mirth at times: malice gleams there when the President recounts to us with harsh animation his difficulties with the press, which has already given us so many reels of wire to rewind; upon the harsh features, normally grave and immobile, this smile reveals an unexpected finesse, which his fine and musical voice accentuates in supple inflections surprising in this stern mouth. The inert face, which seems all of a piece, is full of contrasts, and infinitely complex. One came expecting to see a statesman, severe as the law which he incarnates and who speaks with the implacable authority of ice-cold law, and it is a man which intimacy reveals all at once. This Anglo-Saxon, rigid and distant in appearance, holds at bay the powers of sympathy, cordiality and adaptability of the Celt. This jurist has, in the highest degree, the sense of life. This calculating and achieving politician finds the accents of a prophet, and some of his messages attain a religious elevation. This professor who has lived among his books has achieved the fastest and surest intuition into his country's soul, and no part of its profound humanity is foreign to him. This autocrat who never consults his ministers and confides in no one—during two and half years of outrages and struggles, not one word escaped his lips, even in the intimacy of his home, which did not conform to the principles of absolute neutrality which he has recommended to his people—this lay Pope, separated from everyone by an icy solitude, is attentive to the least movements of the crowd and obedient to its wishes as he perceives them. It is often said that he is a man whose ear is glued to the ground and who hears the approaching footsteps. In this he resembles the great Lincoln, and no one is closer to the living heart of his people than this chief who seems at first to lack all cordiality, and in whom is seen the cold image of abstract justice. This political metaphysician, this ideologue, is nourished by realities. He is a pragmatist, for whom—as he told Miss Ida M. Tarbell who asked the secret of his success—the first thought is: what will be the results? And, in this, he is very much a man of his country—practical and idealistic, realistic and religious, positive and capable of sacrificing everything for an idea. And this American, to whom is given the formulation for the entire world of the principles of that Americanism which up to now have found application only in the United States, comes more from the hardy human stock whose living sap flows in his veins than from his studies, his meditations, his calculations. His strength is there—in the origins of his flesh, in the inspirations of his blood, in the confidence of his people who recognize themselves in him, rather than in the superiority of his mind and the skill of his rare political sense.

"He spoke—and I watched this austere, wise face of a Scottish dialectician, this 'dour and canny Scot'—and suddenly the Celt appeared to me in the rapid flash of a smile, in the sudden humanity of his clear eyes, in the idealism which shone in his stubborn face when he began to expound the principles of that proud peace of equality and liberty which he wishes to give to all men. There are infinite reserves of force in the reticences, the long silences, in the long solitary meditations of this man who asks advice only from his interior genius, which is that of his race, and which nothing can stop on the way which reveals itself to him. No figure more authoritative: it is the last and most absolute autocrat of history. But his authority in no way resembles that of a Napoleon, of a Hohenzollern, or of a Tsar. It does not flow from his individual fantasy and does not end up in any particular or selfish personal goals. It is the issue and the expression of a long history of liberty, of the vast collective will of all of a people who wish for everyone the benefits which they have enjoyed. Behind the President there is, thus, not only all the formidable weight of abstract principles which he formulates and to which all humanity aspires, but the immense force of a country unanimous in wishing that which he wants" Émile Hovelaque, *Les États-Unis et la Guerre de la Neutralité à la Croisade* (Paris, 1919), pp. 227-30.

Washington received May 3, 1917

551. The Minister of Justice to the President of the Council of Ministers.

After the luncheon, when I was alone with the President, he spoke to me of the postwar period. He asked me if the French would not remain in a state of uncontrollable hatred of Germany. I replied that victory, restoration of our provinces, and payment of indemnities would restore and exalt the national spirit, but that the atrocities and foreign devastations of war would leave a prolonged and passionate legacy. He said that no one had been more moved than he by these atrocities, but that he had to think of a durable peace, and he explained to me his formula of "peace without victory." He meant a peace based on a victory that did not mean the annihilation of a nation, for in that case the desire for revenge was always certain and peace was never assured.

I replied that we were in agreement, but that, so long as there was Prussian militarism, there would be no lasting peace. He agreed, and here are his own words: "Two cases are possible. Either Prussian militarism will be beaten and the German nation democratized. Then it must become part of the league of nations. Or we cannot crush it, in which case nothing is possible, and it will be necessary for the nations to outlaw Germany." Signed: René Viviani.   Jusserand

To John Franklin Fort

My dear Governor: [The White House] 4 May, 1917

I am warmly obliged to you for the preliminary report about the coal investigation. I have read it, and read it with great care and interest. I am going to discuss the several suggestions it makes at the earliest possible moment with the Council for National Defense and the Interstate Commerce Commission. We cannot attack these questions too promptly.

May I not express genuine gratification at the enthusiasm and thoroughness with which you have taken hold of your new work?
          Cordially and sincerely yours,   Woodrow Wilson

TLS (Letterpress Books, WP, DLC).

To Henry Clay Hall[1]

My dear Mr. Chairman: [The White House] 4 May, 1917

I am taking the liberty of sending you, because of some of the interesting suggestions it contains, a preliminary personal report to myself by ex-Governor Fort of the Federal Trade Commission concerning the results of his recent investigation of the situation with regard to coal, bituminous coal in particular. I am sure that you will find the suggestions thoughtfully made, and they seem to me thoroughly worth considering.[2]

Cordially and sincerely yours,   Woodrow Wilson

TLS (Letterpress Books, WP, DLC).
  [1] Chairman of the Interstate Commerce Commission.
  [2] Wilson sent Fort's letter also to Baker in WW to NDB, May 4, 1917, TLS (N. D. Baker Papers, DLC).

To John Sharp Williams

My dear Senator: The White House 4 May, 1917

The suggestion made in your letter of April twenty-seventh interests me very much indeed[1] and I am going to take it up at once with the Secretary of War in order to ascertain whether we have any warrant under the existing or the proposed law to organize the several corps you suggest. Thank you for handing these things along.

Cordially and faithfully yours,   Woodrow Wilson

TLS (J. S. Williams Papers, DLC).
  [1] J. S. Williams to WW, April 27, 1917, TLS (WP, DLC). Williams suggested that the United States should have several foreign legions in order to permit foreign nationals domiciled in the United States, such as French, British, Italians, Slovaks, Slovenians, Bohemians, and Poles, to participate in the war against Germany.

To Collins Denny

My dear Bishop: [The White House] 4 May, 1917

May I not acknowledge the receipt of your kind letter of April thirtieth and say how deeply I was gratified by the admirable and patriotic resolutions of the College of Bishops of the Methodist Episcopal Church, South, which accomplished it?[1] I hope that there may be some early occasion when you can express to the College of Bishops my warm feeling in this matter.

Cordially and sincerely yours,   Woodrow Wilson

TLS (Letterpress Books, WP, DLC).
  [1] The letter and resolutions are missing.

To Elizabeth Merrill Bass

My dear Mrs. Bass: [The White House] 4 May, 1917

You certainly seem to have done admirable persuasive work with Miss Addams, Miss Wald, Miss Kell[e]y, and Mrs. Evans, whose scruples, as you know, in all matters I very warmly and unaffectedly respect.

It is hardly necessary for you to make a journey to Washington to get reassurance on the points upon which they most desire it. I have not for a moment lost sight of the danger of the breaking down of the standards of labor, the risk of a relaxation of the enforcement of the Child Labor Law, or the preservation in general of the social structure during hostilities. On the contrary, I think that the Draft Act affords me an unusual power to see that the unfortunate things these ladies dread do not occur, because the idea of the draft is not only the drawing of men into the military service of the Government, but the virtual assigning of men to the necessary labor of the country. Its central idea was to disturb the industrial and social structure of the country just as little as possible.

I have no doubt that great difficulties will be encountered, but I think that we can all here be counted upon to safeguard at every possible point these all-important matters.

Cordially and sincerely yours,   Woodrow Wilson

TLS (Letterpress Books, WP, DLC).

From Harry Augustus Garfield

The Shoreham Hotel
Dear Mr. President: Washington, May 4, 1917

Your letter of April 11 has been following me about and reached me here only this morning. Your address to Congress was most inspiring and convinced me that your way, and not the way I had hoped, was, in the light of the facts in your possession, warranted and necessary, and I accepted the conclusion without further question. The vision to which you have pointed the world illuminates the path we must travel. Too many have eyes only for the sinister figure of war in the foreground. But many who were war-mad see now that this is the last act in the drama of Democracy against Monarchy, begun by our Revolution, in which change in form of government has been the theme. Now you have written the book and set the stage for the next great performance, "The New Freedom," in which the Spirit of Democracy is to inform and unite the peoples of all lands, our own included. I write so much that you may know my support is intelligent as well as from the heart.

I am here over tomorrow to attend the conference of colleges and universities, but shall not impose upon you by calling. I left too hastily to bring messages from your Williamstown family.

With kindest remembrances to Mrs. Wilson, I remain, as always, with affectionate and high regard,

Faithfully yours, [H. A. Garfield]

TCL (II. A. Garfield Papers, DLC).

From Carrie Clinton Lane Chapman Catt

My dear Mr. President: Washington, D. C., May 4, 1917.

As president of the International Woman Suffrage Alliance, in which Russia is one of the countries represented, I feel that it is one of my duties to do all that I can to further the interests of the women of Russia in this crisis in their national reconstruction.

I am sure, therefore, that you will accept in the spirit in which I write, the suggestion that you add to the Commission to Russia a man whose interest in real democracy is in full harmony with your own, Frederic C. Howe, Commissioner of Immigration in New York. As you doubtless know, he has made an exhaustive study of the forms of European government as well as of democracy, and has written a book along broad, liberal lines. He is sincerely interested in the extension of self-government to women as well as to men, and would do all that he could to carry to both men and women in Russia your message of democracy founded upon the consent of all of the governed.

It would be a tragedy, indeed, Mr. President, if there should be fastened upon the Russian women any burden of inferiority to their men before the law because of advice—or the lack of it— from the American Commission. I am sure that you will recognize not only my right but my duty to urge in choosing the personnel of the Commission as large a measure of care for the future interests of those women as you can possibly give.

As president of the National American Woman Suffrage Association also, and in the name of our two million American members, I assure you that the women of America no less than the women of Russia are looking to you with strained and eager eyes, as the leader not only toward a larger democracy for men, but to the first *real* democracy for mankind.

I have the honor to remain,

Sincerely yours,   Carrie Chapman Catt

TLS (WP, DLC).

From Robert Lansing, with Enclosure

My dear Mr. President: [Washington] May 4, 1917.

I enclose a letter I have just received from Mr. Root in relation to the Commission to Russia, and also an article by William English Walling appearing in the GLOBE of May 1st, which apparently Mr. Charles R. Flint[1] sent to Mr. Bertron who must have delivered it to Mr. Root. Judging from this article I should say Walling was very possibly the man who should be selected as the Socialist on the Commission.

Mr. Walling is forty years old, a graduate of the University of Chicago, and a contributing editor to the Independent, Outlook, etc.   Faithfully yours,   Robert Lansing

CCL (SDR, RG 59, 763.72/4524½, DNA).
   [1] Charles Ranlett Flint of New York, industrial capitalist with many international connections, who specialized in supplying munitions, ships, and war machines to foreign governments and in promoting business mergers in the United States.

E N C L O S U R E

Elihu Root to Robert Lansing

Personal

Dear Mr. Secretary,   New York May 3' 1917.

Count Leo Tolstoi has been in to see me. He would be glad to go as Russian secretary of the special Mission. I do not know anything about him, except that he is a son of the great Tolstoi. The name of course is much honored in Russia, and I should suppose that it would be among the very people from whom the greatest danger to the Mission is to be apprehended. A good deal of a drive is being made to excite Socialistic prejudice against the Mission, and particularly against me upon the assertion that I was unfriendly to certain Russian refugees whom the Russian Government sought to extradite when I was Secretary of State, and that I was in favor of extraditing them; the fact being that I had to decide their cases, and I decided both of them in their favor and refused the extradition. This movement proceeds from Morris Hilquitt who is a rabid pro-German Socialist.

Charles Flint has just been in to suggest William E. Walling as a strong pro-Ally Socialist, whose presence in the Commission would have a useful effect upon the Socialists of Russia. He is a nephew of English who was a candidate as Vice President with Mr. Cleveland.[1] He speaks Russian, and is said to be very influential with the Russian Socialists. If the President has not yet found a satisfactory Socialist, perhaps it would be wise for him to consider whether Walling would fill the bill. Flint left with me a copy of an article by Walling, which I enclose.

Has the President thought of George Kennan?[2] I am told that his services in exposing the abuses in Siberia have endeared him to the Russian socialists, and that he would be very useful. He has been ill recently, and I do not know whether his health would permit him to go.

I am getting hundreds of applications, which I am referring to Phillips.

Whenever you get an idea as to when the Commission is likely to start, I wish you would let somebody telegraph me.

With kind regards,

I am,   Always faithfully yours,   Elihu Root

TLS (SDR, RG 59, 763.72/4524½, DNA).
[1] Root was slightly confused. William Hayden English was the Democratic vice-presidential candidate on the ticket with Winfield Scott Hancock in 1880.
[2] Explorer and journalist, best known for his studies of Russia.

From Newton Diehl Baker

My dear Mr President: Washington May 4, 1917

Mr Justice Clarke tells me that Ex Senator Burton of Ohio—now president of a bank in New York—told him that he would like to be a member of the Federal Trade Commission. Justice Clarke felt that Mr Burton rather wanted him to convey the suggestion to you.

Neither Judge Clarke nor I have any interest in the matter, but of course Burton is an able and upright man—barring certain views of his on economic questions, which are abominable!

            Respectfully yours,   Newton D. Baker

ALS (WP, DLC).

From Franklin Knight Lane

My dear Mr. President: Washington May 4, 1917.

I inclose a copy of a joint resolution that may have been brought to your attention,[1] which I think is calculated to do great harm and should be dropped. If it goes into effect I believe that at least one of our large railroads will go into the hands of a receiver and others will cut off their dividends, and this just at a time when it is necessary that they should be stimulated to keep their roads in the very best condition. We are putting an unprecedented burden upon the railroads, and they have got to meet their responsibilities under a popular threat of government ownership. They should be allowed to have money sufficient to meet the necessities of the time. The policy which the Interstate Commerce Commission has adopted in giving a two months hearing upon these necessary rate increases is a wise one, and is, in my judgment, entirely adequate to meet the situation so far as the shippers are concerned. England took over the railroads by guaranteeing the dividends a year before the war began. The high price of materials and supplies bears just as heavily on the railroads as it does upon the individual. It is not merely the wage increase that they have to meet, and it seems to me that this is the time when we ought to be extremely liberal in order to get the service that we need.

Cordially yours,   Franklin K Lane

TLS (WP, DLC).

[1] Printed copy of 65th Cong., 1st sess., H.J. Res. 76, introduced by William C. Adamson on April 30. It alleged that many railroads were taking advantage of the present national emergency to request increases in freight rates on the ground that the Adamson Act had increased their expenses. It directed the Interstate Commerce Commission to suspend all proposed rate increases until after the end of the war and also until after the Goethals commission to investigate the impact of the Adamson Act had made its report. Adamson's resolution also directed the I.C.C. to make an independent investigation to determine which railroads were legitimately in need of increased revenue and to make recommendations to Congress accordingly.

From Michael M. Podolsky[1]

Philadelphia, Pa., May 4, 1917.

Today's demonstration in Petrograd against the Russian provisional government[2] means inevitable disaster to the cause of world democracy as against militarism. Unless you immediately cable to the Russian workmen and soldiers committee, as well as to the provisional government, that the United States agrees in substance with Russian aims for peace; namely recognition of democratic rule and a peace without indemnities or retaliations.

Unless you can impress both the provisional government of Russia and the insurgent factions that aid from the United States is coming speedily and directly, instead of through the kindly offices of the British and French, Russia's fate is sealed. I beg of you to excuse this appeal because of my intense desire to place before you the real temper of the Russian people and I implore you to act speedily; you and you alone in all the world can turn the scale.   Michael M. Podolsky.

T telegram (WP, DLC).

1 Russian mechanical engineer who had come to the United States in 1916 with a Russian governmental mission to purchase munitions and who remained in the United States after the Russian Revolution.

2 The Russian Foreign Minister, Pavel N. Miliukov, on May 1, had transmitted a note to the Allied nations in which he affirmed Russia's determination to continue the war and to fulfill its treaty obligations to the Allies. The publication of this note on May 3 led to antiwar demonstrations on that date by military units stationed in Petrograd and by working-class groups on May 4. Several people, mostly soldiers, were killed or wounded in clashes with other military groups loyal to the provisional government, and a major confrontation was narrowly averted. These disturbances brought about, later in the month, the resignations of Miliukov and the War Minister, Aleksandr Ivanovich Guchkov and were the first of the radical upheavals which were to destroy the provisional government. See William Henry Chamberlin, *The Russian Revolution, 1917-1921* (2 vols., New York, 1935), I, 142-47.

A Memorandum by Joseph Patrick Tumulty, with Enclosure

[The White House] May 4th [1917].

Memorandum for the President

This old man, John D. Crimmins, has been one of our very warm friends. He is not a professional Irishman.

The Secretary.

T MS (J. P. Tumulty Papers, DLC).

E N C L O S U R E

From John Daniel Crimmins

Mr. President: Washington April 28, 1917.

The press this morning leads to the impression that at some timely hour, in your own manner, you will have a word on the Irish problem that at this moment appears to be near solution.

It would be most timely and would have the heartfelt gratitude of millions of people in this and other lands who have long hoped, and many prayed, for Ireland as a small nation to have autonomy, thereby establishing peace with England and among English speaking people. Then if an emergency should arise there would be all for one, and one for all. Mr. President, you have gone a long step in that direction in declaring the rights of small nations—another step may be the means of reaching the goal for the Irish people.

Faithfully and obediently yours,   John D. Crimmins

TLS (J. P. Tumulty Papers, DLC).

From Edward Mandell House

Dear Governor: New York. May 4, 1917.

Hoover, as you know, is just back. I hope you will see him for it seems very important. He has some facts that you should know. He can tell you the whole story in about forty minutes for I timed him.

I trust Houston will give him full powers as to food control. He knows it better than anyone in the world and would inspire confidence both in Europe and here. Unless Houston does give him full control I am afraid he will be unwilling to undertake the job, for he is the kind of man that has to have complete control in order to do the thing well.

Affectionately yours,   E. M. House

TLS (WP, DLC).

From the Diary of Josephus Daniels

May Friday 4 1917

Meeting of cabinet. President talked about the sub-marine task. He returns to his original idea that merchant ships should be convoyed by naval ships, but expressed his view, as he said, without confidence as he is no expert. He also outlined his views as to changing course & ports on trip to England of our ships. Discussed sub-marines. Redfield thought a net could be stretched across the North Sea—250 miles—as nets 5 mi long had been used in Alaska and will talk to Admiral De Chair[1] about it.

[1] Rear Admiral Sir Dudley Rawson Stratford De Chair, at this time naval adviser to the Ministry of Blockade and a member of the British mission to the United States.

To Franklin Knight Lane

My dear Lane: [The White House] 5 May, 1917

I think probably you are right about the Joint Resolution which Judge Adamson has introduced, though I must say that the way in which the railroads are obeying the Eight-hour law does not satisfy me in the least, as far as I understand it. I hope I shall have an early opportunity of speaking of the matter to judge Adamson.

Cordially and faithfully yours,   Woodrow Wilson

TLS (Letterpress Books, WP, DLC).

To Newton Diehl Baker

My dear Mr. Secretary: The White House 5 May, 1917

Thank you for your note conveying ex-Senator Burton's intimation given to Justice Clarke. I am sorry to say I lost all faith in Senator Burton's intellectual integrity during his last days in the Senate; besides, he is a man too far advanced in years for an appointment such as he desires.

But I need not say these things to you, because, as your own note says, neither you nor Justice Clarke is vouching for him.

In haste   Faithfully yours,   Woodrow Wilson

TLS (N. D. Baker Papers, DLC).

To Braxton Davenport Gibson[1]

My dear Mr. Gibson: [The White House] 5 May, 1917

Your letter of May second[2] is certainly most courteous and I respond to it with pleasure.

I do not know that I can give you the best advice about attending the meeting of the League to Enforce Peace, but I may say that I think that the activities of the League are based upon a very much too definite programme which I myself have been very careful not to subscribe to. The general idea of the League I have publicly endorsed in an address at one of the banquets given by the League, but further than that I cannot go and I think it would be very unwise to go at the present time. The agitation conducted by the League has not always been wise, but in view of my concurrence with the general idea they have advocated, I have never felt at liberty to criticise them.

Cordially and sincerely yours,   Woodrow Wilson

TLS (Letterpress Books, WP, DLC).
    [1] A lawyer of Charles Town, W. Va., and an old friend of Wilson from their days at the University of Virginia and in the Jefferson Society.
    [2] It is missing.

To Harry Augustus Garfield

My dear Garfield: The White House 5 May, 1917
    Your letter of May fourth, written from the Shoreham Hotel, has certainly warmed my heart. It is uncommonly generous and gives me a degree of reassurance which adds not a little to the courage and comfort of the day.
    I am heartily sorry I couldn't have a glimpse of you while you were here.
            Cordially and faithfully yours,   Woodrow Wilson

TLS (H. A. Garfield Papers, DLC).

To Robert Lansing

My dear Mr. Secretary: [The White House] 5 May, 1917
    I dare say that our oral conference about releasing Mr. Stevens from the Commission to Russia in order that he may act as one of the Board of Railway Experts who are planning to visit Vladivostok and the Siberian Railway was sufficient to cover the matter, but for the sake of record I am writing to say that I quite approve of the change, knowing how valuable Mr. Stevens' services will be on the Board of Experts.
    I think I understood from you that the matter was being arranged through Mr. Willard.
            Cordially and sincerely yours,   Woodrow Wilson

TLS (Letterpress Books, WP, DLC).

Two Letters to Joseph Patrick Tumulty

Dear Tumulty: [The White House, May 5, 1917]
    You are right about Mr. Crimmins having been a good friend, but I don't like to write any letters on this subject at present. I would appreciate it very much if you would assure him of my interest and of your knowledge of the fact that I am showing in every way I properly can my sympathy with the claim of Ireland for home rule.   The President.

Dear Tumulty: [The White House, May 5, 1917]

Confidentially (for I beg that you will be careful not to speak of or intimate this), I have been doing a number of things about this which I hope may bear fruit.[1]   The President.

TL (J. P. Tumulty Papers, DLC).
  [1] Wilson had suggested to Lansing on April 10 that he instruct Page to urge Lloyd George, in the interest of better Anglo-American relations and coopera-tion, to find a solution to the Irish question. WW to RL, April 10, 1917. Page had accordingly spoken to Lloyd George. WHP to WW, May 4, 1917, TLS (WP, DLC). Wilson had also spoken along similar lines to Balfour. Balfour informed Lloyd George that he had met confidentially on May 4 with a "deputa-tion of Irish Americans of high standing," who had pressed strongly the view that a settlement would insure the future world cooperation of France, the United States, and Great Britain. Balfour had explained the situation at some length and told the deputation that he was not empowered to deal with this question but would faithfully report their views to His Majesty's Government. A. J. Balfour to R. Cecil, May 5, 1917, T telegram (FO 115/2244, p. 161, PRO).

From Joseph Patrick Tumulty, with Enclosure

Dear Governor: [The White House] May 5, 1917.

Do you think the attached letter will answer?   J.P.T.

Yes. Thank you.   W.W.

TL (J. P. Tumulty Papers, DLC).

E N C L O S U R E

Joseph Patrick Tumulty to John Daniel Crimmins

PERSONAL

My dear Mr. Crimmins: The White House May 5, 1917.

Allow me to acknowledge the receipt of your letter of April 28th and to say that I shall be glad to bring it to the attention of the President at the first favorable opportunity. Meanwhile, let me assure you of the President's keen interest in this matter and of the fact that, in every way he properly can, he is showing his sympathy with the claim of Ireland for home rule.

Sincerely yours,   J P Tumulty[1]

TCL (J. P. Tumulty Papers, DLC).
  [1] This letter was published in the New York *World* on May 12, 1917, in a news story which reported, in part, as follows:
"Washington despatches to The World have already told of the conferences between the President and British Foreign Secretary Balfour, at which the Irish question was discussed. Persons who are in a position to speak with authority say that the President has gone as far as the proprieties permit in bringing to the realization of the British Foreign Secretary the importance of the Home Rule proposition in this country.

"The President is said to have told Mr. Balfour that Great Britain's failure to confer upon the Irish people the right to rule themselves constitutes almost the sole obstacle in the way of complete co-operation and sympathy between the British and the American people in the war against the autocracy of Germany."

From Robert Lansing

My dear Mr. President: Washington May 5, 1917.

In our conference yesterday with Mr. Balfour and members of his Commission on the subject of export restrictions, he and Lord Percy[1] called attention to the large amount of commercial information which the British Government had collected in regard to firms doing business in the neutral countries of Europe —information which the British Government was using in discriminating between persons in those countries to whom goods might safely be allowed to be shipped, and another class of persons who were merely channels of trade with Germany. Mr. Balfour thought that, in the enforcement of the pending legislation for the control of exports,[2] it would be a great convenience, if not a necessity, to have the information in London available to the United States, and he suggested, as a means of keeping in touch with the British information, that a person be designated by the United States to represent it in the War Trade Intelligence Department in London.

I think that it is very important to follow out Mr. Balfour's suggestion in this respect, and I am calling the matter to your particular attention for consideration. I think the representative should be somebody from the United States who is familiar with general trade conditions and with the policies of our Government. If you approve Mr. Balfour's suggestion, I will present some names for your consideration, unless you already have some persons in mind.

I should add that, until the Exports Control Bill pending in Congress has been passed, we will have no machinery for using the information from London, in controlling exports from the United States.   Faithfully yours,   Robert Lansing.

TLS (SDR, RG 59, 763.72/4524½A, DNA).
[1] Lord Eustace Sutherland Campbell Percy, a younger son of the Duke of Northumberland, who had served in the British embassy in Washington from 1910 to 1914 and, more recently, under the Minister of Blockade in the Contraband Department of the Foreign Office.
[2] Adamson, on April 16, had introduced a bill (H.R. 3216) to make it unlawful to export any article from the United States whenever, in time of war, the President found that the public safety and welfare so required. This bill was later incorporated into the Espionage Act. Wilson's proclamation of July 9, 1917, putting into effect the provisions on exports, is printed in FR 1917, pp. 1083-84.

From Newton Diehl Baker, with Enclosure

My dear Mr. President: Washington. May 5, 1917.

I attach hereto a very interesting letter from General Pershing to General Scott, which I think you will be glad to read. It gives the best intimate account of the conditions on the border I have yet had from General Pershing, and is very reassuring.

Cordially yours,   Newton D. Baker

TLS (WP, DLC).

E N C L O S U R E

John Joseph Pershing to Hugh Lenox Scott

Dear General Scott: [San Antonio, Tex.] May 1, 1917.

To those of us who really know the weakness of the volunteer system and the failure that would surely follow its continuance, it is gratifying indeed to have the administration insist upon universal selective service for the whole country and put it over accordingly. That means, in plain English, that in the shortest possible time we shall have an army, with which to do the difficult job that has fallen to our lot.

The failure of volunteers is usually due to the inefficiency of their officers. Uneducated and untrained as they are, they cannot appreciate the responsibility that devolves upon them for the instruction of their men. This reason has been generally assigned by the majority of the members of the national guard itself as the real reason for its inefficiency.

Matters in Mexico seem to be shaping themselves rather favorably. The reports of German activities are comparatively few, and I am inclined to believe that the majority of the German element there are minding their own business. Very few Germans are crossing the border in either direction. I do not believe that the German influence, generally, is as strong as it is supposed to be. There are less than twenty of the alien enemy in confinement by the military in this department,[1] and these are held at the request of the Department of Justice.

Insofar as the Mexican situation itself is concerned, there is every reason to believe that our entry into the European war has already had a salutary effect upon the Mexican mind. Having looked upon us as slow, and having mistaken benevolent patience for lack of national spirit, the Mexicans now stand aghast at the immensity and significance of our war preparations. I cannot bring myself to believe that the Mexican government will permit itself to be led astray by scheming Germans. The average Mexican official has already begun to realize the necessity of preserving strict neutrality, and there are those who express the view that Mexico will get in line with the United States in its defense of neutral rights.

This brings us down to a consideration of the border situation. A short time ago I requested the railroads, through their local defense committee, to decline shipments of arms and ammunition to border points, including New Orleans and gulf points west. The railroads have fully agreed to this and no shipments are being made without the approval of these headquarters. In addition, I requested the various Chambers of Commerce of cities and towns located near the border, including gulf coast ports mentioned above, to assist in suppressing the sale of arms and munitions of war to irresponsible persons. They have all displayed a gratifying desire to cooperate and have responded promptly to my request. Based as it was upon the unquestioned patriotism of the average American, the very appeal has had the desired effect. I think we have smuggling more completely in hand now than at any previous time.

With the general attitude of the Mexicans growing more friendly, and with the practical impossibility of obtaining arms and ammunition for filibustering expeditions, it seems to me that we can look with some complaisance upon the Mexican problem. It is gratifying to be able to report this state of affairs, as I realize most emphatically the demands that are to be made upon our regular forces for training the large armies that are to be called to the colors. While I have hitherto rather doubted the advisability of withdrawing regular troops from the border, the situation has recently become very much more favorable.

The papers contain considerable discussion as to the organization of an army for immediate service abroad. If this should be determined upon, I think a division of regulars might be spared for this purpose, their places being filled by national guard if necessary, and two other divisions, fairly well trained, could be organized by selecting one or two of the best regiments of national guard from each state and giving them trained men and such additional officers as might be necessary. This nucleus could probably be taken without too seriously crippling us for further training of new troops. If the moral effect in Germany is considered really important enough all this might be done and possibly should be done. The Mexican situation under such circumstances assumes a secondary place.

I have gone over this hastily, in order to give you the latest aspect of the Mexican situation as it affects the requirements for troops elsewhere.

Enclosed please find a clipping that may be of interest. The remarks were made without any idea they would be published.

With very warm personal regards, I remain as ever,

Yours most sincerely,   John J. Pershing

CCL (J. J. Pershing Papers, DLC).
[1] That is, the Southern Department, United States Army.

From Newton Diehl Baker

My dear Mr. President: Washington. May 5, 1917.

I have your note of May 4th, and herewith return for your files the letter from Senator Williams, which I have read with interest.[1]

Until our pending military legislation is safely passed, I should hesitate very much to suggest legislation looking to any kind of special military organization. There would be obvious differences between it and some of the personal military organizations which have been suggested, but I am afraid one would be an excuse for the other. Would it not be better to get the pending bill actually at work—and unless I am very much mistaken, it will consume all of our training ability and completely use all of the equipment which we can reasonably expect to acquire for the next few months—and then, perhaps, ask Congress, when it reassembles, to authorize some special bodies of the kind suggested by the Senator, and at a time when they can be trained by officers whom we will in the mean time have prepared for the task? In this way, too, these special bodies will fit into a large and existing army. I should be a little afraid if we undertook at this time to get up Slovak groups and Italian groups that there might be a feeling that we were going to use the foreigner in order to excuse our own people.

Respectfully yours,   Newton D. Baker

TLS (WP, DLC).
[1] J. S. Williams to WW, April 27, 1917, cited in WW to J. S. Williams, May 4, 1917, n. 1.

From William Graves Sharp

My dear Mr. President: Paris, May 5, 1917

Although, on account of the imminency of action liable to be taken in the appointment of an American Commission to France, I have taken the liberty to cable you, making certain suggestions affecting the personnel of that Commission, yet I could not set out with any completeness some of the reasons which caused me to cable you.

I shall endeavor in this letter to acquaint you briefly with a few of the conditions existing here, which may possibly serve to indicate some of the needs of the co-operation of such Commission to be located in France; and, further,—to express it in a negative rather than a positive form,—to refer to a class of men who, in my judgment, ought not to be selected.

Not for the moment considering what may be strictly termed "military" needs, I am sure that no Commission could do greater service in France at the present moment than to facilitate the transportation of cargoes of freight as they arrive at the different ports, including expeditious handling of those cargoes at the docks. Great complaint has existed as to the congestion of all kinds of freight, particularly at such ports as Bordeaux and Havre.

During my stay here I have had occasion a number of times to visit both these places, and I know that there is a great lack of any modern appliances for unloading ships, as well as for storing the goods afterwards. It is my belief that a Commission composed in part at least of men experienced in the operations of hoisting apparatus and the construction of docks, the building of warehouses, etc., would quickly be of very great service in bringing about improvements in those directions.

A Frenchman of wide knowledge of industrial conditions recently admitted to me that his people were woefully deficient in organization when it came to handling big industrial problems.

Naturally, also, the demands upon the railways in the transportation of troops, munitions, etc., and the shortage of men, have greatly depleted railway equipment, thereby adding considerably to the difficulties of quick transportation. Materials, particularly of the nature of locomotive engines, freight cars, hoisting apparatus, traveling cranes, and for warehouses are greatly needed. I believe that a Commission made up of men with a practical knowledge of those questions would quickly do much to solve these difficulties.

This would, of course, have a very direct bearing not only upon the prosecution of the war but upon the supplying of necessary food stuffs itself. No better illustration could be given of its effect upon some of the economic conditions existing during the past winter through this lack of transportation facilities than to point to the very great scarcity of coal, and its consequent increase in price, approximating at times $60. per ton.

I am aware that, in making these suggestions, undoubtedly the whole matter has been given some consideration by those who have already visited the United States under one kind of authority or another from the French Government. Within a day or two there will leave a Commission headed by Mr. André Tardieu,[1] one of the ablest and best informed men of France upon all economic questions, and he, too, will be enabled to acquaint our Government with the most pressing needs of the situation as it exists today.[2] In a long talk with him recently I told him that I knew no better way to carry out to the fullest extent his task than to have completely at his disposition information upon every need of France, assuring him that he had but to ask to receive, in so far as our ability would permit.

Now a word as to the personnel of such a Commission: manifestly they should be men of large vision to comprehend in the fullest and most practical manner possible not alone the needs but the way in which best to meet those needs. I have no doubt whatever that such men will be chosen, and I would only express the hope that this Commission, and any other group of men who are to be sent over here to represent the United States in any capacity—even to leading an American contingent of troops—may consist of those who in season and out of season have been heartily in accord with your Administration.

While to one not knowing the unusual and peculiar situation which has existed in Paris—which is France—almost since the beginning of the war, it might seem rather strange to establish such a criterion of useful service, yet no one living at home can appreciate the harm which for a long time was accomplished against your Administration, as well as the putting of our country in a false position in the French mind through the persistent and insidious criticisms of a few men—and, I am sorry to say, Americans.

Whilst their actions have been prompted by the most vicious and bitter kind of partianship, yet, coupled as they have often been with generous gifts to charity, and on account of the more or less prominent position of these men, their baleful work has been of no little effect.

With men more or less conspicuous both at home and in France, one or two of whom, on account of their former high position in the Government, ought to be heartily ashamed of themselves, tripping back and forth between New York and Paris, planting the seed of disloyalty to our Government, and every utterance of a Roosevelt being given the greatest prominence and currency through the columns of the local New York "Herald," and copied extensively in the French papers, there would seem to need no argument to demonstrate that such men, or their sympathizers, should not be given such official recognition as would permit them to covertly continue this kind of work.

It is only because I have lately seen Mr. Roosevelt's name so prominently mentioned in the press despatches as likely to be placed at the head of an American contingent of troops, that I have felt I ought to express to you these convictions. Only your own magnificent course, which you have so consistently followed from the beginning and which now all France so feelingly applauds, has for the time silenced such critics;—I say silenced but, I cannot believe, suppressed.

Fortunately, and to the infinite credit of France, the conditions which need remedying here are not at all of the nature which confront Russia. There are no threatened dangers of a political kind; no industrial troubles and no friction between the military and civil authorities. France presents an example of a united front and unity of action such as, I am sure, is not to be met with in any other belligerent country.

But it is sore distressed and bleeding, the exhaustion is very great—much greater than the world knows—for no other of her Allies has suffered such a drain in men and resources. What undoubtedly Marshal Joffre and Mr. Viviani have already told you as to the heartening effect which the presence of American troops on French soil would exert is completely representative of the sentiment everywhere existing among the French people.

I am sure, however, that there are those who can lead such forces and who, while giving every encouragement and real service, yet, at the same time, would not serve to revive anew partisan feelings or embolden the continuation of the discreditable propaganda to which I have referred. Emphatically, no "knockers" to our Government should be given positions or authority in France.

I have brought this situation to your attention without the slightest personal feeling in the matter, though I have indeed a great contempt for the influence which these people exert; however, I have full confidence that in time the very virulence and malice of that influence will in themselves defeat their purpose.

As a concluding observation, may I express the hope that our people at home may come quickly to realize that the success of their co-operation in this war depends upon the rendering of the greatest and promptest kind of assistance to the Allied

Powers. Germany must no longer be permitted to "break the sticks of the bundle" one by one until all formidable opposition has melted away. Notwithstanding the considerable territory regained during the past few months by the forces of England and France, yet the impasse along the entrenched front, of which I wrote you in a former letter, is still there, and advances from now on must, I fear, be very slow and at great cost of life.

The offensive of the French troops alone last week resulted in the loss to them of more than 90,000 men, one third of whom I understand were killed: the loss to the Germans forces was even greater. Horrible as all this is to contemplate, and great as are these losses, yet the ending of the war even by such attrition is far removed. The cry of France is for men—more men. With a loss in killed of a million and a quarter of men and an equal number of prisoners and seriously crippled, France needs active men for ploughing the fields quite as much as she needs them at the front and today a French General told me that a new supply of men was needed in the overworked munition factories quite as much as they were in the trenches.

In the meantime, the work of drawing the teeth of the enemy submarines and, at the same time, of shutting off outside supplies of food from that enemy, are most assuredly the outstanding features of our task.

With high personal respect and best wishes, I am, believe me, my dear Mr. President,

Most cordially yours,   Wm. G. Sharp.

TLS (WP, DLC).

[1] André Pierre Gabriel Amédée Tardieu, since 1905 the chief political editor of *Le Temps* of Paris and, since 1914, a member of the French Chamber of Deputies. As a captain of infantry, he had taken part in the battles of the Marne, Ypres, Arras, and Verdun. Since June 1916, he had been controller of heavy ordnance.

[2] Ribot had notified Jusserand on April 15 that the French government desired to centralize under a single leadership all its technical missions for cooperation with the United States and was establishing a high commission to direct French missions in France and the United States and to maintain unity of action with the missions of other Allied countries. Tardieu, as high commissioner, Ribot explained, could relieve Jusserand of all technical preoccupations and leave the Ambassador free to carry out his political responsibilities. A. Ribot to J. J. Jusserand, April 15, 1917, T telegram (Guerre 1914-1918, États-Unis, Vol. 512, p. 53, Mission Tardieu I, FFM-Ar). About Tardieu and his mission, see André Kaspi, *Le Temps des Américains: Le Concours Américain à la France en 1917-1918* (Paris, 1976), *passim*.

Charles Richard Crane to Richard Crane

Petrograd, May 5, 1917

The revolution is purely Russian and very characteristic. Practically the whole population took part in it, so there is absolutely no class feeling, no bitterness or resentment even against the old functionaries whose selfullness is welcomed. Even the great landed proprietors unhesitatingly staked all their possessions on the result. The first of May demonstration was remarkable. Notwithstanding a great deal of flammatory oratory and speakers all through the streets, there was not a particle of brutality. The crowds were entirely orderly and good natured. The actual government is practically a peaceful anarchy. There is no method of enforcing its decrees excepting by persuasion or consultation. But nevertheless it is a very orderly government and without the use of force through soldiers or policemen. The jail doors wide open it is perfectly safe to wander around the streets anywhere at any hour of the day or night. It is the most impressive serial picture.

Out through the country the people generally recognize their individual responsibility and carry out in a simple way work formally [formerly] done by officials.

The people seem to be able to get along without any of the old symbols such as the Emperor, the flag, the national hymn or even the cross on St Sofia.

Every one here well, kind and sympathetic and all Russian friends including Miliukoff send affectionate greetings

Father.

Hw telegram (WP, DLC).

From the Diary of William Phillips

Saturday, May 5 [1917].

At twelve o'clock I called for Mr. Balfour and members of his party and escorted them to the House of Representatives. At twelve thirty the delegation entered the Speaker's room to escort us to the House. I was delegated to escort Spring-Rice, and followed Representative Flood and Mr. Balfour. The House was packed. The President and Mrs. Wilson were in the Executive Gallery—the first time that the President has occupied a seat in the Gallery. The Speaker introduced Mr. Balfour, who immediately delivered his speech. His delivery was forceful, his voice was clear and his speech was good; but it was not inspiring.

A reception was held on the steps of the Rostrum. The whole thing was a great success.

This afternoon Jusserand called to inquire why the President had not been present during the reception of the French Commission in the House. I was obliged to take the matter up with the President.

The President called me up on the telephone and said he was astounded at the Ambassador's action and said that if an answer had to be sent that he, the President, did not understand French and did not therefore feel it was necessary for him to go there. That he went there to-day merely on the spur of the moment.

From Edward Mandell House, with Enclosure

Dear Governor: New York. May 6, 1917.

General Goethals took lunch with me today. He is very much disturbed over the delay in getting the ship building program started. He is already two weeks behind what he had counted on. This means a loss of 200,000 tons—if, indeed, the building of tons can be speeded up within six months to 400 000 tons a month as he hopes.

There seems to me to be two vital questions upon which the war, at the moment, hinges upon, the one is Russia and the other is that of replacing ton for ton of the ships that are lost.

Goethals, at my request, made the enclosed memorandum to show what, in his opinion, is immediately needful. If he can know by tomorrow or Tuesday if you favor these proposals he can make a start at once.

The tonnage required cannot be built wholly of timber because, in the first place, there is not enough seasoned timber in the country to anywhere near meet the requirements, and the wooden ships cannot be built as quickly as the steel nor are they as effective when built.

Goethals has gone into the subject exhaustively and he declares there is no other way to meet it. There are an infinite number of firms that have offered to build wooden ships, but he tells me that after inquiry he finds if contracts were let to these firms, they would never be able to carry them through. For instance, Florida offers to deliver a given number of wooden ships but, upon investigation, he says the different companies are counting largely upon the same material and the same labor and they would not be able to carry on construction for more than one tenth of the number contracted for.

Please pardon me for bringing this matter to your attention but it seems so vital, not only to our success in the war, but also to your own success, that I am doing so.

If Russia can be held in line, if the ship building program can be accomplished and the food situation be met, the war must go against Germany.

In order to carry through such a program, I know you will agree, that it is necessary to place these matters almost wholly in the hands of one man, as it will never be possible to do it through boards or divided responsibility.

Affectionately yours,　E. M. House

P.S. Will you not send me a line about this as I am tremendously interested as to the view you take?

TLS (WP, DLC).

E　N　C　L　O　S　U　R　E

(1) Executive order placing the ship yards at the disposal of the Shipping Board or preferably the United States Shipping Board Emergency Fleet Corporation.
(2) Authority of the President to build steel ships in addition to wooden ones.
(3) Appropriation of $500,000,000. for building 3,000,000 tons of shipping.
(4) Appropriation of $250,000,000. to purchase ships now on the ways if found desirable or necessary.

Estimate of $500,000,000. is based on 3,000,000 tons at $155. per ton.

T MS (WP, DLC).

A Memorandum by Jacob Judah Aaron de Haas[1]

Washington, Sunday, May 6th, 1917.

Mr. Brandeis reported at 3.15 P.M. that at 2.15 P.M. he had had an interview with the President lasting three quarters of an hour, in the course of which he explained to the President the general Zionist policy, the changes in American Jewish affairs, the Jewish national problem involved in Polish autonomy, and the difficulties involved in the settlement of the Zionist question in

Palestine as between the French and English policy. The President assured him that he was entirely sympathetic to the aims of the Zionist Movement, and that he believed that the Zionist formula, to establish a publicly assured, legally secured homeland for the Jewish people in Palestine, would meet the situation; that from the point of view of national problems generally, he approved and would support the recognition of the nationality; that he would, at the proper time, make a statement, but that he would first bear in mind the situation arising in France and would exercise his influence in that direction, and that only thereafter would he consider making public his views, and that his utterances under that head would be drafted by Mr. Brandeis.

Further, he expressed his interest in the Polish question, and asked Mr. Brandeis to prepare a memorandum on the Jewish problem involved in it, and to make suggestions as to the forms of administration that might prove useful. Further, the President expressed himself in agreement with the policy, under England's protectorate, for a Jewish Homeland.

T MS (NNZI).
[1] De Haas was a leader of the Zionist movement and editor of the *Boston Jewish Advocate*.

To Edward Mandell House

My dear House,   The White House. 7 May, 1917.

My whole day, nearly, has been devoted to the shipping problem, or, rather, to the ship-building problem. Denman has stated it to me, together with the views of General Goethals, several times, in a series of conferences. It will not be possible to follow General Goethals' program in all its length but I have had Denman on "the Hill" to-day laying the whole situation before the men up there upon whom we shall have to depend and I am arranging for conferences in which I shall take part and use my influence in this all-important matter to the utmost. I think that General Goethals may rest assured that substantially the program he outlines in the memorandum just received in your letter of yesterday will be adopted by the Congress and carried out.

The Shipping Board have prepared a bill which is now ready for introduction and upon it, I think, we can build action which will enable us to do the utmost that our shipyards can do now and can be expanded to do and can be assisted by the structural steel men to accomplish with steel and workmen taken for the time being from bridge work and work on sky-scrapers, with a steady output of standardized freighters.

The English representatives have already agreed to let their contracts with the yards be taken over or thrust aside, and the way is clearing.

This is only a line to say that General Goethals may be sure that I am on the job and that the way will be cleared as fast as possible for what I realize to be immediately and imperatively necessary. I have recently bought some 80,000 tons of Austrian shipping and hope soon to buy as much more; and we are getting the German ships in repair as fast as the shops can repair them.

By the way, we are going to name the two German raiders which were interned here and which have naturally fallen into our possession The STEUBEN and the DeKALB. That seemed to me to have a poetic propriety about it!

Faithfully Yours,   Woodrow Wilson

All of us unite in the most affectionate messages.   W.W.

WWTLS (E. M. House Papers, CtY).

To Robert Lansing

My dear Mr. Secretary,   The White House. 7 May, 1917.

The practicability and wisdom of carrying out this very useful suggestion[1] depends, as in so many other cases, upon finding the right man,—a really capable man who will be equally able and well poised and sensible, not likely to swell with importance and instruct us every day by cable. Have you such a man in mind, or do you think you could find one?

Faithfully Yours,   W.W.

WWTLI (SDR, RG 59, 763.72/4525½, DNA).
[1] See RL to WW, May 5, 1917.

To Breckinridge Long

Personal and Confidential.

My dear Mr. Long: The White House 7 May, 1917

May I not say that I should like very much to be excused from the necessity of seeing Mr. Bakhmetef? I would be very much obliged if you would advise me as to whether it is diplomatically necessary that I should in the circumstances.

The circumstances are these, as you know: Mr. Bakhmetef resigned his position as Ambassador from Russia, saying that he had no sympathy whatever with the things that have recently been happening in Russia, whereas I have the greatest sympathy with them. I do not understand that he has formal letters of recall to present and if he has not, I do not see any necessity for my receiving him. I would very much like your advice and the advice of the department.

Sincerely yours,   Woodrow Wilson

TLS (B. Long Papers, DLC).

From Carrie Clinton Lane Chapman Catt

My dear Mr. President: Washington, D. C., May 7, 1917.

The enclosed clipping[1] will explain itself to you in part only. In a brief talk which my representative, Mrs. Helen Gardener,[2] had with Mr. Tumulty and Mr. Brahany on Saturday, May 5, they asked that I put in writing for you some of the important points she gave to them.

In brief, the National American Woman Suffrage Association did *not* join in the request that you receive this delegation at this time. This movement to reach you on May 14 was brought about by the Congressional Union (National Woman's Party) through men members of the organizations mentioned in the clipping, who secured Mr. Hale[3] as spokesman.

Knowing the overwhelming pressure upon you in pushing through immediate war measures, it seemed to us only fair to you to wait yet a while longer and not press for suffrage during this extraordinary session, however much we feel that it would add to our enthusiasm and usefulness during the war to be equipped with the ballot before we are placed on the firing line. We hoped that our willingness to serve our country even only half armed would appeal to the men with whom you and we must deal in Congress as a good and sufficient reason for our enfranchisement—possibly as a war measure—when you are less pressed than at this moment. However, if this seems to you the auspicious time to make our war appeal, will you not permit the National American Woman Suffrage Association to carry the glad news to the women of America? In that event, will you not receive Dr. Shaw and me, or our representatives, *before* the date of this delegation's call upon you on May 14?[4]

I have the honor to remain,

Very sincerely,   Carrie Chapman Catt

TLS (WP, DLC).

1 It stated that a group of suffragists would visit the White House on May
14 to present to Wilson a resolution adopted by a national convention of
the Progressive party in St. Louis on April 14 asking for an amendment to the
Constitution to enfranchise women. *Washington Post*, May 3, 1917. Also
filed with Mrs. Catt's letter was an undated clipping from *National Suffrage
News*, which reported her remarks on the ill effects of the disfranchisement
of women and quoted her as saying, in part: "The grievance which every
thinking, self-respecting American woman feels is the discrimination which
invites to our land the men of all the nations of earth, naturalizes them after
a five years' r idence, automatically enfranchises them under all State con-
stitutions, and then commands American women to seek the ballot at their
hands."

2 Helen Hamilton Gardener (Mrs. Selden Allen Day), an author and lecturer
of Washington.

3 That is, Matthew Hale.

4 Wilson, on May 14, received the delegation, of which John A. H. Hopkins
was chairman. The committee was intended to represent all parties, but
former Governor David Walsh of Massachusetts failed to appear, and the
Democrats were not represented. Others present included Dr. Edward Aloysius
Rumely, independent Republican and publisher of the New York *Evening
Mail*; John Spargo, Socialist; Virgil Hinshaw, Prohibitionist; and Mrs. Abbey
Scott Baker and Mabel Vernon, National Woman's Party. *New York Times*,
May 15, 1917.

From Robert Lansing

My dear Mr. President: Washington May 7, 1917.

I have just received from Mr. Root the enclosed letter regarding the Railroad Commission which is being sent to Russia.[1]
I judge from his letter that he feels that the usefulness and importance of his commission will be weakened by having in Russia contemporaneously another commission dealing with the
technical side of a topic which he believes he is to discuss with
the Russian Government. I enclose a suggested draft of an
instruction to Mr. Stevens carrying out Mr. Root's idea (Draft
"A").[2] I enclose also another draft of instructions to Mr. Stevens
which would limit his efforts to a particular line, so that he and
Mr. Root would not find themselves embarrassed by dealing
with the Russian Government on an identical matter. (Draft
"B.")[3]

I do not know what your views are, and I simply enclose
these drafts as of possible assistance to you.

In view of the fact that the Railway Commission is to leave
early Wednesday morning, this should receive your very prompt
attention.   Faithfully yours,   Robert Lansing.

TLS (SDR, RG 59, 861.77/97½, DNA).

1 E. Root to RL, May 6, 1917, ALS (SDR, RG 59, 861.77/97½, DNA).

2 It defined the Stevens commission as "subsidiary" to the Root commission
and as a body of experts who should assist the latter in helping Russia
to improve its transportation facilities by supplying men and material from the
United States. Upon the arrival of the Root commission, Stevens would
report to it and work thereafter under Root's direction.

³ It limited the work of the Stevens commission to the supply of men and materials for the construction and operation of railroads, and it instructed Stevens to confer with Root and his commission and to negotiate with the Russian government in accordance with Root's general suggestions.

To Robert Lansing

My dear Mr. Secretary,   The White House. 7 May, 1917.

I think that Mr. Root's mistake about the character and functions of the commission of railway experts is a very natural one, but that it will be removed when Mr. Bertron repeats to him a conversation he (Mr. B.) and I had this afternoon.

This is my understanding of the mission of the railway experts: It bears no resemblance to that of the Commission of which Mr. Root is to act as chairman. It is not going to ask What can the United States do for Russia? but only to say We have been sent here to put ourselves at your disposal to do anything we can to assist in the working out of your transportation problem. They are to report nothing back to us. They are delegated to do nothing but serve Russia on the ground, if she wishes to use them, as I understand she does.

There would, therefore, be no propriety in making them subsidiary to the Commission or in giving them any connection with it of any kind.

If this is not clear to all concerned, I will of course take any course that may seem wise to make it clear.

Faithfully Yours,   W.W.

WWTLI (SDR, RG 59, 861.77/98½, DNA).

From Robert Lansing, with Enclosure

My dear Mr. President: Washington May 7, 1917.

I hasten to send you a memorandum of a conversation which Mr. Polk had this morning with Mr. William English Walling, the socialist. Possibly you would like to speak with me about it tomorrow at Cabinet, or write me earlier in regard to it.

Faithfully yours,   Robert Lansing.

TLS (WP, DLC).

Frank Lyon Polk to Robert Lansing

My dear Mr. Secretary: [Washington] May 7, 1917.

   Mr. English Walling, a leading Socialist, called to see me this morning. He told me that he knows his name has been mentioned in connection with the Russian Mission. He said that, if he should be appointed, of course he would be only too glad to do his part but he thought his appointment would be a mistake as he had been active in the campaign against the German Socialists who are rather in the majority in the Socialist party and if he were appointed they would probably at once start a campaign to discredit him. Under the circumstances he thought it better if a Socialist were to be appointed to take some man who could speak with more authority than he could as he did not have the following that other men in the Socialist party had. He mentioned the following gentlemen and urged their appointment in this order:

   A. M. Simons, born in Wisconsin. (Not Hebrew)
      Active editor of Socialist publications.
   John Spargo.
      The objection to Mr. Spargo is that he was born in England.
   Russell, who has been candidate for Governor of New York.
      Walling says that Russell is not as strong as the other two men in the Socialist party owing to the opposition of the German wing.
   Ghent, of California.
      (I heard some objection to Ghent personally although I must say Walling spoke very highly of him.)

   Walling went on to say that if for any reason Mr. Root could not go as Chairman of the Commission he felt the appointment of Secretary Wilson or Mr. Justice Clarke would meet any possible objection that might be made as to the Commission representing the Conservative feeling in this country.

                                        Frank L Polk

TLS (WP, DLC).

Two Letters to Carrie Clinton Lane Chapman Catt

Confidential.

My dear Mrs. Catt: [The White House] 8 May, 1917

I am sure you will believe that I have as much interest as even you can have not only in putting nothing in the way of the women of Russia, but also in aiding them in any way to the full realization of their rights under the new order of things there; but I have had some pretty intimate glimpses of the situation over there recently and the thing that stands out most clearly to my mind is that they would at the present juncture of affairs not only be very sensitive to any attempt at their political guidance on our part, but would resent it and react from it in a way that would be very detrimental to the interests of the country and to the relations of Russia and the United States.

I am trying to put men on the commission whose popular sympathies and catholic view of human rights will be recognized (at any rate, in the case of most of them), but they are going, not to offer advice or to attempt guidance, but only to express the deep sympathy of the United States, its readiness to assist Russia in every way that can wisely be planned, and our desire to learn how the cooperation between the two countries can be most intimate and effective in the present war.

Cordially and sincerely yours,   Woodrow Wilson

My dear Mrs. Catt: [The White House] 8 May, 1917

You are always thoughtful and considerate, and I greatly value your generous attitude.

In reply to your letter of May seventh, let me say that I candidly do not think that this is the opportune time to press the claims of our women upon the Congress. The thought of the Congress is so much centered upon the matters immediately connected with the conduct of the war that I think the general feeling would be that the time was not well chosen.

I know how many persons whose judgment I greatly value dissent from this conclusion, but my contact with the gentlemen in Congress convinces me that I am not judging wrongly.

With much appreciation,

Cordially and sincerely yours,   Woodrow Wilson

TLS (Letterpress Books, WP, DLC).

To Newton Diehl Baker

My dear Mr. Secretary: The White House 8 May, 1917

    This is indeed a most interesting letter from General Pershing[1] and I thank you warmly for having let me see it. It is reassuring and it throws an interesting light upon Pershing himself.
          Cordially and sincerely yours,   Woodrow Wilson

TLS (N. D. Baker Papers, DLC).
    [1] It is printed as an Enclosure with NDB to WW, May 5, 1917 (first letter of that date).

To Newton Diehl Baker, with Enclosure

My dear Mr. Secretary: The White House 8 May, 1917

    Here is a telegram which has disturbed me a good deal. I am sending it to you in the hope that you may discover through the conferences of the Council for National Defense what may be the best disposition to make of the matter in an attempt to settle it. No doubt Mr. Gompers can enlighten you a good deal as to what is at the bottom of this.
    I am not trying to unload it on you or the Council; I am merely trying to find out where I should turn for the best advice and most immediate action.
          Cordially and faithfully yours,   Woodrow Wilson

TLS (N. D. Baker Papers, DLC).

E N C L O S U R E

Philadelphia, Pa., May 5, 1917.

    We are manufacturing at our plant in Buffalo, N. Y., shell steel for the British and French allies, the railroads have in their yards consigned to us plenty of coal and coke but shipments to and from our plant are being held up by the railroads there at the demand of the railroad unions, no coal or coke has been delivered to us by the railroads for fifty five hours, a continuation of this policy will close down our works and damage the furnaces. We feel this is a situation requiring attention of the highest authority, as the precedent established will be far reaching. The use of a common carrier operated under federal regulation to force in this manner an issue entirely within an independent steel plant is most unfair and suggests dangerous developments. If the railroads will perform their regular duties as common carriers we will have no difficulty in operating. This is a serious situation to confront the steel industry at this time when every pound of steel that can be produced is needed.

Donner Steel Co., Inc., W. H. Donner,[1] President.

T telegram (WP, DLC).
[1] William Henry Donner.

To Ezekiel Samuel Candler, Jr.[1]

My dear Mr. Candler: [The White House] 8 May, 1917

I have your letter of May fifth.[2]

Some instinct tells me that I ought for the present absolutely to refrain from speech-making and, therefore, I feel not only that I must stick to my duties here and deny myself the pleasure of attending the unveiling of the Confederate monument in Shiloh National Park, but also that perhaps I had better not write anything, because if I undertook to write a letter which would be worth reading it would have to be more than a perfunctory compliment. I don't know whether I am right or wrong in following my instinct in this matter, and I need not tell you that it has nothing whatever to do with a thought of the issues between North and South,—there is no longer any trouble in the thought of the country there,—but only with the judgment that since all sorts of extravagant inferences are drawn from everything anyone in authority says, it is just as well not to give the newspapers an opportunity to exercise their ingenuity.

I shall try to send you a telegram on the day of the celebration expressing my interest in the occasion and my sincere regret that I cannot be present.[3]

Cordially and sincerely yours,   Woodrow Wilson

TLS (Letterpress Books, WP, DLC).
[1] Democratic congressman from Mississippi.
[2] It is missing.
[3] Wilson sent the following telegram to Candler at Shiloh National Park, Tenn.: "Will you not express to those assembled upon the interesting occasion of the unveiling of the Confederate monument in Shiloh National Park my very great and sincere interest in the event and my genuine regret that my official duties render it impossible for me to be present and take part in exercises which will revive so many memories of heroic action in the field? Woodrow Wilson." WW to E. S. Candler, Jr., May 17, 1917, T telegram (Letterpress Books, WP, DLC).

To Bernard Mannes Baruch

My dear Baruch:　　　　　　　The White House 8 May, 1917

Colonel House communicated to me the other day the feeling and desire you have with regard to the appointment of Caffey[1] to the District Attorneyship of New York, and I was a good deal disturbed because you may be sure I do not want to do anything that would in the least distress or embarrass you. I, therefore, immediately took the matter up with the Attorney General, only to find that it had gone too far for me honorably to draw back.[2] I think if I could show you the number and character of the approvals of the idea of appointing Caffey to that important office, you would be as deeply impressed as I have been. But this letter is written merely to tell you of my disappointment that I did not learn of your feeling in time to change my direction.

Cordially and faithfully yours,　　Woodrow Wilson

TLS (B. M. Baruch Papers, NjP).

[1] Francis Gordon Caffey, a member of the New York law firm of Clarke, Breckinridge, and Caffey until 1913; Solicitor of the Department of Agriculture, 1913-1917.

[2] William F. McCombs had written to Wilson on April 11 to object to the proposed appointment. McCombs complained that Caffey had unfairly attacked his conduct as counsel in a case tried in New York in October 1912, when McCombs was managing Wilson's campaign for the presidency. W. F. McCombs to WW, April 11, 1917, TLS (WP, DLC). Wilson referred the matter to Gregory, who replied on May 3 that he had reviewed the matter and agreed with a detailed memorandum by Assistant Attorney General Emory Marvin Underwood, who had concluded that McCombs' charges were unjust and unfounded. Gregory added that Caffey had been vouched for by many of the most prominent and reputable lawyers of New York and that the Department of Justice was "thoroughly acquainted with his ability." T. W. Gregory to WW, May 3, 1917, TLS (WP, DLC). Wilson nominated Caffey on May 14 as United States District Attorney for the Southern District of New York; he entered upon his duties on June 4, 1917.

Two Letters from Joseph Patrick Tumulty

My dear Governor:　　　　　[The White House] 8 May, 1917

The Far East is possibly the key to the Russian situation. At any rate, we cannot tell what emergencies will arise in the Far East when we consider that China is in revolution and that Japan is vitally interested in China. We have no Ambassador at present at Tokyo. If we send a new man there, it will take some time for him to become acclimated. He will not be in a position at once to give us advice. We ought to have the most competent counsel from the Far East that we can get. Why would it not be a good idea to designate Mr. Root as Ambassador-at-large to the Far East or Special Envoy to Japan and China? We ought to have someone of his caliber in the Far East in the next six months. A

new Ambassador to Japan could even be on his way and cooperate with him.

Mr. Root could go to Japan on his return journey from
Petrograd. In sending a man who had been formerly Secretary
of State of the United States, the man who negotiated the Root-
Takahira Agreement, we will be indicating to Japan the importance of good relations between Japan and the United States,
and at the same time assuring the people of our own country that
we are leaving no stone unturned to win the war, particularly
by preventing a disturbance of the equilibrium in the Far East.

Sincerely yours,   Tumulty

TLS (J. P. Tumulty Papers, DLC).

Dear Governor: The White House May 8, 1917.

The path of the Espionage Bill will be made more difficult by
the memorandum issued yesterday at the State Department and
distributed broadcast, warning all officials not to talk with newspapermen "even on insignificant matters of fact or detail."[1]

I know how strongly you feel on the matter of a strict censorship but I would not be doing my full duty to you and the
Administration if I did not say to you that there is gradually
growing a feeling of bitter resentment against the whole business, which is daily spreading.[2] The experience of the Administration of President Adams in fostering the Alien and Sedition
laws bids us beware of this whole business. Of course there is a
great difference between the situation which confronts us and
that which confronted some of your predecessors; but the whole
atmosphere surrounding the Espionage Bill is hurtful and injurious, because of the impression which has gained root with
startling intensity that the bill is really a gigantic machine,
erected for the despotic control of the press and that the power
provided for in the bill must of necessity be delegated by the
President and that the press will be controlled by a host of small
bureaucrats who will interpret the President's instructions according to their own intellects.

I have gathered during the last week editorial comment from
various journals throughout the country which have been our
firmest supporters and they are unanimous in condemning what
they consider to be the unjust features of this legislation.

I am sending you clippings from the New York World (1);
Philadelphia Record (2); Washington Evening Star (3); St.
Louis Post Dispatch (4); New York Commercial (5); and New
York Times (6).[3]

I beg to call your attention to the final paragraphs of the editorial written by one of the wisest political observers in the country who writes under the name of "Uncle Dudley" for the Boston Daily Globe.[4] He says:

"The American people could not long endure the necessary war-time conscription of men and property, if the truth were also conscripted. They are the greatest reading public in the world. For nearly three years they have heard every account of the war which their papers could secure for them. They could not stand a shutdown of news just as they enter the war themselves.

"The American people are called to a mighty effort to save the world from an attempt at autocratic domination. Great sacrifices are before them. They are ready to endure whatever is necessary for the work in hand. But if they are to try their hardest, they must know that no effort is wasted; that public offices are administered with faith and efficiency. Public judgment must be passed on those who are weak and those who are strong in the Government. When a department requires reorganization, the people must know it, otherwise it might not be reorganized.

"In fighting for the truth, democracy must know the truth. The more completely the attempt to censor the press is killed, the better for the cause of freedom. The press has no desire to expose military secrets. It wants America to win." I also beg to call your attention to an excerpt from the life of John Adams, (American Statesmen series, p. 283):[5]

"The two grand blunders of the Federal party were committed in these same moments of heat and blindness; these were the famous Alien and Sedition Acts. No one has ever been able heartily or successfully to defend these foolish outbursts of ill-considered legislation which have to be abandoned, by tacit general consent, to condemnation. Every biographer has endeavored to clear the fame of his own hero from any complicity in the sorry business, until it has come to pass that, if all the evidence that has been adduced can be believed, these statutes were foundlings, veritable filii nullius, for whom no man was responsible. But Mr. Adams, it must be acknowledged, did not strangle these children of folly; on the contrary, he set his signature upon them; a little later he even expressed a 'fear' that the Alien Act would not 'upon trial be found adequate to the object intended'; and many years afterward, by which time certainly he ought to have been wiser, he declared, without repentance, that he had believed them to be 'constitutional and salutary, if not necessary.' "   Sincerely yours,   Tumulty

TLS (WP, DLC).

1 By Lansing's order to the State Department, only he and the new Division of Foreign Intelligence should give information to the press. "In order to avoid questions or conference," he directed that this procedure "be applied even to insignificant matters of fact or detail." Lansing, who saw the newspapermen twice a day, said that the current situation was so delicate that the bureau chiefs should not give out information, and that some things which he had not wished published had come out because newspapermen had talked to various officials in the department. *New York Times*, May 8, 1917.

2 The House of Representatives, on May 4, had rejected, by a vote of 221 to 167, the provision, Section Four, in the administration's Espionage bill for censorship of the press. However, after many members had left, the House then reversed itself and wrote into the bill a substitute provision offered by Warren Gard of Ohio, a Democratic member of the Judiciary Committee. The vote on the substitute, which Gard's opponents said was presented in violation of a gentlemen's agreement on the handling of the bill, was 191 to 185. Gard's amendment prohibited, in time of national emergency, the willful and unauthorized publication of information on national defense which was or might be useful to the enemy. It also provided that, in any prosecution, the jury should decide whether the information involved was of such character as to be useful to the enemy. The latter provision was not in the version defeated earlier. Gard's amendment retained language barring any limits on discussion or criticism of acts or policies of the government or its representatives. Following adoption of the Gard amendment, the House debated other provisions of the bill, notably Title XI, Use of Mails, which declared writings in violation of this act, and also those of a "treasonable or anarchistic character," to be nonmailable matter. The House then passed the bill by a vote of 260 yeas, 106 nays, 3 present, and 62 not voting. *Cong. Record*, 65th Cong., 1st sess., pp. 1816-19, 1841.

Before the vote, Burleson had appeared about the House corridors and spoken to various members. Just after he left, Chairman Webb of the Judiciary Committee told the House that he had received a message from Wilson that "the President regards it as essential for the successful conduct of the war that this section be approved." Patrick Daniel Norton, Republican of North Dakota, asked: "Who brought the message—the Postmaster General who is always snooping around here?" Webb did not answer. *New York Times*, May 5, 1917. Louis Seibold, who referred to the Espionage bill as the Lansing-Gregory bill, gave a different version. He quoted Webb as saying: "The President asked me to say to this Congress that the principles of section 4 of this bill are absolutely necessary to the defense and success of this country in the war." Seibold also said that Webb replied to Norton in these words: "I do not think that my friend ought to make an observation of that kind, but in reply I will say that I got the message direct from the President of the United States." New York *World*, May 5, 1917.

Senator Harding announced on May 6 that he would move to strike out the entire censorship section, and Senator Overman, who was handling the bill in the Senate, on May 10 accepted amendments by Senators Cummins and Thomas that would place restrictions only on information about the movement, numbers, descriptions, and disposition of the armed forces of the United States. Two days later, however, the Senate, by a nonpartisan vote of thirty-nine to thirty-eight, cut out the censorship section entirely, and, on May 14, it passed the Espionage bill by a vote of seventy-seven to six. The matter was then referred to a conference committee. *Cong. Record*, 65th Cong., 1st sess., pp. 2073, 2166, and 2270-71.

3 "A Lesson for the Attorney General," New York *World*, May 6, 1917; "Censorship to Suit Sensationalists," *Philadelphia Record*, May [6?] 1917; "The Press Censorship Substitute," Washington *Evening Star*, May 5, 1917; "The Principle of Censorship," *St. Louis Post-Dispatch*, May 4, 1917; "The Censorship Blunder," New York *Journal of Commerce and Commercial Bulletin*, May 7, 1917; and "As Bad As Ever," *New York Times*, May 6, 1917. All of these editorials said that the administration's bill was unnecessarily and unreasonably restrictive of the press and would deprive the public of information needed for sound judgment.

[4] Lucien Price, writing as "Uncle Dudley," in an editorial entitled "Harm From Censorship Greater Than Benefit," *Boston Daily Globe*, May 5, 1917.
[5] John Torrey Morse, Jr., *John Adams* (Boston, 1912), pp. 287-88.

From Edward Mandell House, with Enclosures

Dear Governor: New York. May 8, 1917.

Thank you for your letter of yesterday. I am communicating the substance of it to General Goethals. I know he will be delighted.

I enclose a letter[1] and memorandum received from him this morning.

Cleve Dodge has just telephoned that Davison and his associates are now ready to go ahead with the Red Cross work. He hopes you will announce these appointments at once and make a statement setting forth your plans for the new organization.   Affectionately yours,   E. M. House

TLS (WP, DLC).
[1] G. W. Goethals to EMH, May 7, 1917; TCL (WP, DLC), not printed.

ENCLOSURE I[1]

Washington April 25, 1917.

Memorandum for Mr. Denman, Chairman, U. S. Shipping Board:

It is impossible to carry out the proposed program of supplying 1000 wooden ships in 18 months. It therefore, becomes necessary to augment the fleet of wooden ships by steel ships and this can be done if steel can be secured. I am advised by Mr. Farrell of the Steel Corporation[2] that if an executive order along the lines of the one herewith be issued that the necessary steel for the ships to be constructed by the United States Shipping Board Emergency Fleet Corporation can be provided without interfering in any way with the existing naval program. It is not necessary to call to your attention the advisability of securing steel ships instead of wooden ones if such a course is possible. I recommend that steps be taken to secure the issuance of the executive order at as early a date as practicable in order that we may proceed along the lines indicated.

It is necessary that the Corporation have funds at its disposal for immediate use and that steps be taken to secure additional appropriations. If we are to construct steel ships as well as wood I would suggest that an appropriation of $500,000,000 be secured. It may be noted in this connection that advices from the representatives of the British Admiralty from Canada, who have had experience in construction of wooden vessels, show that the average cost has been $135 per ton with a maximum cost of $147 per ton, so that the estimates of $250,000,000 in addition to the $50,000,000 to be secured from the sale of the Panama Canal bonds would not meet the necessities for wooden ships were it possible to construct them.

1 The following memorandum and Executive Order were drafted by Goethals.
2 James Augustine Farrell, president of the United States Steel Corp.

E N C L O S U R E   I I

EXECUTIVE ORDER

By virtue of authority vested in me under the provisions of the Act of Congress approved March 4, 1917, entitled "An Act Making Appropriations for the Naval Services for the Fiscal Year ending June 30, 1918, and for other purposes" I do hereby require the owners and occupiers of all shipyards in any place subject to the jurisdiction of the United States to place at the disposal of the United States the whole output of such shipyards. In furtherance of this order I direct that no such shipyard shall henceforth accept any contract for or commence the construction of any ship without the consent of the United States Shipping Board; and I direct that the United States Shipping Board, on behalf of the United States, place such orders and take over such existing contracts for the construction of ships in such yards (within the limits of the amounts appropriated) as such Board shall, subject to my approval, deem necessary or expedient.

T MSS (WP, DLC).

Two Letters from Newton Diehl Baker

My dear Mr. President: Washington. May 8, 1917.

The plan for an expeditionary force to France is in this state:

I am directing General Pershing, by cipher despatch, to report in person to me in Washington. He has been confidentially informed of the object of this order. When he arrives here, I will have him select one or two trustworthy aides and go to France at once, sending back word upon important matters in connection with the expeditionary force which in the mean time will be assembled, consisting of about 12,000 men, all of them from the Regular Army, with the possible exception of one regiment of marines, the Marine Corps being particularly anxious to participate in the first expedition, because of a tradition in the Marine Corps that it has always done so in our past history.

I have taken up with Mr. Denman the question of providing the transportation, and he is studying that question. In the mean time, the force will be assembled and ready to send, and will be embarked even before General Pershing arrives in France, unless transportation difficulties intervene.

It has been determined that the force shall cooperate with the French land forces. Our present belief is that for this reason they should be armed in France, both with the French rifle and French artillery, the French Government having offered so to arm them and several other divisions of the same size if we sent them over. The advantage of using French arms and ammunition is in not necessitating the transportation and supply of our own arms and ammunition and the maintenance of an uninterrupted supply, the French having an adequate supply on hand. So small a force would of course be unable to take over for its independent operation a portion of the front, and would have to be used as a mere division of the French army. An entirely different type of weapon and different sizes of ammunition would therefore be an element of confusion which ought to be avoided.

After this division is safely in France and is training, General Pershing can advise us of conditions and of the wisdom of sending other divisions over to be trained in conjunction with the one already there, but my military associates here believe that it will be necessary to have a division of troops on this side ready to follow fairly shortly, so as to get the advantage of the training received by the first division and be able to supplement it should battle losses or sickness diminish its numbers.

The General Staff here believe that the despatch of this force will for a while satisfy the sentimental desire of the French people to see American soldiers on the front, and that it will have an enormously stimulating effect in France. They believe, however, that very constant pressure will be brought to bear from France for further forces, and that the offers of England and France to place their training camps at our disposal to complete the training of partially trained bodies of men will be pressed upon us, so that they urge me to keep in mind the possibility of this sort of insistence from the French and British military authorities.

I would be very glad to have your approval of so much of this program as is involved in the immediate despatch of General

Pershing and his aides to France to study on the ground the conditions and prepare for the reception and arming of our troops which are to follow him. The plan is, however, of course, as yet wholly flexible; and if any feature of it seems to you to need change, it can be conformed to your wishes.

Respectfully yours,   Newton D. Baker

TLS (N. D. Baker Papers, DLC).

My dear Mr. President: [Washington.] May 9, 1917.

I beg leave to return herewith the papers inclosed in your note of the 8th, and a draft of a letter which I have prepared to Mr. Davison, who I understand is to be designated Chairman of the Red Cross War Council.

There is no inconsistency between the creation of this council and the work which it is already doing in cooperation with the War Department.

I have not ventured to prepare drafts of letters for other members of the council, but the one to Mr. Davison is intended as an indication that nothing more than the existing powers of the Red Cross in its cooperation with the Department is intended by the name of War Council.

Respectfully yours,   [Newton D. Baker]

CCL (N. D. Baker Papers, DLC).

A Draft of a Letter to Henry Pomeroy Davison[1]

My dear Mr. Davison: The White House May 9, 1917.

After consultation with my *active* associates in the American Red Cross, it has been ⟨determined⟩ *thought* wise to create a red cross war council of seven members, ⟨two of whom shall be⟩ *including* the chairman and the vice-chairman of the executive committee. ⟨and⟩ I have today created the council. This letter is to ask you to accept the chairmanship (*membership on this council*), a patriotic service which I trust it will be possible for you to perform.

The close cooperation between the American National Red Cross and the military branch of the Government has already suggested new avenues of helpfulness in the immediate business of our organization for war, but the present crisis is larger than that and there are unlimited opportunities of broad humanitarian service in view for the American National Red Cross. Battlefield relief will be effected through Red Cross agencies operating under the supervision of the War Department, but civilian relief will present a field of increasing opportunity in which the Red Cross organization is especially adapted to serve, and I am hopeful that our people will realize that there is probably no other agency with which they can associate themselves which can respond so effectively and universally to allay suffering and relieve distress.   Cordially yours,[2]

T MS (WP, DLC).
    [1] In the following document, Wilson deleted words in angle brackets and added those in italics.
    [2] Wilson sent this letter, *mutatis mutandis*, in this revised form (the words "red cross war council" were capitalized) on May 10 to Henry P. Davison of New York; Cornelius N. Bliss, Jr., of New York; Edward N. Hurley of Chicago; Charles D. Norton of New York; and Grayson H. P. Murphy of New York— all TLS (Letterpress Books, WP, DLC).

From William Bauchop Wilson

My dear Mr. President: Washington May 9, 1917.

In accordance with our conversation yesterday, I have had a talk this morning with Messrs. Walling and Russell, at which Mr. Russell advised me that he would be glad to accept appointment as a member of the Commission to Russia or to perform any other service which you deem him capable of in this crisis.

For your convenience, I am inclosing sketch taken from "Who's Who."[1] His home address is, Charles Edward Russell, 5 East Twenty-seventh Street, New York. His Washington address is 1025 Fifteenth Street, N.W.

Faithfully yours,   W B Wilson

TLS (WP, DLC).
    [1] Not printed.

From Robert Lansing

My dear Mr. President: Washington May 9, 1917.

I send you a copy of a telegram sent to Petrograd on the 2d in regard to publicity in the interests of the United States,[1] together with a reply from Mr. Francis dated the 9th heartily approving of the plan.[2] I also enclose a draft of a telegram for your consideration in regard to the employment of Mr. Bass of the Chicago DAILY NEWS who is now located in London.[3]

I would be pleased if you would give me your judgment

as to the wisdom of this course, and if so, whether the enclosed telegram meets your views.

Faithfully yours,   Robert Lansing.

TLS (SDR, RG 59, 124.61/13, DNA).
¹ RL to D. R. Francis, May 2, 1917, T telegram (SDR, RG 59, 124.61/12a, DNA). In this telegram, Lansing informed Francis that the Department of State was contemplating the establishment of a publicity office in the embassy at Petrograd and asked whether John Foster Bass would be persona grata as director.
² D. R. Francis to RL, May 7, 1917, T telegram (SDR, RG 59, 124.61/13, DNA). This telegram was dated May 7 and received on May 9. Francis also said that the Russian Foreign Minister approved of the plan.
³ RL to WHP, May 2, 1917, T telegram (SDR, RG 59, 124.61/13, DNA). This telegram was a message for Bass which asked if he was willing to go to Petrograd to head the publicity office.

From Paul Oscar Husting

Dear Mr. President: Washington. May 9, 1917.

It is reported that you are considering the appointment of a Socialistic delegate to accompany the Russian Committee which, I understand, will be sent to visit Russia. Among other names mentioned were those of Victor Berger and Morris Hilquitt. These two men are particularly obnoxious to the loyal, or who may be termed, American Socialists.

At St. Louis, Victor Berger and Morris Hilquitt were the leaders in pushing thru the resolution which in effect recommends mass action, or in other words, mass resistance to conscription.

Victor Berger, to my own personal knowledge, has been a rabid pro-German and is still a pro-German and anti-American. His editorials in the Leader,[1] his interviews and his speeches border on, if they do not pass beyond, the line of treason. I have been receiving letters from loyal Socialists in which the[y] tell me the mere report that Berger's name is being considered has done a lot of harm, and I would respectfully suggest than an authoritative statement be given out stating that Mr. Berger's name is not being considered.

The two most prominent Socialists at the St. Louis Convention who opposed the disloyal resolutions were Ex-State Senate [Senator] W. R. Gaylord and A. M. Simons, both of Milwaukee.

I served in the State Senate with Senator Gaylord and know him intimately. He is a recognized leader and has been one of the most active and influential Socialists in Milwaukee, if not in the United States, but his loyalty to the country is unquestioned and he may be thoroly depended upon.

Mr. A. M. Simons was one of the charter members and founders of the Socialist Party in Milwaukee. He is a graduate of the University of Wisconsin "1899" and was prominent as a social settlement worker at Chicago for a number of years. He founded and edited for a number of years "The Coming Nation." Later, he became an associate editor with Victor Berger on the "Milwaukee Leader." He has also been a frequent contributor to "The New Republic." He was one of the American delegates to the International Socialist Convention held one time at Berne, I think.[2] He is also a man of exceptional ability and unquestioned loyalty.

Both of these men have been close to Victor Berger, have been friendly to him and have only broken away from him because of Mr. Berger's disloyalty.

Now, these two gentlemen have asked me to recommend to you Mr. Arthur J. Bullard and I enclose herewith a copy of a letter from Mr. Simons, dated May 4th,[3] and a copy of a telegram from Mr. W. R. Gaylord of May 7th.[4]

I am not acquainted with Mr. Bullard but I believe that the opinion of Messrs. Gaylord and Simons is worthy of consideration in the event that you have not definitely decided upon the man. Among other things, it will be noted in Mr. Simons' letter that Mr. Bullard is the author of the book entitled, "The Diplomacy of the Great War"[5] and that he stands very high in Russia; knows all sections of the Russian Socialist movement and at the same time thoroly understands the intricacies of European diplomacy and has the confidence of every American Socialist except those attached to the pro-German machine. It will also be noted that Mr. Simons' suggestion is spontaneous because he does not even know the present whereabouts of Mr. Bullard but that Macmillian & Co. could give the information if desired. Mr. Simons also suggests that if any more information regarding Mr. Bullard is needed that Ernest Poole,[6] Leroy Scott[7] or Wm. English Walling could give it.

If you should desire anything further upon this matter, I would be glad to confer with you or get Mr. Simons or Mr. Gaylord down here for a conference.

With assurance of my highest respect and esteem, I remain,
                    Respectfully yours,   Paul O Husting

P.S. I almost neglected calling your particular attention to the most important part of Mr. Simons' letter, viz: the fact that Mr. Bullard was active throughout the Russian Revolution of 1906 and knows all the ins and outs of the Russian Socialist movement and that there is no man in the world so highly thought of by the Russian Socialists as Mr. Bullard.

P.O.H.

TLS (WP, DLC).

1 That is, the *Milwaukee Leader*, a Socialist daily.

2 Simons was a delegate to the Seventh International Socialist Congress, held at Stuttgart in August 1907. See Algie M. Simons, "The Stuttgart Congress," *International Socialist Review*, VIII (Sept. 1907), 129-43.

3 A. M. Simons to P. O. Husting, May 4, 1917, TCL (WP, DLC). In addition to the points repeated by Husting, it stated that Bullard would receive an ovation in Russia comparable to that which Lafayette had received in the United States, that Bullard had been active in the Russian Revolution of "1906," and that, although not active in Socialist party politics, he was an active Socialist and would have the confidence of every American Socialist. "The only ones who would be opposed to him would be the pro-German machine." Simons also said that Poole, Scott, or Walling would be acceptable if Bullard was not available.

4 It is missing.

5 Arthur Bullard, *The Diplomacy of the Great War* (New York, 1916).

6 Ernest Cook Poole, Princeton 1902, author and foreign correspondent of New York; a Socialist.

7 Leroy Scott of New York, author and writer for magazines; a Socialist.

From Theodore Hazeltine Price

Dear Mr. President: Washington, D. C., May 9, 1917.

I have never ceased to believe that your suggestion of "Peace without Victory" provided the only practicable means of terminating a struggle that now threatens to destroy civilization before it can be ended by force of arms.

I entirely agree with what you said to me at McAdoo's dinner when you remarked that a fight to a finish might end white supremacy on this planet. I do not mean to quote you exactly, but that was the idea I got from your words.

Ever since my mind has been busy trying to devise some way in which the thoughts of men could be turned from war and vindictiveness and hate and directed toward a contemplation of a possible peace.

So cogitating I have come to have a dream of an unofficial commission composed of a few men of whom the following are types:

> Lord Bryce,
> Joseph H. Choate,
> D'estournelle Constant,[1]
> Maximillian Harden,
> and some leading Social Democrat from Russia.

These men to meet in some neutral country, such as Switzerland and there proceed to paint a word picture of a democratized world at peace and politically confederated for the maintenance of human rights.

This picture as it took shape to be held up to the gaze of the embattled peoples who are now blindly trying to destroy each other.

I feel that the subtle telepathy of liberty would carry the message of the picture to the hearts of the German people, but if I am wrong other methods could be used for getting it before them.

Human ingenuity has never yet devised an obstacle that human ingenuity could not overcome.

In an effort to make mu [my] dream a reality I have discussed it with a few intimate friends and am now in a position to say to you that much of the machinery and all of the money necessary for arranging such a conference will be privately provided if you have no objection to the attempt.

I have not communicated with any of the men named and have no authority to speak for them in any way. They are mentioned simply by way of giving vividness to the picture that I have tried to visualize.

I do not ask for any governmental endorsement. It is highly desirable that any move along these lines should be entirely unofficial, but I would like to try and realize my dream if you have no objection. I believe that I can succeed, for in your "Peace without Victory" I have come to have the sort of faith that can remove mountains.

I am entirely at your disposal if you care to see me.

Yours faithfully,   Theo H. Price

TLS (WP, DLC).

¹ Paul-Henri-Benjamin Balluat d'Estournelles de Constant, French diplomat and statesman; advocate of universal peace; delegate to the Hague Peace Conferences of 1899 and 1907; awarded (with Auguste Beernaert) the Nobel Peace Prize for 1909.

Two Letters from William Cox Redfield

My dear Mr. President: Washington May 9th, 1917.

I was very much interested in your suggestion at the last Cabinet Meeting that the Secretary of the Treasury was making up a plan for what I understood to be combined purchasing by our government and the allied governments. I have since understood from others of my colleagues that the matter has been given a great deal of thought and is perhaps maturing into effect.

It seems, however, not to have occurred to anyone to confer with any representative of the Department of Commerce in con-

nection with the matter although this Department is more closely in touch with the inward movement of necessary government
purchases abroad than any other and is also in constant touch
with our exports. For example, we are in immediate touch with
the British Embassy on the subject of pig tin coming in from
abroad and on the subject of other purchases going out to that
government from here. We are in close relation also to the im-
portations of ferro-manganese through the British authorities
from England and of manganese ore from Brazil, and are consulted by the Canadian and British authorities on the outward
movement of tin cans to supply containers for the allied troops in
the field. In fact I venture to think that there is probably no other
Department with which these matters are more constantly familiar.

Would it not be well, therefore, to have in some small measure
an opportunity afforded to the Department of Commerce to offer
any suggestions that may occur to it and for this purpose to have
knowledge of the plans proposed before they reach finality?

Yours very truly,   William C. Redfield

My dear Mr. President: Washington May 9th, 1917.

In connection with a Senate Resolution asking the Shipping
Board to furnish to the Senate information respecting vessels
now in process of construction in American shipyards, the
Bureau of Navigation of this Department has prepared a summary of the facts for the use of the Shipping Board which I have
transmitted to the latter body today.

It may interest you to learn that on May 1st there were 537
steel ships either building or contracted for to an aggregate of
2,039,261 gross tons, and there were also building or contracted
for 167 wooden ships to an aggregate of 214,753 gross tons—a
total of 704 ships of 2,254,014 gross tons. These ships were all
building or ordered for corporate or private owners save 2 tank
steamers for the Argentine Navy.

During the month of April new contracts were entered into for
102 steel cargo steamers aggregating 417,830 gross tons, which
is probably the largest tonnage of merchant shipping ever contracted for in any month in any country.

Yours very truly,   William C. Redfield

TLS (WP, DLC).

A Statement

May 10, 1917.

I have to-day created within the Red Cross a War Council to which will be entrusted the duty of responding to the extraordinary demands which the present war will make upon the services of the Red Cross both in the field and in civilian relief. The best way in which to impart the greatest efficiency and energy to the relief work which this war will entail will be to concentrate it in the hands of a single experienced organization which has been recognized by law and by international convention as the public instrumentality for such purposes.

Indeed, such a concentration of administrative action in this matter seems to me absolutely necessary and I hereby earnestly call upon all those who can contribute either great sums or small to the alleviation of the suffering and distress which must inevitably arise out of this fight for humanity and democracy to contribute to the Red Cross. It will be one of the first and most necessary tasks of the new War Council of the Red Cross to raise great sums of money for the support of the work to be done and done upon a great scale.

I hope that the response to their efforts will be a demonstration of the generosity of America and the power of genuine practical sympathy among our people that will command the admiration of the whole world.[1]

Printed in the *Official Bulletin*, I (May 11, 1917), 1.
[1] There is a WWsh draft of this statement in the C. L. Swem Coll., NjP.

To Robert Lansing

My dear Mr. Secretary,   The White House. 10 May, 1917.

It seems to me that the wisdom of this depends entirely on the man we employ. I would not like to depend on Francis's judgment in matters of publicity and no newspaper man can rightly interpret us (for that, after all, is the job) who is not really in sympathy with us and of our interest.

I wish you would tell me what you know of Mr. Bass personally. His connection is distinctly against him. He cannot have learned anything of our real thought or purpose through the Chicago DAILY NEWS. If you have had no opportunity to test him directly, I would prefer to choose some man here in America of whose point of view we can be sure of. This seems to me more important than having him there before the arrival of the Commission.   Faithfully Yours,   W.W.

WWTLI (SDR, RG 59, 124.61/15½, DNA).

To Paul Oscar Husting

Confidential.

My dear Senator: [The White House] 10 May, 1917

I am warmly obliged to you for your letter about the appointment of a Socialist representative on the Russian Commission. Before I received your letter, I had gone over the matter as carefully as possible with the advice of those Socialists whose position has been loyal and trustworthy, and the result of the matter has been that I have asked Mr. Charles Edward Russell to go and he has accepted. Mr. Simons himself, I am informed, is of the opinion that this would be the best and wisest choice.

    In haste

        Cordially and sincerely yours,   Woodrow Wilson

TLS (Letterpress Books, WP, DLC).

To Luther Barton Wilson[1]

My dear Bishop Wilson: [The White House] May 10, 1917

I thank you and your colleagues from my heart for the cheering, reassuring message[2] which you have sent to me in their name. Will you not accept for yourself and for them this expression of my deep appreciation of, and warm thanks for, your sympathy, your approbation, and your generous pledge of support?

        Cordially and sincerely yours,   Woodrow Wilson

TLS (Letterpress Books, WP, DLC).
  [1] Bishop Wilson was secretary of the Board of Bishops of the Methodist Episcopal Church and president of the Anti-Saloon League of America.
  [2] It is missing.

To Theodore Hazeltine Price

My dear Mr. Price: [The White House] 10 May, 1917

I have your letter of May ninth and wish I could share your hope that the suggestion it makes would, if adopted, lead to an early contemplation of peace, but I must say that in contact with the grim realities of the situation from day to day it is a hope I cannot share.

I am none the less obliged to you for your thoughtfulness in sending me the public-spirited dream you have had.

        Cordially and sincerely yours,   Woodrow Wilson

TLS (Letterpress Books, WP, DLC).

Two Letters to William Cox Redfield

My dear Mr. Secretary: [The White House] 10 May, 1917

Thank you for your letter of May ninth about organizing the purchasing by our Government and the governments with which we are cooperating in the war. I shall take great pleasure in calling the attention of the Secretary of the Treasury to the useful suggestion you make.

In haste   Cordially yours,   Woodrow Wilson

My dear Mr. Secretary: [The White House] 10 May, 1917

Thank you for your summary of the information furnished by your department through the Shipping Board to the Senate with regard to vessels now in process of construction in American shipyards. I am very glad indeed to have it, and it is very interesting.

Cordially and sincerely yours,   Woodrow Wilson

TLS (Letterpress Books, WP, DLC).

To John Nance Garner

My dear Mr. Garner: [The White House] 10 May, 1917

Your letter of today[1] has given me a good deal of distress, for two reasons:

In the first place, because of the feeling you evidently have that the services, the most loyal and active and constant services, you have rendered the administration in Congress have not been appreciated at their true value, or, rather, have not been in any public way recognized. I can assure you that that impression on your part is entirely unfounded. I have kept in close touch, as you know, with what was going on in Congress and I have valued your assistance all the more highly because you were giving it in circumstances of personal discouragement and without the sligh[t]est expectation of any other recognition than the enhanced reputation you were gaining, and worthily gaining, as a loyal servant of your state and of the country.

In the second place, I must protest very earnestly against the construction you place upon the selection of the gentleman from Tennessee for the Boundary Commission.[2] He has been urged upon the Secretary of State by many other persons than the Senator to whom you allude, and I think the Secretary of State would be as incapable as I am sure you know I would be of making any such appointment for purely political reasons.

I must admit that I have not been able to pay as much per-

sonal attention to appointments of any kind during the last few
months as I formerly endeavored to pay, for reasons which I
am sure will be obvious to you, but I have known enough of this
particular case to be able to exonerate the Secretary of State
absolutely.

I wish, my dear Mr. Garner, that you could know what is really
in my mind and heart in all matters of this sort. I am sure that
if you did, you would not feel that there has been any lack of
appreciation or of genuine admiration for the course you have
pursued.

Cordially and sincerely yours,   Woodrow Wilson

TLS (Letterpress Books, WP, DLC).
    [1] It is missing; see, however, J. N. Garner to WW, Jan. 15, 1917, TLS (WP,
DLC), enclosing J. N. Garner to RL, Dec. 29, 1916, TCL (WP, DLC).
    [2] Lansing had written to Wilson on August 26, 1916, about the vacancy on the
International Boundary Commission, United States and Mexico, with offices
at El Paso, Texas. Brig. Gen. Anson Mills, the Commissioner on the Part of
the United States, had retired in 1913, but, because of the disturbed conditions
in Mexico, the State Department had not asked for a new appropriation to pay
the salary of the commissioner. Congress, however, had voted $22,500 to main-
tain the commission in case it should be deemed advisable to resume its work.
If Wilson wished to appoint a successor to Mills, Lansing recommended Judge
Lucius D. Hill, a lawyer of Sparta, Tennessee, who was strongly supported by
Senator Shields and others. RL to WW, Aug. 26, 1916, TLS (WP, DLC). No
appointment was made at that time, but in April 1917, Lansing, in a letter to
Wilson, noted that conditions had changed and that it would probably be wise
to resume the activities of the commission as soon as possible. Lansing added
that Hill had been highly commended by Senators Shields and McKellar and by
all the members of the House of Representatives from Tennessee. RL to WW,
April 12, 1917, TLS (WP, DLC). In reply, Wilson wrote that he remembered
his conversations with Lansing on the subject, and he asked if Lansing deemed
"the expectation we then held out to the Senators from Tennessee to be conclusive and binding," for, if not, "a much more useful appointment" had
recently occurred to him. WW to RL, April 16, 1917, CCL (WP, DLC). Hill was
appointed and served.

To William Howard Taft

My dear Mr. Taft: The White House 10 May, 1917

Since I had the pleasure of seeing you,[1] I have had several
talks with the other men most active in the Red Cross and with
one voice and very earnestly they protest against your retiring
from the chairmanship of the Executive Committee. My own
preference and instinct, as you know, is to the same effect, and
I am going to take the liberty of asking you to reconsider your
request to me and accede to the desire which we all entertain,
and entertain most earnestly, that you should retain that position. We all think that it would be a very serious detriment to
the Red Cross if you should retire from that post of leadership.

Cordially and sincerely yours,   Woodrow Wilson

TLS (W. H. Taft Papers, DLC).
    [1] Taft had called on Wilson at the White House on April 28, 1917.

To Charles Edward Russell

My dear Mr. Russell: The White House 10 May, 1917

I am very much gratified to learn from the Secretary of Labor that you are willing to serve on the Commission to Russia. It is our desire that the Commission should start at the earliest possible date, and I should like to know the earliest hour at which you could leave for the Pacific Coast.

Cordially and sincerely yours,   Woodrow Wilson

TLS (C. E. Russell Papers, DLC).

To Robert Lansing

My dear Mr. Secretary: The White House 10 May, 1917

I think our list is now complete, namely:

Mr. Elihu Root,
Mr. Charles R. Crane,
Dr. John R. Mott,
Mr. Cyrus H. McCormick,
Mr. S. R. Bertron,
Mr. James Duncan, as the representative of labor,
Mr. Charles Edward Russell.

I have only just learned of the willingness of Mr. Russell to serve and am sending him a note today to learn the earliest hour at which he would be ready to leave. I think it would be wise now to give out the names of the Commissioners and supply the Press with as full information as they desire about the several members. I am enclosing the account of Mr. Russell from Who's Who.[1]

Faithfully yours,   Woodrow Wilson

TLS (SDR, RG 59, 763.72/4673½, DNA).
[1] Not printed.

To Robert Lansing, with Enclosure

My dear Mr. Secretary: The White House 10 May, 1917

Here is Mr. Duncan's letter accepting appointment on the Russian Commission. I would be very much obliged if you would place him in touch with the department and let him have the information which he requests.

Cordially and sincerely yours,   Woodrow Wilson

E N C L O S U R E

From James Duncan

My dear Mr. President: Quincy, Mass. May 7, 1917.

Your very kind letter of May 5[1] received. In it, and in language which in any event would dispel any vestige of lack of co-operation, you ask if it would be possible for me to be a member of the Commission you propose to send to Russia.

I realize the intensity of interest in this great and fraternal undertaking with all of its hopes and responsibilities, but when I read in your letter that you—believe my co-operation would be of the highest value—and being desirous of helping to express the interest and show the sympathy of our great country towards the Russian people at this critical time in their industrial and political development, I readily agreed to conform to your request that I should be a member of the Commission.

I will endeavor to arrange my affairs so that I can be in readiness to travel with the others, and through Secretary Wilson of the Department of Labor or such other source as you may choose to inform me, I hope to receive information where to meet, when to leave and how I may receive the official documents and the essential information to connect me with others of the Commission.

In accepting your kind offer I have in mind the stated object of the Commission, namely,—primarily to show our interest and sympathy at this critical juncture in Russian affairs, and to associate ourselves in counsel and in friendly service with the present government of Russia.

I am in hearty accord with this great purpose, and am very hopeful that the recent humanitarian upheaval in Russia will not only insure a great democratic governmental system representing a new and extensive Republic, but that the inspiring and logical change may have wholesome influence upon some other countries in Europe now unhappily also at war.

Respectfully and sincerely yours,   James Duncan

TLS (SDR, RG 59, 763.72/4670½, DNA).
[1] WW to J. Duncan, May 5, 1917, CCL (WP, DLC).

To Newton Diehl Baker

My dear Mr. Secretary,   The White House. 10 May, 1917.

I have already had the pleasure of speaking with you over the telephone concerning the enclosed,[1] but I am sending this

memorandum to express in a more permanent form my approval
of the programme here outlined, so far as it refers to the immediate despatch of General Pershing and the despatch so soon
as possible thereafter of the Division which he is to command in
France.   Faithfully Yours,   Woodrow Wilson

WWTLS (N. D. Baker Papers, DLC).
  ¹ NDB to WW, May 8, 1917.

From Robert Lansing, with Enclosure

My dear Mr. President: Washington May 10, 1917.
   I send you a copy of a letter which I received last evening from
Mr. Balfour, which I think you will find of interest.
   As to the last paragraph of the letter, will you kindly give me
your opinion?   Faithfully yours,   Robert Lansing

TLS (WP, DLC).

E N C L O S U R E

Arthur James Balfour to Robert Lansing

Confidential.

My dear Mr. Secretary: Washington, D. C. 9th May 1917.
   I think it may interest you personally to know that I received
yesterday a telegram from home saying that the recent submarine returns were rather less heavy and that the reports of
the destruction of submarines were rather more numerous. Of
course these reports of destruction are highly problematical. The
telegram emphasizes that there is nothing to justify the belief
that the situation is less serious.
   German resistance and counter-attacks are fiercely proceeding
on the Western front, but nevertheless the British offensive is
being carried on satisfactorily and methodically.
   A conference held at Paris on May 4 and 5 showed that there
was complete agreement between the military experts of the
two countries. I understand that General Petain[1] has practically
taken the place of General Nivelle.[2] The Conference resulted in
a definite understanding that the war should be prosecuted with
full strength along the whole line. From the other theatres of war
there were practically no reports.
   The attitude of Spain is still unsatisfactory, and Senor Maura's
speech, which we mentioned in our conversation on Sunday,[3]

has given the Germans a strong weapon which they are using to the utmost of their power.

Miliukoff professes that he has prevailed against the Workmen and Soldiers' Committee, but the situation is still critical.

The Foreign Office report that the new Brazilian Minister for Foreign Affairs[4] will only accept office on the condition that Brazil should associate herself with the United States against Germany.

The position of the Ministry in France is said to be weaker. The French Socialist minority have decided to send a representative to the Socialist Conference in Stockholm. If the French Government agree to allow this we shall probably have great pressure exercised on us from *our* Socialist group to allow them also to send delegates. As I understand there is also a question as regards delegates from the United States. I have telegraphed to the Foreign Office proposing that the question should be discussed with Mr Page and the French Ambassador in London.[5]

Believe me,
Yours very sincerely,   Arthur James Balfour

TLS (SDR, RG 59, 763.72/4669½, DNA).
[1] Henri-Philippe Benoni Omer Joseph Pétain.
[2] Robert Georges Nivelle, who had succeeded Joffre in December 1916 as commander in chief of the French armies of the North and Northeast. The "Nivelle offensive" in the direction of Laon had failed in April 1917, and Pétain replaced Nivelle on May 15.
[3] Antonio Maura y Montaner, the former Prime Minister and leader of the Conservative party of Spain, spoke on April 29 to 20,000 persons at the Bull Ring in Madrid. He noted Spain's natural affinity with England and France but pointed out grievances connected with Gibraltar, Tangier, and Morocco. Maura also said that Germany had done nothing to justify a break in Spanish-German diplomatic relations, for all blockades alike were damaging to Spanish interests. He criticized the current Spanish government and insisted that his country must not, could not, and would not enter the war, because Spain was too proud and too great to be the servant of any country whatsoever. London *Times*, April 30, 1917; *New York Times*, May 1, 1917.
[4] Nilo Peçanha, the former President of Brazil, had accepted the post of Foreign Minister, succeeding Dr. Lauro Müller, who had resigned. *New York Times*, May 5, 1917.
[5] That is, Paul Cambon.

From Samuel Gompers

Sir: Washington, D. C., May 10, 1917.

When I learned that the British Government was to send a Commission to this country to discuss matters of common interest to both countries growing out of the war, I cabled to Premier Lloyd George asking that representatives of the British labor movement be sent also. The Premier sent an immediate reply stating that my request would be complied with.

These representatives have arrived in this country. They are Rt. Hon. C. W. Bowerman, James H. Thomas, Joseph Davies and H. W. Garrod.[1]

As you know, each member of the Advisory Commission of the Council of National Defense is chairman of a committee which assists him in his work. My committee consists of about two hundred men and women—representative trade unionists, employers, specialists, publicists, experts in welfare work and other interests. Some of the most prominent men and women in the organized labor movement and most influential financiers and employers of labor constitute this committee upon the welfare of the workers of this country.

I have asked that Committee to come together in this city on May 15, in order that they may have the benefit of the information and experience of the British labor representatives who are here to assist us. Some of these British men have for years been in charge of the affairs of the British labor movement and all have been directly associated with the efforts that have been made in that country to adjust commerce and industries from a peace to a war basis while at the same time maintaining standards which protect the rights and interests of the workers.

Although I appreciate the many demands that are made upon your time and attention in the present emergency, yet I also know that you desire that intimate personal touch with the important movements in this country that will enable you to mobilize the good will of all in working out our common problems. Therefore, I wish to ask if there is any way possible that you could set aside a brief time on May 15 during which to see the members of my Committee on Labor.

I sincerely hope that you will be able to comply with this request.[2]   Very respectfully yours,   Saml. Gompers.

TLS (WP, DLC).

[1] Charles William Bowerman, secretary of the Trades Union Congress, and James Henry Thomas, general secretary of the National Union of Railwaymen, were members of Parliament and the Privy Council. Heathcote William Garrod, a fellow and tutor of Merton College, was Deputy Controller of the Labour Regulation Department, Ministry of Munitions. Joseph Davies, a member of Lloyd George's "Garden Suburb" secretariat, with special responsibility for statistics on commodities and shipping, was part of the labor mission but also was assigned by the Prime Minister to secure dependable information on American merchant shipping. New York Times, May 5, 1917, and Joseph Davies, The Prime Minister's Secretariat, 1916-1920 (Newport, Eng., 1951), 105-10. Wilson had in fact received the British labor committee, escorted by Secretary Wilson, at the White House on May 8.

[2] Wilson received this group, 135-strong, on May 15; his remarks are printed at that date.

From George Creel

Dear Mr. President: Washington, D. C., May 10th, 1917.

The moment I left you I thought of a man for the Russian post we talked about. Arthur Bullard fits the whole idea as skin fits the hand. He graduated at Hamilton College, is a magazine writer and author of the highest reputation, and spent five years in Russia at the time of the first revolutionary attempt. He has been here with me from the first[1] at great personal sacrifice and I owe much to his rare ability, his unflagging zeal, and his clear unfaltering democracy. He is on terms of closest friendship with Mr. Russell, Mr. Crane, Mr. Duncan, and I know that Mr. Root, while opposed to his thought at almost every point, has the highest personal regard for him. I feel that he knows more about the various radical groups of Russia and their leaders than any other American writer, and he brings to this knowledge sympathy and a very wide and understanding tolerance. Colonel House knows him and admires him.

I do not know how I am going to get along without Mr. Bullard, but the conviction grows that he is peculiarly the man for this post. He has literary ability, newspaper experience, democratic ideals, and the sanest sort of outlook.

If you wish I shall be glad to talk with you further about this or have Mr. Bullard see you.

Respectfully,   George Creel

TLS (WP, DLC).
  [1] Bullard was director of the Division of Foreign Correspondents and Foreign Language Publications of the C.P.I.

From William English Walling

Mr. President: Greenwich Connecticut May 10th, 1917.

I received your letter only this morning, having been in Washington the last five days endeavoring to be of assistance in connection with the Russian situation.

From daily talks with the Secretary of Labor I know you are informed as to my views and my personal situation. I was, furthermore, finally assured by the Secretary that you were willing to accept my standpoint as to my possibilities for personal service as being correct.

I hope to be of real service to the cause of internationalism which, like yourself, I place above all else, and also to the American government, by remaining in this country.

Very respectfully,   Wm. English Walling

TLS (WP, DLC).

From Morris Hillquit, with Enclosure

Dear Sir: New York, May 10th, 1917.

I take the liberty of submitting for your consideration a copy of a communication I have this day sent to Hon. Robert Lansing, Secretary of State.

It has been reported in some newspapers that you are personally investigating the character of the proposed International Socialist Conference to be held at Stockholm. If the reports are correct, I shall esteem it a great privilege to be permitted to lay before you authentic facts based on documentary evidence, which I am convinced will assist you in reaching a fair and just conclusion on the subject.

Very respectfully yours,   Morris Hillquit

TLS (SDR, RG 59, 763.72119/594, DNA).

E N C L O S U R E

Morris Hillquit to Robert Lansing

Dear Sir: New York, May 10th, 1917.

The newspapers report that the Committee on Public Information, of which you are a member, has issued a statement signed by Messrs. William English Walling, Charles Edward Russell, Ernest Poole, and others, denouncing the planned International Socialist Conference to be held at Stockholm as "the most dangerous of all the Kaiser's plots for cashing in his military victories" and asserting that the object of the Conference is to bring about a separate peace between Russia and the Central Powers.

According to the same press reports the statement was given to the press by the Chairman of the Committee with the request to give "the largest possible space to this story, as it is of the utmost importance that there be full public understanding of the Stockholm Conference as the base for *further and specific attack.*"

As a member of the International Socialist Bureau, which has called the Stockholm Conference, I am thoroughly familiar with the character, object and plans of the latter, and wish to assure you that there is not the slightest foundation in fact for any of the charges of Mr. Walling, et al. The idea of the Conference did not emanate from German or pro-German interests, and no plan of a separate peace will be suggested or countenanced in its deliberations. I have in my possession facts, correspondence and documents bearing upon the proposed Stockholm Conference which, I believe, will conclusively prove my assertion and I respectfully ask for an opportunity to present them to you.

In view of the unfortunate impression prevailing here and possibly abroad that the intemperate and unwarranted statements of Messrs. Walling, Russell and Poole have received the official sanction of the administration, and particularly in view of the Committee's expressed intention to subject the Conference to "further and specific attack," I sincerely hope that you will grant me such an interview as a matter of fairness and justice.

Very respectfully yours,   Morris Hillquit

TCL (SDR, RG 59, 763.72119/594, DNA).

From Helen Hamilton Gardener

My dear Mr President: Washington, D. C. May 10, 1917

When Mrs Catt and Dr. Shaw were called west they left with me instructions to do whatever I thought best in their absence to further the securing of a Committee on Woman Suffrage in the House of Representatives.

I conferred with Speaker Clark who is willing to do what he can to help us secure such a Committee. I left a letter from Mrs Catt with Mr Kitchen asking for his cooperation.

The matter now seems to hinge upon the good-will of Mr Pou, Chairman of the Rules Committee, who, *I am told*, says that he will report favorably "if the President approves of the creation of such a Committee."

If I might assure him that you do so approve it would, we think, lead to the granting of the *only* request that the National American Woman Suffrage Ass'n has made of this session of the Congress and secure to us the machinery for future work for which we have plead in vain for years.

Surely, Mr President, the women of the country—half of the population—are not asking too much when they urge that they have a committee in the House of Representatives to which they may go freely with their problems and their pleas.

The Judiciary [Committee], to which we have always been sent, is too busy and preoccupied to give more than a very casual and perfunctory "hearing" once a year—and seldom even "reported" on that.

In the Senate, where we secured a committee some years ago our interests are treated with far greater consideration than in the House—or than they formerly received in the Senate.

Is it asking too much, Mr President, at this time to urge you to make known to Mr Pou that you would approve of of [*sic*] this bit of machinery in the interest of the women of America?

I am assuming that you would approve of such a Committee for it seems to me, as a student of your work and career, that it is in line with your progressive democracy.

Before the Rules Committee "turns us down" will you not allow me to say to Mr Pou that you do approve of the appointment of a Woman Suffrage Committee in the House? Then, with the help of the Speaker, which he has promised me (and I believe, also, of Mr Kitchen in that event) I can greet Dr Shaw and Mrs Catt upon their return from their National Defense work with one more forward step in the sane progress of the suffrage movement whose major activities we have placed in abeyance at your call to arms.

With this added bit of legislative machinery working in our interest, as occassion permits, we can all the more freely and happily give of our services in other directions to our country.

I await, with eager anticipation, your reply, and I have the honor to remain,

Yours sincerely,   Mrs. Helen H. Gardener

TLS (WP, DLC).

To William Dennison Stephens[1]

The White House. May 11, 1917.

I hope that in view of certain international aspects which the case has assumed you will not deem me impertinent or beyond my rights if I very warmly and earnestly urge upon you the wisdom and desirability of commuting the sentence of Mooney[2] or at least suspending its execution until the charges of perjury lodged against the witnesses in the case are judicially probed to the bottom. Such an action on your part would I can assure you have the widest and most beneficial results and greatly relieve some critical situations outside the United States.

Woodrow Wilson

T telegram (WP, DLC).

1 Governor of California.

2 Thomas Jeremiah Zechariah Mooney had been convicted of first-degree murder and sentenced to death in connection with an explosion, presumably of a bomb, which had killed nine persons and wounded about forty others on July 22, 1916, during a Preparedness Day parade on Market Street, near the Ferry Building, in San Francisco. Mooney and various associates had been active in the radical labor movement, and charges that they had been falsely accused on the basis of fabricated evidence had aroused international attention. For varying accounts of the explosion, the investigation, the trial, and the aftermath, see *The Mooney-Billings Report: Suppressed by the Wickersham Commission*

(New York, 1932); Ernest Jerome Hopkins, *What Happened in the Mooney Case* (New York, 1932); Curt Gentry, *Frame-up: The Incredible Case of Tom Mooney and Warren Billings* (New York, 1967); and Richard H. Frost, *The Mooney Case* (Stanford, Cal., 1968).

To Robert Lansing, with Enclosures

My dear Mr. Secretary,   The White House. 11 May, 1917.

I agree with you that this is a critical and pregnant matter. I have to-day sent a telegram to the Governor of California in the sense you suggest, and hope that it will bear fruit.

Faithfully Yours,   W.W.

WWTLI (R. Lansing Papers, NjP).

E N C L O S U R E   I

From Robert Lansing

My dear Mr. President: Washington May 10, 1917.

I enclose a few papers in regard to the case of one Mooney, who has been sentenced by a California court to be hanged on May 17th for throwing bombs into the preparedness parade in San Francisco on July 22d last. An attempted demonstration was made on April 24th before the American Embassy in Petrograd protesting against the execution in the United States of Mooney, whom those taking part in the attempted demonstration regarded as an Italian and whom they supposed had been already executed. A demonstration of the same character before the American Consulate at Tampico has been reported to the Department.[1] Mooney appears to be an American citizen and an organizer of labor in San Francisco; and it is supposed, from the incidents at Petrograd and Tampico that there is communication between the labor organizations interested in him in the United States and the labor organizations in Petrograd, Mexico, and other parts of the world. Mr. Gompers tells me that this is no doubt the case.

It appears that the chief witness upon which the prosecution based its case was one Oxman.[2] Upon complaint being filed, Oxman has been investigated by the Grand Jury on the charge of perjury in his testimony against Mooney. The Grand Jury, however, appears to have exonerated Oxman from this charge, notwithstanding, as seems to be the case, that the enclosed photographic letters were before the Grand Jury.[3] It appears that the attorney[4] for Oxman was also the attorney for John D. Spreckles,[5] who was the foreman of the Grand Jury. Another feature of the case is that Judge Griffith,[6] who was the Judge in the Mooney case, and Police Judge Trady,[7] who appears to have heard some of the proceedings in the perjury case, are both up for election this fall. It seems that Trial Judge Griffith wrote an open letter to the Attorney-General of California which he published in the newspapers requesting the Attorney-General to confess error in the Mooney matter and not to await the decision of the Supreme Court on the motion for a new trial which had been made on the basis of new evidence discovered.[8] There appear to be further charges that other witnesses for the prosecution in the Mooney case were also guilty of perjury, but none of them has been arrested or indicted.

In view of the situation in Russia on account of the agitation of the laborites, which has spread over a large part of the disturbed countries of the world, causing at the present moment a very delicate stage not only in the affairs of Russia but in the international situation, and in view of the possibility of a miscarriage of justice in the case of Mooney, I deem it of great importance to bring this case to your special attention for consideration as to whether some action should not be taken by you to prevail upon the Governor of California to suspend the execution of Mooney or to commute his sentence until the charges of perjury against the witnesses used by the prosecution have been thoroughly investigated. It seems to me that if you agree with me in this conclusion, a telegram such as you sent the Governor of Utah in the Hillstrom case[9] would be the most expeditious and most effective means of handling this matter.

As you will see, the Department of Justice has sent me some reports on the case at my request.[10] It may be that the other phases of the matter than the international situation should be taken up with the Attorney-General.

Faithfully yours,   Robert Lansing.

TLS (R. Lansing Papers, NjP).
  [1] Claude Ivan Dawson to RL, May 1, 1917, T telegram (R. Lansing Papers, NjP). It referred to a visit to the consulate by five leaders of the Industrial Workers of the World. Lansing's file also included a telegram to Wilson from the Bricklayers' Union of Tampico, Mexico, in behalf of Mooney and others. Lauro Sandoval to WW, May 2, 1917, T telegram, *ibid.*
  [2] Frank C. Oxman, a wealthy cattleman of Durkee, Ore.
  [3] F. C. Oxman to F. Edward Rigall, Dec. 14 and 18, 1916, both TCL, *ibid.*
  [4] Samuel Morgan Shortridge, a lawyer of San Francisco.
  [5] John Diedrich Spreckels, Jr., son of the president of J. D. Spreckels & Bros. Co., Oceanic Steamship Co., Spreckels Sugar Co., and other companies.
  [6] Franklin A. Griffin, a judge of the superior court of San Francisco County.
  [7] Matthew I. Brady, a judge of the municipal police court, later district attorney in San Francisco. He had bound Oxman over to the superior court for trial

on a charge of attempted subornation of perjury. Oxman was acquitted on September 28, 1917.

8 Griffin's letter of April 25, 1917, to Ulysses Sigel Webb, Attorney General of California, is printed in Henry T. Hunt, *The Case of Thomas J. Mooney and Warren K. Billings: Abstract and Analysis of Record before Governor Young of California* (New York, 1929), pp. 15-16.

9 WW to W. Spry, Sept. 30, 1915, Vol. 34.

10 Along with the letters by Oxman, cited above, Lansing enclosed a copy of a telegram of May 7, 1917, from Don S. Rathbun, a special agent in the San Francisco office of the Department of Justice, to A. Bruce Bielaski, which provided much of the information (including the incorrect spellings of names) incorporated in Lansing's letter to Wilson. Rathbun also noted that the San Francisco *Bulletin* had made serious charges against District Attorney Charles Marron Fickert and his assistants. D. S. Rathbun to A. B. Bielaski, May 7, 1917, TC telegram (R. Lansing Papers, NjP).

E N C L O S U R E   I I[1]

Petrograd. April 24, 1917.

1219. Sunday Evening Embassy was phoned by some official doing police duty that crowds of excited people with black flag were coming to attack American Embassy, having been moved thereto by violent speech of Socialist Lelenin[2] and advised that I phone Miliukoff. I was amused only. Same intelligence was phoned an hour later by another official. On going to Embassy entrance I found seven soldiers who said had been sent to protect Embassy. Was still incredulous but militia official and forty armed soldiers arriving at this juncture tended to convince me that authorities were anxious. Within ten minutes, however, messengers arrived and informed militia official that crowd had been dispersed. Soldiers all departed immediately except seven who remained during night. Miliukoff phoned yesterday that Italian anarchist not Lenin addressed crowd on Nevsky, arousing them by stating that Italian named Muni had been executed in United States. Government acted promptly to protect Embassy, arresting three of threatening crowd and dispersing others. Who is Muni? What crime committed? Wouldn't cable this insignificant incident but four sensational reports may create impression that order not enforced here where quiet prevails and life and property safe.   Francis.

T telegram (R. Lansing Papers, NjP).

1 Lansing also enclosed: (1) A copy of a short reply to Petrograd which identified Mooney and stated that the question of a new trial had not yet been decided. RL to D. R. Francis, April 30, 1917, T telegram (R. Lansing Papers, NjP). (2) An article, "Strange News from Russia," *The New Republic*, XI (May 5, 1917), 8-10. It referred to Francis' telegram, summarized the Mooney case, including the testimony of Oxman and Rigall, and referred to charges "that the state's prosecutors, backed by the Chamber of Commerce, were railroading labor leaders to the hangman in order to end unionism in San Francisco."

2 That is, V. I. Lenin.

To Robert Lansing

My dear Mr. Secretary,　　　　The White House. 11 May, 1917.

Thank you very much for the copy of Mr. Balfour's letter to you of the ninth.

I do not like the movement among the Socialists to confer about international affairs. They are likely to make a deal of mischief, especially in connection with affairs in Russia. I think our own people would warmly resent any encouragement by our government of the American Socialists who may seek to take part, especially after their recent almost treasonable utterances in their convention (at St. Louis, was it not?). It is their own lookout what they do. We should neither give them leave nor seek to restrain them. My own view is, that they will make themselves either hated or ridiculous.　　　　Faithfully Yours,　W.W.

WWTLI (SDR, RG 59, 763.72119/632½, DNA).

To Stanley Hubert Dent, Jr.

My dear Mr. Dent,　　　　The White House. 11 May, 1917.

Now that the Army Bill has been successfully brought out of conference I want to express to you my sincere appreciation of the service you and your colleagues have rendered in helping to bring the Bill to a final consideration free from any feature that would embarrass the system of draft upon which it is based.

I trust that the conference report may be very promptly adopted. Every hour counts in these critical times and delay might have very serious consequences.[1]

　　　　　　　　Sincerely Yours,　Woodrow Wilson

WWTLS (S. H. Dent, Jr., Coll., A-Ar).
　[1] Wilson wrote the same letter, *mutatis mutandis*, to Senator George E. Chamberlain, chairman of the Senate Committee on Military Affairs. There are WWsh drafts of the letters to Dent and Chamberlain in WP, DLC.

To William Gibbs McAdoo

My dear Mac.,　　　　　　Washington. 11 May, 1917.

I of course approve of both of the enclosed,[1] but I would like to be sure that the practical steamship men are certain that the second, third, and fourth class passenger spaces on the steamers PENNSYLVANIA, PRESIDENT GRANT, and PRESIDENT LINCOLN can be used for freight without destroying the sea balance of the boats, which were, of course planned to carry passengers in those spaces and not dead weight freight.

Faithfully Yours,   W.W.

WWTLI (W. G. McAdoo Papers, DLC).
¹ The enclosures are missing.

From Edward Mandell House, with Enclosures

Dear Governor: New York. May 11, 1917.

Last week the Japanese Ambassador[1] took lunch with me. Before the end of our conversation he wanted to know if I did not think it a good time to take up the differences existing between our two governments.

I asked him what particular differences he had in mind. He spoke of the immigration and land questions. I feared that any official move in this direction would have the appearance of trying to take advantage of our entrance into the great war. He disclaimed such a purpose, stating that he was led to ask the question because of your public declarations that all international differences should be met and removed in a spirit of justice.

I insisted that an official move at this time would be miscon[s]trued and suggested, if they had anything in mind, it would be best to state it informally. I requested him to let me have in writing just what they wished to bring before this Government.

I am enclosing you a copy of his letter and the memorandum and my reply. When you have leisure, will you not advise me concerning this. If Russia swings back to autocratic government, I think a close alignment between Germany, Japan and Russia is certain.

Walter Rogers[2] has just returned from the Far East. He tells me that what news of our army and navy program has leaked into Japan has changed their openly expressed antagonism to the United States into a more friendly tone.

He strongly advises a better news service to Japan, China and Russia. I will not go into details, but, from what I learn not only from Rogers but from others, this is one of the crying needs at the moment.

The general public in both Japan and China regard us as being almost as unwilling to fight as China herself, and none of our war preparations and but little of your addresses have reached the people.

This can all be changed at very little cost and I should be glad to undertake its direction if you approve.

Affectionately yours,   E. M. House

TLS (WP, DLC).
¹ Aimaro Sato.
² Walter Stowell Rogers, formerly assistant to Charles Richard Crane. He became director of the Division of Foreign Cable News Service of the C.P.I. in 1917.

E N C L O S U R E   I

Aimaro Sato to Edward Mandell House

My dear Colonel House: Washington. May 8, 1917.

For your kind reception and open-hearted talk which I had the pleasure of enjoying in New York, I wish you to accept my warm and sincere thanks.

According to your suggestion, I have since prepared a memorandum succinctly setting forth the point which formed a part of our conversation and I am taking the liberty to send it to you for whatever you may see fit.

Mr. Oscar S. Straus called on me two days after I had the pleasant interview with you, and he was telling me about his idea of making the most of the present trend of things for fostering better relations between our countries. It is indeed gratifying to find evidences indicating that a more serious interest in our relations is actually being taken in this country and especially among men of great influence.

With high regard and cordial wishes, I beg you, Dear Colonel House, to believe me,

                    Very sincerely yours,   Aimaro Sato.

TCL (WP, DLC).

E N C L O S U R E   I I

The Japanese-American question which calls for an immediate adjustment, is that of the treatment of the resident Japanese in this country. What Japan desires is nothing more than the enjoyment of the most favored nation treatment. That desideratum may be attained in my personal opinion, by the adoption of some of the following means.

1. By Treaty.

a. By concluding an independent treaty, mutually guaranteeing to the citizens and subjects, the most favored nation treatment, in matters of property and other rights relative to the exercise of industries, occupations, and other pursuits. Negotiations in this line were for some time conducted between Secretary Bryan and Ambassador Chinda, which, however, for reasons I need not here state, have since been in abeyance.

b. By revising the existing commercial treaty between our two countries, so as to conform, in its stipulations, to similar engagements between Japan and various European powers, which guarantee, in principle, the most favored nation treatment, in the enjoyment of property rights and in all that relates to the pursuit of industries, callings and educational studies.

2. By American legislation.

Although the subject is not fit for international discussion, it may be mentioned that a constitutional amendment restraining any state from making and enforcing any law discriminatory against aliens in respect to their property and other civil rights, will prove a far-reaching remedy. In fact a resolution with the same object in view has, I understand, been introduced in Congress lately.[1]

In this connection, I may state the fact that the provisions of racial distinction in the present naturalization law, were, in a number of instances, made use of for the purpose of depriving Japanese subjects of the rights and privileges of a civil nature. Although the wisdom of the law is in itself a matter of national and not international concern, the unfortunate circumstance that certain provisions of that law furnish a pretext for the impairment of alien rights, should, I may be allowed to remark, constitute a fit subject for legislative attention.

The comparative merits of each means should be studied by both Governments in the light of expediency and feasibility. Whether the adoption of any one means will be sufficient to cover the whole ground is a matter upon which precaution forbids me to pass a final judgment at present, but I am strongly convinced that each means will go a long distance towards a complete solution of the question.

Before concluding, I desire to touch upon the subject of immigration. The question whether Japanese laborers shall be admitted or not has been consummately solved by the continued faithful observance by Japan of the so-called Gentleman's Agreement. So far as the Japanese Government is concerned, it is no longer in the realm of living questions, and, in my view, it would serve the best interests of both nations to leave the question as it is.

T MS (WP, DLC).
[1] H.J. Res. 386, introduced on March 1, 1917, by James William Husted, Republican of New York. It proposed an amendment to the Constitution, as follows: "SECTION 1. That no State shall, without the consent of the Congress,

make or enforce any law which shall discriminate amongst aliens in respect to the holding of property or the enjoyment of any civil privilege or immunity. SEC. 2. That the Congress shall have power to enforce this article by appropriate legislation." *64th Congress, 1st 2nd and 3rd Sessions, 1915-1917* . . . (Washington: Library of Congress Photoduplication Service, 1970).

ENCLOSURE III

Edward Mandell House to Aimaro Sato

My dear Mr. Ambassador: New York. May 10, 1917.

Thank you for your letter of May 8th enclosing the memorandum.

I shall take up the matter informally with Washington when the time seems opportune. At the moment, I am afraid, it could not be given that calm consideration which its importance justifies.

Please be assured that I shall always do what I can to help maintain the good relations which exist between our two countries.

I shall remember with much satisfaction our conversation of the other day, and I shall look forward to seeing you soon again.

I am, my dear Mr. Ambassador,

Your very sincere,   [E. M. House]

TCL (WP, DLC).

From William Gibbs McAdoo

Dear Mr. President: Washington May 11, 1917.

I have your memorandum of the 11th instant in reference to the removal of the second, third and fourth class passenger accomodations of the German Steamships PENNSYLVANIA, PRESIDENT GRANT, and PRESIDENT LINCOLN. I have assumed that the Shipping Board was satisfied that the stability of the ships would not be affected by the proposed change, or that they would not have made the recommendation. I think your inquiry is very pertinent and I have brought it to the attention of the Board.

Cordially yours,   W G McAdoo

TLS (WP, DLC).

From William Dennison Stephens

Sacramento, Calif., May 11, 1917.

Replying your wire of today Mooney sentence stayed indefinitely by appeal pending in state supreme court subordination [subornation] of perjury charges now pending in superior court.[1]

Wm. D. Stephens.

T telegram (WP, DLC).

[1] In reply, Wilson thanked Stephens for his telegram and added: "It relieves a rather serious anxiety." WW to W. D. Stephens, May 14, 1917, TLS (Letterpress Books, WP, DLC).

Two Letters from Newton Diehl Baker

My dear Mr. President: Washington. May 11, 1917.

On the receipt of your note of the 8th, with the telegram from Mr. W. H. Donner, of the Donner Steel Company, which is herewith returned for your files, I took the matter up with the Secretary of Labor, who is, of course, a member of the Council of National Defense. For my information, and in order that I may transmit it to you for your information, the Secretary of Labor made the inclosed memorandum, which I think covers the entire situation.[1]   Respectfully yours,   Newton D. Baker

[1] W. B. Wilson to NDB, May 11, 1917, TS memorandum (WP, DLC). It reported that W. L. Chambers and the United States Board of Mediation and Conciliation had, on the previous day, met in Buffalo with the parties concerned, and that prospects for a solution were favorable.

My dear Mr. President: Washington. May 11, 1917.

I return herewith the preliminary report from ex-Governor Fort, of the Federal Trade Commission, which Secretary Wilson and I have read with great interest. Some of the facts stated by the Governor had already been canvassed in the Council of National Defense, but this very well considered report throws new light on the whole subject, and we will await with interest its further treatment by the Federal Trade Commission.

Respectfully yours,   Newton D. Baker

TLS (WP, DLC).

From Bernard Mannes Baruch

My dear Mr. President: New York May 11, 1917.

I am in receipt of your letter of May 8th and, although I regret your decision, please do not think of it again. Rest assured of one

thing, I shall never be distressed or embarrassed for one single minute by anything done by you. I know your clear head, your conscience and kind heart too well to feel anything but happiness in submitting to any decision that you may make. It is always such a pleasure to do anything for you. You always show a greater sense of gratitude and appreciation than anyone I have yet met.

I was so glad to do the ship business for you.[1] That was easy. Give me something real hard.

Cordially and faithfully yours,   Bernard M Baruch

TLS (WP, DLC).
[1] He probably had made the arrangements for the purchase of the Austrian ships mentioned in WW to EMH, May 7, 1917.

From Charles Edward Russell

Dear Mr. President: Washington, D. C. May 11, 1917.

I am profoundly grateful to you for the opportunity your kindness has conferred upon me to serve the country we love and the great cause in which, under your leadership, we are enlisted. To be able to fill any post at such a time, or to render any service, whether great or small, must fill us with solemn joy.

But for the intervening of Sunday I should be ready to start in forty-eight hours. In the existing conditions I shall be ready Monday evening, or earlier if earlier departure be desired.

In thanking you, Mr. President, may I not wish for you all health, strength and fervent, loyal support in the great task that God has put into your hands for the freedom and advancement of man and the eternal vindication of democracy?

I am, dear sir, with great respect and gratitude
Yours very truly   Charles Edward Russell

TLS (WP, DLC).

From Cleveland Hoadley Dodge

My dear President   New York. May 11th 1917

Just a line to thank you for the "perfectly bully" way in which you put out the appointment of the Red Cross War Council, and to let you know how keenly we all appreciate what you have done.

As the terrible needs on the other side become more apparent, the serious question arises, whether they can be met entirely by the voluntary gifts of the American people & it may be that the Red Cross may be compelled to ask for the assistance of the Government.

We are having high old jinks in New York these days, and the enthusiasm of the people is most thrilling. I am just leaving the office to meet the Englishman.[1]

Trusting that you may soon be able to get a little rest with warm regards to you all

Yours affectionately   C H Dodge

ALS (WP, DLC).
[1] Balfour.

From the Diary of Josephus Daniels

1917 Friday 11 May

Cabinet. President was most amusing describing how John Barrett[1] elbowed him at Balfour reception & said not to swear at him proved his Christian character. Wanted to tell him to go to — Lansing said B was very energetic. President told story of woman who praised the devil by saying "You know he is very energetic." President talked of Russian mission & gave names of men appointed—3 may be said of capitalistic turn of mind & 4 Democratic—one of them a Socialist. They leave next week on Buffalo[2]—not to tell Russians how to manage their business, but to be ready to co-operate with them.

[1] That is, the Director General of the Pan American Union.
[2] U.S.S. Buffalo, an auxiliary cruiser.

Remarks at the Dedication of the Red Cross Building[1]

12 May, 1917.

Mr. Chairman, Mr. Secretary, ladies and gentlemen: It gives me a very deep gratification, as the titular head of the American Red Cross, to accept in the name of that association this significant and beautiful gift, the gift of the government and of private individuals who have conceived their duty in a noble spirit and upon a great scale. It seems to me that the architecture of the building to which the Secretary alluded suggests something very significant. There are few buildings in Washington more simple in their lines and in their ornamentation than the beautiful building we are dedicating this evening. It breathes a spirit of modesty and seems to adorn duty with its proper garment of beauty. It is significant that it should be dedicated to the women who served to alleviate suffering and comfort those who were in need during our Civil War, because their thoughtful, disinterested, self-sacrificing devotion is the spirit which should always illustrate the services of the Red Cross.

The Red Cross needs at this time, more than it ever needed before, the comprehending support of the American people and all the facilities which could be placed at its disposal to perform its duties adequately and efficiently. I believe that the American people perhaps hardly yet realize the sacrifices and sufferings that are before them. We thought the scale of our Civil War was unprecedented, but, in comparison with the struggle into which we have now entered, the Civil War seems almost insignificant in its proportions and in its expenditure of treasure and of blood. And, therefore, it is a matter of the greatest importance that we should, at the outset, see to it that the American Red Cross is equipped and prepared for the things that lie before it. It will be our instrument to do the works of alleviation and of mercy which will attend this struggle. Of course, the scale upon which it shall act will be greater than the scale of any other duty that it has ever attempted to perform. It is in recognition of that fact that the American Red Cross has just added to its organization a small body of men whom it has chosen to call its War Council—not because they are to counsel war, but because they are to serve in this special war those purposes of counsel which have become so imperatively necessary. Their first duty will be to raise a great fund out of which to draw the resources for the performance of their duty.

And I do not believe that it will be necessary to appeal to the American people to respond to their call for funds, because the heart of this country is in this war, and, if the heart of the country is in the war, its heart will express itself in the gifts that will be poured out for these humane purposes. I say the heart of the country is in this war because it would not have gone into it if its heart had not been prepared for it. It would not have gone into it if it had not first believed that here was an opportunity to express the character of the United States. We have gone in with no special grievance of our own, because we have always said that we were the friends and servants of mankind. We look for no profit. We look for no advantage. We will accept no advantage out of this war. We go because we believe that the very principles upon which the American republic was founded are now at stake and must be vindicated. In such a contest, therefore, we shall not fail to respond to the call to service that comes through the instrumentality of this particular organization.

And I think it not inappropriate to say this: there will be many expressions of the spirit of sympathy and mercy and philanthropy. And I think that it is very necessary that we should not disperse our activities in those lines too much; that we should keep constantly in view the desire to have the utmost concentration and efficiency of effort; and I hope that most, if not all, of the philanthropic activities of this war may be exercised, if not through the Red Cross, then through some already constituted and experienced organization. This is no war for amateurs. This is no war for mere spontaneous impulse. It means grim business on every side of it, and it is the mere counsel of prudence that, in our philanthropy as well as in our fighting, we should act through the instrumentalities already prepared to our hand and already experienced in the tasks which are going to be assigned to them. This should be merely the expression of the practical genius of America itself, and I believe that the practical genius of America will dictate that the efforts in this war in this particular field should be concentrated in experienced hands as our efforts in other fields will be.

There is another thing that is significant and delightful to my thought about the fact that this building should be dedicated to the memory of the women both of the North and of the South. It is a sort of landmark of the unity to which the people have been brought so far as any old question which tore our hearts in days gone by is concerned. And I pray God that the outcome of this struggle may be that every other element of difference amongst us will be obliterated, and that some day historians will remember these momentous years as the years which made a single people out of the great body of those who call themselves Americans. The evidences are already many that this is happening. The divisions which were predicted have not occurred and will not occur. The spirit of this people is already united, and, when effort and suffering and sacrifice have completed the union, men will no longer speak of any lines either of race or of association cutting athwart the great body of this nation. So that I feel that we are now beginning the processes which will some day require another beautiful memorial erected to those whose hearts uniting, united America.

T MS (WP, DLC).

1 William Howard Taft presided at the dedication ceremonies, which were held in the auditorium of the nearby Constitution Hall of the D.A.R. He and Wilson ascended the platform together. Secretary of War Baker formally presented the new building to the Red Cross Society, and Wilson accepted it for the nation in this speech. Senator John Sharp Williams spoke for the women of the South, and the Rev. Horace Percy Silver, chaplain of the United States Military Academy, spoke for the women of the North. After the exercises, Wilson and Taft reviewed a parade of about 1,000 members of the Women's Volunteer Aid Corps led by Mrs. Hugh L. Scott, Mrs. Baker, and Mrs. Josephus Daniels. *Washington Post*, May 12 and 13, 1917.

From Robert Lansing, with Enclosure

My dear Mr. President: Washington May 12, 1917.

I enclose a memorandum on Mr. John F. Bass.

I do not think, from this memorandum which is prepared by Mr. Patchin,[1] that Mr. Bass' connection with the Chicago NEWS would materially affect his usefulness in Petrograd. I am quite strongly of the opinion that it would be wise to have a publicity man in Petrograd.   Faithfully yours,   Robert Lansing.

TLS (SDR, RG 59, 124.61/15½, DNA).

[1] Philip Halsey Patchin, head of the Bureau of Information of the Department of State.

E N C L O S U R E

MEMORANDUM FOR THE SECRETARY OF STATE RE JOHN F. BASS.

He was originally recommended to the Department for the work proposed by Mr. Stanley Washburn.

Mr. Bass was born in Chicago in 1866. He is a brother of former Governor Bass of Vermont. He speaks French fluently, is a well-known war correspondent, has independent means and has an attractive wife, concerning whom the French Government lately issued a special order thanking her for Red Cross work. Mr. Bass has spent most of this war in Europe. When with the Russian forces he was wounded. His correspodence has had almost exclusively to do with military operations and not politics. He is very well known to Judge Advocate General Crowder, who went through the Russo-Japanese war with him. General Crowder gives him a strong recommendation. He has lately been in the service of the Federal Trade Commission, to which he was "loaned" by the CHICAGO DAILY NEWS, with which he has been connected, off and on, for a number of years.

Mr. Bass is a graduate of Harvard and a member of the New York bar. He is a member of the Royal Geographical Society, and has been a leading official of the National Conservation Association. During the political campaign of 1912 he was the Progressive Party's national committeeman for Illinois, and was chairman of the Illinois Progressive State Committee in 1913.

He began his war correspondence with English troops in Egypt in 1895. He "covered" the Cretan insurrection the same year. He was in Armenia in '96 during the massacres. In 1898 he saw the Cretan rebellion and the Turko-Greek war. He was a war correspondent in the Spanish-American war, the Philippine insurrection and, in 1900, the Boxer trouble, during which he accompanied the relief column to Peking. He "covered" the Bulgarian uprising in Macedonia in 1903 and the Russo-Japanese war in 1904. He was six months in the field with Kuroki.[1]

Concerning his politics or his attitude toward the administration's policies and aims I can ascertain little further than that he has devoted himself during the war essentially to military developments. Mr. Washburn knows him exceedingly well—they are, in fact, very close friends—and his recommendation for this particular work was very strong.   P.H.P.

T MS (SDR, RC 59, 124.61/15½, DNA).
[1] Tamemoto Kuroki, commander of the Japanese First Army.

From George Earle Chamberlain

My dear Mr. President: Washington, May 12, 1917.

I appreciate your note of the 11th inst. You express the hope that the Army Bill may be pressed to a speedy passage. It is my disposition to urge it in the Senate, but the Conference Report must first be considered by the House of Representatives. This report is being taken up there today, and I hope it will be adopted. I assure you that when it comes over to us from the House it will be urged with all possible energy in the Senate, though quite a number intend to oppose it because the volunteer feature has been left out. May I suggest that you get some of our Democratic friends to give me all possible assistance in the Senate?
                    Yours very sincerely,   Geo E Chamberlain

TLS (WP, DLC).

From William Gibbs McAdoo

STRICTLY CONFIDENTIAL.

Dear Mr. President: Washington May 12, 1917.

I gathered from what you said at the Cabinet meeting yesterday that you had the impression that I had been consulted by the Shipping Board concerning the plan announced in the papers for the expenditure of $1,000,000,000 in the construction of merchant ships. As I then stated, I was not consulted about this matter and knew nothing of it until I read about it in the papers. I, of course, have no right to expect that I will be consulted about matters of policy, which are solely within your own determination, such as the policy involved in this measure, but do you not think that your Finance Minister should have an opportunity to be heard where such huge expenditures are concerned before the policy is adopted? It is not possible for me to properly conduct this Department and to deal effectively with the really prodigious problems of finance which now confront the country unless I can be informed about the larger policies that may be in contemplation and be permitted to advise whether or not the necessary moneys can be raised before final decisions are made. In almost every Department large estimates are being made and transmitted to the Congress without the slightest consideration as to how the money is to be provided. In every country in Europe the Minister of Finance is one of the War Council, because it is everywhere recognized that money is a fundamental problem in war and that the Finance Minister must be able to advise about ways and means before commitments to great expenditures are made. Please do not take this as a suggestion that your Secretary of the Treasury should be on the Council of National Defense. I prefer not to be a member of that body—my only point is that the Secretary of the Treasury should be consulted before we enter upon policies requiring enormous expenditures of money.

Perhaps you may recall that I suggested in our conference April 30th, that you request the Shipping Board to act in the closest cooperation with this Department, but that you did not look upon it with favor. The more I see of the progress of events here, the more I am convinced that this Board ought to be related closely to some one of the Executive Departments, unless you can, yourself, take the burden of keeping in direct and intimate touch with its activities. The future will demonstrate, I am sure, the correctness of this judgment. I do not want the job myself, but I think the matter so important that I would suggest that the proposed amendment to the Shipping Bill contain a provision making either the Postmaster General or the Secretary of Labor Chairman Ex-Officio of that Board for the period of the war. Either of these men would be very helpful—more so than the Secretary of Commerce under existing conditions. I have found that these independent commissions work much better with the Administration if a Cabinet officer is at their head. The Federal Reserve and Farm Loan Boards are cases in point. The present Shipping Board has developed some weaknesses to which it will be a grave mistake to shut our eyes. My advice may be worthless, but I shall, at least, have discharged my duty in bringing these matters to your attention.

I beg you to believe that this is written in no captious spirit; it is prompted solely by a desire to secure effective cooperation

in the work in hand and to conserve the credit resources of the
Nation for the colossal demands of the war.

Cordially yours, W G McAdoo

TLS (WP, DLC).

From Henry Burchard Fine

My dear Tommy, Princeton, May 12th, 1917

Last evening at the Enos'[1] I met a young American surgeon,
Dr. Malco[l]m C. Grow,[2] who interested me very much. He is
just back from Russia after two years service in the medical
corps of the Russian army. He was under Brusyloff[3] in the bril-
liant campaign of that general last summer and rose to the rank
of chief of the medical staff of one of the Russian regiments. I
was especially impressed by the clear, succin[c]t, & vivid accounts he gave of the engagements he had witnessed, but even
more by what he had to say regarding the strong desire for peace
which during the last months he has heard expressed by the
Russian soldiers among whom he has been thrown. He has
come back filled with concern lest this sentiment, which he
fears is growing, may lead to Russia's dropping out from active
participation in the war, and is naturally eager that the steps
which America is taking to help avert this catastrophe be the
most effective possible. He found that the best known & most
admired American private citizen, among all classes of men with
whom he talked, is Roosevelt—to whom they seemed to feel
especially grateful because he helped stop the war with Japan—
and he is so fully possessed of the idea that the addition of
Roosevelt to the U. S. Commission about to be sent to Russia
would immensely add to the influence of that Commission with
the rank and file of the Russian people that he feels he cannot
rest until he has done his best to see you & tell you the grounds
of his belief. He therefore begged me to write you that he is to be
in Washington this coming week, probably on Wednesday, his
address there being c/o H. Ralph Burton, Union Trust Co. At my
suggestion, that you may be saved the trouble of sending him
any word, he is to call at the White House (on Wednesday, I
think) and learn from Mr. Tumulty whether you are willing to
see him and, if so, when.

There is nothing for me to add, except that I am convinced
that Dr. Grow is thoroughly sincere & not acting under the influence of his own personal admiration for Roosevelt—if indeed
he possesses any, for he said nothing to indicate it. His sugges-

tion may be wholly impracticable, but, on the other hand, it may, as he thinks, have promise enough to warrant meeting serious difficulties to have it or something like it carried into effect. You will know.

With love from us all, as ever,

Affectionately Yours,   Henry B. Fine

ALS (WP, DLC).

[1] Alanson Trask Enos, Princeton 1878, a retired businessman who at this time was living at 159 Nassau St. in Princeton. His wife was Jeannette Taylor Enos.

[2] Malcolm Cummings Grow described his experiences as a lieutenant colonel in the Imperial Russian Army's medical corps in *Surgeon Grow: An American in the Russian Fighting* (New York, 1918). He entered the United States Army as a medical reserve officer in 1917 and became Air Surgeon General in 1946.

[3] That is, Gen. Aleksei Alekseevich Brusilov.

From Edward Mandell House

Dear Governor: New York. May 13, 1917.

Mr. Balfour took lunch with me today and we had a very interesting talk.

I suggested that it would be well to use his influence towards limiting the members of the peace conference to a minimum and I expressed the hope that you would consent to go from here as our only representative. He concurred in the wisdom of having a body small enough for it not to be unwieldly.

I asked him what would be his inclination in the event Germany made a tentative offer of peace on the basis of the status quo ante. He thought it would largely depend upon the condition of the u-boat warfare and also upon the condition of Russia, France and Italy.

It was my opinion that we ought not to let our desires run away with our judgment in the matter of making peace. For instance, if Turkey and Austria were willing to break away from Germany, or were willing to force Germany to make peace, I thought certain concessions should be made to them other than what we would have in mind in the event we had our complete will. He agreed to this.

He also agreed to the proposal that there should be no insistence that the makers of the war should be punished before a settlement should be even tentatively discussed.

He asked me to express to you his very great appreciation of your coming to Congress to hear him speak. He understands what an unprecedented compliment it was and is deeply moved. He thought to write you himself but hardly knew how to do so.

He is very happy over his visit and considers it a great success from every viewpoint.

Sometime ago I had a letter from Page proposing that we start a propaganda in England to improve the feeling towards us. I spoke to Balfour about this and suggested that it would be better if this were done by the English themselves. He agreed to take it up with his government and see that it was properly done.

Affectionately yours,   E. M. House

TLS (WP, DLC).

To Robert Lansing

My dear Mr. Secretary,   The White House. 14 May, 1917.

I have no personal objection to Mr. Bass of course, but I do not think that it would be wise to send a man who has had his connections.

I have hit upon a man, however, whom I deem eminently fitted for the task. It is Mr. Arthur Bullard, who is now working with Mr. Creel, at such personal sacrifice to himself as to show what stuff he is made of.

He is a magazine writer and an author of excellent reputation, and spent five years in Russia at the time of the last revolutionary attempt. He is on terms of close friendship with Mr. Russel[l], Mr. Crane, and Mr. Duncan and enjoys the warm personal regard of Mr. Root, I am told. He probably knows as much as any other man in America about the various radical groups in Russia and their leaders and adds to this knowledge sympathy and an understa[n]ding tolerance. I am quite willing that he should be commissioned and sent at once.   Faithfully Yours,   W.W.

WWTLI (A. Bullard Papers, NjP).

To Charles Allen Culberson

My dear Senator: [The White House] 14 May, 1917

I am taking the liberty of sending to you with the earnest hope that it may commend itself to your committee and to the Senate a Joint Resolution authorizing me to direct that certain kinds of traffic or particular shipments shall from time to time have preference or priority in transportation by common carriers by railroad or water.[1] The exercise of such authority has become imperatively necessary because there is at present no authority in existence by which such decisions can be made. The railroads of the country have in a very practical and patriotic way consented to the formation under the guidance of the Council of National

Defense of an Executive Committee presided over by Mr. Daniel Willard, through which they undertake to serve the interests of the Government and of the country in the best and most effective way possible under our guidance. Of course, one department thinks the shipments in which it is most interested the most important and deserving of immediate transportation, while another department thinks it an imperative necessity that other shipments should take priority. What this resolution would provide, if adopted, would be some authority by which competitive questions of this sort could be determined. It would cause no friction, indeed, it would remove it, and it would relieve a very great embarrassment arising out of the existing conditions.

In asking the Attorney General to draw up the enclosed resolution I did not request him to prescribe a penalty because I had in mind the following provision which is already law and is contained in the Army Act of August 29, 1916:

"The President, in time of war, is empowered, through the Secretary of War, to take possession and assume control of any system or systems of transportation, or any part thereof, and to utilize the same, to the exclusion as far as may be necessary of all other traffic thereon, for the transfer or transportation of troops, war material and equipment, or for such other purposes connected with the emergency as may be needful or desirable."

I assumed that this furnished sufficient sanction if sanction were needed, as I think it would not be.

With warm regard,

Cordially and sincerely yours,   [Woodrow Wilson]

P.S. Inasmuch as I had some doubt as to the committee jurisdiction in this matter, I have taken the liberty of communicating to the same effect with Senator Newlands.[2]

CCL (WP, DLC).
[1] Wilson's enclosure is missing.
[2] WW to F. G. Newlands, May 14, 1917, CCL (WP, DLC). Wilson sent the same letter, *mutatis mutandis*, on May 14 to E. Y. Webb and W. C. Adamson.

Two Letters to George Creel

My dear Creel: [The White House] 14 May, 1917

Thank you for your memorandum about Bullard. It is fine of you to be willing to part with him and I think the suggestion a splendid one. I have just sent a note over to the Secretary of State about it.

Cordially and faithfully yours,   Woodrow Wilson

TLS (Letterpress Books, WP, DLC).

My dear Creel: The White House 14 May, 1917

In the estimate you submitted the other day for the Committee on Public Information, I found no provision, at any rate no definite provision, for yourself. I cannot be content with that arrangement and write to beg that you will do me the favor to provide a proper compensation for your own services. I could not be content with anything less.

Faithfully yours,   Woodrow Wilson

TLS (G. Creel Papers, DLC).

To Robert Kilburn Root

My dear Professor Root: [The White House] 14 May, 1917

Your letter of May eleventh warms my heart.[1] It is certainly conceived in the most generous spirit and you may be sure that I shall not forget its offer. Just at present it is impossible to say whether it will be possible to find a place in which to ask you to serve the Government, but I shall be very happy to keep in mind the offer, for I know how genuinely it is made.

Cordially and sincerely yours,   Woodrow Wilson

TLS (Letterpress Books, WP, DLC).
[1] It is missing.

To William English Walling

My dear Mr. Walling: The White House 14 May, 1917

Your letter of May tenth and your entire action throughout the recent consultations with which the Secretary of Labor has kept me in touch have given me the greatest gratification, and I want to thank you very warmly for your unselfish and patriotic attitude.

Cordially and sincerely yours,   Woodrow Wilson

TLS (W. E. Walling Papers, WU).

To Josephus Daniels

My dear Mr. Secretary: The White House 14 May, 1917

Section 2 of the Joint Resolution recently passed authorizing me to take over to the United States the possession and title of the German merchant vessels now in American waters provides that the Secretary of the Navy shall appoint, subject to my approval, a board of survey for the purpose of assessing the apparent present value of these vessels.

I would very much appreciate it if you could make early arrangements to have this done.

Cordially and sincerely yours,   Woodrow Wilson

TLS (J. Daniels Papers, DLC).

To Newton Diehl Baker

My dear Mr. Secretary: [The White House] 14 May, 1917

The enclosed papers[1] interest me immensely. Doctor Fitch[2] is one of the most remarkable men in the United States. He has extraordinary force and eloquence and personal magnetism, and has won my admiration and affection. That he should be willing and even desirous of playing the part of chaplain in this war strikes me as one of the most interesting indications of the influences abroad in the country that I have known. I hope sincerely that it will be possible to find some place for Doctor Fitch such as he desires.

Cordially and faithfully yours,   Woodrow Wilson

TLS (Letterpress Books, WP, DLC).
  [1] They are missing.
  [2] The Rev. Dr. Albert Parker Fitch, Bartlet Professor of Practical Theology and president of the faculty at Andover Theological Seminary, 1909-1917, whom Wilson and Ellen Axson Wilson had known at Cornish, N. H.

To Henry Burchard Fine

My dear Harry: [The White House] 14 May, 1917

I wish I could see Doctor Grow, but it is really impossible. My days are so full now as to come near to driving me to distraction and I could not in any circumstances consider the suggestion of sending Mr. Roosevelt anywhere to represent the administration.

I am none the less obliged to you for your letter and hope that you will not regard this as a discouragement for writing me anything it comes into your head to write.

Affectionately yours,   [Woodrow Wilson]

CCL (WP, DLC).

To Helen Hamilton Gardener

My dear Mrs. Gardener: [The White House] 14 May, 1917

I have your letter of May tenth and beg to assure you that it will give me pleasure to write to Mr. Pou as you suggest. I have always found Mr. Pou ready to respond in the most generous way to every call of public duty.

Cordially and sincerely yours,   Woodrow Wilson

TLS (Letterpress Books, WP, DLC).

To Edward William Pou

My dear Mr. Pou: The White House 14 May, 1917

My attention has been called to the question as to whether it was desirable to appoint a Committee on Woman Suffrage in the House of Representatives. Of course, strictly speaking, it is none of my business, and I have not the least desire to intervene in the matter, but I have a letter written in admirable spirit from Mrs. Helen H. Gardener, in which she says that she has been told that you had said that you would report out a proposal for such a committee if I should approve. On the chance that I may be of some slight service in this matter, which seems to me of very considerable consequence, I am writing this line to say that I would heartily approve. I think it would be a very wise act of public policy, and also an act of fairness to the best women who are engaged in the cause of woman suffrage.

Cordially and sincerely yours,   Woodrow Wilson

TLS (E. W. Pou Papers, Nc-Ar).

To William Henry Donner

My dear Mr. Donner: [The White House] 14 May, 1917

Immediately upon the receipt of your telegram of May fifth, I took the matter it referred to up with the Chairman of the Council of National Defense and have pleasure in sending you enclosed a copy of a memorandum furnished him by the Secretary of Labor.[1]   Sincerely yours,   Woodrow Wilson

TLS (Letterpress Books, WP, DLC).
[1] See NDB to WW, May 11, 1917 (first letter of that date), n. 1.

From David Franklin Houston

Dear Mr. President: Washington May 14, 1917.

I am sending you herewith a copy of the Food Production Bill, which has been printed,[1] and a typewritten copy of the regulatory bill. This is the latest revision of the regulatory bill.[2]

I am also sending you two memoranda which give an indication of the powers requested, and their nature.[3]

Faithfully yours,   D. F. Houston.

TLS (WP, DLC).

[1] The printed text of H.R. 4188, introduced on May 4 by Representative Lever, as reported with amendments and committed to the Committee of the Whole House on May 7, 1917 (WP, DLC). The bill provided for "the national security and defense by stimulating agriculture and facilitating the distribution of agricultural products." To this end, it authorized the Secretary of Agriculture to summon witnesses, inspect premises, procure seeds and supply them to farmers, and to take various other steps for increasing production and reducing waste. The authorization would remain in effect not later than one year after the end of the war with Germany.

[2] A typewritten copy (WP, DLC) of the latest version of H.R. 4125 (*the* Lever bill). It provided sanctions, with penalties, against the waste or hoarding of food, shoes, clothing, fuel, and other "necessaries of life" and articles required for their production. It authorized the President, whenever he found it essential, to establish standards, prescribe regulations, and issue licenses concerning these "necessaries," and, in certain cases, to establish fair rates and prices, require their sale, or requisition them, with just compensation. It also authorized the President to act against market manipulation or other "evil practices" and to determine what, under specified conditions, was "a reasonable minimum price for any necessaries, in order to assure the producer a reasonable profit," this price in certain cases to be guaranteed by the United States Government. In addition, under certain conditions, the President could establish maximum prices that would be enforceable by fines and imprisonment but that would safeguard, insofar as possible, the "equities and bona fide investments" of all concerned. Finally, the President could also regulate the use of food materials in alcoholic beverages and make exceptions to the mixed-flour law of 1898 (but not in violation of the food and drugs law of 1906). This authority would expire no later than one year after the end of the war with Germany. H.R. 4125 had met such strong opposition in debate on May 8 that Lever, on June 11, introduced a revised bill, H.R. 4961, about which see the White House Staff to WW, June 16, 1917, n. 1.

[3] "Production Bill H.R. 4188" and "Control Bill (Revision of H.R. 4125)," T MSS (WP, DLC).

From William Gibbs McAdoo

Dear Mr. President: Washington May 14, 1917.

Everybody connected with the Liberty Loan is convinced that if you would issue a brief proclamation to the country, asking all good citizens to subscribe to the extent of their means to these bonds, it would have a powerful effect. I am really concerned about the success of the Loan unless we can get the people generally aroused to its importance. No one can bring it so forcibly to their minds and hearts as you can. I earnestly hope you may be willing to do this. I enclose a brief statement I gave to the press last night,[1] which may be of use to you as suggesting an idea.

It is with extreme reluctance that I have felt obliged to accept a few invitations to make speeches in a number of places in the Central West. It has been represented to me as being essential that I should do so, as interest in the Loan seems very slight throughout that section. A failure would be disastrous from every point of view. I am leaving Wednesday, the 16th, and shall be gone about ten days.   Cordially yours,   W G McAdoo

TLS (WP, DLC).
[1] Office of the Secretary of the Treasury, mimeographed press release (WP, DLC).

From Newton Diehl Baker

Dear Mr. President: Washington. May 14, 1917

While I was away yesterday, General Scott had a long confer-ence with General Marti and others of the Cuban military mis-sion now here. As a result General Marti cabled President Menocal and later gave General Scott a memorandum of which I inclose a copy.[1] From this it will be observed that according to President Menocal the situation in Oriente Province is far from bad and is steadily improving. After receiving this message from General Marti I inclosed a copy of it to the Secretary of State, telling him that the War Department is ready to send any force deemed desirable to Cuba, but is waiting his further advices in view of General Marti's advice. I inclose a copy of my letter to the Secretary of State.[2]

Respectfully yours,   Newton D. Baker

TLS (WP, DLC).
[1] T MS (WP, DLC). It conveyed information from a telegram from Menocal which stated that 800 men with their leaders had surrendered during the previous week in Oriente, where the government's forces now totaled over 8,000, and that the revolution was "completely under control."
[2] NDB to RL, May 14, 1917, TCL (WP, DLC).

From William Howard Taft

My dear Mr. President: New Haven, Conn May 14th 1917.

I have your kind note of May 10th and of course yield to your suggestion.

The very competent committee whom you have elected to do the extraordinary work to be done in the war will make weekly meetings of the Executive Committee less important.

It was a great pleasure to see and talk with you and Mrs. Wilson on Saturday.   Sincerely yours   Wm H Taft.

ALS (WP, DLC).

Sir Cecil Arthur Spring Rice to the Foreign Office

                                        Washington May 14th. 1917.
Urgent. Secret.

Following for Prime Minister from Mr. Balfour.

Large United States programme for capital ships makes construction of any considerable number of additional destroyers impossible. We have suggested abandonment for the present of capital ships but fear of Japan is so great both in the Navy Department and elsewhere that we have made no progress. In discussion with Colonel House yesterday latter suggested that programme might be modified in direction we desire if United States could receive a guarantee from us that if necessity arose they could call on us for assistance in capital ships to a not less extent than number which would have been completed under present programme. Danger to which United Kingdom might be exposed in such conditions from German fleet was pointed out (? to him). He then developed the idea and suggested arrangement might take a wider form and be mutual, in short a defensive alliance on the sea between United States and ourselves. He was in favour of a secret agreement on these lines but I doubt whether this is consistent with United States Constitution and in any case it is a violent departure from United States practice.

If however you agree to general principle I would consult him as to best method of carrying it out. Personally I consider that apart from all important need for more destroyers there would be a great advantage in obtaining anything in the nature of a defensive alliance with United States. Of course Japan's susceptibilities will have to be spared but this should not be difficult to manage.

T telegram (FO 371/3119, No. 97867A, pp. 293-94, PRO).

Remarks to the Labor Committee of the Council of National Defense[1]

                                        15 May, 1917.

Mr. Gompers and ladies and gentlemen: This is a most welcome visit because it means a most welcome thing—the spontaneous cooperation of men from all walks of life interested to see that we do not forget any of the principles of our lives in meeting the great emergency that has come upon us.

Mr. Gompers has expressed, already, one of the things that have been very much in my mind of late. I have been very much alarmed at one or two things that have happened—at the apparent inclination of the legislatures of one or two of our states to set aside, even temporarily, the laws which have safeguarded the standards of labor and of life. I think nothing would be more deplorable than that. We are trying to fight in a cause which means the lifting of the standards of life, and we can fight in that cause best by voluntary cooperation. I do not doubt that any body of men representing labor in this country, speaking for their fellows, will be willing to make any sacrifice that is necessary in order to carry this contest to a successful issue, and in that confidence I feel that it would be inexcusable if we deprived men and women of such a spirit of any of the existing safeguards of law. Therefore, I shall exercise my influence, as far as it goes, to see that that does not happen and that the sacrifices we make shall be made voluntarily and not under the compulsion which mistakenly is interpreted to mean a lowering of the standards which we have sought through so many generations to bring to their present level.

Mr. Gompers has not overstated the case in saying that we are fighting for democracy in a larger sense than can be expressed in any political terms. There are many forms of democratic government, and we are not fighting for any particular form. But we are fighting for the essential part of it all, namely, that we are all equally interested in our social and political life and all have a right to a voice in the government under which we live; and that, when men and women are equally admitted to those rights, we have the best safeguard of justice and of peace that the world affords. There is no other safeguard. Let any group of men, whatever their original intentions, attempt to dictate to their fellow men what their political fortunes shall be, and the result is injustice and hardship and wrong of the deepest sort. Therefore, we are, just now, feeling, as we have never felt before, our sense of comradeship. We shall feel it even more because we have not yet made the sacrifices that we are going to make; we have not yet felt the terrible pressure of suffering and pain of war; and we are going presently to feel it. And I have every confidence that, as its pressure comes upon us, our spirits will not falter but rise and be strengthened, and that, in the last, we shall have a national feeling and a national unity such as never gladdened our hearts before.

I want to thank you for the compliment of this visit and say if there is any way in which I can cooperate with the purposes of this committee or with those with whom you are laboring, it will afford me a sense of privilege and of pleasure.

T MS (WP, DLC).

[1] About 135 members of the Committee on Labor of the Advisory Commission of the Council of National Defense met in Washington on May 15 at the call of Samuel Gompers, chairman of the committee. Those present included officials of the A.F.L. and of the railroad brotherhoods, leading employers, financiers, publicists, educators, and representatives of the army and navy. Gompers had convened the meeting to receive the British and Canadian labor representatives. Wilson received the entire committee at the White House at 2:30 P.M.

From Bernard Mannes Baruch

My dear Mr. President: [New York] May 15, 1917.

The general policy of determining the prices which our Army, Navy, Shipbuilding and Allies are to pay, must necessarily come before you. Before you determine this I should like to have you keep in mind the following facts:

(a) We must win the war.

(b) To win the war we must have the men and materials.

(c) The United States is the last reservoir of credit upon which we can draw to win the war.

Materials must be had in unceasing and ever increasing amounts.

Beyond a certain point, restriction of profits will restrict the production of these vital materials.

Wages cannot and must not be reduced.

QUESTION: How far can we reduce prices, yet keep wages up and keep production at full blast?

A proper decision of the price policy, in my opinion, would untie and set lose the great machinery of the Government, and clarify the situation tremendously.

Before you come to a decision, and if you desire, I am entirely at your service to give you my thoughts and experience.

Yours very truly,   B. M. Baruch

TCL (B. M. Baruch Papers, NjP).

From Edwin Yates Webb

My dear Mr. President: Washington, D. C. May 15, 1917.

I have just received your letter enclosing Joint Resolution conferring upon you power to direct certain shipments by water and by rail, and I beg to inform you that I introduced the resolution this afternoon in the House and, under the Rules, it was referred to the Committee on Interstate and Foreign Commerce.

I think the resolution is the most direct and practical proposition in the effort to solve the immediate food problem that has so far been suggested, and I beg to assure you that I will use every effort to have it speedily considered both in the Committee and in the House. I feel quite sure that Judge Adamson will co-operate with equal heartiness.

With great respect, I am,   Sincerely,   E. Y. Webb.

TLS (WP, DLC).

From Charles Allen Culberson

Dear Mr. President,   Washington, D. C. May 15, 1917.

Your letter of yesterday with enclosed joint resolution authorizing the President to control transportation during the present war was duly received. In view of the suggested doubt of the jurisdiction of the Committee on the Judiciary and that of Interstate Commerce, I took a poll informally of the Committee, and a decided majority expressed the belief that the joint resolution should go to the Committee on Interstate Commerce. Accordingly, this morning I notified Senator Newlands of the decision of the Committee on the Judiciary, and he will take charge of the matter.   Very sincerely yours,   C. A. Culberson

TLS (WP, DLC).

Jean Jules Jusserand to the Foreign Ministry

Washington, reçu le 15 mai 1917

No. 619. Le Ministre de la Justice à Président du Conseil Paris.

Nous sommes arrivés au terme de notre voyage et nous embarquons ce soir à New-York pour être sans doute à Paris mercredi soir 23 mai à 5 heures. Je suis venu présenter mes adieux au Président Wilson qui m'a reçu avec une cordialité marquée. Après m'avoir félicité du succès de la mission, il m'a ouvert la voie à la discussion politique. J'ai interprété vos télégrammes concernant le resserrement du blocus dont il est partisan en se gardant d'exaspérer les neutres. Il serait bon qu'il soit tenu au courant minutieusement de tous les incidents et de toutes les nécessités du blocus afin de pouvoir faire pression sur le point désirable sans commettre d'erreurs. En ce qui concerne l'envoi des troupes, il m'a déclaré qu'il enverrait le plus tôt possible, très rapidement, le troupes par petits détachements sur des bateaux qui porteront le frêt afin, non pas de partager les risques, mais de montrer à l'Allemagne, par la suite continuelle des envois, la persistance dans le dessein.

En nous séparant, il m'a dit: "Nous sommes frères dans la même cause."

La mission française a reçu un accueil qui a dépassé les espérances. Aucun incident. Pas une fausse note. Tous ont travaillé à la cause commune. Nous ne pouvions plus faire et je crois que la France aura le droit d'être fière de sons admirable situation ici.

Je vous serai reconnaissant de vouloir bien faire exercer une censure implacable sur les télégr. de presse en ce qui concerne notre départ et notre arrivée. A notre départ de France toute la ville de Brest était à la gare. Il n'est pas possible de laisser cette situation se continuer.

Je serai prêt, dès le jeudi 24 mai, à discuter la question des loyers. Si par impossible, je subissais un retard Desplas[1] pourrait me remplacer dans la discussion qui lui est familière. Signé Viviani.   Jusserand.

T telegram (Guerre 1914, 1918, États-Unis, Vol. 115, pp. 115-16, FFM-Ar).
[1] Georges Desplas, Minister of Public Works.

T R A N S L A T I O N

Washington, received May 15, 1917

619. The Minister of Justice to the President of the Council Paris.

We have come to the end of our stay and embark this evening at New York, to be in Paris no doubt on Wednesday evening, May 23, at 5 o'clock. I have just said my farewells to President Wilson, who received me with marked cordiality. After congratulating me upon the success of the mission, he opened the way for a political discussion. I explained your telegrams on tightening the blockade, an issue on which he wants to avoid exasperating the neutrals. It is desirable that he be kept minutely informed of all incidents and of the urgent necessity for the blockade so as to be able to apply pressure on the desired place without committing errors. As for the sending of troops, he told me that he will send, as soon as possible, very quickly, troops in small detachments on ships carrying freight, not in order to spread the risks, but, through a continuous procession of troop movements, to show Germany the dead seriousness of the plan.

As we parted, he told me: "We are brothers in the same cause."
The French mission has received a welcome exceeding all hopes. No incident. Not a false note. All have worked in a common cause. We could not have accomplished more, and I believe that France can be proud of its admirable situation here.

I will appreciate your keeping a tight censorship on press dispatches concerning our departure and our arrival. At our departure from France, the whole city of Brest was at the railway station. We cannot permit this situation to recur.

I will be ready, Thursday, May 24, to discuss the question of interest rates. If by some remote chance I am delayed, Desplas is familiar with the discussion and can take my place. Signed Viviani.   Jusserand.

To Josephus Daniels

Dear Daniels,   [The White House, May 16, 1917]

This is all right;[1] but I hope Creel will remind the newspaper men of their agreement *not* to publish news of the movements of our naval vessels.   W.W.

ALI (J. Daniels Papers, DLC).
[1] The Enclosure printed with WW to G. Creel, May 17, 1917.

To Bernard Mannes Baruch

My dear Baruch: The White House 16 May, 1917

Thank you for your letter of yesterday. I realize to the full the force of your suggestions and shall certainly try to keep them in mind in the difficult matters that are ahead of us.

    Cordially and faithfully yours,   Woodrow Wilson

TLS (B. M. Baruch Papers, NjP).

To Asbury Francis Lever

My dear Mr. Lever: [The White House] 16 May, 1917

I thought it important that you should see the enclosed, if it has not already been brought to your attention.[1]

    Cordially and sincerely yours,   Woodrow Wilson

P. S. I felt that the conference of last evening[2] did a great deal of good in clearing up the situation and I hope you felt the same way.   W.W.

TLS (Letterpress Books, WP, DLC).

1 Wilson's enclosure is missing. It was a telegram from Jonathan Ogden Armour, president of Armour & Company, packers, and others at a meeting in Chicago of the State Council of Defense of Illinois on May 12 about the conservation of foodstuffs.

2 Wilson and Houston had met at the White House with members of the Senate and House committees on agriculture to try to get them to agree on a bill that could be passed. Several bills were pending. Houston explained the administration's intentions concerning price controls. It did not intend to fix maximum prices generally, but only in specific instances to force the unloading of hoarded stocks of food. Minimum prices might be set if necessary to encourage production, but maximum price fixing would be resorted to only to prevent extortion and corners on food.

Wilson told the committeemen that, in his opinion, the three crucial factors in the conduct of the war, in the order of their importance, were the fighting forces themselves, control of the food situation, and control of the country's transportation facilities. Senator Kenyon and Representative Lever urged Wilson to issue a statement defining what was understood by the proposal for maximum prices in the pending legislation. Wilson said that he would consider issuing such a statement. *Washington Post*, May 16, 1917. His statement is printed at May 19, 1917.

To Caroline Dutcher Sterling Choate

My dear Mrs. Choate: [The White House] 16 May, 1917

May I not join in expressing what I believe to be the grief of the whole nation at the death of your honored and distinguished husband?[1] The news of it came as a great shock to me and I wish to convey to you my most heartfelt sympathy.

Cordially and sincerely yours,   Woodrow Wilson

TLS (Letterpress Books, WP, DLC).

1 After taking a leading part in several public events in honor of the French and British missions visiting in New York, Joseph Hodges Choate had suffered a heart attack and died on May 14 at the age of eighty-five.

Two Letters from William Gibbs McAdoo

Dear Mr. President: Washington May 16, 1917.

I am going away, as you know, today, to be gone ten days. Meanwhile, the amendments to the Federal Reserve Act have gone to conference.[1] I have succeeded, I am glad to say, in reconciling Mr. Glass to the provisions for issues of Federal Reserve notes against gold, which we all think is highly important in view of the situation created by the war. The only stumbling block now is the amendment tacked on by the country banks and non-member banks of the Federal Reserve System, authorizing them to make an exchange charge of not exceeding one-tenth of one per cent. Hardwick, of Georgia, put it on in the Senate and Kitchin championed it in the House. This is a most unfortunate amendment, and unless materially changed in the conference will, I think, produce some unhappy effects. Mr. Glass is trying to have the amendment reshaped in the conference and doubtless will be able to do so. If, however, the Senate and the House should put the bill through with this amendment in a form that is thoroughly unsatisfactory, I wish you would send for Mr. Glass and discuss the matter with him fully before you approve or disapprove the bill. I am really distressed that this issue has been raised at this time when it is so important to have all of the banks of the United States cooperating heartily in the effort to place the large issues of Government bonds. Therefore, I should be sorry to see the bill vetoed unless the reasons for that course are very convincing. Mr. Glass will, however, go over the matter with you thoroughly and if you need to talk with anybody on the Federal Reserve Board about it I would suggest that you send for Williams and Warburg. Of course you will not forget to confer with Senator Owen also, if you have to face the question of vetoing the bill.[2]   Cordially yours,   W G McAdoo

[1] Various amendments recommended by the Federal Reserve Board and others had failed of passage in the Sixty-fourth Congress and were reintroduced in the Sixty-fifth. The House of Representatives, on May 5, 1917, passed a bill (H.R. 3673), which provided, among other things, for an increase of the gold reserves in Federal Reserve banks by approximately $350,000,000, with a proportional increase in their rediscount facilities. *Cong. Record*, 65th Cong., 1st sess., p. 1888. The Senate, on May 9, accepted Hardwick's amendment (described below by McAdoo), passed the bill, and called for a conference with the House. 65th Cong., 1st. sess., *Journal of the Senate*, p. 83.
[2] Glass, having succeeded in incorporating various qualifying provisions in the Hardwick amendment, accepted it, and the conference was able to agree. The House passed the bill on June 14, the Senate on June 18, and Wilson approved it on June 22, 1917.

My dear Mr. President: Washington May 16, 1917.

In connection with your note of a few days ago as to whether the second, third and fourth class passenger spaces on the steamers PENNSYLVANIA, PRESIDENT GRANT and PRESIDENT LINCOLN can be used for freight without destroying the sea balance of the boats, I took the matter up with Mr. Donald of the United States Shipping Board, who is a practical steamship man, and I send you herewith a copy of his reply.[1]
                    Faithfully yours,   W G McAdoo

TLS (WP, DLC).
[1] John A. Donald to WGM, May 14, 1917, TCL (WP, DLC). Donald, president of the Donald Steamship Co., said that the proposal was feasible.

From William Henry Donner

My dear Mr. Wilson: Philadelphia May 16th, 1917.

Acknowledging receipt of your letter of May 14th,—your interest and assistance in righting conditions affecting our Works at Buffalo, referred to in my telegram of May 5th, are very much appreciated.

Judge Chambers, Commissioner of Mediation and Conciliation, after several conferences arranged a temporary adjustment satisfactory to all concerned which I believe will result in restoring normal conditions. Permit me to compliment the practical and diplomatic manner in which Judge Chambers handled the situation.[1]   Very respectfully yours,   W. H. Donner

TLS (WP, DLC).

[1] Chambers reported to Wilson on May 12 that the "trouble arose from the discharge by the Donner Steel Company of all of its Union engineers, firemen and switchmen." Officials of the company had told Chambers that they had learned that the organized employees were attempting to unionize all the others, some two thousand in number. Chambers had been able to work out a temporary solution which all parties hoped would become permanent. W. L. Chambers to WW, May 12, 1917, TLS (WP, DLC).

To George Creel, with Enclosure

My dear Creel: The White House 17 May, 1917

I have suggested a few changes in this, but aside from the changes suggested it seems to me excellent. I hasten to return it.
          Cordially and sincerely yours,   Woodrow Wilson

TLS (G. Creel Papers, DLC).

E N C L O S U R E[1]

COMMITTEE ON PUBLIC INFORMATION
PRELIMINARY STATEMENT TO THE PRESS

"I can imagine no greater disservice to the country than to establish a system of censorship that would deny to the people of a free republic like our own their indisputable right to criticise their own public officials. While exercising the great powers of the office I hold, I would regret in a crisis like the one through which we are now passing to lose the benefit of patriotic and intelligent criticism."   WOODROW WILSON.

[1] Words in angle brackets in the following document deleted by Wilson; those in italics, added by him. Creel read this statement to the Washington press corps on May 23. See D. Lawrence to WW, May 24, 1917.

FOREWORD.

⟨Various⟩ Belligerent countries are *usually* at pains to veil in secrecy all operations of censorship. Rules and regulations are issued as "private and confidential," each pamphlet ⟨being⟩ *is* numbered, and the recipient held to strict accountability for its safe and secret keeping. The Committee on Public Information has decided against this policy, and the press is at liberty to give full publicity to this communication. It is well to let people know just what it is that the Committee proposes and desires, so that there may be the least possible impairment of public confidence in the printed information presented to it.

GEORGE CREEL,
Chairman, Committee on Public Information.

TO THE PRESS OF THE UNITED STATES:

The committee on Public Information, created by Executive order of April 14, 1917, desires to lay before the press of the nation the common task imposed upon press and Committee alike by the exigencies of war. It does this in the full faith that a common understanding of mutual responsibilities and duties will assure the co-operation essential to the patriotic discharge of all obligations, whether implicit or defined.

Neither in peace nor in a time of national peril can the national welfare be wholly secured or completely explained by any statute or order. The best defense is an enlightened and loyal citizenship. The *representatives of* [*the*] press ⟨is⟩ are at one with the Committee in regarding its [*their*] great responsibilities in creating loyalty through enlightenment as *being* only heightened by existing conditions, for war is not entirely a matter of armed force. Public opinion is a factor in victory no less than ships and guns, and the creation and stimulation of a healthy, ardent national sentiment is the kind of fighting that the press alone can do. The Committee feels that it can best serve this common purpose by a statement as clear as may now be made of the ways in which modern war, and this war in particular, necessitate readjustments in the gathering and distributing of news.

Before the Committee on Public Information was established, definite steps in this direction had already been taken. On [blank] at a conference between the secretaries of ⟨the⟩ State, *of* War and *of* the Navy on the one part and representatives of the press on the other, a voluntary agreement was reached regarding the censorship of the press during the period of the war. It is possible for the Committee to profit by the experience gained *else-where* in the ⟨general⟩ satisfactory working of this plan. It is already clear that this communication will serve a large purpose if it removes needless misapprehensions which have led the conscientious many to omit matters freely open to discussion, and sweeps away such misrepresentations as have served to shelter the unscrupulous few.

BULLETINS FROM TIME TO TIME.

It is impossible to lay down in advance hard and fast rules. The experience of the press bureaus in belligerent countries in Europe has shown a need for constant amendment. All the European censors are now passing for publication news which at first they thought it advisable to stop. It will be necessary to issue from time to time new bulletins advising the press of the country of changing policy as new conditions arise.

None of the press bureaus in Europe has functioned without friction. None has been entirely successful in attaining its objects. We cannot expect perfection from ours. All we can hope for is that the Committee on Public Information, while working out a satisfactory solution to the problem, will avoid the more obvious blunders of others. The staff to be employed will naturally be inexperienced in this work and must acquire skill with practice. It will have to face problems one at a time and work out definite rules from experience.

Every report at our disposal emphasizes the willingness of the press of European countries to join with their governments in the effort to prevent the use of the newspapers by the enemy. There is the hope and belief that the printed word in the United States will equally realize the obligations of patriotism as keenly as those who take the oath of service in army and navy. The policies of the Committee will be based upon this assumption. Co-operation is the vital need, not grudging obedience to resented orders, and there will be earnest effort to frame all rules ⟨with a view of⟩ *in such a way as to* appeal to common sense as well as to patriotism.

We have for our guidance the experience of two and a half years of war. We have before us the reports of our military and naval attaches and a large number of reports from civilian observers. Some of the governments already at war with Germany have referred to us official and confidential documents relating to the routine work of their press bureaus.

The problem facing the Committee on Public Information is, in most respects, different from ⟨those⟩ *that* of the press bureaus of Europe. The habitual peacetime relations between the government and the newspapers has been different in the United States from what it was in any European country. Also, from a military point of view, speed in transmission of news is of vital importance and military censorship is immensely simplified for us by the fact of our distance from the enemy. Even the worst newspaper indiscretions here will not be so serious in helping the enemy as is the case in Europe. French journals can be read by German spies in Switzerland or British papers in Holland within twenty-four hours of publication. It will be ten days at least before our newspapers reach a neutral country in direct communication with Germany.

It is not all news which we wish to keep from the enemy. Almost all information which we regard as "good" would be "bad" news for the enemy and would exercise a depressing effect on the morale of their people. We wished, for instance, to give the widest possible publicity in Germany to the fact that Congress had voted the War Credit Bill, including the loan to the Allies, without a dissenting voice.

The only news which we wish to keep from the authorities of Berlin is the kind which would be of tangible help to them in their military operations.[2] At the moment more than half of such news has to do with naval operations, including the movements of merchant ships. The remainder is of such subjects as Coast and Harbor defense, new inventions, information confided to us by our Allies, details of diplomatic proceedings, etc.

It will be some ⟨months⟩ *time* before our army grows to the point where successful censoring on its behalf becomes of vital importance. The staff of the Committee will have gained much valuable experience before this more formidable problem of shielding the army from undesirable publicity becomes pressing.

THE THREE CATEGORIES OF NEWS.

It will facilitate the work of the Committee if a sharp distinction is made between three categories of news.

   I. Matters which obviously must not be mentioned in print.
   II. Matters of a doubtful nature which should not be given
       publicity until submitted to and passed by the Committee.
   III. Matters which do not ⟨interest⟩ *affect* the conduct of ⟨the⟩
       war, do not concern this Committee and are governed only
       by peacetime laws of libel, defamation of character and so
       forth.

2 Creel's emphasis.

Under Category I, would fall locality of warships ⟨,⟩ *and* mine-fields; location and description of Coast and Harbor Defenses or photos giving clues on these matters, date and port of sailing of merchant ships, etc.

Under Category II, would come such matters as narrative descriptions of units in the Army or Navy or of their operations. We will want many such stories published, but they should be first submitted for visë, as it is extremely easy to give inadvertant information of great value in such narratives. The Kipling stories of the Destroyers in the Battle of Jutland were very carefully scrutinized by the Admiralty experts before release. The Committee will strive to meet the wishes of the publishers in this matter as far as possible and so to encourage them to submit all doubtful items and manuscripts.

The mass of "copy" will fall under Category III, which can be freely published as it is innocent of any connection with the conduct of the war.

There is the further problem of preventing the transmission to the enemy of information not appearing in the public prints. The news most desired by the Enemy General Staff will not be collected from our newspapers but will be gained by high grade and highly placed spies. This *is* not a matter of unintentional newspaper indiscretions such as is the prime consideration of any press censorship but of malicious and criminal conspiracy and comes directly under the jurisdiction of the Department of Justice and the Secret Service.

Despite the greatest care on all hands a certain amount of spy communication will, in all probabilities, be maintained. None of the belligerent countries ⟨have⟩ *has* been able to eliminate the spy. There has been much senseless hysteria abroad in regard to naturalized waiters and nurserymaids. The really dangerous spies are high officials or officers in high command. Damaging information is hard to come by and, in spite of the cleverness of the code makers, hard to communicate.

Our problem in America is (1) to stop the source of such information by preventing leaks and (2) to interfere with its transmission. An adequate censorship of all outgoing cables has already been established, but self-restraint on the part of the newspapers in publishing news deemed dangerous by our military authorities will immensely increase the difficulty of spies in collecting the information they desire. A matter may be of common knowledge in a New England port but if it is not published it will be more difficult for an enemy spy on the Mexican border to learn of it.

FREE FLOW OF NEWS TO NEUTRALS.

Not content with striving to keep dangerous information from the enemy, all the belligerent governments have tried to keep objectionable news from neutral countries. The object of such efforts has been diplomatic rather than military. We, in America, have experienced this treatment during the period when we were neutral. It would be extremely difficult to prove any concrete utility from the attempts to censor news going to neutral nations. When it is known that news is being withheld it inevitably rouses suspicion that there is something really serious to hide. It is, therefore, not the intention of this Committee to exercise such a censorship against the neutral nations of South and Central America. The free flow of news will not be checked, effort being concentrated to prevent the transmission of the specific information set forth in these rules and regulations.

Nearly all the European belligerents have also tried to prevent the publication of news likely to offend their Allies or create friction between them. The Committee is of the opinion that the more full the inter-Ally discussion of their mutual problems the better. Matters of high strategy and so forth will of course have to be kept secret by the war council, but the more the people of the Allied countries get acquainted with each other through their newspapers the better.

If any case arises where one of our papers uses insulting or objectionable language against our comrades in arms it had best be dealt with individually. But ⟨as⟩ *so* far as possible this Committee will maintain the rule of free discussion in such matters.

Regularly accredited correspondents from Allied nations will be allowed to cable to their papers free from interference by our Censors. We can, and should, rely on the discretions of their editors. If cases arise of foreign correspondents sending to their home papers false, misleading or intentionally discourteous despatches, a word to their Ambassadors would certainly bring down the necessary reprimand. It will be a great loss of prestige to us if we let the feeling get abroad among our Allies that we are hiding the truth from them.

The European Press Bureaus have also attempted to keep objectionable news from their own people. This must be clearly differentiated from the problem of keeping dangerous news from the enemy. It will be necessary at times to keep information from our own people *in order to keep it from the enemy*,[3] but most of the belligerent countries have gone much farther.

---

3 Creel's emphasis.

In one of the confidential documents submitted to us there is, under Censorship Regulations, a long section with the heading "News likely to cause anxiety, dissent or distress." Among other things forbidden under this section are the publication of "reports concerning outbreaks of epidemics in training camps," "Newspaper articles tending to raise unduly the hopes of the people as to the success" of anticipated military movements. This sort of suppression has obviously nothing to do with the keeping of objectionable news from the enemy.

The motive for the establishment of this internal censorship is not merely fear of petty criticism, but distrust of democratic common sense. The officials fear that the people will be stampeded by false news and sensational scare stories.

The danger feared is real, but the experience of Europe indicates that censorship regulations do not solve the problem. A printed story is tangible even if false. It can be denied. Its falsity can be prove. It is not nearly so dangerous as a false rumor.

⟨There has been some immediate gain in these efforts to "preserve the public morale" by suppressing sensational and false stories. But in the long run the ill effects have definitely outweighed the "immediate gain." The clearest example of this in Europe is the dis-array of French and British opinions in regard to the Balkans. The censors forbade any frank discussion of this problem. Fantastic hopes were allowed to grow in the public mind and the reaction was dangerous when the house of cards fell down. The forced retirement of certain ministers was one result. The public had been so ill informed in regard to this problem that they were made the scapegoats for a policy they had consistently opposed.⟩

The atmosphere created by common knowledge that news is being suppressed is an ideal "culture" for the propaganda of the bacteria of enemy rumors. This state of mind was the thing which most impressed Americans visiting belligerent countries. Insane and dangerous rumors, some of obvious enemy origin, were readily believed and they spread with amazing rapidity. This is a greater danger than printing scare stories. No one knows who starts a rumor, but there is a responsible editor behind every printed word.

NO SHIELD AGAINST CRITICISM

But the greatest objection to such censoring of the news against the home population is that it has always tended to *create* the abuse of shielding from public criticism the dishonesty or incompetence of high officials. While it certainly has never been the policy of any of the European Press Bureaus to accomplish this result, the internal censorship has generally worked out this way. And there are several well established instances where the immense power of the Censor has fallen into the control of intriguing cliques. Nominally striving to protect the public from pernicious ideas, they have used the censorship to protect themselves from legitimate criticism.

In so far as the censorship is felt by the public to be withholding news of interest which could do the enemy no good, in so far as the public suspects that the censorship is being used to further personal ambitions or to influence internal politics, the objects of this Committee will be defeated. The field will be left open for the wildest and most disintegrating rumors. If it is known that the papers are forbidden to mention outbreaks of epidemics in training camps, every German sympathizer in this country will be whispering stories of cholera, smallpox, and plague and they will be believed.

While the Committee has no intention of instituting such a drastic censorship on internal affairs, it is within its province to seek to protect the people—and the great mass of reputable editors—from the publication of maliciously conceived and clearly false reports.

Keeping to this one example of possible epidemics in the training camps, we can deduce a rule of procedure. Every editor in the country will probably have "copy" on this subject submitted to him. While military sanitation has been immensely improved of late, more or less serious epidemics have broken out in every army in Europse [Europe]. In the Western Armies they have been ⟨suppressed⟩ *checked* with amazing ease. Very few have gotten in any way out of hand. In Surgeon General Gorgas, Surgeon General Braisted and Surgeon General Blue,[4] we have the three great sanitarians of the world, and there is every reason to expect a very high efficiency in the health programs of Army, Navy and Marine Corps. But some sporadic epidemics will in all probabilit⟨ities⟩*y* break out.

The Committee will not try to suppress information on this subject, but to assure accuracy and a proper perspective. We can expect our editors to co-operate in this matter and refrain from publishing unverified or exaggerated reports.

The same general rule can be applied to the publication of falsehood in other matters. "Our special correspondents" are at

4 Rupert Blue, M.D., Surgeon General of the United States Public Health Service.

the moment a serious problem. Their despatches are anonymous and often absurdly and dangerously false. This Committee believes that it would be to the public good if such despatches were signed so that the reader would be able to distinguish between the honest reports of people who were willing to stand for their statements and the alleged "news" which is often sent from the Mexican Border for instance, by agencies known by our Secret Service to be supported by the enemy.

Section II. QUESTIONABLE MATTER.

There are many other news items which, while not so obviously dangerous as those listed in Section I., may be dangerous. In all cases of doubt, editors are requested to seek advice of the Committee on Public Information. The following are some examples of such doubtful news:

(1) Narrative accounts of naval or military operations, including descriptions of life in training camps. While it is desir⟨ous⟩-*able* that the public should be kept interested in these subjects, there is always a chance that a reporter, narrating facts, may unconsciously mention something which the military authorities particularly desire to keep from the enemy; all such articles should be submitted to the Committee on Public Information.

(2) Technical Inventions. It is desired that the subject of possible new military inventions should be kept before the public, but great care should be exercised in publishing any definite statements as to experiments or accepted inventions.

It is of peculiar importance that all government experiments in war material should be veiled in absolute secrecy. This request has particular application to the search for means to combat the submarine. Therefore all articles and news stories along these lines should be submitted for vise.

The name of every well-known inventor is connected with a single kind of work and may not be mentioned without conveying to the enemy a hint as to the nature of the invention upon which he is working.

An instance of the menace of the specific mention of the work of an inventor was afforded by the result of the publication of a newspaper story that the well-known inventor in question had discovered a "U-Boat Killer." The story was followed the next day quite naturally by another story that police protection against German agents had been immediately required to guard both the man and the works where the experiments were supposed to be conducted. That the report of the invention had been promptly denied did not lessen the peril to life and property caused by this piece of editorial inadvertence.

(3) Many sensational and disturbing rumors will be brought to the attention of newspaper men. It is to be desired that they should not be given publicity until they have been most carefully verified; for example, sporadic epidemics may break out in some of our training camps. It would be most unpatriotic to give credence to exaggerated accounts of such inevitable mishaps. Editors are requested to submit information which they may receive on such subjects to the Committee for verification. Daily reports from the chief sanitary officers will be available. And this Committee will arrange to have parties of newspaper men and reputable doctors sent to camps where sickness occurs to check up these reports.[5]

T MS (G. Creel Papers, DLC).
[5] This statement was released for publication on May 28 as *Preliminary Statement to the Press of the United States* (Washington, 1917).

To William Leonard McEwan[1]

My dear Mr. McEwan: [The White House] 17 May, 1917

I am very sorry indeed that you did not find me accessible when you were in Washington, but I am sure you understood.

The resolution unanimously adopted by the Presbytery of Pittsburgh on May fourteenth, which you were kind enough to leave for my consideration,[2] of course carries with it very great weight indeed.

I am not clear, and shall not be until I have thought the matter over a little further, whether it would be wise at this juncture and on the particular date suggested to set a day of prayer. My feeling is that when such a day is set the object for which our prayers should be offered should be a very definite one indeed, and it is in the confidence that such objects will presently present themselves that I feel like waiting. I am sure the weight of such considerations will be obvious to the members of the Presbytery.

With sincere regard,

Faithfully yours,   Woodrow Wilson

TLS (Letterpress Books, WP, DLC).
[1] The Rev. Dr. William Leonard McEwan, pastor of the Third Presbyterian Church of Pittsburgh since 1894.
[2] "Resolution Unanimously adopted by the Presbytery of Pittsburgh May fourteenth, Nineteen Hundred and Seventeen," T MS (WP, DLC), enclosed in W. L. McEwan to WW, May 14, 1917, TLS (WP, DLC). It petitioned Wilson to designate Decoration Day as a national Day of Prayer.

To Thomas Pryor Gore

My dear Senator: The White House 17 May, 1917

My attention has been called to Senate Joint Resolution No. 62, introduced by yourself, empowering me to appoint a Controller General of Supplies. I take the liberty of asking whether this idea preceded in your mind the conference we had the other evening?

We are in danger, I fear, of multiplying unrelated pieces of machinery, and I would greatly appreciate an expression of your thought with regard to this resolution.

Sincerely yours,   Woodrow Wilson

TLS (T. P. Gore Papers, OkU).

From Robert Lansing, with Enclosure

My dear Mr. President: Washington May 17, 1917.

I enclose a memorandum of a conversation which Mr. Polk had day before yesterday with the Brazilian Ambassador.

I believe Brazil is inclined to enter the war but is disposed to obtain guarantees of continued commercial facilities in case war is declared.

In so far as protecting the coasts of Brazil from hostile attack, I believe that under the Monroe Doctrine we would be bound to do that if the occasion required.

On account of the large German population in some of the southern states of Brazil I understand that the Brazilian Government would not weaken its military forces by sending troops to Europe. I doubt if that would be advisable in any event.

My own view is that it would have a decided influence on Argentina and Chile if Brazil declared war, as it would on other American Republics. If you agree with this view what assurance can I give the Ambassador as to transportation and general trade?   Faithfully yours,   Robert Lansing.

TLS (SDR, RG 59, 763.72/13420, DNA).

ENCLOSURE

Department of State May 17, 1917.

On May 15 the Brazilian Ambassador read me despatches from his President[1] and from his Minister of Foreign Affairs[2] bearing on the future attitude of Brazil in this war. The gist of both messages was that Brazil was prepared to abandon its position of neutrality towards Germany. One note stated that they would be willing to grant our warships the right to refit in their ports, and the Brazilian Government might take over a portion of the patrol of the northern coast of Brazil. As the Minister of Foreign Affairs put it, Brazil would give their moral, economic and political support to the United States in exchange for some trade guarantees and for some agreement, not necessarily a treaty, covering the position that this Government would take in case Germany should later consider Brazil an enemy as a result of this action.

The Ambassador said he realized that it would be difficult to be specific as to what this Government would do to protect Brazil in case of attack by Germany, but he would like to bring the matter up for discussion and consideration. I asked him what he meant by trade guarantees, and in substance they mean that this Government would see they continued to receive from the United States necessary supplies, particularly wheat and coal, and that shipping used in trade with Brazil would not be withdrawn for use in transatlantic trade to a degree that would seriously embarrass Brazil. I asked him if he had any details as to the amount of shipping and foodstuffs and merchandise they would require. He said he had not but would make some investigations and let me know. He said that he had received this telegram last week and he would like to have some sort of message to send his Government this week.

In course of conversation he suggested that it might be advisable to send an expert to Argentina to find out what that Government was doing with their supplies, that is to say, whether the embargo that had been put on foodstuffs was really justified.

The Ambassador returned today and said that, although he did not yet have information as to food supplies necessary, he would like to have some message to send his Government as they were holding Congress until they could get a reply from us.

F.L.P.

TI MS (SDR, RG 59, 763.72/13420, DNA).
  ¹ That is, Wenceslao Braz Pereira Gomes.
  ² That is, Nilo Peçanha.

From Robert Lansing

My dear Mr. President: Washington May 17, 1917.

I had yesterday two conversations in relation to Turkey which are worthy of consideration because any possibility of alienating an ally of Germany ought not to be ignored even if accomplishment is doubtful.

In the morning Mr. Elkus' private secretary (Mr. Alsberg,[1] I believe) called to see me and I spent sometime questioning him as to conditions in Turkey. He left Constantinople on April 6th and, therefore, brought the latest information.

He said that the food situation was as bad it could possibly be, that he thought 200,000 people were starving in the city, and that in the interior the condition was even worse; that the people were most anxious for peace but without leadership could do nothing; and that all classes were bitter against the Germans who were being gradually removed as officers in the army.

He said that even the Government was becoming irritated at the arrogance of the Germans and feared German control after the war; that they did not want to become a vassal of Germany; that they saw in American capital the only hope of rebuilding their ruined fortunes and desired to remain on friendly terms but were compelled by the Germans to break off relations, which increased Turkish ill-feeling toward the German Government. Alsberg said that he believed the Turks would listen to terms of a separate peace if they dared.

I asked him what prevented them, and he replied the GOEBEN and BRESLAU, which were anchored before Constantinople with their guns trained on the city, and that to the Turks the preservation of Constantinople was the all-important thing, that he believed that they would give up Palestine, Syria and Armenia in order to hold Constantinople, even though it were under a practical protectorate like Egypt.

He believed that it was possible, on account of the attitude of Turkey toward the United States, for us to approach the Turkish Government with suggestions for a separate peace, and that it might be brought about if the German cruisers could in some way be destroyed by bombs or other means.

When he spoke of the Turkish Government he referred of course to the Triumvirs, Enver, Talaat and Djemel,[2] who possess practically absolute power. He felt that these three were beginning to chafe under German control and to resent the insolent manner in which they were being treated, while the possibility of rebellion among the Turks was increasing as a result of the famine and suffering of the people.

I had been impressed with these statements, when Mr. Morgenthau came to see me in the afternoon and said that he had been thinking over the situation and believed that the time was ripe to make secret overtures to Turkey for he was sure that by this time the Turkish leaders were heartily sick of their German masters.

I asked him why they submitted and he said that the cruisers and some of the forts were in the hands of the Germans, which prevented the people from acting against the Government, and the Government from acting against the Germans. He said that he believed if the three Turkish leaders were properly approached (meaning undoubtedly by bribery or promises) he thought that they would allow some submarines to enter the Dardanelles and destroy the German vessels, and that if that was done and the Turks relieved of their fear of the Germans, they would be willing to make peace on very favorable terms for the Allies.

I asked him how he would get in touch with Enver, Talaat and Djemel. He replied that he believed that he could do it by going himself to Switzerland where two members of the former Turkish Cabinet were at the present time, men, whom he knew intimately, to whom he could talk freely, and who would act as intermediaries. He said that he did not court this service but was willing to undertake it if it seemed desirable. He suggested that we (he and I) confer with Mr. Balfour on the subject. I told him that I would think it over and if it seemed feasible would communicate with him later.

Of course it would be a tremendous blow to the Central Powers to have Turkey withdraw as no doubt Bulgaria would be forced to follow the same course. But has this plan the slightest prospect of success? It seems very doubtful, and yet, if the chance was one in fifty, I think it should be taken, but has it that chance? Of course we could well afford to spend a large sum to accomplish such a result. To make the attempt would cost very little. Is it worth trying? That is, is it worth while to send Morgenthau to Switzerland and let him make the attempt?[3]

The other day I asked Mr. Balfour what chance he thought there was of making a separate peace with Turkey. He replied that he had nothing very definite on the subject, but that he had been advised that they were "nibbling" and that Bulgaria was also.

This may be the opportune time, but I am not at all sure that it is. The only thing is that I do not like to leave any stone unturned which will lessen the power of Germany, and I have therefore felt that I should submit the matter to you in detail for your consideration.   Faithfully yours,   Robert Lansing

Ans. orally W.W.

TLS (WP, DLC).
[1] Henry Garfield Alsberg, a lawyer and editorial writer for the New York

Evening Post, joined Elkus in 1916 and became his intermediary for Jewish relief work throughout Turkey and later in Palestine.

2 General Enver Pasha, Minister of War; Talat Pasha, Grand Vizier and Minister of the Interior; Djemel Pasha, Minister of Marine.

3 This was the beginning of what came to be known as the Morgenthau mission, about which there will be many subsequent documents. The standard account of this subject is William Yale, "Ambassador Henry Morgenthau's Special Mission of 1917," *World Politics*, I (April 1949), 308-20. See also Laurence Evans, *United States Policy and the Partition of Turkey, 1914-1924* (Baltimore, 1965), pp. 43-45.

From Robert Lansing, with Enclosures

My dear Mr. President: Washington May 17, 1917.

I enclose a telegram of the 16th from William English Walling to Mr. Polk and also two telegrams (No's 1270 and 1288) from Francis which bear on the same subject.

It would seem that certain phrases uttered by you are being used by the radical socialists (probably under German influence) to force the Provisional Government to declare a policy which will remove the chief incentive to Russian offensive operations, namely control of the Dardenelles and possession of Constantinople. It is an adroit scheme to advance argument of what is the use of Russia continuing the war and why should she not make a separate peace, if neither in territory nor in indemnity she can be compensated for the enormous expenditure of life and money which a vigorous prosecution of the war will entail.

It is an insiduous and ingenious plan to win over the Russian people to the idea of a separate peace, which seems to me a very real danger and one that ought to be avoided, if possible.

Cannot some interpretation of the language, which is being used, be given which will remove the idea so industriously circulated in Russia before it has gone too far to counteract the effect?

Of course the only way in which that can be done is by a message from you to Francis for the Russian Government and for publication in Russia. I realize the difficulty of doing this, but the harm which is being done seems to me very great. It may cost this country millions of men if this movement for a separate peace cannot be checked. I feel that every day that the argument remains unanswered increases the peril.

Faithfully yours,   Robert Lansing.

TLS (WP, DLC).

ENCLOSURE I

Greenwich Conn 1917 May 16

Immediate renunciation of no annexations no indemnities program by President may save Russia Nothing else will

William English Walling.

ENCLOSURE II

Petrograd, May 11, 1917.

1270. Confidential for Secretary.

Thomas,[1] *acting* French Ambassador here, tells me he advised his government to reply to Provisional Government's note of May third reiterating statement of April tenth giving ends of war and thinks President Wilson, whom he considers most powerful influence in the world today, should also make reply. I concur because workmen's committee using "peace without victory" and other expressions in the President's address to Senate of January 22nd to justify their advocacy of peace. They do not wish separate peace but desire proletariat of belligerent countries to conclude peace "without annexation or contribution" claiming such is President's position. Provisional Government contends that wrong construction is being placed on President's utterances and believes as I do that noble ends for which he is striving can only be (#) by decisive victory over Germany. I am persistently calling attention to prompt action of congress and liberal subscription to loan as evidence that we mean prosecution of war to victorious ending. Workmen furthermore maintain that existing arrangement[s] between allies were effected on the part of Russia by Government which no longer exists. Thomas suggested conference between representatives here of allied Governments for joint reply to Provisional Government but I discouraged same in absence of definite understanding between ourselves and other countries fighting Germany as such conferences likely to open discussion concerning Dardanelles and possibly Panama Canal to say nothing of problems involving annexation, restitution of territory, and indemnification. Believes reply to Minister for Foreign Affairs[2] from President or yourself would greatly clarify situation.   Francis.

1 Albert Thomas, French Socialist leader and Minister of Munitions, had recently been sent to Russia to improve relations with the provisional government.
2 That is, Miliukov.

ENCLOSURE III

Petrograd, May 14, 1917.

1288. RUSSKO SLAVO, Moscow morning daily, with circulation one million two hundred thousand perhaps the most influential Russian journal, desires statement or interview from the President on the following: First, objects of the war. Second, peace without annexations or contributions. Third, is it possible to treat with the actual German Government. Paper says will ask same questions of Lloyd George, Riband [Ribot and] Italy provided President consents to make reply. If suggestion of Thomas that President reply to Minister for Foreign Affairs made in my 1270 of May eleventh is followed no necessity for such interview. Received note from Thomas May twelfth urging such reply from President. Made unavailing efforts to see Goutchkoff[1] all day. Rumored Minister for Foreign Affairs and Minister of Justice[2] will also resign but not confirmed.   Francis.

T telegrams (WP, DLC).
[1] Aleksandr Ivanovich Guchkov, Minister of War and Navy since March 1917, had just resigned.
[2] Miliukov resigned on May 15 and was succeeded as Foreign Minister by Mikhail Ivanovich Tereshchenko. Aleksandr Fedorovich Kerenskii resigned as Minister of Justice and succeeded Guchkov as Minister of War and Navy.

From George Creel

Dear Mr. President: Washington, D. C. May 17, 1917.

The attached telegram[1] speaks for itself. Mr. Polk also tells me they have suggested a statement from you for one of the Russian papers. In the event that you make it, might I ask a copy so that we may give it to the press of the United States?
                    Sincerely,   George Creel

TLS (WP, DLC).
[1] W. E. Walling to W. B. Wilson, May 16, 1917, T telegram (WP, DLC). Its text was the same as Walling's telegram just printed as Enclosure I with RL to WW, May 17, 1917.

From Edward William Pou

Dear Mr. President: Washington, D. C. May 17, 1917.

I am very glad indeed to know that the efforts of those of us who have been urging the establishment of a Committee on Woman Suffrage have your approval.

The Committee on Rules will hold a hearing on the subject

tomorrow morning at ten o'clock. While I am convinced of the wisdom of favorable action, I doubt very much if a majority of the membership of the Committee on Rules is of like opinion.[1]

Assuring you that any suggestion from you is always welcome, I beg to remain,

Cordially and sincerely yours,   Edwd W. Pou.

TLS (WP, DLC).
[1] The Committee on Rules, on June 6, reported favorably on the resolution to establish a Committee on Woman Suffrage. The House, on September 24, voted, 180 to 107, to establish the committee. *Cong. Record*, 65th Cong., 1st. sess., p. 7384.

From Newton Diehl Baker, with Enclosure

My dear Mr. President: Washington. May 17, 1917.

I return herewith the letter of J. Milton Waldron of May 11.

I was called upon many times by Mr. Waldron and representatives of his committee of one hundred. After considering their request I came to the conclusion that a training camp for colored people ought to be established, and took up with representative colored men the location of such a camp. It has now been definitely fixed at Fort Dubuque, Iowa, with the full concurrence of the authorities of Howard University, Hampton Institute and Tuskegee Institute, all of which educational institutions offered their facilities, but finally realized their lack of adaptation. So far as I know the question is settled wisely from the point of view of the army, and certainly from the point of view of the colored men.

As they have already been notified of the consideration, and concurred in it, it seems likely that no further acknowledgment from you is necessary.

Respectfully yours,   Newton D. Baker

TLS (WP, DLC).

E N C L O S U R E

From John Milton Waldron
and Thomas Montgomery Gregory[1]

Honored Sir: Washington, D. C. May 11, 1917.

The undersigned, representing "The Committee of 100 Colored Citizens on the War," composed of representatives of numerous civic and religious organizations, Howard, Atlanta, Fisk, Lincoln and Virginia Union Universities; Hampton and Tuskegee and other representative schools and colleges are petitioning the War Department to establish a special officers' training camp for the training of Colored officers for the Colored regiments in the New Federal Army. Secretary Baker now has the matter under consideration and has promised a decision this week.

The War Department deemed it in-advisable to admit Colored men to the fourteen regular training camps and suggested a separate camp. Our young men are so anxious to serve their country in this crisis that they are willing to accept a separate camp. Fifteen hundred qualified men have already made application for admission to such a camp and their applications are in the hands of the Secretary of War. Howard University, a government Institution offers the use of its Buildings and grounds for its camp in case other situations are not available.

This opportunity for our representative young men to receive training as officers is not only necessary for the proper efficiency of the army but it is also essential to the active and hearty patriotism of ten million Colored citizens. They stand ready to give themselves and all they possess, to this noble cause to which the nation has dedicated itself but they need the encouragement of a fair opportunity to demonstrate their loyalty on the field both as privates and as officers.

We feel assured that you will sympathize with us in our petition and we most respectfully request you to bring the matter favorably to the attention of Secretary of War Baker before it is finally settled to-morrow.

Assuring you of the united support and loyalty of the Colored race in this great crisis, we have the honor to remain,

Most respectfully yours,

THE COMMITTEE OF 100 CITIZENS ON THE WAR.

J. Milton Waldron,
President

CENTRAL COMMITTEE OF NEGRO COLLEGE MEN
Chairman.
Montgomery Gregory.

TLS (WP, DLC).

[1] Thomas Montgomery Gregory, Harvard 1910, was assistant professor of English at Howard University and a teacher of dramatics. The Central Committee of Negro College Men included students and graduates of Howard, Lincoln, Fisk, Atlanta, Morehouse, Morgan State, Virginia Union, Columbia, Harvard, Yale, and Brown universities and colleges. Rayford W. Logan, *Howard University: The First Hundred Years, 1867-1967* (New York, 1969), pp. 180-83.

From Irving Fisher

My dear President Wilson: New Haven, Conn. May 17, 1917.

At the advice of Secretary Daniels and Admiral Grayson I have been waiting until the Army bill should be out of the way before asking for an appointment with you for myself and the other members of the Sub-Committee on Alcohol under the Council of National Defense.

This time has apparently arrived.

Could you, then, spare us a few moments to present to you in person the arguments which have led us to favor National Prohibition during the war and one year thereafter? Could you see us (with a few others whom we may bring) on the morning of Wednesday, May 23rd, or Thursday, May 24th, or any other day before or after, and any other hour, of which you can notify me by letter or wire a day ahead so that I may get the members together?[1]

The members of the Committee are:

Irving Fisher, Chairman

Dr. Alonzo Taylor, Expert, Department of Agriculture

Dr. Haven Emerson, Health Commissioner, New York City

Dr. Eugene L. Fisk, Medical Director, Life Extension Institute, New York

Charles Stelzle, Authority on relations of alcohol to labor[2]

I have also consulted Congressman Lever and Mr. Hoover both of whom concur in the conclusions of the Committee.

As you know, there has been much backing and filling in Congress on this matter. It will, I believe, be very easy for you to clear the air.   Very sincerely yours,   Irving Fisher

TLS (WP, DLC).

[1] Wilson received the committee on the afternoon of May 23.

[2] Irving Fisher, Professor of Political Economy at Yale University and president of the Committee of Sixty on National Prohibition; Alonzo Englebert Taylor, M.D., distinguished pathologist, at this time assistant to the Secretary of Agriculture; Haven Emerson, M.D., president of the Board of Health and Commissioner of the Department of Health, New York City; Eugene Lyman Fisk, M.D., Medical Director of the Life Extension Institute and author of *Alcohol: Its Relation to Human Efficiency and Longevity* (New York, 1917); and the Rev. Charles Stelzle, Presbyterian leader in the social-gospel movement and, at this time, field secretary of the Federal Council of Churches of Christ in America.

From James Thomas Heflin

My dear Mr. President: Washington, D. C. May 17, 1917.

You have been misquoted or misunderstood, I am sure, in regard to what you said to the Red Cross ladies a few nights ago. Representative Hill, of Connecticut,[1] and others are quoting you as saying that "we have no special grievance against Germany, etc.," and that you said "we are fighting to establish world Democracy."

I am sure that the first of these statements does not represent your views on the war with Germany and I know that you will agree with me that the circulation of such a report of your speech will do harm.

I will thank you to write me a note, explaining the matter so that I can read it on the floor of the House.

With best wishes, I am,

Yours sincerely,　J. Thos. Heflin.

TLS (WP, DLC).
　[1] That is, Ebenezer J. Hill, Republican.

From Theodore Roosevelt

Oyster Bay, New York, May 18, 1917.

I respectfully ask permission immediately to raise two divisions for immediate service at the front under the bill which has just become law and hold myself ready to raise four divisions if you so direct. I respectfully refer for details to my last letters to the Secretary of War. If granted permission I earnestly ask that Captain Frank McCoy be directed to report to me at once. Minister Fletcher has written me that he is willing. Also if permission to raise the divisions is granted I would like to come to Washington as soon as the War Department is willing so that I may find what supplies are available and at once direct the regular officers who are chosen for brigade and regimental command how and where to get to work.

Theodore Roosevelt.

T telegram (WP, DLC).

A Statement

[May 18, 1917]

I shall not avail myself, at any rate at the present stage of the war, of the authorization conferred by the act to organize volunteer divisions. To do so would seriously interfere with the carrying out of the chief and most immediately important purpose contemplated by this legislation, the prompt creation and early use of an effective army, and would contribute practically nothing to the effective strength of the armies now engaged against Germany.

I understand that the section of this act which authorizes the creation of volunteer divisions in addition to the draft was added with a view to providing an independent command for Mr. Roosevelt and giving the military authority an opportunity to use his fine vigor and enthusiasm in recruiting forces now at the Western front.

It would be very agreeable to me to pay Mr. Roosevelt this compliment and the Allies the compliment of sending to their aid one of our most distinguished public men, an ex-President who has rendered many conspicuous public services and proved his gallantry in many striking ways. Politically, too, it would no doubt have a very fine effect and make a profound impression. But this is not the time or the occasion for compliment or for any action not calculated to contribute to the immediate success of the war. The business now in hand is undramatic, practical, and of scientific definiteness and precision. I shall act with regard to it at every step and in every particular under expert and professional advice from both sides of the water.

That advice is that the men most needed are men of the ages contemplated in the draft provision of the present bill, not men of the age and sort contemplated in the section which authorizes the formation of volunteer units, and that for the preliminary training of the men who are to be drafted we shall need all of our experienced officers. Mr. Roosevelt told me, when I had the pleasure of seeing him a few weeks ago, that he would wish to have associated with him some of the most effective officers of the regular army. He named many of those whom he would desire to have designated for the service, and they were men who cannot possibly be spared from the too small force of officers at our command for the much more pressing and necessary duty of training regular troops to be put into the field in France and Belgium as fast as they can be got ready.

The first troops sent to France will be taken from the present forces of the regular army, and will be under the command of trained soldiers only.

The responsibility for the successful conduct of our own part in this great war rests upon me. I could not escape it if I would. I am too much interested in the cause we are fighting for to be interested in anything but success. The issues involved are too immense for me to take into consideration anything whatever except the best, most effective, most immediate means of military action. What these means are I know from the mouths of men who have seen war as it is now conducted, who have no illusions, and to whom [the whole][1] grim matter is a matter of business. I shall centre my attention upon those means and let everything else wait.

I should be deeply to blame should I do otherwise, whatever the argument of policy for a personal gratification or advantage.

Printed in the *New York Times*, May 19, 1917.
 1 Added from the T transcript (WC, NjP) of Wilson's shorthand draft of this statement in WP, DLC.

To George Creel

My dear Creel: The White House 18 May, 1917

Thank you for your letter of yesterday. I dare say that I shall attempt some statement to correct the misapprehension apparently existing in Russia, but it is the opinion of the Secretary of State, and I dare say he is right, that I should communicate the statement direct to our Ambassador in Petrograd and let him make it public there. I will, of course, furnish you with a copy with the suggestion that it be withheld from publication until the date of its probable arrival in Petrograd, or until after it has been acknowledged by Mr. Francis.

Cordially and sincerely yours,   Woodrow Wilson

TLS (G. Creel Papers, DLC).

To James Thomas Heflin

My dear Heflin: [The White House] 18 May, 1917

I am sorry that any misunderstanding should have arisen as to the meaning of what I said at the Red Cross the other day. I thought the meaning was obvious. I meant merely that we were not making war against Germany because of any special and peculiar grievance of our own but because her actions had become intolerable to us as to the rest of free mankind and, therefore, we had found it necessary to make common cause against her. Of course, our own people have suffered grieviously at her hands. It would certainly be a most extraordinary interpretation of my meaning to read it otherwise.

Cordially and sincerely yours,   Woodrow Wilson

TLS (Letterpress Books, WP, DLC).

Leading the parade in honor of the men drafted in the District of Columbia

General Pershing arriving in Boulogne, France, June 13, 1917

Arthur James Balfour and Robert Lansing

Admiral William S. Sims

George Creel

Stockton Axson

Raymond B. Fosdick

Alexander F. Kerensky

To Robert Ferdinand Wagner

My dear Senator Wagner: [The White House] 18 May, 1917

I was extremely sorry that I did not have the pleasure of meeting the committee[1] which conveyed to me the admirable patriotic resolutions adopted by the Tammany Society. I should have liked to express to them in person, as I now wish to express in this acknowledgment, my very deep sense of the admirable spirit of patriotism and cooperation manifested by these unusual resolutions. May I not beg that, if an opportunity occurs, this expression of my appreciation may be conveyed in very warm and sincere terms to the members of the organization?   Sincerely yours,   Woodrow Wilson

TLS (Letterpress Books, WP, DLC).

[1] Wagner was chairman of a committee of five Tammany leaders who had called upon Wilson to present copies of resolutions adopted by the New York Democratic County Committee and the Tammany Society on April 25 which pledged support for Wilson's war program.

From Arthur James Balfour, with Enclosure

Dear Mr. President,   Washington. 18th May, 1917.

I beg now to fulfil, though in somewhat belated fashion, my promise to send you the text of the various Agreements which Great Britain has come to with the Allied Powers.[1] I found that we had not copies with us and it has taken some time to obtain them from England.

I do not think that they will add much to the knowledge which you already possess of our negotiations since the War began, nor do I think they are likely to modify your general views.

Perhaps it might also interest you to read the enclosed note, which gives the main points of a statement which I made on foreign policy to the Imperial War Council.[2] The proceedings of the Imperial War Council are of course absolutely secret. I feel that many of the problems dealt with are inadequately treated, but I trust that you may find it of some value.

Pray believe me, dear Mr. President,

    Yours very sincerely,   Arthur James Balfour

TLS (WP, DLC).

[1] Balfour enclosed the following printed texts, but he did not include any of the Allied treaties with Japan relating to the postwar settlement in the Far East:

Treaty Series. 1915. No. 1. Declaration between the United Kingdom, France, and Russia, Engaging Not To Conclude Peace Separately during the Present European War. Signed at London, September 5, 1914. Cd. 7737.

Treaty Series. 1915. No. 9. Exchange of Notes Respecting the Accession of Japan to the Declaration of September 5, 1914, between the United Kingdom, France, and Russia, Engaging Not To Conclude Peace Separately during the Present European War. London, October 19, 1915. Cd. 8014.

Treaty Series. 1915. No. 14. Declaration between the United Kingdom, France, Italy, Japan, and Russia Engaging Not To Conclude Peace Separately during the Present War. Signed at London, November 30, 1915. Cd. 8107.

Agreement between the Three Powers and Italy. Secret. Printed for the War Cabinet. April 1917.

Sir G. Barclay to Viscount Grey. Received September 6. [A letter to transmit the "Political Agreement and the Military Convention" signed on Aug. 17, 1916, at Bucharest by representatives of the British, French, Italian, Russian, and Rumanian governments.]

Télégramme circulaire russe du 4 mars, 1915, au sujet de Constantinople et des Détroits, Pétrograde, le 4 mars, 1915. Aide-mémoire communicated to Russian Government, Petrograd, March 12, 1915. Memorandum, Petrograd, March 12, 1915. Note verbale remise par M. Paléologue à son Excellence M. Sazonof, le 12 avril, 1915, en réponse au précédent.

Memorandum Communicated by Sir M. Sykes, May 8, 1916. Secret. [It transmitted the texts of letters exchanged on April 26, 1916, between Sergei Dmitrievich Sazonov, the Russian Minister of Foreign Affairs, and Maurice Paléologue, the French Ambassador to Russia, concerning the "Arab question."]

M. Cambon to Sir Edward Grey. May 9, 1916. [A letter to confirm the agreement reached by Sir Mark Sykes and Georges Picot on the "Arab question."]

Sir Edward Grey to M. Cambon. Secret. May 15, 1916. [A letter to propose mutual assurances of each other's rights in the Arab regions which were to become British or French.]

M. Cambon to Sir Edward Grey. May 15, 1916. [A letter to accept the terms outlined in Grey's letter of the same date.]

Sir Edward Grey to M. Cambon. Secret. May 16, 1916. [A letter to set forth terms of agreement between the French and British governments on the "Arab question."]

Sir Edward Grey to Count Benckendorff. Secret. May 23, 1916. [A letter concerning agreement on the annexation of certain Ottoman territories by Russia.]

M. Cambon to Viscount Grey. August 25, 1916. [A letter to clarify certain terms in the letters exchanged on May 9 and 16, 1916.]

The Marquess of Crewe to M. Cambon. August 30, 1916. [A letter to accept the proposal in Cambon's letter of Aug. 25, 1916.]

Count Benckendorff to Viscount Grey. September 1, 1916. [A letter to accept the agreement proposed in Grey's letter of May 23, 1916, with a reservation concerning Russian rights of coastal navigation in the Black Sea.]

Viscount Grey to Count Benckendorff. October 23, 1916. [A letter to take note of the reservation contained in Benckendorff's letter of Sept. 1, 1916.]

2 That is, the Imperial War Cabinet, which began its meetings in Downing Street on March 20, 1917. The Imperial War Conference met more or less concurrently at the Colonial Office. For accounts of the two groups, see Lord Hankey (Maurice Pascal Alers Hankey), *The Supreme Command, 1914-1918* (2 vols., London, 1961), II, 657-63, and Stephen Roskill, *Hankey: Man of Secrets* (3 vols., London, 1970-74), I, 365-79.

E N C L O S U R E

Confidential: [March 22, 1917]

THE PRIME MINISTER. I will now ask Mr. Balfour to give his statement on Foreign Policy.

MR. BALFOUR. I do not think it is necessary really for me to say much about either of the two important foreign countries, America and Russia, at this moment, because about America some of the gentlemen here have more direct knowledge than is possessed by the Foreign Office. The Canadian representatives have a knowledge of America which we hardly possess, while as regards Russia we have already discussed the situation, and I think the Cabinet understands it as well as anybody can understand this rapidly moving cinematograph of Russian politics. The real thing that is important to us I think is to know whether, if, as we hope, the reasonable and moderate reformers win, they will be able successfully to administer the country. If you look back upon Russian history you will see that every great movement of reform has come when the administrative inefficiency of the autocracy has been followed by some great calamity. The Crimean War, which broke the heart of Nicholas I, was immediately followed by the greatest of all revolutions, the freeing of the serfs, and other great legal reforms of the early reign of Alexander II. The calamity of the Japanese War was followed by the establishment of the Duma, and the administrative disgraces of the present war are followed by the revolution which is now going on before our eyes. But we have to notice that while the general feeling of disgust and discontent with the inefficiency of the autocracy has always been able to produce these reforms, we have never had the opportunity of seeing whether the democracy will be able to do what the autocracy utterly failed to do, which is to administer this enormous country and to organize it for purposes either of war or peace. The total failure of the autocracy is amazing if you look back, and my fear is whether these new people will do so much better than the old. In Russia there is no middle class. Corruption has eaten deeply into their vitals and we must not hope for too much. It seems certain, however, that they cannot do worse than their predecessors. I think that is quite clear.

The Central Powers, as we all know, have an enormous military advantage over us in their central position. They have a corresponding advantage from the point of view of their aims. Germany dominates the aims of the whole of the coalition against us, but none of the other Powers have aims which are inconsistent or even divergent from those of Germany. Austria, for example, has, or had, in the earlier days of the War, nothing except to gain by German successes. Germany's desire to press on in the East was not only good for Germany but for Austria. Turkey, of course, was promised hegemony in the farther East, which certainly, when it came to the point, Germany would never have allowed her to exercise. But Turkey felt that her objects were identical with Germany, so there has been not only a central direction but a central motive. Now we and our Allies, on the other hand, are not only not contiguous with each other, but we are as widely separated as we well can be. Our most important Ally, next to France, is Russia, and we cannot get at Russia. Even to take away a single individual or a single mission from Russia is a matter which the Admiralty has seriously to consider, and steps for which they have to work out with the utmost caution. Japan is at the extreme end of the world, we are separated geographically; but there is a much more important separation, and that is the separation of temperament, and the separation of history and tradition. It is really an extraordinary thing on which to reflect that of the five Great Powers now fighting on the Entente side, Japan and Russia were in death grips about ten or eleven years ago. France and England were on the edge of war more than once, and on more than one subject, until the Entente arrangement was finally made in the year 1904. Italy was actually joined by treaty with the Central Powers as a counterpoise to France and Russia, whilst we and Russia were regarded as almost traditional enemies. I remember quite well in the first days of the Committee of Imperial Defence, which started in the year I think 1902 or 1903, we worked out the many problems with which the Empire was then faced. What were they? How to prevent Russia getting to India and how to deal with a war with France. That was twelve or more years ago. Now the change which has been brought about largely by German ambition backed by German diplomacy, which is the worst diplomacy in the world, has welded all those nations into one coalition determined to put down this world tyranny. We have to accept the fact that residues of the old condition of things must to a certain extent remain, and one of the diplomatic troubles which we have to deal with for example, is the eternal jealousy between Italy and France. It is curious that these two Latin nations, one of which owes so much to the other because, without France, Italy would hardly have gained her unity, in spite of that they cannot get on with each other. We are the link between the two. I think if you were to ask the First Lord of the Admiralty,[1] he would tell you that one of our difficulties in the Adriatic is that the French will not work under the Italians. We ourselves are quite ready to do so. We have sent ships to help them and our ships work under an Italian Admiral; but the French will not do this. In the Eastern Mediterranean there is jealousy at this moment which is hampering our diplomacy, I do not say in a serious way, but it is vexatious and irritating. Greece, which is the scandal of contemporary diplomacy, is a

---

[1] Sir Edward Carson.

scandal because three nations—the French, the English and the Italians—are trying to manage her, all of whom have divergent views. The Italians detest M. Venizelos—I do not know why—but they appear to think that under M. Venizelos Greece might attain to a position of influence in the Aegean Sea, which is inimical to the ambitions of Italy. Merely as a characteristic mark of what is going on, the Italians have been sending troops to Corfu, but nobody knows why. We cannot get any explanation. The French say, "Cannot you send even a corporal's guard so that the British flag may be hoisted there as well as the French, the Greek and the Italian." Broadly speaking, however, everything is working well with the exception of these little elements of discord, which are very vexatious to the Foreign Office but which I hope will not profoundly modify the general course of the War.

I do not want to go at length into the question of Japan because that is too large, but perhaps I ought to say a little about it. The great Dominions and the United States of America are naturally, and I think rightly, jealous of Japan's obtaining any footing within their territories. Japan, on the other hand, at present quite genuinely believes that what has been the sheet anchor of her policy for the last twelve years, namely, the British alliance, is still the sheet anchor of her present policy and they still cling to that. Of course, we are talking quite privately and I do not think we can conceal from ourselves that there is in every quarter of the Eastern world a certain uneasiness as to whether Japan is in the future going to try and play the part in those regions which Prussia has played in Europe,—whether she is not going to aim at some kind of domination. That fear hangs over the world. I do not venture to give any opinion on that at all. Lord Grey held the view that if you are going to keep Japan out of North America, out of Canada, out of the United States, out of Australia, out of New Zealand, out of the islands South of the Equator in the Pacific, you could not forbid her to expand in China. A nation of that sort must have a safety valve somewhere, and although I think Lord Grey carried his doctrine to excess, I think there is something in it. I do not, however, propose to touch further on this question.

As regards the War in the immediate future, I have myself no doubt that Japan, with an eye to her own interests, is quite genuinely helping the Allies, and helping the Allies to the best of her ability. She is making money, unlike the rest of us, she is going well: but I do not think we ought to underrate the services she has given or the services she is giving, and the present administration so far as I can judge is incomparably more reasonable in its Chinese policy than the ministry which immediately preceded it. They are making great professions of leaving China to work out her own salvation. Whether these professions will be carried out to the full remains to be seen, but certainly I have not observed anything at present which ought to inspire us with suspicion. I do not believe suspicion is well placed. The only reason for which I mention that is I am told that at this moment the Germans still have hopes of detaching Japan. That telegram which was sent to Mexico and which produced all that excitement, you remember, suggested that Mexico should act as an intermediary between Japan and Germany. I do not know whether you have that in your minds. The plan was to bring in Japan on the German side. I believe that was one of Germany's extraordinary blunders which she is always making, and I do not myself look forward with the least apprehension to anything that Japan is likely to do during the course of the War.

If I turn from these considerations, which affect the Allies, to the diplomatic relations between the Allies and the Central Powers other than the immediate military relations between the Allies and the Central Powers, the most important question is,—are the Terms of Peace to which we are committed of a kind which are unnecessarily going to prolong the War? There is no doubt that Germany, as we have heard today, is in very great peril. How are they keeping up the spirits of their people? They are keeping them up in two ways. They are saying in the first place that England will succumb under the submarine warfare. They are saying in the second place, "You must go on fighting at whatever sacrifice, because, if you do not win, our enemies are determined not merely to beat us but to destroy us"; and every nation worth anything, of course, will fight to the last crust of bread and to the last cartridge, if its actual destruction is going to be the result of an unsuccessful war.

The practical destruction of the Turkish Empire is undoubtedly one of the objects which we desire to attain. The Turks may well be left—I hope they will be left—in a more or less independent position in Asia Minor. If we are successful unquestionably Turkey will be deprived of all that in the larger sense may be called Arabia; she will be deprived of the most important portions of the Valley of the Euphrates and the Tigris; she will lose Constantinople; and Syria, Armenia and the southern parts of Asia Minor will, if not annexed by the Entente Powers, probably fall more or less under their domination.

If we turn from Turkey, however, to Austria, the position is somewhat different. According to rumours, which you must all have heard, Austria is so exhausted that she would desire to have a separate peace; but, again, one of the difficulties about a separate peace is what, by the terms as interpreted in our Note to President Wilson, will be left of Austria if we do make a separate peace? We have entered into treaties with Italy, Roumania and Serbia, all of which affect Austrian territory. Italy, who came into the war in April, I think it was, of 1915, opened her mouth rather widely: that is Italy's way; and she not only got the Allies to promise her *Italia Irredenta*, the populations bordering upon her frontier, who are of Italian origin, speak Italian and possess Italian culture, but she asked also for parts of Dalmatia which neither ethnologically nor for any other valid reason can be regarded as a natural part of Italy. Her justification, however, was not ethnological, it was purely military, or rather, naval. Italy is very unfortunately situated in the Adriatic; she possesses the whole of the western seaboard of that sea, but along her coasts from Venice to Brindisi there really is nothing which deserves to be called a harbour at all. But opposite, threatening her, within easy striking distance and within a few hours' steam, there is the coast of Dalmatia with its islands and its harbours contrived by nature to suit modern submarine warfare, and it is most natural that Italy should say: We should like, in our own interests and for our own protection, to possess this coast. Except from that military point of view I am not aware that it is easy to justify handing over the Dalmatian coast, which is not Italian, to Italy. But there it is, it is in the Treaty to which we are bound. We, the French, the Russians and the Italians, are bound to each other never to make peace without the other, and among the conditions which we have mutually promised are these cessions of territory which so far as Italy is concerned I have just described.

If you turn to Serbia, we promised Serbia Bosnia and Herzegovina, and I think that it is a most legitimate promise. They are of the same race, of the same language, and of the same religion. They are not old provinces of Austria; they were Turkish provinces up to the Treaty of 1878 in the full sense of the word, and after 1878 until 1908 when Austria broke through the Treaty of Berlin they were still Turkish provinces in name, though not in administration or in any other substantial sense. Still, they are not old provinces of Austria and if Austria lost them nobody could say that Austria was destroyed. If you go a little further north and ask how you are going to treat the Slav population which also speaks the same form of Slav language, the

Croat and other Slav communities to the south of the Danube, you undoubtedly are going to make a great breach in the traditional Austrian Empire. But I am not aware that we are by treaty bound in any sense to do that.

THE PRIME MINISTER: The promise to Serbia was conditional.

SIR ROBERT BORDEN: Did we promise anything more than Bosnia and Herzegovina?

MR. BALFOUR: We promised an outlet to the Adriatic.

THE PRIME MINISTER: We wanted Serbia to give up a certain portion of Macedonia to Bulgaria, and then we said, if you do this when the settlement comes we will give you these provinces the populations of which are more or less akin to your own. If the war is won by the Allies then we will give you access to the Adriatic.

MR. BALFOUR. I do not see that so far as Italy and Serbia are concerned it can be said that even if we had the sort of peace we liked it could be said that we had destroyed Austria, certainly not historic Austria, the Austria of the 18th century, in any sense of the word at all.

When you come to our promises to Roumania and our promises in connection with Poland, in connection with which I shall speak presently, the case is different. We promised Roumania, if she came in, that that part of Hungary which is predominantly Roumanian in race and in language should be handed over to Roumania. There are people who say that there are Roumanians in Hungary who do not wish to be handed over to Roumania. I do not know whether that is true or not; I should doubt it. But at all events it is undeniable that to take away the Roumanian part of Hungary, namely Transylvania, and hand that to Roumania is to break up historic Hungary. That does touch the historic kingdom of Hungary.

As regards another historic Kingdom with an important past, Bohemia. Bohemia is predominantly Slav in language and in civilization. It differs of course from the Southern Slavs, from the Serbs, for instance, in being Roman Catholic in religion and in speaking a language of a variety of Slav which is very different from that spoken by their brothers further South. It has a history and a tradition of its own. It has been quite abominably used by Austria in this war. If all accounts are true Bohemia has a hatred of German civilization and German propaganda which is intense and I think inextinguishable. Whether, however, all those feelings could not be adequately satisfied by giving Bohemia some form of autonomy in the Austria Empire I am not so clear. I happened to meet a few months before his assassination with the poor man who was the beginning of all our troubles. He was then heir to the Austrian Throne, and he had a view that the only way to keep Austria together was to make it a triple State instead of a dual State.

At present it is a dual State which is the AustroHungarian Empire. He wanted to make a third element in the Empire, namely a Southern Slav. It seems to me that if you made it a quadruple Empire and gave Bohemia autonomy, it would be a very curious construction, but not more curious than Austria has been through all these centuries and it might really meet the views of the populations without absolutely destroying Austria as history knows it. But I am afraid that does not touch the Roumanian difficulty. I do not see any way out of that at present.

With regard to Poland, I do not think you can call the Polish part of Austria—in fact, it would be absurd to call it a part of historic Austria; it became Austrian because Frederick the Great, Catherine II, and Maria Theresa chose to cut up Poland and divide it among themselves. Galicia is not part of historic Austria, and might and ought to go to the Poland of the future. But what is the Poland of the future? That, I think is now, as it has been ever since the great crime of partition was accomplished, the greatest crux of European diplomacy. A very distinguished Pole came to see me yesterday, whose name I will not even venture to pronounce, (Lord R. Cecil: Mr. Dmowski) but he is a man of very high character and great position. He is an ardent advocate for a completely independent Poland which should include all the Poles. But, I asked him: "What relations does the Poland that you desire, the Polish Poland that you desire created, bear to the Poland of 1772, the year of the first partition?" "Well," he said, "I quite agree you cannot precisely follow those old frontiers." Part of what was then Poland is more Russian than Polish—the Eastern part of it—and we could not ask that it should be taken from Russia and handed over to Poland. On the other hand, there is a part of Upper Silesia which had been taken from ancient Poland before the partition; Frederick the Great, in fact, took it from Austria. "That," he said, "is quite genuinely Polish." I think, he said, 80% of the inhabitants of the Polish area of Silesia were Poles by birth and Poles by language; and in his view that ought to be added to Poland. Then I said to him, "Well, what about Dantzig?" Dantzig, as you will remember, is one of the old Hanseatic towns, and undoubtedly, subject to its municipal independence, it was part of the Polish kingdom. But I suspect, myself, it has been practically German for many centuries; it is certainly predominantly German at this moment. The country immediately around it, or a great deal of the country in its immediate neighbourhood, is just as Polish as other parts of Poland; at any rate, more than 50% are Poles. But here comes the difficulty. He said, without Dantzig, Poland is impossible. Dantzig is the one outlet, the one adequate outlet to the sea, which the restored Poland would have, and unless you are prepared to give back Dantzig to Poland it is useless to try and create a really flourishing modern State. Of course, you will remember Dantzig belonged to Poland at the time of the Partition. In fact, it belonged to Poland after the first Partition. Frederick the Great was content not to take it at that time because he said, with great truth, that "Anybody who has the Vistula, or the upper waters of the Vistula, will become in time the owner of Dantzig"; as indeed he did become; but still, I think everybody must admit that to take away Dantzig from Germany would be to deprive Germany of a town which is predominantly German; but if you have the map in your mind, it cuts off Konigsberg, and all East Prussia from the rest of the Prussian State, and therefore undoubtedly that is a thing which would touch German emotions and German interests very quickly. Konigsberg and East Prussia would become a kind of enclave, separate from Germany, but remaining German, embedded in a Polish and Russian framework. The difficulties of that are very great, but you see you are in a dilemma, according to my friend, whether Poland is absolutely independent, as he desires, or whether it becomes an autonomous State, bound more or less closely to Russia. However that may be, whether you include Dantzig or not, any idea to make a Poland which does not include Posen is, in his view, destroying Poland. On the other hand, Posen is, at present, a very integral part of Germany, and Germany, no doubt, would feel that if Posen were taken by a Power which was potentially a great power it would bring it very close up to the gates of Berlin. And yet, supposing we are successful, can we allow this war to come to an end without doing something substantially to get rid of the Polish scandal? It is true that Poland brought it upon herself. If Poland had understood the elements of reasonably good government, the idea that she could be partitioned like an inert mass, as she was, is out of the question. But that is in the past, and it is quite possible that the Poland of the future will be a useful member of the European community; but until she is satisfied you will have this nucleus of bitter discontent, and a nation going back to great and glorious memories, when it was the most powerful State in Eastern Europe. I frankly admit that when the Germans say that we are fighting for a cause which means their destruction, it is not true in one sense; we are not destroying a German Germany, but we are trying to destroy the rather artificial creation of the modern Prussia, which includes many Slav elements which never belonged to Germany until about 140 years ago, and ought, really, not to belong to Germany at this moment.

I am afraid I am merely stating difficulties; I am sorry to say I am not solving them. If we are not successful in the war, there is no hope of solving them. If the war is a drawn battle, these great causes, I am afraid, will never be satisfactory dealt with by us. If we win triumphantly, then we shall be able to deal with them. Let me return for a moment to my Polish friend. He urged me very strongly to make a public appeal now on behalf of Poland. "Now," said he, "that the Tsar has gone, the Entente Nations ought to announce publicly that they are going to establish an independent Poland; and if you do not do that," he said, "there is great danger that the Germans may succeed in the future in doing what they have failed to do in the past, which is to raise a Polish army."

His view was, that the recruiting of this Polish army had largely failed because the magnates whether ecclesiastical or lay in Poland had taken the oath of allegiance to the Tsar and were not prepared to break it. The Tsar has gone, the oath has gone, and he declared that his view was that the constant pressure of Germany, after this particular doubt had been removed, might succeed in producing this great addition to her man-power. If it did, the effect upon the Allied cause would undoubtedly be more serious. He put the numbers down at between 700,000 and 1,000,000. Supposing Poland came in, in that way, on the side of the Central Powers, and supposing Russia fell into disorganization and military chaos, the whole of the position in the East would be changed disastrously for the worse. Whether we are in a position to proclaim our intentions with regard to Poland and whether, if we did, it would have the effect which he says, I do not know; I think, very likely, it would. I put this question to him: "The Tsar has gone, and with the Tsar one obstacle may have gone, but can you ask this new Russian Government to begin its career by handing over what the Russians regard as an indisputable part of their territory?" He seemed to think it would be possible. I confess I have my doubts. I am sending an account of this conversation to Sir George Buchanan[2] and I shall be interested to hear what he says about it.

2 Sir George William Buchanan, British Ambassador to Russia.

Personally, from a selfish Western point of view, I would rather that Poland was autonomous under the Russians, because if you make an absolutely independent Poland, lying between Russia and the Central States, you cut off Russia altogether from the West. Russia ceases to be a factor in Western politics, or almost ceases. She will be largely divided from Austria by Roumania. She will be divided from Germany by the new Polish State; and she will not be coterminous with any of the belligerents. And if Germany has designs in the future upon France or the West, I think she will be protected by this new State from any action on the part of Russia, and I am not at all sure that that is to the interests of Western civilization. It is a problem which has greatly exercised my mind, and for which I do not see a clear solution. These are disjointed observations in regard to Poland; they lead to no clear-cut recommendation on my part. I am not pleading for a cause; I am trying to lay before the Cabinet the various elements in the problem as they strike me.

The next branch of the subject on which I have anything to say is the smaller neutrals.

SIR ROBERT BORDEN: "Is there any point about Belgium?

MR. BALFOUR: With regard to Belgium, I think I can very shortly describe the position to the Cabinet. It is more an economic than a diplomatic problem. I take it, that whatever we fight for, we fight for the restoration of Belgium to her old limits and her old condition of independence and prosperity. The Belgian Minister[3] has more than once been to see me and has put to me this problem. He says: "All of us, every nation, will, after the War, have to face a whole series of new and difficult questions, social, economic, military; the upsetting of everything is so complete, that there is not a nation in the world that will not have to face a new set of things, and do their very best to solve the problem raised." All that is true of Belgium. But what is true of Belgium is true to some extent of no other country. Unless the Allies will, while the war is going on, make preparation to help Belgium, when peace comes, even though its independence be restored and its old frontiers established, she will be left derelict; it is an industrial community, thickly populated, depending for its very livelihood and bread for its people upon mining and upon manufactures. The Germans have not only over-run the country, but they have taken away all the machinery, all the raw material, they have practically taken

---

[3] Paul Hymans, Belgian Minister to the United Kingdom.

away everything for the carrying on of the elementary economic effort of the country, and it is impossible for Belgium to make itself again a going concern unless the Allies are prepared at the moment of peace, at the first moment possible, to pour in the raw material, to supply the machinery to make Belgium, in other words, something like what it was before the Germans overwhelmed it. I have no answer to that: I believe what he said is perfectly true, and I believe the appeal which the Belgian Minister makes to the Allies is one which ought to be considered. We are overwhelmed with work; my office can do nothing; I am not sure what [my] office ought to do it. So great is the pressure that I have not had time to put this case before the Prime Minister and our smaller Cabinet. I only circulated an account of my conversation with the Belgian Minister, but the question must be raised and it must be faced. I think it is one of the most important things, outside the war itself, but how it is to be done, other Ministers and other Departments must say.

SIR JOSEPH WARD:[4] In regard to that restoration of machinery, do you mean prior to the re-building of the devastated Belgium?

MR. BALFOUR: I think we ought to be ready to pour it into the country if we can.

THE PRIME MINISTER: It is impossible for the simple reason that all our available manufacturing capacity is put to urgent war work. If we have anything to spare, we put it into agricultural work.

MR. BALFOUR: Perhaps I should add that in my view, the notion which is going through the German mind that they can restore Belgian independence enough to satisfy the world, and yet keep a grip upon Belgian economic life and Belgian ports, I regard as absolutely inadmissable. I think that is almost as bad as annexing Belgium, and I would fight against it to the last drop of my blood. I do not think that is arguable.

As regards the Neutrals—the small Neutrals I mean—Sweden and Royalist Greece, which must be regarded as more or less hostile; Spain and Holland, which I think are friendly, but more doubtful, Norway and Denmark, which are certainly very weak, especially Denmark—there is a great deal of important diplomatic work and Foreign Office work done with these countries; but most of that work really belongs to my colleague, the Minister of Blockade,[5] and measured by telegrams it is far greater,

---

[4] Sir Joseph George Ward, representative for New Zealand in the Imperial War Cabinet.

[5] Lord Robert Cecil.

I believe, than that of all the other Offices of State put together; but he will make a statement upon the subject. I do not believe I have anything more to say except this one observation.

MR. AUSTEN CHAMBERLAIN: Are you going to say anything more about German aims in the Middle East and their consequence to us?

MR. BALFOUR: I feel intensely upon that question. It was referred to, I think, by the Prime Minister in his statement the day before yesterday,[6] but I am quite ready to say something about it if you think it desirable. This War has been described, and quite accurately I think, as a war against the world domination of Germany, but I think that Germany after all was not equally anxious to have world domination in every direction at one and the same time. What Germany wanted to do was not to make every country equally subservient to her economic designs; I think her economic ambitions in these later years were largely directed, not, of course, wholly, but largely directed to developing the communications between Germany, through Austria, through subordinate States like Bulgaria and Turkey to the Persian Gulf and ultimately to India and the Far East. All the German literature of the last ten years is full of these dreams. Germany has borrowed a great deal from Napoleon, almost always the worst things of Napoleon's. These are the dreams and they have eaten very deeply into the social imagination of the whole community. They picture to themselves Asia Minor, the Valleys of the Euphrates and the Tigris and beyond, India and the East; they picture that as a happy field where German enterprise can reign undisturbed. They found Great Britain and the United States had got before them in entirely new countries. South America they were nibbling at, but they had never made up their minds to deal with it. But they thought they had a really fair field in these Oriental regions, and I believe that it was within their power to do it. I believe that if they were successful in this war, they would do it and that their success would undoubtedly adversely affect the British Empire. I will not say the British Empire would fall, I do not think it would, but it would have a very severe struggle for existence and the whole balance of the world's trade and the world's power would be altered. The Dominions like Australia and New Zealand would be in an entirely different position from what they are now. India would be in an entirely different position from what it is now, and I am not at all sure that among the dangers of German

---

[6] It is printed in *War Memoirs of David Lloyd George* (6 vols., Boston, 1933-36), IV, 37-52.

domination, which every country has to fear, the particular dangers that arise through their being able to establish an unbroken avenue of influence from the North Sea to the Persian Gulf is not the greatest of all. I think whatever else happens in the war, that recent events have upset that dream, and I do not think that things could possibly go so badly that Germany could piece together the scattered fragments of this structure which they are striving to complete. In that particular I think we have been successful. I wish I could feel that our success was as complete in other fields of operations and that we could look forward with equal confidence to breaking the designs of Germany in Europe as I hope we have been now in breaking her designs in Turkey and the Middle East generally.

MR. MASSEY:[7] Can you tell us anything with regard to the French provinces of Alsace and Lorraine?

MR. BALFOUR: The importance of Alsace and Lorraine is two-fold. In the first place, if we could transfer them back to France we should, I think, do something to improve the equilibrium of Europe. You would remove a population which does not wish to be under Germany to France which it does wish to be under. You would further increase the population of France relative to the population of Germany, which undoubtedly must make for the equilibrium of Europe, and because it makes for the equilibrium of Europe, makes also for the peace of the world. Then there is another point. Since Alsace and Lorraine were taken by Germany, means have been found to utilise the great iron deposits of Lorraine to an extent which makes them a very formidable adjunct to Germany's industrial power. I frankly admit that I should very much like to see these great fields of industrial enterprise restored to their original owners. Germany's strength in coal and steel is an absolutely new phenomenon, you must remember, since the war of 1870, and it is one of the most formidable factors in her success in this War.

THE PRIME MINISTER: And it is one you cannot touch by the Blockade.

MR. BALFOUR: I was told that when the war broke out, Germany had a greater power of producing munitions at the moment than the whole of the rest of the world put together. She owed that, of course, partly to her desire to be prepared in a military sense, but partly to these enormous resources which she has developed since 1870, of which the iron and coal fields west of the Rhine are an important part and, therefore, from that point of view as well as from the more strictly political and diplomatic

7 William Ferguson Massey, Prime Minister of New Zealand.

point of view, I should be most desirous to see Alsace and Lorraine restored to France. I am told that the French are not so eager about them as they were. Or let me put it rather differently; I am told that the war-weariness in certain sections of French society in consequence of their terrific losses and the general burdens which the war has thrown upon them are so great that if they could get an honourable peace, even without Alsace and Lorraine, or even a small fragment of Alsace and Lorraine, they might be content to take it. I should be very disappointed if this War ends without the complete restoration of the ancient frontiers of France.

The only other thing I have to say is that German atrocities have really had an important diplomatic effect. I think that when Lord Robert Cecil comes to speak, he will tell you how great an effect upon allied diplomacy has been the terrorism which Germany has inspired and produced in Holland, Denmark and Norway. These countries are trembling at the German terrorism. They hate Germany, they hate the domination of Germany, but they feel that if they quarrel with Germany, they will be as Belgium is, and that is undoubtedly a very great diplomatic weapon in the hands of Germany. It is painful to have to admit it, but I think it is true.

THE PRIMER MINISTER: I am sure we are very much obliged to the Secretary of State for Foreign Affairs for his most illuminating exposition. I do not know whether any members of the Cabinet would like to ask any further questions.

T MS (WP, DLC).

From Newton Diehl Baker

Dear Mr. President: Washington. May 18, 1917

I inclose with the bill the proclamation modified as you directed when it was previously submitted to you.[1] It fixes the fifth day of June as Registration Day. It is desired to save time, and therefore I submit the proclamation for signature on the same day with the bill. If you prefer to have the official copy of this proclamation written more formally and on legal-cap paper with the usual margins, I will be very glad to have a substitute copy made for your signature tomorrow, but if you approve, would like to have your signature on this paper as authority for the promulgation of the proclamation tonight.

Respectfully yours,   Newton D. Baker

TLS (WP, DLC).
[1] It is printed at May 1, 1917.

From Albert Sidney Burleson

Personal

My dear Mr. President: Washington May 18, 1917.

Enclosed please find the list of Senators prepared by Senator Martin; those checked are the Democrats with whom he desires you to confer.[1] He suggests that you urge upon them the importance of the speedy passage of the pending Deficiency Appropriation Bill in which is carried authorization for the new army, as well as appropriations to carry into effect the program with reference to the new ships. He also would appreciate it if you would impress upon the Senators the importance of regular attendance at the meetings of the Senate, in order to expedite the legislation necessary for the prosecution of the war.

I also conferred with Mr. Webb, imparting to him your views with reference to the Gard amendment, pertaining to the censorship of the press.   Faithfully Yours,   A. S. Burleson

TLS (WP, DLC).
[1] They were Senators Fletcher, Gore, Jones (New Mexico), Kendrick, McKellar, Phelan, Thomas, Thompson, and Park Trammell of Florida.

From the Diary of Josephus Daniels

May Friday 18 1917

Cabinet—The delay of action by Congress. Baker said Panama RR, though entirely owned by Government, could bring nitrates from Chili, though a Gov. vessel could not. "Nobody but a lawyer" said the President, "could say that with a straight face." President told of Dr McCosh. Committee called to protest against his action. Chairman tried to give rebuke. Dr McC quoted appropriate scripture about men receiving rebuke in proper spirit (would have served father right if boy had parted), & turned to the Chm. & said "let us pray Gods lead." It was a hard prayer & the Com left after the prayer without a word. Lecture on Plato (Flaps open) Checks & balances were carefully adjusted and promptly kicked over. All questions revolve around a dictum or phrase. When Constitution was formed Newtons ideas possessed the thought of the world. Centrifugal & centripetal forces marked references to those who discussed the Constitution. Later came Darwin & all the talk was of evolution. The President very interesting & illuminating.

A Statement on the Lever Bill

[May 19, 1917]

It is very desirable, in order to prevent misunderstandings or alarms and to assure cooperation in a vital matter, that the country should understand exactly the scope and purpose of the very great powers which I have thought it necessary in the circumstances to ask the Congress to put in my hands with regard to our food supplies. Those powers are very great indeed, but they are no greater than it has proved necessary to lodge in the other governments which are conducting this momentous war, and their object is stimulation and conservation, not arbitrary restraint or injurious interference with the normal processes of production. They are intended to benefit and assist the farmer and all those who play a legitimate part in the preparation, distribution, and marketing of foodstuffs.

It is proposed to draw a sharp line of distinction between the normal activities of the government represented in the Department of Agriculture in reference to food production, conservation, and marketing, on the one hand, and the emergency activities necessitated by the war in reference to the regulation of food distribution and consumption on the other.

All measures intended directly to extend the normal activities of the Department of Agriculture in reference to the production, conservation, and the marketing of farm crops will be administered, as in normal times through that department, and the powers asked for over distribution and consumption, over exports, imports, prices, purchase, and requisition of commodities, storing, and the like which may require regulation during the war will be placed in the hands of a commissioner of food administration appointed by the President and directly responsible to him.

The objects sought to be served by the legislation asked for are: full inquiry into the existing available stocks of foodstuffs and into the costs and practices of the various food producing and distributing trades; the prevention of all unwarranted hoarding of every kind and of the control of foodstuffs by persons who are not in any legitimate sense producers, dealers, or traders; the requisitioning when necessary for the public use of food supplies and of the equipment necessary for handling them properly; the licensing of wholesome and legitimate mixtures and milling percentages; and the prohibition of the unnecessary or wasteful use of foods. Authority is asked also to establish prices, but not in order to limit the profits of the farmers, but only to guarantee to them when necessary a minimum price which will insure them a profit where they are asked to attempt new crops and to secure the consumer against extortion by breaking up corners and attempts at speculation when they occur by fixing temporarily a reasonable price at which middlemen must sell.

I have asked Mr. Herbert Hoover to undertake this all-important task of food administration. He has expressed his willingness to do so on condition that he is to receive no payment for his services and that the whole of the force under him, exclusive of clerical assistance, shall be employed so far as possible upon the same volunteer basis. He has expressed his confidence that this difficult matter of food administration can be sucessfully accomplished through the voluntary cooperation and direction of legitimate distributors of foodstuffs and with the help of the women of the country.

Although it is absolutely necessary that unquestionable powers shall be placed in my hands in order to insure the success of this adminstration of the food supplies of the country, I am confident that the exercise of those powers will be necessary only in the few cases where some small and selfish minority proves unwilling to put the Nation's interests above personal advantage and that the whole country will heartily support Mr. Hoover's efforts by supplying the necessary volunteer agencies throughout the country for the intelligent control of food consumption and securing the cooperation of the most capable leaders of the very interests most directly affected, that the exercise of the powers deputed to him will rest very successfully upon the good will and cooperation of the people themselves, and that the ordinary economic machinery of the country will be left substantially undisturbed.

The proposed food administration is intended, of course, only to meet a manifest emergency and to continue only while the war lasts. Since it will be composed for the most part of volunteers, there need be no fear of the possibility of a permanent bureaucracy arising out of it. All control of consumption will disappear when the emergency has passed. It is with that object in view that the administration considers it to be of preeminent importance that the existing associations of producers and distributors of foodstuffs should be mobilized and made use of on a volunteer basis. The successful conduct of the projected food administration by such means will be the finest possible demonstration of the willingness, the ability, and the efficiency of democracy, and of its justified reliance upon the freedom of individual initiative. The last thing that any American could contemplate with equanimity would be the introduction of anything resembling Prussian autocracy into the food control in this country.

It is of vital interest and importance to every man who produces food and to every man who takes part in its distribution that these policies thus liberally administered should succeed and succeed altogether. It is only in that way that we can prove it to be absolutely unnecessary to resort to the rigorous and drastic measures which have proved to be necessary in some of the European countries.[1]

Printed in the *Official Bulletin*, I (May 21, 1917), 4, 6.
[1] There is a WWsh draft of this statement in the C. L. Swem Coll., NjP.

To Theodore Roosevelt

[The White House May] 19 [1917]

I very much regret that I cannot comply with the request in your telegram of yesterday period The reasons I have stated in a public statement made this morning[1] and I need not assure you that my conclusions were based entirely upon imperative considerations of public policy and not upon personal or private choice   Woodrow Wilson

T telegram (T. Roosevelt Papers, DLC).
[1] He meant published in the newspapers "this morning."

To Arthur James Balfour

My dear Mr. Balfour,   The White House. 19 May, 1917

Thank you very much indeed for your kindness in sending me the important papers accompanying your kind note of yesterday. I shall study them with the greatest interest,—particularly your statement to the Imperial War Council.

Cordially and sincerely Yours,   Woodrow Wilson

ALS (A. J. Balfour Papers, FO 800/208, PRO).

To Thomas James Walsh

My dear Senator: [The White House] 19 May, 1917

Knowing Secretary Lane's sentiments towards you, I am sure that it must have been as much of a distress to him as it is to me that any misunderstanding should have arisen between you with regard to appointments in Montana.

I sought Mr. Lane out so soon as I received your letter[1] and obtained from him a full statement of the character of the appointment to which he designated Mr. Goodwin[2] and of the circumstances which led him to choose Mr. Goodwin.

I must say, my dear Senator, that it seems to me that the Secretary acted with a very careful regard for the public service and upon a principle of Civil Service with which I very warmly sympathize. When I read your letter, I assumed that the appointment was one requiring Senatorial confirmation, but it seems that it was not and that Secretary Lane was merely seeking to put the best man at his disposal within the service into the position that had been made vacant by the resignation of Mr. Ralston.[3]

I am sure that Secretary Lane feels the utmost desire to consider your wishes in every matter of appointment in Montana when it is possible to do so, and you may rest assured, Senator, that my own feeling is the same, but in this particular case I really cannot see that he has been guilty of a discourtesy, though I wish, and no doubt he wishes, that he had informed you of his purpose before making the appointment.

With much regard,

Cordially and sincerely yours, Woodrow Wilson

TLS (Letterpress Books, WP, DLC).

[1] It is missing.

[2] Probably George E. Goodwin, a civil engineer at large in the field service of the National Park Service.

[3] Oliver Caldwell Ralston, a metallurgist with the Bureau of Mines, who had resigned to direct confidential wartime studies for the Hooker Electrochemical Co. of Niagara Falls.

To Vance Criswell McCormick

My dear McCormick: [The White House] 19 May, 1917

I hope that you and Morris won't worry about the leakage with regard to the appointment to Japan.[1] I, of course, knew that neither of you was responsible for it. Goodness knows how these things happen!

I have just received your letter of yesterday enclosing letters from the State of Washington recommending Mr. Ole Hanson for appointment.[2] I am sorry to say that Senator Poindexter has served notice on me that the appointment of Hanson would be highly objectionable to him, and you know what happens in such circumstances through the so-called "courtesy" of the Senate. This is a great life we are living here!

In haste

Cordially and faithfully yours, Woodrow Wilson

TLS (Letterpress Books, WP, DLC).
  ¹ Wilson's selection of Roland Sletor Morris as Ambassador to Japan had been reported in the newspapers on May 16. He was commissioned on August 1 and presented his credentials on October 30, 1917.
  ² V. C. McCormick to WW, May 18, 1917, TLS (WP, DLC). Hanson had been recommended for appointment to the Federal Trade Commission.

From William Cox Redfield

My dear Mr. President: Washington May 19th, 1917.

Some days ago at a Cabinet Meeting I spoke of a hope that means might be found of fencing in the North Sea. I am now glad to hand you copy of communication to me of the 15th inst. from the Superintendent of the Coast and Geodetic Survey¹ embodying the results of a study of a committee of technical and sea officers of that Service on this important matter.² A copy of this communication has been sent to Admiral deChair³ at the British Embassy and a copy to the Secretary of the Navy, accompanied by data sheets, diagrams and photographs of the apparatus suggested to be used. You will note that I have advised both the British authorities and the Secretary of the Navy that subject to your approval I will, if desired, instruct the officers of the Coast and Geodetic Survey whose duties have for years made them thoroughly familiar with this class of work, to proceed to Great Britain either under the auspices of the Navy Department or direct as you may prefer.

I have also said that an electrical expert of the Bureau of Standards will be sent if that is deemed wise.

The matter has received careful thought at the hands of men who have made a practical and scientific study of such problems. We have now carried the matter as far as is possible within our scope and have left it in the hands of those by whom the decision must be made. If, however, it is deemed best to put the matter into practical form, I have no doubt that it can be carried into effect.   Yours very truly,   William C. Redfield

TLS (WP, DLC).
  ¹ (Ernest) Lester Jones.
  ² E. L. Jones to W. C. Redfield, May 15, 1917, T MS (CGSR, RG 23, Office of the Director, War Files, 1917-19, DNA). It presented tentative plans for laying wire nets, for antisubmarine purposes, across the Skagerrak between Norway and Denmark (ninety miles) or across the North Sea between Norway and Scotland (270 miles), at estimated costs of $4,500,000 and $13,500,000, respectively, exclusive of mines and electrical equipment. The plan envisaged using light nets with explosive mines rather than nets heavy enough to stop a submarine. In order to carry out the operation before the enemy could take countermeasures, Jones and his committee recommended using about twenty-four specially equipped vessels, which should be able to complete the entire task in from twenty to thirty hours.
  ³ W. C. Redfield to D. R. S. DeChair, May 19, 1917, TCL (CGSR, RG 23, Office of the Director, War Files, 1917-19, DNA).

From Edward William Pou

Dear Mr. President: Washington, D. C. May 19, 1917.

I know you are so busy it would amount almost to an imposition to ask for opportunity to talk with you unless it becomes absolutely necessary to do so about a matter of public importance. I think, however, you should be informed of criticism, unjust and unfair as I believe, which is being made of a part of your Red Cross address.

I beg to enclose herewith what purports to be copy of excerpt from that address. The criticism I refer to is this; it is being said that you admit in your address on that occasion that our nation has gone to war with Germany without a grievance. Those who make such criticism, I am glad to say, are few in number, and if I did not feel the matter were of the very greatest importance I would not write concerning it.

I did not understand you to mean at all that we had entered a world war without just grievance, or to put it in plain language, without just cause. I have supposed you meant that our grievance while entirely sufficient was the same as that of other neutral nations.

Surely those who heard or read your address to Congress on April 2nd, in which you recited, in language never to be forgotten, the crimes of Germany against the entire neutral world, America included, ought not to make such a criticism, and yet it is being made.

You are the head of the Government and the leader of the party to which I belong. Everybody despises the gratuitous news carrier, but I have no apology to make to any one for letting you know how your address upon the subject of our participation in the war is being criticized. Surely the subject is of vital interest to every man, woman and child in America, and I would feel that I had not done my duty as a loyal American if I did not let you know the charge is being made that "the President himself admits we have gone to war without a grievance." I would even feel that I were lacking in loyalty to my Country, a loyalty which I believe I would feel to the same extent if the President of my Country in this hour of stress belonged to a different political party.   Sincerely yours,   Edwd W. Pou

TLS (WP, DLC).

From Robert Lansing, with Enclosure

My dear Mr. President: Washington May 19, 1917.

I have just had a talk with Morris Hil[l]quit, the socialist, who is seeking a passport to go abroad and attend the Stockholm conference. I gained the impression from the few minutes spent with him that he is a natural intriguer and utterly unreliable; that in spite of his profession of sympathy with the cause which we support in the war, he would favor any means to aid in forcing peace. I may misjudge him for I know that Secretary Baker thinks highly of him and believes him sincere in purpose.

But whether he is sincere or not makes comparatively little difference so far as the conference is concerned. I do not see how it can result in good and it may do much harm. I understand that the British are greatly disturbed over it and are disposed not to issue passports to their socialists who wish to attend and that the French have the same view. They feel if we issue passports to our socialists that they will be forced to do the same.

The question is shall we issue passports to men who are avowedly going to the Conference. If we refuse, it may make them martyrs. If we do issue them, we may encourage a dangerous pro-German movement and permit agitators near Russia who are frankly hostile to the Commission to Russia and will seek every means to discredit it and weaken their influence with the socialistic and labor element.

Will you be good enough to give me your opinion as to the action which we should take?[1]

I enclose a letter which I received yesterday from Mr. Russell and which bears on this subject.

Faithfully yours,   Robert Lansing

TLS (WP, DLC).
[1] Wilson wrote at the top of this letter: "Ans. orally W.W." Without issuing a formal statement, the State Department on May 23 expressed strong disapproval of the peace propaganda of the European socialists, denied passports to American delegates to the Stockholm conference, and warned that any Americans taking part in that conference would be liable to severe punishment under the Logan Act, about which see n. 1 to the extract from the House Diary printed at Dec. 15, 1915, Vol. 35.

E N C L O S U R E

Charles Edward Russell to Robert Lansing

Dear Mr. Secretary: Washington, D. C. May 15, 1917.

In the course of the interview you were good enough to give me yesterday I overlooked one point I had desired to make and that is concerning the Stockholm conference. I observe strong denials that this is of either proGerman origin or proGerman significance, but my long acquaintance with controlling influences in the Socialist movement enables me to judge of these with accuracy and I am perfectly certain that the entire conception of the Stockholm conference is of the most sinister nature. The Socialists in America that are not ready to put their Socialism before their Americanism and just as unready to see their country menaced by German autocracy have no illusions on this subject. All the denials I have seen come from men that previous to the declaration of war by Congress were outspoken German champions. For myself I doubt very much whether human nature is so constituted that one can be vehemently proGerman from August 1, 1914, to April 6, 1917, and then become equally earnest on the side of the Allies. I think that if all the letters written in the last three weeks from New York City to Russia had been censored there would have been some rather remarkable revelations. The task before the American Commission to Russia is extremely difficult. The Stockholm conference enormously increases the difficulty. I trust you will pardon me if in this exceedingly critical situation I venture to express the hope that your own clear vision concerning it will be unaffected by denials of its true character. If this were in any way related to one of those factional quarrels in the Socialist party that are quite a familiar episode or if it went no farther [sic]. But I do assure you, dear sir, that the significance here is quite otherwise. Unfortunately a certain element in the Socialist movement is essentially proGerman and proGerman sympathy is the mainspring of the Stockholm conference, which meets to endorse a policy that would mean the defeat of the Allies' cause and the triumph of the basic principles of German imperialism.

I am giving to Mr. Long at the station a cable message that I believe should be sent to Petrograd and is submitted for your judgment.

I hope you will bear with me if I venture at this time to express my appreciation of your extreme kindness and courteous patience.

I am, my dear sir, with great respect
    Yours very truly Charles Edward Russell

TLS (SDR, RG 59, 763.72119/603, DNA).

From Newton Diehl Baker

Dear Mr. President: Washington. May 19, 1917

Your statement with regard to an independent Polish nation[1]
has, of course, been brought to the attention of Poles everywhere in the world. In Russia its value in securing Polish soldiers
for Russia and discouraging Polish enlistments in the German
and Austrian armies is deemed very great. As a consequence, the
Russians are said to be separating out the Poles who are in their
army and organizing them into exclusively Polish regiments with
a view to having on the Eastern front a Polish army as a visible
representative of the Polish nation which is to be. This, it is
thought, will attract Poles now in Austria and Germany to cross
the line and affiliate themselves with the Polish army.

Mr. Alexander Znamiecki, of the Foreign Trade Department
of the National City Bank of New York, a very impressive and
enthusiastic man, came to see me last week and introduced to me
Count Jean Marie de Horodyski. Together they present a proposition which I attempt to summarize as follows:

Count Horodyski has been in Switzerland, Paris and London
during the entire war, at the head of a Polish secret service. He
has apparently been in close touch with the French and British
war offices. With their approval he comes to this country to urge
the formation of an American-Polish army for use on the Western front, in order that the Polish nation may thus have its
only [own] army on each of the battle fronts, the thought being
that the German and Austrian Polish regiments, as soon as they
learn of the presence of a Polish army, will be disposed to cross
the line and join their own nationals. There are in France now
about 700 Polish officers and about 4,000 Polish soldiers. This
number is deemed too small to be sufficiently representative
of the Polish nation, and it is therefore suggested that the Polish
Falcons and the various Polish societies in this country be
authorized by you to enlist Polish Americans to the number of
perhaps 60,000, send them to Canada to be trained under British
and French officers who would be sent for the purpose, and
formed into an American army made up exclusively of Poles, but
commanded and officered by Americans appointed by you. When
trained, this force shall take its place on the Western front under
the American flag, as a part of the American army, but for
sentimental reasons known as the Polish army, the expense
of this undertaking to be paid by the United States as a loan
to the future independent Polish nation, to be guaranteed by
the present entente allies. The suggested training in camp is for

the purpose of saving the expense of new training camps, since those in Canada are in part idle, and also to prevent any difficulty in this country from the fact that an American army would be in training under British and French officers.

The advantages of this suggestion are, of course, largely the effect which such a movement would have upon Poles in Germany and in Austria. It would be difficult to secure the necessary clothing and equipment within any short space of time without prejudicing the preparation of our own forces, but not impossible.

It occurs to me that there would have to be considered the likelihood of a desire on the part of the Czechs, Serbians, Irish and others who might want to emphasize their hope of future independent nationality by such military segregation. Indeed, I have already had a letter with regard to the propriety of organizing a Serbian legion.

It is possible also that our American army ought to be as homogenous as possible and that we would lose a good deal by allowing nationalist divisions and distinctions to be made in it, rather than to have it a common enterprise of Americans of all extraction merge all other distinctions in their Americanism.

Even assuming it a wise thing to organize such nationalist groups, I have felt that it ought in no case to be done until our own large army is fairly well organized, fearing that it might be said that we were planning to fight America's part of this war by using our foreign-born citizens as soldiers, and I can imagine German emissaries spreading the notion that such a use of foreign-born people implied an under-valuation of them and a willingness to risk them in order to save our native people.

To the extent that any such force contained Poles of German allegiance not yet naturalized citizens of the United States, their presence in such a force would, of course, be very hazardous for them, as in the event of capture they would not be prisoners of war, but executed for treason.

I submit the suggestion as made with these reflections upon it for your decision.

Respectfully yours,   Newton D. Baker

TLS (N. D. Baker Papers, DLC).
¹ In his "Peace without Victory" address to the Senate, printed at Jan. 22, 1917, Vol. 40.

The Foreign Office to Sir Cecil Arthur Spring Rice

[London] May 19th, 1917.

Personal. URGENT. Secret.

Following for Mr. Balfour from Lord R. Cecil. Personal.
Your telegram of May 15th. to the Prime Minister.

If we were to undertake to give naval aid to the United States in a future war I feel that the spirit of our Treaty with Japan would make it incumbent on us to inform her of what we were doing. She might regard such a step as making valueless the whole treaty and this might lead to prolonged negotiations. Indeed it might be necessary to recast the alliance altogether. All this requires very careful consideration by the War Cabinet since a false step might throw Japan into the arms of our enemies. At the same time it is very important to induce the United States to concentrate on building destroyers and speaking for myself and I believe all my colleagues the idea of a defensive alliance with the United States is so attractive to us that any step which would lead in that direction we should desire to take. We are therefore examining very carefully what is the best way of reconciling Japan to such proposed action. In the meantime would it be of any use to point out to the United States Government that with or without a guarantee popular opinion here would undoubtedly force us to go to the assistance of America if she were attacked by Japan. It would therefore be perfectly safe as a matter of practical politics for the United States to forego building capital ships at the present time.

T telegram (FO 371/3119, No. 110785(A), p. 309, PRO).

From Edward Mandell House

Dear Governor: New York. May 20, 1917.

Sir Eric Drummond has been here for two days. We have gone over the situation of the Central Powers and he has given me the views of his Foreign Office on many points.

I have been trying to pin Balfour and him down to what they would consider the minimum terms upon which the Allies would consent to go into a peace conference. I am satisfied they would be willing to begin parleys on the basis of complete evacuation of Belgium and France. He at first suggested a like restoration of Russian territory. I showed him this would involve a delineation of the new Poland, which all agree must be created, and that if we began to discuss boundaries before a conference was called, the discussion would be interminable.

It saddens me to remember that when I first went to Europe in January 1915, I urged the Allies to consider some such terms as these. After the Battle of the Marne Germany was more depressed than she is today. She had failed in her objective and was fearful of the combined strength which the Allies could bring against her.

I convinced Drummond that the most effective thing we could do at present was to aid the German Liberals in their fight against the present German Government.

The idea is for you to say, at a proper time and occasion, that the Allies are ready at any moment to treat with the German people, but they are not ready to treat with a military autocracy—an autocracy which they feel is responsible for the troubles that now beset the world. It is not fair to the peoples of Russia, of Great Britain, of France, of Italy and of the United States to be asked to treat with a military caste that is in no way representative of the German people themselves.

Both Drummond and I think that care should be used not to include the Kaiser. He has a very strong personal following in Germany, and if he is shorn of his power as the King of England, he could be rendered as harmless. In not designating the Kaiser, the hands of the Liberals will be strengthened because there is an element in Germany that would like to see a democratic Germany under a limited monarchy. The situation in Russia will accentuate the feeling that it is better not to make a too violent change from an autocracy to a republic.

If Balfour is sympathetic to this suggestion, he will ask you for an interview in order to get your mind.

Your affectionate,   E. M. House

TLS (WP, DLC).

Sir Cecil Arthur Spring Rice
to Lord Robert Cecil, with Enclosure

Washington, May 20th [1917]

Following for Genl Macdonogh[1] from Drummond

Horodyski would like following message in his name communicated to Erasme Piltz,[2] St. James Hotel Paris. He hopes you will arrange with Dmo[w]ski to take necessary action on penultimate paragraph.

Hw telegram (FO 115/2302, p. 232, PRO).
    [1] Maj. Gen. George Mark Watson Macdonogh, director of Military Intelligence, Imperial General Staff.

2 Piltz was a member of the Polish National Committee, at Paris, of which Roman Dmowski was president. For background and information, see Jacek R. Wedrowski, *Stany Zjiednoczone a odrodzenie Polski* [The United States and the Rebirth of Poland] (Warsaw, 1980).

ENCLOSURE

Your cablegram received. Many thanks. We have made substancial progress and the issue of the creation of the army has already been made known to the President by very influential men. His word will be final but we are hopeful that it will be a favorable one.

The issue is clouded for the time being by the dispute which has been raging in Congress over the Roosevelt army. That situation however will clear shortly.

We are now anticipating a call from the President for definite information as to our plans and our ability to fulfill such promises as we may make. When that call comes we must be prepared to inform the President as to the exact number of officers who can be raised in Europe to help train the Poles recruited in America. We must have as many as we can.

To that end I think you should get together with Count Zamoyski[1] and secure from the War Office in Paris the names of all the officers with their rank who can come to this country on cable notice to help train the Polish recruits.

Tell them that in the case of a satisfactory reply from the President our plans call for the establishment and maintenance of from three to four divisions to serve for the period of the war. Therefore you can estimate how many officers we will need for training purposes.

I would also suggest that you endeavor to learn whether it would be practicable for Seyda[1] to select from the prisoners of war in France and England some NCOs who could assist us on this side also in training the rec[r]uits.

I am also cableing London to get the list of all the Polish officers connected with the Russian Commissions who could come over here and assist.

This information is not only vital for presentation to the President but it is of importance to ourselves so that in the event of securing a favorable reply from the President we can move with speed.

T MS (FO 115/2302, p. 233, PRO).
1 Count Maurice Zamoyski, a member of the Polish National Committee in Paris.

2 Marjan Seyda, formerly editor of a leading newspaper in Posen; director of the Central Agency of Lausanne and a member of the Polish National Committee in Paris.

To Newton Diehl Baker

My dear Mr. Secretary: The White House 21 May, 1917

This is a most interesting proposition but I think your own reflections upon it are very wise and that it would be a mistake, at any rate at this stage of our own preparations, to organize a force of the sort proposed. I agree with you that there are many advantages in this plan and many striking and impressive things about it, but this is not the stage at which to act upon the suggestion. We must keep this in store for later action.

Cordially and sincerely yours,   Woodrow Wilson

TLS (N. D. Baker Papers, DLC).

To Edward William Pou

My dear Mr. Pou: The White House 21 May, 1917

Certainly no apology was necessary for your letter of May nineteenth. It was an act of friendship on your part to write it and of loyalty also to the great cause we are engaged in.

Your interpretation of my message I supposed would be the interpretation everybody would give it. I meant just what you say, that our grievance, "while entirely sufficient, was the same as that of other neutral nations," perhaps aggravated by the fact that Germany had made us special promises which she had grossly ignored.

I would be very much obliged to you for any steps you might take to correct this damaging and erroneous and, I must believe, insincere interpretation of my address to the Red Cross.

Cordially and sincerely yours,   Woodrow Wilson

TLS (E. W. Pou Papers, Nc-Ar).

To John Milton Waldron

My dear Sir: [The White House] 21 May, 1917

I dare say that by this time you have learned of the plans of the War Department to establish a training camp for colored men at Fort Dubuque, Iowa, but in order to acknowledge again your letter of May eleventh, I write to call your attention to the decision, which I warmly approve.

Sincerely yours,   Woodrow Wilson

TLS (Letterpress Books, WP, DLC).

To William Cox Redfield

My dear Mr. Secretary: The White House 21 May, 1917

I sincerely value your letter of May nineteenth about the fencing in of the North Sea and am very glad that you have handed the suggestion on to the active authorities in this all-important matter.

Cordially and sincerely yours,   Woodrow Wilson

TLS (CDR, RG 40, No. 75024/94, DNA).

From Robert Lansing, with Enclosures

My dear Mr. President: Washington May 21, 1917.

I enclose to you a communication which I had from the Argentine Ambassador, dated the 17th, in response to a request which I made him in conversation.

This proposed conference of American Nations is creating a very bad impression in this country as its purpose is not understood. Mr. Naón appreciates this and is greatly concerned about it. He is most anxious for Argentina to take a decided stand against Germany, even to the extent of a declaration of war.

I think that the matter is of sufficient importance for you to see Mr. Naón as soon as possible in order that he may communicate direct with his Government your views. It is a matter which seems to me should be handled without delay as it may have a very decided effect upon all the Latin Americans.

Will you please let me know at your earliest convenience when it will be possible for you to see Mr. Naón?

Faithfully yours,   Robert Lansing.

TLS (SDR, RG 59, 763.72119/587½, DNA).

ENCLOSURE I

Rómulo Sebastian Naón to Robert Lansing

My dear Mr. Secretary: Washington, May 17th, 1917.

As I promised you this morning, I have the pleasure of sending to you a paraphrase of the cable received by me today. As I stated to you, I am most interested in discussing this subject thoroughly and if the President and you yourself would think advisable, I would be very glad and highly honored to pay a visit to the President with that object in view.

As I stated to you this morning the most earnest desire both of my Government and of myself would be completely to remove any misunderstanding no matter how slight it might be, that may have arisen by the initiative to which that cable refers. I beg you to advise me whether an interview with the President could be arranged.

With my kindest regards, I remain,
                         Very sincerely yours,   R. S. Naón.

TLS (SDR, RG 59, 763.72119/587½, DNA).

ENCLOSURE II

PARAPHRASE.

The Argentine Embassy has received official information in regard to a meeting of the American nations at the initiative of the Argentine Government with the purpose of trying to come to an understanding between them on the occasion of the present war and its aggravation from day to day. The Argentine Government thinks that the American nations should concrete an uniform judgment in that regard, bringing into realization the earnest desire of establishing ties capable of strengthening their situation and personality in the general concert of the nations. The idea has been accepted by Bolivia, Brazil, Colombia, Chile, Mexico, Paraguay, Peru, Uruguay, Guatemala, Nicaragua, San Salvador, Ecuador, Honduras, Costa Rica and Haiti, and the Department of Foreign Affairs is expecting the responses of the other nations in order to propose the date for the international meeting. The Argentine Government will be desirous to know the thought of the Government of the United States about this initiative and thinks that it is most interesting that it realizes the true

spirit and purposes of such a meeting, lending to it its moral adherence.

The fact that the Government of the United States of America
was already in war with Germany when the idea of this meeting was initiated was the reason why it did not receive the same
invitation sent to the other American nations.

It is unnecessary to say that in initiating this idea the Argentine Government has not been prompted in any way or shape
whatsoever to separate itself from its traditional policy toward
the United States which has always been consequent [candid?]
and frank. The most constant cordiality and friendship of our
relations with the American people as well as our plain recognition of the justice of its position publicly stated when the state
of war with Germany was declared, are facts conclusive enough
to prove that any act initiated or seconded by the Argentine Government cannot be interpreted as in any way unfriendly by it
toward the United States.

T MS (SDR, RG 59, 763.72119/587½, DNA).

From Robert Lansing

Dear Mr. President: Washington May 21, 1917.

Sir Joseph Pope, Under Secretary of Foreign Affairs of Canada,
called this morning and left with Mr. Phillips an inquiry which
he asked to have transmitted to you. The inquiry comes from Sir
Robert Borden, Premier of Canada, and is as follows:

"To what extend [extent] does the United States desire or
propose to co-operate with Canada in matters pertaining to
the war, and what co-operation do they desire from us?"

With assurances of respect, etc, I am, my dear Mr. President,
          Faithfully yours,   Robert Lansing.

TLS (WP, DLC).

Two Letters from Joseph Patrick Tumulty

Dear Governor: The White House May 21, 1917.

The German propaganda wears various disguises and the one
now being worn with great effect is that of a separate peace in
the spread of which the socialistic movement throughout the
world is being daily utilized. The most dangerous thing about this
whole movement is its insidious character, and its contagious effects threaten soon to touch our own shores. How best to handle

this movement and thus retard its progress should now be challenging our best thought and attention, for peace is the principal plank in the socialistic platform and is the web and woof of its life as an international organization.

The demand for a separate peace is now most insistent in Russia, the weakest link in the whole line of the Allied cause. Russia is the very crux of the whole situation. Silence and indifference on the part of the Allied statesmen is the only answer to the socialistic demand throughout Russia and elsewhere for a separate peace. The Allied statesmen have insisted upon "subordinating political questions like that of a separate peace to military questions" because their statesmen insist that a "knockout" blow must precede negotiations. To retard this movement, therefore, some move by the President is necessary, for if the spread of this separate peace movement is not prevented, it will promote currents of peace throughout the world, much to our injury and embarrassment. It is admitted that any move on our part to retard the progress of this movement at this time would be dangerous but when one considers what the affect of a separate peace would be on our own fortunes, the alternative, i.e., of discussing the evils of a separate peace, might well be considered before the spread of the contagion touches us. With the situation in Russia as it is and with this movement looking to a separate peace gathering momentum with the hours, "daring diplomacy" on the part of the western Allies and especially the United States in handling this matter must be attempted.

"Something needs to be done at once," as the New Republic says, "which will strengthen the devotion of Russia to the cause of the Allies and will cause dissension in Central Europe. Von Bethmann-Hollweg's refusal to speak has given the initiative to the Allies and the United States. The thing which is needed is a powerful re-affirmation of the international purposes for which the war is waged, so far as the cause of the United States embraces those purposes."[1] (See attached article from New York Times, May 21st, by Herbert Bailey.)[2] "The statement should be aimed directly at Russia, Austria-Hungary, and the German Radicals in the same spirit and temper of the President's address to the Senate. No doubt such a statement will cause reaction among certain groups in France, England, and America, but the cost of this is not so great as the danger of the situation in the East. We cannot stand pat diplomatically speaking. *We must give the discontented peoples of Central Europe material with which to answer the Chancellor's statement that we are aiming at the conquest and destruction of the German people. That same material could be used to reassure the Russian Revolution against the suspicion which they undoubtedly entertain,—that we are in this war for the purpose of aggression and self-aggrandizement."*

As the New Republic says, "The final victory must be won by diplomacy. The German government has been exhibiting a clearer understanding of this strategic condition than have the governments of France and Great Gritain [Britain]. The strategy seems to be to fight the enemies which cannot be divided, and to divide those which it is unnecessary to fight. The submission of terms of peace which would have a fair chance of acceptance by eastern Europe as a prospectively permanent settlement would be worth more to the cause of the Allies than another two millions of trained soldiers and a new fleet of merchant shipping. If the Russians can be divided from one another and from their allies by German diplomacy, the Germans can at least to an equal extent be divided from one another and from their allies by a diplomacy of liberalism. Austria-Hungary is almost as disorganized and is probably as ripe for revolution as was Russia. These causes of internal dissension within and among the Central Powers have been fermenting for a long while and have been prevented from obtaining any overt expression chiefly because the diplomacy of the western Allies has insisted upon subordinating political to military considerations. Let them abandon their past insistence upon an absolute military decision as a condition of peace, and the result will be a rapidly progressive diminution of the military morale of Central Europe." The initiative must come from the President rather than from the governments of France and Great Britain. This movement for a separate peace has been gaining momentum because there has been no clear expression by British and French statesmen. The responsibility is with the President. It is his business to obtain the consent of the Allies to the publication of a statement embodying the reasons which impelled us to take up arms against the autocratic forces of Germany. "The American people did not enter this war to add to the sum of human goods and beings which were being calamitously annihilated"; they entered it chiefly in order to make a promising and indispensable contribution to a scientific and just settlement. "Such a settlement cannot be obtained merely by working for victory. Victory itself can best be obtained by working for the settlement."

In this statement of the President reiterating the purposes of the United States, he should lay particular stress upon the dangerous character of a separate peace so far as Russia is concerned, warning the democratic and progressive forces of Russia that such a peace is one behind which lie the intrigues of autocratic governments. If the Germans triumph through separate peace, it means the triumph of a despotic order. (See the attached article by Mr. Herman Bernstein.)[3]

Emphasize the utter fatuity of a separate peace as a step toward permanent peace. Emphasize the purpose for which America engaged in this struggle; why she has ranged her forces with the other *progressive* forces of the world,—to establish bases upon which permanent peace might be laid. Show that separate peace would lead only to a continuance of the war and would provoke other wars. It would lead to resentments and hatred which experience has shown to be prolific breeders of war; that a separate peace now would only stifle and hold in check the energies of free peoples everywhere; that our goal is permanent peace by striving to set up and to encourage and maintain democratic standards of government and to hold in check those influences in government which have been the breeders of war.

Re-state the fundamental purpose the Government of the United States had in mind in going into this war and in adding its forces to the other democratic forces of the world; that it could in this way best accomplish the great object of the Socialists, namely, permanent peace; that our great hope is for the establishment of a permanent world peace, based upon "democratic republicanism"; that the whole trend of events is toward a world peace, and that out of this war will come this great consummation and that the only thing a separate peace will do will be to offer resistance to that great movement. That the United States wishes no indemnity; wishes no annexation; has in her heart no purpose of aggression. The President's object should be to show that a separate peace would mean the continuing of autocracy. What we are fighting for is democracy. "My purpose is to warn the democratic peoples of the world against the evils of a separate peace."   Sincerely yours,   Tumulty

[1] *The New Republic*, XI (May 19, 1917), 62, 65-67.
[2] See n. 1 to the next letter.
[3] Herman Bernstein, "The 'Conscience' of Russia Against a Separate Peace," *New York Herald*, May 21, 1917. In this editorial-page article, Bernstein wrote that, to those who knew the new Russia, current rumors about a separate peace lacked the slightest foundation of fact and were "a slander against the people who have thrown off the yoke of the Romanoffs and who would not now place Russia at the mercy of the Hohenzollerns."

Dear Governor: The White House. May 21st [1917].

Since I dictated this letter last night, I found this article by Herbert Bailey, published in the New York Times,[1] which emphasizes the necessity for "re-creating enthusiasm for the war against Germany." Mr. Bailey says "that it is essential that the proletariate should know why it is absolutely necessary to fight to a finish; they should receive clear and definite proof that the Allies have no imperialistic aims, or what the Russians consider, —nationalistic aims."   Sincerely yours,   Tumulty

TLS (WP, DLC).

[1] A dispatch from Petrograd, May 19, 1917, in which Bailey quoted a leading Russian diplomat as saying that the Russian proletariat regarded the war as "a war of the old régime" and did not feel threatened by Germany. Tumulty quoted a portion of the dispatch in the *New York Times* of May 21, 1917.

From William English Walling, with Enclosure

Mr. President: Greenwich Connecticut May 21, 1917.

In our conversation of last Friday the so-called International Socialist Peace Conference summoned by the Russian Council of Workmen's and Soldiers' Deputies was referred to. This Conference has been postponed, but there seems little question that it will be held within a month or two.

The important meeting of the National Council of the French Socialist Party on May 27th will probably decide upon participation and will also fix the conditions of participation. The same presentation of the case against the German government that would impress the Russian people would also, undoubtedly determine the position of the French Socialists at this critical moment.

The peace policy of the French Socialists as well as the Socialists of other countries is indicated in the enclosed memorandum, I believe in the briefest practicable form. I think I can guarantee the strict accuracy of this statement. I am also able to support it with evidence at every point, if required.

                    Very respectfully,   Wm. English Walling

TLS (SDR, RG 59, 763.72119/612, DNA).

E N C L O S U R E[1]

Commencement 1915, les socialistes des pays neutres, à Copenhague, les socialistes des pays alliés, à Londres, et les socialistes austro-allemands, à Vienne, avaient affirmé
                              (2 lignes censurées)
                    le droit pour les peuples à disposer librement d'eux-mêmes * * * *

Aujourd'hui, les principes affichés par les socialistes de tous les pays trouvent de nouveaux et puissants adeptes. C'est, d'abord, le Président Wilson et, avec lui, le grand pays qui l'a placé a sa tête et qui est entré dans la guerre pour faire triompher ces principes. C'est, ensuite, la Russie qui, par la voix de son gouvernement provisoire et par celle du Conseil des délégués des ouvriers et soldats, déclare vouloir une paix générale, sans annexions, sans indemnités de guerre, sur les bases du libre développement national des peuples.

En Allemagne, avec un courage admirable, les socialistes minoritaires se sont élevés, à maintes reprises, contre toute annexion et pour le droit des peuples à disposer d'eux-mêmes!

From Le Populaire, organ of the French Socialist Minority, May 6.

T MS (SDR, RG 59, 763.72119/612, DNA).
[1] Our translation follows:
"Beginning in 1915, the socialists of the neutral countries, at Copenhagen, the socialists of the Allied countries, at London, and the Austro-German socialists, at Vienna, have affirmed (two lines censored) the right of peoples to free self-determination * * * *

"Today, the principles stated by the socialists of all countries are once again winning new and powerful followers. First, President Wilson and, with him, the great country that put him at its head and that has entered the war to make these principles triumph. Also, Russia, which, through the voice of its provisional government and that of the Council of Delegates of Workers and Soldiers, declares that it wants a general peace, without annexations, without war indemnities, on the bases of the free national development of peoples.

"In Germany, with admirable courage, the Minority Socialists time and again have come out against any annexation and for the right of peoples to self-determination."

From Le Populaire, organ of the French Socialist Minority, May 6.

To the Provisional Government of Russia[1]

NO DISTRIBUTION.

Washington, May 22, 1917.

1426. You will deliver a verbatim copy of the following communication from the President to the Provisional Government and confer with them as to the propriety of giving it publicity simultaneously in both countries. You will please telegraph me promptly of any agreement which is reached as to the time when the publication will take place.

Paragraph. The President's communication is as follows: Quote:

In view of the approaching visit of the American delegation to Russia to express the deep friendship of the American people for the people of Russia and to discuss the best and most practical means of cooperation between the two peoples in carrying the present struggle for the freedom of all peoples to a successful consummation, it seems opportune and appropriate that I should state again, in the light of this new partnership, the objects the United States has had in mind entering the war. Those objects have been very much beclouded during the past few weeks by mistaken and misleading statements, and the issues at stake are too momentous, too tremendous, too significant for the whole human race to permit any misinterpretations or misunderstandings, however slight, to remain uncorrected for a moment.

PARAGRAPH. The war has begun to go against Germany, and in their desperate desire to escape the inevitable ultimate defeat those who are in authority in Germany are using every possible instrumentality, are making use even of the influence of groups and parties among their own subjects to whom they have never been just or fair or even tolerant, to promote a propaganda on both sides of the sea which will preserve for them their influence at home and their power abroad, to the undoing of the very men they are using.

PARAGRAPH. The position of America in this war is so clearly avowed that no man can be excused for mistaking it. She seeks no material profit or aggrandizement of any kind. She is fighting for no advantage or selfish object of her own but for the liberation of peoples everywhere from the aggressions of autocratic force. The ruling classes in Germany have begun of late to profess a like liberality and justice of purpose, but only to preserve the power they have set up in Germany and the selfish advantages which they have wrongly gained for themselves and their private projects of power all the way from Berlin to Bagdad and beyond. Government after government has by their influence, without open conquest of its territory, been linked together in a net of intrigue directed against nothing less than the peace and liberty of the world. The meshes of that intrigue must be broken, but cannot be broken unless wrongs already done are undone; and adequate measures must be taken to prevent it from ever again being rewoven or repaired.

PARAGRAPH. Of course, the Imperial German Government and those whom it is using for their own undoing are seeking to obtain pledges that the war will end in the restoration of the *status quo ante*. It was the *status quo ante* out of which this iniquitous war issued forth, the power of the Imperial German Government within the Empire and its widespread domination and influence outside of that Empire. That *status* must be altered in such fashion as to prevent any such hideous thing from ever happening again.

PARAGRAPH. We are fighting for the liberty, the self-government, and the undictated development of all peoples, and every feature of the settlement that concludes this war must be conceived and executed for that purpose. Wrongs must first be righted and then adequate safeguards must be created to prevent their being committed again. Remedies must be found as well as statements of principle that will have a pleasing and sonorous sound. Practical questions can be settled only by practical means. Phrases will not accomplish the result. Effective readjustments will; and whatever readjustments are necessary must be made.

PARAGRAPH. But they must follow a principle and that principle is plain. No people must be forced under a sovereignty under which it does not wish to live. No territory must change hands except for the purpose of securing those who inhabit it a fair chance of life and liberty. No indemnities must be insisted on except those that constitute payment for manifest wrongs done. No readjustments of power must be made except such as will tend to secure the future peace of the world and the future welfare and happiness of its peoples.

PARAGRAPH. And then the free peoples of the world must draw together in some common covenant, some genuine and practical cooperation that will in effect combine their force to secure peace and justice in the dealings of nations with one another. The brotherhood of mankind must no longer be a fair but empty phrase: it must be given a structure of force and reality. The nations must realize their common life and effect a workable partnership to secure that life against the aggressions of autocratic and self-pleasing power.

PARAGRAPH. For these things we can afford to pour out blood and treasure. For these are the things we have always professed to desire, and unless we pour out the blood and treasure now and succeed, we may never be able to unite or show conquering force again in the great cause of human liberty. The day has come to conquer or submit. If the forces of autocracy can divide us, they will overcome us; if we stand together, victory is certain and the liberty which victory will secure. We can afford then to be generous, but we cannot afford then or now to be weak or omit any single guarantee of justice and security. WOODROW WILSON. UNQUOTE. Lansing

T telegram (SDR, RG 59, 763.72/5171A, DNA).
[1] There is a WWsh draft and a CLST draft with WWhw emendations of this document in WP, DLC. It was sent by Lansing as telegram 1426, May 22, 1917, to the American embassy in Petrograd.

To Robert Lansing, with Enclosures

My dear Mr. Secretary,   The White House. 22 May, 1917.

I am very glad to approve this message. I have suggested only a few verbal changes.   W.W.

ALI (SDR, RG 59, 763.72/5078E, DNA).

ENCLOSURE I

From Robert Lansing

My dear Mr. President: Washington May 19, 1917.

If it meets with your approval I will send forward the enclosed telegram. I hope, if you think it advisable to send a message of this sort at the present time, that you will give me the benefit of any suggestions which you may have as to the subject matter or language.   Faithfully yours,   Robert Lansing

TLS (SDR, RG 59, 763.72/5078E, DNA).

ENCLOSURE II[1]

Washington, May 18, 1917

Amembassy PETROGRAD.

You may state to the Minister of Foreign Affairs for the information of his Government that the High Commission now on its way from this country to Russia is sent primarily to manifest to the Russian Government and people the deep sympathetic feeling which exists among all classes in America for the adherence of Russia to the principle of democracy which has been the foundation of the progress and prosperity of this country. The High Commissioners go to convey the greetings of this Republic to the new and powerful member which has joined the great family of democratic nations.

Paragraph. The commissioners, who will bear this fraternal message to the people of Russia, have been selected by the President with the special purpose of giving representation to the various elements which make up the American people and to show that among them all there is the same love of country and the same devotion to liberty and justice and loyalty to constituted authority. The Commission is not chosen from one political group but from the various groups into which the American electorate is divided. United, they represent the Republic. However they may differ on public questions they are one in support of democracy and in hostility to the enemies of democracy throughout the world.

Paragraph. This Commission is prepared, if the Russian Government desires, to confer upon the best ways and means ⟨to cooperate⟩ *to bring about effective cooperation between the two governments* in the prosecution of the war against the German autocracy which is today ⟨a⟩ *the* grave*st* menace to all democratic governments ⟨in the world⟩. It *is the view of this Government that it* has become the solemn duty of those, who love democracy and individual liberty, to render harmless this autocratic Government whose ambitions, aggressions, and intrigues, have been disclosed in the present struggle. Whatever the cost in life and treasure the supreme object ⟨must be⟩ *should be and can be* attained *only* by the united strength of the democracies of the ⟨earth,⟩ *world, and* ⟨for⟩ only thus can come that permanent and universal peace which is the hope of all people.

Paragraph. To the common cause of humanity which Russia has so courageously and unflinchingly supported for nearly three years, the United States is pledged. To cooperate and aid Russia in the accomplishment of the task, which as a great democracy is more truly hers today than ever before, is the desire of the United States. To stand side by side, shoulder to shoulder, against autocracy will unite the American and Russian peoples in a friendship for the ages.

Paragraph. With this spirit the High Commissioners of the United States will present themselves in the confident hope that the Russian Government and people will realize how sincerely the United States hopes for their welfare and desires to share with them in their future endeavors to bring victory to the cause of democracy and human liberty.   Lansing

T telegram (SDR, RG 59, 763.72/5078E, DNA).
[1] Words in angle brackets in the following document deleted by Wilson; words in italics added by him.
[2] This was sent as RL to D. R. Francis, No. 1428, May 22, 1917.

To Edwin Yates Webb

My dear Mr. Webb: [The White House] 22 May, 1917

I have been very much surprised to find several of the public prints stating that the administration had abandoned the position which it so distinctly took, and still holds, that authority to exercise censorship over the Press to the extent that that censorship is embodied in the recent action of the House of Representatives[1] is absolutely necessary to the public safety. It, of course, has not been abandoned, because the reasons still exist why such authority is necessary for the protection of the nation.

I have every confidence that the great majority of the newspapers of the country will observe a patriotic reticence about everything whose publication could be of injury, but in every country there are some persons in a position to do mischief in this field who cannot be relied upon and whose interests or desires will lead to actions on their part highly dangerous to the nation in the midst of a war. I want to say again that it seems to me imperative that powers of this sort should be granted.

Cordially and sincerely yours,   Woodrow Wilson

TLS (Letterpress Books, WP, DLC).

[1] The House members were still fighting in the conference committee to save some form of newspaper censorship, such as the Gard amendment. Wilson's letter to Webb was printed, *inter alia*, in the *New York Times*, May 23, 1917.

The conference committee, on June 4, approved the elimination of any provision for censorship; the House approved the conference report on June 7; the Senate approved it on June 12; and Wilson signed the Espionage bill on June 15. *Cong. Record*, 65th Cong., 1st sess., pp. 3307 and 3498; *New York Times*, June 5 and 16, 1917.

To James Thomas Heflin

My dear Mr. Heflin: [The White House] 22 May, 1917

It is incomprehensible to me how any frank or honest person could doubt or question my position with regard to the war and its objects. I have again and again stated the very serious and long-continued wrongs which the Imperial German Government has perpetrated against the rights, the commerce and the citizens of the United States. The list is long and overwhelming. No nation that respected itself or the rights of humanity could have borne those wrongs any longer.

Our objects in going into the war have been stated with equal clearness. The whole of the conception which I take to be the conception of our fellow-countrymen with regard to the outcome of the war and the terms of its settlement I set forth with the utmost explicitness in an address to the Senate of the United States on the twenty-second of January last. Again in my message to Congress on the second of April last those objects were stated in unmistakable terms. I can conceive no purpose in seeking to becloud this matter except the purpose of weakening the hands of the Government and making the part which the United States is to play in this great struggle for human liberty an inefficient and hesitating part. We have entered the war for our own reasons and with our own objects clearly stated, and shall forget neither the reasons nor the objects. There is no hate in our hearts for the German people, but there is a resolve which cannot be shaken even by misrepresentation to overcome the pretensions of the autocratic government which acts upon purposes to which the German people have never consented.

Cordially and sincerely yours,   Woodrow Wilson

TLS (Letterpress Books, WP, DLC).

From Frank Irving Cobb

Dear Mr. President: New York May 22, 1917.

George Harvey has a solution of the censorship problem which seems wholly sane and practical.[1]

He went to Washington today, but I do not know whether he intends to call at the White House or not.[2] I am writing this to you because we discussed the matter last night and I was deeply impressed by the reasonableness of his plan. It ought to be possible to unite the Administration and the press in a common cause, and Harvey has found a way.

The censorship controversy has been so unfortunate that I know you will be eager to consider any proposal that gives promise.

Incidentally let me congratulate you on the magnificent way in which you have planned your war policies, and the sure judgment you have shown.

Sincerely yours   Frank I. Cobb.

ALS (WP, DLC).

[1] In an editorial, "Fair Play for the Government and Whole Truth for the People," *North American Review*, CCV (June 1917), 817-25, Harvey reviewed the accomplishments and problems of the government since the United States had entered the war. One of the most serious problems was the administration's attempt to secure the enactment of an "unprecedentedly drastic and quite indefensible" censorship bill. And, yet, Harvey pointed out, there was need for "a legitimate and serviceable censorship." The President (following precedents set by Lincoln) had ample authority to deal effectively with notorious offenders, but, Harvey said, for ordinary cases a statute was needed as authority to issue sensible rules and regulations—not the unreasonable ones now proposed to be administered by subordinate officials. Congress would approve censorship by the President or a disinterested person responsible only to him. This person, Harvey continued, obviously had to be a journalist "of the highest recognized standing in his profession," who would in effect have cabinet rank. Harvey urged the creation of "a real Department of Public Information," whose head would be a member of the President's official family.

[2] Harvey's name does not appear in the Executive Appointment Diary or the Head Usher's Diary for this period.

From Edward Mandell House, with Enclosure

Dear Governor: New York. May 22, 1917.

I am enclosing you a memorandum which Paderewski prepared concerning the advisability of your permitting the raising of a Polish army.[1]

I have talked to General Bridges and to Balfour about this and they both heartily approve—particularly General Bridges. Bridges suggests that they be given training in Canada where camps are already equipped and ready.

I am enclosing a letter from George Gordon Moore.[2] Moore was with General French for a year on the Western Front. His advice is the "other side of it," but is largely concurred in by Frederick Palmer the war correspondent who was at the front in France for so long.

My third and last enclosure is a memorandum made by Stettinius.[3] Spring-Rice, for some reason, wanted me to see him which I did the other day. This memorandum is the result. I presume his conclusions are approved by the Allies.

Affectionately yours,   E. M. House

TLS (WP, DLC).

[1] It is missing in all collections and archives.

[2] Moore, a retired wealthy businessman of New York, was a close friend of Gen. Sir John French and, following the outbreak of the war, had visited him frequently at the headquarters of the B.E.F. in France.

[3] Unsigned memorandum by Edward Reilly Stettinius, May [22?], 1917, TC MS (WP, DLC). Stettinius, a member of the firm of J. P. Morgan & Co., had, in 1915, organized its department for the purchase of munitions and matériel for the British and French governments. His memorandum made the following points: The aggregate purchases in the United States by the Allied governments of munitions and war matériel, exclusive of grain, foodstuffs, cotton, and other products, was estimated to have been more than $4 billion since 1914. Each of the Allied governments maintained missions in the United States. Many of the purchases were made through J. P. Morgan & Co. Interpreters were needed for many transactions. The United States Government was directly interested in the prices and available supplies of practically all the materials involved. "Theoretically, it would appear logical to create immediately a Central Buying Organization to buy all munitions and all supplies for all the Allies and for all Departments of the United States Government." Practically, however, such a body would be unwieldy and would disrupt the existing programs of the War and Navy departments. A better solution would be to coordinate purchases of the more important raw materials. Legislation was needed to give the President the same powers over the control of output, manufacturing facilities, and prices for the Allied governments as he already had on behalf of the United States Government. A standard was needed by which the reasonableness of prices could be determined. For these purposes, a board or department, judicial rather than administrative in character, might be established to control prices and to set and enforce priorities. At the outset, it would not necessarily be required to deal with more than a relatively small number of materials, such as steel, copper, spelter, aluminum powder, and explosives.

ENCLOSURE

George Gordon Moore to Edward Mandell House

Dear Colonel House: New York May 17th, 1917.

I hope the President will not be stampeded by the clamor to rush troops to France. While I believe that every American should die, if necessary, to defeat Germany, my rather intimate contact with the War from its beginning compels a contrary conclusion as to the method of achieving this result. I have a vivid memory of the Dardanelles Expedition conceived with the same enthusiasm and lack of sanity and military thought. Modern artillery gives overwhelming superiority to the army on the defensive and three years of warfare have shown the impossibility of an offensive succeeding against an army possessed of artillery and machine-guns adequately manned. For this reason Ypres, Verdun, the Somme and the Dardanelles were German and British failures. To-day if England and France would go upon the defensive and stop the needless wastage of men, they can maintain their lines indefinitely. This condition may only be altered when economic distress or internal disorders have so weakened the German army that the application of overwhelming superiority in men and material may break their lines and defeat their army. To wait until we have carefully prepared such an army should be our national objective. Political urgency and the personal ambition of commanders have caused a hideous wastage of the man-power of England and France in attacks from which there was no intelligent hope of success, and the fighting of the past thirty days shows that the Germans have learned this lesson but our Allies have not.

I suggest that before any troops are sent to France it should be determined:

(1) That the man-power of France and England is inadequate, fighting a defensive fight to maintain their lines and that our man-power is needed for this purpose; or

(2) That if the troops requested are for the purpose of taking part in an offensive, that the President, upon the advice of his military advisers, is warranted in concluding that there is reasonable hope that the application of the forces of the American army shall produce victory.

I believe the higher wisdom lies in perfecting an army of at least two million men with adequate reserves and completely equipped, and when such force is ready, the application of this force of fresh men against the war-wearied Germans will give some real hope of success.

I recognize that at the moment this course is unpopular, but the certainty that such forces are coming will be a stimulant to our Allies and a depressing influence upon the Germans, and will avoid the needless wastage of American lives until the time when the sacrifice is warranted. I have seen the steady dissipation of the man-power of England without any intelligent plan and pray that this may not happen here.

Most sincerely,   George G. Moore

TLS (WP, DLC).

From the Diary of Josephus Daniels

May Tuesday 22 1917

Cabinet—Decided to hold united Flag day celebration at foot of monument. President to speak. He was not favorable to the temporary chicken coops Lansing suggested we put up.[1] Burleson opined Congress would not permit.

Baker & I took up copper & lead with President. Baruch said copper cos. thought they ought to have 25¢ instead of 19. Baker said, & all agreed, we should get same price for allies. President said we should offer good prices—10 to 20 per cent—offer that, if they declined, let them do so in writing & he would appeal to the country & demand they sell to all at fair prices. Baker to see Baruch and convey President's idea.

[1] That is, the "temporary" wooden-frame office buildings erected along the mall between the Capitol and the Lincoln Memorial, some of which remained in use until the 1960s.

André Tardieu to Alexandre Ribot

Washington, sans date reçu le 22 Mai 1917

No. 19 Haut Commissaire à Président du Conseil.

J'ai été présenté aujourd'hui par l'Ambassadeur au Président.

J'ai sommairement exposé à M. Wilson le but et l'organisation de ma mission: donner aux États-Unis, pour toutes les formes de la coopération le tableau exact et total de nos besoins et placer ce tableau dans le cadre plus général des besoins interalliés.

J'ai ajouté que la France pour organisation raisonnable comptait de façon particulière sur le concours américain: d'abord parce qu'elle a pendant plus de 2 ans servi d'armée de couverture à la coalition ensuite parce que dans l'effort commun, les

2 démocraties la France et l'Amérique ont un intérêt solidaire à démontrer que les Républiques ne sont pas inférieures aux monarchies quand, attaquées, elles ont à se défendre.

L'accueil du Président a été très cordial, après m'avoir indiqué les mesures que les États-Unis envisagent pour coordonner les fabrications et les transports en évitant une concurrence sans règle, il m'a dit qu'il ferait tout pour faciliter ma tâche et celle de mes services et que je pourrais toujours m'addresser à lui.

J'en ai profité pour lui demander s'il m'autorisait à lui envoyer l'exposé sommaire, avec (mot passé) à l'appui de nos principaux besoins. Il m'a répondu qu'il serait heureux de le recevoir et je vais le lui adresser.

Cette première entrevue confirme l'impression de parfaite bonne volonté que j'ai recueilli, depuis mon arrivée, dans les divers Ministères. L'état d'esprit dont la mission Viviani a recueilli la manifestation enthousiaste demeure et ne demande qu'à se traduire en actes.

Le premier contact avec les Anglais a été également satisfaisant. Je vous l'exposerai dans un télégramme consacré aux questions techniques, dont nous poursuivons l'examen dans des réunions quotidiennes.   Tardieu.

T telegram (Guerre 1914-1918, États-Unis, Vol. 512, pp. 184-85, FFM-Ar).

T R A N S L A T I O N

Washington, no date
received May 22, 1917

No. 19 High Commissioner to President of the Council of Ministers.

I was presented today to the President by the Ambassador.

I gave Mr. Wilson a summary description of the goal and organization of my mission: for all the forms of cooperation, to give to the United States the exact and total picture of our needs, and to place this picture in the more general framework of inter-Allied needs.

I added that, as an equitable arrangement, France counted particularly on American cooperation: first, because for more than two years the French army has provided the cover army for the coalition, and second, because in the common effort the two democracies, France and America, have a common interest in showing that republics are in no way inferior to monarchies when they are attacked and have to defend themselves.

The President's greeting has been very cordial. After outlining for me the measures that the United States envisages for co-ordinating manufactures and transport to avoid unbridled competition, he told me that he would do everything to ease my task and that of my staff, and that I could always come and see him.

I took the opportunity to ask if he authorized me to send him the summary exposition with (word missing) indicating our principal needs. He said that he would be glad to receive it, and I shall send it to him.

This first interview confirms the impression of perfect good will that I have gained, since my arrival, in the various departments. The spirit that gave the Viviani mission such an enthusiastic impression remains, and it only needs to be translated into acts.

The first contact with the English has been equally satisfying. I shall describe it for you in a telegram devoted to technical questions, which we are examining in daily meetings.

Tardieu

To Robert Lansing

My dear Mr. Secretary,   The White House [c. May 23, 1917].

I have fully informed you orally, of what I said to Ambassador Naon,[1] but return his letter for your files.

The despatches show a very poor chance for Argentina to pull anything off!   Faithfully Yours,   W.W.

WWTLI (SDR, RG 59, 763.72119/587½, DNA).
[1] Wilson saw Naón at the White House on May 23.

To Frank Irving Cobb

Personal.

My dear Cobb: The White House 23 May, 1917

Thank you for your letter of May twenty-second. You may be sure I am willing to consider any reasonable solution of the censorship question. With ninety-nine out of every hundred papers the question would not arise, but, as I am sure you know better than I do, there are some papers and some news agencies which we simply cannot trust and I felt it absolutely essential for the safety of the country that I should have some power in the premises.

I am greatly obliged to you for the kind last paragraph of your letter. I think you know how I value your friendship and approval.

In haste

Cordially and faithfully yours,   Woodrow Wilson

TLS (IEN).

To Newton Diehl Baker

Personal and Confidential.

My dear Mr. Secretary: The White House 23 May, 1917

House has just sent me the enclosed memoranda which I take the liberty of sending over to you. The one from George G. Moore about defensive and offensive warfare on the western front in Europe makes a considerable impression on me and I should very much like to discuss it with you when we have the next opportunity.

Cordially and faithfully yours,   Woodrow Wilson

TLS (N. D. Baker Papers, DLC).

From Robert Lansing, with Enclosure

My dear Mr. President: Washington May 23, 1917.

I had a talk a few days ago with Mr. Bullard about going to Russia. He seemed disposed to accept the appointment and I asked him to consult with Mr. Patchin as to the specific line of work to be done at Petrograd, carrying out the general plan of useful publicity there.

I received the enclosed letter from him this morning, in which he seems disposed to decline the position. I also enclose a memorandum by Mr. Patchin of the conversation which he had with Mr. Bullard on Monday.[1] Will you please return the letter and memorandum to me, and also kindly advise me what you think we should do in the circumstances?

Faithfully yours,   Robert Lansing.

[1] P. H. Patchin, "MEMORANDUM FOR THE PRESIDENT," May 23, 1917, TI MS (SDR, RG 59, 124.61/28½, DNA).

ENCLOSURE

Arthur Bullard to Robert Lansing

My dear Mr. Secretary: Washington, D. C., May 22, 1917.

After talking with Mr. Patchin, as you requested, I find that I entirely misunderstood the situation and I would not care to accept the position he offers me, except at the direct request of the President.

When Mr. Creel first spoke to me of the matter, he said that the President had asked him to suggest some one to accompany the Mission to Russia to facilitate their contact with the Press, and that he had proposed my name. A few days later he showed me a letter from the President, which indicated that Mr. Wilson had decided to appoint me.

I could get no very clear idea from Mr. Patchin of the work it is now proposed for me to do. As nearly as I could understand, it is a permanent position which he has in mind and the duties limited to distributing to the Russian press such bulletins of official news as the Department sends out and the writing of reports for the Department. The salary which Mr. Patchin proposed is liberal,[1] but that is not what interests me. Such limited work for the Department is not attractive to me.

I am a journalist, and feel that whatever usefulness I can offer must be along that line. Having been in Russia a good deal, I was anxious to get back. It seemed to me that there was in the President's offer an opportunity for this kind of service for which I am fitted in the work with the Mission. But I have no desire to enter the diplomatic career permanently.

I would not have allowed the matter to drag on so long if I had not been under a misapprehension. I understood that the President's intention was that I should be offered an opportunity for real work in my profession.

I am, Mr. Secretary,   Very truly yours,   A. Bullard.

TLS (SDR, RG 59, 124.61/28½, DNA).
[1] It was $5,000 a year and travel expenses.

From William Phillips, with Enclosure

Dear Mr. President: Washington, May 23, 1917.

At the request of Mr. House I am sending you a copy of a letter which he has recently received from Mr. W. H. Buckler of the American Embassy in London. It is a very pessimistic letter in regard to the submarine situation.

With assurances of respect, etc., I am, my dear Mr. President,

Faithfully yours, William Phillips

TLS (WP, DLC).

ENCLOSURE

William Hepburn Buckler to Edward Mandell House

Dear Colonel House: London, May 4, 1917.

Many thanks for your letter of April 19th (received May 1) about the change in peace terms, and for your kind messages through Mr. Whitehouse with whom I had a long talk yesterday. He thoroughly appreciates his luck in having been spectator of events—from a "stage box" so to speak—at that great crisis, and is filled with gratitude to the President and to yourself.

His escapes on the BALTIC were narrower than he could have wished: at 250 miles from Ireland one torpedo was dodged, at 25 miles out another; clothes were kept on all night, and a boat-load of torpedoed sailors could not be picked up. The captain saw only the wake of the oncoming torpedoes, but in neither case any sign of the submarines, so that gunnery was of no avail.

The gravity of this warfare of "U against you" (to quote the Daily Mail) is but partly revealed to the public here, the tonnage figures are still withheld and one of the best naval critics, Pollen[1] —a great friend of Symington,[2] our Naval Attaché—has been muzzled, as you will see from the enclosed "Star."

I had a long talk yesterday with Walter Runciman[3] who does not hide his profound anxiety, and whose views are of special interest because he has within the last fortnight been visiting the great shipbuilding works on the Wear and the Tyne—i.e. Sunderland and Newcastle—,as well as Cardiff and Bristol. Also his wife's brother-in-law, Sir Kenneth Anderson, is now head of a big department under the Shipping Controller (Sir Joseph Mclay). For the first time I learnt that all British freight steamers in the Indian and Far Eastern trades, as well as in other parts of the world, have for the past six weeks been withdrawn in order to carry foodstuffs. This is a great blow to British Commerce as well as to manufactures, for it means that the Lancashire Cotton-Mills will shortly close down.

As to new output of British tonnage it was the consensus of

opinion among the big builders whom R. consulted that for 1917 this could hardly exceed one million tons. The men all work with unflagging energy but are handicapped by a loss of 25% of the skilled hands; in other words the yards have barely 75% of the skilled staffs of peace time.

It seems incredible that the War Office cannot be induced to release such men at the present crisis, but R. failed last year in persuading them to do this, and his successors at the Board of Trade seem to succeed no better. A month ago the total loss of world tonnage was at the rate of six million tons a year; now it is at the rate of over ten million tons a year (1,700,000 tons for the two months February and March, multiplied by six = 10,-200,000) and the loss of British ships alone is at the rate of about six million tons a year.

Thus, even if there be no increase in rate of losses this summer, England is annually losing 6 million and replacing only 1 million tons. Runciman says—and these figures say it even more plainly—that everything depends on what *the U. S. can do.*

Five things are important for us to produce as quickly as possible: (1) fast sea-going destroyers, (2) small freight-carrying steamers for running foodstuffs through the blockade, (3) guns for arming merchant ships, (4) gunners to serve these guns—four to a gun (5) engineers trained to operate merchant ships' engines. The explanation of this last need is that within the past fortnight at Cardiff ships' engineers have shown a disquieting tendency to seek munition-jobs on shore instead of going to sea in a death-trap, i.e. the engine-room of a tramp-steamer slow enough to be torpedoed.

This same tendency has for some time been growing among firemen, but they are readily replaced. The defection of the engineers is a far more serious symptom, yet not surprising; occupants of the engine room are more likely than are deck hands to be killed by the explosion or drowned if their ship sinks quickly. The seriousness of all this is painfully obvious, especially when one hears from Captain MacDougall (our Naval Attaché)[4] that the type of destroyer required takes a year to turn out, and that the gears of their high powered turbines can only be cut in this country where the gear-cutting machines are already in arrears with their work. How long, I wonder, will it take American energy to produce at home these essential gear-cutters? One feels that the saving of the situation is literally a race against time.

May our press face these facts and not copy the self-complacent clap-trap about sea-power, invincible fleets, etc., with which the British public has so long been drugged.

This morning's TIMES account of things in Washington gives
one hope, yet I cannot imagine that our people as a whole have
yet grasped what they are up against.

I cannot help wondering whether a realization that the Entente
were "all in" did not have much to do with our entrance into the
war, for it is fairly clear that but for this intervention it would
soon be over and that peace would be by no means "without victory."

This inevitable increase in our burdens will have the great
advantage of making our voice more potent in the Peace Conference. I am glad that Mr. Whitehouse will disabuse his Liberal
friends of their fears, which I mentioned last week, as to our un-
pacific tendencies.

This month's ENGLISH REVIEW is interesting for the complete
conversion of Austin Harrison[5] (son of Frederic Harrison)[6] from
ultra-smashing jingoism to the ideals of the President's speech.
By way of contrast I am enclosing Blackwood's, with an article
about us and the Russians that might almost have been written
before 1789 but is none the less amusing.[7]

I call your attention to the letter of welcome from Liberal
M.P.s to Russia, which was cabled by the Embassy and widely
published there.

Nabokow,[8] their Chargé d'Affaires, a decided progressive, is
rather hurt, I understand, by the official coolness shown here
to the Revolution and by the fact that Lloyd George is holding
meetings with members of the Entente regarding foreign affairs
without the attendance of any Russian representative.

Rosen,[9] the new Ambassador to Washington, seems an excellent appointment, as he is moderate and anti-annexationist—so
far at least as Constantinople is concerned.

Yours very sincerely,   W. H. Buckler

W.R. expressed surprise at the recent German estimate of
total Allied and neutral tonnage sunk in February and March
being so near the actual figures: 1,800,000 tons instead of 1,700,-
000 the true amount. He said it showed how accurate the wireless reports from submarines must be and how well the submarine captains size up the dimensions of the ships which they
torpedo.

TLS (WP, DLC).
    [1] Arthur Joseph Hungerford Pollen, a writer on naval affairs for the London
Star and other publications.
    [2] Comdr. Powers Symington, U.S.N., naval attaché at London, 1912-1916.
    [3] Walter Runciman, President of the Board of Trade, 1914-1916; M.P.
for Hartlepool; son of Sir Walter Runciman, Bart., shipowner.
    [4] Capt. William Dugald MacDougall, U.S.N., naval attaché at London since
September 1916.

[5] Austin Harrison, "Germany *versus* the World," *The English Review*, XXIV (May 1917), 461-69. Harrison wrote: "The entry of America following on the Russian Revolution gives the war a spiritualism which distinguishes it from all other wars. It has become a crusade. Everywhere doors are opening; all over the world men are conscious of an intellectual growth which is the one great hopeful sign in this gigantic madness."

[6] Frederic Harrison, author, president of the English Positivist Committee, 1880-1905.

[7] An unsigned article, "Musings Without Method," *Blackwood's Magazine*, CCI (May 1917), 808-20. It criticized Wilson's policies, asked whether the world was safe *from* his type of democracy, reviewed German penetration of Russia since the eighteenth century, and commented that, if only Russia had "discovered at the beginning a Mirabeau of her own, there would have been no danger."

[8] Konstantin Dmitrievich Nabokov, Chargé d'Affaires of the Russian embassy in London.

[9] Baron Roman Romanovich Rosen, Russian Ambassador to the United States, 1905-1911, and one of Russia's plenipotentiaries at the peace negotiations at Portsmouth, N. H., following the Russo-Japanese War (1904-1905). As it turned out, Rosen did not become Ambassador to the United States to succeed George Bakhmet'ev.

From David Starr Jordan

Stanford University, Calif., May 23, 1917.

Feel greatly heartened by your Heflin letter reiterating adherance to principles address January twenty second. Opposition of Metropolitan press to that address gives expectations they will later try vigorously to defeat international principles thus enunciated. Seems to me well that you should make categorical statement you regard message as covenant with American people and would declare explicit aim to help rescue people oppressed by intolerable system securing world peace and justice to Belgium, France, Alsace, etc., thus to clarify would command support from many hitherto morally reluctant or distrustful of war results.   David Starr Jordan.

T telegram (WP, DLC).

From Thomas Pryor Gore

My dear Sir: Washington. May 23, 1917.

I beg to acknowledge your note of May 17th, inquiring whether my idea in relation to Senate Joint Resolution No. 62 preceded the recent conference at the White House.

Answering, permit me to say that the Joint Resolution in question was introduced in the Senate on May 14th, and the conference, as you will remember, was held on May 15th. Perhaps I ought to acquit any one else of responsibility by saying that the measure was drafted and presented upon my sole responsibility.

There are several ideas which influenced me in preparing and presenting this resolution.

In the first place, it was necessary to choose between devolving the duties of a food controller on the Secretary of Agriculture or creating an independent and separate agency. As Chairman of the Committee on Agriculture and Forestry I was unwilling to devolve such duties on the Secretary of Agriculture. This Department enjoys and should continue to enjoy the confidence and favor of the people. If the powers of a food controller are ever exercised with rigor it must of necessity occasion more or less disappointment and criticism. I felt that this criticism ought not to be directed toward the Department of Agriculture, which is a permanent institution, but should rather be concentrated upon a transient agency which will pass with the occasion. It was intended as a sort of lightning rod for the protection of the Department of Agriculture.

In the second place, it was necessary to make choice between a single administrative officer and a commission consisting of several members. I have a strong predilection in favor of the former system. A single executive officer for a single task undoubtedly insures greater efficiency and despatch. It also centralizes and fixes the responsibility.

In the third place, it was necessary to make a choice between the plan of conferring general power on the President to erect such agency as he might deem necessary, or expressly and directly creating such an agency, fixing in a general way the powers to be conferred and the duties to be performed. Personally, I prefer the latter plan, because it is more direct and definite. It is possible, however, that the Congress may prefer the former plan, because it is indefinite and general. The important point, however, was to have both plans accessible so that we can take choice of tracks and pursue the line of least resistance.

Further I may say that the proposition conferring power to fix prices will encounter most stubborn opposition in the Senate. I can not foretell whether it will pass or fail, but even if it should fail there are many important functions which could be performed by a food controller or administrator. It is a matter of the first importance that there should be cooperation and not competition between the United States and the Allies in the markets of the world. Senate Joint Resolution No. 62 contains ample raw materials and conveys ample powers for the erection and operation of a pretty complete system. It enables the President to transfer the duties of any officer or agency of the Government to the food controller, and to direct any officer or agent of the Government to render him such assistance as may be found necessary. It conveys a maximum of power in a minimum of language.

At the time it was drafted I had not examined the Defense of the Realm Act nor the Order in Council establishing a ministry of foods and providing for a food controller. Upon comparison I was surprised not only at the many points of similiarity but at the many points of identity.

Permit me to say finally, that much as I was opposed to the war I shall do whatever is necessary to be done to carry our arms to a speedy and complete triumph, subject only to the limitations of the Constitution and to the obligations of international law and humanity. We are now waging war against the spirit of absolutism and the doctrine of state necessity. I agree with you entirely that we must avoid not only the substance but even the semblance of Prussian autocracy. I hope it will not be necessary to confer autocratic power on any officer or department of the Government. It would be unfortunate to familiarize the people even with the forms and phrases of depotism. As a matter of tactics and prudence I think it of the highest importance that we should not go so far so fast as to occasion a revulsion of public sentiment that would be prejudicial to the vigorous prosecution of the war.

Assuring you of my earnest desire to cooperate within these limitations, I am   Truly yours,   T. P. Gore

P.S. Please pardon my delay. (Dictated May 21st)

TLS (WP, DLC).

From Cleveland Hoadley Dodge

Dear President   New York May 23d, 1917

I have been looking forward to seeing you tomorrow or Friday at the Red Cross meetings but for the first time in my life I am completely hors de combat. I never had a trained nurse before but now I have one to care for the streptococci in my throat (familiarly known as "quinsy")

I am not seriously sick but the miserable bugs make me weak as a cat. I wouldn't bother you with this lugubrious tale, except that I don't want you to think that I am shirking my Red Cross duties after all your splendid help & cooperation. My great joy is to read about the glorious way in which you are handling all the big problems which you have tackled. I wish I could do more to help you, but about all I can do now is to think of you and pray for you.

There will be no Corona this year but when the Summer comes if you can ever get a day off, & sail up the Hudson, come & bide a wee with us & get a little golf at St Andrews.

Grace joins with me in warmest regards & wishes for you all
Yours affectionately   C H Dodge

The way you handled the Colonel was simply out of sight

ALS (WP, DLC).

Arthur James Balfour to Lord Robert Cecil

Washington. May 23rd [1917].

Personal & Secret

President is taking advantage of despatch of mission to Russia from U. S. to issue manifesto which he read to me[1] in order to counteract effect which some of his earlier ⟨pacifist⟩ pronouncements have apparently had in Russia. ⟨He consulted me as to language he proposed to hold.⟩ This manifesto is also designed to encourage liberal opinion in Germany. I think it will do good. This was interpreted as meaning that at the peace [conference] there was to be no transfer of territory & no indemnities. This is by no means his view. For example he would like to restore Poland & Alsace Lorraine: and to exact compensation for Belgium & Northern France.

Hw telegram (FO 115/2317, p. 343, PRO).
    [1] That is, Wilson's message to the Russian Provisional Government, printed at May 22, 1917. Wilson had had a long conference with Balfour at the British embassy during the late afternoon of May 21.

Arthur James Balfour to the Foreign Office

Washington, 23rd May 1917.

Following from Mr. Balfour.

In conversation with Mr Lansing yesterday I raised the question of a Polish army consisting of about one hundred thousand men recruited in the United States fighting in France under the American flag but definitely described as Polish. Quite apart from the fighting value of such an army its creation ought to have a very favorable effect upon the international situation in central Europe and it would greatly hamper if not entirely defeat any German attempts to get an important section of the Poles either to fight for them or to work for them.

Mr Lansing informed me that the scheme had been agreed to

in principle by his Government. I expressed great satisfaction at this result adding that the sooner the affair was made public the better would be its effect.   A.J.B.

T telegram (FO 115/2302, p. 234, PRO).

From David Lawrence

PERSONAL and CONFIDENTIAL

My dear Mr. President: [Washington] May 24, 1917

I think I may be of service to you in straightening out the censorship tangle. I believe, as do many who have thought the thing out, that there should be a censorship law to prevent the revelation to the enemy of military information. I believe such a law can be obtained if the proper strategy is pursued.

Today several things happened which you ought to know about and which I am telling you not as a correspondent but as a friend in the hope that an amicable solution can be reached. First, I will set forth briefly the situation and then suggest a remedy.

George Creel submitted some regulations.[1] With the greater part of them, most correspondents agreed. They would have been approved today but the effort in Congress to revive the censorship provision in the espionage law stopped such action. Such was the temper of the correspondents that at a meeting today even a motion which I made to secure the adoption of the regulations as a *tentative basis* was defeated. The argument was made that the Administration purposed to enact the regulations into law anyway and that the approval by the correspondents would be used as a means of bringing that about in Congress. It was argued that George Creel was all right, that he had the right point of view and promised much but apperantly he had no authority. The correspondents claimed that they had been assured at their Monday meeting that if the regulations submitted were approved there would be no censorship law. They claimed that Mr Lansing has one set of ideas, Mr Creel another, and now Congress is to be asked to enact a law superseding all. In view of what was termed a chaotic situation, the point was made that the Washington correspondents ought not go on record at all. As I said before, a few of us tried to have some action taken which would indicate our approval of the regulations in principle. I tried finally to secure the appointment of a committee of ten correspondents to confer with you personally and learn your views as well as exchange ideas. The point was made that you might not desire to receive such a delegation and finally the motion was not acted on at all, a motion to adjourn having been adopted.

Now, I think there is a distrust which ought not to exist, an antagonism that has no just foundation and a beginning of friction that will kill the very spirit of cooperation which must prevail in order to enable the people to understand thoroughly what their government is doing. My remedy would be this:

I would suggest that *you invite* the Washington correspondents to the White House, the whole body of them, so that they may express to you their viewpoint. Similarly, I am sure they will not fail to be impressed by such information as you must have which prompts you to ask for some kind of a censorship law. If there is an understanding, even of a general nature, the obstacles to legislation will have been removed. I do believe, however, that the censorship provision should be detached and separately introduced after conferences with the leading newspaper editors. The moment the necessity for some legislation is thoroughly understood and the desire of the Administration to consult the editors is manifest, I think the latter will voluntarily indicate the lines on which a bill could be drawn that would cover the needs of the situation.

The trouble now is that the correspondents here and the editors outside believe there has not been good faith on the part of the Government. The promises made at the Department of Justice that the editors would be consulted before legislation was introduced are held up as proof of the charges. In a situation like this, I am confident that only you can bring harmony out of confusion. And instead of an irritated press, ready to pounce on every slight thing and hammer men who are trying only to do their best with a machinery and a people unused to war, we will have a press that will be charitable in its criticisms and will inspire the people with a confidence in their government. I write you very infrequently and only when I think something is going to happen that should not happen, when I think, indeed, trouble for you can be avoided. I believe that in the censorship situation lies enough danger of every kind to make your task twice as difficult as it would otherwise be. Prompt action, the introduction of a spirit of cooperation and mutual trust, will bring about a better atmosphere all around. With best wishes,

I am,   Very sincerely yours,   David Lawrence

P.S. The meeting of the correspondents with you would afford a splendid opportunity to indicate how completely you are behind George Creel whose work will be much easier if you touch on the confidence you have in him, etc.

TLS (WP, DLC).

¹ Creel had just held a confidential conference with the Washington press corps in the Senate press gallery on May 23 and had read to them the "Preliminary Statement to the Press" printed as an Enclosure with WW to G. Creel, May 17, 1917. The *New York Times*, in reporting about the meeting, said only that the correspondents had responded that they wished to consider the matter further. *New York Times*, May 28, 1917. Creel, on May 27, gave out the statement for publication. A summary of the "Preliminary Statement," with long quotations, is printed in *ibid.*

From Edward Mandell House, with Enclosure

Dear Governor: New York. May 24, 1917.

I am enclosing a letter which I asked Raymond E. Swing to write in order to summarise the main points he made in a conversation with me.

Swing has been regarded as one of the most reliable American correspondents in Germany. He has represented the Chicago News in Berlin for the past five years. I am sure you will be interested in what he says.

Affectionately yours,   E. M. House

TLS (WP, DLC).

ENCLOSURE

Raymond Edwards Swing to Edward Mandell House

My dear Colonel House: New York, May 23, 1917.

With your permission I shall summarize what I said today.

The liberal movement in Germany has grown steadily in power. Its chief support, naturally, comes from the socialist parties, but practically the entire Progressive-Popular Party, half of the Centrists and a third of the National Liberals wish moderate peace terms, while even a greater political backing is behind the demand for franchise reform in Prussia and responsible ministry in the Empire.

The greater political ability and more unified organization of the conservatives is responsible for the external view of a half-and-half division on these questions.

The German people wish peace at any acceptable price. Scheidemann told me a week before I left Berlin that if the Allies offered a peace which left German territory intact and her commercial growth unhampered, and if, then, the Government should refuse these terms, there would be a revolution in twenty-four hours, "and I should place myself at the head of it." He has made the same statement in numberless speeches. It is the only basis upon which Germany can continue the war, this belief that the Allies insist on taking German soil and on shackling her commercially.

Should such moderate terms be announced by the Allies I doubt whether the Government would dare refuse. Such leaders as Scheidemann, Naumann,[1] Delbrück,[2] Dernburg, Bernstorff, Erzberger and the minority socialists would be too formidable. The public behind them could not be defied.

It seems to me that the jingoes in Germany are getting too much help from the Allies. All statements about "no peace with the Hohenzollerns" bring the instantaneous reaction, even among backsliders from monarchy, of uniting support for the Emperor. I have witnessed it time and again. I saw the answer of the Allies to President Wilson[3] stop a process of swift disintegration and make grim patriots out of hopeful pacifists.

I doubt not Lord Cecil's recent reply to Bethmann Hollweg[4] was worth more to the war party in Germany than the next potato crop. The Germans are taking care of their own domestic affairs; they resent interference, or the threat of it. Such threats can only retard the constitutional reform movement in the Reichstag and delay the fulfilment of the Kaiser's pledge of universal and equal suffrage.

The great thing, of course, would be the announcement of liberal terms by the Allies. A clear and exalted word spoken on this subject, spoken so the whole world would hear, would bring about the almost instantaneous collapse of the war. For it is not British, nor French, nor German jingoism which keeps the war going, it is the belief in each of these countries that liberal terms are impossible. Once let the people know—how *could* the war go on?

Let me, in closing, speak only one more point. The illusion prevails throughout the allied countries that the Scheidemann group are dupes of the Government and that Scheidemann is Bethmann's alter ego. On the contrary, Scheidemann's strength has forced the Chancellor to appear to be supporting a Scheidemann program. In the meantime the majority socialists have consistently, and with startling success, worked for making the Reichstag a true, popular assembly. These men are for democracy to the death. But they do not believe they must fight for it. "But if we must," Scheidemann told me once, "don't forget the Government has taught millions of men to make and throw hand grenades."

The old Germany is gone. Delbrück, Treitschke's successor,

was the first to announce his conversion to pacifism and to advocate the peace league. I talked with thirty editors in the Empire last fall, men of all shades of political thought, and not one dared predict that the next Reichstag would not be overwhelmingly radical. The new Empire is there already, the new Empire of popular rights. It needs only be enacted into law. To say incessantly that these great and genuinely democratic movements are merely tricks of an astute autocracy, subtle deceits, Prussian lies, is to do the cause of democracy in Germany immeasurable harm.

But the German people will never believe in our interest in them so long as the answer of the Allies to President Wilson remains unmodified.

I thank you once more for your kindness, and, with all my respects, beg to remain,

Faithfully yours,   Raymond E. Swing.

TCL (WP, DLC).

1 Friedrich Naumann, a publicist, Protestant theologian, and leader of the left-liberal Progressive Popular party (Fortschrittliche Volkspartei), editor of *Die Hilfe* and *Die Zeit*, author of *Mitteleuropa* (Berlin, 1915), and other works.

2 Hans Gottlieb Leopold Delbrück, Professor of History at the University of Berlin, editor of the *Preussische Jahrbücher* and writer on military and political history and affairs.

3 See W. G. Sharp to RL, Jan. 10, 1917, Vol. 40.

4 Bethmann Hollweg, who had addressed the Reichstag on May 15, had refused to go beyond what he had previously said about Germany's war aims but had proffered an olive branch to the new government in Russia if it would renounce all plans of conquest. *New York Times*, May 16, 1917. Lord Robert Cecil replied in the House of Commons on May 16 that, judging from the speech, there was "no inclination on the part of the Germans even to state what terms of peace" they were willing to accept. The Germans, Cecil went on, had a long record of having reforms thwarted by the "immediate surrender of the Government to the Junkers." Until the Junker spirit had been "exorcised," Cecil said, it was "ludicrous, apart from its want of dignity, to suggest that we should ask for terms from the German Emperor." Referring to the phrase then being widely circulated, "no annexation and no indemnity," Cecil denied that Great Britain had any idea of "Imperialistic conquest or aggrandisement," but he would not rule out an indemnity to Belgium, or territorial changes affecting (for example) the Near East, Africa, Poland, Alsace-Lorraine, and Italia Irredenta. He concluded by saying that the Allies were determined not to accept a peace "which will be no peace." *Parliamentary Debates: Commons*, 5th Ser., XCIII, Cols. 1665-76.

From Robert Langton Douglas[1]

London, May 24, 1917.

The Board of Governors of the National Gallery of Ireland and the Trustees of the Dublin Municipal Gallery unanimously and respectfully request Dr. Wilson to agree to sit for a portrait by Sargent. At the Red Cross sale held in London in 1915 the late Sir Hugh Lane,[2] Director of the National Gallery of Ireland, bought for ten thousand pounds the right to nominate a sitter for a portrait by Sargent and the right to possess the portrait. As legatees of Sir Hugh Lane these bodies, which include representatives of all parties in Ireland, ask you to sit for portrait.

Please reply to Captain R. Langton Douglas, the National Gallery Merrion Square, Dublin.   (Not signed)

T telegram (WP, DLC).
  [1] Director of the National Gallery of Ireland in Dublin.
  [2] He had perished on *Lusitania*.

A Proclamation[1]

[May 25, 1917]

Inasmuch as our thoughts as a nation are now turned in united purpose toward the performance to the utmost of the services and duties which we have assumed in the cause of justice and liberty;

Inasmuch as but a small proportion of our people can have the opportunity to serve upon the actual field of battle, but all men, women, and children alike may serve and serve effectively by making it possible to care properly for those who do serve under arms at home and abroad;

And inasmuch as the American Red Cross is the official recognized agency for voluntary effort in behalf of the armed forces of the nation and for the administration of relief:

Now, therefore, by virtue of my authority as President of the United States and president of the American Red Cross, I, Woodrow Wilson, do hereby proclaim the week ending June 25, 1917, as Red Cross Week, during which the people of the United States will be called upon to give generously and in a spirit of patriotic sacrifice for the support and maintenance of this work of national need.   Woodrow Wilson.

Printed in the *Official Bulletin*, I (May 25, 1917), 1.
  [1] There is a WWsh draft of the following document in the C. L. Swem Coll., NjP.

A News Report

[May 25, 1917]

YOUNG GENERALS FOR FRANCE

Following the final conference between President Wilson and Maj. Gen. Pershing at the White House[1] it was announced unofficially that Secretary of War Baker is searching for young officers to be made brigadier generals for service in France.

After having discussed the problems which will confront our

arms in France with British and French military commanders both the President and the head of the first expeditionary force were prepared to make their preliminary plans for joining the allies in the trenches.

Printed in the *Washington Post*, May 26, 1917.

[1] Pershing later wrote about this meeting as follows: "On the afternoon of May 24th, the Secretary of War and I called on President Wilson for my first and only meeting with him until he came to France after the Armistice. After engaging in conversation with Mr. Baker for a few minutes on the subject of shipping, he turned to me and said, 'General, we are giving you some very difficult tasks these days,' to which I replied, 'Perhaps so, Mr. President, but that is what we are trained to expect.' Mr. Wilson spoke of my recent expedition into Mexico and inquired about my acquaintance with France. I had naturally thought that he would say something about the part our Army should play in the war in coöperation with the Allied armies, but he said nothing.

"Upon leaving, I said, 'Mr. President, I appreciate the honor you have conferred upon me by the assignment you have given me and realize the responsibilities it entails, but you can count upon the best that is in me.' His reply was, 'General, you were chosen entirely upon your record and I have every confidence that you will succeed; you shall have my full support.' The President then asked me to convey to His Majesty the King of Great Britain and to the President of France his greetings and best wishes. His manner was cordial and simple and I was impressed with his poise and his air of determination. His assurance of confidence in me was gratifying, but in the difficult situation that arose later regarding the manner of giving military aid to the Allies he was inclined to yield to the persistent importunities of the Allied representatives in Washington. In the actual conduct of operations I was given entire freedom and in this respect was to enjoy an experience unique in our history." John J. Pershing, *My Experiences in the World War* (2 vols., New York, 1931), I, 37.

To Robert Seymour Bridges

My dear Mr. Bridges: [The White House] 25 May, 1917

It was certainly most gracious of you to send me the verses, "To the United States of America," which have given me, as I am sure they will give all Americans, so much gratification, and I particularly thank you for the gracious note which accompanies them. It is very delightful to exchange such greetings of genuine sympathy and correspondence of thought, and I beg to be permitted to send you my warmest personal greetings and good wishes.

Cordially and sincerely yours,   Woodrow Wilson

TLS (Letterpress Books, WP, DLC).

To Robert Lansing, with Enclosure

My dear Mr. Secretary: The White House 25 May, 1917

The writer of the enclosed letter, Doctor Mackenzie, is a man whose quality I have so thoroughly tested that I know that he speaks with knowledge whenever he gives information such as the enclosed letter contains concerning the Reverend Alexander Francis,[1] and I would be very much obliged if in sending matter to Petrograd, if you are sending anything thither, you would have conveyed to Doctor Mott in quotation the portion of this letter which is under the caption, "First."

Cordially and sincerely yours,   Woodrow Wilson

TLS (SDR, RG 59, 861.404/3, DNA).
[1] The Editors have been unable to add anything to the identification of the Rev. Mr. Francis given in the Enclosure.

E N C L O S U R E

From William Douglas Mackenzie

Hartford, Conn.

My dear Mr. President: May twenty-third 1917

Although I have thought it wiser and kinder not to trouble you with any letter during the past anxious months you have been constantly in my thought and in my prayer. It is a great satisfaction to know that one has had confidence in you all through these trying months, and that you have now led the country to its momentous decision with marvellously united conviction and devotion of spirit.

I write now on two practical matters:

First; I am deeply interested in your appointment of John R. Mott. I wrote him a letter which I fear did not reach him before he left, as I got the enclosed reply from his Secretary, Mr. Barber.[1] In this letter I told him that probably of all living men the one who could most help him in his particular concerns with the religious problems of Russia, the best equipped and most influential is the Rev. Alexander Francis. He was for fifteen years or more minister of the American Church in Petrograd, and is intimately known to Mr. Breckenridge, former ambassador to the Russian Court.[2]

Mr. Francis is a really great authority on things Russian. He made himself famous by his chairmanship of the American Relief Committee at the time of the great famine in 1892. I know that Sir Donald Mackenzie Wallace[3] said that he would like Francis to take over his library and carry on his work when he lays it down.

He is not only thoroughly acquainted with Russia, but has the confidence of many prominent people in that country. He is a man of great executive ability, and speaks Russian, French and German fluently. He would be of immense value to Mott.

At present Francis is chaplain in the British force in France. I imagine that a cable would send him flying to Russia, unless, indeed, he has gone there already, as in his last letter to me he said he might be. His address is A.P.O. 3, B.E.F., France.

A second matter I wish to trouble you with.

If the war is prolonged, the strain will ultimately lie upon the intelligent convictions of the great democracies, especially those of America, England and Russia. It is of the utmost, indeed vital importance, to enlighten the minds of the people who are called upon to make prolonged sacrifices of the severest kind. This can only be done by a much more systematic course of instruction than has been attempted. I suggest that it is as important to mobilize the educational forces of these countries for this purpose as to raise money, manufacture munitions and train soldiers. I think you will agree with me.

It seems to me that one outcome of the visit of the British Commission might well be an agreement that such a system of popular education should be deliberately undertaken on an extensive scale by each government. It could be done at comparatively small expense. I see that a movement of this kind has been inaugurated by some educators in New York; but their program does not go deep enough. Popular lectures ought to be given throughout the country dealing with the spirit and purpose of the German Empire. For this, of course, the literature is abundant; but especially ought attention to be given to Cheradame's "Pangerman Plot Unmasked,"[4] and Dr. Bang's "Hurrah and Hallelujah."[5] A series of maps made from the former book, and the story of Pan-Germanism simply and frankly told would awaken any democracy in the world today to see this extreme danger. There should be no attempt to sow hatred of the Germans, no mere denunciation even of their war methods, except so far as these illustrate and fulfil the purposes embodied in their imperialistic program. I am deeply convinced that if the strain on our great democracies lasts long only such a work as this will give them the depth of conviction sufficient to sustain them in the great trial.

I have often pictured you and Mr. Arthur Balfour together, knowing that you would understand each other and have far more in common if leisure allowed than the present stifling war interests. It is a great many years since I met him, when, indeed, I was the means of introducing him to those relations to my old University of Edinburgh[6] which have been so fruitful to the University and, I think, to himself.

I trust his health will stand the extraordinary demands which he is making upon it in these awful days.

With ever warm regards,

Yours sincerely, W. Douglas Mackenzie

TLS (SDR, RG 59, 861.404/3, DNA).

¹ Benjamin Russell Barber, private secretary of John R. Mott. His letter, B. R. Barber to W. D. Mackenzie, May 19, 1917, TLS (SDR, RG 59, 861.404/3, DNA), is not printed.

² Clifton Rodes Breckinridge, Minister to Russia, 1894-1897.

³ Long-time journalist in various capacities with the London *Times*; editor of the tenth edition of the *Encyclopaedia Britannica*; author of a pioneering study, *Russia* (2 vols., London, 1877), which is still considered a classic.

⁴ André Chéradame, *The Pangerman Plot Unmasked: Berlin's Formidable Peace-Trap of "The Drawn War,"* trans. Lady Frazer (London, 1916; New York, 1917).

⁵ Jacob Peter Bang, *Hurrah and Hallelujah: The Spirit of New-Germanism, A Documentation*, trans. Jessie Bröchner (London, 1916; New York, 1917).

⁶ *Sic!*

To William Douglas Mackenzie

My dear Doctor Mackenzie: [The White House] 25 May, 1917

I have your important letter of May twenty-third and wish that I had time to send a reply worthy of its importance.

In the few minutes at my disposal, I can only say that I shall certainly try to convey to Doctor Mott in some way your information about the Reverend Alexander Francis, and, in the second place, that my attention is already being centered upon a feasible plan of popular instruction as to the meanings and exigencies of the war. I hope with all my heart that a plan can be worked out that will be effective. A good deal has been done in this direction already in Great Britain, and I think we can profitably follow some of the methods they have developed there.

I am always thankful for suggestions from those who, like yourself, really have thoughtful suggestions to make, and I want you to believe me always

Your sincere friend, Woodrow Wilson

TLS (Letterpress Books, WP, DLC).

To David Lawrence

My dear Lawrence: [The White House] 25 May, 1917

Thank you for your letter of May twenty-fourth. I fear that it would not be wise for me to pursue the course you suggest, just at present at any rate, because it might look as if I were trying to straighten it out when there is really nothing to straighten out; or, it might look as if I were trying to correct mistakes which Creel is thought to have made when I do not in my heart believe that he has made any.

I cannot help believing that continued intercourse with Creel such as the newspaper correspondents will have will more and more convince them of his unusual qualities, not only of sense but of trustworthiness. I depend upon their perceptions and their candor to find those qualities out, and I have very little doubt as to the result.

In haste　　　　　Faithfully yours,　Woodrow Wilson

TLS (Letterpress Books, WP, DLC).

To Cleveland Hoadley Dodge

My dear Cleve:　　　　　　The White House 25 May, 1917

I am deeply distressed to hear that you are laid up, and beg that you will take care of yourself. I don't think you know how indispensable you are to all of us.

It was generous of you to write, notwithstanding your weakness, and I thank you with all my heart for your letter.

All unite with me in affectionate and sympathetic messages.
　　　　　　Affectionately yours,　Woodrow Wilson

TLS (WC, NjP).

From Robert Lansing, with Enclosure

My dear Mr. President:　　　　Washington May 25, 1917.

I enclose a copy of a confidential memorandum which I received today from Mr. Balfour and which he asked me to transmit to you.　　　　Faithfully yours,　Robert Lansing.

TLS (WP, DLC).

ENCLOSURE

Washington May 24 1917.

MEMORANDUM.

The following are some brief notes on certain subjects of great importance which have been discussed during the stay of the British mission at Washington, but on which no final decision

appears to have been come to. Their enumeration may be con-
ve[n]ient to the Departments of both Governments.

(1). *Purchase of war materials, etc.,*

(a). The entry of the United States into the War has been of
incalculable benefit to the Allied cause, but has brought with it
some disadvantages which are inevitable, but I hope temporary.
When the United States of America were a great producing country but not a belligerent, the problem before the European Allies
as buyers in the American market was to prevent undue competition among themselves and to arrange for the financing and
transport of what they purchased. Very elaborate organisations
were devised for these purposes which on the whole worked fairly
well. The fact that most of the tonnage and most of the credit
were in one hand probably made it easier to come to a working
arrangement.

A new state of things, however, immediately arose on the
declaration of war by the United States. They became a fighting
country as well as a producing one. In the former capacity they
necessarily compete in their own markets with the Allies; and in
the absence of specific arrangements they inevitably obtain a
priority, both of manufacture and transport, undoubtedly injurious to the armies fighting in Europe and not necessarily of
advantage to the army which is being created in America.

Evidently therefore some co-ordination is urgently required by
which delays, whether in the execution of orders or in the transport of material may be avoided.

(b). There seems to be a general desire to obtain this co-
ordination by making all war purchases through a single channel: and this appears, as far as I can judge, to be the best, if not
the only method, of reaching the desired end. But if all purchases are to be made by one authority they must surely be also
made at one price; and to such a uniformity of procedure some
objection has I understand been raised by certain Departments in
the United States. I hope however that these objections will be
got over. Evidently the question is not a departmental one. It
must be treated as a whole. The U. S. A. are not merely great
sellers of war material; they are also great purchasers of war
material. All the wool, all the jute, and a very large part of the
rubber tin and ferro-manganese which they require come, I believe, from the British Empire. Evidently we have here a case in
which the policy to be adopted is one of reciprocal rationing—and
reciprocal rationing between allied Governments seems to carry
`with it as a practical, if not a logical, corollary, identity of price
to all purchasers.

II. *Military equipment.*

The subject of Munitions has been much debated by the experts in the United States War Department and those attached to the Mission. But points of the first importance seem still undecided; nor is there at present, so far as I am aware, any single authority in the Administration which has power to deal with them in their practical as well as their theoretical aspect. The discussions which have taken place have indeed been of great value; but evidently decisions are urgently needed. Delay in determining types necessarily involves delay in producing guns and ammunition; and this in turn must hamper the rapid equipment of a large American army. I need not say that I fully recognise that the equipment of United States troops is a matter for the United States Government alone; but in so far as the problem is looked at merely from the point of view of the Allied Armies in France, it seems fairly clear that the best and quickest results could be obtained by employing for the United States army the weapons on which the United States manufacturers have been engaged in producing for the British forces since the beginning of the war. It is believed that the immense quantity of material required for a new army could be more quickly produced in this way than in any other, and that when produced its management and transport at the front would be attended with fewer difficulties and complications than if a third type of equipment were introduced in addition to the two already in use. It is moreover evident that if the American Army in France could on emergency draw upon British reserves, their position would be much more secure than if they depended solely on their line of communication across the Atlantic.

III. *Merchant Tonnage.*

The vital importance of this to the Allied Cause is universally recognised, and admirable results seem likely to be produced as soon as Congress supplies the necessary funds.

Nevertheless I gather from Mr. Secretary Denman that in some quarters a misunderstanding has arisen on which perhaps it is desirable to say a word.

When the full scope of the danger arising from submarine warfare was realised by the Shipping Controller in London he set to work to contract for ships wherever ships could be built. Practically this meant the placing of orders in United States yards on a very large scale, since the yards of Great Britain and Canada were already utilised to their full capacity. The result has been that orders placed by the British Government, in addition to the large number that had been already placed by Norwegian ship-owners, practically filled up all the private yards in the United States. So far no distinction could be drawn by the least friendly critic between the procedure of Great Britain in respect of ships and its procedure in the case of shells or guns. But after the United States had come into the war the Shipping Board and General Goethals set to work to devise methods by which the great capacity of the United States for the manufacture of constructional steel could be diverted by Government action to the rapid construction of cargo steamers; and I learn from Mr. Denman that certain critics, taking these two facts together, have argued that the industry of the United States is to be upset in order that Great Britain may at the end of the war find itself in possession of a mercantile marine built in United States yards by United States labour, with the assistance of the United States Government, and at the cost of the United States public.

It need hardly be said that for this suggestion there is no foundation whatever. The ships were ordered (at very unremunerative prices!) before the United States were themselves involved in the war and therefore without consultation with them. But the British Government had & have no other interest than that mercantile tonnage should be produced as quickly as possible and in as large quantity as possible and that when produced it should be used to carry on the trades necessary for the effective conduct of the war. The question of ownership is one of very secondary importance; and in no circumstances whatever would the British Government allow themselves to enter into any controversy on such a matter with the Government of the United States who have a right to dictate the policy which, in their somewhat unusual circumstances, should be pursued and on whose justice the British Government entirely rely.

IV. *Naval questions.*

As regards Naval matters I have only two obser[v]ations to make. The way in which the Navy Department have met and are meeting out of their existing resources the request of the British Admiralty for destroyers and other anti-submarine craft has earned our profound gratitude; but the need for increasing the number of destroyers is one of the most urgent in the whole field of naval enterprise, and it would be a great misfortune if the Naval yards in the United States could not give material aid in carrying out this policy. This view I understand to be fully shared by the Navy Department and their technical advisers; but unfortunately both the space and the labour of the dockyards are largely occupied with the construction of ships on which the Government is naturally reluctant to stop work since they may be required to meet possible contingencies at the end of the present war. The only way, it would seem, of meeting this difficulty is to give the United States some kind of call upon Allied Capital ships should the need for them arise. I have spoken about this to Mr. Secretary Lansing; and it ought not, I think, to be impossible to devise some scheme for consideration by the Governments concerned.

The only other point which I need mention under this heading is the urgent necessity for finding tankers to carry oil for the British Navy. That Navy, so far as its newer type of fighting ships are concerned, is now much more dependent upon oil than upon coal; and it is absolutely necessary that oil in sufficient quantities should be supplied from overseas. For this additional tankers are urgently required. I add details in a note at the end of this paper.[1]

V. There is one other subject which I approach with great diffidence, fully appreciating the fact that the problem is one very largely of internal military administration, and that the difficulties of carrying out the policy which, on purely military grounds, the military members of the British Mission would desire to see adopted, might well seem insuperable to any Government which has to consider its army organization as a whole.

The facts, as I understand them, are as follows: The United States are sending out a small but well trained body of troops to take an immediate share in the fighting on the French front, where their presence is most important morally and materially. At the same time they are making arrangements for training an important Army in America which they hope to use with decisive effect at a later stage of the war.

Now I gather that, in the opinion of those competent to speak from experience, it will not be possible to train and get to the front this new Army until next Spring. But on the other hand they point out that if, altogether apart from this Army, recruits could be sent out for training in France or in England, a really important addition could be made to the fighting man-power of the Allies in the course of the present year and before the winter season hampers military operations. The art of rapidly training recruits has, under the stern pressure of necessity, been brought to the highest pitch of perfection in the French and British armies. I am assured that average recruits can, under the new system, be turned into good soldiers in nine or ten weeks. A whole body of training experts has been created, just as experts have been created in artillery or in aviation; while the atmosphere in which the training is carried on, in close proximity to the fighting line, makes it speedily effective. In these circumstances, and remembering that time is the essence of the problem, I venture to suggest that it may be worth while for the Military Authorities of the U. S. A. to consider whether the great and obvious difficulties in the way of sending over important numbers of American citizens to be trained abroad under conditions which make it difficult to see how they are, *for the moment*, to form part of an organized force under the Stars and Stripes, can in some way or another be surmounted.

T MS (WP, DLC).
¹ This "note" is missing.

From John Skelton Williams

Dear Mr. President: Washington May 25, 1917.

I am taking the liberty of handing you with this a copy of a statement which I am giving to the press tonight for publication in Sunday's papers, in regard to the banking situation and our financial preparedness, (especially with reference to the Liberty Bonds) showing conditions which I am sure must be gratifying to you.¹

My deepest concern at the moment is the enormously reduced purchasing power of the dollar. I cannot help feeling that it is very much like selling our Liberty Bonds at 25 cents on the dollar when we have to invest their proceeds in material and supplies at four times the prices prevailing three years ago, as in the case with the steel billets, or that we are selling them at $33\frac{1}{3}$ cents on the dollar when we invest their proceeds, in coal for example, at 300 per cent advance.

For steel billets which were quoted at $19 per ton just before the outbreak of the European War, July, 1914, manufacturers are now demanding $80 per ton. An advance of $60 per ton of course means an increase, on a production of 40 million tons, or 2.4 billion dollars.

In my railroad days I was accustomed to buy a million or two tons of coal a year at about 70 cents to 90 cents a ton, and I understand that the operators are now demanding for this coal from $4 to $6 per ton. An advance of $4 per ton on our coal output the last year of, say 600 million tons, accounts for just 2.4 billion dollars additional.

This means that coal men and steel men on basis of today's prices are demanding for a year's output of their product 6.2 billion dollars for the SAME QUANTITY (and quality) that in 1914 was selling on the basis of 1.4 billion dollars.

Unhappily, these enormous additional profits on coal and steel and iron are not being evenly distributed among the people. Things are becoming unbalanced and the intervention of your strong hand is greatly needed.

I have the utmost confidence that, however great the difficulties of the problems may seem to be, you will find the solution, and that, in the language of the old hymn, we may find that "the clouds we so much dread are big with mercies, and shall break, with blessings on our head."

Respectfully and faithfully yours,

Jno. Skelton Williams

TLS (WP, DLC).
¹ J. S. Williams, press release dated May 25, 1917, to be published May 27, T MS (WP, DLC). The release called attention to the vast new wealth in the form of bank deposits which had come to the United States since the beginning of the war and explained the advantages of investing this money in Liberty bonds.

Jean Jules Jusserand to the Foreign Ministry

Washington, reçu le 25 Mai 1917

CONFIDENTIEL

No. 695 M. Balfour et la mission anglaise quitteront ce soir Washington se rendront au Canada d'où, après une visite au Gouverneur, ils partiront pour l'Angleterre. Au cours d'une visite d'adieu que je lui ai faite M. Balfour s'est montré fort satisfait des dispositions rencontrées ici. Le Président est certainement résolu à continuer la guerre jusqu'à ce que la sécurité des nations libérales soit assurée. Comme les États-Unis ne revendiquent rien pour eux-même et que l'aide qu'ils donnent à la cause commune est gratuite, nous (fe)rions une politique dangereuse si nous nous montrions chicaniers ou exigeants. Le Ministre anglais a montré une confiance absolue dans l'issue de la guerre et dans une paix pas trop éloignée. "Vous viendrez sans doute alors en Europe (a-t-il) dit et nous la célébrerons ensemble." (1 gr. fx.) conditions de cette paix, il a les appréhensions que, je suppose, nous avons tous, spécialement en ce qui concerne le probleme Adriatique et celui de Constantinople; il m'a paru incliner pour cette ville pour le régime internationale, mais ne pouvoir d'ailleurs citer de cas où un tel régime ait réussi.

Personnellement M. Balfour a beaucoup plu; le Président qui se rapproche de lui par le côté réfléchi de son caractère, a eu pour lui maintes attentions; son séjour aura certainement fait du bien à la cause de son pays.

Jusserand

T telegram (Guerre 1914-1918, États-Unis, Vol. 507, p. 78, FFM-Ar).

Washington, received May 25, 1917

CONFIDENTIAL

695 Mr. Balfour and the English mission will leave Washington this evening for Canada, from whence, after visiting the Governor-General, they will depart for England. In the course of my farewell visit to Mr. Balfour, he showed himself very pleased with the arrangements arrived at here. The President is surely resolved to continue the war until the security of the liberal nations is assured. Since the United States wants nothing for itself, and since the aid it gives to the common cause is free, we would pursue a dangerous policy if we showed ourselves to be quibbling or demanding. The English Minister showed absolute confidence in the outcome of the war and in a peace not too far distant. "You will no doubt come then to Europe," he said, "and we shall celebrate together." [As for] the conditions of this peace, he has apprehensions which, I suppose, we all have, especially on the problem of the Adriatic and the problem of Constantinople. Concerning that city, he seems to me to incline toward internationalization, but, however, he cannot cite a single case where such an administration has succeeded.

Personally, Mr. Balfour has made a fine impression. The President, who is drawn to the reflective side of his character, has paid him a great deal of attention; his visit has certainly done much good for his country's cause. Jusserand

From Robert Langton Douglas

Dear Sir, [Dublin] May 26, 1917

On the 23rd instant, acting upon the instructions of the Board of Governors of the National Gallery of Ireland, and also of the Lord Mayor[1] and the Corporation of Dublin who are Trustees of the Dublin Municipal Gallery, I cabled to you Sir, respectfully requesting you to agree to sit for your portrait to Mr. Sargent R.A, who is now in America (Hotel Vendome, Boston). This invitation is unanimous. It comes from the representatives of all creeds and parties in Ireland. The Board of Governors of the National Gallery includes, on the one hand such men as the Earl of Mayo, Lord Rathdonnell and the Protestant Archbishop of Dublin,[2] & on the other hand such men as the Right Honble. Lawrence Waldron[3] and Mr. Desmond O'Brien.[4] Mr. James Stephens,[5] I may add, is Secretary to the Board.

It was Sir Hugh Lane, the late Director of the Gallery, who bought the right to nominate a sitter for the portrait, at the Red Cross sale of 1915. Mr. Sargent had said that he would paint a portrait for the Red Cross Society if a very high price were bid for it. Sir Hugh Lane bid £10,000 sterling. A few weeks later, he was drowned in the Lusitania. Except for a few small legacies, he left all his property (including the right to nominate a sitter for this portrait, and the right to the portrait when painted) to the Irish Galleries.

I have already had a reply to my cable to Mr. Sargent. He cables "Am most willing. I suppose you will communicate with President, then with me * * * *"

I earnestly trust that I may be able to tell my Board at their next meeting, and also the Lord Mayor of Dublin and the Trustees of the Municipal Gallery that you have kindly consented to do as they ask.

I am, sir,

Your obedient servant,   R. Langton Douglas.

ALS (WP, DLC).
  1 Laurence O'Neill.
  2 Dermot Robert Wyndham Bourke, 7th Earl of Mayo; Thomas Kane Mc-Clintock-Bunbury, 2d Baron Rathdonnell; and the Rt. Rev. John Henry Bernard, Archbishop of Dublin.
  3 Laurence Ambrose Waldron, stockbroker, Independent Nationalist M.P., 1904-1910, Privy Councilor for Ireland since 1911.
  4 Actually Dermod O'Brien, an artist who lived in Limerick.
  5 Poet and novelist, at this time registrar of the National Portrait Gallery in Dublin.

Newton Diehl Baker to John Joseph Pershing

Washington, May 26, 1917.

From: The Secretary of War.
To: Major-General J. J. Pershing, U. S. Army.
Subject: Command, authority and duties in Europe.

The President directs me to communicate to you the following:

1. The President designates you to command all the land forces of the United States operating in continental Europe and in the United Kingdom of Great Britain and Ireland, including any part of the Marine Corps which may be detached for service there with the army. From your command are excepted the Military Attaches and others of the Army who may be on duty directly with our several embassies.

2. You will proceed with your staff to Europe. Upon arrival in Great Britain, France and any other of the countries at war with the Imperial German Government, you will at once place yourself

in communication with the American Embassy and through its agency with the authorities of any country to which the forces of the United States may be sent.

3. You are invested with the authority and duties devolved by the laws, regulations, orders and customs of the United States upon the commander of an army in the field in time of war and with the authority and duties in like manner devolved upon department commanders in peace and war, including the special authorities and duties assigned to the commander of the Philippine Department in so far as the same are applicable to the particular circumstances of your command.

4. You will establish, after consultation with the French War Office, all necessary bases, lines of communication, depots, etc., and make all the incidental arrangements essential to active participation at the front.

5. In military operations against the Imperial German Government, you are directed to cooperate with the forces of the other countries employed against that enemy; but in so doing the underlying idea must be kept in view that the forces of the United States are a separate and distinct component of the combined forces, the identity of which must be preserved. This fundamental rule is subject to such minor exceptions in particular circumstances as your judgment may approve. The decision as to when your command, or any of its parts, is ready for action is confided to you, and you will exercise full discretion in determining the manner of cooperation. But, until the forces of the United States are in your judgment sufficiently strong to warrant operations as an independent command, it is understood that you will cooperate as a component of whatever army you may be assigned to by the French government.

6. You will keep the Department fully advised of all that concerns your command, and will communicate your recommendations freely and directly to the Department. And in general you are vested with all necessary authority to carry on the war vigorously in harmony with the spirit of these instructions and towards a victorious conclusion.   Baker

TS MS (WP, DLC).

From Newton Diehl Baker, with Enclosure

My dear Mr. President: Washington. May 27, 1917.

I return herewith the letter of Mr. Moore which was sent to you by Colonel House, and with it a memorandum drawn for my information by General Bliss, in which very warm concurrence is expressed with Mr. Moore's views. I confess, however, a belief that it is not going to be possible for us to act on the theory advocated by Mr. Moore, and to some extent at least approved by General Bliss, for the reason that our own country will not be willing to continue here a long drawn out process of training with the ultimate intention of doing fighting on a large scale at some later time.

I think it essential to keep the country in the spirit which made it necessary for us to go into this war. That spirit, I think to be a compound of two motives; first, the determination express[ed] by you to make the world safe for democracy, and second, the desire to bring the war to the earliest possible conclusion.

For us to sit by and allow the French and British to be worn down by further attrition would start three kinds of criticism; first, it would be said that our part in the war was too slow, and that the red tape of the General Staff was prevailing over the impetuous wish of Americans to be of present assistance, and this would be based upon statements made by the English and French, and also by soldiers in our own Army, to the effect that a long drawn out period of training in this country is unnecessary. Second, it would be said that we were running the chance of the French or Russians breaking down, and thus immeasurably increasing the size of our own task later. Third, it would be said that the immediate and overwhelming aggregation of forces, including our own, is the way most speedily to terminate the war, and not to feed nations to the German machine in detail.

I confess my own mind inclines to sympathize in some part with the last view expressed. As it seems to me the paramount objective ought to be the early conclusion of the war, and even if our men are not prepared to the highest point, I think we can trust the discretion of our own officers to assign them to less important tasks in the fighting until their preparation is perfected, but their mere presence on the fighting front relieves better prepared men of the French and English armies for the more trying operations.

I have this morning been going over the question of building cantonments for the forces which we are proposing to train. Originally it was estimated that $77,000,000 would be needed for this purpose. A committee of officers aided by the most eminent and upright experts in construction, have this morning told me that in their judgment a minimum of $140,000,000 would be needed for that purpose. This, of course, is on the theory of building thirty-two separate cantonments, and having in training at one time in the United States 1,250,000 men. I think the task is impossible. I do not believe the supplies of lumber and building material are in existence to build thirty-two cities of this size between now and the first of September. I do not believe the carpenters and other workmen are in the country for any such building program, and I have therefore just directed the General Staff to restudy with these experts the whole problem, with a view to cutting the program in half, building sixteen cantonments rather than thirty-two, and proceeding on the theory that sixteen large divisional camps thus constructed will be successively occupied; being filled with new levies as those which have had three or four months training in them are sent either to England or France for the completion of their training.

As a matter of fact we are going to spend very large sums of money in France providing shelter and accommodations for our men there. One of the great difficulties in France has been the housing question. The attempt to use the ill ventilated and unsewered houses of the French Peasants as army quarters has undoubtedly greatly increased the prevalence of disease, and on every ground our American forces there ought to be adequately houses [housed]. It would seem, therefore, bad economy to duplicate these buildings, one set in France and another set here, and rather in the interest of both speed and economy to make our constructions in this country of such character as to insure the health of our troops in training, and of such a size as to enable us by successive use of them to send our troops in a continuous flow from this country to France and England where they could at the outset occupy existing camps used by the French and English for the training of their own reserves and ultimately coming into prepared housing during the period of their remaining as reserve battalions to supply the actual force at the front.

This memorandum calls for no decision from you, but I will ask the opportunity of bringing to your attention the result of the General Staff's study now in progress since the adoption of any determination with regard to cantonment building will require a determination of our general policy in the matter of dispatching troops overseas at the present and in the near future.

Respectfully yours,   Newton D. Baker

TLS (WP, DLC).

E N C L O S U R E

Tasker Howard Bliss to Newton Diehl Baker

Dear Mr. Secretary: Washington. May 25th, 1917.

It is very refreshing to read such sound and well-considered views as those expressed by Mr. Moore in his letter, herewith, to Colonel House, and which you have permitted me to see.

Of course, you know what has been the consistent and oft-repeated view of our General Staff. Until the arrival of the English and French Missions it was not assumed by anyone that we would do anything else than be guided by what, up to that time, had been the repeated recommendations and hopes expressed by many high officials, both civil and military, in England and France. These hopes and recommendations were to the effect that we would avoid what proved to be the grave error on the part of the English in attempting to take a decided part in the land warfare before they were ready. They sacrificed their regular army,—their only means for training raw levies,—in the early days of the war,—and perhaps this was a necessity. But you can imagine what a helpless mob a body of a million or more of men is when it has not an ample leaven of trained officers and veteran troops to organize and train it and England found herself with such a mob on her hands after the practical destruction of her regular forces. It caused the larger part of the long delay which ensued before this mob could be gotten into shape for field service.

We assumed that, taking advantage of the experience of the English and believing that it would not be necessary to send away a part of our small regular army needed for the training of raw troops at home, we would have a considerable period for careful and intensive training and that none of our troops would go abroad until next spring. We did not assume that the Entente Allies were in such a condition as to make any other course desirable or necessary. As you know, all our estimates, carried in the pending large appropriation bill, were based on the assumption of this somewhat prolonged period of training. They did not include the huge expenses that will be incurred when we actually begin to engage in the war with its corresponding enormous loss and waste of expensive materiel of all kinds.

Our knowledge of what seems to be the real situation began to clarify shortly after the arrival of the English and French Missions. The gentlemen belonging to these Missions at first were very reserved in their conferences with us. At first they laid stress only on the desirability of having a small body of troops go to the European theatre of war for the mere purpose of producing a moral effect. At first they spoke of this moral effect as being one to be produced on the troops and people of the Entente Allies. As they began to speak more unreservedly they let it appear that they wanted also to produce a moral effect upon our own people. They did not seem to think that we, as a nation, were interested enough in the matter, and that we needed something to wake us up. It was not long before they said quite openly that we would not feel that we were in the war until we were well "blooded"; that what we needed was to have a large casualty list telegraphed home and that that would stir our fighting blood.

As you know, these views did not change the belief of our General Staff that we should properly train and organize and thoroughly equip and prepare for war a real and formidable force before we attempted to go across the water, but as the foreign gentlemen spoke more and more freely it became evident that what they want and need is *men*, whether trained or not. They have urged us to send small organizations, even companies, as rapidly as they can be organized, and allow them to be trained abroad. They have told us that while it requires a long time to train a large army so that it will play its part properly on the firing line, the *recruits* that must be fed in in order to keep that line at its full strength do not require so much training. This, of course, is quite evidently true; an untrained man between two veterans will soon get to do his work well, whereas if all three are untrained they are helpless.

It seemed to most of us that what both the English and French really wanted from us was not a large well-trained army but a large number of smaller *units* which they could feed promptly into their line as parts of their own organizations in order to maintain their man power at full strength. General Bridges told us that the French man power has for some time been steadily going down and that it will never reach its former strength unless it is reinforced in some such way as indicated above. He also told us that the English man power will never exceed its present strength and that with the present campaign it will steadily decline. He told us that if the French receive no such reinforcements they will now have to consolidate two divisions into one in order to obtain one of reasonably full strength. He said that England and France could keep up their supply of materiel but not men; that in fact they were sure to have an excess of materiel because new rifles were unused for lack of men to fire them and batteries of artillery were going out of action not for want of field guns but for want of men to serve them. His idea seemed to be that we could feed in large numbers of organizations, going to Europe unarmed and using materiel already there for which they had no men and for which in the near future they would have still fewer men.

All of these considerations raise a very grave question in my mind; shall we wait to train, equip and arm our troops, or shall we feed them in as reinforcements to the English and to the French, taking with us such arms as we have and such as we may be able to manufacture and also using such as we can obtain in Europe? If we follow the latter course it will be at a greatly disproportionate sacrifice of life and suffering on our part and it is problematical whether it will, after all, produce a decisive result. When the war is over it may be a literal fact that the American flag will not have appeared anywhere on the line because our organizations will simply be parts of battalions and regiments of the Entente Allies. We might have a million men there and yet no American army and no American commander. Speaking frankly, I have received the impression from English and French officers that such is their deliberate desire. I do not believe our people will stand for it.

I and many other General Staff officers have expressed, in our discussions, the same view as that held by Mr. Moore in his letter to Colonel House; to wit, that the time has come for the English and the French to stand fast and wait until our reinforcements can reach them in such a way as to give the final, shattering blow. I doubt if the Allies will contemplate with satisfaction such a course so long as they can hope to get our men rapidly, whether trained or not, but I think it is a course which our Government should urge upon them with all the force at its disposal.   Very sincerely,   Tasker H. Bliss

TLS (WP, DLC).

To Robert Lansing

My dear Mr. Secretary,   The White House. 28 May, 1917.

I have already conferred with you orally about the enclosed, and return Mr. Bullard's letter. Thank you for letting me see it.
          Faithfully Yours,   W.W.

WWTLI (SDR, RG 59, 124.61/29½, DNA).

To John Skelton Williams

My dear Mr. Comptroller: [The White House] 28 May, 1917

Thank you for your courtesy in sending me a copy of your statement given out to the Press for yesterday's papers in regard to the bank situation and our financial preparedness. I feel as you do about the effect of the present cost of materials. It is a situation which has caused me the deepest concern and I wish I knew more thoroughly than I do just how to meet it.

Cordially and sincerely yours,   Woodrow Wilson

TLS (Letterpress Books, WP, DLC).

From Newton Diehl Baker, with Enclosures

Dear Mr. President: Washington. May 28, 1917

I inclose a memorandum on purchasing for the Allies, and price fixing. Mr. Baruch, Mr. Daniels and I are ready to attend at your pleasure a meeting to determine the question of price fixing for raw materials. In the meantime, it is suggested that Secretary McAdoo ought to be at such a meeting. If you will indicate the time at which you care to see us, I will get the word to Secretary Daniels, Mr. Baruch and Mr. McAdoo.[1]

Respectfully yours,   Newton D. Baker

TLS (WP, DLC).
[1] Baker, Daniels, McAdoo, Baruch, and Hoover met with Wilson at the White House at 8 P.M. that evening. See the extract from the Daniels Diary printed at this date.

E N C L O S U R E   I

From Newton Diehl Baker

Dear Mr. President: Washington. May 28, 1917

I have thought earnestly upon the question of a centralized purchasing agent for the Allies in the United States. The task is, of course, larger than any similar task ever undertaken. It involves necessarily the creation of an organization which will assemble and order, with regard to each commodity from its raw material or production state to the finished product, all the commercial and industrial information available. It will necessarily be integrated with the purchase of supplies for the public departments of the United States and the maintenance of adequate supplies and proper price levels in the United States. I believe that no one man can properly be such a purchasing agent for the reason that no matter how patriotic, disinterested and wise his determinations, the conflicts of interests will be such as to engender about him complaints and doubts which he cannot withstand. I believe, therefore, that a Board having a certain constant personnel to which are added from time to time for the consideration of special cases the persons interested in those cases and in no others, affords the best machinery.

There is already in existence as a subordinate body of the Council of National Defense the General Munitions Board, and similarly the General Supply Commission. These two bodies are studying practically the entire industrial and commercial situation in the United States and advising the War and Navy Departments upon sources of supply, priorities, and prices. If from these two bodies three or four members were selected, and to the number thus chosen were added representatives of the State and Treasury Departments, the Treasury representative being the general representative of the Allied Governments for purchases in this country, or at least the medium through which allied needs would become known for correlation with our domestic needs, such a Board would, by a mere enlargement of its present functions, be able to perform all the duties now under consideration, and its determinations made after hearing all the conflicting needs and desires of the several possible purchasing authorities would be less likely to encounter criticism than the determinations of a single individual.

Basis of Price Fixing.

The War and Navy Departments have attempted to make certain contracts for urgently needed ordnance supplies on the basis of cost plus. This, however, is not a rule susceptible of universal and uniform application. A plant which makes a turn-over of its product every week and receives two per cent profit on the cost of its product would be paid fifty-two times as well on its capital investment as a plant which made a product capable of but one turn-over per year on the same basis of percentage of profit on cost of product. A varying percentage of profit is, therefore, necessary to be fixed with relation to the character of work, etc.

The cost plus mode of contracting requires joint accounting and joint approval upon all items of cost and still leaves open the question of a method of price regulations of raw materials entering into product, and the question which Mr. Baruch is especially concerned to have determined is a policy of price regulation for raw materials entering into industrial products.

It has been suggested that the cost plus method could be applied to the production of raw materials. The difficulties, however, are that in dealing with minerals which are mined you find no two mines of equal richness of product or ease of mining. Labor conditions vary in different parts of the country and the wages of labor vary both absolutely and in their method of determination: in some mines a day rate; in others an hour rate; in some a ton-of-ore rate, and in some a rate per ton which varies with the market price of the smelted mineral. Any attempt to apply the cost plus principle to such a situation would inevitably lead to widely varying prices for the same product from different mines.

The needs of the Government for certain minerals are so great, and particularly when taken in conjunction with the needs of the Allied Governments for the same mineral, that competition for the residue of the available supply will greatly enhance its market value. It would seem, therefore, that some method of price fixing ought to be determined upon which will have the effect of supplying the need of the Government and Allies first, and of the general market second, at a fixed price, relying upon the excess profits tax to equalize the profits of the various and varying mines. I believe this can best be done by calling in, in each instance, those who control trade in a particular metal or raw material product and agreeing with them upon a price which will be less than the present artificially enhanced market, and which will have a tendency to go down rather than to go up. This I think possible to accomplish because in all lines of trade the prices are at present recognized to be upon an unwholesome and unsafe high level. I think it necessary to try this method because there is no other alternative, so far as I can think it out, except to seize the mines and control the raw material supply directly through the Government. This I think neither Congress or the public are ready to sanction, and I therefore recommend that Mr. Baruch be directed to try the other course. It will result in fixing a level of price below the present market, probably not so low as in justice it ought to be, but with a downward tendency, and if that process fails, Government control will be obviously necessary as the only other recourse.

Respectfully yours,   Newton D. Baker

TLS (WP, DLC).

ENCLOSURE II

Memorandum by Mr. Baruch.

It is abhorrent to think, that in a struggle of the nature such as faces us, when blood will flow so freely and suffering will become so great, that we have even to discuss the question of prices and profits, but do not let our hearts and sentiments, our feelings and desires close our minds to the experience of others and the hard and cruel fact that our effectiveness will depend in part on the handling of these questions.

THE WINNING OF THE WAR IS THE SOLE THING TO BE CONSIDERED.

To win the War, we must have the materials in unceasing and ever increasing amounts.

We must unite, solidify and increase the support and enthusiasm of the people.

Wages cannot and must not be reduced.

The United States is the last reservoir of credit from which we can draw to win the war. It is imperative to preserve this.

A fair and just price should be paid. That price is usually the market price, but a fair market price does not mean a fictitious or unduly inflated market price, such as exist[s] now in many cases & I am absolutely opposed to any one growing rich from the war.

The country has not yet realized the titanic struggle in which we are engaged, nor the efforts and sacrifices we must make. While indeed for three years, this greatest of all struggles has been going on—far removed from it as a people and a nation, we have endeavored to be neutral and it would be too much to expect that suddenly every sacrifice would be made and that the unanimous and unstinted effort and support of the people would be forthcoming. Nothing must be done to discourage the people, but everything done to encourage them.

Lloyd George insisted that in all his contracts, there should be a "buck-up" clause.

Whatever the justice or injustice of arbitrarily low prices, experience has shown that production has followed stimulation. Maximum production in every industry is essential. Beyond a certain point, restriction of profits will restrict production of the vital materials. We must find that point.

Question: How can we reduce prices to the point we believe proper, yet keep wages up, preserve our financial strength, keep production of these absolutely vital materials at full blast and increase our resolution and determination to conduct the war to a successful conclusion.

Prices to be paid to manufacturers are more readily determined upon a basis of cost plus a profit, although personally I am opposed to that method, because I think in the end it costs more. This profit it is contended is more or less equal to what the profits are in normal times.

The determination of a price for a raw material is entirely different. Not alone must the given conditions in each industry be taken into consideration, but the known amount of the deposit of the raw materials from which the supply is to be drawn, with the proper amount of amortization taken into consideration.

There is a mistaken idea that the raw materials are controlled by a few, but actually they are derived from innumerable sources, far greater in number than in the case of most manufactured goods.

In fact, I think it is impracticable and I am almost inclined to say impossible to determine the cost of the given raw materials, except in a very few instances. In few cases does the property which produces raw materials rest with the original owners. Shall the cost be based on the cost to original owners, cost of duplication, or the cost to those who only recently have become owners or part owners of the properties.

Undoubtedly prices are now abnormally high and excited competitive bidding by nations fighting for their existence is one of the chief causes.

The subject is so great and the consequences so far-reaching, affecting the necessary elements to win the war—the success of loans and the maintenance of the reservoir of credit, the increasing supplies of materials, the solidifying of the purposes of the people, that we should approach the subject slowly. But our necessities for immediate wants are pressing and action on them must be taken.

I do not believe a fixed principle should be adopted or followed generally, but I believe rather that a flexible method or procedure used, which will lead towards lower prices.

Experience and time will develop a better policy than any one person can now formulate.

I respectfully suggest that the prices for the following basic materials:

Aluminum, Iron and Steel, Coal and Coke, Copper, Lead, Zinc, Lumber and Chemicals

so far as the purchases of our government and our allies are concerned, be determined as follows:

Purchase only for the needs of the first four or six months at the most. Do this by moral suasion and the help and co-operation of the producing interests. These are now organized in committees, whose perso[n]nel is such as to command the co-operation of the industries. This has already been done successfully to a small extent.

Of course prices cannot be obtained such as were obtained before, but prices which are eminently satisfactory considering the increased costs and the requirements of the general situation.

We thus can get our immediate needs, which are only a small part of the total needs, at prices much below those now prevailing. With this will come, I believe, the enthusiastic support of the producers *and there will be no lessened production*.

The business interests will feel encouraged and stimulated by the knowledge that they have been advised with and not forced.

To get enthusiastic co-operation from National Industry the country should be impressed with the intention to treat all fairly and considerately.

If then we find that production does not lessen, we can gradually further decrease the prices.

With these basic prices fixed on the levels, which I believe can be arranged, the whole price structure may commence to fall, but not in a way that will destroy confidence of business or lessen production.

Gradually and promptly the less needful activities should be eliminated in favor of war purposes. (Stop building roads, enterprises—public and private, not necessary to winning the war.) This shifting of activities will involve considerable financial and commercial strain and price policy should therefore not be too rigid in the beginning.

This will have a tendency to lessen the prices. I believe this will be found to be a constructive and practical method of meeting a most difficult situation.

The price we set for ourselves will have a great bearing upon the prices that are made to the civilian population of the United States and the rest of the world. Even though we do not take into consideration our civilian population (who must be kept satisfied) we must think of the grave effects, it would have upon our export trade.

This is the principal market for not alone the borrowing warring Allies, but Japan and all of the neutral countries. The things they must have, they will purchase no matter what the price.

England even now in the midst of her great struggle has an eye to the future.

SUMMARY.

1. In regard to price, I recommend a flexible method of procedure, that will I believe lead towards lower prices. The administration should deal with the situation tentatively and not make itself responsible for an arbitrarily fixed low price. 2. That strongly centralized purchasing power should be promptly established and put into effect with a Priority Committee co-operating. The present governmental media of establishing the wants of each department can be used.

T MS (WP, DLC).

From Robert Lansing, with Enclosures

My dear Mr. President: [Washington] May 28, 1917.

I enclose a memorandum which I received today from Mr. Phillips, transmitting the translation of a telegram of the 21st received by the Russian Chargé d'Affaires from the Minister of Foreign Affairs at Petrograd. I am sure you will find it of much interest.   Faithfully yours,   Robert Lansing

CCL (SDR, RG 59, 861.00/362½, DNA).

E N C L O S U R E   I

William Phillips to Robert Lansing

Dear Mr. Secretary: Department of State May 28 [1917].

I learned of this very important communication from the Russian Government to the Embassy here through Prof. Samuel Harper, who was permitted to see it; and I asked Mr. Onou if he would be kind enough to send me a copy of it. He could not be prevailed upon to present it officially, because he did not receive explicit instructions to do so. It is a very significant communication.   Sincerely,   W Phillips

TLS (SDR, RG 59, 861.00/362½, DNA).

E N C L O S U R E   I I

TRANSLATION.

May 8/21, 1917.   No. 2050

The Minister of Foreign Affairs to the Chargé d'Affaires. No. 2.

The Provisional Government which has just been reorganized and strengthened with new representatives of revolutionary democracy[1] declares that it will bring into decisive play the ideas of liberty, equality and fraternity that have been inscribed on the banner of the great Russian revolution.

In the field of foreign policy the Provisional Government is joined by the whole people in spurning any idea of a separate peace and openly aims at arriving as speedily as possible at a universal peace that would imply neither the enslaving of other peoples, nor the taking away of their national patrimony nor the forcible occupation of foreign territories—at a peace without annexation or indemnities leaving the nations free to guide their destinies as they see fit. Firmly convinced that the fall of the Czarist régime and the consolidation of democratic principles in the domestic and foreign policies of Russia have given birth to a new factor inciting the allied democracies toward lasting peace and brotherhood of peoples, the Provisional Government will take preliminary measures to bring the ideas expressed in the Provisional Government's note of March 27/April 9 of this year[2] into harmony with those of our allies.

2. Satisfied that the defeat of Russia and her allies would not only prove the source of the greatest evils to the nations, but would also put off if not do away with the conclusion of a universal peace on the above mentioned basis, the Provisional Government is of the strong belief that the Russian revolutionary army will not let the German forces crush our allies on the Western front and then fall upon us with the full strength of their armies. The consolidation of the principles of democratizing the army, organizing and increasing its fighting strength both for defense and offense will constitute the main duty of the Provisional Government. Paragraphs 3, 4, 5, 6, 7 and 8 deal with the domestic policy. Setting up the energetic execution of the above mentioned program as its goal the Provisional Government categorically declares that productive labor can only be performed by it on condition that the whole nation will testify its full and absolute confidence and enable it actually to exercise to its full extent the power it needs to consolidate the conquests of the revolution and expand them in the future. In this its strong press-

ing appeal to all citizens that they preserve the unity of power exercised by it, the Provisional Government declares that it will adopt, for the salvation of the country, the most energetic measures against any attempted counter-revolution or violence that would disorganize the country and pave the way for a counter-revolution. The Provisional Government is confident that on that path it will find the unswerving support of all to whom the freedom of Russia is dear. Signed: Prince Lvoff. Minister President and of the Interior; Kerensky, Minister of War and Marine; Pereversev, Minister of Justice; Terestchenko, Minister of Foreign Affairs; Nekrasow, Minister of Ways and Communications; Konovalow, Minister of Commerce and Industry; Manouelow, Minister of Public Instruction; Chingarew, Minister of Finance; Tchernoff, Minister of Agriculture; Tseretelli, Minister of Posts and Telegraph; Scobelew, Minister of Labor; Pechehonoff, Minister of Supplies; Lvoff, Procurator of the Holy Synod; Godneff, State Comptroller.[3]   Signed: Terestchenko.

CC MS (SDR, RG 59, 861.00/362½, DNA).

[1] Following the antiwar demonstrations of May 3 and 4 (about which see M. M. Podolsky to WW, May 4, 1917, n. 2), a coalition provisional government had been formed which included six socialists from the Petrograd Soviet. The names and offices of the new ministers are listed at the end of the document and in n. 3 below. The socialist ministers were Kerenskii, Pereverzev, Chernov, Tseretelli, Skobelev, and Peshekhonov. See William Henry Chamberlin, *op. cit.*, I, 146-49.

[2] Actually, the so-called proclamation of April 9, 1917 (New Style), was first published as a message from the provisional government to the Russian people and only later was included in a diplomatic notice sent to the Allies on May 1. The most important portion of the proclamation is quoted in translation in the first paragraph of J. R. MacDonald *et al.* to WW, May 29, 1917. However, that translation contains one serious error. An accurate translation of the last sentence reads as follows: "In the name of the higher principles of equity it [the Russian people] has removed the shackles that weighted down the Polish people." C. Onou to RL, May 3, 1917, *FR-WWS 1917*, 2, I, pp. 53-55. For another, somewhat differing, translation and notes on the origin of the proclamation, see Robert Paul Browder and Alexander F. Kerensky, eds., *The Russian Provisional Government, 1917: Documents* (3 vols., Stanford, Cal., 1961), II, 1045-46.

[3] Georgii Evgen'evich L'vov, Aleksandr Fedorovich Kerenskii, Pavel Nikolaevich Pereverzev, Mikhail Ivanovich Tereshchenko, Nikolai Vissarionovich Nekrasov, Aleksandr Ivanovich Konovalov, Aleksandr Appollonovich Manuilov, Andrei Ivanovich Shingarev, Viktor Mikhailovich Chernov, Irakli Georgievich Tseretelli, Mikhail Ivanovich Skobelev, Aleksei Vasil'evich Peshekhonov, and Ivan Vasil'evich Godnev.

From the Diary of Josephus Daniels

May Monday 28 1917

At night McAdoo, Baker, Baruch, & Hoover & I went to talk with the President about the best method of purchasing for us and for the allies. It was agreed both must get the same price & price must if possible be fixed so that it would not be high &

that it would be high enough to keep up production. Hoover wanted to control food purchases & felt it necessary to have that power. McAdoo wanted B to be the purchaser for all. The President wished to find a way by which citizens should get the same price as the government. Complicated & difficult Baruch to draw a chart & meet again on Wednesday.

From James Ramsay MacDonald and Others

Mr. President,   London May 29th. 1917.

Since the entry of the Government of the United States into the War, the Provisional Government of Russia has issued an official pronouncement of its war-aims, which, as published in this country, reads as follows:

The Government deems it to be its right and duty to declare now, that free Russia does not aim at the domination of other Nations, at depriving them of their national patrimony, or at occupying by force Foreign Territories, but that its object is to establish a durable Peace on the basis of the rights of Nations to decide their own destiny.

The Russian Nation does not lust after strengthening its power abroad at the expense of other Nations. Its aim is not to subjugate or humiliate anyone. In the name of the higher principles of equity the Russian people has broken the chains which fettered the policy of the Nation, but it will not suffer that its own country shall emerge from the great struggle, mutilated or weakened in its vital forces.

(April, 9th. last)

This Pronouncement, the Provisional Government repeated in identical terms in an explanatory note issued on May 1st. last.

In the course of the present month the Provisional Government has been strengthened by the inclusion of six Representatives of the Council of Workmen and Soldiers' Delegates. These representatives took office under certain conditions, of which the first is reported to be that the new Provisional Government shall pursue an:

Active foreign policy directed towards the speediest possible attainment of a general peace without annexation or indemnity, based upon the express will of the people, and negotiations with the Allies for a revision of their agreements with Russia on the basis of the declaration of the Provisional Government of April 9th.

On May 19th. the new Provisional Government issued a declaration of which the first clause reads as follows:

In its foreign policy the Provisional Government rejecting, in concert with the entire people, all thought of a separate peace, adopts openly as its aim the re-establishment of a general peace which shall not tend towards either domination over other nations, or the seizure of their national possessions, or the violent usurpation of their territories—a peace without annexations or indemnities, and based on the rights of nations to decide their own affairs. In the firm conviction that the fall of the regime of Tsardom in Russia and the consolidation of democratic principles in our internal and external policy will create in the Allied democracies new aspirations towards a stable peace and the brotherhood of nations, the Provisional Government will take steps towards bringing about an agreement with the Allies on the basis of its declaration of April 9.

We recognize that the conditions indicated by the Provisional Government of Russia as providing the basis for negotiations, do not constitute in themselves a complete formula.

But they show a divergence so profound and far-reaching from the avowed war aims of the late political *régime* in Russia, as to suggest that the Allies ought to revise the note addressed to you, Mr. President, on January 10th. last[1]—or agree to such an explanation of it as will remove all implications and suspicions of a policy of imperialistic aggrandisement, or of systematic economic warfare after peace has been signed.

The now declared aims of the Russian Provisional Government so accurately embody the real ideals of the democracies of the World, and are in so close an accord with your own pronouncements, that we are encouraged to believe that the Allies will be constrained without delay to put themselves in touch with, and give definite voice to those sentiments of freedom and nationality, and those methods of democratic diplomacy which have been inaugurated by the Russian Revolution, and now find expression through the Provisional Government's declaration.

The emancipation of the Russian Democracy from the evil traditions and the hampering commitments of the old *régime* invest it with a greater freedom and initiative and with a clearer vision than, in the nature of the case, can be enjoyed by the peoples whose minds have become dulled by the habitual thoughts of war, and whose liberties generally, have been increasingly curtailed under the stress and strain of this unparalleled conflict.

We can assure you, Mr. President, that any action taken by the

Government of the United States in the direction indicated, with the object of securing a general declaration by all the belligerent States renouncing aggressive aims, would receive an enormous volume of grateful support in this country, and would have an immediately beneficial effect in encouraging democratic resoluteness in all countries to end this war in such a way as to remove for ever its various causes, and to guarantee an abiding peace.

We have the honour to be, Mr. President, with great respect,

Your obedient servants,

Executive Committee of the Union of Democratic Control,

Norman Angell	J. Ramsay Macdonald
Charles Roden Buxton	E. D. Morel.
Irene Cooper Willis	F W Pethick Lawrence.
J. A. Hobson.	Arthur Ponsonby
F. W. Jowett.	Philip Snowden
Charles Trevelyan.	H. M. Swanwick.[2]

This is interesting because of the signatures   E.M.H.

TLS (WP, DLC).

[1] Again, see W. G. Sharp to RL, Jan. 10, 1917, Vol. 40.

[2] Those persons not heretofore identified are Charles Roden Buxton, lawyer, former Liberal M.P., brother of Noel Buxton; Irene Cooper Willis, later author of several biographical and literary studies; John Atkinson Hobson, prolific author of works in economics and the social sciences; Frederick William Jowett, Labour M.P.; Edmund Dene Morel, journalist, organizer of the Congo Reform Association in 1904, secretary of the Union of Democratic Control; Frederick William Pethick Lawrence, a leader in the British woman-suffrage movement; and Helena Maria Sickert (Mrs. F. T.) Swanwick, journalist, active in the woman-suffrage movement.

An Address at Arlington Cemetery on Memorial Day[1]

30 May, 1917.

Mr. Commander, fellow citizens: The program has conferred an unmerited dignity upon the remarks I am going to make by calling them an address, because I am not here to deliver an address. I am here merely to show, in my official capacity, the sympathy of this great government with the objects of this occasion, and also to speak just a word of the sentiment that is in my own heart.

Any Memorial Day of this sort is, of course, a day touched with sorrowful memory, and yet I, for one, do not see how we can have any thought of pity for the men whose memory we honor today. I do not pity them. I envy them, rather; because theirs is a great work for liberty accomplished, and we are in the midst of a work unfinished, testing our strength where their strength has already been tested. There is a touch of sorrow, but there is a touch of reassurance also in a day like this, because we know how the men of America have responded to the call of the cause of liberty, and it fills our minds with a perfect assurance that that response will come again in equal measure, with equal majesty, and with a result which will hold the attention of all mankind.

Thus, when you reflect upon it, these men who died to preserve the Union, died to preserve the instrumentality which we are using to serve the world—a free nation espousing the cause of human liberty. In one sense, the great struggle into which we have now entered is an American struggle, because it is in defense of American honor and American rights. But it is something even greater than that—it is a world struggle. It is the struggle of men who love liberty everywhere, and in this cause America will show herself greater than ever because she will rise to a greater thing. We have said in the beginning that we planted this great government that men who wished freedom might have a place of refuge and a place where their hope could be realized. And now, having established such a government, having preserved such a government, having vindicated the power of such a government, we are saying to all mankind, "We did not set this government up in order that we might have a selfish and separate liberty, for we are now ready to come to your assistance and fight out upon the field of the world the cause of human liberty." In this thing, America attains her full dignity and the full fruition of her great purpose.

No man can be glad that such things have happened as we have witnessed in these last fateful years, but perhaps it may be permitted to us to be glad that we have an opportunity to show the principles that we profess to be living principles that live in our hearts and to have a chance, by the pouring out of our blood and treasure, to vindicate the thing which we have professed. For, my friends, the real fruition of life is to do the thing we have said we wished to do. There are times when words seem empty and only action seems great. Such a time has come, and, in the Providence of God, America will once more have an opportunity to show to the world that she was born to serve mankind.

T MS (WP, DLC), with corrections from a reading of the CLSsh notes in the C. L. Swem Coll., NjP.

1 Wilson spoke to a large audience which included many veterans of the Civil and Spanish-American wars, as well as many National Guardsmen and members of the regular army. Aaron H. Frear, Commander of the Department of the Potomac, Grand Army of the Republic, presided. *Washington Post*, May 31, 1917.

From Bernard Mannes Baruch

My dear Mr. President: [New York] May 30, 1917.

I am sending herewith by special delivery the chart you desired.[1] Study and experience will undoubtedly cause many changes both by elimination and addition, but it embodies my idea of centralization.

I have endeavored, as far as possible, to use the present media now established and in use by the Council of Defense, the Advisory Commission, the Army and Navy and the allied purchasing missions and agencies. I have not carried the chart out in details because I did not want to burden your mind with them. It is not intended to show the relative importance of any department or activity. For instance, I have the Shipping Board on the chart; not that it would come under the Central Agency. But no purchase, for instance, for the Allies of whatever nature should be made unless the shipping could be furnished by the purchasing nation itself or by our own shipping board. Constant touch with the shipping board will help to avoid congestion in our manufacturing and transportation and at our seaboard. Of course you understand that unless the Central Purchasing Agency has authority as to prices and the closing of contracts nothing much will be gained.

I would have brought this myself but I wanted to definitely complete the price arrangements for the basic materials which were discussed. Too much is held up for lack of this determination. Owing to the fact that the Committees were scattered (the Chairman of the Copper Committee being out of town) I was unable to get definite prices and I will not return to Washington until I have done so. However, much progress has been made and I expect to be in Washington on Friday morning, with definite results. Any time after that I am at your service to give you the result of my negotiations and explain any questions that may arise concerning the chart. It is natural to expect that any plan made now would have to be changed, but this one will work.

Let me assure you there is no pride in its originality because it is not original. Let me also assure you that no part in it is too small or insignificant for me to undertake.

Very sincerely yours,   [B. M. Baruch]

CCL (B. M. Baruch Papers, NjP).
[1] It is missing in both WP, DLC, and the Baruch Papers, NjP; however, Baruch explains it in B. M. Baruch to WW, June 4, 1917.

From Edward Mandell House

Dear Governor: New York. May 30, 1917.

It is, I think, evident that the German Military Clique have no intention of making peace upon any other basis than that of conquest. They hold Middle Europe from Bruge to Constantinople, and Belgium, Poland. A[u]stro-Hungary and European Turkey are almost as much under the domination of Prussia as Saxony and Bavaria.

The Kaiser and his civil government are taking the gambler's chance. If they are able to hold what they have, then the German liberals can be defied, for the mass of the German people will be satisfied with the outcome of the war.

If, on the other hand, military reverses come, the Kaiser and his ministers will lean towards the liberals and give Germany a government responsive to the people. In the meantime, they will give no terms because they hope to hold what they have seized, and if their intentions were known, there would be near revolution in Germany because a majority of the people want peace even if it should be without conquest.

The pacifists in this country—in England and in Russia are demanding a statement of terms by the Allies which shall declare against indemnities or territorial encroachments. They believe, and are being told, that Germany is willing for peace on these terms.

It seems to me important that the truth be brought out, so that everyone, both in and out of Germany, may know what the issue is. I hope you will think it advisable to take some early occasion to do this. Unless you lead and direct the liberal Allied thought, it will not be done.

Such utterances as those recently made by Lord Robert Cecil and Ribot[1] play directly in the hands of the German imperialists. There seems to be no intelligent or coordinate direction of Allied policy. Imperial Germany should be broken down within as well as from without. The German liberals justly complain that they not only have had no help, but that their cause is constantly hurt by the statesmen and press of the Allied countries.

My address after this week will be Magnolia, Massachusetts
Affectionately yours,   E. M. House

TLS (WP, DLC).

[1] Both Cecil and Ribot were responding to the declaration of the Russian provisional government against imperialistic conquest and aggrandizement. About Cecil's speech, see n. 4 to the Enclosure with EMH to WW, May 24, 1917. Ribot spoke in a similar vein to the Chamber of Deputies on May 22. France

had to recover her "lost provinces," and the Central Powers would have to pay suitable indemnities, not only to France, but also to Belgium, Serbia, Rumania, and Montenegro. *New York Times*, May 23, 1917.

A Last Will and Testament

LAST WILL AND TESTAMENT OF WOODROW WILSON.

[May 31, 1917]

I, Woodrow Wilson, being of sound and disposing mind and in every respect in full vigour of mind and body, do declare the following to be my last will and testament:

I will and devise all my property, of whatever kind, real and personal, after the payment of any just debts that may constitute a claim upon it at the time of my death, to my beloved wife Edith for her lifetime, with the request that she distribute among my daughters such articles of clothing, jewelry, personal ornament, or art material as may have been the personal belongings of their mother, and with the direction that my daughter Margaret shall receive out of the income of my estate, so long as she remains unmarried, the sum of twenty-five hundred dollars annually, unless that amount should at any time exceed one-third of the entire annual income of my estate; in which case I direct that she shall receive one-third of that income annually.

Upon the death of my beloved wife Edith, it is my will and direction, should she die without issue, that the whole of my estate, real and personal, or so much of it as shall remain unexpended or undispersed, shall revert to my children, share and share alike; and that, should she die leaving issue, her child or children shall inherit, share and share alike, with my daughters living at the time of the execution of this instrument.

I do hereby also name and appoint my beloved wife Edith sole executor and administrator of this my last will and testament.

Duly signed and acknowledged in the City of Washington, in the District of Columbia, on the thirty-first of May, in the year of our Lord one thousand nine hundred and seventeen, in the presence of the witnesses whose signatures are below inscribed.

In the Presence of: Woodrow Wilson
Helen Woodrow Bones
I. H. Hoover.
Ralph M. Rogers.[1]

WWTS MS (WP, DLC).
[1] Clerk at the White House. There is a fragment of a WWsh draft of this document in WP, DLC.

To Joseph Patrick Tumulty, with Enclosure

Dear Tumulty: [The White House, c. May 31, 1917]

I have had a conversation with the Secretary of War about this and he has promised to get Mr. Sherley on the telephone and express the opinion which both the Secretary and I hold about this, namely, that it would be very dangerous.

The President.

TL (J. P. Tumulty Papers, DLC).

E N C L O S U R E

From Joseph Patrick Tumulty

Dear Governor: The White House May 31, 1917.

Swagar Sherley called this morning and said that he is serving as a member of the conferees' committee which is handling the Military Appropriation Bill. He said that one of the points of difference between the conferees now is that brought forward by the amendment of Senator Hoke Smith, providing that the army now being organized shall be disbanded four months after the termination of the war. Sherley is opposed to this and thinks that his opinion is representative of your views. He says it is necessary that the Committee should know just what your attitude is on this matter. He thinks that you ought to write or telephone him today.

I do not think you ought to write a letter on this matter, but think it would be wise for you to give your views to Sherley over the telephone.   Sincerely yours,   Tumulty

TLS (J. P. Tumulty Papers, DLC).

From Joseph Patrick Tumulty

Dear Governor: The White House May 31, 1917.

It is very discouraging to find a spirit of indifference abroad with reference to the attitude of the general mass of people toward the war. Their "righteous wrath" seems not to have been aroused, and the thought has occurred to me that if it is possible, Brand Whitlock should be brought to this country to relate to the people just what has happened in Belgium, and to show the character of the beasts we are fighting. A speech by Mr. Whitlock about German outrages in Belgium would help the people to visualize just what poor Belgium has suffered and what our own people might suffer if German autocracy should triumph.

This is just a suggestion that I pass on to you for your consideration.   Sincerely yours,   Tumulty

TLS (WP, DLC).

From Edward Mandell House, with Enclosure

Dear Governor: New York. May 31, 1917.

Spring-Rice came in this morning, just back from Canada, and very much perturbed.

Balfour received the enclosed (paraphrased) cable from the British Government. I saw the original. This is the sense of it, but the other had some sentences which they have thought best to eliminate.[1]

Spring-Rice also showed me Balfour's reply, which was a very earnest argument against sending any such representative here at this time. He also added that if it was intended to send Northcliffe or anyone else your consent should first be obtained, for "you and you alone were the Government of the United States."[2]

I told Spring-Rice that I thought you would agree with Balfour that it would be best not to send anyone at present. Will you not confirm this if it reflects your views?

The Ambassador knows and wishes this communication to go to you, but he especially requests that it go no further, provided Mr. Balfour's cable results in preventing the appointment being made.

I shall not be leaving until Saturday afternoon and a word from you tomorrow will reach me.

                    Affectionately yours,   E. M. House

TLS (WP, DLC).
    [1] R. Cecil to C. A. Spring Rice and A. J. Balfour, May 26, 1917, T telegram (FO 115/2295, pp. 162-64, PRO). The only sentence which House omitted from his paraphrase was the following: "Reply 'Urgent' as all departments press for appointment to be made immediately."
    [2] [A. J. Balfour to R. Cecil], May 27, 1917, T telegram (FO 115/2295, pp. 165-66, PRO). Balfour's comments were much blunter than House suggests. "The American Government and people," Balfour wrote, "know Lord Northcliffe as the owner of a great group of newspapers which are more characteristically represented by the Daily Mail than by the Times. This is a type of politician with which they suppose themselves to be well acquainted, which they are obliged to tolerate, but do not greatly admire. If they form a concrete picture of Lord Northcliffe other than in his character of newspaper proprietor, they probably think of him as a vigorous hustler and loud voiced propagandist; one who will tell them with the utmost emphasis not merely what the Allies would like to see done, but what America ought to do. Whether this is the best way to treat our new Allies is a matter for argument. Personally I think it is not. There are no doubt the very gravest defects in their administrative organization. It is only suited for peace and is not easily or quickly modified to suit conditions of war. But whether it is likely to be improved by aggressive lecturing

is another matter. I am myself disposed to think that reform must come from within; and that the last thing that is likely to secure the rapid mobilisation of America's resources is anything that can be represented as external pressure. . . . The Government of the U. S. A. is the President, and nobody but the President. Would it not therefore be desirable, indeed all important, to find out confidentially what he thinks of the proposal[?] Colonel House could doubtless obtain the necessary information."

E N C L O S U R E

War Cabinet think that it is desirable to have some system of generally supervising and co-ordinating work of representatives of various British Departments in United States who are employed there on matters connected with shipping, food supply, munitions, and War Office and Admiralty business. If there is no such co-ordination, representatives of these Departments would waste much valuable time and power, and especially interfere with each other by mutual competition.

In view of these circumstances, and this danger which the War Cabinet consider as serious, they consider it essential that for some months to come they should have in the United States an energetic and influential man of good business capacity and wide knowledge for purposes of general supervision and co-ordination.

Mr. B's mission has done excellent work, but it is strongly felt that much still remains to be done, especially with a view of bringing home to the United States Government the realities of the present war situation, and the necessity of immediate active and strenuous co-operation in the war with the least delay possible.

The War Cabinet therefore propose that they should have a representative in United States charged with the duty of insuring to the best of his ability that all possible measures are taken in order to render America's resources available in the most effective manner and with the least possible delay.

He would have no diplomatic duties. Diplomatic relations would remain in the same hands as heretofore, and the War Cabinet representative would apply to the British Embassy should he require diplomatic support for the purpose of carrying out the duties connected with his mission.

In the opinion of the War Cabinet Lord Northcliffe is suited for such an appointment, and they propose making the appointment at once with the duties above enumerated. Before doing so, however, they would be glad to receive the views of Mr. B. on the proposal.

T MS (WP, DLC).

From Herbert Clark Hoover

Dear Mr. President: Washington May 31, 1917.

I have had an opportunity, at the request of various Senators and Congressmen, of discussing with them the Lever bill[1] and the proposed methods of giving administration to it. I find the general feeling that the whole matter can be expedited in Congress and a great deal of opposition overcome if certain provisions of the bill are deleted.

In particular, Section 5, which provides for the establishment of standards and grades in all sorts of foodstuffs. This is a reform which is of very minor importance from a war point of view and is a power which could not be executed by the Food Administration and would necessarily be put upon the Department of Agriculture. It would seem to me undesirable to establish the large administrative measures necessary to give it effect unless this administration is established for a longer period than the war, and if in your judgment it is desirable that such measures should be taken, they might be separated from the Lever bill,— a war measure.

Another clause which is arousing a great deal of opposition is Section 16, allowing mixtures of wheat flour with other cereals. It is my belief that we would probably not want to take advantage of this section because it will open the doors to adulteration which we could not control without a very large administrative staff embracing a representative in every milling plant in the United States. On the other hand we can accomplish the problem of securing consumption of other cereals in substitution for wheat by such voluntary methods as the establishment of corn-bread days and other devices of this kind. If these voluntary methods should fail we could then come back for powers at a later stage.

Somewhat the same argument applies also to Section 15 which provides for the establishment of minimum percentages of wheat milling. Inquiry into the mechanical situation of milling in the country indicates that this could not be accomplished in the smaller mills without imposing a great deal of expense upon them and will arouse a great deal of opposition. The national saving to be made therefrom is of somewhat doubtful importance when we weigh all the various factors that enter into the question. Moreover, there are a great number of misguided faddists in the country who will bring constant pressure to bear upon us to take drastic action along these lines and whose antagonism we will certainly incur if we have the powers and do not make use of them. I am somewhat in doubt as to whether this clause should be deleted as it has its certain value in enabling us to force the millers to do certain other things we want by threatening the use of these powers, but if any very considerable fight is made over it, it is my view that it is not critical.

Another matter in connection with the bill seems to me of vital importance and that is that we should have an appropriation of at least $100,000,000 as working capital in purchase and sale of foodstuffs and to supplement the minimum guarantee provisions of the bill.

I am informed by various Congressmen with whom I have discussed the matter that there would be no difficulty in the inclusion of such an appropriation and I cannot conceive that it would result in any financial loss to the country. Probably we would never call upon the appropriation at all, but the fact that we had it would enable us to establish banking credits on a much more positive scale.

I do not wish to take any particular attitude with regard to the bill without your kindly counsel as to whether or not the above ideas should be put into action.

Yours faithfully,   Herbert C. Hoover

TLS (WP, DLC).
1 The first Lever bill, H.R. 4188, described in D. F. Houston to WW, May 14, 1917, n. 1.

From Newton Diehl Baker

My dear Mr. President: [Washington.] May 31, 1917.

Mr. Paderewski called upon me to-day, further to explain the project which I took up with you some days ago, with regard to the formation of a Polish army. At that time the problem was complicated by my feeling that it was necessary to concentrate our entire effort upon supplies, equipment and training for our own Army. In this view you concurred; both of us, I believe, feeling that very large sentimental value was to be found in the suggestion of an independent Polish army, but that it would have to be taken up later.

Mr. Paderewski now tells me that as a result of conferences between him and Mr. Balfour, the British Government has placed at the disposal of the Poles two Canadian training camps, one near Toronto and one near Montreal, and has undertaken to supply the needed equipment, subsistence and training forces for a Polish force aggregating perhaps a hundred thousand men. Mr. Paderewski now suggests that the Polish Committee be authorized, with the formal approval either of the President or of the Secretary of War, to enlist resident but non-citizen Poles in the United States, take them to Canada, and train them, under the following conditions:

1. The approval of the President or of the Secretary of War is to say that the Government of the United States looks with approval and favor upon the project, and that the service performed by these Polish contingents will be a contribution to the general cause which the United States represents, and incidentally a benefit to the Polish nation.

2. That the troops, when trained, are to be permitted to fight in conjunction with American troops in France, under the control of American military commanders.

3. That the sole cost of equipping, transporting and subsisting these forces is to be provided without a present call upon the resources of the United States.

Mr. Paderewski presses upon my attention the very great sentimental value in the presence of such a force on the fighting front, its effect upon Polish soldiers now reluctantly composing parts of the armies of the Central Powers, and the very earnest urgings of both the British and French Governments that such a force be speedily organized and used. He tells me further that there are about six thousand Poles in France who have been taken out of their general fighting forces and segregated with a view to making them a part of the larger forces herein contemplated, and that on the Russian front five or six hundred thousand Poles are to be organized as a distinctive Polish army.

I am very happy to submit this modified suggestion to your judgment, the only request now being made of the Government of the United States being its formal endorsement and approval of the project.

Mr. Paderewski thinks it likely that Poles beyond the age of thirty years, and therefore not eligible for selection under our present law, might also desire to enlist in the proposed force.

Respectfully yours,   Newton D. Baker

CCL (N. D. Baker Papers, DLC).

A Telegram and a Letter to Edward Mandell House

The White House [June] 1 [1917]

Action mentioned in your letter of yesterday would be most unwise and still more unwise the choice of the person named

Woodrow Wilson.

T telegram (E. M. House Papers, CtY).

My dear House,   The White House. 1 June, 1917.

Your letter of May thirtieth chimes exactly with my own thoughts, and I wish that you would follow it up with advice on these points:

I would like to say in substance just what you say in your letter, that the present military masters of Germany "have no intention of making peace upon any other basis than that of conquest," that they already hold Middle Europe from Bruges to Constantinople, that Belgium, Poland, Austria-Hungary, European Turkey, and a portion of the Balkan states are completely in their power, and that they intend that they shall remain so, meaning to take a gambler's chance, stand pat if they win, yield a parliamentary government if they lose;

But when shall I say it (on Flag Day?), And how shall I say it without seeming directly to contradict Cecil and Ribot if I am to add, as I feel that I must, the terms (in general phrase, as in the address to the Senate) upon which we in this country think that a settlement should be made when we win?

I would be immensely grateful to you if you would write me fully in reply to these questions. You are closer in touch with what is being said and thought on the other side of the water than we are here and could form a much safer and surer judgment than I could on how the necessary things ought to be said.

I am grateful to you all the time, for that matter, and every thing you do makes me more so.

I am both glad and sorry that you have got off to the Massachusetts shore,—glad for your sake, sorry for ours, who would wish to be much nearer to you.

All unite in affectionate messages. We are going to have the pleasure of having Mr. and Mrs. Auchincloss in for lunch to-day. We have just discovered that they are in town.

                    Affectionately Yours,   Woodrow Wilson

WWTLS (E. M. House Papers, CtY).

To Frank Irving Cobb

                    [The White House] 1 June, 1917

I would be very much pleased if you could spend Sunday here and lunch with me to discuss a very important matter.[1]

                    Woodrow Wilson.

T telegram (Letterpress Books, WP, DLC).
  [1] Cobb lunched at the White House on June 3. They undoubtedly discussed, among other things, the problem of newspaper censorship.

To Robert Lansing

My dear Mr. Secretary,   The White House. 1 June, 1917.

I have read the attached paper with the profoundest interest.[1] I hope with all my heart that the new forces in Russia may be guided by the principles and objects it sets forth!

Faithfully Yours,   W.W.

WWTLI (SDR, RG 59, 861.00/383½, DNA).
  [1] That is, the message from the new Russian Provisional Government, printed as Enclosure II with RL to WW, May 28, 1917.

From Martin Grove Brumbaugh[1]

Sir: Harrisburg June 1, 1917.

I dislike much to take even a moment of your time in these burdened days, but I need your counsel in a matter of moment. Our Legislature is in session. Many Bills have been introduced that in one way or another attempt to modify existing laws relating to labor and industry. The main idea in most of them is suspension of existing laws during the war or such absolute setting aside of the same as to allow all sorts of procedure not now permitted by law in Pennsylvania.

I have only one desire—to do here what will best serve the Nation, and my whole wish is to be loyally in cooperation with National thought and purpose. A word from you will be guidance to me. It will be a help to hear soon.

Our prayers and our efforts are for you daily.

Very respectfully,   M. G. Brumbaugh

TLS (WP, DLC).
  [1] Governor of Pennsylvania.

From William Phillips, with Enclosure

Dear Mr. President: Washington June 1, 1917.

I am sending you at the request of Mr. House an interesting letter which he has recently received from Mr. W. H. Buckler who is attached to the Embassy at London.

With assurances of respect, etc., I am, my dear Mr. President,

Faithfully yours,   William Phillips

TLS (WP, DLC).

ENCLOSURE

William Hepburn Buckler to Edward Mandell House

Dear Colonel House: London May 10 1917.

Ramsay MacDonald, whom I met today at luncheon, was as much tickled as I by the TIMES admission (see clipping herewith[ )], that the two British Labor Delegates to Russia—carefully chosen by a prudent Government—were not sympathetic to the powers that be in Petrograd. In point of fact the Russian revolution has worried this "fight-to-a-finish" Government even more than our entrance into the war has cheered them up. Here is an instance: The Soldiers and Workmen's Delegates, ultra U.D.C. and I.L.P.[1] in sentiment, have just invited the I.L.P. to send to Petrograd representatives duly elected—not selected by Lloyd George. This was told me explicitly by MacDonald and is implied in today's TIMES. Can this Government now refuse passports to such representatives without discourtesy to Russia?

Another instance, still more awkward: On Wednesday, 16th, several U.D.C. members will move in Parliament a resolution inviting the Government to endorse the declared policy of their great ally by affirming their opposition to all conquests and annexations.

Which can this Government more safely snub, its Russian allies or its jingo supporters? The official handling of this dilemma will be a curious spectacle. Formerly we used to marvel how a nation so democratic as England could get on with Nicolas II. The question now is how a country so democratic as Russia can get on with Curzon and Milner. The U.D.C. and I.L.P. may be relied on to point out this yawning chasm, and the danger of alienating Russian sympathies.

I enclose the prospectus of a new French weekly, LES NATIONS,[2] which is to start next month on the independent lines of the NATION and the NEW REPUBLIC. The editor, M. de Marmande,[3] whom I met at Trevelyan's house, thinks it not improbable that his review may share the fate of the NATION, i.e. have its export forbidden.[4] I have subscribed, as there seems to be no other similar French organ of moderate views.

I have lately heard, on what seemed good authority, that if France should go on for another year she would be ruined for the next quarter of a century. So the point of view of M. de Marmande and his moderates will obviously be anti-"knock out" and pro-negotiation.

The opinion that, except at Bagdad and Salonika, the Eastern struggle is already over becomes, I find, more and more general. And if Russia drops out Italy can hardly remain in to bear the full weight of Austrian blows. Among all sorts of people I find the impression that the Russian armies are "dissolving" (Lord Parmoor[5] has this direct from a Russian correspondent) and that even if this tendency should be exaggerated by rumor Russia will no longer be an effective fighting force (see article of the TIMES military expert today). People's minds are actually being prepared for this by the view which I now sometimes hear: "Never mind; we are already fighting all the best German armies, so we needn't care what Russia does." M. de Marmande says this same "discounting" theory is beginning to circulate in France. The really consolatory feature is that Russian democracy can hardly cease fighting without the cooperation of the German Social Democrats, and that anything which increases their prestige is a defeat for Prussian militarism.

May 11th.

I regret to appear always pessimistic but viewing the situation objectively I do not see how one can well be otherwise. More and more it seems to me that the role to be played by the U. S. is that of deliverer, in other words of helping the Entente out of a serious hole.

I enclose some confidential notes on the two principal speeches made at yesterday's secret session. The remarks of Churchill represent to my mind much more faithfully than do those of the Prime Minister the views and feelings of the people here who are "in the know." The sinkings of British tonnage for last month were 500,000 tons, or at the rate of 6,000,000 tons a year, as I told you. The total of British and Allied tonnage sunk in April was strangely enough not mentioned.

Buxton was much impressed and evidently surprised by the fact (1) that Miliukow has taken up informally with Sir George Buchanan the question of detaching Bulgaria, and (2) the Government speakers showed willingness to consider this proposal. This was the only topic on which Buxton spoke; and Lloyd George was so much interested that he asked him to breakfast this morning to discuss the matter further, and is going to Buxton's house next Tuesday week for further discussion. B. thinks that an American Agent would be the best medium for sounding the Bulgars, say in Switzerland, and he would be very glad to know what view our Government would take of such an attempt. The present idea seems to be that it would be best not to make definite offers to Bulgaria but merely to listen at first to what she has to say.

B. regards this willingness to negotiate as a very material step
forward on Lloyd George's part.

Yours sincerely,   W. H. Buckler

TCL (WP, DLC).
¹ That is, the Union of Democratic Control and the Independent Labour
party.
² Apparently only nine numbers of the periodical appeared, from June 15 to
August 10, 1917.
³ R. de Marmande cannot be further identified.
⁴ That is, *The Nation* of London.
⁵ Charles Alfred Cripps, 1st Baron Parmoor, noted lawyer, opponent of British
participation in the war, and advocate of a league of nations.

Herbert Clark Hoover to Joseph Patrick Tumulty

My dear Tumulty,   [Washington, June 1, 1917]

The President asked me for a sketch of proposed Food Administration. I send a preliminary note and family tree herewith.¹
It needs an apology as to the drafting but we havent a draftsman
yet, and we will get out another in a few days as the organization develops.   Sincerely   H. Hoover

ALS (WP, DLC).
¹ "Preliminary Note on the Organization of the Food Administration," June
1, 1917, T MS (WP, DLC). Hoover proposed the creation of a conservation division; a division of food utilization; federal commissioners to encourage, and
to act as liaisons with, state food administrations; officers, or groups of officers, to cooperate with other governmental departments such as Agriculture,
Commerce, Labor, Justice, and State; commodity executives, who might buy,
sell, and distribute basic food commodities such as grain, sugar, and meat, both
at home and abroad; and committees of volunteer experts to advise on such
subjects as the setting of reasonable prices, accounting, banking and credits,
and the participation of women in the process.

Arthur Hugh Frazier to Edward Mandell House

Dear Mr. House: Paris, June 1, 17.

I have not written for the last two mails because so many
events were in course of development that I thought it better to
wait for something definite to report.

The second American commission has arrived, the railroad
commission, and the French appear to be a little bewildered by
the succession of two commissions with apparently full powers,
each acting independently of the other and independently of the
Military Mission in Paris. No doubt this will be changed with
the arrival of Gen. Pershing. Both Logan¹ and I believe that some
great American administrator, acting as the personal representa-

tive of the President, should have sole and undivided authority in France in all matters pertaining to the conduct of the war.

As far as the military situation is concerned the French are practically marking time waiting for the Russians to do something before continuing the offensive begun in April; General Pétain I am confidently told, is absolutely opposed to any piecemeal attack. The French are also perplexed about the shipment of munitions to Russia; there are vast quantities ready to be loaded on ships but they cannot decide whether to let them go out of the country or to hold on to them.

Internally there is a good deal of unrest in Paris which is manifesting itself in the shape of strikes. This is partly due to the high cost of living which bears very heavily on the poorer classes exhausted by the severest winter Paris has known for years, and partly to a growing distrust of the Government. It was notorious, for instance, that the hospital service of the army broke down lamentably during the last offensive in the Champagne after nearly three years of experience. I fear it must be reluctantly admitted that the French have no conspicuous talent for organization.

I am glad to learn that our troops will soon arrive as their presence will have a stimulating effect upon the French morale which is drooping at the present time. If it were possible to take over the management of some of the French public services, such as transportation, provisioning, distribution of coal etc., it would be an enormous help. A great many Frenchmen think as I do on this subject but unless our people exhibited great tact there would be danger of wounding national pride.

I do not think too much importance should be attached to the decision of the minority group of the Socialist Party to send delegates to the Peace Congress at Stockholm. These delegates, in case they are allowed to go, will not represent the Government and I doubt whether they will represent any considerable section of the population.

Relations with Spain are a little strained just now as the French are satisfied that German submarines are being supplied with gasolene by Spanish agents. In this connection the French Navy Department have requested that the tanks of all ships (tank steamers) sailing from the United States for Spanish ports be inspected and sealed up before leaving the United States, the seals to be broken by consular representatives on arrival at destination.

They have also requested that Cristobel Morales, commanding the Spanish liner Alfonso XIII, be denied access to the ports and territories of the United States as they believe him to be an agent of the Germans who has furnished them valuable information since May 1917. This is of course for your information as it has already been communicated to our Navy Department.

Sincerely yours,   Arthur Hugh Frazier

TCL (WP, DLC).
[1] Maj. James Addison Logan, Jr., U.S.A., chief of the American military observers with the French army since September 1914; in April 1917, Logan's group had been reconstituted as a mission.

A Statement[1]

[*June 2, 1917*]

We should have scant capital to trade on were we to throw away the wisdom we have inherited and seek our fortunes with the slender stock we ourselves have accumulated. This, it seems to me, is the real, the prevalent argument for holding every man we can to the intimate study of the ancient classics. What you cannot find a substitute for is the classics as literature; and there can be no first hand contact with that literature if you will not master the grammar and the syntax which convey its subtle power. Your enlightenment depends on the company you keep. You do not know the world until you know the men who have possessed it and tried its wares before you were ever given your brief run upon it. And there is no sanity comparable with that which is schooled in the thoughts that will keep. All literature that has lasted has this claim upon us—that it is not dead; but we cannot be quite so sure of any as we are of the ancient literature that still lives, because none has lived so long. It holds a sort of primacy in the aristocracy of natural selection.

Printed in the *New York Times*, June 3, 1917.
[1] A message sent to a conference on classical studies in liberal education called by Princeton University and arranged by Andrew F. West.

To Robert Lansing, with Enclosure

My dear Mr. Secretary: The White House 2 June, 1917

I have just read Ambassador Morgan's dispatch of May thirty-first from Rio de Janeiro[1] about an appreciative telegram from myself to the President of Brazil upon the completion of the action of the Brazilian Congress with regard to neutrality. I think it an excellent suggestion and am glad to enclose a message which I would be very much obliged if you would have forwarded at the time he suggests.

Cordially and sincerely yours,   Woodrow Wilson

TLS (SDR, RG 59, 763.72/5120, DNA).
1 E. V. Morgan to RL, May 31, 1917, T telegram (SDR, RG 59, 763.72/5015, DNA). Morgan reported that the Brazilian Senate was about to pass legislation to revoke the decree of neutrality in the war between the United States and Germany and to authorize the Brazilian government to seize and utilize interned German merchant vessels. Morgan added: "An appreciative telegram from the President to the President of Brazil upon the completion of this legislation would produce admirable impression especially should this telegram indicate the President's hope that all the South American powers should cooperate in a continental movement to check the German menace."

E N C L O S U R E

May I not convey to your Excellency on behalf of my Government the feeling of deep appreciation and admiration with which the recent action of the Brazilian Congress with regard to the present struggle for peace and liberty has been received in the United States? I am sure that I speak for my fellow-countrymen in expressing my warm admiration of that action and in expressing the hope that it is prophetic of the action which will be taken by all the American States. I look forward with confident hope to their cooperation in a united movement to check the German menace.[1]

T MS (SDR, RG 59, 763.72/5120, DNA).
1 This was sent in RL to E. V. Morgan, June 4, 1917, T telegram (SDR, RG 59, 763.72/5015, DNA).

From William Gibbs McAdoo, with Enclosure

Dear Mr. President: Washington June 2, 1917.

I send you herewith, for your information, copy of a letter I have just sent to the Attorney General. This is, in part, an answer to the Attorney General's letter to you of April 17th.[1] I also enclose sample badge which the "Secret Service" Division of the American Protective League is using.

I dislike more than I can express to burden you with matters of this character, but I regard this organization as having very harmful possibilities. It seems to be very much in line with the "Sons of Liberty" organized during the American Revolution and through which many injustices and abuses resulted.

Cordially yours,   W G McAdoo

TLS (WP, DLC).
1 TWG to WW, April 17, 1917, TLS (WP, DLC).

E N C L O S U R E

William Gibbs McAdoo to Thomas Watt Gregory

Dear Mr. Attorney General: [Washington] June 2, 1917.

I have been under such exceedingly great pressure that I have not had the time to reply to your letter of the 17th of April, enclosing a copy of your letter to the President in regard to my suggestion for the establishment of a Bureau of Intelligence.[1] That suggestion was made solely in a spirit of helpfulness and cooperation, based upon an intense desire that this important function of the Government be organized along the most efficient and effective lines possible to cope with German intrigue and propaganda. If the existing organization is sufficient, all well and good; but you evidently misunderstood the purport of my letter and you have been so much misinformed as to the activities of the Secret Service of the Treasury Department, as indicated by inaccuracies in your letter to the President, that I shall reply at length as soon as I get the time. I am sorry I cannot do so now.

There is one important matter, however, which I must draw to your attention at once and that is the organization and operation, with the approval of the Department of Justice, of the *Secret Service Division* of the American Protective League.[2] I cannot believe that you have personally sanctioned the formation and activities of this private association operating under the name of "Secret Service," a name that at once falsely identifies it in the public mind with a branch of the public service in the Treasury Department. The scheme is fraught with the gravest danger of misunderstanding, confusion and even fraud, and in the public interest I am sending you my serious protest against its continuation under its present designation.

"The Secret Service Division" is the title by law of that division in the Treasury Department and the term "Secret Service" has a very definite meaning in the public mind; and for that reason the Treasury Department has always strongly discouraged its use by private parties. I am consequently astonished to learn that the Department of Justice has officially approved the use by a private organization of a title, a badge and a card of identification that confer the designation of "Secret Service." The Department of Justice has no right in law or reason to grant any such authority, especially when it opens the door to possible widespread deception of the public through the misuse of the name of a well known and distinct governmental agency.

This League is described by your Bureau of Investigation as a volunteer private organization cooperating with and following the wishes of the Department of Justice. It has been organized on a nation-wide scale with headquarters in most of the large cities of the country. In one of its letters which I have seen it is stated that its badges are sold to its employes at $1.00 each. In another city I am told that the charge is 75 cents each. In other words, for 75 cents or $1.00, membership may be obtained in this volunteer organization and authority conferred, with the approval of the Department of Justice, to make investigations under the title of "Secret Service." Apparently the agents of this association are not selected by the Government. The Government does not exercise the absolute control over these appointments that is essential to guarantee the integrity of the organization and its activities. They are simply private citizens who, with no official status, are authorized to perform official functions. In one instance at least I know of the appointment of a man in whom I personally have no confidence.

The Government cannot escape responsibility for their activities whatever they may be, and my serious complaint is that by the use of the title of "Secret Service," officially conferred by the Department of Justice, a private organization has been armed with a power the very existence of which in private hands is detrimental to the public interest and the public service. Not only will the public be confused by this improper use of the title "Secret Service," but information of great value to the United States Secret Service may, under misapprehension, be given to these volunteer investigators and through them reach sources inimical to the interests of the United States. The ends of justice may easily be defeated in this manner.

Not only does this private organization use the title "Secret Service Division," but its cards of membership contain the same designation prominently displayed, and the words "Secret Service" are written in large letters across the face of the badges it distributes. Its literature contains such terms as "operative" and "chief," which naturally further tend to identify it with the Secret Service of the Government. If it were not for the fact that this organization had received the definite approval of the Department of Justice, I would think that its name, badge and card of membership were designed for the deliberate purpose of deceiving the public.

In order to avoid this sort of confusion and deception of the public, a serious effort has been made for some time past to prevent private detective agencies and organizations from using the words "Secret Service" in transacting any of their businesses or voluntary services. For instance, through the assistance of United States Attorney Marshall, the State Comptroller of New York issued orders to all private detective agencies to discontinue the use of these words, and 32 agencies in that state announced their intention to comply with these instructions.

If this Association had been called "American Protective League, Bureau of Investigation," or some similar appellation identifying it with the Department with which it is associated and not confusing it with a Division of the Treasury Department, of course I would have no complaint. Already much confusion has resulted, and this Department has received many inquiries from various parts of the country in regard to this Association. These inquiries show conclusively the false impression the situation is creating.

I am writing to you fully and frankly in order to invite your personal attention to the situation which is sure to lead to confusion, misunderstandings and complications. With this statement of my views before you, permit me to request that steps be taken at once to check the activities of this organization under a name to which it has no right and the use of which is fraught with so much danger to the public and the Government. I urgently ask that you give immediate instructions that the Association change its designation and withdraw and destroy at once all badges, cards and literature referring to the "Secret Service" or the "Secret Service Division."

You will recall that during the American Revolution a voluntary organization similar in character, I imagine, to the one in question was formed under the title of "Sons of Liberty." It committed grave abuses and injustices. This "Secret Service" division of the American Protective League contains the same evil potentialities, especially since it is operating under the sanction of the Department of Justice. I am, of course, not advised as to whether or not there is authority of law for such sanction on your part.

When any citizen can become a member of such a "Secret Service" as that formed by the American Protective League by making application and buying a badge at a cost of 75 cents or $1, you can readily see that thoroughly irresponsible and untrustworthy people may be taken into the Service.

I am sending a copy of this letter to the President.

Faithfully yours, [W G McAdoo]

CCL (WP, DLC).
[1] WGM to WW, April 16, 1917, TLS (WP, DLC).
[2] About this organization and its activities, see Joan M. Jensen, *The Price of Vigilance* (Chicago, 1968).

From Robert Lansing

My dear Mr. President: Washington June 3, 1917.

Senator Owen called to see me yesterday and left with me a copy of a resolution which he had drafted and which is embodied in a speech which he proposes to deliver in support of the resolution.[1]

While he did not say so I assume that he wished me to submit it to you for comment as to the desirability of introduction at the present and as to the terms of the resolution.

I did not have time to read the Senator's speech until today. I think that is based on the essential principles which will be the foundation of a permanent peace, but I am not at all sure that this is the time to invite controversy over the terms of peace in Congress and, as a consequence, throughout the world. I am not sure how the various Allied Governments would view this formal declaration on our part of arrangements, in which they are so vitally interested, without our consulting them or giving them an opportunity to object to one or more of the provisions.

In fact I believe that any resolution at the present time would precipitate a debate in Congress which might give opportunity to those hostile to you to criticize your declarations as to the purposes which we seek to accomplish in the war. That would be very undesirable and might cause serious differences with our co-belligerents.

I do not know quite how to explain this to Senator Owen who has evidently given much thought to the subject and is strong in the belief that Congress should declare our purposes. I am afraid that my objection alone would not restrain him from acting.

It seems to me that the best way is for you to ask Senator Owen to come and see you, and then give him orally your views rather than write them to me for transmission to him.

I will tell the Senator that I have sent you his resolution and speech for your consideration.

Faithfully yours,   Robert Lansing

TLS (WP, DLC).

[1] *International Peace: Speech of Hon. Robert L. Owen . . . in the Senate of the United States, May, 1917* (WP, DLC). The heart of Owen's proposed speech was the following resolution:

"*Resolved by the Senate and House of Representatives of the United States of America in Congress assembled,* That it is the opinion of the Government of the United States that an early peace might be obtained based on the following principles:

"*First.* The establishment of the right of self-government of the people of Germany and Austria through parliaments chosen by and representing the people and through ministers directly responsible to the parliaments or to the people, and the termination of the military autocracy governing the people under the pretense of 'divine right.'

"Second. There should be no forcible or involuntary annexations on the continent of Europe or punitive indemnities imposed against Germany or other nations as a result of this war unless the German people, after reasonable notice, persist in waging war in support of annexations and punitive indemnities against other nations.

"Third. Belgium, northern France, Poland, east Prussia, Servia, and Roumania should receive such contributions and credit as may be necessary to provide for the restoration of the devastated areas in such countries, to be raised by international agreement, as part of an international settlement providing for world peace.

"Fourth. The people of Alsace and Lorraine should have local self-government, and determine, by a referendum vote of their own people, whether they shall be attached to Germany or France, or neither.

"Fifth. There should be an international agreement providing for the freedom of the seas and free access to the sea for the goods of all nations having no seaports, by the shipment of their goods in bond to ports of other nations.

"Sixth. There should be no peace with the Imperial Government of Germany until the actual sovereignty of the German people shall have been completely established, either by the German people themselves or as the result of the pending war.

"Seventh. There should be no separate peace with the Imperial German Government by any of the allies."

Arthur James Balfour to Lord Robert Cecil

Halifax. R. 11 a.m. June 3rd. 1917.

Personal and Secret.

Sir C. Spring Rice has had conversation with Colonel House on various matters. Following is a summary of latter's views.

If British Government wish to get special naval and military officers to help United States Government best plan would be to offer to invite United States officers to London to serve as special representatives of War and Navy Departments and at the same time to offer to send corresponding officers here; he thinks matter should be arranged with Navy and War Departments and not through President. It would be safer not to offer to send special officers here unless Departments concerned express willingness. He thinks British Government is in quite special position here and should not conclude that because French Government could safely send man like Tardieu we could do the same. Position is in high degree delicate and only great tact and skill of Mr. Balfour and Mission has prevented energetic press campaign against an "English War." President is very sensitive on this point. Danger is that this essential difference between French and British position here may not be understood in England. Should His Majesty's Government send anyone corresponding in position to Tardieu his activities should be strictly limited to control over British officers here. Even this should be done in an inconspicuous way and the less prominent the (?place) the better. House thinks present arrangement with Sir R. Crawford and

Polk acts admirably but said he understands that public opinion in England may demand something more positive. But position of a prominent person here would be so unpleasant owing to probability of press attacks and necessary aloofness of United States Government that he would probably soon return home.

T telegram (FO 371/3119, No. 110899, pp. 358-59, PRO).

To Martin Grove Brumbaugh

[The White House]

My dear Governor Brumbaugh:　　　　　　　　4 June, 1917

I take pleasure in replying to your letter of June first.

I think it would be most unfortunate for any of the states to relax the laws by which safeguards have been thrown about labor. I feel that there is no necessity for such action, and that it would lead to a slackening of the energy of the nation rather than to an increase of it, besides being very unfair to the laboring people themselves.

Sincerely yours,　　Woodrow Wilson

TLS (Letterpress Books, WP, DLC).

To Thomas Watt Gregory

[The White House]

My dear Mr. Attorney General:　　　　　　　4 June, 1917

Has your attention been called to the enclosed association? It seems to me that it would be very dangerous to have such an organization operating in the United States, and I wonder if there is any way in which we could stop it.

Cordially and faithfully yours,　　Woodrow Wilson

TLS (Letterpress Books, WP, DLC).

To Josephus Daniels

Confidential.

My dear Daniels:　　　　　　　The White House 4 June, 1917

The other day you wrote me a note about an undertaking of the Scripps' newspapers which they have put in the hands of Mr. H. P. Burton.[1]

Can you tell me who this Mr. Burton is?[2]

A man of that name was recently sent over here by Lord Northcliffe, and I want to have as little to do with him as possible, because I don't believe in Lord Northcliffe any more than I do in Mr. Hearst and I wonder if this Mr. H. P. Burton is the man.

In haste

Cordially and faithfully yours,   Woodrow Wilson

TLS (J. Daniels Papers, DLC).
¹ JD to WW, May 28, 1917, TLS (WP, DLC). Daniels reported that the Scripps newspaper chain had commissioned Harry Payne Burton to edit a "publication," to be sent gratis to all the newspapermen of America who wanted it, for the purpose of instilling "patriotism in the newspaper offices." Burton had suggested that Wilson contribute to this "magazine" a statement on "the patriotic duty of the American editor . . . in war time."
² Daniels said that Burton was a long-time employee of the Scripps chain and "an old friend of ours." He was, Daniels continued, in no way related to Pomeroy Burton, the man reportedly sent over by Northcliffe. Pomeroy Burton, formerly with the New York World, was at this time general manager of Associated Newspapers Ltd., the holding company for Northcliffe's newspapers. He had been sent to the United States by the Foreign Office to investigate ways to improve British propaganda. JD to WW, June 12, 1917, TLS (WP, DLC).

To Jacques A. Berst[1]

My dear Mr. Berst: [The White House] 4 June, 1917

Several times in attending Keith's Theatre here I have seen portions of the film entitled "Patria," which has been exhibited there and I think in a great many other theatres in the country. May I not say to you that the character of the story disturbed me very much? It is extremely unfair to the Japanese and I fear that it is calculated to stir up a great deal of hostility which will be far from beneficial to the country, indeed will, particularly in the present circumstances, be extremely hurtful. I take the liberty, therefore, of asking whether the Pathe Company would not be willing to withdraw it if it is still being exhibited.[2]

With much respect,

Sincerely yours,   Woodrow Wilson

TLS (Letterpress Books, WP, DLC).
¹ Vice-president and general manager of Pathé Exchange, Inc.
² See WW to F. L. Polk, June 9, 1917.

From Bernard Mannes Baruch

My dear Mr. President: Washington, D. C. June 4th, 1917.

I have been wondering whether in my desire to avoid burdening your mind with too many details, I had not left some things without an explanation, to which you might care to give some thought before you saw me again. For instance, the following things shown on the chart:

FOOD CONTROL. The Food Controller would purchase all food

supplies coming to the Central Purchasing Agency, needed by the Army, the Navy, the Allies and perhaps the neutral nations. Contracts would be made direct for the purchaser by the Food Controller,—the Central Purchasing Agency being the clearing house.

LABOR. The Labor Section would naturally fall under the head of Secretary Wilson to whom the labor disputes affecting the industries furnishing supplies would be referred for settlement.

COST OF PRODUCTION. This section might have better been called "Cost of Production and Adjudication or Fixing of Prices," or some simular title. Where a price was made that did not meet with the satisfaction of both sides, it could be referred to this section for adjudication. This body would hear the evidence and have at its command the cost of production, the economic situation and all the necessary information required to fix fair prices.

I would suggest, that it be composed of five men of such character as Professor Goodenow, head of John Hopkins University; the head of the Tariff Commission or a member of the Tariff Commission like Mr. Roper; the head of the Federal Trade Commission or a commissioner like Mr. Colver; Judge Lovett, President of the Union Pacific and a labor man of the character of John Mitchell. It might be well to have as Chairman of the Committee, a man like Ex-President William H. Taft, if he would work.

Prices made or approved by a committee of this nature would avoid the criticism and nasty investigation that might come after the war. The more I think of it, the greater its importance appears.

The responsibility of fixing or adjusting prices from time to time would be referred to this body. After the adjudication of a few items, the work of the committee would grow less and less, because the industries would fall in line very quickly on the basis established by its decisions. With the advice and suggestion of the Central Purchasing Agency, this body would not resolve itself into a debating society and its decisions could be made quickly.

The consumers, the producers and the government could well accept the decisions of such a body and it seems to me its conclusions would meet with the approval of all.

The Priority Committee here is a different body from the Priority Committee sitting in London, establishing the priority of the orders forwarded by the Allies. The Priority Committee here would not alone decide the priority between our Allies and the Army and Navy, but would make certain decisions when the supplies of raw materials was less than the demands. For instances, there is a shortage of lead. The Priority Committee might decide that certain uses of lead would have to cease, like the making of lead soldiers, bird shot, etc., lopping off the less essential for the more essential.

The Priority Committee might decide that a man could not build a greenhouse or it might be well to postpone the building of a public library or a skyscraper, because of the inability to obtain steel for the purpose. The Priority Committee might decide that it would be unwise to build new roads, because of the demands for materials and the demands of the labor market. The Priority Committee might decide that it would be better not to open new coal mines, but to use all of the labor on the present coal mines. The continuance of the War might necessitate the licensing of the use of certain scarce raw materials and this the Priority Committee could do.

The chart is by no means carried out in detail and I shall refrain now from going further into it. No names are on the chart as heading the various divisions. Making use of the materials we already have at hand, I would suggest the following:

For instances, Legal and Accounting, Thomas L. Chadbourne, Jr.;[1] Aviation, Howard Coffin; Munitions, Frank Scott; General Supplies, Julius Rosenwald; Transportation, Daniel Willard, etc.

Awaiting your further commands, I am

Very sincerely yours,   Bernard M Baruch

TLS (WP, DLC).
[1] Thomas Lincoln Chadbourne, Jr., corporation lawyer of New York.

From the White House Staff

The White House.

Memorandum for the President: June 4, 1917.

Assistant Secretary Roosevelt is very anxious to see the President at the President's convenience to take up with the President the matter of meeting the submarine menace—upon which matter the Navy Department and the Department of Commerce have been working for some time. Mr. Roosevelt states that both Secretary Daniels and Secretary Redfield are anxious that he should see the President.[1]

T MS (WP, DLC).
[1] Wilson saw Roosevelt at 3 P.M. that afternoon. Roosevelt strongly supported the plan to prevent German submarines from reaching their hunting grounds by creating a barricade of mines and nets across the North Sea between Scotland and Norway. See Frank Freidel, *Franklin D. Roosevelt: The Apprenticeship* (Boston, 1952), pp. 312-17.

Lord Robert Cecil to Sir Cecil Arthur Spring Rice

F. O., 4th. June 1917.

My personal and secret telegram of May 19 for Mr. Balfour.

Question of future naval cooperation with the U. S. has now been carefully considered by War Cabinet who are in general agreement with the views which I expressed in above telegram, but, much as they would like to be in a position to give forthwith a formal guarantee of naval aid to the U. S. for the future and out of that to develope a definite naval alliance, they are of opinion that its announcement at Tokio, which could not justifiably be withheld, must inevitably raise in a highly dangerous form the whole extent of Anglo-Japanese relations and would certainly be interpreted by Japan as primarily aimed at blocking her ambitions in China, the Pacific and the Far East generally.

The U. S. Govt must, however, be aware that, quite independently of any diplomatic agreements that might be concluded, this country would be unable to refrain from going to America's assistance in case of need, and they can hardly feel that they are incurring any serious risk in shaping their naval policy on that assumption and foregoing the formal guarantee which, as stated, the present international situation makes it difficult for HMG to give, short of a general recasting of existing agreements.

HMG have indeed been primarily impressed by the prospect of the possible development of Anglo-American naval cooperation in the future, but they have also given their attention to the technical consideration which gave rise to this larger question, namely the reluctance of the U. S. Govt. to alter their naval programme in favour of the construction of additional destroyers.

With some important exceptions, the American fleet is much superior to the Japanese numerically and otherwise. Of the larger capital ships, both constructed and under construction, with the exception of Battle Cruisers, the U. S. have already a considerable preponderance. On the other hand, their number of fast light cruisers is in the opinion of our Naval auths. quite inadequate for the operations of a fleet of the dimensions of that of the U. S., while their superiority in destroyers over the Japanese is also insufficient.

The most urgent requirements of the American navy as against Japan are in fact for Light Cruisers, destroyers and anti-submarine craft, and, with the exception of the Battle Cruisers, it would be a waste of resources for the U. S. Govt to build more capital ships. The same requirements apply to the present war, and it seems essential that the U. S. Govt. should concentrate on building the classes of vessels required even at the cost of postponing the completion of the Dreadnought Battleships.

Y. E. should take an early opportunity of resuming the discussion begun by Mr. Balfour with Col. House, or elsewhere, and developing the arguments in favour of the U. S. modifying their naval programme as desired by us, and, with regard to the ultimate question of a naval guarantee from us or an alliance, you should, while explaining our difficulties, make it clear that we are extremely disappointed at being unable at once to surmount them and that only the sensitiveness of the Far Eastern situation under present circumstances prevents us from tackling the problem immediately.   R.C.

Hw telegram (FO 371/3119, pp. 312-13, PRO).

Remarks to Confederate Veterans in Washington[1]

5 June, 1917

Mr. Commander, ladies and gentlemen: I esteem it a very great pleasure and a real privilege to extend to the men who are attending this reunion the very cordial greetings of the Government of the United States.

I suppose that, as you mix with one another, you chiefly find these to be days of memory, when your thoughts go back and recall those days of struggle in which your hearts were strained, in which the whole nation seemed in grapple, and I dare say that you are thrilled as you remember the heroic things that were then done. You are glad to remember that heroic things were done on both sides, and that men in those days fought in something like the old spirit of chivalric gallantry. There are many memories of the Civil War that thrill along the blood and make one proud to have been sprung of a race that could produce such bravery and constancy. And yet the world does not live on memories. The world is constantly making its toilsome way forward into new and different days, and I believe that one of the things that contributes satisfaction to a reunion like this, and a welcome like this, is that this is also a day of oblivion. There are some things that we have thankfully buried, and among them are the great passions of division which once threatened to rend this nation in twain. The passion of admiration we still entertain for the heroic figures of those old days, but the passion of separation, the passion of difference of principle, is gone—gone out of our minds, gone out of our hearts. And one of the things that will thrill this country as it reads of this reunion is that it will read also of a rededication on the part of all of us to the great nation which we serve in common.

These are days of oblivion as well as of memory, for we are forgetting the things that once held us asunder. Not only that, but they are days of rejoicing, because we now at last see why this great nation was kept united, for we are beginning to see the great world purpose which it was meant to serve. Many men I know, particularly of your own generation, have wondered at some of the dealings of Providence. But the wise heart never questions the dealings of Providence, because the great long plan, as it unfolds, has a majesty about it and a definiteness of purpose, an elevation of ideal, which we were incapable of conceiving as we tried to work things out with our own short sight and weak strength. And now that we see ourselves part of a nation, united, powerful, great in spirit and in purpose, we know the great ends which God, in His mysterious Providence, wrought through our instrumentality. Because, at the heart of the men of the North and of the South, there was the same love of self-government and of liberty, and now we are to be an instrument in the hands of God to see that liberty is made secure for mankind. At the day of our greatest division, there was one common passion amongst us, and that was the passion for human freedom. We did not know that God was working out in His own way the method by which we should best serve human freedom—by making this nation a great united, indivisible, indestructible instrument in His hands for the accomplishment of these great things.

As I came along the streets a few minutes ago, my heart was full of the thought that this is Registration Day. Will you not support me in feeling that there is some significance in this coincidence—that this day, when I come to welcome you to the national capital, is a day when men, young as you were in those old days, when you gathered together to fight, are now registering their names as evidence of this great idea—that in a democracy the duty to serve and the privilege to serve falls upon all alike? There is something very fine, my fellow citizens, in the spirit of the volunteer, but deeper than the volunteer spirit is the spirit of obligation. There is not a man of us who must not hold himself ready to be summoned to the duty of supporting the great government under which we live. No really thoughtful and patriotic man is jealous of that obligation. No man who really understands the privilege and the dignity of being an American citizen quarrels for a moment with the idea that the Congress of the United States has the right to call upon whom it will to serve the nation. These solemn lines of young men going today all over the Union to the places of registration ought to be a signal to the world—to those who dare flout the dignity and honor and rights of the United States—that all her manhood will flock to that standard under which we all delight to serve, and that he who challenges the rights and principles of the United States challenges the united strength and devotion of a nation.

There are not many things that one desires about war, my fellow citizens, but you have come through war, you know how you have been chastened by it, and there comes a time when it is good for a nation to know that it must sacrifice, if need be everything, that it has to vindicate the principles which it professes. We have prospered with a sort of heedless and irresponsible prosperity. Now we are going to lay all our wealth, if necessary, and spend all our blood, if need be, to show that we were not accumulating that wealth selfishly but were accumulating it for the service of mankind. Men all over the world have thought of the United States as a trading and money-getting people, whereas we who have lived at home know the ideals with which the hearts of this people have thrilled. We know the sober convictions which have lain at the basis of our life all the time. And we know the power and devotion which can be spent in heroic ways in the service of those ideals that we have treasured. We have been allowed to become strong in the Providence of God that our strength might be used to prove, not our selfishness, but our greatness, and, if there is any ground for thankfulness in a day like this, I am thankful for the privilege of self-sacrifice, which is the only privilege that lends dignity to the human spirit.

And so it seems to me that we may regard this as a very happy day, because a day of reunion, a day of noble memories, a day of dedication, a day of the renewal of the spirit which has made America great among the peoples of the world.[2]

T MS (C. L. Swem Coll., NjP).
 [1] Wilson spoke at the Arcade Auditorium to the twenty-seventh annual convention and reunion of the United Confederate Veterans and other related groups, such as the Sons of Confederate Veterans and Daughters of Confederate Veterans. Hilary Abner Herbert, Secretary of the Navy, 1893-1897, presided, and General George Paul Harrison, former congressman from Alabama and commander in chief of the United Confederate Veterans, was one of the speakers. *Washington Post*, June 5 and 6, 1917.
 [2] There is a WWsh outline and a WWT outline of this speech in WP, DLC.

From Robert Lansing, with Enclosure

My dear Mr. President: Washington June 5, 1917.

I enclose a memorandum which Mr. Phillips handed me today in regard to an interview which he had with a Pole by the name of

Horodyski. In view of the opinion of Sir Eric Drummond I believe that Mr. Horodyski's statements are worthy of careful consideration.   Faithfully yours,   Robert Lansing.

ENCLOSURE

William Phillips to Robert Lansing

Dear Mr. Secretary: Department of State June 4, 1917.

Sir Eric Drummond, before leaving, asked me to receive Horodyski, a very influential Pole who has been for a long time in close touch with the British Foreign Office. Drummond described him as having the complete confidence of the Foreign Office, and that he was an authority on Polish questions. I have also asked Mr. Paderewski about Horodyski, who agrees with Drummond's estimate of him. According to Paderewski Horodyski is now the principal agitator for the Polish army to be raised in the United States; that he is here for that purpose, etc., etc. Paderewski spoke cordially of him.

Mr. Horodyski called upon me a day or two ago and made an excellent impression. Among many other things he dwelt upon the importance of this country having a very active and efficient Legation at Berne, and a Minister who would have access to the hundred and one different sources of information there. In this connection he referred to the "Central Polish Agency," composed of patriotic Poles who offered their services without remuneration, whose work is to send information secretly into Poland and to receive information regarding Poland through the same secret channels. He said that the British Government had at last realized that the "Central Polish Agency" was an organization of great importance; and that they had offered to pay for the privilege of utilizing it. The Central Agency, however, refused to accept any British remuneration, but was one of the principal mediums which the British had for communicating with Poland. He said he had information from Berne that Mr. Stovall, partly because he had no knowledge of foreign languages, did not have an open door to the many sources of information regarding Germany which are to be found in Switzerland; that it was almost of the first importance that we should have a Minister there who was capable of getting in touch intimately not only with his colleagues in the diplomatic corps, but with the underground channels of communication with Germany. Horodyski said that it was not until a year after the war broke out that the British Government appreciated the importance of having a man with these qualifications in Berne; but that they had an excellent man there now who was very much a live wire.[1]

It seems to me that the importance of having exceedingly active and efficient ministers at Berne, Copenhagen and The Hague & Stockholm cannot be over-estimated; that during the war we shall have to rely upon these Legations for all the intelligent information regarding the situation in Germany and German occupied territory, and that we should place these missions upon a *war basis* as speedily as possible.

Sincerely,   W. Phillips

TLS (SDR, RG 59, 763.72119/636½, DNA).
[1] Sir Horace George Montagu Rumbold.

From William Gibbs McAdoo

Dear "Governor":   En route, June 5, 1917.

The House has passed the War Risk Insurance bill amendments, providing for the insurance of the lives of the masters, officers and seamen of merchant ships, and providing, also, for indemnity insurance. The Senate will, I understand, concur in the House amendments, which are immaterial, so that the bill may reach you in a few days. I write merely to say that the measure is, in form and substance, entirely satisfactory to the Treasury Department, and that I earnestly recommend that the bill be approved.

We have had wonderful meetings in New York and Boston on the Liberty Loan and find the spirit of the people all that could be desired. The draft registration, as far as I am able to learn, has proceed[ed] quietly and most satisfactorily throughout the country. It is a great achievement and I congratulate you and the Secretary of War.

I believe that the excellent campaign for the Liberty Loan bonds which is now being carried on in almost every town and precinct in the country, is having a most helpful effect upon public opinion with respect to the war. I hope you are all well. This speech-making is gruelling work for me and I am glad to think that it will soon be over.

Affectionately yours,   W G McAdoo

TLS (WP, DLC).

From Edward Mandell House

Dear Governor,   Magnolia, Massachusetts. June 5th 1917.

Upon my arrival here I find your letter of June 1st.

I am glad you think well of the suggestion to define in some near by address the purposes of the German Government, and to state the objects for which the Allies are at war. June 14th—Flag Day—I think would do if you will arrange for wide publicity. I would get the world on tip-toe beforehand, and then arrange to have what you say cabled to the ends of the earth.

You have come to be the spokesman for Democracy, as indeed the Kaiser is the spokesman for Autocracy. However, I would caution against mentioning him. He is nearly as unimportant as the Tsar was before he was dethroned—both merely representatives of systems.

It will vastly accelerate liberalism in Germany to ignore the Kaiser, and let the German people work out their own details. I would advise care in phraseology so that neither France nor Italy may see their respective hopes for Alsace and Lorraine and the Trentino endangered. England will not be offended. She is interested in having German hopes for a Middle Europe under Prussian control forever shattered. I have talked this out witl [with] Balfour.

A kindly word for Austria-Hungary, Bulgaria and Turkey would help the purpose in mind. The two points I would bring out are

1. To make clear Imperial Prussia's purpose of conquest,

2. the unwillingness of the democracies to treat with a military autocracy.

I would emphasize the thought of a world at arms, not against the German people, but against a Prussian military oligarchy. If you would send me in advance a copy of the address, I think I would know if there was a word or line which might offend sensibilities. If you also think well I can ask Sir William Wiseman to come here, so that he may take a word of explanation to the Ambassadors of England, France and Italy.

For your information only let me say that Balfour has given Wiseman his confidence to an unusual degree, and they have arranged a private code that can only be unraveled by Drummond and Wiseman themselves.

Affectionately yours,   E. M. House

Thank you for your kindly thoughts of me. My only concern is that I cannot do more.

TLS (WP, DLC).

From Franklin Delano Roosevelt

My dear Mr. President: Washington. June 5, 1917.

In confirmation of what I said to you about the North Sea question, I have thought over the composition of a Board or Commission to make a speedy report on the advisability of making the attempt to carry out this plan on a large scale. I do not think that such a Board should be composed wholly of line officers of the Navy and would, therefore, suggest its composition somewhat as follows:

One officer from the mine force of the Atlantic Fleet, possibly Captain R. R. Belknap,[1] its commanding officer.

One officer from the Bureau of Ordnance.

One officer from the Bureau of Yards & Docks; for instance, Civil Engineer Kirby Smith,[2] who has given the whole subject much study.

One representative from the Coast and Geodetic Survey, because the Department of Commerce has had much experience with buoys, wire drags, etc.

One representative of the Naval Consulting Board. I would suggest Mr. Thomas Robbins, the secretary, as Mr. Robbins represents no special group in the Board and is in touch with all the members.

It is not my idea that a Board or Commission of this kind should carry on extensive experiments. There is enough data in regard to mines, nets, buoys, currents, etc., to enable them to report on the advisability of making the attempt on a large scale, and I cannot help feeling that time is of the essence of the plan, especially because during the next three or four months the weather conditions will be good for carrying out the preliminary work.

I am showing this to Mr. Daniels, and I feel sure that the whole Department will approve the initiation of the project. May I say, however, that it is a matter which is bigger than any mere Department, and that in the execution of the work the usual department routine and red tape should be cut to a minimum, and that outside of the actual patrol of such a barrier the work to be done has a distinctly civilian and industrial character.

Faithfully yours,   Franklin D Roosevelt

TLS (WP, DLC).

[1] Reginald Rowan Belknap.

[2] Lt. Comdr. Kirby Smith.

To Joseph Patrick Tumulty, with Enclosure

Dear Tumulty: [The White House, c. June 6, 1917]
    I would by no means associate myself with this crowd.
                                                The President.

TL (WP, DLC).

E N C L O S U R E

From Joseph Patrick Tumulty

                                            The White House
Memorandum for the President: June 6, 1917.
    Professor Henry D. Thompson, formerly a member of the New
Jersey Legislature, has asked me to permit the use of my name
as a member of the Board of Control of the Summer Military
Camp, at Princeton, having been delegated by President Hibben to
invite me. The other members of the Board are President Hibben,
some members of the Princeton faculty, Governor Edge, Wallace Scudder, Melvin Rice, Dr. Kendall, Governor Stokes, Thomas
McCarter and several others. Princeton has placed all of its buildings and equipment, dining halls, ete., at the disposal of the Summer Military Camp, which is to be used for training college and
high school men of all ages, from 17 years up. It is believed that
after the two months' course at Princeton they will be better able
to go into the service—either in the training camps or the enlisted
ranks. Preference is to be given to Jerseymen and there is to be no
cost to the Government. Each member of the camp will be
charged $80 for the two months' training.
    I shall be obliged if you will tell me frankly what answer you
think I should make to Professor Thompson's invitation. I have
no special desire to serve on this Board and shall be guided entirely by what you think best in the circumstances. My own
opinion is that we ought not to help this crowd in any way.
                                                Tumulty.

TLS (WP, DLC).

From Joseph Patrick Tumulty

Dear Governor: The White House June 6, 1917.
    I have seen the Russian note.[1] I know what you intended by the
phrase: "Remedies must be found as well as statements of prin-

ciple that will have a pleasing and sonorous sound." But I am afraid that the average man will not catch your meaning. I fear that it may give the impression that we are proposing high-sounding remedies just because we like to hear them and they are pleasing to the ear.

Would we not convey a better impression by making the sentence read thus: "We ought not to consider remedies merely because they have a pleasing and sonorous sound."

I do not think there will be any difficulty in changing the copy.[2]   J.P.T.

TL (WP, DLC).
[1] That is, WW to the provisional government of Russia, printed at May 22, 1917.
[2] The change was made before publication.

From Joseph Patrick Tumulty, with Enclosure

Dear Governor: The White House. June 6, 1917.

A great deal of publicity has been given to this letter from John P. White, President of the United Mine Workers of America. I merely acknowledged it and said I would call it to your attention. Evidently there is a feeling that because of the important part the mine workers of America are going to play in the war, it might be worth while considering the suggestion Mr. White makes. I think the letter is important enough for you to acknowl[edge] personally, and possibly you may wish to take up with the Council of National Defense the suggestion of having the United Mine Workers of America represented in the Council of National Defense by Mr. White.   Sincerely yours,   J P Tumulty

TLS (WP, DLC).

ENCLOSURE

From John Philip White

                                        Indianapolis, Ind.
Sir: May twenty-third, Nineteen Hundred Seventeen.

Knowing your deep concern for the national welfare, as exemplified both in the material matter of the coal supply and in the maintenance of righteous and safe standards of work and service, I have the honor to submit to you a copy of a statement (accompanied by a resolution adopted by our Executive Board), which I have just sent to the Council of National Defense.[1]

Assuring you of my deep solicitude that this matter be placed quickly on the right basis of national welfare and security, I am
Very respectfully,   John P. White

TLS (WP, DLC).

[1] J. P. White to Council of National Defense, May 23, 1917, enclosing statement, May 21, 1917, TLS and T MS (WP, DLC). These documents are summarized and quoted at length in the *New York Times*, May 27 and June 3, 1917. The letter and statement protested against the creation of the Council of National Defense's Committee on Coal Production with broad powers to control the coal industry. The committee, the protests asserted, not only contained no representative of organized labor but also included such a well-known enemy of the labor movement as Jesse Floyd Welborn. The United Mine Workers was both ready and eager to cooperate wholeheartedly in the war effort; however, in order to do so, it had to be permitted to continue its normal activities on behalf of the miners and had to be represented on any federal commission which dealt with the coal industry.

From James L. Davidson

Birmingham, Ala., June 6, 1917.

For the past nine years the coal mines of Alabama have been operated on the open shop basis without discriminating between union and non-union workmen, and during that time the relations between the operators and the workmen have been universally harmonious. Except in a few isolated instances, all of which were promptly adjusted to the satisfaction of the workmen, affected. The industry has grown under the open shop until the coal mines now are producing a much greater tonnage than ever before. Better working and living conditions and better sanitation obtains and much higher wages are being paid than ever before. If the coal cars were returned to the owning lines in the south, the output of the Alabama mines could be largely increased, provided no extraneous influence intervenes to cause dissatisfaction and disaffection among the workmen. Such an effort is now being made, the organizers of the United Mine Workers of America have been sent here to organize the workmen and put the mines in this district on the closed shop basis and drive the non-union workmen from the mines of this district to other non-union coal fields or into other lines of industry. These organizers make the statement that if the operator opposes their efforts to organize and close[s] the mines to non-union workmen, that they will furnish transportation for union mine workers and carry them to other coal fields where the closed shop prevails. These organizers are appealing to the workmen to join their organization, stating that they were sent here "to aid the President in keeping the miners at work steadily." However they propose to call a convention and make demands as soon as their organization is perfected. This means cessation of operations while wage agreements are being negotiated and if the operator is unable to meet the demands his mine will be closed down.

These organizers also state that they were sent here to agitate organization and "closed shop," having first obtained the approval of the government and of Congress to the plan, implying that the President approves the same and intimating that they were sent here at the instance of the governmental authorities for such purpose. The above being in effect the only argument that appeals to the loyal workmen to join the organization. They have offered no other argument worth mentioning.

We respectfully beg to inquire if the statements of these union organizers and officials above set out are correct. We will appreciate it if you will kindly reply by wire at our expense as early as your convenience will permit.

Alabama Coal Operators Association,
By Jas. L. Davidson, Secretary.

T telegram (WP, DLC).

From Edward Mandell House

Dear Governor: Magnolia, Mass. June 7, 1917.

I am sorry that Northcliffe is coming. I thought Balfour's cable had headed him off.

Wiseman did not dare communicate with his Government during Balfour's absence. We framed a cable together which was to reach him upon his arrival, but the Northcliffe faction in the Government evidently wanted to act upon it before Balfour arrived and could stop it.

In Balfour's cable, he urged that they ascertain your wishes either through Page or through me. They concluded to use Page since he was more convenient. Wiseman tells me that Page approved his coming and thought he would be acceptable to you.

There are two factions in the British Cabinet. With Balfour away the Northcliffe faction dominates. With Balfour there, he is generally able to control. Lloyd George is more or less neutral—inclining, however, towards the Northcliffe crowd. I hope this does not result in Balfour's resignation.

It is to be remembered that Northcliffe comes apparently with your approval and of course expects to be cordially received. I am afraid his visit may stir up the anti-British feeling here that at present is lying dormant.

Affectionately yours,   E. M. House

TLS (WP, DLC).

From Francis Griffith Newlands

My dear Mr President,   Washington, D. C. June 7th, 1917.

I enclose herewith the bill regarding priorities and the proof of the Report which I propose to present to morrow with a supplement added since the date of the original report containing the letter of Mr Willard and the address of Mr Howard Elliott.[1]

As the letter which you originally sent me on the subject of this legislation referred only to governmental priorities[2] I would be glad to receive from you another letter which will show the necessity of the pending bill and which I can present to the Senate for publication in the Record.

The bill is the unfinished business for to morrow (Friday). I would suggest that you read the short discussion of this measure in the Record of last Monday.[3] Believe me

Very sincerely yours   Francis G. Newlands.

ALS (WP, DLC).

[1] They are missing but they were S. 2356, the bill about railroad priorities, and 65th Cong., 1st sess., *Senate Report No. 48*. The bill as reported consisted of two sections: one forbade the obstruction or retardation of the orderly movement of trains in interstate transportation; the other gave the President power, whenever necessary for the public security and defense, to direct that certain kinds of traffic or particular shipments should have preference or priority under such rules as he might prescribe. The accompanying report consisted of a brief explanation of the bill, together with the supporting letter of Daniel Willard and an address by Howard Elliott.

[2] WW to F. G. Newlands, May 14, 1917, CCL (WP, DLC). For the same letter, *mutatis mutandis*, see WW to C. A. Culberson, May 14, 1917.

[3] *Cong. Record*, 65th Cong., 1st sess., p. 3258.

From Henry Morgenthau

My dear Mr. President: Washington June 7, 1917.

My object in wishing to see you was to explain to you the desirability of having Mr. Felix Frankfurter accompany me. When I asked for the appointment Justice Brandeis was somewhat opposed to it. He is now quite reconciled to it but wants an opportunity to discuss the matter with you for a few minutes. He wants you to decide whether this commission is more important than the services that Frankfurter can render in the War Department. I hope you can grant him an early interview so as to settle the matter and give Frankfurter a chance to prepare himself.[1] Our intention is to leave on June 16th on the Spanish steamer.

Captain Williams,[2] who is Military Attache in Constantinople, has just returned and brought me the following message from Enver:

"Please tell Mr. Morgenthau he had won the confidence of the Turkish people, and would always be welcomed in Turkey. That if Mr. Morgenthau ever returned to Turkey, in either an official or private capacity, he would be received by the Turkish people with open arms. He said further, please take to Mr. Morgenthau my warm personal regards and best wishes."

I think this is quite significant.

I shall not see you before leaving unless you so wish it.

Faithfully yours,   H Morgenthau

TLS (WP, DLC).
1 There is no record of a meeting between Wilson and Brandeis at this time.
2 Capt. Richard H. Williams, U.S.A., had been military attaché in Constantinople in 1915-1916.

From Robert Lansing, with Enclosure

My dear Mr. President: Washington June 8, 1917.

I submit for your consideration a memorandum which was handed to Mr. Polk by one of the British representatives, and which contains suggestions which appeal very strongly to me.

If we adopt the suggestions this Government would not have to appear in the matter at all, but we would work through the connections which the British have made in this country. I estimate it would cost us approximately $100,000.

On account of the situation in Russia I feel no stone should be left unturned to counteract the German propaganda which is being carried on there.

Faithfully yours,   Robert Lansing.

Approved by Prest orally 6/15/17 RL

TLS (SDR, RG 59, 861.00/423½A, DNA).

ENCLOSURE

RUSSIA

It is important that everything possible should be done to counteract present German intrigues in Russia.

It is common knowledge that the Germans are counting on their propaganda to bring about a separate peace with Russia; but the details of their intrigues are not so well-known.

We have reliable information that the Germans are organizing from every neutral country parties of Russian refugees, largely Jewish socialists. These parties are sent to Petrograd where they are organized by German agents posing as advanced Socialists.

The United States is the best situated country from which to organize a counter-propaganda. The Germans have been able to make the Russian people somewhat suspicious of the aims of the French and English, while the activities of the German agents in Holland and Scandinavia make these countries difficult as an organizing centre.

German agents have already been at work in the United States, and are sending Russian-Jewish Socialists back to Petrograd who are either knowingly or unknowingly working in the German cause.

The counter-propaganda proposed would have to be entirely unofficial, and very secretly organized, as any idea of Government support would ruin the scheme. The propaganda should be organized under one head in America, who would be the only person knowing the details. The other people working in the scheme would, under no circumstances, be allowed to know of each other's existence.

The scheme would involve sending six or seven different missions to Petrograd, each entirely unknown to the other, and all working along distinct lines towards a common object.

None of these parties would attempt to interfere in any way with Russian domestic questions. The whole object of the scheme to which all these parties would be working would be, first, to expose present German intrigues and their undoubted connection with the late reactionary Government. Secondly, to persuade the Russians to attack the Germans with all their might, and thus accomplish the overthrow of the Hohenzollern dynasty and autocracy in Berlin.

Very briefly the missions and their various lines of work would be as follows:

1. The leader of the most important CZECH secret Society in America would go with the object of organizing the Czechs and Bohemians in Russia. Incidentally, it should be noted that there are 220,000 Bohemian prisoners of war who surrendered to Russia early in the war, about 50 per cent. of whom are skilled mechanics, and almost all of them entirely reliable from the Allied point of view. If these prisoners could be released they, with the other Czechs now in Russia, would form the nucleus of one of the most important and most bitterly anti-German societies. It should be remembered that the Germans have managed to secure control of the most important secret Societies in Russia, and it is necessary that this German influence should

be exposed and counter-Societies organized, if necessary. It must not be forgotten that the Russian people are accustomed to regard the secret societies as the most important part of their Liberal political machinery.

2. A similar leader from the chief SLOVAC Society in America would proceed to Petrograd and work on similar lines.

3. The MONK ILLIADOR[1] should go without delay. This man has an extraordinary influence over the peasants, and his name is known from one end of Russia to the other. His close association with RASPUTIN, and subsequent quarrel and flight, set him up as definitely opposed to the old regime. He is a wonderful mob orator and bitterly anti-German.

4. One or two leaders of the POLISH societies from Chicago should go. The chief of these men is a Lithuanian by descent and a noted Socialist. They are looked upon in Russia as honest socialists whose opinions would be listened to.

5. There are in America several notorious NIHILIST refugees, the leaders of the Russian BUNDTS. One of these men in particular could be relied upon, and is an able organizer. The late Russian Government set a high price on his head. He is anxious to expose German influence in the Nihilist secret societies.

6. A considerable party of intelligent Russian working men—not necessarily revolutionary leaders but Russians who have come to this country and made good—could be induced to proceed to Russia and lecture along the right lines. A party of 20 or 30 of these men would go in charge of a leader.

7. We should endeavor to do in Russia what we have done successfully elsewhere; namely to place Germans who are working for us among the real German agents. There are one or two here, both men and women, who would not be known to the Germans in Russia and have special facilities for getting into the confidence of German agents. It is, of course, never certain that these people will succeed, but the effort should be made.

The lecturers and propagandists of the above parties would have apparently been sent to Russia by different philanthropic Americans who were anxious to assist the new Russian Republic. They would carry with them details of the German intrigues in America, and warn their Russian comrades against similar traps. They would emphasize the necessity for the two great republics working together for the freedom of the World, and, above all, they would seek to warn the Russian people of the plot to enslave them again which is being carried out by the combined efforts of the old reactionary Government and the Military Party in Germany.

T MS (SDR, RG 59, 861.00/423½A, DNA).

1 Sergei Mikhailovich Trufanov, commonly known by his monastic name, Iliodor. Born in 1880, he had become a very popular religious leader in Russia in the early 1900s by leading a fundamentalist crusade for God and the Czar against the alleged corruption of the Russian government and culture. Following Iliodor's break with Rasputin in 1912, he was defrocked by the Holy Synod of the Russian Orthodox Church. Iliodor was sentenced to prison in 1914 for attempting to foment a revolution but escaped to Norway by way of Finland. He came to New York in 1916. His autobiography is *The Mad Monk of Russia, Iliodor* (New York, 1918).

From Sun Yat-sen[1]

Shanghai, June 8, 1917.

Since America was foremost in welcoming us as a democracy and her example was the chief factor that influenced China to terminate her neutrality with the Central Powers America is morally bound to assist our Republic at this critical juncture. A band of traitors under the pretext of declaring war for the benefit of China's interests, but whose real purpose is the restoration of the monarchy are endeavoring to enlist the sympathies and support of the Entente Allies and to obtain from them loans, nominally by joining them as faithful allies, but actually for attaining their own selfish ends. The people knowing the real motive for their sinister action bitterly opposed China's entering the war with the result that militarism, the very evil that is now being fought out in Europe, is employed to subjugate the people and abolish our parliament, although the militarists have the upper hand we are able to vanquish them for ever and preserve our Republic provided Your Excellency will only now make known the real situation to those friendly powers and exert your influence to gain their cooperation in preventing China from being dragged into the European war. By doing this friendly act we can easily destroy militarism and anarchism in China. May I not count upon Your Excellency's assistance on behalf of the cause of humanity.　　　　　　　　　Sun Yat Sen.

T telegram (SDR, RG 59, 893.00/2631, DNA).

1 Having been driven into exile in Japan by Yüan Shih-k'ai in December 1913, Sun returned to Shanghai in April 1916 during the revolutionary uprisings against Yüan. He remained there until July 1917 and spent much of his time writing on the subject of how to achieve genuine popular sovereignty in China. He was opposed both to the regime of President Li Yüan-Hung and to the military uprisings against it under way at this time.

To the American Embassy, Petrograd

Washington, June 9, 1917.

1472. Your 1373, June 7, 8 P.M. President's communication being given to press for publication morning papers June tenth without alteration. The President desires me to express to the Provisional Government of Russia his gratification at the way it has received his communication and is especially pleased that the Russian authorities appreciate the spirit which inspired it.

Lansing

T telegram (SDR, RG 59, 763.72/5213, DNA).

To Frank Lyon Polk

My dear Mr. Polk: [The White House] 9 June, 1917

I wrote the other day to Mr. Berst, the writer of the enclosed letter,[1] asking him if it was not possible to take off the film play, entitled, "Patria," and the letter is his reply. I would be very much obliged to you if you would tell me exactly what was eliminated that you thought objectionable. As I saw the play, it did not seem to me possible to cut out the offensive parts without changing the whole motive and action of the story, but I did not know the circumstances to which Mr. Berst calls my attention in this letter and do not feel qualified now to form an opinion until you post me.

    In haste

Cordially and faithfully yours,   Woodrow Wilson

TLS (Letterpress Books, WP, DLC).
[1] J. A. Berst to WW, June 8, 1917, TLS (WP, DLC). Berst reported that International Film Service, Inc., producer of *Patria*, had "changed the picture entirely" by eliminating several scenes which portrayed Japanese people and flags and also by changing most of the explanatory titles. The new version had been submitted to several officials, including Polk, all of whom had declared that all that was objectionable had been removed "and that they were satisfied that the showing of same be resumed and so it had been." A great deal of money had been invested in the production, Berst went on, and it was likely that suits for damages would be filed by exhibitors if the film was withdrawn. Berst concluded by asking Wilson to modify his request and by expressing willingness to come to the White House at Wilson's "command.

To James Hamilton Lewis

My dear Senator: [The White House] 9 June, 1917

I have your letter of June seventh about the kind desire of certain gentlemen representing the large commercial bodies of Chicago to have me make an address in Chicago upon the general issues of the war.[1]

I feel that for me to go away from Washington upon such an errand at this time would be a blunder. I do not myself believe that the country needs very much enlightenment or stimulation.

I believe that it is thoroughly awake and quietly dead in earnest, and I should dislike to play into the hands of those who are trying to muddy the waters by lending color to what they are already saying, namely, that we have to beat the waters to get what we want in the way of a response from the country. Such an impression is most unjust to the country, of course, and I think that anything that it may be necessary for me to say from time to time will best be said from Washington.

I am encouraged to believe from the latter part of your letter that your judgment concurs with mine.

Cordially and sincerely yours,   Woodrow Wilson

TLS (Letterpress Books, WP, DLC).
[1] It is missing.

From Sun Yat-sen

Shanghai Received June 9, 1917.

Your Excellency: At the same time I despatched my appeal to you came Your Excellency's advice to our statesmen. In the name of my countrymen I beg to express deepest gratitude for Your Excellency's foresight and timely warning.[1] China can never be united or at peace so long as she is held in the grip of militarism and enemies of democracy. We are ready to sacrifice our lives for the extermination of these evil factors and look expectantly to Your Excellency to keep all powers neutral and give us fair play.

Sunyatsen.

T telegram (WP, DLC).
[1] Sun referred to the following "communication from Washington" which Reinsch had given to the Chinese press on June 7:

"The United States Government learns with the most profound regret of the dissensions in China and expresses a sincere desire that tranquility and political co-ordination be forthwith established.

"The entry of China into the war, or the continuance of the status quo in her relations with the German Government, are matters of secondary importance. China's principal necessity is to resume and continue her political entity and proceed along the road to national development. In China's form of Government, or the personnel which administers the Government, America has only the friendliest interest, and desires to be of service to China.

"America expresses the sincere hope that factional and political disputes will be set aside, and that all parties and persons will work to re-establish and co-ordinate the Government and secure China's position among nations, which is impossible while there is internal discord." New York Times, June 8, 1917. The complete version of this telegram, RL to P. S. Reinsch, June 4, 1917, is printed in FR 1917, pp. 48-49.

From Robert Lansing, with Enclosure

My dear Mr. President: Washington June 9, 1917.

I enclose a letter which I have received from Mr. Edward N. Smith,[1] one of my most intimate friends, who is the owner of the most influential paper in northern New York[2] and controls its editorial policy.

While Mr. Smith is a staunch Republican he is a sincere patriot and a man whose opinions I always consider carefully although I frequently do not agree with him.

In this letter I think that the marked portions[3] express a view which is gaining favor with many and which is worthy of attention. It seems to me that many, probably the very large majority, of the American people require stimulus to keep them up to the proper pitch of earnestness and determination, which is necessary for a nation entering upon so great an adventure as the prosecution of a war which does not immediately affect the individual. To overcome the natural tendency "to run down" an appeal to the emotions seems to me justifiable and wise. While the decision of peace or war was in the balance an appeal of this sort would have been improper since it would have affected the sober judgment of the nation. But now that the decision has been made I feel that every agency should be employed to arouse patriotic fervor and that whole-hearted devotion to the cause which springs from the emotions even more than from the intellect.

May I then ask you to give consideration to the matter and to the best means of appealing to the patriotism of the people and increasing the spirit of zeal and determination which should inspire them? Faithfully yours, Robert Lansing

Returned to me at Cabinet meeting
June 12/17 with approval. RL

[1] Edward North Smith, a lawyer of Watertown, N. Y.
[2] The *Watertown Standard*.
[3] The third and fourth paragraphs.

E N C L O S U R E

Edward North Smith to Robert Lansing

Dear Duke: Watertown, N. Y. June 7th, 1917.

I think every citizen of Watertown is entitled to take a just pride in the attitude of the city towards the war and its responsibilities.

As to the army and the navy, we have furnished a company for the Naval Reserve, which is now in service; we have furnished a company of the militia, recruited up to war strength; fifty-five of our young men for months were preparing for membership in the Officers' Reserve Corps, and are at Sackets Harbor, and we have been a fertile ground for recruiting for the regular army and the navy in addition. In other words, without regard to the question of draft, Watertown has already furnished all the men that it could be called upon to furnish as a quota for an army of over one million. This same spirit has been exhibited in the attitude of the people towards the liberty loan. We were called upon to contribute two million dollars. Binghamton, twice the size, was called upon to contribute one million eight hundred thousand dollars. Our quota will be more than subscribed for and I am inclined to think that the final returns will show that Watertown has subscribed for two million five hundred thousand dollars of the bonds. Based upon population, this would mean a subscription adequate to take care of a bond issue of nine billions of dollars, and I do not think we have yet scratched the surface. It has all been done in a splendid spirit of cooperation and support, and yet the great body of the people are ignorant of their responsibilities and of the duties of the hour. This has been disclosed in many ways.

I realize the purpose of the administration to base positions upon judgment, but I do think that the time is near at hand when that conviction which has been brought home to many of our people should be fanned into an active enthusiasm, due to a conscious realization of what this struggle means. Patriotism is not a matter of mathematics. I think that the time is at hand when the President could properly appeal to and arouse, while at the same time keeping within the bounds of restraint, the patriotic spirit of the country, based upon the meaning of the institutions of the republic to the world and the serious threat which is made upon these institutions of liberty as the theme. I was very much in doubt about the Roosevelt matter, and have been on both sides of the question. I assume that if I had been in the President's position I should have followed the advice of the army experts, but looking to the other side of the picture, I would like to see a little real American spirit aroused. Our people like to spread the eagle a little, and a brass band well played has always done wonders. Don't let the boys go into this thing as a matter of drudgery, but let them go into it as a matter of joy and a consciousness of devotion.

It is a terrible thing to offer one's life for others, and the beauty and poetry and justification of the sacrifice should not be lost.

Sincerely yours,   Edward N. Smith.

TLS (R. Lansing Papers, DLC).

Two Letters from William Bauchop Wilson

My dear Mr. President: Washington June 9, 1917.

Referring to the letter from Mr. John P. White, which you handed me Friday, I do not believe it will be necessary for you to give it your further personal attention. I am just in receipt of a communication from Mr. White, in which he accepts, on behalf of the United Mine Workers, the invitation of the Council of National Defense to attend a conference for the purpose of arriving at a mutual understanding. The facts in the case, as I understand them, are these:

The Council of National Defense had been impressed with the belief that the high prices demanded for bituminous coal for immediate delivery were due in a large measure to the shortage of transportation facilities. It came to the conclusion that the selection of a Committee on Coal Production, which would cooperate with the Committee on Transportation, would result in the elimination of delays in the handling of cars at the mines and at points of delivery, thereby increasing the number of times the same car could be used and helping in the solution of the transportation problem. Accordingly on April 21st a Committee on Coal Production was created by the Council of National Defense. Mr. Francis S. Peabody, of Chicago,[1] was named as its Chairman and given authority to select the other members of the Committee, with a suggestion from the Council that labor should be represented on it. Mr. Peabody consulted with Secretary Lane, Mr. Gompers and myself relative to the selection of the labor members, and finally named John P. White, President of the United Mine Workers of America, James Lord, President of the Mining Department of the American Federation of Labor, John Mitchell, former President of the United Mine Workers and at present a member of the Industrial Commission of the State of New York, and my Private Secretary, Mr. Hugh L. Kerwin,[2] to represent labor on the Committee. Notice to that effect went out on the 15th day of May.

On the 16th day of April the coal operators and miners, representative of Western Pennsylvania, Ohio, Indiana and Illinois, in joint conference in the City of New York, adopted a resolution proposing the appointment of a committee of five coal operators and five mine workers from that field, and tendering their services in cooperation with the Council of National Defense. No notice of the action of the joint convention was given at that time, but on May 4th in a conference held in the City of Indianapolis, Indiana, the representatives of the miners and operators met and selected the members of the proposed committee, and on that date sent a communication to the Council of National Defense, tendering their cooperation in accordance with the resolution adopted on April 16th. The communication was referred by the Director of the Council to the Committee on Coal Production, and no further action was taken by the Council at that time.

In the meantime on the 14th of May, the Chairman of the Coal Production Committee issued a circular to those engaged in the coal trade, in which several statements occurred that were objectionable to the representatives of the Mine Workers. Their Executive Board was in session in Indianapolis at that time.

A number of labor disputes existed in the coal mines in West Virginia, and with a view to securing an adjustment of them, I sent two mediators to consult with the members of the Executive Board. They reported to me orally the result of their visit on May 17th, and in that report I learned for the first time of the tender of cooperation that had been made and the issuance of the circular by the Coal Production Committee, which had given rise to the objections. Learning from that source of the intention to issue a protest, Mr. Gompers was consulted, who, in conjunction with Mr. Lord, sent a telegram to Mr. White and the Executive Board of the Mine Workers, advising that no such protest be issued until they could come to Washington and learn the circumstances at first hand. The statement was nevertheless issued, and, as Mr. Tumulty says in his note to you, has been given wide publicity.

The matter was then immediately brought to the attention of the Council of National Defense, as a result of which the Council sent a very courteous letter to Mr. White, explaining the circumstances, acknowledging that it was a mistake for the Coal Production Committee to have issued any statement affecting labor before the labor men had been added to the Committee, and inviting the Mine Workers to a conference in Washington, on such date as they might select, with representatives of the Council of National Defense, the Department of Labor, the Coal Production Committee and the American Federation of Labor. A letter was also sent to Mr. White by Mr. Peabody, in which he acknowledged the mistake and suggested a conference, and one was sent from this Department along the same lines. Today I am in receipt of a communication from Mr. White, accepting the invitation to such a conference, on some date yet to be named.

For these reasons, as I said in the beginning, I do not believe it will be necessary for you to give the subject matter your further personal attention.

I am returning the correspondence herewith.

Faithfully yours,   W B Wilson

1 Francis Stuyvesant Peabody, founder and president of the Peabody Coal Co., with headquarters in Chicago.
2 Hugh Leo Kerwin.

My dear Mr. President: Washington June 9, 1917.

Referring to the telegram from James L. Davidson, Secretary of the Alabama Coal Operators Association, which you handed to me Friday, in the absence of more definite information relative to the exact language used, care should be exercised in making reply to avoid any statement that might be construed as either an approval or disapproval of the activities of the organizers referred to.

The desire of workers to organize will undoubtedly manifest itself more strongly during the period of industrial activity growing out of the war than at other times. It would be folly, in my judgment, to undertake to repress it. It would be screwing down the safety valve to the point where an explosion would be almost certain. The desire of employers to prevent the establishment of unions and avoid collective bargaining will be just as intense as heretofore, though the unusual demand for labor makes it more difficult for them to enforce their own will.

Because of the war emergency through which we are passing, the Government is vitally interested in these differences being composed in such a manner that a stoppage of work will not take place. In adjusting labor disputes in the Tin Plate Mills at Wheeling, West Virginia, and in the copper mines at Jerome, Arizona, I took the following position: In the present emergency capital has no right to interfere with labor organizing into unions, just as labor has no right to interfere with capitalists organizing capital into corporations. If you can get a condition where efforts to organize the workers are not interfered with and where a scale of wages is recognized that maintains the present standard of living, it occurs to me that for the time being no stoppage of work should take place for the purpose of forcing recognition of the union. Of course, that would not interfere with the employers and the workers entering into any arrangement for recognition that might be mutually agreeable. My judgment is that where our workers have been unable to force recognition of their unions in normal times, they should not take advantage of the country's necessities to force recognition of the unions now, if the workers are left free to organize and conditions of employment secured which will maintain the standards of living existing before war was declared. For the same reason employers who have heretofore recognized and dealt with trade unions should not take advantage of the country's necessities to force abandonment of collective bargaining.

As a result of this attitude, settlements were reached in both cases by the workmen withdrawing the demand for recognition of the union on the one side, and the employers removing the discrimination against employees for belonging to the union on the other.

Beyond these statements, I do not know of any expression on the subject matter by any of the Departments of the Government.

Faithfully yours,   W B Wilson

TLS (WP, DLC).

From Helen Hamilton Gardener

My dear Mr President: Washington, D. C. June 10, 1917

It is with hesitation that I come to you a second time for help in the matter of our Suffrage Committee in the House of Representatives, but I am told that a word or a note from you to Mr Heflin would be the means of swinging in our favor one of the two most dangerous and persistent opponents on the floor.

If Representative Heflin and Representative Glass can be made to realize that this small measure of justice from the Democratic party to the women of America is, at this time, as much in the interest of that party as it is in the interest of women, it now looks as if the recommendation of the Rules Committee would, within the next few days, carry on the floor of the House.

If these gentlemen do not feel that they can consistently vote for this small measure of justice to the women of America at a time when almost every other civilised country has given, or is now preparing to give their women full suffrage, it will surely not reflect glory upon the Democratic party in its present declared purpose of carrying real democracy and self-government to the world. Perhaps these gentlemen can be made to see this point, at least.

Can you, will you, Mr President, add the powerful weight of your influence in securing either cooperation or silence from one or both of these men when the question comes on the floor? Mrs Catt is not here and it, therefore, becomes my duty to secure, if we can, this further help from you before the report of the Rules Committee comes upon the floor, which we hope, and they tell us, will be within the next few days.

Thanking you again for your continued and invaluable aid in our struggle for an honorable and full citizenship and a voice in our own government, I have the honor to remain,

Yours Sincerely,   Helen H. Gardener

TLS (WP, DLC).

To Felix Frankfurter

My dear Mr. Frankfurter: [The White House] 11 June, 1917

May I not express my sincere gratification that you have consented to go with Mr. Morgenthau on the important errand which he is undertaking? I shall feel the greater confidence in the success of his errand because you are lending your aid, which I am sure will be invaluable to him.

Cordially and sincerely yours,   [Woodrow Wilson]

CCL (WP, DLC).

From George Washington Goethals

My dear Mr. President: Washington June 11, 1917.

It is nearly two months since I took hold of the shipbuilding project at your request. At that time, I acquainted you with the views which I held, and you learned further concerning them from Colonel House. Since then, I have received your permission, through the United States Shipping Board, to supplement the number of wooden ships that it is possible to build by the construction of steel ships, which I hoped would enable us to secure the total tonnage provided by the program of 3,000,000 tons in eighteen months.

In the time which has elapsed, a central organization has been created, and decentralization of the work has been effected by dividing the country into districts, placing a man experienced in ship construction in charge of each, and providing in addition such local assistance as will enable all of the shipbuilding work in his section or district to be satisfactorily handled. These organizations have been completed.

Generally speaking, the art of wooden shipbuilding is a thing of the past. Those constructed of late years have been for the most part schooners, with auxiliary power, though within the past year or two wooden ship construction has revived to some extent. Conditions surrounding our problem, however, are peculiar, for in order to have a fair chance against a submarine, the speed must be not less than 10½ knots, with reserve power for speeding up an additional knot or so through the danger zone, thus necessitating a much stronger construction than is required for sailing vessels. It was also necessary that the plan adopted should be for the largest vessel that can be safely and economically constructed, because of the fuel problem, and the difficulty of procuring requisite crews, as well as the limit to the output of machinery and equipment. By standardization, greater results can be accomplished in a shorter time.

The preparation of the plans and specifications for the standard type of ship to meet the requirements took longer than I had anticipated, due partly to the fact that the representative of the British Admiralty desired the standard plans to conform with the ideas obtained from recent experience with the submarines. The plans and specifications for the standard wooden ships to be constructed on the coasts were completed and issued to prospective bidders on May 21. Those for ships to be constructed on the Lakes, which must be smaller, being limited to the dimensions of the Welland Canal, will, I expect, be ready for issue this week.

Pending the completion of the standard plans and specifications, time being an essential element, contracts were made with those builders of wooden ships who had already constructed vessels of about the size contemplated, and whose own plans and specifications were generally satisfactory to our naval architect, or could be made so. For the reasons stated hereinbefore, no ships were considered of less than 3000 tons deadweight carrying capacity. While numerous general designs were presented, with applicants promising quick construction, investigation developed defects which did not warrant their adoption for overseas traffic.

A general survey of existing shipyards indicated very little hope of getting much assistance, unless the construction of steel ships already on the ways could be pushed to permit launching at earlier dates than the contracts provided, or unless extensions could be made to the yards. Because of the scarcity of labor, there is apparently very little to be gained by the latter method. The "fabricated" ships, using structural steel employed in bridges and buildings, together with the forces engaged thereon, held out possibilities of increasing the tonnage, and though the representatives of the shipyards did not look upon the idea with favor at first, the sentiment has changed, so that three of them are now desirous of cooperating in this method of securing tonnage. Mr. Sutphen, of the Submarine Boat Corporation,[1] who made a record in completing submarine chasers for the British Admiralty, cooperating with Mr. Worden of the Lackawanna Bridge Company,[2] took hold of the proposition, and, after investigation, they have become so enthusiastic over the prospect that they are ready and anxious to begin on a program by which they anticipate producing two hundred 5000-ton steel ships, complete in all details, in eighteen months. The idea and enthusiasm have so spread that the Chester Shipbuilding Company and the New York Shipbuilding Company also have become interested. The first named company expects to be able to turn out some 600,000 tons in the eighteen months period and the latter in excess of 1,000,000 tons in the same period. A new company, which is to organize at Charleston, S. C., for erecting material to be furnished by the Birmingham mills, hopes to supply 350,000 tons. If the Emergency Fleet Corporation assists the Maryland Shipbuilding Company in extending its facilities, which I am willing to consider favorably when the money becomes available, the foregoing tonnage will be still further increased.

On the Great Lakes, the American Shipbuilding Company stands ready to contract with us for 15 ships to be delivered before navigation closes, each between 3000 and 4000 tons deadweight carrying capacity, all of steel, provided it can get the material and start at an early date. There are also other concerns on the Lakes which will undertake similar construction for us. These latter vessels, while relatively small, are good cargo carriers and are the largest that can make the transit of the Welland Canal.

Summing up the situation, therefore, I feel very much encouraged, and anticipate, even assuming that there be considerable shrinkage in hoped for tonnage by the "fabrication" method, that we will be able to go well beyond the 3,000,000 tons in the eighteen months period, if the money is available.

[1] Henry Randolph Sutphen, engineer and a director of the Electric Boat Co.

[2] Beverly Lyon Worden, founder and president of the Lackawanna Bridge Co. of Buffalo.

In order to secure funds to carry out the project, it was necessary to have something fixed and definite to present to the committees of Congress, and I accordingly proposed the program of 3,000,000 tons in eighteen months, including both wood and steel, estimating that $500,000,000. would be required.

Of this tonnage, I hope that we may be able to secure wooden ships to the amount of 1,000,000 tons, but I am not so optimistic of this because of the change of policy concerning contracts. I did not regard with favor the idea of building on a cost-plus percentage basis. There are few yards capable of undertaking the work, and the security against loss, and the certainty of profit no matter what the cost would lead many to undertake contracts, who were not sufficiently skilled, and who lacked other qualifications. While the outstanding contracts thus made might be sufficient to cover the tonnage desired, there would be no certainty of producing the ships; no possibility of securing the greatest efficiency by employing the services of the limited number of shipwrights; and no way of limiting the total cost to a reasonable amount, or the time of completion to eighteen months. With the desire of getting greater speed and economy, the policy was therefore changed from a cost-plus percentage basis to a cost plus fixed fee basis.

Commissioner Brent, of the Shipping Board,[3] after a tour of the Pacific Coast in company with our naval architects who are now engaged in that section of the country, looked with strong disfavor on this method, and the lump-sum basis was thereupon adopted for that coast in lieu of the cost-plus basis. This led to charges being made of discrimination in favor of the Atlantic and Gulf coasts, and, finally, as the result of the hearings before the House Committee on Appropriations, where the whole matter was threshed out, the cost-plus fee basis was eliminated and the lump-sum form of contract was adopted for all sections of the country, for both wood and steel ships. With the varying labor conditions and the constantly increasing cost of materials, it was felt that the Government, or in this instance the Corporation, should assume contingencies arising from fluctuating prices of labor and material, which in these times cannot be estimated in advance, so an arrangement has been made whereby the Corporation agrees to take care of any increase in labor and material above the rates used by the bidder in the preparation of his proposal. This eliminates the more important contingencies from this form of contract, and therefore no hardship is imposed on those who have the proper organizations to carry the work

3 Theodore Brent.

through to successful completion. In the case of wooden ships, whenever necessary, the Corporation is willing to pay for the ways and the machinery required to properly equip the yard.

The completion of steel ships on the ways under private contracts is impeded to some extent at the present time by the inability to secure materials in time to enable the existing shipyards to work to their full capacity, and for the most part no provision is made in contracts for these ships for overtime work. A large quantity of steel will be required, and arrangements with the steel companies whereby they will cooperate to secure the necessary material and distribute it to the various ship plants in time to meet requirements have been effected. The Railroad Committee will assist in its transportation.

Because of the existing conditions, and in order to expedite the work now on the ways, there seems but one course open—consider the shipyards as component parts of a whole and distribute material where and when it is needed, thus avoiding overstocking one plant to the detriment of another, endeavoring to keep all properly supplied through coordination and cooperation. This will necessitate the Corporation taking over all commercial ships that are now on the ways. For the purpose of ascertaining the value of such ships, arrangements are in contemplation for the appointment of an Appraisal Committee, on which the shipping interests will have representation.

To date, we have contracted for 104 ships, of which 18 are steel; 32 are composite (steel ribs with wood sheathing); 30 are wood to be delivered complete by the contractor, and 24 are wood hulls, for which the Corporation is to supply the necessary machinery and equipment, giving a total tonnage (deadweight carrying capacity) of 497,400 tons. In addition, contracts are ready for signature for 10 steel ships and 20 wooden hulls. The aggregate cost of all work thus far pledged approaches $80,000,-000. The sum of money thus far available is only $50,000,000., and I adhered to this limit prior to the hearings held by the Committee on Appropriations in order that I might truthfully say that I had not obligated the United States to a greater amount than already authorized; but subsequent to these hearings, in view of the extraordinary emergency confronting the country, I took the responsibility, in order to avoid delaying construction, to accept proposals for ships of wood and steel, in limited numbers, in excess of the $50,000,000. limit, and I am now awaiting additional funds before launching forth into the construction of a greater number of steel units, in accordance with the "fabricated" idea, which must be combined into a small number of larger contracts.

Various estimates have been made as to the time within which wooden and steel ships can be constructed. Based on contracts which have been made for wooden and steel ships with companies that have constructed such ships and whose plans have been accepted, each company being fully equipped and ready to begin work, I find that the shortest time within which the wooden ship complete (3500 tons) is to be delivered is eight months, whereas the shortest time for the steel ship (8800 tons) is five months. The shortest time for the delivery of a wooden hull is seven months, and it is estimated it will require two months to complete the erection of the machinery on wooden hulls. It is also estimated it will require from 60 to 90 days to equip a yard to undertake the construction of wooden hulls.

As regards cost, based on the contracts already let, complete wooden ships average $143. per ton deadweight carrying capacity, while the steel ships contracted for average $160. per ton deadweight carrying capacity, with steel plates at $4\frac{1}{4}$ cents per pound and steel shapes at $3\frac{3}{4}$ cents per pound. There is of course no comparison as to the commercial value of the wooden and steel ship.

I trust that I have not gone into the matter in too much detail; but as I am in hopes that the appropriation bill may soon become a law, I felt desirous of acquainting you with the shipbuilding program that has been arranged, so that if it is not in accordance with your wishes, I can make any changes in it that you desire.

Very respectfully,   Geo W. Goethals

TLS (WP, DLC).

From Herbert Clark Hoover, with Enclosures

Dear Mr. President: Washington June 12, 1917.

In case it may be of interest to you for reference purposes, I enclose herewith copies of the memorandums which we discussed yesterday:

First, one on the necessity of early legislation;

Second, on the question of the organization of commodity controls;

Third, on the organization of voluntary conservation;

Fourth, some preliminary lists of names of purely technical men to be assembled for the assistance of the conservation committees.

I also enclose copy of brief which has been presented to me by William C. Edgar,[1] of Minneapolis, with the backing of the principal millers of the country, which is some indication of both the sentiment with regard to control and also the desire on the part of this trade to support the proposed Food Administration.

I beg to remain,

Your obedient servant,   Herbert Hoover

TLS (WP, DLC).

[1] William Crowell Edgar, editor of *The Northwestern Miller*. The enclosure was *Brief Submitted to Mr. Herbert Hoover by William C. Edgar* (WP, DLC). Edgar alleged that uncertainties about proposed legislation for food control were causing millers to take on as little business as possible at a time when they should be working at capacity to meet the emergency needs of the country. He proposed the creation of a "Milling Executive," to be assisted by eight heads of regional divisions and twenty-nine heads of subdivisions, to cooperate voluntarily with Hoover in the regulation of the industry. All these positions should be filled by experienced millers, and the "Milling Executive" should be a western miller.

E N C L O S U R E   I

June 12 1917

I

MEMORANDUM ON NECESSITY OF EARLY FOOD LEGISLATION.

Owing to the discussion and uncertainty throughout the country as to the character of food administration and the objective which will be sought in the administration of commodities and prices, we are rapidly drifting toward an acute crisis.

The harvest is already started and in consequence, the farmers will wish at once to realize their crops. The middlemen are unable to make committments or even secure credits until the policy of the Government is announced. The Allied governments are withholding their purchases at my request pending the solution of administrative questions and they are keenly desirous to enter the market to secure orders for September and October deliveries of wheat. The principal millers of the country are also withholding their hands in the provision of supplies, partially because they do not wish to embarrass the administration by a mass of contracts and partially because they are uncertain as to the action which will be taken as to such contracts. The nominal price of the new wheat harvest is already at from $2.00 to $2.25 per bushel, and if all the forces now desirous of securing this supply, would enter today into a general scramble to secure it, we can see $3.00 wheat and $19.00 flour in a month. Furthermore, in such a scramble, the earlier portion of the harvest would be absorbed for immediate export and immediate milling purposes in centers removed from their normal production, and at a later period in the year it will be necessary to re-ship into these localities and thus our whole transportation problem greatly increased.

Beyond this, speculation is forming continually in this country in connection with the new harvest. In particular, agents of various distributors are endeavoring to enter contracts for the purchase of rice from the farmers. The same phenomenon is appearing in potatoes, the consequence of which will be a considerable looking up of the country's food resources and the creation of a mass of contracts which will present the utmost difficulties for solution in any endeavor to prevent speculation and combination.

Again, we are on the threshold of the harvest and the proper utilization of the foodstuffs during the coming year must be taken in hand at once. For instance, we shall have a surplus of vegetables and it is critical that we secure at once a complete voluntary organization of the people in order that we may obtain an increased proportion of vegetable consumption in the national diet to the saving of staples for winter use and export.

Neutral governments and their agents are endeavoring to make contracts for supplies and are, by their competition, already effecting our prices and creating disturbing currents into the whole problem of price control.

The cost of living is steadily increasing and unless amelioration can be secured out of the proper handling of the new crop it will entail an early reorganization of the wage scale of the country and consequent social disorganization, to the loss of national efficiency.

Altogether, the necessity for immediate and quick action or total abandonment of the Food Administration is imperative. A delay beyond the first of July in securing the necessary legislation and even the creation of the necessary administration ready for that date may render nugatory a large part of the value of the Food Administration itself.

E N C L O S U R E   I I

June 12 1917

II

ORGANIZATION OF COMMODITY CONTROLS.

The time which will be required to complete the legislation pending is likely to delay the passage of such legislation to the last moment when effective administration can be installed and possibly even delay it until too late to properly grapple with the problems entailed by the movement of the harvest in the country. In order, however, to minimize as much as possible, it is desirable to complete the organization, so that when legislation is effected the Administration can enter upon its duties within twenty-four hours. The proposed organization of the cereal controls involves two different types of administration. The first type are bodies which will be engaged in buying and selling operations on behalf of the government and the Allies. In these cases I am convinced that the entire personnel should be free and independent of any business association or interest in the commodities with which they must deal. The second type are bodies composed of the principal members of various trades whom we shall call upon to regulate themselves as to business methods but who will not be engaged in handling government money. Of the first type the most critical commodity is wheat and in order to create an administration by which the price of wheat may be stabilized and speculation eliminated it becomes necessary to set up a Grain Executive with its necessary branches in the larger terminal centers and to arrive at the entire method of control of interior terminals and the purchase and sale of wheat both for domestic and export consumption.

From the many men in the country skilled in this matter, I have to propose Mr. Julius Barnes of New York[1] as head of this executive with a directorate representing banking, economic and transportation and business interests and sub-organizations in the principal grain centers.

Of the second type the most immediate importance is the control of flour. Here I propose to set up a flour committee embracing millers throughout the country, it being my desire to impose upon them the duty of seeing that the price of wheat, whatever it may be, is reflected directly in the price of flour to the consumer.

My suggestion for the head of this flour committee is Mr. James Bell,[2] and I have insisted that should he undertake the work he will resign his position and disassociate himself from his present business in the same manner which Mr. Barnes has voluntarily agreed to do. I believe Mr. Bell is the ideal man for the work.

As a necessary part of the machinery for the control of wheat and flour, it is necessary that we set up a price committee to determine a range of prices toward which the efforts of the wheat and flour executives should be directed in maintenance. It is my view that this committee should come under the Chairmanship of some leading Economist and be composed of say two representatives from the agricultural element; say two from the labor element as best representing the consumer; one or two men from the agricultural institutions of the country; one or two men of business experience in this branch of trade; and one or two leading economists.

Generally, in the creation of these bodies, I would suggest that I submit the names of the heads of such organizations as above for the President's approval and that the other principals should be assembled by us for final ratification, but that the secondary committees or assistants should be left to the principals for selection, subject to my approval.

1 Julius Howland Barnes, president of the Barnes-Ames Co., a wheat brokerage firm.
2 James Ford Bell, vice-president of the Washburn Crosby Co., a merchant milling concern of Minneapolis.

E N C L O S U R E   I I I

III

ORGANIZATION OF VOLUNTARY CONSERVATION.

The general plan is to ask every person in the country who presides over household and public eating of food to join the Food Administration as an actual "member." All members to sign a a pledge to follow the advice and directions given, in so far as his or her circumstances permit. Each member to be issued a certificate, a house tag, and some form of insignia to indicate membership, and to be given concise instructions as to saving, substitutions, and domestic economy generally. These instructions to be formulated by the committees on Domestic Economy, Food Utilization, Alimentation, and Public Health, under the guidance of the departmental heads.

It is proposed to use the services of the Press, all the women's organizations, Boy Scouts, Hotel Associations, etc. of the country

in recruiting this membership and to use the State Food Administrations and various other associations in its management. While
it is intended ultimately to decentralize the administration into
the states, it is nevertheless considered vital that in recruiting
membership the organization should be national in character and
thus better appeal to the imaginative side of national service.

It is imperative that no time should be lost, because:

(a)   It should be possible to reduce national food expenditure
at least to the extent of $1,000,000,000 per annum, i.e.–the
individual expenditure by 3 cents per diem.

(b) The wide propaganda and the service implied will contribute very largely to bringing the realization of war and the
self-sacrifice required into every home.

(c) The growing season is now rapidly drawing to a close and
if we are to save the surplus of vegetables by urging their consumption in substitution of staples and their preservation, we
must act at once.[1]

T MSS (WP, DLC).
[1] Here follow the names of suggested members for a "General Advisory
Committee, to assist in the organization of the Home Economics Section,"
a committee to conduct research on "Food Vitalization," an "Advisory Committee on Alimentation," an "Advisory Committee on Public Health," a "Food
Conservation Division," and a "Food Utilization Division."

To Herbert Clark Hoover

My dear Mr. Hoover: [The White House] 12 June, 1917

It seems to me that the inauguration of that portion of the
plan for Food Administration which contemplates a national
mobilization of the great voluntary forces of the country which
are ready to work towards saving food and eliminating waste
admits of no further delay.

The approaching harvest, the immediate necessity for wise
use and saving, not only in food but in all other expenditures,
the many undirected and overlapping efforts being made toward
this end, all press for national direction and inspiration. While
it would in many ways be desirable to await complete legislation
establishing the Food Administration, it appears to me that so
far as voluntary effort can be assembled, we should not wait any
longer, and therefore I would be very glad if you would proceed
in these directions at once.

The women of the nation are already earnestly seeking to do
their part in this our greatest struggle for the maintenance of
our national ideals, and in no direction can they so greatly assist

as by enlisting in the service of the Food Administration and cheerfully accepting its direction and advice. By so doing, they will increase the surplus of food available for our own Army and for export to the Allies. To provide adequate supplies for the coming year is of absolutely vital importance to the conduct of the war, and without a very conscientious elimination of waste and very strict economy in our food consumption, we cannot hope to fulfill this primary duty.

I trust, therefore, that the women of the country will not only respond to your appeal and accept the pledge to the Food Administration which you are proposing, but that all men also who are engaged in the personal distribution of foods will cooperate with the same earnestness and in the same spirit. I give you full authority to undertake any steps necessary for the proper organization and stimulation of their efforts.

Cordially and sincerely yours,   Woodrow Wilson[1]

TLS (Letterpress Books, WP, DLC).
[1] Hoover drafted this letter, and Wilson signed it. There is a TC of it in the H. Hoover Papers, HPL.

From Felix Frankfurter

My dear Mr. President: Washington. 12 June 1917.

May I convey to you the depth of my thanks for the confidence implied in your selection. These days we are all soldiers. As such I go obedient to the duty with which you have generously charged me.   Respectfully,   Felix Frankfurter.

ALS (WP, DLC).

From Edward George Lowry

My dear Mr. President: Washington, D. C. June 12, 1917.

Will you be good enough to see me some afternoon or evening and talk with me about the war for quotation directly or indirectly in an article for the Saturday Evening Post? I would not request this draft upon your time and energies if I did not know so certainly that it would answer a definite need and be a real service. I have been about over the country in recent months—as far West as the Coast and up and down the Mississippi Valley twice. People do not yet understand fully why we are in the war, and that we must "see it through." This lack of full understanding exists despite your several clear utterances. They are eager to learn. You are the only person in public life or office who has their complete trust and confidence. I don't know whether you fully realize how much they do look to you for guidance and direction. As we become more deeply involved and send more men to France this desire for communication with you, the leader of us all, deepens and strengthens. Anyone who goes out into the country is instantly and acutely made aware of this.

The root of the so-called pacifism and apathy in the Mississippi Valley and beyond has been largely a lack of information about our vital stake in the war. My justification in seeking access to you at this time is to help meet this need and satisfy this thirst for further light on our duties and the true nature of the conflict between Prussianism and the ideals of free peoples. What you might say in an hour's talk with me will be brought home to five or six million men and women. I hope you can find a time to talk to them.

I am, Mr. President,

Yours very sincerely,   Edward G Lowry

TLS (WP, DLC).

From Edward Mandell House

Dear Governor: Magnolia, Massachusetts. June 12, 1917.

I want to congratulate you upon the success of your message to Russia. It well deserves the praise it is getting throughout the world. I hope you will cover the tender spots as well in your Flag Day speech. What you are saying is having a profound influence everywhere, including Germany.

J. K. Ohl of the New York Herald[1] writes that George Bronson Rea, proprietor of the Far Eastern Review published in Peking has written you a letter which he hopes you will find time to read.[2]

I had a long talk with Wiseman over the telephone yesterday about Northcliffe. Northcliffe was not received by any of the staff of the British Embassy and he was angry beyond words. He told Wiseman that he had been offered the Ambassadorship but had declined it.

His Government requested him to get in touch with Sir William upon his arrival and suggested that he be guided by him. This Northcliffe seems willing to do.

Following Wiseman's counsel, he has given up the idea of opening offices in New York and will probably make his headquarters in Washington. The British Government have given him the widest possible powers and it would therefore seem necessary to give him proper consideration.

At my suggestion, Wiseman is advising him not to talk through the press and not to attempt to force his opinions upon our people. Sir William's purpose is to keep him away from the Wall Street influence, and to bring him in close touch with Administrative [Administration] circles. If he follows this course his visit will probably be of service.

Northcliffe and Andre Tardieu are great friends. While Sir William was with Northcliffe yesterday, Hearst sent a representative to the hotel. Northcliffe refused to see the representative and sent word to Hearst to come himself if he desired. In the event he comes Northcliffe indicated his intention of telling him some home truths which may be good for his soul.

Northcliffe will ask for an interview through the Embassy.

Affectionately yours,   E. M. House

TLS (WP, DLC).
    ¹ Josiah Kingsley Ohl to EMH, June 10, 1917, TLS (E. M. House Papers, CtY). Ohl had been the correspondent for the *New York Herald* in the Far East, 1907-1913. He was on the editorial staff of the *Herald* in 1917.
    ² G. B. Rea to WW, June 1, 1917, TLS (E. M. House Papers, CtY). This letter was primarily a diatribe against Paul S. Reinsch; it accused the Minister of subverting Wilson's policies toward China.

From Samuel Gompers

Sir: Washington, D. C. June 12, 1917.

Yesterday when the delegation which waited upon you were discussing the food regulation for them, there was one particular feature which I omitted to present to you for consideration.

The people of the United States hold you in reverential respect, have confidence in you, in your wisdom, your courage, your sense of justice and your leadership in this great crucial time, all that it implies and carries with it. The magnificent response of the young manhood to the country's call in defense of fundamental principles and ideals of justice, freedom and democracy must have brought joy to you, as well as to other men and women of understanding in our country.

The masses of the people of the United States are ready to do their full duty, and in its performance yield to your leadership. If in your position of potential influence and leadership you were to address yourself in person to a joint session of both houses of the Congress of the United States upon the necessity for immediate consideration and action by Congress to control and administer the food supplies; to standardize prices by regulative action, that action and utterance on your part would not only secure the enactment of the specific legislation on or before the essential, pivotal day, July 1st, but every man and woman of our nation would realize that you are the sentinel on duty to safeguard the masses of the people of the country against the food speculators gambling the peoples' needs.

Last evening, some hours after the interesting conference we had the honor of having with you, the same men and a number [of] other representatives in Congress and additional labor men met to consider the necessary next effort which should be put forth in the campaign to secure protection for the people against their exploiters. I wish you could have heard the splendid encomiums of appreciation for the course you have pursued, and these came from the lips of men who are your political adherence [adherents], as well as political opponents. However, there was a unanimity of feeling and judgment expressed that it lies within your power to solve the problem in the most direct and effective manner as suggested yesterday and herein repeated and emphasized, by addressing a joint session of both houses of the Congress of the United States.

Acting upon the judgment already mentioned, I address this letter to you in the hope that it may meet with your approval and action.

I have the honor to remain,

Respectfully yours,   Saml. Gompers.

TLS (WP, DLC).

From Frank Lyon Polk

Dear Mr. President: Washington June 12, 1917.

I have the honor to acknowledge the receipt of your letter of June 9th regarding the film play entitled "PATRIA."

In reply I beg to say that upon having its attention called by the Secretary of War and the Attorney General to this motion picture, portions of which were thought to be objectionable to the sensibilities of the Japanese and Mexicans, the Department wrote to Mr. Berst under date of April 6, 1917, inquiring whether he would not, through patriotic motives, voluntarily withdraw the films from display. Subsequently, Mr. G. S. McFarland,[1] counsel for the International Film Company, owner of "PATRIA," called in person at the Department and explained that the Company would suffer such severe financial losses by the complete withdrawal of the film that he found it impossible to meet the Depart-

ment's request. He offered, however, to make the same altera-
tions in the film and in the advertisements for the film as had
been required by the Canadian censor, i.e., elimination of Japanese names and all references to Japan, both in the play itself
and in the advertisements of the play.

Mr. McFarland promised to make these modifications just as
soon as possible. I understand, however, from those who saw
the last episodes of the play at Keith's, that there appeared to be
little change for the better. For instance, while the principal
Japanese conspirator had been given a Mexican name, at the
very end of the play he is shown to commit Harikiri. Moreover,
the original objections to the play as far as offending the sensibilities of the Mexicans is concerned, still remain.

As to our legal right to interfere in the matter, the Attorney
General has informed the Department that there is so far as he
knows no Federal legislation which makes the production of this
play in any way unlawful. Moreover, Assistant Attorney General
Warren is of the opinion that the suppression of improper motion pictures is a matter entirely within the control of the State
and local authorities.

I have just had a conversation over the telephone with Mr.
McFarland, now in Boston. He tells me that he will visit Washington next week and will call upon me.

I would therefore beg to suggest that further action in the matter be postponed until after I have an opportunity of seeing Mr.
McFarland. I shall be very grateful if you will let me know if this
meets with your approval.

Yours faithfully,   Frank L Polk

TLS (WP, DLC).
¹ Grenville Stanley Macfarland, lawyer of Boston.

Robert Lansing to Edward North Smith

My dear Ed: [Washington] June 12, 1917.

I received your letter of June 7th and am very proud indeed
of the patriotic spirit exhibited by Watertown, both in the matter of men and money. If other communities would do half as
well they would lessen the burden of anxiety felt here in
Washington at the apparent apathy in certain quarters of the
Republic.

The second part of your letter—which deals with the propriety
of an appeal to the emotions at the present time—voiced in a
very excellent way my own thought and I therefore took the

liberty of marking that portion of your letter and sending it to the President, recommending to him its careful consideration. He returned the letter to me today at Cabinet meeting and said that he felt that what you said was justified and that he should act along those lines. He said that he thought it was a decided advantage to appeal to the higher emotions, but that we must avoid the emotion of hate. On Flag Day, June 14th, he will deliver an address which will give him opportunity to make an appeal to the patriotism of our people and will, I trust, excite their enthusiasm to renewed efforts in the great struggle upon which we have entered.

I thank you for your letter and for what it contains. I hope that in another month I may be in Northern New York preparing to go with you all to the Galloos.[1] These are uncertain times but we have to make our plans as if they were normal. I hope very much that I shall be able to carry out the plans I have made.

Very sincerely yours,   Robert Lansing

CCL (R. Lansing Papers, DLC).
[1] Galloo Island in Lake Ontario, about twenty miles west of Watertown, N. Y.

To Robert Lansing, with Enclosure

My dear Mr. Secretary: The White House 13 June, 1917

The enclosed letter from Mr. Sosnowski which my classmate, Wilder, sends me, contains some things worth thinking about.

Cordially and faithfully yours,   Woodrow Wilson

TLS (SDR, RG 59, 763.72119/672½, DNA).

E N C L O S U R E

From George Jan Sosnowski

Dear Mr. President: New York, June 5, 1917.

The military power of Russia is now so disorganized that it cannot be of any substantial assistance to the Allies for a long time. I doubt whether the Russian army will ever again take a serious offensive in this war unless some heroic measures are taken by the Allies. The blame for this unfortunate condition can be laid to the Russian Provisional Government and the Allies. With the outbreak of the revolution there should have been given to the Russian army a watch-word which would have stimulated further fighting. *The moral fighing efficiency of an army of democracy (a revolutionary army) must be upheld by the highest ideals*, but this was not done.

No Russian land is occupied as yet by the Central Powers. The eastern battlefield is still on the soil of the former Republic of Poland and consequently does not arouse any patriotism or anger in the breast of the Russian peasant soldier. This is one of many reasons why the German army is not attacking the Russian line and pushing into Russia proper.

The whole of Russia, including the Russian army, want peace.

The Central Powers have been successful in convincing a large proportion of the Russian people that they do not want their land by stopping their offensive and proposing peace.

The Allies, on the other hand, have not laid bare this hypocrisy of the Central Powers. This could have been done if the Allies had announced their terms of peace, as advocated by you. Peace on such terms would have been rejected by the German Government and their rejection would have demonstrated to the Russian democracy the insincerity of the Central Powers and the necessity of Russia's fighting to preserve their newly won liberty, to abolish Prussian militarism and dethrone the Hohenzollerns.

The men who are now at the head of Russian affairs took part in the Russian revolution in 1905, but they have not learned by experience. I was hopeful of seeing these men exert a strong policy after the revolution, but in the eleven weeks of Russian freedom I have become convinced that they and their methods have not changed in these last twelve years. No strong man has as yet come to the front in new Russia. They have failed because they are *soft-hearted humanitarians*, carrying [currying] favor with all parties, believing in government by soft words and persuasion and do not believe in the virtue of applying stern justice. To them the enforcement of law is the oppression of liberty, so they avoid everything in the way of strong action.

It is not too late to remedy this situation. The aims of the war, as well as the terms of future peace, can still be proclaimed to the world in joint declaration, but if diplomacy is to accomplish something it must be done without further delay.

The self-satisfied speech of the Austrian Emperor opens the way.[1] From the attitude taken by Emperor Charles and the leaders of the Poles, Bohemians, Slovaks and Southern Slavs to form a federation of different free nations on equal rights, we can safely assume that Count Tarnowski has already presented the project of the United States of Europe to all interested parties.

This project, the success of which will preserve for a short time the shadow of Hapsburg Imperialism, carries with it the condition of a separate peace with the Allies, the abandonment of Germany by Austria and the dismemberment of Prussia, and for this reason it should be embodied in the terms of future peace. Even if rejected by Austro-Hungary, it will serve its purpose to assure the Russians of the insincerity of the Central Powers and it will promote revolution in Austro-Hungary. Now that Russia has achieved, by the revolution, more than she could ever have expected to achieve from this war, and has no object for a further offensive (only to defend her newly gained liberty), the Poles are very much aggravated by the attitude of the Russians. The Poles are politically ripe; they understand that with the collapse of the Eastern offensive victory is assured for Germany, and they realize that they must therefore go under the Teutonic yoke. There are at present from 600,000 to 800,000 Poles in the Russian army. They have formed, since the revolution, a military society of Polish soldiers and officers. They have recently held mass meetings in Petrograd, Moscow, Kieff, Kazan, Charkoff, Oddessa and at many places at the front. They passed resolutions to preserve discipline and order in the army and expressed the desire to be formed into a separate Polish army, the formation of which may be even on the way. Inquiry made recently among the war prisoners, Poles, soldiers and officers of German and Austrian armies, held in Russia, revealed the real character and feelings of the Poles, when they consented to serve in the Polish army if such would be formed, for the liberation of Poland from the Huns.

Here lies the salvation of the Eastern front. The Poles are a most patriotic people; they are the finest soldiers—perhaps better than the French. They have all of the French dash, but are physically stronger, more cool headed and have more endurance. *Above all, they want to fight to liberate* their beloved motherland. All the Polish peasants, contrary to the Russians, are landed proprietors, they love their soil and they are willing to die for their homes. The Poles, having an *object* to fight for, will carry the Germans before them. Of this I am positive. The Russians do not hate the Germans, but the Poles do. *One million Poles could be enrolled in Russia into a Polish Army.* Any Polish army should *not be dependent on Russia—it must be organized and financed by the Allies.*

The Poles are now the only nation on the eastern front which is eager to fight, and they are too valuable material to be wasted under Russian management and disorganization.

The United States of America, France, England, Russia and Italy should form a committee of able generals and officers who have been in actual war to organize this army and to serve as its staff after organization. For patriotic reasons, any Polish army should be led if possible by a Pole. This army should be organized, prepared and supplied with the greatest care. *It would prove a winning card in the hands of the Allies and such an army would put backbone into the Russian army, would serve as an example of order, discipline and efficiency and would arouse patriotism among Russians.*

If the Poles advance, the Russians will not stay in the trenches, but will follow the Poles. I know the Russian character better than many Russians, and I know the Polish character. *You will not take the slightest risk, Mr. President, in promoting this enterprise.*

It is a physical impossibility to smash the Central Powers on the western front except through Holland, as there is no room for manoeurering [manoevering]. The crushing blow must come from the eastern front and by the formation of a Polish army, and this is the *only solution* and the *only remedy* by which new life and new activity can be restored and new impetus given for the success of the Allies.

I am, Your Excellency,

Most respectfully,   G. J. Sosnowski.

TLS (SDR, RG 59, 763.72119/672½, DNA).
    ¹ Charles had spoken at the opening of the Imperial parliament on May 31. His speech was rambling and couched in generalities. However, he did throw out a few suggestive hints. He urged the parliament to cooperate with him to "create conditions" within the empire to give "scope to free national and cultural development of equally privileged people." He hailed the apparently conciliatory foreign policy of the Russian provisional government and declared that the Central Powers stood ready to make peace with nations which abandoned threatening intentions. However, Charles also reasserted the determination of the Central Powers "to force, if necessary by arms, a good end to the war." For a lengthy report of and extensive extracts from the speech, see the *New York Times*, June 1, 1917.

To Herbert Clark Hoover

My dear Mr. Hoover: The White House 13 June, 1917

Thank you very warmly for your letter of yesterday with the accompanying memoranda.

After you left, I wondered why when you spoke of Doctor

Hadley of Yale I had not thought of President Garfield of Williams, a man of fine capacity and of the finest principle and spirit.

In haste

Cordially and faithfully yours,   Woodrow Wilson

TLS (H. Hoover Papers, HPL).

To Joseph Patrick Tumulty, with Enclosure

Dear Tumulty: [The White House, c. June 13, 1917]

Of course I will see these men, and since they generally need ample notice, perhaps we had better fix Thursday, June 21st at 2:15.   The President.

TL (WP, DLC).

E N C L O S U R E

Henry French Hollis to Joseph Patrick Tumulty

Dear Joe: [Washington] 12 June, 1917.

The heads of the Railroad Brotherhoods saw me in Washington about a fortnight ago. I persuaded them that there was nothing critical in their affairs which required a personal call on the President and I advised them not to see him until they had an errand of real importance. They agreed to this heartily.

They have now written me a letter regarding the general labor situation and they want me to see the President and present their views to him. I think this ought to be done and I should be very glad to do it, if it is agreeable to the President.

I wish you would kindly arrange for me to see the President for about fifteen minutes some day this week, morning preferred.   Sincerely,   Henry F. Hollis

TLS (WP, DLC).

To Newton Diehl Baker, with Enclosure

My dear Mr. Secretary: The White House 13 June, 1917

You may find a good deal of weight in what Mr. Glass says in the enclosed letter; at any rate, I know that you will be willing to consider his suggestion.

In haste

Cordially and sincerely yours,   Woodrow Wilson

ENCLOSURE

From Franklin Potts Glass

My dear Friend: [Birmingham, Ala.] June 11, 1917.

I am exceedingly desirous of seeing Birmingham selected for one of the military training camps. Enclosed is an editorial I wrote on the subject, which summarizes Birmingham's case.[1] I hope you may spare the time to read it.

From one standpoint especially it seems to me to be greatly to the advantage of the Government to place a camp here—protection for the numerous industrial plants whose output is so essential to the prosecution of the war. The steel plants, the benzol plants, the coking plants, the coal mines, all require the utmost precautions for their safety. The Steel Corporation has just announced the expenditure here of many more millions for plants for the Government's use. The few hundred Guardsmen now patrolling these plants are nothing compared to many thousands under trained officers. Their proximity would be a blanket policy of insurance.

Confidentially, there is another important point. This District has been out of control of the Unions for ten years, when the last great strike and riots occurred. Notwithstanding all the coal, iron and steel plants have advanced wages *three* times in the last year, the reorganization of unions is now going on actively: it is said that five thousand men were organized last week. One of the arguments the leaders are advancing is that *you* have expressed the desire that all laboring men will join. Of course, intelligent men know this is not true; but there is great apprehension among industrial leaders here. Nothing would give so much reassurance as a training camp.

On Saturday I talked fully with Secretary McAdoo on this matter, and he stated that he appreciated thoroughly the whole situation, that he had already talked to Secretary Baker about it, and that he would again do so.

I venture the suggestion that if you could say a friendly word to Secretary Baker, it would settle the matter. I believe that in so doing you would not merely do my home town a good turn, but that you would also serve the Government's best interests as well.

Sincerely yours,   Frank P. Glass

TLS (N. D. Baker Papers, DLC).
    [1] It is missing.

To Edward George Lowry

My dear Mr. Lowry: [The White House] 13 June, 1917

I warmly appreciate the spirit of your letter of June twelfth and fully understand the object you had in mind, but, frankly, I do not think that I ought to handle such matters in interviews to particular papers or groups of papers, but that I ought rather to speak out in my own person in public addresses. It is in pursuance of this idea that I am going to make an address, which I hope will be illuminating and stimulating, tomorrow, Flag Day.

This is a policy which I have so often had to consider that I feel tolerably certain that I am right.

Cordially and sincerely yours,   Woodrow Wilson

TLS (Letterpress Books, WP, DLC).

To James Thomas Heflin

Personal.

My dear Heflin: [The White House] 13 June, 1917

May I without taking too great a liberty suggest to you that it would be a very wise thing, both politically and from other points of view, if you and the others in Congress who feel like you would consent to the constitution of a special committee of the House on woman suffrage? I perhaps am more in the storm center of this question than you are, and I think I can give this as my mature counsel; and I am sure that you will understand why I do it and forgive me if I have taken too great a liberty.

Cordially and faithfully yours,   Woodrow Wilson

TLS (Letterpress Books, WP, DLC).

To Samuel Gompers

My dear Mr. Gompers: The White House 13 June, 1917

Thank you for your letter of yesterday. You may be sure I will do anything that is necessary to get this legislation through and through speedily, and it may be that it will be unnecessary for me to adopt the particular suggestion you make.

Thank you warmly for your cordial and generous letter.

In haste   Sincerely yours,   Woodrow Wilson

TLS (photostat in RSB Coll., DLC).

From Newton Diehl Baker

My dear Mr. President: Washington. June 13, 1917.

The attached papers[1] present in graphic form the study so far made by the Council of National Defense for the reorganization of the committees. The first paper is the proposed plan. The relations are indicated by the diagram.

The plan contemplates an immediate subordination of all committees to the Council of National Defense, with the Advisory Commission acting in a purely advisory capacity. The main committees of the Council are immediately subordinated to it. The War Industries Board would be what is now the General Munitions Board. It would consist of a civilian chairman, with Army and Navy representatives, and the proposed purchasing agent of the Allies, with such additions to its membership as might be appropriate for the consideration of special subjects. For instance, if a transportation subject were under consideration, the Chairman of the Transportation Committee would sit with the War Industries Board as a member.

This plan contemplates the appointment of a chairman of the War Industries Board, a chief of raw materials, a chief of priority, a chief of finished materials, and a purchasing agent of Allies. When this number of official representatives of the Government shall have been appointed all subordinate committees report to them in the manner indicated in the diagram.

The other charts indicate the organizations maintained in France, England and Germany, and the last diagram indicates roughly the present organization of our own general government as at present organized.

These charts and this explanatory note are sent in order that you may give the scheme proposed a glance before the cabinet meeting on Friday, if it is convenient.

Respectfully yours,   Newton D. Baker

TLS (WP, DLC).

[1] These enclosures are missing in both the Baker and Wilson Papers, DLC; however, Baker describes them well.

A Flag Day Address[1]

14 June, 1917

My Fellow Citizens: We meet to celebrate Flag Day because this flag which we honor and under which we serve is the emblem

[1] Wilson spoke at 3 P.M. at the outdoor Sylvan Theater near the Washington Monument. He was introduced by Robert Lansing. A heavy rainstorm before and during his speech kept the crowd down to an estimated 1,000 persons. *Washington Post*, June 15, 1917.

of our unity, our power, our thought and purpose as a nation. It
has no other character than that which we give it from generation to generation. The choices are ours. It floats in majestic
silence above the hosts that execute those choices, whether in
peace or in war. And yet, though silent, it speaks to us,—speaks to
us of the past, of the men and women who went before us and of
the records they wrote upon it. We celebrate the day of its birth;
and from its birth until now it has witnessed a great history, has
floated on high the symbol of great events, of a great plan of life
worked out by a great people. We are about to carry it into battle,
to lift it where it will draw the fire of our enemies. We are about
to bid thousands, hundreds of thousands, it may be millions, of
our men, the young, the strong, the capable men of the nation,
to go forth and die beneath it on fields of blood far away,—for
what? For some unaccustomed thing? For something for which
it has never sought the fire before? American armies were never
before sent across the seas. Why are they sent now? For some
new purpose, for which this great flag has never been carried before, or for some old, familiar, heroic purpose for which it has
seen men, its own men, die on every battlefield upon which Americans have borne arms since the Revolution?

These are questions which must be answered. We are Americans. We in our turn serve America, and can serve her with no
private purpose. We must use her flag as she has always used it.
We are accountable at the bar of history and must plead in utter
frankness what purpose it is we seek to serve.

It is plain enough how we were forced into the war. The
extraordinary insults and aggressions of the Imperial German
Government left us no self-respecting choice but to take up arms
in defense of our rights as a free people and of our honour as a
sovereign government. The military masters of Germany denied
us the right to be neutral. They filled our unsuspecting communities with vicious spies and conspirators and sought to corrupt the opinion of our people in their own behalf. When they
found that they could not do that, their agents diligently spread
sedition amongst us and sought to draw our own citizens from
their allegiance,—and some of those agents were men connected
with the official Embassy of the German Government itself here
in our own capital. They sought by violence to destroy our industries and arrest our commerce. They tried to incite Mexico to take
up arms against us and to draw Japan into a hostile alliance with
her,—and that, not by indirection, but by direct suggestion from
the Foreign Office in Berlin. They impudently denied us the use
of the high seas and repeatedly executed their threat that they

would send to their death any of our people who ventured to approach the coasts of Europe. And many of our own people were corrupted. Men began to look upon their own neighbours with suspicion and to wonder in their hot resentment and surprise whether there was any community in which hostile intrigue did not lurk. What great nation in such circumstances would not have taken up arms? Much as we had desired peace, it was denied us, and not of our own choice. This flag under which we serve would have been dishonoured had we withheld our hand.

But that is only part of the story. We know now as clearly as we knew before we were ourselves engaged that we are not the enemies of the German people and that they are not our enemies. They did not originate or desire this hideous war or wish that we should be drawn into it; and we are vaguely conscious that we are fighting their cause, as they will some day see it, as well as our own. They are themselves in the grip of the same sinister power that has now at last stretched its ugly talons out and drawn blood from us. The whole world is at war because the whole world is in the grip of that power and is trying out the great battle which shall determine whether it is to be brought under its mastery or fling itself free.

The war was begun by the military masters of Germany, who proved to be also the masters of Austria-Hungary. These men have never regarded nations as peoples, men, women, and children of like blood and frame as themselves, for whom governments existed and in whom governments had their life. They have regarded them merely as serviceable organizations which they could by force or intrigue bend or corrupt to their own purpose. They have regarded the smaller states, in particular, and the peoples who could be overwhelmed by force, as their natural tools and instruments of domination. Their purpose has long been avowed. The statesmen of other nations, to whom that purpose was incredible, paid little attention; regarded what German professors expounded in their classrooms and German writers set forth to the world as the goal of German policy as rather the dream of minds detached from practical affairs, as preposterous private conceptions of German destiny, than as the actual plans of responsible rulers; but the rulers of Germany themselves knew all the while what concrete plans, what well advanced intrigues lay back of what the professors and the writers were saying, and were glad to go forward unmolested, filling the thrones of Balkan states with German princes, putting German officers at the service of Turkey to drill her armies and make interest with her government, developing plans of sedition and rebellion in India and

Egypt, setting their fires in Persia. The demands made by Austria
upon Servia were a mere single step in a plan which compassed
Europe and Asia, from Berlin to Bagdad. They hoped those
demands might not arouse Europe, but they meant to press them
whether they did or not, for they thought themselves ready for
the final issue of arms.

Their plan was to throw a broad belt of German military power
and political control across the very centre of Europe and beyond
the Mediterranean into the heart of Asia; and Austria-Hungary
was to be as much their tool and pawn as Servia or Bulgaria or
Turkey or the ponderous states of the East. Austria-Hungary, indeed, was to become part of the central German Empire, absorbed
and dominated by the same forces and influences that had
originally cemented the German states themselves. The dream
had its heart at Berlin. It could have had a heart nowhere else!
It rejected the idea of solidarity of race entirely. The choice of
peoples played no part in it at all. It contemplated binding together racial and political units which could be kept together only
by force,—Czechs, Magyars, Croats, Serbs, Roumanians, Turks,
Armenians,—the proud states of Bohemia and Hungary, the
stout little commonwealths of the Balkans, the indomitable
Turks, the subtle peoples of the East. These peoples did not
wish to be united. They ardently desired to direct their own affairs, would be satisfied only by undisputed independence. They
could be kept quiet only by the presence or the constant threat
of armed men. They would live under a common power only by
sheer compulsion and await the day of revolution. But the German military statesmen had reckoned with all that and were
ready to deal with it in their own way.

And they have actually carried the greater part of that amazing plan into execution! Look how things stand. Austria is at their
mercy. It has acted, not upon its own initiative or upon the choice
of its own people, but at Berlin's dictation ever since the war
began. Its people now desire peace, but cannot have it until leave
is granted from Berlin. The so-called Central Powers are in fact
but a single Power. Servia is at its mercy, should its hands be
but for a moment freed. Bulgaria has consented to its will, and
Roumania is overrun. The Turkish armies, which Germans
trained, are serving Germany, certainly not themselves, and the
guns of German warships lying in the harbour at Constantinople
remind Turkish statesmen every day that they have no choice
but to take their orders from Berlin. From Hamburg to the
Persian Gulf the net is spread.

Is it not easy to understand the eagerness for peace that has been manifested from Berlin ever since the snare was set and sprung? Peace, peace, peace has been the talk of her Foreign Office for now a year and more; not peace upon her own initiative, but upon the initiative of the nations over which she now deems herself to hold the advantage. A little of the talk has been public, but most of its has been private. Through all sorts of channels it has come to me, and in all sorts of guises, but never with the terms disclosed which the German Government would be willing to accept. That government has other valuable pawns in its hands besides those I have mentioned. It still holds a valuable part of France, though with slowly relaxing grasp, and practically the whole of Belgium. Its armies press close upon Russia and overrun Poland at their will. It cannot go further; it dare not go back. It wishes to close its bargain before it is too late and it has little left to offer for the pound of flesh it will demand.

The military masters under whom Germany is bleeding see very clearly to what point Fate has brought them. If they fall back or are forced back an inch, their power both abroad and at home will fall to pieces like a house of cards. It is their power at home they are thinking about now more than their power abroad. It is that power which is trembling under their very feet; and deep fear has entered their hearts. They have but one chance to perpetuate their military power or even their controlling political influence. If they can secure peace now with the immense advantages still in their hands which they have up to this point apparently gained, they will have justified themselves before the German people; they will have gained by force what they promised to gain by it; an immense expansion of German power, an immense enlargement of German industrial and commercial opportunities. Their prestige will be secure, and with their prestige their political power. If they fail, their people will thrust them aside; a government accountable to the people themselves will be set up in Germany, as it has been in England, in the United States, in France, and in all the great countries of the modern time except Germany. If they succeed they are safe and Germany and the world are undone; if they fail Germany is saved and the world will be at peace. If they succeed, America will fall within the menace. We and all the rest of the world must remain armed, as they will remain, and must make ready for the next step in their aggression; if they fail, the world may unite for peace and Germany may be of the union.

Do you not now understand the new intrigue, the intrigue for peace, and why the masters of Germany do not hesitate to use any agency that promises to effect their purpose, the deceit of

the nations? Their present particular aim is to deceive all those
who throughout the world stand for the rights of peoples and
the self-government of nations; for they see what immense
strength the forces of justice and of liberalism are gathering out
of this war. They are employing liberals in their enterprise. They
are using men, in Germany and without, as their spokesmen whom
they have hitherto despised and oppressed, using them for their
own destruction,—socialists, the leaders of labour, the thinkers
they have hitherto sought to silence. Let them once succeed and
these men, now their tools, will be ground to powder beneath the
weight of the great military empire they will have set up; the
revolutionists in Russia will be cut off from all succour or cooperation in western Europe and a counter revolution fostered
and supported; Germany herself will lose her chance of freedom;
and all Europe will arm for the next, the final struggle.

The sinister intrigue is being no less actively conducted in
this country than in Russia and in every country in Europe to
which the agents and dupes of the Imperial German Government
can get access. That government has many spokesmen here, in
places high and low. They have learned discretion. They keep
within the law. It is opinion they utter now, not sedition. They
proclaim the liberal purposes of their masters; declare this a
foreign war which can touch America with no danger to either
her lands or her institutions; set England at the centre of the
stage and talk of her ambition to assert economic dominion
throughout the world; appeal to our ancient tradition of isolation
in the politics of the nations; and seek to undermine the government with false professions of loyalty to its principles.

But they will make no headway. The false betray themselves
always in every accent. It is only friends and partisans of the
German Government whom we have already identified who utter these thinly disguised disloyalties. The facts are patent to all
the world, and nowhere are they more plainly seen than in the
United States, where we are accustomed to deal with facts and
not with sophistries; and the great fact that stands out above all
the rest is that this is a Peoples' War, a war for freedom and
justice and self-government amongst all the nations of the world,
a war to make the world safe for the peoples who live upon it
and have made it their own, the German people themselves included; and that with us rests the choice to break through all
these hypocrisies and patent cheats and masks of brute force
and help set the world free, or else stand aside and let it be
dominated a long age through by sheer weight of arms and the
arbitrary choices of self-constituted masters, by the nation which

can maintain the biggest armies and the most irresistible armaments—a power to which the world has afforded no parallel and
in the face of which political freedom must wither and perish.

For us there is but one choice. We have made it. Woe be to
the man or group of men that seeks to stand in our way in this
day of high resolution when every principle we hold dearest is to
be vindicated and made secure for the salvation of the nations.
We are ready to plead at the bar of history, and our flag shall wear
a new lustre. Once more we shall make good with our lives and
fortunes the great faith to which we were born, and a new glory
shall shine in the face of our people.[2]

Printed reading copy (WP, DLC).
    [2] There is a WWsh draft and a WWT outline of this address in WP, DLC.

To James L. Davidson

My dear Sir: [The White House] 14 June, 1917

I have read with a great deal of interest and solicitude your
telegram relative to the activities of the representatives of the
United Mine Workers of America in attempting to organize the
coal miners of Alabama. In the absence of more definite information than is contained in your communication as to the exact
language used by these men, I do not feel justified in commenting
on their attitude. Of course, however, it should be definitely understood that the administration is not engaged in directing or
suggesting the organization of either capital or labor, except in
so far as may be necessary to coordinate their energies for the
promotion of the public welfare.

It is very generally acknowledged that our laws and the long
established policy of our Government recognize the right of work-
ingmen to organize unions if they so desire, just as we recognize
the right of capital to organize co-partnerships and corporations.
In so organizing each is exercising a natural and legal right.
When, negotiating with each other in the exercise of these rights,
they come to a disagreement concerning the terms of employment, which threatens to cause a stoppage of work, the rest of
the public is interested in an adjustment of their differences, because the conflict may interfere with the supplies needed for the
sustenance of the people, or the safety of our institutions.

Congress has consequently created mediation agencies which
may be utilized to bring about a mutually satisfactory adjustment of disputes of this character, and I am sure the Department of Labor, which is entrusted with the administration of

this work, would be glad to use its good offices in endeavoring to find a common ground acceptable to both sides if any situation develops which is likely to interfere with the production of coal. May I not venture to express the hope, however, that the operators and miners in Alabama may be actuated by a common purpose in the present emergency and both exhibit that fine spirit of cooperation which is so essential for the common defense to the end that the greatest measure of production shall be secured without the need of calling upon the mediation agencies of the Government?   Sincerely yours,   Woodrow Wilson

TLS (Letterpress Books, WP, DLC).

To Joseph Patrick Tumulty, with Enclosure

Dear Tumulty: [The White House, June 14, 1917]

I don't like to handle this matter directly, but I would be very much obliged if you would get Senator Newlands on the telephone and tell him that I consider any suggestions that come from the Senators whose names I have underscored on this memorandum as distinctly hostile, and I should be very much chagrined and disappointed if their suggestions were acted upon, because I believe them to be intended to prevent the very things that are now absolutely necessary. I believe that the granting of the power suggested direct to the Executive is the only wise and feasible thing that can be done in the existing circumstances.

Please, at the same time, explain to the Senator that my not seeing him this morning was due to the fact that I was so engaged that it was not possible to reach me in time to make the engagement.

(I think on the whole I had better not be mixed up in these negotiations.)   The President.

TL (WP, DLC).

E N C L O S U R E

The White House. June 14, 1917

Memorandum for the President:

Senator Newlands called this morning and stated that a conference was held yesterday between himself and Senators Cummins, Robinson and Kellogg[1] on the one side, and Senators Smith of Georgia, Reed and Hardwick, on the other, with a view to adjusting differences on the Priorities Bill. After much discussion, the opponents of the bill in its present form suggested Amendment "A" as a substitute for the first part of Section 2.[2] The other members of the committee indicated that this provision would be satisfactory to them if it was satisfactory to the chairman, Senator Newlands. Senator Newlands has not yet given his assent and would like the views of the President.

In view of the probability that Senator Norris' amendment would carry, giving to the shippers the right to make claims for damages under the proviso on Page 5, the Senator said that it was thought advisable by the conference to strike out the two provisos on pages 5 and 6.

T MS (WP, DLC).
[1] Frank Billings Kellogg, Republican of Minnesota.
[2] For the main provisions of the railroad priorities bill, see F. G. Newlands to WW, June 7, 1917, n. 1. The proposed "Amendment A" (T MS [WP, DLC]) took the emergency powers over railroad priorities away from the President and gave them instead to the Interstate Commerce Commission.

To Joseph Patrick Tumulty, with Enclosure

Dear Tumulty: [The White House, June 14, 1917]

I don't like to answer this with a letter. Won't you get Mr. Wolf on the telephone and tell him that I entirely agree with his judgment about this matter?   The President.

TL (WP, DLC).

E N C L O S U R E

From Simon Wolf

To the President: Washington, D. C. June 11, 1917.

I have read with great admiration and patriotic fervor, your admirable letter to the Russian people. Nothing could be clearer or sincerer, and the passage about expending our blood and treasure, and that we must be victorious now, I am sure will have a great effect upon all the people of the world. It is providential that in a crisis like this, we have at the head of our great Government, a man whose brain and heart are so completely woven together for the common good of humanity.

I would like very much indeed to have your opinion—confidential if you choose, otherwise for publication—as to the feasibility and practicability of American citizens of Jewish faith holding a Congress at this present juncture. Personally, I am utterly opposed to it. I think it is bound to embarrass the Government and thwart the very objects for which the Congress is to be convened. There might have been a reason before Russia acted, but there certainly is none at this present moment. Besides this, the reckless utterances of some of the delegates to this Congress might seriously effect the situation, and instead of helping the Jews or the United States, might have the reverse effect.

I shall await your answer with great solicitude.

Very sincerely yours,   Simon Wolf

TLS (WP, DLC).

From Robert Lansing, with Enclosure

My dear Mr. President: Washington June 14, 1917.

I had a conversation yesterday with Mr. Bullard in regard to a proposed trip which he and Mr. Poole intend to make to Russia. At the close of the conversation I requested him to write me a letter on the subject, which he has done, and which I told him I would submit to you for your consideration.

You will perceive Mr. Bullard's idea is that he and Mr. Poole should have a semi-official position, which would give them the entrée in Petrograd and an opportunity to see some of the leading men there.

My own view is that such a position might cause us some embarrassment. At the same time I did not feel that I should reject his suggestion without submitting it to you for consideration.

As you will see by the last paragraph of Mr. Bullard's letter, he plans to sail a week from Saturday, so that he desires a prompt decision as to whether he can obtain official recognition.

Faithfully yours,   Robert Lansing.

Prest returned this objecting to Bullard's holding such a position   RL   June 15/17

TLS (SDR, RG 59, 124.61/30½, DNA).

ENCLOSURE

Arthur Bullard to Robert Lansing

My dear Mr. Secretary: Washington, D.C. June 13th, 1917.

In resumé of my conversation with you this afternoon:

We all are in accord, I believe, that it is well for Mr. Poole[1] and myself to go to Russia. The question to settle is how we can be of greatest service to our Government. There are three possibilities, being sent officially, being sent semi-officially or going as private citizens.

Mr. Poole and myself are both writers and it is in that way—especially by writing in the Russian press—that we can accomplish most. We have both been in Russia and have some influential friends there.

For the reasons I explained to you, I do not consider the official connection with the Embassy desirable. The Ambassador and our Mission will do all the official speaking and writing which is necessary. The best journalistic work can be done independently.

The semi-official arrangement seems more advisable to me. My proposal is that Mr. Poole and myself be appointed delegates from The Committee on Public Information to present greetings to the similar organization in Russia. There is a good text for a discourse in the name of our Committee. Public information must be the foundation of public freedom. Our credentials should be explicitly limited. Our mandate should be simply to seek to produce a cordial accord between the press, and the officials who supervise the press, in the two countries: just as Lieutenant-Colonel Chambers,[2] the Chief Censor for Canada, came to Washington and conferred with us on mutual problems. His mission was not in any way diplomatic, but it was official and he brought official introductions.

Judging from the meager press dispatches, a section of the Russian press is distinctly hostile to America. Maxim Gorki[3] had a very bad time when he was in this country and he now seems hostile. I know him well enough to have a large degree of certainty that I could get some articles into his paper. A week spent in Russia with representatives of the press in Petrograd and Moscow could I am sure have a beneficial result. We would both be interviewed. We could keep to the safe subject of democracy and the hope of the future and do our bit to persuade the Russians that the United States really is interested in such subjects and has not been adequately represented by our travelling salesmen; that there is another and more sympathetic America than Gorki knew.

And when this short and precise mission was finished, we could stay on as private citizens to do what we could both in spreading a juster idea of America in Russia and also in informing our people at home of the trend and meaning of events there.

If this project meets with your approval, neither Mr. Poole nor myself would care to receive any other remuneration than the one dollar a month which is required by law for public employees.

The third possibility is that we should go on our own responsibility as private citizens. In the long run it would be almost the same, but we would not get an audience so quickly. And would probably never get quite as many points of contact as if we at first had some official standing.

I wish to assure you once more, Mr. Secretary, that Mr. Poole and myself wish only to make whatever influence we can have in Russia count as strongly as possible. I understand that you agree with me that the first possibility—a permanent official connection with the Embassy—is undesirable. The decision lies between the short term semi-official arrangement or the private enterprise. In either case we would want to work in accord with the Embassy. I do not think that either of us know personally any of the present staff, but we know several of the Commission.

We are planning to sail if possible on the "Bergensfiord" which is announced for a week from Saturday, so it would be a great favor if you could give us your decision as soon as may be.

Very truly yours,   A. Bullard.

TLS (SDR, RG 59, 124.61/30½, DNA).
    [1] DeWitt Clinton Poole, career officer in the Foreign Service, at this time on duty in Washington.
    [2] Ernest John Chambers.
    [3] Maksim Gor'kii [Aleksei Maksimovich Peshkov] (1868-1936), the distinguished Russian writer.

From Thomas Watt Gregory, with Enclosure

Dear Mr. President: Washington, D. C. June 14, 1917.

I acknowledge receipt of yours of June 4th enclosing one of the identification cards and application blank for enrollment in the American Protective League. You state that your attention has been called to this association and that it seems to you it would be dangerous to have such an organization operating in the United States, and you ask if there is any way in which we could stop it.

On June 2d I received a letter from the Secretary of the Treasury in regard to this League in which the Secretary stated he was sending a copy to you.

Briefly stated, the American Protective League is a patriotic organization, composed of from eighty to one hundred thousand members, with branches in almost six hundred cities and towns, was organized with my approval and encouragement, and has been tremendously helpful in the work of the Bureau of Investigation of the Department of Justice. It has no official status and claims none. Its members serve without the slightest expense to the Government, and not a single officer or member receives compensation from any source.

I herewith enclose copy of my reply to Secretary McAdoo's letter and sincerely hope that in the midst of your many burdens you may find time to read this complete statement of the organization, purposes, work and character of the American Protective League. On reading this I am sure you will agree with me that it should be encouraged and that its work is not subject to any real criticism.

I herewith return the two enclosures which accompanied your letter.   Faithfully yours,   T. W. Gregory

TLS (WP, DLC).

ENCLOSURE

Thomas Watt Gregory to William Gibbs McAdoo

Dear Mr. Secretary: [Washington] June 12, 1917.

I acknowledge receipt of yours of the 2d in regard to the American Protective League.

On the severance of diplomatic relations with Germany the work of my Bureau of Investigation began to increase tremendously. Then came the declaration of war, the President's proclamation in regard to alien enemies, the spy, conscription and other problems. There have been days when as many as one thousand letters came to my Department purporting to give more or less detailed information as to spies, disloyal citizens and plots to destroy ships, factories, railroad bridges, munition plants, waterworks, arsenals, etc., etc., etc. In perhaps ninety per cent. of these cases the information furnished was of no value, but in a small number of them it proved to be very valuable indeed, and it thus became necessary to investigate everything called to our attention. This involved the keeping under observation of a very large number of citizens and situations throughout the United States. When the war began I had three hundred agents in my Bureau of Investigation scattered from San Francisco to New York, and since then only about one hundred have been added.

Numbers of letters came to the Department, many from men of distinction and well established loyalty, offering the help of volunteer patriotic organizations. All were advised that I approved of the formation of such bodies and that I would put the investigating agents of my department in touch with them with the view of receiving information from them, especially as to local situations, but that it must be clearly understood that membership in these bodies did not make their officers or members officers of the Government in any sense; that the organizations possessed no Governmental powers and must not attempt to exercise any. At a cabinet meeting at which, I think, you were present, I stated the situation and the policy which I was adopting, and it seemed to meet with general approval.

A number of these organizations have been formed, they have been of great help to this Department within the lines prescribed, and it would have been very difficult for my Department to have successfully coped with the situation without their valuable assistance.

The American Protective League is the largest, best organized, and most effective of these bodies. It has branches in almost six hundred cities and towns, and a membership of between eighty and one hundred thousand. It has no Constitution, by-laws or charter. As to its purposes, I have before me a form of the circular issued last March by its General Superintendent A. M. Briggs[1] from the National Headquarters at Chicago at a time when he was organizing branches of the League throughout the country, and this shows just what activities were contemplated and being carried on. It contains the following language:

"The object of this organization, which is entirely a patriotic one, is to work under the direction of the local offices of the Bureau of Investigation for the purpose of assisting the local agents of the government in securing information of the activities of agents of foreign governments or persons unfriendly to this government, for the protection of public property, etc."

The circular states that the organization "will be composed of American citizens of high moral character and good standing

1 Albert M. Briggs, vice-president of Outdoor Advertising, Inc., of Chicago.

who are willing to serve from a purely patriotic motive and without compensation; further that the chief of each local organization will report daily or as often as necessary to the local government agent from whom he will receive instructions for the work of his organization, using great care at all times that the activities of his organization be under the entire control of the local government agent, as the entire object of each local organization is to do everything possible to assist the local government agent of the Bureau of Investigation in securing information on such matters as may be presented by the local government agent for investigation." It also directs that great care be taken by the entire organization "at all times that nothing is done by it or any member of it to unnecessarily alarm aliens in this country or cause them any apprehension as to the fair manner in which they will be treated, and that no arrests should be caused excepting after consultation with the local government agent or his assistants."

A circular letter issued to all special agents of my Bureau of Investigation on March 22d last by the Chief of that Bureau[2] indicates the status of the American Protective League and the purpose of its organization, and reads as follows:

"This note will introduce to you Mr. A. M. Briggs, of Chicago, Illinois, who, with the approval of the Department, is organizing confidentially a volunteer committee or organization of citizens for the purpose of cooperating with the Department in securing information of activities of agents of foreign governments or persons unfriendly to this Government, for the protection of public property, etc.

"It will be the aim of such organization to supply to you information and to assist you in securing information as to any matters which you may present to it, and it is planned that some one in the organization will be designated to deal with the agent in charge of this service in each city.

"Mr. Briggs understands fully that this arrangement must be kept as confidential as practicable and that great care must be taken that nothing is done by it to unnecessarily alarm aliens in this country or cause them any apprehension as to the fair manner in which they will be treated and that no arrests should be caused except after consultation with the Federal authorities.

"Please assist Mr. Briggs in any way practicable and arrange to take advantage of the assistance and cooperation which he may offer through this organization."

2 That is, A. Bruce Bielaski.

To this should be added that the Bureau of Investigation, through its agents, has kept in close touch with the various branches of this League and have found the organization in all cases loyal, patriotic and self-sacrificing, and I know of no complaint because of the acts of any member of the organization. I, of course, do not claim to read all the letters which have come into my Department, but I have had the correspondence relating to this organization looked up, and am impressed with the care that has been taken to prevent any misapprehension as to its service, powers and authority.

I note specially a letter addressed by the Chief of my Bureau of Investigation to Mr. William M. Offley, in charge of the New York Division of the Bureau, in which the following language is used:

"* * *While the American Protective League is organized and operated with our approval, it is a volunteer organization without any direct official status. That is to say, its members are not officers, agents, or employes of the United States.

"It is quite important to preserve this distinction and one of the greatest merits of the League over similar volunteer organizations is that it at no time assumes any authority to act as a government agency. We have not had a single complaint with respect to any over-stepping of the proper bounds by any member of this organization. * * *

"The success of this organization is largely dependent on keeping its exact relations with the Government clear in the minds of its members.

"Government officials, especially in other Departments, have anticipated some difficulty along these lines, but because of the very high character of the men in the League and the care with which its exact relations have been explained to everybody, no such difficulties have arisen, and I am confident that they will not arise. * * *"

None of its officers or members receive any compensation whatsoever from any source, and its letterheads, stationery and clerical help are paid for by voluntary contributions made by its General Superintendent, Mr. Briggs, and other patriotic members. Among the prominent citizens and business men belonging to the New York branch are acquaintances of mine who are among the leading men of the country.

It has been useful in sifting out thousands of charges and complaints reaching this Department; it has kept under observation thousands of alien enemies and other individuals, giving my Department information as to their antecedents, whereabouts and activities, and on registration day it quietly performed services for the Government which entitle it to the thanks of the nation.

Merely for the purpose of illustration, I will state that in Chicago alone two thousand of its members were at and around the registration booths, encouraging good citizens to register, securing the names and addresses of those who appeared to be evading registration, and taking particular note of any attempt to influence against registration. About two hundred were actively engaged in promptly reporting information obtained to the division superintendent of my Bureau of Investigation at Chicago; also they assisted the registration officials in many instances through almost the entire night and furnished numbers of automobiles which were used in the distribution of registration cards and keeping up with the work in the various precincts.

In the city of New York they had one or more men on duty at each of the 2,125 election districts and several hundred in outlying districts near New York, the work being similar to that performed in Chicago.

As indicating the manner in which the League assisted in handling the registration problem, I quote the following portion of a letter issued by the New York Headquarters to its members on June 4th.

"*Instructions to your men.* The members of the League are not expected to quell disturbances or enforce arrests, but to ascertain the cause of the disturbance, the names of those causing the disturbance, as far as possible locating any important individuals or organizations which are furthering any opposition to registration, collect any pamphlets or other printed matter used in urging men against conscription, and ascertain as far as possible which men in the election districts, of the required age, are not presenting themselves for registration.

"The necessary assistance from any Federal, State, or local official should be immediately sought when any violator has been discovered. The Department of Justice desires the summary 'arrest of any individual or individuals who urge or endeavor to pursuade persons not to register or who in any manner interfere with the proper performance of the duties placed upon the Registration Officers.'"

No instance has come to my attention where Governmental authority has been claimed by virtue of membership in the organization. It has no official Governmental status, and if such has been claimed I am not aware of it.

The personnel of the organization seems to be very high, and my attention has not been called to any member who might be characterized as irresponsible or untrustworthy. Membership is not secured by the mere purchase of a badge, as suggested by you, and the badge is only the indicia of membership, each member paying a small sum for it after he has become a member. All assistance given by this and like organizations has been without the slightest expense to the Government.

To sum up the whole situation, the work of the League has been of the very highest character, inspired by the most patriotic motives, and tremendously helpful to the National Government, as I am sure it will continue to be in the future.

You will excuse me for thus having gone into detail in regard to the organization and work of this League, as a proper reply to yours of June 2d should necessarily present these facts.

As to the character of applications for enrollment, identification cards, letterheads and badges of the American Protective League, I knew nothing of these up to the time I received your letter. Since then I have procured samples, and they are now before me.

The application has the following heading:

> "Application for Enrollment as a Volunteer
> in the Secret Service Division
> AMERICAN PROTECTIVE LEAGUE"

It is addressed to the "Chief of Bureau of Enrollment" and is "for enrollment as a volunteer in the Secret Service Division of Investigation in the American Protective League."

Attached to some of the applications is the oath of the applicant as follows:

> "I _____, do solemnly swear that I will support and defend the Constitution of the United States against all enemies, foreign and domestic; that I will bear true faith and allegiance to the same; that I take this obligation freely, without any mental reservation or purpose of evasion; and that having read the regulations, I will well and faithfully discharge the duties of a Volunteer in the American Protective League, under these regulations; So help me God."

The following is a sample of the stationery:

> "National Headquarters
>
> A M Briggs   AMERICAN PROTECTIVE LEAGUE   Telephone
> General Supt.   Secret Service Division   Harrison 2075
> Room 1307 Peoples Gas Building
> Chicago"

(Of course, the stationery used in New York and other offices is slightly different because of the different locations of the offices.) A sample identification card reads as follows:

"Badge No. _____
New York Headquarters
SECRET SERVICE DIVISION
American Protective League

This is to certify that

_____

_____

_____

has been appointed a _____
in this Service.

The badge issued with this certificate is the property of the League and can be recalled at any time and certificate cancelled."

(A reproduction of the badge hereinafter referred to appears on the upper left hand corner of the card. The cards issued, of course, differ with the locality.)

The badge is of metal, and on it are inscribed the words:

"American Protective League
Secret Service
Chief"

(This evidently is the badge used by one of the officials of the organization and I understand the badge of an ordinary member would not have on it the word "Chief.")

In this connection, it should be stated that the badge of the League is colored to resemble brass and is oval-shaped, while that used by your Secret Service is a five-pointed star of silver. The wording on the badge of your Department is "Secret Service U. S." In size, material, color, shape, and wording the two badges are utterly dissimilar, and the most casual observer would note the difference at a glance. Below is a photographic reproduction of the two badges, from which you will observe how entirely unlike they are.[3]

To my mind, the expressions "Secret Service" and "Secret Service Division" appearing on the application, stationery and

[3] Not reproduced.

badge are intended to relate, and on their face appear to relate, entirely to the activities of the American Protective League, and no instance has come to my notice in which a member of the organization has attempted to give them any Governmental significance.

About April 26th last Mr. Moran,[4] Assistant Chief of the Secret Service Division of the Treasury Department, informally inquired over the telephone of the Chief of the Bureau of Investigation of my Department regarding the enrollment card of the American Protective League, and on that day Chief Bielaski of this Department addressed a letter to Mr. Moran calling his attention to the manner in which the words "Secret Service" appear on the enrollment card of that organization and asked him to please note any suggested changes on the card enclosed which he thought desirable; this letter was written more than five weeks ago and no reply thereto has yet been received.

On April 25th last Mr. Flynn, Chief of your Secret Service Division, wrote a letter to Mr. Bielaski protesting against the use of the term "Secret Service Division" by the American Protective League, and on April 28th, five weeks ago, Mr. Bielaski replied at some length, giving general information in regard to this organization, and closing the letter as follows:

"You will, of course, realize that we wish to do nothing or have the American Protective League do nothing to which you might object, and if you will indicate such changes on the enrollment blank as you think desirable, we will, in so far as practicable, endeavor to bring them about."

To this letter there appears to have been no reply.

If, by your references to the sanction of the Department of Justice as applied to this organization, you mean I have utilized the information it has furnished, have encouraged it to furnish that information, and have expressed my appreciation of its patriotic efforts, then I have sanctioned it, and have done so without any idea that the work of your Secret Service Division would thereby be embarrassed or interfered with.

In fact, I do not see how any activities of this league could affect the work in which your Secret Service is engaged, i.e., suppressing counterfeiting and other felonies relating to the pay and bounty laws, and protecting the person of the President. After diligent inquiry, I have what I consider the most satisfactory evidence that this League has never had the remotest connection with either of the duties with which your Secret Service

[4] William Herman Moran, who succeeded William James Flynn as Chief of the Secret Service on January 1, 1918.

is charged, and has no intention of ever having any, and if you have any proof to the contrary, I will be glad to receive and consider it. This League is organized for the clearly expressed purpose of giving assistance to the Bureau of Investigation of the Department of Justice in the performance by the latter of the duties with which Congress has charged it.

You ask that I give immediate instructions that the association change its designation and withdraw and destroy at once all badges, cards, and literature referring to the "Secret Service" or the "Secret Service Division."

On yesterday, General Superintendent Briggs of the American Protective League, who is at the head of this organization, was in my office, and in deference to your views I expressed the hope that the League would eliminate from their literature and badges the expressions you object to. He stated that there would be no difficulty in having new stationery, identification cards and literature prepared and the old ones destroyed. As to the badges he stated that thousands of these had been issued, each member paying something like seventy-five cents for his badge, and he did not see how he could properly take them up without paying for them and that the organization did not have the thousands of dollars which would be required to furnish new badges or pay for the old ones. I confess that his point of view appeals to me strongly, as I trust it will to you. I think I would have no difficulty in having the expressions referred to eliminated from all the badges issued in the future, and will be glad to feel that this and the suggested change in the identification card and the literature would reasonably meet your views. I know of no authority I have to instruct this organization to destroy these badges, and on account of the efficient work they are doing and the tremendous importance of having good citizens of the class involved cooperate with the Government in the manner in which these people are doing, I should hesitate to issue such instructions even if I had the power. I am sure you will agree with me that this is a peculiarly bad time to discourage citizens who are spending their time and money in patriotic and effective service for the common good.

Following your example, I am sending a copy of this letter to the President.　　　Faithfully yours,　[T. W. Gregory][5]

CCL (JDR, RG 60, No. 44-03-2, DNA).
　[5] Gregory wrote to McAdoo in February 1918, as follows:
　"I am sorry that you still appear to be hostile to the activities of the American Protective League, as indicated on the second page of your letter of January 5th.
　"On June 2d last you wrote me complaining of this organization, and on

June 12th I replied at great length, sending a copy of the letter to the President. I gave you the history of this organization, its purposes, the tremendously important work it had performed for the government, and explained its total lack of any governmental authority.

"This letter was written with a very earnest desire to meet your objections to the badges, cards and literature used by this organization and especially to the terms 'Secret Service' and 'Secret Service Division' appearing thereon. I conferred with the General Superintendent of the League and was assured by him that there would be no difficulty in eliminating from their literature the expressions you objected to and having new stationery, identification cards and literature prepared and the old ones destroyed. I explained to you the difficulty of taking up all the old badges, but stated that I would have no trouble in having the expressions eliminated from all new badges, and that I would be glad to know if this and the suggested change in the identification cards and literature would reasonably meet your objections.

"Though written almost eight months ago, that letter is still unanswered. However, I proceeded to have the suggested changes made in the cards and literature, and have arranged that no new badges bearing the expressions referred to shall be issued. I have also perfected an arrangement which, I trust, will in a short time result in the calling in of all the old badges which met with your disapproval.

"This organization now has about 250,000 members. It is intensely patriotic and extremely valuable. With such a large membership there is likely to occur from time to time some assumption of authority not warranted and some interference which must not be permitted. The head of the League has an office in Washington. I keep in close touch with him, and any complaints made to me of improper acts on the part of any member of the organization will be promptly taken up with the head of the League and discipline administered where necessary. Under no circumstances have the officers or members of the League been given authority to make arrests or to exercise governmental powers.

"In Exhibit C which accompanies your letter of January 5th, three instances are complained of in which members of the American Protective League are charged with having done unauthorized acts. I have referred these three cases to the head of the League for a prompt and thorough investigation and will appreciate any assistance your agents may give in developing the facts fully.

"The mere fact that only three instances are suggested in which members of an organization of 250,000 men have done something objectionable during the past ten months is of itself indicative that there has been little cause for complaint." TWG to WGM, Feb. [blank], 1918, CCL (JDR, RG 60, No. 44-03-2, DNA).

In his letter of January 5, McAdoo had written: "The fact that the Department of Justice has organized and accepted the services of a volunteer organization, the American Protective League, which has assumed to issue badges to its members and to advertise itself as a 'Secret Service,' expressly sanctioned by the Department of Justice, is, in itself, evidence of the need [for a coordination of internal intelligence work]. Many abuses have already arisen out of the unfortunate situation created by this voluntary organization. I am frank to say that if I were a German spy I should want nothing better than the opportunity of joining this organization, getting one of its 'Secret Service' badges, and carrying on my nefarious activities under the guise of this organization. My own emphatic judgment is that in a matter of such grave importance to the country as this whole Intelligence service is, the Congress should make the necessary appropriation to create a sufficient force to cope with it. A Government controlled and directed organization would be responsible and would, in itself, protect the people of the country against possible gross impositions and injustices. No volunteer organization should, in my opinion, be entrusted with power of this character, which can be irresponsibly exercised with resultant injustices of the gravest sort to the people." WGM to TWG, Jan. 5, 1918, TLS (JDR, RG 60, No. 44-03-02, DNA).

Exhibit C in McAdoo's letter, mentioned by Gregory, is missing.

From Edward Mandell House

Dear Governor: Magnolia, Massachusetts. June 14, 1917.

I can hardly express the pleasure your speech of today has given me. It has stirred me more than anything you have ever done.

For two years or more I have wanted someone high up in the Allied governments to arraign Germany as she deserved. You have done it, and done it so well that she will be centuries freeing herself from the indictment you have made.

I am happy beyond measure, and I wish I was near enough to say more.

With deep affection, I am,

Your devoted,   E. M. House

TLS (WP, DLC).

Sir Cecil Arthur Spring Rice to the Foreign Office

Washington 14 June 1917

Horodyski tells me S of War said today President approved of following plan. A Polish committee to be formed in London or Paris to act as provisional Polish Govt with power to conduct all Polish affairs, borrow money etc. He will speak to S of S tomorrow. I said that if USG has a formal proposal to make it will doubtless be made through U S Ambassador in London and that all the Allies will be consulted before a decision is made.

Hw telegram (FO 115/2302, p. 237, PRO).

To Edward Mandell House, with Enclosure

My dear House,   The White House. 15 June, 1917.

The Secretary of State and I have conferred, in as acquiescent a mood as possible, about the enclosed (though we both think, with you, that it is most unwise and inconsiderate of Gerard to publish a book at this juncture) and our joint judgment is, that Nos. 1, 2 and three (numbered in blue) are harmless, *provided* he does not include the statement attached to 2[1] which the Emperor is said to have had written out for me (it would, among other things, seem to give the lie to Grey). With regard to 4, we did not have the text before us and could not form an opinion. It is hardly safe to print anything that forms part of the official record of the Department.

I hope you liked yesterday's speech. I was very much delayed in getting at the composition of it and so did not have a chance to let you see it beforehand. I do not think that it contains anything to which our Associates in the war (so I will call them) could object.

I delivered the speech in a downpour of rain to a patient audience standing in the wet under dripping umbrellas.

All join me in warmest messages.

Affectionately Yours,   Woodrow Wilson

I am to see Northcliffe to-morrow.   W.W.

WWTLS (E. M. House Papers, CtY).

1 Actually, Gerard did print this statement in his book, *My Four Years in Germany* (New York, 1917), pp. 200-202.

ENCLOSURE

MEMORANDUM—MR. GERARD'S BOOK

With the consent of the President and the State Department, could the following interviews with the Emperor be incorporated into Mr. Gerard's forthcoming book:

①1   1. June 27, 1914, on board the Emperor's yacht "Hohenzollern" at Kiel, the Emperor said, referring to the fact that Socialist members of the Reichstag, when the Emperor's name was cheered at the closing session, had remained in the Reichstag and refused to rise:

"Did you see what those Socialists did at the close of the Reichstag session? You wait about three weeks, and you will see something that will be done that will fix those fellows."

②   2. August 10, 1914, in the garden of the Castle, Berlin, when Mr. Gerard interviewed the Emperor on President Wilson's willingness to mediate at any time, the Emperor said that the coming into the war of England was unexpected and made an entirely new proposition, and he feared that on that account it would last a long time, but that otherwise victory would have been easy.

(Permission is also asked to print the statement which the Kaiser wrote out for President Wilson that day and which has never been published, copy of which is enclosed herewith.)2

③   3. Interview with the Emperor at Potsdam on October 25, 1915, in the course of which the Emperor stated that America had better look out after this war. "I will stand no nonsense from America after the war is over." The Emperor also said that

he would not have torpedoed the "Lusitania," and that no gentleman would have torpedoed a ship so full of women and children.
He referred to the war as a "Lawyer's war," citing Asquith, etc.

④   4. May 2nd or 3rd, (1916?). An interview in the garden at
Charleville about settlement of the submarine controversy, given
in detail in two dispatches to the State Department.[3]

T MS (E. M. House Papers, CtY).
  [1] Wilson's numbers.
  [2] J. W. Gerard to WJB, Aug. 14, 1914, Vol. 30.
  [3] See the Enclosures printed with RL to WW, May 3 and May 5, 1916,
both in Vol. 36.

From Newton Diehl Baker

My dear Mr. President: Washington. June 15, 1917.

I have your letter of June 13, and have carefully read the statements of Mr. Frank P. Glass with regard to the advisability of
selecting Birmingham as a site for one of the training camps.
Frankly, I doubt very much the advisability of selecting Birmingham, and chiefly for the reasons which Mr. Glass thinks operate
the other way. There have been a good many labor disturbances
there. If we were to locate 25,000 soldiers immediately in the
midst of that great industrial district it would not be long before
the notion would get abroad, however well-founded, that the
soldiers were there for the purpose of preventing the free action
of labor in its relation to the steel plants and mining industries
at that point. In addition to that, my own observation of Birmingham would hardly lead me to select it. It is, like most industrial
districts, smoky, and the ground about it too intensively used to
be very suitable for the maneuvering of large bodies of troops.

General Wood, with the assistance of a board of officers, is
considering these questions very actively, and, of course, he
may recommend Birmingham. If he does I shall very willingly
forego any doubt I have on the subject; but there are certainly
a number of places, both in Alabama and Georgia, which would
seem better adapted than this region.

                 Respectfully yours,   Newton D. Baker

TLS (WP, DLC).

From Herbert Clark Hoover

Dear Mr. President: Washington June 15, 1917.

I am greatly obliged for your note with regard to President
Garfield and I have telegraphed him today asking him if he

would be willing to accept the position suggested; that is, as chairman of the committee for determination of prices of food commodities.

I remain,   Your obedient servant,   Herbert Hoover

TLS (WP, DLC).

From Edward Mandell House

Dear Governor: Magnolia, Massachusetts. June 15, 1917.

I hope you are seeing the reception your Flag Day speech has been given. The hide-bound, bilious Transcript had the enclosed editorial last night.[1] The Boston Herald (but little better) says editorially: "Every American ought to read it and in doing so rejoice that we have at the head of the Republic in such a crisis as this a man of preeminent capacity for clear and convincing statement of public policies."

While, of course, you will not want to make another speech of this kind soon, yet when it is necessary, what do you think of challenging Germany to state her peace terms in the open as the other nations have. She should be driven into a corner and made to express her willingness to accept such a peace as the United States, Russia and even England have indicated a willingness to accept, or put herself in the position of continuing the war for the purpose of conquest.

Affectionately yours,   E. M. House

TLS (WP, DLC).
  [1] It is missing.

From George Washington Goethals

My dear Mr. President: Washington June 15, 1917.

The report on "Rapid Emergency Construction of Shipping," which received your approval, contained the provision that:

"to secure the speed of production, which is all-important, we feel that the task of securing and equipping these ships should be put in the hands of one man. Centralized control is essential for rapid and efficient work."

In order to carry out this policy, the United States Shipping Board Emergency Fleet Corporation was organized under the authority contained in the general Act establishing the United States Shipping Board, and the responsibility for the construction work placed on the General Manager, who was given the necessary authority to carry the responsibility.

Under the Act, approved June 15, 1917, you are authorized and empowered to take over plants of various kinds, shipyards, vessels built and in process of construction, and material. The same Act also authorizes incurring obligations to certain amounts for the construction of ships, for completing ships now in the course of construction, and for other purposes. It authorizes the President to

"exercise the power and authority hereby vested in him and expend the money herein and hereafter appropriated through such agency or agencies as he shall determine from time to time; Provided, that all money turned over to the United States Shipping Board Emergency Fleet Corporation may be expended as other moneys of said corporation are now expended."

In my letter of June 11th, I outlined the work that had already been accomplished, together with the program for future construction, and I now submit for your consideration draft of an Executive Order by which, if approved, you will exercise the power and authority vested in you through the agency of the United States Shipping Board Emergency Fleet Corporation, fixing the responsibility definitely upon the General Manager and giving him the authority which will be necessary to enable him to carry on the construction work, thereby confirming the existing status.[1]

The Act contemplates two separate and distinct functions, one relating solely to construction; the other relating to requisitioning and taking over completed ships, and the operation, management and disposition of the ships so acquired and constructed. The Executive Order submitted herewith covers the construction features only.

The next to the last paragraph of the proposed Order relates to the cost of material entering into the construction of ships, a matter which has given me some concern. Arrangements have been made with the Lumber Committee of the Council of National Defense for lumber for our wooden ships so far as fixing a maximum price at which it can be obtained is concerned, but no arrangement has yet been made for definitely fixing the price for steel, though purchases have been made for some of the ships under contract. The Council of National Defense has also appointed a committee to fix the prices of materials of all kinds, and the work of ship construction should secure whatever advantages may result therefrom. If a central purchasing agency is established, as I have been informed is under advisement, I should be very glad to avail myself of its facilities in making purchases for the Emergency Fleet Corporation.

I trust the Executive Order proposed may commend itself to your approval.   Very respectfully,   Geo. W. Goethals

TLS (WP, DLC).
1 Goethals well summarizes the proposed Executive Order.

From Walter Lippmann

Dear Mr. President: Washington. June 15, 1917.

I hope I am not presuming upon you when I say that your speech yesterday was the most adequate and searching expression of the meaning of this war that has yet been uttered.

I simply wish to express my personal gratitude for it.
                    Very sincerely yours,   Walter Lippmann

TLS (WP, DLC).

From Gavin McNab

San Francisco, Calif., June 15, 1917.

The importance of this subject to California and the United States is my justification for telegraphing you during this time of great pressure of world events on your time. I telegraph you as a citizen only as were I interested as an owner of oil land or stock in oil companies or as attorney for any oil interest whatever I would consider such action indelicate if not improper. I have been asked by all oil industries concerned by ownership or use to go to Washington to implore your attention in their serious concerns. I deem the highest duty that a citizen can perform at this time to be that not molesting the Executive or Legislative Departments of the Government in this great crisis that the best service he can render his country is to remain away from Washington so that those charged with those vast responsibilities may perform them without embarrassment from importunity or annoyance. The transcendent importance of the oil situation from the consumers and producers standpoint warrants the question being considered of prime importance in this crisis. Unless this matter is adjusted the industries of California and Pacific States will be seriously paralyzed. It certainly is not going to benefit the Government or any of the people if these vast petroleum deposits should be left idle in natures embrace when there is a crying need for them in industrial use. There is sufficient wisdom and skill at the command of the Government to solve this problem with justice to all and advantage to the nation. No one less than myself would advocate or countenance that any holding obtained by fraud should be recognized by the Government but the Government should take steps to immediately distinguish the innocent from the guilty to recognize equities and apportion rights; that the powers of the earth in this emergency be liberated. With due respect to Secretary Daniels I believe that he is in error in assuming that any adjustment of this question would reduce the reserves of oil necessary for the operation of the navy; on the contrary I am satisfied that a proper adjustment would insure the navy a permanent and abundant supply. The oil situation from the producers standpoint and from the position of the consumer including manufacturing and transportation and the public demands rapid action on the part of the government. With the multitude of responsibilities pressing upon you I would not urge this subject upon your attention were I not cognizant of its vast importance. A suggestion from you to the legislative power would insure action that would lead to a speedy solution. I therefore, as one interested, as a citizen in the public welfare respectfully pray your consideration of this, to us, all important subject.

Gavin McNab.

T telegram (WP, DLC).

From the Diary of Josephus Daniels

June Friday 15 1917

Cabinet. Hannis Taylor[1] had written pamphlet alleging it was unconstitutional to send soldiers to fight across the water. Is not that treasonable—certainly discouraging enlistment & Pres thought some examples must be made of men who circulated statements calculated to aid the enemy or discourage &c "I have a mind to go to G—[2] & say 'I have come to consult with you, as I never have any support from your Senators[.']" Burleson no— Congress had acted well & better than ever, & it was best not to have any conflict. But they always contrary? "I don't mind them hitting if I can hit back" said W.W.

McAdoo reported bonds fully subscribed & happy.

Farm conservation more important to push than revenue measure.

Banks & why I issued Wine Mess order[3]

[1] Lawyer of Washington, author of numerous works on constitutional law, Minister to Spain, 1893-1897.
[2] Georgia.
[3] On June 1, 1914, Daniels had issued a general order which prohibited

the use of alcoholic beverages aboard naval vessels and in navy yards and stations. In effect, it extended to officers the prohibition on enlisted men which had existed since McKinley's administration. The order created a furor both within and without the navy and brought a storm of abuse and ridicule upon Daniels. See Josephus Daniels, *The Wilson Era: Years of Peace —1910-1917* (Chapel Hill, N. C., 1944), pp. 386-403, and Arthur S. Link, *Wilson: The New Freedom* (Princeton, N. J., 1956), p. 123.

From the Diary of Colonel House

June 15, 1917.

Frank Polk telephones me good news this afternoon. The President has agreed to join the British Government in the work which Wiseman and I planned to do in Russia. He has also accepted my plan to take over certain British warships at the end of the war, and has come to an agreement with Balfour about the matter before he left.

To William Gibbs McAdoo

Personal

My dear Mac: The White House 16 June, 1917

Here is a proposition which is made, I dare say, in good faith and which I think I ought to refer to you with the request that you tell me what reply you think ought to be made.[1]

Always   Affectionately yours,   Woodrow Wilson

TLS (W. G. McAdoo Papers, DLC).
[1] E. D. Duffield to WW, June 13, 1917, TLS (W. G. McAdoo Papers, DLC). Edward Dickinson Duffield, Princeton 1892, vice-president of the Prudential Insurance Co. of Newark, said that his company was prepared, either alone or in conjunction with other insurance companies, to issue a group life insurance policy to cover the entire personnel of the United States Army and Navy. He argued that this would be much cheaper and more efficient than for the government to create a new department for the purpose.

To Frank Lyon Polk

My dear Mr. Polk: [The White House] 16 June, 1917

Thank you for your letter about the film play, "Patria." I quite agree with you that the mere change in the language used does not alter the character of the play. I have seen it and the persons depicted are too clearly Japanese to need label of any sort. I shall await your further conference with Mr. McFarland with a great deal of interest.

Cordially and sincerely yours,   Woodrow Wilson

TLS (Letterpress Books, WP, DLC).

To Walter Lippmann

My dear Mr. Lippmann: [The White House] 16 June, 1917
  Certainly no apology was needed for your letter of June fifteenth, which has cheered me mightily. I thank you for it most warmly.
  In haste
        Cordially and sincerely yours,   Woodrow Wilson

TLS (Letterpress Books, WP, DLC).

From William Patterson Borland

My dear Mr. President: Washington, D. C. June 16, 1917.
  I believe Congress is thoroughly in accord with the proposals of the Administration to provide adequate legislative machinery to deal promptly and effectively with the food problem. I join with you in feeling that the vital question of this hour is to provide means to marshal the full resources of this nation in the way of food and forage, and make it count in our industrial and military preparedness and in the early triumph of ourselves and our allies in the casue [cause] of democracy. The evils of waste, extortion and hoarding must be eliminated not only in the interest of our army in the field and of our allies but in the interest also of the great body of American wage-earners who must be relied upon to provide the supplies and munitions of war. I am convinced that the effective way to do this is by the flexible method of Executive control through men of recognized experience and ability rather than by the rigid method of legislative restrictions and penalties.
  The business men of the Missouri Valley, even those whose business will be directly affected by such regulations, concede the necessity for such control. The wage-earners are united in demanding it, and the farmers recognize that it cannot result otherwise than as a spur to production. It cannot have escaped your notice, however, that systematic efforts are being made to prejudice various classes of our people against the proposed legislation ostensibly on the ground that it is despotic in character and is intended to be put to unjust and oppressive usage. I am inclined to think that below the surface some of the real objections are that it will curb the special interests and make the rights of the people paramount, and that it will not lend itself to the ordinary uses of politics.
  I am quite satisfied that the people will understand that the

whole system has been initiated and will be conducted in the white light of public opinion, and that it must and can justify itself by its results in this important national crisis. In view of the fact, however, that a special effort has been made in the central West to forestall by attack and misrepresentation the benefits of any adequate method of food control, I should be very glad, if possible, to have a word from you to our people on the subject.

With kindest regards, I remain,

Yours very truly,   Wm. P Borland

TLS (WP, DLC).

From the White House Staff

The White House.

Memorandum for the President: June 16, 1917

Senator Gore telephones that the Senate Committee on Agriculture at its meeting this morning decided to report out at once without amendment and without recommendation the Lever Food Bill.[1] The bill will be reported to the Senate today, but under the rules it will have to go over until Monday before it can be taken up for discussion. This, he says, is in accordance with the wishes of the President as expressed to him.

The Senator did not understand whether the President desired the Food Bill substituted for the Newlands preferential shipment bill as the unfinished business and would like to have advice on this.

T MS (WP, DLC).

[1] That is, H.R. 4961. The revised Lever bill had been changed to give the President broad authority to carry out its provisions and to delegate its administration to individuals or to agencies which he might create. For a good summary of the bill, see 65th Cong., 1st sess., *House Report No. 75.*

Sir William Wiseman to Sir James Eric Drummond[1]

[New York] 16th June 1917

Following message No. 1 for Sir Eric Drummond in a private code. Message begins:

Polk and Caesar [House] have asked me if I have heard from you regarding proposal we discussed of sending special agents to Russia.

Caesar understood that you would put proposal before proper person in London and advise him through me of result.

On this side the proposal is known only to Ajax [Wilson] Caesar Janus [Lansing] and Polk. It has not been mentioned to Plato [Spring Rice].

It appears that certain reports from Root as to Euclids [Germany's] intrigues in Russia have made Ajax anxious to try the scheme as soon as possible.

Remus [The United States Government] has paid over seventy five thousand dollars to me. Will you place an equal amount to my credit at Morgans here.

I will arrange to submit reports regarding Russian scheme to Caesar.

Shall I also send you detailed reports or will periodical reports as to general progress suffice.

I shall of course not report to Caesar or anyone here as to methods employed but only as to results.   W.[2]

T telegram (W. Wiseman Papers, CtY).
  [1] Hereinafter, referred to as Sir Eric Drummond. He was, at this time, Private Secretary to Balfour.
  [2] The reply to this telegram was E. Drummond to W. Wiseman, June 19, 1917, T telegram (W. Wiseman Papers, CtY). Drummond reported that the Foreign Office was "entirely in favour" of sending special agents to Russia but much preferred that the United States handle the matter alone. "Dual control is difficult," he continued, "and we feel it would be better that we should not in any way appear even unofficially."

From Edward Mandell House

Dear Governor: Magnolia, Massachusetts. June 17, 1917.

This war, I think, can be won in one of two ways. It must either be by artillery or by superior air craft. It seems as if the maximum has been reached in the artillery branch. Anyway, we are not prepared, and cannot be for a long time, to compete with the other belligerents in artillery.

We can, however, overwhelm the enemy by superiority in the air. It is our one chance of putting the finishing touches on the war in the Spring of 1918. We can do to Germany more than she is doing to the Allies through her submarines.

I have gone into this matter exhaustively, not only through my experience on the other side, but I have discussed it in detail with General Bridges and other members of the British and French Missions and also with our own people including many fliers who have seen service in France.

Unless the war is to drag along indefinitely we must do something original and radical.

Secretary Baker, through General Squier, has an admirable organization started. What it now needs is assurance from you that you desire the thing done on the biggest scale possible. If you will give the word, and will stand for an appropriation of one billion dollars, the thing is done.

England, I am told, spent a billion last year on her air service. We can do three times as much with the same amount, because we have their mistakes to profit by, and because our industrial conditions are peculiarly fitted for the building of air craft. Their construction will not in any way interfere with our other preparations. This has been carefully looked into.

It is the only expenditure that will be made during the war for war purposes, other than the building of merchantmen, that will be of any lasting benefit to this country or the world.

Page has just sent through the State Department this message to Howard Coffin:

"General Smuts[1] on his own initiative requested me to transmit following message: 'The decision of this war lies in the air and complete victory can only be won by ten or more thousand airplanes with which enemy aircraft can be annihilated. This achievement would be worthy of America, is a contribution which she alone is capable of making, and would enable her to dictate peace.'"

General Smuts, as you know, is a very able, liberal minded, far-seeing man.

I have not written you about this before because I wanted to be satisfied that the suggestion was worthy of your personal consideration and attention.

Affectionately yours,   E. M. House

TLS (WP, DLC).
[1] Jan Christiaan Smuts, Afrikaner general in the Boer war; Minister of Defence of the Union of South Africa, 1910-1919; at this time a lieutenant general in the British army and member of both the Imperial War Cabinet and the British War Cabinet.

To William Patterson Borland

My dear Mr. Borland: [The White House] 18 June, 1917

You are quite right about the Food Administration measure. In my opinion, it is one of the most important and most imperatively necessary of the measures which have been proposed in connection with the war.

A certain disservice has been done the measure by speaking of it as the Food Control Bill. The object of the measure is not to control the food of the country but to release it from the control of speculators and other persons who will seek to make inordinate profits out of it, and to protect the people against the extortions which would result. It seems to me that those who oppose the measure ought very seriously to consider whether they are not playing into the hands of such persons and whether they are not making themselves responsible, should they succeed, for the extraordinary and oppressive price of food in the United States. Foodstuffs will, of course, inevitably be high, but it is possible by perfectly legitimate means to keep them from being unreasonably and oppressively high.

I hope and believe that the Congress will see the measure in this light, and that it will come to an early passage. For time is of the essence. The legislation should be secured by the first of July to make the country safe against the dangers it is meant to guard against.

Cordially and sincerely yours,   Woodrow Wilson

TLS (Letterpress Books, WP, DLC).

To Joseph Patrick Tumulty, with Enclosure

Dear Tumulty: [The White House, June 18, 1917]

Please let Mr. Hoover know that I have exerted my influence to the best of my ability in exactly the direction he here suggests.[1]

The President.

TL (WP, DLC).
[1] Wilson had conferred with Senators Martin, Gore, Hollis, and Kenyon on June 15.

ENCLOSURE

From Herbert Clark Hoover

Dear Mr. President: Washington June 15 1917.

Senator Kenyon informs me that he believes great expedition could be accomplished with the Food Bill in the Senate by the introduction of the Lever Bill at once from the Senate Agricultural Committee to the floor of the Senate as the Senate measure. I understand from him that the Committee, owing to its internal divisions, would only be likely to do this "by request" and that the request would need come from yourself. If it were done it would place the Food Bill in front of the discussion on the Revenue Bill and would probably save a month or two in time.

I am.   Your obedient servant,   Herbert Hoover

TLS (WP, DLC).

To Franklin Knight Lane

My dear Mr. Secretary: [The White House] 18 June, 1917

I know, not only from the enclosed telegram[1] but from other sources, how serious the situation which this telegram refers to has become, and I would very much like your advice as to the means of relieving the situation, if there be any, and relieving the state without going too far in opening the door to those who have been trying to get a foothold in the oil fields in a way we cannot approve or sanction.[2]

        Cordially and faithfully yours,   Woodrow Wilson

TLS (Letterpress Books, WP, DLC).
    [1] G. McNab to WW, June 15, 1917.
    [2] Wilson wrote the same letter, *mutatis mutandis*, to Daniels and Gregory on June 18.

From Newton Diehl Baker

Dear Mr. President: Washington. June 18, 1917.

Mr. Justice Brandeis has spent two evenings talking with me about the general labor situation throughout the country and feels very strongly that, as our munitions contracting business, both on our own account and that of the Allies, increases in volume, very special arrangements will have to be made to prevent the labor conditions from being lost sight of in the agitation for hurried quantity production.

Justice Brandeis, as you may know, has determined to remain in Washington over the summer so as to be available for any help he can give to any of us who are dealing with labor problems. He has kept himself pretty well informed of the workings of the advisory committees of the Council of National Defense.

I am writing this note merely to suggest that, if you want a disinterested view of the whole situation from a man who is thinking hard and seeing it all from the outside, I feel very sure that the Justice would be glad to come to you at any time you cared to see him.[1]

        Respectfully yours,   Newton D. Baker

TLS (WP, DLC).
    [1] There is no record of a meeting between Wilson and Brandeis before August 29.

From Josephus Daniels

My dear Mr. President: Washington. June 18, 1917.

I notice in the papers this morning the question raised about the price that ought to be paid for steel plates, etc., for the steel ships that are being built by the Shipping Board. You no doubt saw the statement last week of the abnormal profits and absurdly large dividends which the steel people were declaring. I feel that these people should be required to furnish steel for these ships at a reasonable profit. What is a reasonable profit? Will you permit the suggestion that the Government should order the steel plates, etc., from the companies who make them, at a reasonable price, the reasonable price to be fixed by the Trade Commission?

You will recall my telling you about the various interviews we had before we obtained steel plates for the Navy. The Steel Committee, of which Judge Gary was chairman, held a meeting of the Steel Institute in New York and decided that in view of the fact that they could sell the plates, etc., for five, six, and even seven cents under the abnormal markets created by demands from this country and abroad, the Navy ought to pay 3.50. I wrote back and told them that we could not pay this price, because we had only paid 1.70 a year and a half ago, which gave them a good profit, and that they themselves had sold these identical plates to us in the present year for 2.90. They held another meeting and agreed to 3.30; and then you will recall Mr. Farrell, President of the Steel Corporation, came to Washington and agreed to give the Navy these plates for the ships authorized by Congress at three cents. We discussed the matter in Cabinet, and you indicated that my contention for 2.90 was right. I returned to the Department immediately after the meeting of the Cabinet and made an agreement for 2.90.[1] Three cents gives a large margin of profit. I am recalling your attention to this transaction in the Navy Department, thinking you might like to have these facts before final action is taken in the very big contract to be placed for the merchant ships.

In connection with the above, I may add that during the last week I have been unable to secure what Redfield, Wilson and I thought was a fair price for coal. I gave the order for it at a price to be fixed, and the Trade Commission is now, at my request, working to ascertain the cost of coal so that in fixing a reasonable profit we may have a correct basis. I have also given a like order as to oil, and the Trade Commission is investigating the cost of oil. In my own opinion it will be necessary to pursue this course with reference to all the larger items which must be bought by the Government, or some other course having relation to the cost of production.

Sincerely yours,   Josephus Daniels

TLS (WP, DLC).
  [1] See the extract from the Diary of Josephus Daniels printed at April 6, 1917, Vol. 41.

An Address and a Reply[1]

[June 19, 1917]

[Radcliffe][2] On behalf of the commission, I want simply to express our very deep appreciation of your courtesy and kindness in granting us this interview with you today. Dr. Chapman[3] has already assured you of the support of the church, which you knew. Before any action was taken by the General Assembly, one of the functions assigned to this commission has been that of assisting, in every way possible, the President of the United States with the prosecution of this war. Those are the phrases in the memorial adopted at the commission meeting this morning. It has adopted a program—quite a large one. The commission is composed of about 160 of the selected men of our Presbyterian Church,[4] many of whom are present here today.

We propose, Mr. President, to go throughout the country, and, in the Providence of God, our Moderator is able to give his entire time and counsel to the continuing work of this commission, holding meetings in all the cities of our country, and holding meetings in the rural districts, because we know in our Presbyterian constituencies some conception of the great principles, as outlined by yourself, which have led America into this war, [are not understood] and [we want] to get our people into line with the splendid idealism that you have announced as the great purpose and ideal of America.

These meetings will be addressed by Dr. Chapman and by other speakers selected by a committee of this commission, with the one great purpose of quickening the interest of the Christian people of America in the great purpose for which America is standing under your leadership.

In addition, we are asking very earnestly of you and of the government that there should be a day of prayer, or days of prayer, designated by yourself or others, one you might select for that purpose, in order that the Christian people of America may be brought to realize our utter dependence upon God and upon His grace and power to make successful our army and our navy in this great contest. We are prepared to relate the entire Presbyterian Church to these services of prayer and, in addition to that, Mr. President, we are very anxious, for the boys who are going forth from our homes and from our churches with such a clear sense of the purposes to which you are calling them, that they may be protected against the dangers and the temptations which are incident to the military spirit and the establishment of that spirit, the establishment of such a wide zone around all our training camps as would ease them from the temptations that would naturally befall them where a great company of boys are. And we are prepared, through our committee, to do what we can to cooperate with you and with the government in this purpose, backing you to the very last of the ability and strength of the Presbyterian Church and in the country through other committees.

We are going to cooperate with the Young Men's Christian Association and other agencies in being in most of the camps in every way possible, and, then, we are endeavoring to fire the interest of all Presbyterian ministers, especially, and, incidentally, all of the residents in the vicinity of the training camps, in the welfare of the boys—their physical and intellectual and moral and spiritual welfare—asking our people to open their homes to these boys that they may be received in their homes at times when they are at leisure and, through our churches, giving them that social spirit and life that will make them more efficient for the service.

These are the bare outlines, Mr. President, of some of the plans our commission has. We are ready to spend money. We are ready to give our money and our bonds, in saying to the commission, "Today you can have our securities to use in every way that may be required in this service."

Mr. President, we would be delighted to have from you any suggestion that you may make to us as to any way in which we can help to make possible the realization of the high ideals and purposes that you have.

[Wilson] Mr. Moderator and gentlemen: I am sure I need not express my appreciation of this visit and of the spirit and plans which have prompted it. That appreciation is very profound. I doubt whether I can give you suggestions that are more fertile than those which have come to you without intimation from me. The truth is that, in this tremendous undertaking, I am borrowing all the plans I can borrow, and I am delighted to be supported and supplemented by so splendid a body as this, and by plans such as have been outlined.

It is a singular thing to draw a church into the support of a war, and yet I feel with you that this is a war which any great spiritual body can support, because I believe if ever a nation purged its heart of improper motives in a war, this nation has purged its heart, and that, if there ever was a war which was meant to supply new foundations for what is righteous and true and of good report, it is this war.

Now, as for the things that a church can do, the thing that it can best do—and that you evidently have in mind—is to constantly interpret the spirit of our actions and to see to it that there is no touch of those things which have brought this war to so intolerably low a level in the methods employed, in the passions excited, in the things engendered which I feel it will take more than one generation to eradicate and destroy. Because, as I have repeatedly said on other occasions, we are fighting, not people, but a system—one of the most hateful systems that has ever been built up into strength by the mistaken plans of men. And if we can keep that constantly in mind, that what threatens the world is not the aggression of any great nation but the aggression of a system which has been imposed upon a great nation, we shall assist properly to interpret this war. And, after all, blood is the necessary purchase price for almost everything that is precious—blood either literally or figuratively.

And I feel that, so far as I myself am concerned, whereas I tried to keep this nation out of war, I can now say with a clear conscience about the war that it was necessary that we should enter it. It was inevitable that we should enter it.

It heartens me, therefore, very much, gentlemen, that a body of men like yours, reaching a great spiritual community, should come to give me this word of cheer and of sustenance. This is the clearinghouse for difficulties—this office—and, therefore, anything that brings me a wealth of additional strength, like a visit of this sort, is more than welcome and cheers me more than I can say.

May I not assume this attitude towards the offers that you have made? I can't now use or know how to use half the fine instrumentalities that have been put at my disposal, but, from time to time, I shall see channels of employment which I can avail myself of, and I shall rejoice to feel that there is this great body that I can turn to for some of the most fundamental service that can be rendered.

I thank you with all my heart for this visit and for your help.[5]

JRT transcript (WC, NjP) of CLSsh (C. L. Swem Coll., NjP).
[1] The 129th General Assembly of the Presbyterian Church in the United

States of America, which met in Dallas, Texas, adopted, on May 22, a resolution creating a National Service Commission which was instructed "to make formal offer to the Government of the United States of the services of the Presbyterian Church" in the present emergency. The commission was further instructed "to exert its utmost influence to secure Governmental action that shall protect this country from the dangers arising within the nation out of the liquor traffic and of commercialized vice, to safeguard the morals of our young men and young women, and to call upon all ministers and other teachers and leaders to set before the youth of our land the high duty of sobriety and chastity." The commission was also to deliver to the President the following message:

"We pledge to you our support in holding the American people to the high idealism with which we entered this war, and to the keeping of our hearts free from hate and from revenge.

"We are heartily grateful for the action already taken by the National Government in creating a zone around the training camps from which the saloon and other incentives to immorality are excluded.

"Convinced that war, in itself, as a method of settling international disputes is irrational, inhuman and unchristian, and that it must finally be abolished by the spiritual force of international good will, we appeal to you to use your great office to secure an early but honorable peace, and that when the time comes to end the war, in harmony with the principles you have laid down, you help to secure such terms of peace as shall prepare the way for an organization of the world that will make war impossible." *Minutes of the General Assembly of the Presbyterian Church in the United States of America*, New Series, Vol. XVII, August 1917 (Philadelphia, 1917), pp. 156-57.

[2] The Rev. Dr. Wallace Radcliffe, pastor of the New York Avenue Presbyterian Church in Washington, who brought the group to the White House.

[3] The Rev. Dr. John Wilbur Chapman, Moderator of the General Assembly; Executive Secretary of the General Assembly's Committee on Evangelistic Work since 1903.

[4] The commission consisted of eighty-one clergymen and eighty laymen. For a complete list, see *ibid.*, p. 448.

[5] There were brief reports of this meeting in *The Presbyterian*, LXXXVII (June 28, 1917), 7-8, and in the *Washington Post*, June 20, 1917. The latter report said that Wilson urged his listeners "to give their support to the maintenance of lofty ideals among the people and in keeping the hearts of Americans free from the spirit of hate or revenge."

To Josephus Daniels

My dear Mr. Secretary: The White House 19 June, 1917

Thank you very much for your letter about the steel prices. I hardly know how to spell the word!

Faithfully yours,   Woodrow Wilson

TLS (J. Daniels Papers, DLC).

From Bernard Mannes Baruch, with Enclosure

My dear Mr. President: Washington, D. C. June 19th, 1917.

The letter of Mr. Hoffstot is very much to the point.

The establishment of a Central Purchasing Agency with a committee with priority powers as outlined in my diagram to you would meet and was meant to meet exactly the conditions complained of by him. This is only one of many complaints. Until there has been a thorough re-organization, which perhaps the people are not yet ready for and would not permit, you will hear more and more of this thing in each and every industry and trade.

The success of any scheme or plan depends more upon the method and wisdom of execution that [than] upon the plan itself. There are many who are very adept in telling what can or should be done or criticising what is done, but there are few who can do it.

It is not generally realized that the problem, which faces us in steel and other things is the same as the one that is facing us in food products. Indeed I think the steel situation is the most serious of all our products but it is not felt because it does not effect the stomach.

The less necessary will have to give way to the more necessary and in steel as in other things, an allotment of the production must be made to those who can make the greatest use of it for the winning of the war and the benefit of the general community. No competition for any product should be permitted to interfere with this purpose or to cause the unjustifiable high prices now prevailing. I am firmly convinced that much of this is caused by hysteria.

If you desire you can reply to these complaints by referring them all to me and I will endeavor to satisfy them by answering as below. If this is not satisfactory, I would suggest your replying to Mr. Hoffstot along the same lines:

"That the authorities were well aware that when they withdrew from the steel industry, steel and steel products necessary for its immediate needs, there would be a derangement or dislocation of the steel business and the consequent supply to the consumers of steel. The state of War necessitated this.

A readjustment will have to take place either through the mutual efforts of the producers and consumers of steel or through some governmental action, which this condition will necessitate. Patience and sacrifice will be required of all during this readjustment.

The whole subject is being given serious thought. It is well understood that the price of iron and steel as well as many other products are inordinately high and a readjustment must be made all along the line, but made with extreme care."

Very sincerely yours,   Bernard M Baruch

Please do not hesitate to shift anything on to me.   BMB

TLS (WP, DLC).

From Frank Norton Hoffstot[1]

Sir: Washington, D. C., June 14, 1917.

Believing that it is of the utmost importance at the present time that the country immediately obtain a maximum output of steel and steel products at prices which do not reflect the present deranged condition of business and secure a prompt delivery thereof, I take the liberty of submitting for your consideration the following suggestion.

It is my firm belief that the present high prices of most commodities are caused, to a large extent, by the failure to secure transportation of both the raw and finished product and, further, by the unscientific method which now obtains in the placing of orders. It is unnecessary to waste your time with setting forth the deficiency of cars and the consequent almost paralyzation of deliveries. This has been a matter of common knowledge for some months past and the condition has been over and over again forecasted by railroad officials, by reason of the present shortage of rolling stock and terminals even for normal times. I would respectfully, however, point in support of this proposition, to two clippings taken from this morning's "New York Times."[2]

I desire to respectfully draw your attention to the serious results that flow from the present unscientific ordering of steel and steel products. At this time, while the steel companies are loyally and energetically making their best efforts to produce as large an output as the transportation facilities will permit, that output so produced has been so allotted by reason of the lack of the orderly methods which would result from the action of a centralized Board with adequate power, that the car business is now in a serious state. The Company I represent is now only able to produce about thirty-five per cent of its normal output, this by reason of the steel long since ordered being diverted to other uses. As a result, our organization is being impaired and our efficiency diminished and yet we are being severely criticized by the railroads for our failure to deliver. They pointing out to us that we must get steel because the producer must see that cars are necessary to carry plate shapes, angles and other products.

The producer when reproached for his failure to deliver as required, says he has been ordered by Washington to do thus and so. When we attempt to get relief in Washington we find no Board has the power of allottment of steel products.

I am confidently of the opinion if a scientific method of allottment were made by a Board clothed with sufficient powers, all industries would get nearly their normal requirements. I am confident that there is ample capacity to secure a reasonably near normal output if proper allottment were made. I am confident such a course would immediately result in a considerable fall in prices, yet the fair profits necessary for a proper business operation would remain.

Therefore, I respectfully request that you use your offices in causing to be created a Priority Board with power to, among other things, allot the deliveries of steel and various other products from producers. Such a Board would have the loyal and patriotic support of every producer and would inject into the present deranged steel industry, a sound business condition that would appeal to every interest. Furthermore, such a Board would be instrumental in causing the products of steel, including ships, cars, bridge material, to be not only manufactured quicker and in greater quantities but also delivered sooner than is possible under the present headless system.

Very respectfully,　F N Hoffstot

TLS (WP, DLC).
   1 President of the Pressed Steel Car Co. of Pittsburgh.
   2 "Roads Want Federal Aid" and "Pig Iron Up to $55 in Rush for Steel," *New York Times*, June 14, 1917. The first article detailed a proposal by Fairfax Harrison, president of the Southern Railway System and chairman of the Railroads' War Board, that the federal government alleviate the critical shortage of rolling stock by investing in 50,000 to 75,000 railway cars, which the railroads would then use as they used privately owned cars. The second article discussed the rapid rise in the prices of both pig iron and scrap steel in the preceding two weeks, as well as the increasing demands of the United States Government and the Allied governments for finished steel products. The article emphasized that the lack of railroad equipment to handle ore, coal, and coke was a basic cause of the problems of the steel manufacturers.

From Newton Diehl Baker

Dear Mr. President:　　　　　　　　Washington. June 19, 1917.

I beg to quote the following cablegram received from Governor-General Harrison:

"Please offer to the President specifically one infantry division as National Guard unit in accordance with tables of organization of 1914, including changes and as modified by national defense act with reduction or omission of artillery and cavalry as may be desired, additional personnel organized as may be desired, an aggregate of 25,000; organization rapidly progressing, to be completed by September 30th. An early acceptance is desirable as quality of personnel will be improved when it is known that foreign service is certain. A majority of officers and men have had previous service, volunteers, scouts, or constabulary organizations."

This cablegram is indicative of the fine spirit of the Filipino people which has been shown in many ways since the entry of the United States into the present war.

The War Department has submitted to the Senate Committee on Military Affairs the draft of a provision, which, if enacted into law, would authorize you to call into the service of the United States a division of Filipino troops which is now being organized by the Governor General in accordance with an act of the Philippine Legislature.

I am,   Very sincerely,   Newton D. Baker

TLS (WP, DLC).

From Edward Mandell House, with Enclosure

Dear Governor: Magnolia, Massachusetts. June 19, 1917.

Here is a letter from Sir Horace in which he says some nice things about you.

And this reminds me that you charmed Northcliffe in your few minutes talk with him the other day. I have heard from many directions of his enthusiastic praise of you. You seem to have been a revelation to him.

I am glad you treated him so kindly for he has shown a desire to work in harmony with everyone.

Affectionately yours,   E. M. House

TLS (WP, DLC).

ENCLOSURE

Sir Horace Plunkett to Edward Mandell House

My dear Colonel House: Dublin. 1st June, 1917.

I hope to see Arthur Balfour when he returns and then I shall, very likely, write you pretty fully on the subjects we have discussed together in recent years.

I want now to send you my heartiest congratulations on the magnificent part the President is playing in the great world struggle for peace in our time and after. I have not yet been about in England but have met a good many Englishmen. I think it is not too much to say that, in the British regard, the President now occupies the foremost place among the world's statesmen. What a marvellous effect this one individual is having upon the life of the hundred million people who have chosen him as their leader, and how small all the political machinery looks in the national decisions compared with this one man's will.

Much as I regret not being in the United States at such an amazingly interesting crisis, I realize that I was bound to come back to my own country. I am inclined to think that the Convention[1] we are about to hold will get the Irish question out of the way, so far as it is a disturbance to the world at large, for some years to come. I should, however, speak with more confidence if the Government would only make up their minds and let us know what they intend to do about the composition and chairmanship of this body, and also the precise Terms of Reference to it.

You will be glad to hear that my health is steadily improving and I hope, before long, to be in first-rate working form.

Believe me,   Yours sincerely,   Horace Plunkett.

TCL (WP, DLC).

[1] In a letter sent to the leaders of various Irish parties on May 16, David Lloyd George had suggested the possibility of "a convention of Irishmen of all parties for the purpose of producing a scheme of Irish self-government." Enough favorable replies were received to make it possible for Lloyd George to announce in the House of Commons on May 21 that the government intended to summon a convention of representative Irishmen which would prepare and submit to Parliament a scheme for the government of Ireland within the empire. As it turned out, ninety-five representatives of various nationalist and unionist groups assembled at Trinity College, Dublin, on July 25 and Sir Horace, himself, was elected chairman. See Robert Brendan McDowell, *The Irish Convention, 1917-18* (London, 1970), pp. 76-77, 103-104.

Sir William Wiseman to Sir Eric Drummond

[New York] June 19, 1917.

Following for Sir Eric Drummond from Horodyski.

Secretary Baker told me last Thursday most confidentially that the President and War Department are very much in favor of National Polish Army here and State Department has been asked to find out in London and Paris some way to make it a legal international affair. Your co-operation in hastening the final decision most desirable as told already my people getting impatient further delay would prove fatal politically and also strategically on account of serious troubles and unrest in Poland. Stop. There is undeniable evidence that French Government approached by some Polish leaders is planning formation of a provisional Polish Government which certainly will meet with the approval of Washington for it will provide a responsible institution capable of negotiating loans necessary for army. In principle it would be a great advantage because it would consolidate forces and simplify action. The difficulty, however, is very serious. Such Government must be strong consequently very popular in the whole country; it must consist of representatives of all three parts and most important political parties of Poland. Its formation exclusively of members of the national democratic party in spite of excellent organization and services rendered by that body to the Allies Cause would be positively injurious. Stop. Inclusion of DMO[W]SKI and especially SEYDA would be sufficient. A national democratic government headed by DMO[W]SKI besides provoking inevitable protests on the part of opponents both in Poland and here would also meet with most violent opposition from the element now extremely powerful in international politics in America, France and Russia. The Jews would fight it desperately therefore I strongly advise you to use your influence and prevent the formation of Provisional Polish Government of such a dangerous uniformity which will lead to complete failure.[1] Stop. As all parties have to be included I suggest that you inform your Ambassador Petrograd to get in contact with Polish leaders in Russia: SZEBEKO, ALEXANDER LEDINCKI, STANISLAS LOPACINSKI LADISLAS GRABSKI COUNT LADISLAS SOBANSKI[2] in order to decide whom they would select as two delegates to take part in the proposed Government; further give instructions to RUMBOLD[3] to inform SEYDA about absolute necessity of inducing either PRINCE WITOLD CZARTORYSKI[4] or COUNT LEON PININSKI[5] to accept the presidency of the proposed Government any of them would be accepted by all the Poles. Stop. As the creation of that Provisional Government will undoubtedly take considerable time and the Polish Army from America is of primary importance not only to the Poles but still much more to the Allies it is of absolute necessity that the Entente Governments should at once address a note to President Wilson asking him to issue an appeal to the Poles calling upon them to enlist in National Polish Army created by the United States of America and the Entente Powers and nominate the Commander. The Financing of that enterprise ought to be accomplished by the Allied Governments in common as a loan advanced to the future State of Poland which loan will be formally accepted by the proposed Provisional Government when definitely established.

Kindly cable at once the stand you will take in the matter and answer my question concerning technicalities of the Army also please ask Gregory[6] to inform DMO[W]SKI I am awaiting his answer to my letter and remind ALMA TADEMA[7] send immediately translations encyclopedia.   W

T telegram (W. Wiseman Papers, CtY).
  [1] Dmowski was well known as a reactionary and an anti-Semite.
  [2] Persons in this group who can be identified are Ignacy Szebeko, a member of the Polish State Council; Aleksander Lednicki, influential lawyer in Moscow, chairman of the joint committees of the Polish associations in Russia; Wladyslaw Grabski, economist, member of the Russian Duma, 1905-1917, Prime Minister of Poland, 1920, 1923-1925; and Count Wladyslaw Sobanski, later the representative of the Polish National Committee in London.
  [3] That is, Sir Horace Rumbold.
  [4] Prince Witold Czartoryski, scion of a Polish-Lithuanian noble family influential in Polish affairs since the fifteenth century.
  [5] Unidentified.
  [6] John Duncan Gregory, a clerk in the British Foreign Office.
  [7] Miss Laurence Alma-Tadema, British author and translator.

To Robert Langton Douglas

My dear Mr. Douglas: [The White House] 20 June, 1917

My delay in replying to the generous suggestion of the Board of Governors of the National Gallery of Ireland, joined in by the Lord Mayor and the Corporation of Dublin, has been due entirely to my doubt as to whether I could at this particular time afford Mr. Sargent sufficient opportunity to paint my portrait.

The suggestion of the Board of Governors and of the Lord Mayor and Corporation has gratified me very deeply. I would be very proud indeed to have a portrait of myself by so eminent an artist as Mr. Sargent placed in the National Gallery of Ireland, and I am sincerely desirous of affording Mr. Sargent an opportunity to make the portrait. I am sorry to say I shall have to delay the decision in order to see whether after the adjournment of the present session of the Congress I may not command sufficient leisure to make the necessary arrangements for sittings.

With warm appreciation and many apologies for my delay in replying,

Cordially and sincerely yours,   Woodrow Wilson

TLS (Letterpress Books, WP, DLC).

To Thomas Watt Gregory

[The White House]

My dear Mr. Attorney General: 20 June, 1917

Here are some things[1] which I think you will find pertinent to the actions of the department. I would like very much to "get" these fellows.

Always   Faithfully yours,   Woodrow Wilson

TLS (Letterpress Books, WP, DLC).
[1] The Editors have been unable to find them.

From Walter Hines Page

London, June 20, 1917.

6503. PERSONAL VERY CONFIDENTIAL FOR THE SECRETARY AND THE PRESIDENT.

I have hesitated to telegraph more about the submarine situation but the condition so increases in danger that in addition to Sims' reports to Navy Department I cannot refrain from sending the following facts. The British reports are incomplete and to a degree misleading. They fail to report tonnage. Of course they do not include the other Allies' or neutral vessels. The British alone last week lost 194,000 tons. The destruction is thought to exceed merchant vessel building in all countries. Rate of destruction is therefore a cumulative net gain for the enemy. The British naval and military authorities while partially concealing rate of destruction from the public view the situation with utmost gravity. The only known method of reducing loss is to provide, if possible, enormous anti-submarine patrol far larger than any now in existence or in sight or hitherto thought of and thus force submarines from attacks on shipping to attacks on anti-submarine craft. Would it be possible for our Government to send over hundreds of armed sea-going tugs, yachts, and any kind of swift small ships to supplement the existing inadequate patrol? Unless some such help come from some quarter naval supplies and material for the British Army and Navy will soon fall below requirements and the present fighting efficiency [efficiency] be impaired. Certain kinds of such material, such as lubricating and fuel oils will be exhausted before a serious food shortage occurs as time goes on. The need of safe transportation of our army and its needs will greatly increase required shipping and even with greatly expected output of our shipyards the total tonnage afloat will constantly decrease. This critical situation demands the fullest and most prompt action possible. It seems to me to be the key to any possible early end of the war. It may well be that the issue of the war is itself involved unless such aid come. The fighting power of the allies will inevitably be lowered within a few months and be very seriously impaired before we have an army to come and to be maintained in the face of constantly increasing dangers. The Germans are making such positive gains by submarines that they can afford to withdraw gradually in France and to hold on until the Allied fighting power is thus weakened. It is the most serious situation that has confronted the Allies since the battle of the Marne.   Page.

T telegram (WP, DLC).

From Josephus Daniels

My dear Mr. President: Washington. June 20, 1917.

I am in receipt of your letter and copy of a telegram sent you by Mr. Gavin McNab of San Francisco.

He is mistaken in supposing that I had opposed any adjustment of this question. As a matter of fact, during the last session of Congress, I expressed a willingness to accept a compromise which would have partially relieved the situation.

The land claimed by the Navy in Navy Petroleum Reserve No. 2, the one in dispute, represents less than 9% of the proven oil land in California, and contains less than 5¾ per cent. of the total estimated oil content of the California fields and about 28¼ per cent. of the estimated total content of all the unpatented withdrawn oil lands in California. I have never opposed the opening up of the withdrawn oil lands outside of the Naval Petroleum Reserves, and in my opinion such a course would relieve the situation, but the claimants of these lands are in my opinion taking advantage of the situation to demand the opening up of this Reserve because it is a very valuable field.

This morning I had a conference with the Federal Trade Commission regarding the oil question and explained to them that there was a very strong effort being made by people in California to have the Government consent to the taking over of these lands at a small rental by parties who had entered upon them, some illegally and some through dummies. I told them that I was greatly troubled because it is alleged that there are no other fields in America to furnish the oil we need. At my request the Commission is making an investigation of the possible supply of oil from other districts. As soon as I receive their report I will furnish it to you.

I am to have a conference this afternoon with Mr. Bedford,[1] Chairman of the Oil Committee of the Council of National Defense, regarding the supply of oil for the Navy.

Sincerely yours,   Josephus Daniels

TLS (WP, DLC).

[1] Alfred Cotton Bedford, president of the Standard Oil Co. of New Jersey.

Robert Lansing to Joseph Patrick Tumulty, with Enclosure

My dear Mr. Tumulty: Washington June 20, 1917.

It affords me pleasure to enclose, for the President's information, a translation of a note by which the Brazilian Ambassador has communicated to the Department the reply of the President of Brazil to the President's recent telegram congratulating Brazil on its attitude in support of the United States in the war with Germany.

I am, my dear Mr. Tumulty,

Very truly yours,   Robert Lansing

TLS (WP, DLC).

E N C L O S U R E

Domicio da Gama to Robert Lansing

Mr. Secretary of State,   Washington, June 14, 1917

By order of my Government I have the honor to transmit to your Excellency with a request that you be pleased to cause to be delivered to President Wilson the reply to His Excellency's telegram to the President of the United States of Brazil. It reads as follows:

I acknowledge with thanks to your Excellency the memorable words in which, in the name of the people and government of the United States, you congratulate Brazil on its frank attitude at this historical time. In again standing by the side of the United States at this time, Brazil remained true to its political and diplomatic traditions of continental solidarity, and, like the great American nation, we are not moved to take that step by either hatred or selfish interest, but by international judicial order, nay, by the defence of those principles which, if at issue or in peril in the Old World, must find their shelter and equipoise among the free peoples of the two Americas. Brazil has resolved all its foreign questions, cherishes no ambition in the present, suffered nothing in the past and prizes as a great boon the friendship of the United States. More than any outward manifestation, no occasion could like this one of uncertainty and strife bring so close together the hearts of Brazil and of the United States.

(Signed)   Wenceslau Braz.

I avail myself of this opportunity to reiterate to Your Excellency, Mr. Secretary of State, the assurances of my highest consideration.   Domicio da Gama.

TCL (WP, DLC).

From Newton Diehl Baker

Dear Mr. President: Washington. June 21 [20], 1917

The Aircraft Production Board created by the Council of National Defense to advise with reference to the possibility of rapidly increased quantity production of aircraft and personnel for aircraft work, has among its members the foremost experts in aircraft production in the country, and has for some time been working in immediate association with General Squier of the Army, Admiral Taylor of the Navy and the air personnel of both Departments. The work of the Board has been under constant inspection of the War College Division of the General Staff, and the upshot of their work can be said to be that they have reached the conclusion that perhaps America's most speedy and effective contribution to the Allied cause from a military point of view will be the complete and unquestioned supremacy of the air.

For a variety of reasons the contribution of an army to the French front from America, at all proportionate to the forces now there from France and England, will be a matter of long delay. But it is believed that in a very much shorter time, under the plans which have been matured, a practically overwhelming contribution to the Allied supremacy in the air can be made. Our peculiar opportunity here arises from the fact that in our country suitable personnel ought to be found in much greater abundance and also because our industrial resources are not so exclusively demanded for forms of military production as they are in both France and England. The program, therefore, worked out involves the immediate training of large numbers of air men and the immediate production of large numbers of air machines.

Recent appropriations have been generous as compared with earlier ones to this new service. There are now established in eight colleges of the country preliminary training courses in which, in all, at present about 800 young men are receiving theoretical preparatory training. This course is eight weeks in length and will be repeated with fresh bodies of students continuously. There are in process of construction four large training fields with others projected to which these students will come from the collegiate schools for training in actual flight. After four months' residence in these training camps, the graduates will be ready for a completion of their training in France under actual battle conditions and with combat machines.

The production end involves large industrial activity in this country with certain finishing processes carried on in France, so that the latest improvements in aircraft can be installed upon the machines and use can be made of the experienced mechanics of France who have been working since the beginning of the war in this art. In order to secure a diversion of adequate industrial capacity from present occupations to this new production, a continuing program is necessary, as a long period is needed to revamp an industrial establishment and supply it with the necessary special tools, jigs, dies, etc. for quantity production of a new device. It may, therefore, well be that should the war terminate before a completion of the program, some part of the expenditure involved would turn out to be unnecessary, but that, of course, is true of all productions of war materials.

The total amount proposed to be asked from Congress for the program involving training fields, personnel, production of training machines, production and arming of combat machines, maintenance in France, repairs and duplication of parts, etc. aggregate $639,000,000. I have gone over the figures with General Squier, General Kuhn[1] and Mr. Coffin and am satisfied that their plan will lead to the immediate and effective speeding up of our contribution to this essential phase of war activity, and I think the General Staff are without dissent in favor of undertaking a program and pressing it rapidly to completion.

The General Staff has had the advantage of constant consultation with the English and French air experts who accompanied their respective missions and remained to work out the details of their proposed work. Before presenting the matter to the two Houses of Congress, I beg leave to submit the matter to you for your approval, which I recommend be given.

Respectfully yours,   Newton D. Baker

TLS (WP, DLC).
[1] Brig. Gen. Joseph Ernst Kuhn, President of the Army War College since December 1916.

From Jessie Woodrow Wilson Sayre

Siasconset Nantucket Island Mass.

Dearest Father,   June 20, 1917

Here we are, all safe and sound, at Siasconset. Our house is cozy and comfortable and we are all recovering from our journey and the transplanting as quickly as might be expected.

We have as yet secured no male protector to take care of me, and Frank will not leave until we do, for of course he respects your advice. So I imagine we shall have a peaceful, happy, lazy, month down here together. My garden is well started and I have been working in it all day, 'cultivating the ground.' It is all a strange language to me, but I hope to have something before I get through. If my spinach grows we shall have enough for one meal!

It was good to see you all, and that happy, quiet, Sunday will linger long in our memories.[1]

Give my love to all the dear ones

Ever devotedly your daughter   Jessie.

ALS (WC, NjP).
[1] The Sayres spent the weekend of June 9-10 at the White House.

Sir William Wiseman to Sir Eric Drummond

[New York] June 20, 1917.

In reply to yours of the 19th I submit following points for your consideration:

1. Caesar [House] seems to have assumed that the matter of joint action was accepted in principle. It is on that basis he explained the scheme to Ajax [Wilson] who has become particularly interested since receiving messages from Root.

2. I do not think they will proceed unless we participate because the scheme depends on help of certain Slavic Societies here with whom Remus [the United States Government] has no means of dealing without me.

3. It is possible that by acting practically as a confidential agent for Remus I might strengthen the understanding with Caesar that in future he will keep us informed of steps taken by Remus in their foreign affairs, which would ordinarily not be a matter of common knowledge to the Government of the two countries.

4. I do not think the question of dual control will be difficult as they will leave everything to me. You may be sure that great

discretion will be used and that Minos [the British government] will not even unofficially appear.

Please consider above points and cable me as soon as possible and if you decide not to participate I will withdraw tactfully. Stop.

Apropos of the general situation Cobb, who is an intimate friend of Ajax and has recently stayed with him, informs me that the regard and admiration of Ajax for Damon [Balfour] is quite remarkable and I submit this should not be forgotten as a factor in any political situation which may arise.

Message ends.   W.

T telegram (W. Wiseman Papers, CtY).

To Newton Diehl Baker

My dear Mr. Secretary: [The White House] 21 June, 1917

I have your letter of yesterday about the production of aircraft and the training of men to operate them, and want to say that I am entirely willing to back up such a programme as you suggest. I hope that you will present it in the strongest possible way to the proper committees of the Congress.

Cordially and sincerely yours,   Woodrow Wilson

TLS (Letterpress Books, WP, DLC).

From Robert Lansing

My dear Mr. President: Washington June 21, 1917.

I have been turning over in my mind in what way we can best utilize the intense longing of the Poles for the restoration of Poland as an independent nation.

It seems to be recognized by all the Allies that Polish independence should be one of the results of the war and that the Poles should as far as possible be segregated into military units so that they would feel their nationality and be inspired to fight for the freedom of their country.

It is my understanding that France has already taken steps to form a skeleton on which to build up a Polish army to fight on the Western front; and that something of a like nature could be organized on the eastern front. This latter plan will require discreet handling because the Russians may be at first loath to release troops already incorporated in the Russian armies, but I think that it can be done by starting with a movement to call

Poles not already in military service to join a Polish army for independence. When this step is taken I believe the separation of the Poles in the Russian armies will follow as a matter of course.

To gain the full benefit of the loyalty of the Poles to their country it seems to me that, in the first place, this government and those of the Allies should announce in separate but identic declarations that they recognize the legitimate nature of Polish desire for self-government and that they purpose to devote their energies to free Poland and restore the nation to full sovereignty, in contradistinction to a nation under the protection or control of any neighboring power.

In the second place, the matter of financing the Polish military establishment is most important. Of course it will have to be done by this country. My suggestion is that a Polish Provisional Government [be] set up in this country, that it be recognized by this Government and the Allied Governments, and that it send diplomatic representatives to all the powers with which it is associated in the war. After formal recognition of this Government of an independent Poland we could legally loan the Government for military purposes the necessary funds secured by Polish bonds underwritten by this country and the Allies.

I have carefully considered the place where the Provisional Government should be located and have come to the conclusion that to avoid all suspicion as to the genuine purpose of this step looking to the rebirth of Poland this country is the only place. Furthermore, in view of the fact that this country will have to supply the money for this enterprise, I believe that the new Government should be where we can keep a watchful eye on the expenditures.

If this plan or one along the same lines meets with your approval, shall I sound the diplomatic representatives of the Allies on the subject?   Faithfully yours,   Robert Lansing.

TLS (SDR, RG 59, 763.72119/673½a, DNA).

From Edward Mandell House, with Enclosure

Dear Governor: Magnolia, Massachusetts. June 21, 1917.

Lincoln Colcord saw Goethals yesterday and he sends me this dispatch this morning. I thought it would be of use to you to know his attitude.

Denman and Goethals are both positive characters and I am

afraid are too much alike to ever work in harmony. Is it not possible to divide their authority so as to avoid conflict?

Affectionately yours,   E. M. House

TLS (WP, DLC).

E N C L O S U R E

Washington, D. C. June 20, 1917.

He said to me "If the Chief thinks I am going to him to argue my case it is a mistake for I am a soldier and do not work that way. An erroneous statement was put out about me here last Monday.[1] I wanted to see the Chief on an entirely different matter from that taken to him by the other man,[2] and they knew this when they put out the statement. That looks bad to me. I shall take up this other matter on Friday and say nothing more. I am waiting to see how the pendulum swings."

Lincoln Colcord.

TC telegram (WP, DLC).

[1] Newspapers reported on June 18 that, on the previous day, Denman had issued a statement to the effect that he would not sign shipbuilding contracts to pay $95 a ton for steel, a price that he called "absurd." The statement was seen as a further challenge to Goethals, one that might force Wilson to decide whether Denman, as president of the Emergency Fleet Corporation, or Goethals, as its general manager, would have authority over the ship-building program. The two men disagreed over procedures for determining prices. The price of steel was tentatively reduced to $56 a ton, subject to adjustment. *Washington Post* and *New York Times*, June 18, 1917. Following a long conference with Wilson on June 18, Denman told reporters that the conference "had nothing to do with the reported differences between myself and Gen. Goethals," and that there was no real difference in their views. "There never has been anything but a smile between us," Denman added; he and Wilson had talked about "U-boats and the need of merchant ships." Goethals had also requested an appointment with Wilson, it was reported, but none would be available until June 22. *Washington Post*, June 19, 1917. For further information on the issues involved, see Joseph Bucklin Bishop and Farnham Bishop, *Goethals: Genius of the Panama Canal* (New York, 1930), pp. 271-370, and William Denman, *Shipping Board Operations. Testimony of William Denman, Esq., First Chairman of the United States Shipping Board, relating to the policies and activities of his administration and reviewing shipping conditions in general . . . December 13, 14, and 15, 1920* (Washington, 1920).

[2] That is, Denman.

From Edward Mandell House

Dear Governor: Magnolia, Massachusetts. June 21, 1917.

Since writing you this morning Mezes has telephoned from New York very much what Colcord wired, except that General

Goethals hopes you will indicate to him tomorrow that he is free to talk with you about his difficulties.

Unless you do, he thinks as your subordinate he ought not to initiate it himself.

Colcord's telegram and Mezes' telephone must have been inspired by the General, and indicate much feeling on the subject.   Affectionately yours,   E. M. House

TLS (WP, DLC).

From William Denman

My dear Mr. President: Washington June 21, 1917.

I was rather taken by surprise this afternoon to hear that the question of the delegation under the commandeering Act[1] was to be taken up within twenty-four hours. I had understood from our last conference that it was to be delayed until after the Food Bill had progressed further in the Senate. I beg of you that this matter be held over until I have had another opportunity to discuss it with you. If the commandeering power with regard to steel ships is to be decided immediately, I beg that it be given to the Corporation,[2] and that the power follow the line of the use of the money indicated in the legislation, namely, through the Corporation.

With regard to the suggestion that we go to the bottom of the wooden ship matter, I am gathering documentary evidence together showing a definite expressed intention to depress wooden ship construction and to discourage it;—this at a time when the rate of destruction by the Germans was three times greater than the highest estimated hope of reproduction of steel vessels. There is, for instance, a stenographic report of General Goethals' instructions to men who would place wooden ship contracts.

Is Colonel House within reach? I have never met him, but I wish I could have his counsel, advice, and a chance to give him all the facts. In any event, we should not commandeer the British steel tonnage, and then abandon our wooden ship program. One of the chief arguments I urged with Mr. Balfour was our intention of going in for non-commercial wooden ships, and I offered this as a pledge of our good faith in taking over all our steel commercial cargo ships on the stocks. I have not seen a copy of General Goethals' proposed scheme of commandeering, and beg that before it is acted upon I have a chance to consult with you concerning it. The General announced at a public meeting in our office here recently that it was intended to commandeer all foreign tonnage, including the British. Perhaps we should consider the question of accepting Mr. Balfour's offer before doing this.

With reference to the attitude of the press on certain phases of the wooden ship controversy, I am inclosing two editorials, one from the New York Times, and the other from the Springfield Republican.[3]

We have only the reports of the sinkings of English vessels for the last two weeks, but considering the total sinkings of all nations in the proportion in which the British sinkings bore to the total in the first two months the rate of sinkings the past fortnight amount to twelve million tons dead weight a year. Our program, including the few wooden ships we intend building, will not give us over four millions of tons in both English and American construction in that time. No matter how long it may take to build wooden ships, even if it were longer than steel, we must have them for supplements to the steel program. The rate of reproduction will then be far behind the rate of destruction.   Very faithfully yours,   William Denman.

TLS (WP, DLC).
[1] The section of the Urgent Military and Naval Deficiency Appropriations Act, approved on June 15, which empowered the President to order and acquire ships and material and, if their owners refused, to take possession of ships and plants, for just compensation.
[2] That is, the Emergency Fleet Corporation.
[3] "A Fine Old Saying," New York Times, June 20, 1917. This editorial referred to a statement by Goethals to the American Iron and Steel Institute on May 25 to the effect that birds were still "nesting in the trees from which the great wooden fleet was to be made." The editorial pointed out that the figure of speech about the trees had been used twice before in American history, in 1814 and in 1862, but not to prove the hopelessness of the American wartime efforts then. In both of these cases, the editorial noted, wooden ships had been built and had served to "illustrate Yankee energy, Yankee dauntlessness, the Yankee scorn for impossibilities."
"The Wooden Ship Controversy," Springfield Republican, May 29, 1917. This editorial said that it was "satisfactory" to know that the shipping board did not intend, because of Goethals' opposition, to drop the construction of wooden ships entirely. The sooner the General was left free to forget wooden ships and give his whole attention to steel ships the better; meanwhile, however, the experiment with wood was "worth pressing with the utmost energy."

From Francis Bowes Sayre, with Enclosure

Dear Father,   New York City [c. June 21, 1917]

I expect to sail for France to help in the Army Y.M.C.A. work a week from next Saturday on the "Touraine" of the French line. Because of your advice I have refused to go until I could secure some mature man to stay with Jessie and the children; I have just succeeded in getting a Dr. Wilson S. Naylor,[1] who has travelled widely, written on Africa, lectured rather extensively, and is at present Professor of Biblical Literature in Lawrence College, of Appleton, Wis. Those who know him speak of him in the highest terms, and, on meeting him, I felt he was just the man for what I want. At present he is working in the Y.M.C.A. offices here; but Mr. Brockman[2] generously promised to lend him for staying with Jessie till Aug. first when Nevin[3] comes. My mother[4] will also be with her through the summer. This satisfies my own mind about Jessie during the three months I will be gone; but more important is the freeing of *your* mind from any anxiety about her. If this arrangement is going to cause you anxiety or worry, dear father, please send me word at once, and I will cancel all my arrangements to go, and understand perfectly. Please do not hesitate.

I took Jessie and the children to Siasconset last Saturday, and there they are most pleasantly established. Little Frank, who had never seen sand before, was at first afraid to walk on it. It was his first experience in a boat, too; he kept asking to get out and walk on the water.

You asked for the name of the man in Williamstown who was heard to utter threats against the children. He is A. H. Rosenburg, living on "Bee Hill Road" (Telephone, Williamstown 68-3). So far as I know he has made no similar threats recently.

If it would not unduly bother you, would you give me a letter of identification (unless for some reason you feel it wiser not to) which I might carry abroad? I would not want to use it except in some emergency; then it might prove a life-saver.

I enclose a copy of the letter Kitchener wrote to his troops. I was wondering whether you had thought of writing a letter to our troops, which would be a letter still finer. So many stirring temptations await our soldiers in France!

I return to Siasconset tomorrow.

With dearest love,   Ever devotedly your son, Frank

ALS (WP, DLC).

[1] Wilson Samuel Naylor.

[2] Fletcher Sims Brockman, associate general secretary of the International Committee of the Y.M.C.A. and of the National War Work Council of the Y.M.C.A.

[3] That is, the Rev. John Nevin Sayre.

[4] Martha Finley Nevin (Mrs. Robert Heysham) Sayre.

ENCLOSURE

COPY OF LORD KITCHENER'S LETTER
TO THE TROOPS ORDERED ABROAD.

"You are ordered abroad as a soldier of the King to help our French comrades against the invasion of a common enemy. You have to perform a task which will need your courage, your energy, your patience. Remember that the honor of the British Army depends upon your individual conduct. It will be your duty not only to set an example of discipline and perfect steadiness under fire, but also to maintain the most friendly relations with those whom you are helping in this struggle. The operations in which you are engaged will, for the most part, take place in a friendly country, and you can do your own country no better service than in showing yourself, in France and Belgium, in the true character of a British soldier.

Be invariably courteous, considerate, and kind. Never do anything likely to injure or destroy property, and always look upon looting as a disgraceful act. You are sure to meet with a welcome and to be trusted; and your conduct must justify that welcome and that trust. Your duty cannot be done unless your health is sound. So keep constantly on your guard against any excesses. In this new experience you may find temptations both in wine and women. You must entirely resist both temptations, and while treating all women with perfect courtesy, you should avoid any intimacy."   Do your duty bravely.
                                Fear God.
                                Honor the King.
                                     Kitchener, Field-Marshal.

T MS (WP, DLC).

A Draft of an Executive Order[1]

[c. June 22, 1917]

By virtue of authority vested in me by Title VII of the Act of June 15 1917 entitled, "An Act to punish acts of interference with the foreign relations, the neutrality, and the foreign commerce of the United States, to punish espionage and better to enforce the criminal laws of the United States, and for other purposes," I hereby vest in the Secretary of Commerce the *executive* administration ⟨and execution of⟩ *of the instructions of the President under* Title VII and proclamations issued thereunder, and the said Secretary is hereby authorized and directed to take such measures as may be necessary to administer and execute the same, and to grant and refuse export licenses thereunder, in accordance with the policies and recommendations formulated ⟨and made by the Exports Council⟩ *by the Exports Council* herein established *and approved by the President.*

I hereby establish an Exports Council, to be composed of one or more representatives of the Department of State, assisted by advisers representing the Department of Commerce, the War Department, the Navy Department, *and* the Food ⟨Control⟩ *Administration,* and by such other advisers as the ⟨Secretary of State and the Secretary of Commerce shall select⟩ *President may designate*; and I hereby authorize and direct the Exports Council thus constituted to formulate the *necessary* policies and make the *necessary* recommendations *to carry out the purposes of the Act,* subject to the approval of the ⟨Secretary of State, under which the export licenses above referred to shall be granted or refused⟩ *President.*

T MS (WP, DLC).
¹ Words in angle brackets excised by Wilson; words in italics added by him. This Executive Order, as amended by Wilson and with further changes, is printed at June 26, 1917.

To Josephus Daniels

My dear Mr. Secretary: The White House 22 June, 1917

Thank you for your letter of June twentieth about the oil. I hope with all my heart that amongst us we can work out some relief for the West in particular.

Cordially and faithfully yours,   Woodrow Wilson

TLS (J. Daniels Papers, DLC).

To Francis Bowes Sayre

My dear Frank: The White House 22 June, 1917

Thank you for your letter. I know I can trust you to make sure that Doctor Naylor is the right man to leave on guard, and I am very much pleased that your mother is going to be with Jessie all summer.

How I wish I could drop in on the dear ones there and see them for a few quiet days, but that is past praying for.

I, of course, am glad to send you such a "letter of identification" as you suggest, and I am enclosing it.¹

In haste, with great affection and warmest messages from us all,   Faithfully yours,   Woodrow Wilson

TLS (WC, NjP).
[1] It reads as follows: "22 June, 1917. To Whom It May Concern: The bearer of this letter is Prof. Francis Bowes Sayre. Mr. Sayre is my son-in-law and I take pleasure in commending him to the confidence and assistance of all whose advice or cooperation he may desire." CCL (WP, DLC).

To Jessie Woodrow Wilson Sayre

My darling Daughter: [The White House] 22 June, 1917

Thank you with all my heart for your letter from Siasconset. It eased my heart not a little, and along with it came a letter from Frank in New York which spoke of the arrangements he has been making for the summer, which look as if they were satisfactory as far as one can judge from this distance. At any rate, I am quite willing to trust his choice.

It is delightful to think of you and the little ones successfully transplanted to that quiet place. My heart longs to come up and be with you all, but apparently that is something I must not allow myself to hope for even.

Do let us know, my dear girlie, from time to time how you are all faring, because our hearts will wait anxiously for news. We are all well, over head and ears in work of course but keeping our heads above water by hard swimming. Edith and I have resumed horseback riding and I am sure it is going to do both of us a great deal of good.

I dare say you heard of the fracas raised by the representatives of the Woman's Party here at the gates of the White House.[1] They certainly seem bent upon making their cause as obnoxious as possible.

It was indeed a delight to see you and Frank, and the only trouble of it was that it was too short. Nell was quite broken-hearted that she was not here to see you. Mac is overworking himself as usual and the dear girl is very anxious, but I am depending on Mac's extraordinary powers of recovery. He seems tough in spite of his high-strung nerves.

All unite in sending you and the little ones and Frank messages full to overflowing with love.

                    Lovingly yours,   [Woodrow Wilson]

CCL (WC, NjP).
[1] To greet the newly arrived Russian mission on June 20, when it called on Wilson at the White House, a group of militant suffragists displayed a ten-foot-wide banner on which was printed: "To the Russian Mission: President Wilson and Envoy Root are deceiving Russia. They say: 'We are a

democracy. Help us win a world war, so that democracies may survive.' We, the women of America, tell you that America is not a democracy. Twenty million American women are denied the right to vote. President Wilson is the chief opponent of their national enfranchisement. Help us make this nation really free. Tell our Government it must liberate people before it can claim free Russia as an ally." "Angry men in a crowd of several hundred persons" tore down the banner. *New York Times*, June 21, 1917.

From Thomas James Walsh

Mr. President: [Washington] June 22, 1917.

You were good enough to send word that you would see me to-morrow afternoon, Saturday, at four o'clock. The occasion for my conferring with you will then have passed. The Public Lands Committee has been holding hearings on the mining leasing bill. The testimony thus far adduced, particularly that given by Mr. Manning,[1] Director of the Bureau of Mines, and Mr. Peabody, of the Coal Committee, discloses a desperate situation so far as our supply of coal and petroleum is concerned. Senator Pomerene apparently acquainted you with the seriousness of the situation in Ohio. The price of coal has more than doubled in Montana in the past eighteen months. A witness testified at the last hearing in substance that the industries of the middle West will be paralyzed unless the production of coal is speedily materially enhanced. The Secretary of the Navy and the Attorney General are requested to appear before the Committee to-morrow morning. It was my purpose to acquaint you before they were heard with the substance of what has been said heretofore going to show that immediate legislation is vitally necessary to unlock the western fuel supplies. It is to be regretted that the whole vast western country must remain tied up until the controversy concerning the naval reserves is settled. Personally, I am convinced that the Navy never will need the oil in those reserves so badly as it does just at this very hour, but if the differences about them are utterly insoluble I thought you might be induced to urge immediate action on the bill which, as it stands, leaves untouched the controversies referred to.

I can assure you, Mr. President, that the food situation is no more critical than the fuel situation and the fuel situation would be relieved enormously by the immediate passage of the leasing bill.

I await your pleasure in this matter, but, as stated above, there will be no occasion for me to go to see you at four o'clock to-morrow, though I shall be glad to do so if you shall indicate your desire.   Very sincerely yours,   T. J. Walsh

TLS (WP, DLC).
1 Vannoy Hartrog Manning.

From Key Pittman

My Dear Mr President: Washington, D. C June 22nd, 1917

I feel it my duty to you and to myself to speak to you about a matter which I know has never come to your attention, but which has become so noticeable to some of my constituents and friends that it causes me embarrassment.

I have never had the honor of receiving an invitation to any of the official entertainments at the White House other than the regular public receptions, altho many have been given since my election to the Senate on the 29th January 1913.

Nor would I allude to the matter, were it not your custom to officially invite Senators and Representatives to such functions.

As a member of the committee on foreign relations and by virtue of my seniority to some forty nine senators, I expected, and the people of my State had a right to expect, that I would be honored by an invitation to some of the official dinners and receptions given in honor of the various foreign missions accredited to our Government.

You have shown me such substantial evidence of your friendship and I have so openly expressed and proven my sincere appreciation, that I am certain that I am not listed with those who by their own acts have forfeited your friendship confidence and respect.

These reasons, and the belief that this apparent neglect of my State and my official position was the error of those to whom you must entrust such matters seem to justify me at this time in burdening you with this subject.

Very sincerely yours   Key Pittman.

ALS (WP, DLC).

From William Bauchop Wilson, with Enclosure

My dear Mr. President: Washington June 22, 1917.

I am sending you herewith copy of a letter which I have today written to Secretary Baker, the contents of which I am sure you will be interested in reading.

Faithfully yours,   W B Wilson

TLS (WP, DLC).

ENCLOSURE

William Bauchop Wilson to Newton Diehl Baker

CONFIDENTIAL.

My dear Mr. Secretary: Washington June 22, 1917.

I am in receipt of your note, transmitting a communication from Secretary Lane, inclosing a letter received by him from Mr. Walter Douglas, President of the Phelps Dodge Corporation, relative to the labor situation in the mines in Arizona.

Our reports indicate that the situation in Arizona is very well in hand. The I.W.W. have been making a big drive in that state and a great deal of unrest has existed. The adjustments we recently negotiated in the Jerome, Morenci and Clifton districts seem to have had a steadying influence on the mining situation. There are still some irritating circumstances which I feel sure we will be able to handle without any serious stoppage of work taking place.

The labor situation as a whole is very much better than could have been expected in view of the tremendous increase in the cost of living and the fact that only in a limited number of instances have the wages kept pace with the upward trend of commodities. One of the annoying features of the situation, and one that I know would lead to a great deal of friction among the workmen if it became generally known, is that whenever any disposition is shown by the workers to demand an increase of wages commensurate with the increased cost of living, the employers immediately assume that the action is inspired by traitors or spies and is therefore treasonable. I am under obligations to the Attorney General and yourself for the broad view you have taken of this situation and the promptness with which communications from employers calling for troops or secret service men in connection with labor disputes have been referred to this Department so that these difficulties could be taken up by Conciliators in the regular way.

When the employers say to the consuming public, "You must pay more money or you don't get the goods," and pat themselves on the back for their wonderful display of business acumen, and then when the workers say to the employers, "You must pay more money or you don't get the labor," denounce it as treason, the contrast strikes me as decidedly unjust and an unfair reflection upon the patriotism of the wage-workers of the country.

Our only serious labor disputes, either in the strike stage or impending, are in the metal mining industry at Butte, Montana, and Tooele, Utah; the marine building trades in the vicinity of New York, and the possibility of I.W.W. troubles in the State of Washington. We are endeavoring to keep in touch with each of these situations. It may be of interest to you to know that since the declaration of war on April 6th we have handled one hundred and sixty labor disputes, involving hundreds of thousands of workmen, most of which never reached the strike stage. We have adjusted ninety-eight of these, failed to adjust two, and have sixty at the present time in the process of negotiation, the large number pending being due in a great measure to our shortage of funds and the consequent necessity of withdrawing our Conciliators until the beginning of the new fiscal year.

I am returning the correspondence to you herewith.

Cordially yours,   W B Wilson,

TCL (WP, DLC).

To Sir Cecil Arthur Spring Rice

My dear Mr. Ambassador,   The White House. 23 June, 1917.

I must within the next day or two decide the final details of our shipbuilding programme, but I cannot do so without the following information:

1) Great Britain's present remaining tonnage available for the sea-carriage of supplies;

2) The present remaining tonnage of the other Allies available for the same purpose;

3) The neutral tonnage available for that purpose; and

4) The actual destruction of tonnage by submarines since the first of January last, listed month by month.

I would be very much obliged to you if you would be good enough to let me have this information in as full detail as possible. I would, of course make only confidential use of it, but it is absolutely necessary to me for this reason: The Congress has given me full powers in this matter of shipbuilding and I can act intelligently and effectively only if I have the information which will enable me to judge whether, in order to tide us over the time between this and the first of next year, I shall go in for quantity regardless of kind or whether I shall be at liberty to confine our construction to the safest and soundest models.

I know that you will see the necessity and I hope that you will have or can get the facts I need.

With the highest consideration and sincere regard,

Very truly Yours,   Woodrow Wilson

WWTLS (FO 115/2333, pp. 2-3, PRO).

From William Gibbs McAdoo

Dear Mr. President: Washington June 23, 1917.

I have been laid up for a few days and therefore have been unable to answer sooner your letter in reference to the suggestion of the Prudential Insurance Company of Newark about insurance upon the lives of our soldiers and sailors. I regard this as a most important matter and I think insurance upon the lives of our soldiers and sailors, if effected upon the right basis, is not alone a humane and wise provision for the men and their families, but that it will contribute immensely to the effectiveness of the Army and Navy. Whenever the fighting men are made to feel that if the worst happens to them their families will be provided for, a great load is taken off their minds. The idea appeals to me tremendously and I should like to see it carried out. It never has been done before by any Nation, which is all the more reason why this great progressive Nation should set the example. It is in line with what we have just done for the officers and seamen of our merchant vessels. Our War Risk Insurance Bureau is now granting insurance upon their lives and providing indemnities for injuries arising out of the war. It does not seem to me, however, wise to let any one insurance company take hold of this matter. Any one company would be glad to do what the Prudential Insurance Company offers to do in its letter to you. The advertising value would be tremendous. Again, I think the jealousies of other insurance companies would be aroused and it might be difficult to get their effective cooperation.

I had in mind a plan which I was going to discuss with you for the enlargement of our present War Risk Insurance Bureau so as to permit insurance on the lives of officers and men of the Army and Navy. This is a big problem, but not too big for us to tackle. I shall not, at the moment, discuss the merits of the proposition. That can, I think, be deferred until we can take the step I now propose, namely, that you permit me to call a conference of the leading life insurance companies to meet me at the Treasury Department in Washington at an early date for a full discussion of the question of insurance upon the lives of the officers and men of the Army and Navy. If, as a result of that conference, a satisfactory plan is not devised for such insurance, then we can consider seriously enlarging the present War Risk Insurance Bureau to perform this service.

I enclose, for your information, copy of a letter from Mr. William C. DeLancy, Director of the Bureau of War Risk Insurance, bearing upon the matter.[1]

Cordially yours,   W G McAdoo

TLS (WP, DLC).
  ¹ W. C. DeLancy to WGM, June 20, 1917, TCLS (WP, DLC).

From William Bauchop Wilson, with Enclosure

My dear Mr. President: Washington June 23, 1917.

I am sure you will be interested in the inclosed communication, relative to deserting British seamen, which I have forwarded to the Secretary of State.   Faithfully yours,   W B Wilson

TLS (WP, DLC).

E N C L O S U R E

William Bauchop Wilson to Robert Lansing

My dear Mr. Secretary: Washington June 21, 1917.

I am in receipt of your letter of June 13th, inclosing memorandum from the British Embassy, relative to the desertion of seamen from British merchant vessels in United States ports, especially at Galveston, and requesting an expression of the viewpoint of the Department of Labor thereon.

One of the purposes sought to be accomplished by the enactment of the Seamen's Law was the equalization of the operating expenses of American vessels with those of foreign vessels trading in our ports. By virtue of our treaty arrangements, through which we used our police powers to arrest and return deserting seamen of foreign vessels in American ports, we enabled the foreign ship-owner to maintain a decided advantage over American owners in that part of operating expenses represented by wages. The foreign ship-owner could sign his seamen at the prevailing rate of wages in a foreign port, with the assurance that they would be compelled to return with the vessel to the port from which it sailed on the same terms of employment as they started with, whether the conditions were satisfactory to them or not. The American ship-owner being compelled to sign his seamen at the rate of wages prevailing in American ports was thereby placed at a competitive disadvantage. It was believed that that was one of the important reasons for the decline of the American merchant marine. The Seamen's Law gave the American seaman the right to quit at any time when his vessel was in a safe harbor, and it gave the foreign seaman the right to quit whenever his vessel was in a safe harbor in the United States. The natural operation of such a law is that the wages and conditions of employment on all vessels, foreign and domestic, trading in American ports must be approximately equal, else desertions will take place. If the wages and conditions out of our ports are higher and better than those out of foreign ports, the foreign seamen will desert when they come into our waters. If their wages and conditions are higher and better than ours, our seamen will desert when they go into their waters. My information is that the wage rate for sailors on American vessels going out of American ports is $60.00 per month, with a bonus of fifty per cent. when the vessel is to pass through the danger zone, making a total rate in that trade of $90.00 per month, while the wage rate on British vessels engaged in the same trade is $42.00 per month. Of course there will be desertions under such circumstances. The remedy would seem to be either lower rates for American seamen or higher rates for British seamen.

Personally, I do not believe there is any more justification for compelling the services of seamen for private profit than there is for compelling the services of employees on land for private profit. I realize that the situation is a serious one, as it affects furnishing the necessary supplies to our Allies. It may ultimately be necessary to conscript the vessels needed for carrying supplies, and when that time comes we may properly consider the conscription of men to man them, but until that time is reached, I doubt the wisdom of the conscription of seamen any more than the conscription of workers on land.

When your communication of May 24th to the Secretary of Commerce on the same subject was brought to my attention, I immediately started to make arrangements for a conference of representatives of the Department of State, the Department of Commerce, the Shipping Board, the ship-owners, the seamen, and the Department of Labor, with a view to threshing out the whole question to a working basis. From the progress already made in that direction, I am hopeful that such a conference can be held at an early date.   Cordially yours,   W B Wilson

TCL (WP, DLC).

From Willard Saulsbury

Dear Mr. President: [Washington] June 23d, 1917.

I am delighted to see in the morning papers that you have determined to place the matter of the ship building programme in the hands of General Goethals.[1] I only know General Goethals as I do Mr. Denman very slightly but since boyhood I have been in a general way familiar with ship building from the time my grandfather had wooden ship yards, three I think, until I have represented steel ship building companies in Wilmington. General Goethals' characterization of the wooden ship building programme as hopeless was I think a mild and polite way of characterizing it and I want to congratulate you most sincerely in placing him in control of the matter as I do not believe we will build a thousand wodden [wooden] ships in this country of a thousand tons upward in the next thousand years. Our wooden ship industry in Delaware has practically ceased to exist except for the smallest and most easily built vessels, much to my regret, but I think the progress of the times has made it apparent to anyone familiar with the condition of things that wooden ships of necessity must give way to the more easily built steel vessels. I thought of saying this much to you before but was satisfied that when the matter came to a crisis you would do what you have done—the proper thing.

Yours very truly,   Willard Saulsbury

TLS (WP, DLC).

[1] Under the headlines, "Wilson Upholds Goethals in Row over Steel Ships" and "Goethals Wins Fight," the *New York Times* and the *Washington Post* reported that Wilson, after a long conference with Goethals on June 22, had given the General full power over the shipbuilding program and had instructed him to build all the ships possible, both steel and wooden. Goethals would be authorized to commandeer all shipping under construction, speed up the work, and spend the funds appropriated by Congress. Denman would retain the powers needed for operating and chartering vessels, and, as president of the Emergency Fleet Corporation, he would continue to pass finally on contracts for construction. *New York Times* and *Washington Post*, both June 23, 1917.

On the day after he saw Wilson, Goethals wrote to his son and daughter-in-law, as follows: "Of course Denman has the entré to the White House and I have not. From the publicity given to the fact that I had asked for an appointment last Monday and it wasn't given to me I'm inclined to think the W. H. is rather antagonistic. I phoned for the appointment—Denmans statements were not the cause nor the reason, so that the fact that I had asked was given out at the W. H.

"I had my interview yesterday afternoon. I hadn't heard anything about the report I made two weeks ago Monday next; so I branched into a full outline of my program and for the first time he evinced enough interest in the subject under discussion between us to ask a number of questions, so that I straightened out a variety of matters and impressions. In this respect it was the most satisfactory interview I have ever had. When we finished that I told him the statements in the press concerning my having fixed the price of steel or that I had contracted for any at $95 a ton were false. I had bought some after haggling over the price at $85 a ton so that we might get things started and subsequently used this as a basis protecting both ourselves and the contractor. I never mentioned Denman, didn't argue or ask for the authority to be placed on me. I had written him about the latter and it would be *infra dig* for me to take it up. We parted." G. W. Goethals to George Rodman Goethals and Priscilla Goethals, June 23, 1917, ALS (G. W. Goethals Papers, DLC).

ADDENDA

To Edward Rogers Bushnell[1]

"The Bluff," Judd Haven, Muskoka District,

My dear Sir,   Canada. 1 September, 1904.

In reply to your letter of August twenty-seventh, forwarded to me here, I would say,

1. That it is certainly best, whenever it is possible, for a young man who wishes to work his way through college to enter with at least enough money to pay a part of his expenses; otherwise, he will not be able to devote a sufficient proportion of his time to his studies. Moreover, it is seldom possible for such a man, necessarily a stranger at first in the college town, to get enough outside work at once to cover his expenses. He must gradually get acquainted and adjusted.

2. I do not think that the proportion of students trying to work their way through college is greater now than it was, say, ten years ago, though of course the absolute number is much larger. The college should, when possible, remit the tuition of such men and furnish them with full information with regard to the opportunities for self-help, as well as with all friendly assistance in getting the necessary introductions; but it ought not to make wards of them and sap their self-reliance; and it ought, for the sake of their moral fibre, to put them under obligations to pay their tuition as soon after graduation as they may be able to earn it over and above their living expenses. There ought to be no touch of "charity" about the transaction, but only full friendliness and helpfulness.

3. It is generally safe to assume that a man who is working his way through college, if he does not seek "charity" but only opportunity, is taking his life seriously and will be one of the world's successful workers after graduation; but I do not think that it would be safe to say that that [sic] such a man is always more apt to succeed than a more fortunate fellow student who is not obliged to support himself while studying.

Very truly Yours,   Woodrow Wilson

WWTLS (WC, NjP).

[1] Editorial writer for the Philadelphia *North American*, who had worked his way through the University of Pennsylvania.

To William DeWitt Hyde[1]

My dear President Hyde: Princeton, N. J. March 29th, 1910.

It goes very hard to be obliged to tell you how highly we think of men whom we wish to retain and you wish to draw to you at Bowdoin. You certainly would make no mistake either in the case of Mr. McIlwain[2] or Mr. Adriance.[3] They are admirable men. McIlwain is the broader and more accomplished scholar, but Adriance is thoroughly fit for promotion of the best kind. It would distress me to lose either of these men, and to lose both would be serious. I cannot stand in their way and unhappily I cannot at present increase the budget of the University to retain them.

With much regard,

Sincerely yours,   Woodrow Wilson

TLS (W. D. Hyde Papers, MeB).
  [1] President of Bowdoin College, 1885-1917.
  [2] Charles Howard McIlwaine, Princeton, 1894, at this time preceptor in history and politics at Princeton.
  [3] Walter Maxwell Adriance, preceptor in history and politics at Princeton. McIlwaine received and accepted the call from and to Bowdoin.

Two Letters to Lyman Abbott

My dear Doctor Abbott: [Trenton, N. J.] April 12, 1911.

I wish sincerely that I had brains enough in the midst of my daily rush to send you something that would be worth reproducing in the Outlook, but I really have not. These are the closing days of our Legislature and I am not left alone for five minutes at a time.

I can only thank you for the compliment you pay me by desiring it.

In haste, and with the most delightful recollections of the evening spent with you recently,

Cordially and faithfully yours,   Woodrow Wilson

My dear Doctor Abbott: Sea Girt, N. J. August 31, 1912.

You are very kind and I know just the generous spirit as well as the enlightened purpose which prompts your urgency in the matter of a statement of my views through the Outlook. But I am in the grip of days which render it *literally* impossible for me to write anything. Sometimes when a day has ended and late evening has come, I try to dictate advance matter for an important speech and the result is always entirely unsatisfactory because of the fatigue of the day and absence of everything that is necessary for clear thinking. I have found my own limitations and must decline in mere justice to myself.

I am nonetheless warmly obliged to you for I know that your kindness is prompted by genuine friendship and not by the mere instincts of the editor.

All join me in warm regard.

Cordially yours,   Woodrow Wilson

TLS (L. Abbott Papers, MeB).

INDEX

NOTE ON THE INDEX

THE alphabetically arranged analytical table of contents at the front of this volume eliminates duplication, in both contents and index, of references to certain documents, such as letters. Letters are listed in the contents alphabetically by name, and chronologically within each name by page. The subject matter of all letters is, of course, indexed. The Editorial Notes and Wilson's writings are listed in the contents chronologically by page. In addition, the subject matter of both categories is indexed. The index covers all references to books and articles mentioned in text or notes. Footnotes are indexed. Page references to footnotes which place a comma between the page number and "n" cite both text and footnote, thus: "418,n1." On the other hand, absence of the comma indicates reference to the footnote only, thus: "59n1"–the page number denoting where the footnote appears.

The index supplies the fullest known form of names and, for the Wilson and Axson families, relationships as far down as cousins. Persons referred to by nicknames or shortened forms of names can be identified by reference to entries for these forms of the names.

All entries consisting of page numbers only and which refer to concepts, issues, and opinions (such as democracy, the tariff, the money trust, leadership, and labor problems), are references to Wilson speeches and writings. Page references that follow the symbol Δ in such entries refer to the opinions and comments of others who are identified.

Two cumulative contents-index volumes are now in print: Volume 13, which covers Volumes 1-12, and Volume 26, which covers Volumes 14-25. Volume 39, covering Volumes 27-38, is in preparation.

INDEX

Woodrow Wilson, cont.

autocracy can divide us, they will overcome us; if we stand together, victory is certain and the liberty which victory will secure. We can afford then to be generous, but we cannot afford then or now to be weak or omit any single guarantee of justice and security, 367; on objects in going into war, 370-71; There is no hate in our hearts for the German people, but there is a resolve which cannot be shaken even by misrepresentation to overcome the pretensions of the autocratic government which acts upon purposes to which the German people have never consented, 371; The real fruition of life is to do the thing we have said we wished to do. There are times when words seem empty and only action seems great. Such a time has come, and, in the Providence of God, America will once more have an opportunity to show to the world that she was born to serve mankind, 423; on studying the ancient classics, 439; There is something very fine, my fellow citizens, in the spirit of the volunteer, but deeper than the volunteer spirit is the spirit of obligation, 452; I am thankful for the privilege of self-sacrifice, which is the only privilege that lends dignity to the human spirit, 453; We are ready to plead at the bar of history, and our flag shall wear a new lustre. Once more we shall make good with our lives and fortunes the great faith to which we were born, and a new glory shall shine in the face of our people, 504; We are fighting, not a people, but a system—one of the most hateful systems that has ever been built up into strength by the mistaken plans of men. And if we can keep that constantly in mind, that what threatens the world is not the aggression of any great nation but the aggression of a system which has been imposed upon a great nation, we shall assist properly to interpret this war, 537; on working one's way through college, 569

RECREATION

plays golf, 13, 31; attends theater, 13, 64, 158; reads Ordeal by Battle, 161,n5; goes horseback riding, 560

RELIGION

and Wilmington, N.C. Presbyterian Church's Centennial, 86-89; Spring Rice sends verse from Isaiah, 112-13; But the wise heart never questions the dealings of Providence, because the great long plan, as it unfolds, has a majesty about it and a definiteness of purpose, an elevation of ideal, which we were incapable of conceiving as we tried to work things out with our own short sight and weak strength, 451

WRITINGS

69,n2; intention to write when retires from office, 161-62; last will and testament, 426;

Woodrow Wilson, cont.

has no time to write article for Outlook, 570-71

End of Woodrow Wilson entry

Wilson Era: Years of Peace—1910-1917 (Daniels), 526n3
Wilson: The New Freedom (Link), 526n1
Wilson Upholds Goethals in Row over Steel Ships (New York Times), 567n1
Wisconsin, University of, 254
Wise, Stephen Samuel, 41-42, 44-45, 124-25, 152
Wiseman, William George Eden, 18, 120, 142n1, 143, 169, 456, 461, 543-45; and Northcliffe, 487-88; and plan to send special agents to Russia, 527, 529-30, 551-52
Wolf, Simon, 506-507
Woman's party: see National Woman's party
woman suffrage, 215-16, 237,n1,4, 293, 474-75, 497; and Maryland, 124,n1, 138-39; establishment of committee in House of Representatives on, 241, 269-70, 320-21,n1; demonstration before newly arrived Russian mission, 560,n1
women: in Russia, 215, 241; and dedication of Red Cross Building, 281,n1, 283; and Food Administration, 437n1, 485-86
Women's Volunteer Aid Corps, 281n1
Wood, Leonard, 120, 158, 522
Wooden Ship Controversy (Springfield Republican), 556n3
wooden ships: see shipbuilding program
Woodrow Wilson as I Know Him (Tumulty), 29n1
Woolley, Robert Wickliffe, 158
Worden, Beverly Lyon, 477,n2
World Politics, 317n3
World War: and civil service precautions, 3; coordination of secret service work, 16-17; Cuba enters, 41,n1, 51,n1; and Guatemala, 46-47; and contraband list, 101-102, 106; and German ships in U.S. ports, 133-34, 292; and mail censorship, 195-96; idea of educational program for populace on, 394, 395; Brazil enters, 439-40,n1; WW on how Germany forced U.S. into, and U.S. purpose in, 499-504
atrocities and war crimes: Balfour on German, 342; Tumulty suggests Whitlock publicize, 427-28
economic impact: and Liberty bonds, 25-27, 294-95, 401,n1; and shipbuilding program, 32, 233-34, 235-36, 248-49, 249, 285-87, 475-80; WW's appeal to the American people, 71-75; and food, 73-74, 108-109; and labor, 135-38, 205-208, 564; and export restrictions, 224,n2; and Red Cross appeal, 282; and priority shipments, 289-90; Lever bills and, 294n1,2, 344-46; and prices and price control, 298, 301,n2, 372,n2, 374, 411-13, 414-17, 419-20, 424, 447-49, 534; and Centralized Purchasing Agency, 256-57, 397, 411-13, 414-17, 424, 447-49; McAdoo on amendments to Federal Reserve Act, 302,n1,2; and British commerce and manufacture, 379-80; J. S. Williams